I AM BECAUSE WE ARE

I AM BECAUSE ·WE ARE

Readings in Black Philosophy

Edited with an introduction by

Fred Lee Hord (Mzee Lasana Okpara)

and Jonathan Scott Lee

University of Massachusetts Press   A M H E R S T

Printed in the United States of America

LC 95–1249

ISBN 0–87023–964–3(cloth); 965-1(pbk.)

Designed by David Ford

Set in Adobe Utopia by Keystone Typesetting, Inc.

Printed and bound by Thomson-Shore

Library of Congress Cataloging-in-Publication Data

I am because we are : readings in Black philosophy / edited with an
   introduction by Fred Lee Hord (Mzee Lasana Okpara), and Jonathan
   Scott Lee.

         p.   cm.

     Includes bibliographical references.

     ISBN 0–87023–964–3 (cloth). — ISBN 0–87023–965–1

     1. Blacks—Race identity.   2. Identity.   3. Social groups—
Philosophy.   4. Philosophy, Black.   I. Hord, Fred L.   II. Lee,
Jonathan Scott.

     DT15.I15   1995

     305.8'96—dc20   95–1249
                                                                 CIP

British Library Cataloguing in Publication data are available.

For my parents,
Reverend Noel E. Hord
and
Jessie Tyler Hord,
who taught me by precept and example
that I am because we are.

F L H

For Peggy Berg,
for her strength,
her spirit, and her love.

J S L

 CONTENTS

Acknowledgments

With much appreciation and gratitude:

To Knox College and The Colorado College, and Deans John Strassburger and Timothy Fuller, for their generous financial support.

To our librarians, Sharon Clayton (Knox College) and Mary Johnson (The Colorado College), for their time and assistance.

To John Riker for his thoughtful reading.

To Terry Duffy, Nancy Fennig, and Rory Maikoski for their secretarial assistance.

At the University of Massachusetts Press: to Clark Dougan for his unflagging enthusiasm and support for this project, to Janet Benton for her exemplary work as editor, and to our anonymous readers for their valuable criticism.

I AM BECAUSE WE ARE

INTRODUCTION

 "I am because we are": An Introduction to
Black Philosophy

The volume you hold in your hands offers itself as a highly selective overview
of a central tradition of black philosophy, a tradition extending over more
than five thousand years and stretching geographically from Africa to the
Caribbean and North America.[1] This tradition includes a rich diversity of
texts, including the Egyptian *Book of Coming Forth by Day;* essays on negritude by Léopold Sédar Senghor and Wole Soyinka; practical reflections on
revolution, political reform, and the relation between culture and identity in
texts by Julius Nyerere, Amilcar Cabral, Malcolm X, and Frantz Fanon; and
sophisticated proposals for the transformation of Western worldviews and
theoretical assumptions in the works of bell hooks, Cornel West, and Molefi
Kete Asante. These texts and the others included here—despite their remarkable diversity of origin, style, and of method—constitute a tradition, we suggest, because in them it is made more or less explicit that the fundamental
philosophical or intellectual concern is that of the meaning of individual life
in community.

Our claim that there is a black philosophical tradition effectively defined
by the range of texts included here is, of course, quite controversial. Indeed,
the question of whether or not one can even speak of an *African* philosophy
remains a central question among many black thinkers,[2] so the claim that a
tradition of black philosophy—in fact, more than one tradition—can be discerned across the great temporal and spatial reaches of the African diaspora
is bound to be greeted with some skepticism.[3] Nevertheless, we offer this
anthology as substantive evidence for the existence of a black philosophical
tradition. In this introduction we mean to explore some objections that have
been or might be raised to the very idea of a black philosophical tradition,
hoping to make a case for our own approach to the material included herein
while also opening up the possibility that there are other ways of thinking
about these texts.

As a point of departure, it is worth emphasizing that in the expression "a
black tradition of philosophy," each of the salient terms raises important
questions and problems. The term "black" immediately raises the question

of whether or not the tradition introduced here is in any respect tied to race. In using the term "philosophy" to characterize the intellectual work of these thinkers, questions about what constitutes philosophy are bound to come up. Finally, in writing of a "tradition," we face any number of problems about what makes possible the transmission of traditions through history, and particularly through a history as complex as that of Africa and the African diaspora. Using these problematic terms as our framework, we will now pursue some of these issues in greater depth.

"Black"

The idea of a *black* philosophical tradition raises two quite different kinds of objections. On the one hand, there is the irreducibly racist contention that people of African descent simply are not capable of producing works of philosophy comparable to those of the European tradition. On the other hand, there is the more sophisticated objection, most forcefully developed by Kwame Anthony Appiah,[4] that identifying a philosophical tradition in terms of race runs the double risk of tying this tradition to false theories of race and of homogenizing the remarkable variety in beliefs, attitudes, and values characteristic of thinkers of African descent.

In response to the racist objection to the notion of black philosophy, it is crucial to note that black philosophy is not the only black intellectual tradition that has been dismissed by the dominant European culture. Black literature has until recently been declared virtually nonexistent, excepting those rare works that met a proposed set of "universal" criteria. Black theatre was similarly discharged unless it contained the "universal" elements of great tragedy. And although the uniqueness of black music could not be ignored, it was relegated to the realm of "popular" culture because it did not meet the "standards" of the classics. Similarly, as William R. Jones has argued, black philosophy has been subjected to the particularly virulent criticism of having its very legitimacy called into question.[5]

To what extent does it make sense to speak of black philosophy? Can we give any concrete meaning to an idea covering such an historical sweep and so many different thinkers of diverse backgrounds? Demonstrating that each standard objection to the notion of a black philosophy simply begs various questions about what counts as legitimate philosophical activity, Jones rightly suggests that "to advance the category of a black philosophy inaugurates a crucial and unavoidable *philosophical* debate about the nature of philosophy itself."[6] The notion forces a rethinking of philosophy precisely because philosophy in the West, at least since Plato, has defined itself in terms of exclusions, in terms of what it is not. Philosophy has constituted itself as neither science nor religion nor literature, and Europeans have effectively used this exclusionary definition of the discipline to exclude further the works of non-European thinkers, works rather casually categorized as religion, literature, or (proto)science. To propose that a selection of black thinkers, then, makes up a black philosophical tradition is to call into question the absolute legitimacy of the current European philosophical canon and to suggest that the European tradition of philosophy itself suffers from ethnocentrism, at the very least.

Although Jones does not go on to suggest his own conception of the nature of philosophy in general or of black philosophy in particular, he does note that "all philosophies are particular,"[7] and we believe the discipline of philosophy will only enrich itself through coming to the realization that all its positions, arguments, and texts are themselves products of a particular context and history. In the light of this, we agree with Jones that "an ethnic approach may well become the catalyst for a more accurate, comprehensive, and less angular picture of reality, including our understanding of the nature of philosophy."[8]

Even if we grant that racist objections to the possibility of a black philosophy need not be taken seriously, our claims for such a tradition must be defended against the important arguments of Appiah. Twin themes of Appiah's recent book, *In My Father's House,* are the dangers of promoting false theories of race, even (and especially) in the development of pan-Africanism, and the problems of treating Africa as possessing any sort of cultural unity and thereby underestimating the significance of both the wide range of African cultures and the multiple identities of African people.

While we agree generally with Appiah's arguments concerning the impossibility of satisfactorily defining the concept of race—arguments he develops in his reading of W. E. B. Du Bois's changing perspectives on race[9]—the framework sketched in his book for dealing with questions of Africa and the African diaspora fails to deal adequately with the impact of the admittedly false concept of race on these questions. When Appiah remarks at the very beginning of his book that he is accustomed "to seeing the world as a network of points of affinity,"[10] we fear that Appiah may not be fully alive to the ways in which the affinities of which he writes must themselves be constructed in the light of a modern history dominated by Europe and its racism, a racism both affinity-constructing and affinity-denying. It is necessary to recognize the importance of the concept of race in any attempt to deal with Africa and the diaspora, even while insisting that the concept of race is itself inherently false. This belief grounds our use of the term "black."

The notion of race—itself a European export to Africa—is inextricably linked with notions of culture. Thus, we think it useful to distinguish three stages in the development of African and diaspora thought. The first is a precolonial stage, in which philosophical themes more or less directly reflect the diversity of Africa's cultural environment. While this precolonial period is essentially lost today (and we therefore run the risk of romanticizing its alterity both to Europe and to contemporary black cultures), we think that Jacques Maquet is on the right track in seeing African *cultures* as categorizable in terms of a relatively small number of what he calls *civilizations,* ways of life integrally linked to geography and climate.[11] Thus the diversity of sub-Saharan African cultures is grounded in commonalities of civilization, and such commonalities might well be expected to show up at the level of philosophical reflection as well. In the second stage, Africa's cultural heterogeneity has imposed upon it the social construction of race as a result of European (and also Arab) colonial intrusion. The concept of race—a concept the ambiguity of which reflects its essentially ideological role—serves to homogenize the native population of Africa so as to justify the slave trade and, later, to ground the racist policies of colonial governments. The concept of race—despite its philosophical flaws—serves in myriad ways to construct both the social reality of colonial Africa and the identities of people of African descent caught up in this colonial reality. The third and postcolonial stage is one of a *claiming* of race at both the political and the psychological level, a claiming meant to facilitate the reconstruction of the very idea of race. We see this operating ideologically in the negritude and black aesthetic movements and politically in pan-Africanism.[12]

In short, we are inclined to accept the current dominant concept of race, according to which people of sub-Saharan African descent are categorizable as "black," but only so as to deconstruct or decenter it: while certainly not interested in leaving nineteenth and twentieth century ideas of race intact, we think it crucial not to ignore this social construction. We begin by focusing on African *culture,* not on race, but we believe it crucial to forge connections between the precolonial and the postcolonial; the notion of race as a social construction is fundamental to this endeavor.

In responding to Appiah's concerns about race, we have in effect responded as well to his insistence on the diversity of African and diaspora cultures. In trying to articulate a black philosophical tradition, we are in no way denying the range of sub-Saharan African cultures and thinkers. Rather than focus on the perhaps excessively European dualism of unity and diversity, we endorse a position that makes plain the way cultures develop uniquely on the basis of broad commonalities—that cultures, in Maquet's terms, belong to civilizations. Moreover, Maquet's positing of "Africanity" as "a conceptual tool that enables us to grasp what the various African civilizations have in common"[13] provides a method for exploring the possibility of one or more African (and Africana) philosophical traditions.

"Philosophy"

To make explicit what exactly we mean here by the term "philosophy," we turn to Kwame Nkrumah's notions regarding the vital relationships between philosophy and society. Asserting that "philosophical systems are facts of history . . . [and more than] statements standing in logical relation to one another,"[14] Nkrumah points up the ways in which philosophy, like history, can enrich and illuminate the concrete experiences of human beings in their communities. "The evaluation of one's own social circumstance is . . . as good a starting point of the inquiry into the relations between philosophy and society as any other," he writes. "Philosophy, in understanding human society, calls for an analysis of facts and events, and an attempt to see how they fit into human life, and so how they make up human experience."[15] In other words, for the purposes of this anthology, we are construing the discipline of philosophy in a way that brings social and ethical questions into the foreground, along with issues about the nature of human identity. This is not to deny the importance of other kinds of philosophical questions—be they epistemological, metaphysical, or aesthetic—within African and diaspora thought. However, as we argue in the next section of this introduction, these other sorts of questions find their ultimate significance in the context of the social issues which seem to us to dominate the black philosophical tradition introduced here.

A reading of the thinkers included in this anthology suggests an initial characterization of philosophy within this tradition as essentially an intellectual power of *mediation*. It is the philosopher's role, for example, to mediate the desires and expectations of the individual with the interests of the social collective, interests that the philosopher will be quick to acknowledge are themselves largely responsible for the particular contour of the individual's desires and expectations. Given the historical facts of European slave-trading, colonialism, and postcolonialism as dominant features of the history of Africa and the African diaspora, the philosopher's mediating role takes on a second dimension: not only must the black thinker work out systematically ideals that help shape the individual's relation to the life of his or her community, but this thinker must also help mediate the complex relationships between colonizer and colonized, between European cultural demands and the authentic interests of black culture. In short, philosophy is here called upon to evaluate and counter the dehumanization to which people and ideas of African descent have been subjected through the history of colonialism and of European racism. Central to this legacy of dehumanization and resistance to it are the intraracial dilemmas of black people. At the same time, philosophy also holds the promise of helping to counter the white person's self-dehumanization, a dehumanization that is the product of that same history of racism and manifests itself in the false universalism of so much European thought.

It is at this juncture, perhaps, that philosophy's role as mediator becomes most problematic, since philosophy itself has been in important senses a European abstraction, an intellectual weapon wielded by the colonizer against black traditions of reflection and analysis. There can be no question but that European conceptions of appropriate philosophical discourse have tended to hold sway and erode loyalty to more traditional modes of reflective discourse within the African, Caribbean, and African-American, university-based, intellectual communities.[16] We trust this volume will suggest some of the richness of at least one black philosophical tradition, which has flourished largely beyond the walls of universities founded by and in the interests of the colonizers. Certainly many of the texts found here—in the challenges they pose to political and intellectual elites and in the images of personal identity and social organization they elaborate—pursue themes far removed from those canonized within the European philosophical tradition.

Philosophy can play the role of mediator that we have outlined precisely because it is at its best a discipline sensitive to the values of both *universality* and *cultural particularity*. Philosophy—again, at its best—is able to uncover, articulate, and nurture precisely those aspects of a particular cultural tradition that seem best suited to universalization for the purpose of building bridges between various distinct cultural traditions. This universalizing tendency of philosophical reflection ideally carries within it a critical tendency that helps make it possible for the philosopher to play the mediating role we have described. At the same time, both the tendency to universalize and the tendency to criticize are somewhat double-edged: the dangers of philosophy include naive and false claims to universality, as well as ungrounded and sterile attempts at destructive criticism.

A fundamental principle, then, guiding our selection of texts for this volume has been the wish to illustrate this conception of philosophical activity as essentially a matter of building bridges between diverse cultures and individuals, between individuals and their multiple communities: in an important sense, the texts included here are meant to be *used* in our joint construction of a better future.

However, it must be clear from the start that the tradition of black philosophy introduced here is but one of a number of more or less distinct philosophical traditions to be found within Africa and its diaspora. There has been, for example, a tradition of Christian philosophy in North Africa since the beginning of the Christian era (perhaps reaching its peak in the texts of Augustine), and—with the rise of the slave trade and colonization—this tradition has worked its way throughout Africa and the New World. Similarly, there has been a lively tradition of Islamic thought in Africa, perhaps most notably in Ethiopia, as documented by C. Sumner.[17] Because both of these traditions work essentially with issues, problems, and themes deriving from sources outside of Africa, they are arguably more integrally related to the broader Christian and Islamic intellectual traditions than to specifically African currents of thought.[18] However, since the coming to independence of the majority of African nations, new traditions of African philosophizing have developed, owing their methods to contemporary French and English philosophy in particular but often pursuing themes directly relevant to the political and economic situation of contemporary Africa. Thus, in the texts of Anthony Appiah and Kwasi Wiredu, the method of Anglo-American conceptual analysis is turned towards issues of pan-Africanism and "development,"[19] while in the work of Paulin Hountondji, the "scientific" method of French structuralist marxism (as elaborated in the texts of Louis Althusser) is directed to questions about the nature of philosophizing in Africa.[20] The texts of these thinkers certainly constitute an important African philosophical tradition—and thinkers working within the same tradition can be found in the Caribbean and in North America as well—but their special and explicit emphasis on European methods and modes of analysis distinguish these philosophers and their tradition from the black philosophical tradition to be found in these pages.

"Tradition"

At this point, we think it useful to try to sort out similarities and differences among the thinkers included in this volume and to articulate what we call the common *generative themes* which give birth to the diverse methods, styles, and interests of the philosophical texts included here.[21] Yet in introducing this notion of generative themes, we are in no way implying that we adhere to what Paulin Hountondji has described as "unanimism," the claim that Africa is (in Appiah's words) "culturally homogeneous."[22] Rather, we have chosen the term "generative" precisely to reflect our sense that, although the themes may be common, the products that grow out of these themes—the texts and philosophies that sprout—will often be strikingly different. We do not intend these generative themes to serve as reductionistic specifications of the "essence" of black philosophy; we recognize in them, rather, the seeds from which an astonishing number of different gardens have grown.

The first generative theme constitutive of the black philosophical tradition highlighted herein is the idea that the identity of the individual is never separable from the sociocultural environment. Identity is not some Cartesian abstraction grounded in a solipsistic self-consciousness; rather, it is constructed in and at least partially by a set of shared beliefs, patterns of behavior, and expectations. In place of Descartes's "I think; therefore I am," we find in this black tradition, "I am because we are; and since we are, therefore I am."[23] If individual identity is grounded in social interaction, in the life of the community, then that individual's good life is inseparable from the successful functioning of his or her society. Hence, in this black philosophical tradition, ethics and moral reflection tend to focus much more on collective structures than on individual decision-making.

The second generative theme we find recurring through the history of this black intellectual tradition is a fundamentally relational conception of reality. In the same way that individuals and communities are inextricably related, so too are all other dimensions of reality. Physical objects, for example, cannot truly be separated from the uses to which they are put, uses that are themselves necessarily essentially human. Nor can such objects be separated from the natural materials of which they are made, from the geographical and temporal references of their existence, or from their specific relations to what, for want of a more accurate term, we might describe as the divine. Dona Richards has captured this theme of black thought, making special reference to its spiritual aspect. "The traditional African view of the universe is as a spiritual whole in which all beings are organically interrelated and interdependent," she writes. "The cosmos is sacred and cannot be objectified. Nature is spirit, not to be exploited. . . . All beings exist in reciprocal relationship to one another; we cannot take without giving. . . . The mode of harmony (rather than control) which prevails does not preclude the ability to struggle. Spirit is primary, yet manifested in material being."[24]

We should note that this relational conception of reality—at least in its explicitly metaphysical and cosmological form—remains pretty much in the background in most of the texts we have chosen for this volume: in effect, this conception provides the metaphysical foundation for much of the philosophical reflection of this black tradition without itself being a central focus of such reflection. A more common dimension of this relational conception found in the texts included here is the remarkable way in which black thinkers such as Frederick Douglass, Frantz Fanon, and Martin Luther King, Jr., have *extended* the notion of community to ground a genuinely universal humanism as opposed to the typically partial humanisms of the European tradition. Thus for these thinkers, all human beings are related, beyond the ties of kinship and community, by bonds of reciprocity founded on the inherent interweaving and interdependence of the world's populations.

The third recurring theme in this tradition of black philosophy is the central importance of religion and religion-based ethics as dominant forms for the fundamentally social expression of core philosophical ideas. This does not mean, to be sure, that no black thinkers in this tradition have self-consciously separated philosophical inquiry from religious belief; far from it.

What it does mean is that religious conceptions of human identity, portrayals of excellence in the community, and expectations concerning the ultimate value of life are themselves powerful sources of philosophical reflection, sources intimating that even social collectives can only be understood properly in relation to realities transcending them. To put this point in another way, the community—which provides the basis for individual identity and serves as the metaphysical ground for interconnectedness—itself includes certain realities that transcend particularities of culture, realities that thereby both extend and transform community.

We suggest that these three generative themes can be seen to give birth to a diverse but coherent tradition of black philosophical thought. Echoing V. Y. Mudimbe's reflections on tradition,[25] we would emphasize that our calling this collection of texts the heart of a tradition is itself an attempt to transform the system of values that currently structures the discipline of philosophy. In highlighting this black tradition, we are encouraging others to take seriously the idea of a tradition of doing philosophy that engages the world in order to *change* it.[26] Moreover, we see in this tradition the flowering of a humanism that places the community rather than the individual at the center and thereby offers us, among other things, a framework for a humanism of the *decentered* human subject. For the black philosophers included in this volume, the primary decentering force has been the social construction of race in the colonial era, and we see their continuing use of the concept of race as a means towards the reclamation of a new sense of identity in these postcolonial, postmodern times. The deconstruction of the colonial concept of race and the reconstruction of the role of race in the postcolonial period—tasks characteristic of many texts included here—together promise new possibilities for thinking about the complex relations between individuals and their (multiple) communities in the troubled times in which we now live.

In articulating some distinctive features of this black philosophical tradition, we must pay attention as well to intra-African history and to the impact of the Arab and European incursions into Africa. The tradition of thought presented in this anthology begins in ancient Egypt (Kemet), and we would suggest that it is likely that philosophy itself begins there. This should come as no surprise for, regardless of the extent of Egypt's influence on Greek philosophy,[27] it is only reasonable to suppose that reflective thought about the primordial questions of being and fundamental realities of the human community would begin where civilization as we define it begins. Archaeological evidence in Africa reveals that philosophical reflection was born at least five thousand years ago in Egypt. In the earliest texts of the Egyptian tradition, the writers, although seeming to be entirely concerned about admission into the afterlife, were "actually articulating a set of values and a code of behaviors by which to live one's life in the world before death,"[28] a code reflected in the concept of *Maat*. As Maulana Karenga asserts, "The Maatian stress on moral social practice is rooted in the assumption that self-actualization of humans is best achieved in *morally grounded* relations with others. . . . The perfectability and authenticity of the human person lie in her/his sociality, i.e., rootedness in social relations and practice. Maatian ethics, like African ethics in general, then, stress the practical dimension."[29]

Cheikh Anta Diop has argued in turn that the leading ideas of Egyptian thought are essentially at one with the fundamental notions of traditional sub-Saharan African thought in general. He traces these ideological connections to issues of environment in what he calls the "first cradle" of civilization. He concludes that there is, thus, "a consistent cultural unity, resulting from similar adaptations to the same material and physical conditions of life,"[30] identifying some of these material conditions as agricultural sedentarism, natural phenomena such as the floods of the Nile Valley, and the general mildness of the physical surroundings of Africa. The philosophical concepts promoted by adaptation to these conditions include, Diop suggests, "a sort of social collectivism, . . . an ideal of peace, of justice, goodness and an optimism which eliminates all notions of guilt or original sin in religious and metaphysical institutions."[31] He goes on to claim that the institutionalization of such values had beneficent consequences for the community without any lessening of individual welfare. "The individual is subordinated to the collectivity," he writes, "since it is on the public welfare that the individual welfare depends: thus private right is subordinated to public right. This does not mean that the individual is a negligible quantity and that the Meridional [i.e., African] civilizations, in contrast to the Northern ones, put little value on human individualities or on human personality."[32] While Diop's claims are controversial and likely to remain so,[33] we believe his work represents a particularly striking challenge to earlier and largely colonial notions of African tradition. We see Diop's challenge as that of encouraging us to consider the possibility of "a different system of values" (in Mudimbe's words) when it comes to thinking about African traditions of thought and culture, and we hope that our readers will approach the Egyptian texts in this collection with a mind open to the possibility of their relevance to the other texts included herein.

Sage/Griot

In an effort to make more concrete our conception of black philosophy, we suggest as an emblem of the black philosopher a composite of the traditional roles of the *sage* and the *griot*.[34] Like the sage or moral teacher, the black philosopher has often assumed a visionary role; looking into dimensions of reality or aspects of ordinary problems not ordinarily experienced, the philosopher offers a fundamentally new redescription. This redescription, in turn, carries elements of a prescriptive critique of the social and intellectual status quo, a critique that itself offers a new vision of the future. As H. Odera Oruka claims, "In a strict sense, a sage has at least two abilities, insight and ethical inspiration. So, a sage is wise, he has insight but he employs this for the ethical betterment of his (her) community."[35] Like the griot, the black philosopher is charged with preserving the cultural memory of his or her people; in the retelling of his or her tradition, however, the philosopher as griot inevitably offers a substantive critique of aspects of the community's situation, aspects that perhaps reflect a degree of forgetfulness of the richness and intellectual power of the community's tradition. Such a critique, of course, itself involves a revisioning of the future, a future in which memory is both preserved and transformed.

What we are suggesting with this image of the black philosopher as sage/griot is that, in the tradition we are exploring here, the black philosophical enterprise has been and continues to be a sophisticated mediation between what Okondo Okolo has powerfully described as *tradition* and *destiny*,[36] a mediation balancing the competing claims of memory and of renewed vision and insight. It is worth emphasizing that this enterprise of intellectual mediation has both a collective and an individual thrust: while the sage/griot's work is essential to the continued smooth functioning of the community, this work of vision, critique, and re-vision provides a model for the lifelong activity of shaping and reshaping individual identity. At the same time, our image of the philosopher as sage/griot resonates with ideas and images found in the oldest philosophical texts of Africa. Thus, the "Memphite Theology"—dating back perhaps to 3000 BCE—asserts that the fundamental and divine reality is in fact speech,[37] and the notions that speech is divine and that gifted speakers—among whom we must include the sage and the griot—are inspired by the divine are notions found in a variety of forms and contexts throughout the history of Africa and the African diaspora.

Inclusions/Exclusions

A team-taught course in black philosophy represented the beginnings of this anthology. Both of us saw sources of wisdom in the work of certain black philosophers that might prove quite valuable in rethinking the lives of individuals in Western societies and in provoking philosophical critiques of the subtle (and not-so-subtle) effects of colonialist and neocolonialist thinking on issues of personal identity and community. At the moment of our course's conception, we thought that the texts we had brought together might challenge students to engage the world and so to engage the ostensible differences among them. We did not, and do not, believe that the inglorious history of violent racism over the last half-thousand years has blinded us to our similarities or has crippled us so as to make us need our own infirmities and those of others. This anthology grows out of and reflects our shared concerns and hopes for a future that might be post-Western, postexploitative, postmodern, postcolonial, and postracist.

We do not intend our editorial selections to be thought of as definitive of a canon for black philosophy. Rather, the texts in this collection are meant to help define and further the ongoing discussion about the nature of black philosophical traditions. Guided by our understanding of philosophy as a discipline of mediation and by our recognition of generative themes linking a rich diversity of texts, we have tried to offer a representative selection of black philosophers and their work, knowing full well that others would choose to constitute a black philosophical tradition in other ways. We ask of our readers only that they approach this anthology in the spirit with which it is offered: we hope this volume may serve as an incitement to new questions and analyses, to new conversations, and to the creation of new philosophical texts.

Notable among texts excluded are those of Plotinus and Augustine, as well as selections from the tradition of Ethiopian Islam. Here we have been guided by our sense that these texts are ultimately more representative of their respective, particular intellectual traditions—Platonism, Christianity, and Islam—than of the African tradition that seems to link the other texts. Again, we have excluded the works of philosophers such as Hountondji, Wiredu, and Appiah, largely because we see their work as constituting a tradition of philosophical method alternative to that which is represented by the figures we have gathered together. Finally, we have tried to sidestep the enormous philosophical literature on ethnophilosophy, "the attempt to explore and systematize the conceptual world of Africa's traditional cultures,"[38] even though the work of many ethnophilosophers and their critics would be consistent with the general tenor of our collection. We trust that readers interested in the ethnophilosophy debate will quickly turn to sources devoted to these issues.[39] Related to the exclusion of ethnophilosophy is our omission of examples of traditional African and diaspora folklore, on the grounds that such texts are not explicitly and self-consciously reflective, although they often embody profound philosophical insights. We have done this reluctantly, recognizing that such an omission reinforces a Western bias in favor of written texts over products of oral traditions. We do not mean to suggest that oral "texts" should be excluded from the realm of philosophy; rather, we think such sources of traditional African thought warrant their own anthology.[40]

Pragmatic concerns have also shaped our choices. For example, we have tried to offer relatively substantial texts from our chosen authors, in part because we hope this anthology might help give new directions to the exciting and even revolutionary debates currently surrounding the question of the nature of philosophy. In general, the shorter the selection, the easier it will be to assimilate it and its contents to some prior conception of a philosophical genre or a "properly" philosophical issue. The longer the selection, the more likely it is that the text's distinctive contribution to the ongoing process of philosophical self-definition will be seen.

In short, we have tried to assemble a collection of texts that shows itself as constituting a tradition of black philosophy. The proof of the pudding here lies in the texts themselves. While we have tried in this introduction to set them in a context, we hope that this anthology will prove useful for those who disagree radically with our interpretation of philosophical trends in Africa and the diaspora.

Beyond our intention to make possible the exploration of the interpretative questions concerning black philosophy discussed in the preceding pages, we hope that this anthology might effect more immediate forms of mediation, in keeping with the spirit of this black philosophical tradition as a mode of doing philosophy that engages the world in order to change it. We suggest that there are at least five different areas of current cultural conflict the intellectual mediation of which might be aided by reflection on the texts included here. (1) These texts should help disabuse representatives of culturally dominant groups of their claims to cultural universality, helping them see that their cultural dominance does no more than mask the particularity of their culture. (2) They should also help both black and non-black people develop ways of approaching questions of homogeneity and heterogeneity within the current black situation in North America. (3) These texts certainly should provide a framework to help black people mediate the reclamation of race and identity. (4) They should, moreover, help to develop new ways of thinking about the current global situation, in which points of conflict appear to configure themselves more and more along lines of color. (5) Finally, the texts included here should help those interested in black philosophical traditions realize that black philosophy is itself becoming more intertextual, thus making the philosophical task one of mediating among varying texts. This growing intertextuality of black philosophy helps ground our claim that these texts constitute something that deserves to be called a tradition. If these selections can help effect, shape, or nurture intellectual mediation at these levels—if they can help build bridges between black and white people, between all American citizens and the black community, between black people and their identities, between peoples of different nations, and between philosophical texts of varying traditions—no further argument in defense of the legitimacy of seeing these texts as constituting a tradition will be necessary.

Finally, we must acknowledge that the act of putting together such an anthology is itself a philosophical gesture: we are quite self-consciously attempting to reclaim and document the memory and vision of some of the greatest black thinkers; we are as well counting on our readers to take our act of reclamation and documentation and use it to help critique existing institutions and practices. The work of critique accomplished, we trust that the inspiration of this centrally important black philosophical tradition may help guide us all to a re-visioned future of authentic emancipation.

[1]Our title comes from an often-cited proverbial phrase formulated by John Mbiti, "I am because we are; and since we are, therefore I am." See John S. Mbiti, *African Religions and Philosophy*, 2d ed. (Oxford: Heinemann, 1989), 141.

[2]This question is put most forcefully in Paulin Hountondji, *African Philosophy: Myth and Reality*, trans. Henri Evans with Jonathan Rée, introduction by Abiola Irele (Bloomington: Indiana University Press, 1983).

[3]This skepticism constitutes one of Kwame Anthony Appiah's themes in *In My Father's House: Africa in the Philosophy of Culture* (New York: Oxford University Press, 1992). For a stimulating assessment of the issues involved here, see also Lucius Outlaw, "African, African American, Africana Philosophy," *The Philosophical Forum* 24, nos. 1–3 (fall–spring 1992–1993): 63–93.

[4]Appiah, *In My Father's House*, especially 3–46.

[5]William R. Jones, "The Legitimacy and Necessity of Black Philosophy: Some Preliminary Considerations," *Philosophical Forum* 9, nos. 2–3 (winter–spring 1977–1978): 149–60.

[6]Ibid., 151.

[7]Ibid., 155.

[8]Ibid., 158.

[9]Appiah, *In My Father's House*, 28–46.

[10]Ibid., viii.

[11]Jacques Maquet, *Africanity: The Cultural Unity of Black Africa*, trans. Joan R. Rayfield (New York: Oxford University Press, 1972), 8–10.

[12]That the conceptual framework of colonialism remains an integral feature of postcolonial discourse is but one of the themes in Edward W. Said, *Culture and Imperialism* (New York: Knopf, 1993).

[13]Maquet, *Africanity*, 10.

[14]Kwame Nkrumah, *Consciencism: Philosophy and Ideology for Decolonization and Development with Particular Reference to the African Revolution* (New York: Monthly Review Press, 1964), 3.

[15]Ibid., 2.

[16]V. Y. Mudimbe incisively makes this point with regard to twentieth century African philosophy, noting that "[m]odern African thought seems somehow to be basically a product of the West" and that "[t]he conceptual framework of African thinking has been both a mirror and a consequence of the experience of European hegemony. . . ." See V. Y. Mudimbe, *The Invention of Africa: Gnosis, Philosophy, and the Order of Knowledge* (Bloomington: Indiana University Press, 1988), 185.

[17]See Mudimbe's review of the sources for Ethiopian philosophy in *The Invention of Africa*, 201–3.

[18]Our claim here remains controversial. For the claim that the Abrahamic religious traditions themselves owe much to traditional African thought, see Yosef ben-Jochanan, *African Origins of the Major Western Religions* (New York: Alkebu-Lan Press, 1970); Yosef ben-Jochanan, Modupe Oduyoye, and Charles Finch, eds., *African Origins of the Major World Religions* (London: Karnak Press, 1988); and, most recently, Paul Boyd, *The African Origin of Christianity*, vol. 1 (London: Karia Press, 1991).

[19]See Appiah, *In My Father's House* and J. E. Wiredu, *Philosophy and an African Culture* (Cambridge: Cambridge University Press, 1980); for Appiah's most explicit defense of the tradition of Anglo-American conceptual analysis, see K. Anthony Appiah, "African-American Philosophy?," *Philosophical Forum* 24, nos. 1–3 (fall–spring 1992–1993): 11–34.

[20]See Hountondji, *African Philosophy*.

[21]Our notion of "generative themes" has its origins in Paulo Freire's discussion of "thematic universes" and "generative themes" in his *Pedagogy of the Oppressed*, trans. Myra Bergman Ramos (New York: Continuum, 1970), 86–101.

[22]See Appiah, *In My Father's House*, 24–26, and Hountondji, *African Philosophy*, especially 56–62 and 170–83.

[23]Mbiti, *African Religions and Philosophy*, 141.

[24]Dona Richards, "European Mythology: The Ideology of 'Progress,'" in Molefi K. Asante and Abdulai S. Vandi, eds., *Contemporary Black Thought: Alternative Analyses in Social and Behavioral Science* (Beverly Hills: Sage, 1980), 76–77.

[25]See Mudimbe, *The Invention of Africa*, 191–92; in his discussion of Jahn and the relation between tradition and history, Mudimbe goes so far as to claim that "[h]istory is a legend, an invention of the present. It is both a memory and a reflection of our present" (195).

[26]Although resonating with the eleventh of Marx's "Theses on Feuerbach"—"The philosophers have only *interpreted* the world, in various ways; the point, however, is to *change* it"—this tradition clearly offers an alternative notion of the relation between the individual and the community to that found in most marxist traditions. For the text of the "Theses," see Robert C. Tucker, ed., *The Marx-Engels Reader*, 2d ed. (New York: Norton, 1978), 143–45.

[27]Fundamental references for this very controversial issue include: George G. M. James, *Stolen Legacy* (New York: Philosophical Library, 1954), Henry Olela, "The African Foundations of Greek Philosophy," in Richard A. Wright, ed., *African Philosophy: An Introduction*, 3d ed. (Lanham, MD: University Press of America, 1984), 77–92; Cheikh Anta Diop, *Civilization or Barbarism: An Authentic Anthropology*, trans. Yaa-Lengi Meema Ngemi, eds. Harold J. Salemson and Marjolijn de Jager (Brooklyn: Lawrence Hill Books, 1991); Théophile Obenga, "African Philosophy of the Pharaonic Period (2780–330 B.C.)," in Ivan Van Sertima, ed., *Egypt Revisited* (New Brunswick: Transaction, 1989), 286–324; and Martin Bernal, *Black Athena: The Afroasiatic Roots of Classical Civilization*, 2 vols. thus far (New Brunswick: Rutgers University Press, 1987, 1991).

[28]Asa G. Hilliard, III, Larry Williams, and Nia Damali, eds., *The Teachings of Ptahhotep: The Oldest Book in the World* (Atlanta: Blackwood Press, 1987), 12.

[29]*The Book of Coming Forth by Day: The Ethics of the Declarations of Innocence*, trans. and commentary by Maulana Karenga (Los Angeles: University of Sankore Press, 1990), 32–33.

[30]Cheikh Anta Diop, *Black Africa*, trans. Harold Salemson (Westport, CT: Lawrence

Hill, 1978), 7. Diop's position is clearly more "unanimistic" than is that of Maquet in *Africanity.*

[31]Cheikh Anta Diop, *The Cultural Unity of Black Africa: The Domains of Patriarchy and of Matriarchy in Classical Antiquity,* introduction by John Henrik Clarke, afterword by James G. Spady (Chicago: Third World Press, 1978), 195.

[32]Ibid., 144.

[33]On Diop, see Appiah, "African-American Philosophy?," 25–28, and *In My Father's House,* 101–2.

[34]These roles are reflected as well in Maulana Karenga's discussion of the *Seba* or moral teacher in ancient Egyptian thought and in Henry Oruka's concept of the sage in traditional African culture; see, respectively, Maulana Karenga, "Towards a Sociology of Maatian Ethics: Literature and Context," in Van Sertima, *Egypt Revisited,* 352–95; Henry Odera Oruka, "Sagacity in African Philosophy," in Tsenay Serequeberhan, ed., *African Philosophy: The Essential Readings* (New York: Paragon House, 1991), 47–62; and H. Odera Oruka, ed., *Sage Philosophy: Indigenous Thinkers and Modern Debate on African Philosophy* (Leiden: E. J. Brill, 1990).

[35]Oruka, *Sage Philosophy,* xxvii.

[36]Okondo Okolo, "Tradition and Destiny: Horizons of an African Philosophical Hermeneutics," in Serequeberhan, *African Philosophy,* 201–10.

[37]"The Memphite Theology," in Miriam Lichtheim, ed., *Ancient Egyptian Literature: A Book of Readings,* 2 vols. (Berkeley: University of California Press, n.d.), 2:51–57. For an introduction to the context of this difficult text, see Théophile Obenga, "African Philosophy of the Pharaonic Period," 309–16.

[38]Appiah, *In My Father's House,* 94.

[39]Serequeberhan's *African Philosophy* offers many of the important recent articles in this debate, while Appiah's review of the issues in *In My Father's House* is exemplary.

[40]For an important consideration of the special issues involved in working with oral traditions in philosophy, see Oruka, *Sage Philosophy.*

A F R I C A

It is in the texts from Africa included here that the three generative themes discussed in our introduction are most clearly articulated. From the beginnings of recorded African thought in *The Book of Coming Forth by Day* (better known as the Egyptian *Book of the Dead*) to the stirring words of Nelson Mandela, there is a repeated emphasis on the relation between the individual and his/her community. This emphasis is grounded in turn in an ontological framework stressing a fundamentally relational conception of reality. This ontological conception simultaneously positions the human being in a network of relationships with all aspects of the world and situates his/her community in a further network of relations (including relations to God or gods) that transcend the particularities of any culture. These texts can be seen, then, to outline and develop a sophisticated version of humanism—what might be called relational humanism—in which the human being is essentially a web of relationships both social and cosmic. We suggest that this distinctively African take on humanism offers answers to the problem of grounding ethical commitments faced by postmodern theories of the decentered human subject.

In "The Declarations of Innocence," a text that may represent the first stage of a shift towards the popularization of the tenets of Kemetian (Egyptian) ethics and religion, we find a particular emphasis on truth, righteousness, and justice. Appearing here ostensibly as testimonies meant to bolster the deceased's case for eternal life, the "declarations" effectively define a set of standards for moral conduct in the community. Intimating obligations both to the gods and to other people, the declarations offer a relatively concrete presentation of the concept of Maat, the code of conduct for life in the community that assures each individual a place in the eternal network of the universe after his/her death. It is precisely this notion of Maat that is spelled out with greater richness in *The Teachings of Ptahhotep*, one of the earliest ancient Kemetian "books of instruction" apparently articulating a moral code to be taught to the masses. Central to the framework of this text is the valorization of principles of egalitarianism, peace, harmony, sharing, deliberate speech, and humility. Taken together, these principles constitute the framework of a moral community in which relationships—between classes, between women and men, and between people and gods—make up the substance of human life.

A similar vision of moral community is found in the reflections of Paul Mbuya Akoko (ca. 1891–1981), the moral/spiritual elder of the Luo people (in what is now Kenya). We include the interview with Akoko to offer something of a transition between ancient African thought and the twentieth-century texts that make up the bulk of our African selections, although we realize that—given the parameters of this anthology—there is simply no way for us at present to provide significant documentation of precolonial philosophical traditions in Africa. Akoko clearly articulates ways in which one system of traditional African wisdom parallels leading ideas of our Kemetian texts, while at the same time he is working in a colonial/postcolonial context that requires him to take into account the presence of Europeans. Akoko is but one of many traditional African sages whose philosophical work exists only in oral form, and we hope this brief interview gives our readers a sense of the philosophical richness of African oral traditions.

The next three texts, written by leaders of three newly independent African nations—Léopold Sédar Senghor of Senegal, Kwame Nkrumah of Ghana, and Julius Nyerere of Tanzania—provide three distinctive approaches to the problem of theorizing community in the context of the economic and cultural constraints of the modern nation state. In his essay, "Negritude: A Humanism of the Twentieth Century," Senghor elaborates a profoundly relational worldview echoing earlier African thought. Moreover, he explicitly uses this worldview to ground and articulate a form of humanism adequate to meet the collapse of traditional Western versions of humanism in the twentieth century. For Senghor, negritude is neither a racialist creed nor evidence of African inferiority; rather, it is a form of self-confirmation, a notion of African personality that brings feeling and intuition to the incomplete notion of rationality found in Europe. Centering his theory in traditional African culture with its complex relationships binding individual and community, Senghor encourages an enlarged dialogue and reciprocity between Africans and Europeans, suggesting that contemporary humanism must ground itself in interdependency.

Kwame Nkrumah, too, endorses a form of humanism, but he takes as his fundamental point of departure the present conflicts in the African conscience. In his essay "Consciencism," Nkrumah shows how a social revolution can simultaneously revive traditional African notions of egalitarianism and foster the integration of Christian and Islamic elements into a postcolonial concept of African identity. He argues that the basic ethical position of humanism and socialism—the Kantian claim that all people are ends in themselves and not simply means—is itself congruent with traditional African ideas that human equality proceeds naturally from the unity and interdependence of everything making up the universe.

Julius Nyerere advocates yet another form of socialist humanism, but it is one grounded in the traditional notion of *ujamaa* or "familyhood." Seeing the extended family as the basic structure of African society, he articulates a vision of socialism that avoids the class conflict models of European socialist thinkers. Socialism is, rather, "an attitude of mind," an ethos of avoiding domination and fostering hospitality. Nyerere maintains that this ethos effectively undermines the conflictual assumptions underlying the development of European theories of both capitalism and socialism.

While Senghor, Nkrumah, and Nyerere came to their positions of power through relatively peaceful processes of political transition, Amilcar Cabral served as the leader of the armed struggle that eventually—only after Cabral's assassination—liberated the nation of Guinea-Bissau from Portuguese rule. Cabral focuses here on the ways in which the armed struggle for liberation serves to construct postcolonial African identities. While Cabral calls famously for a "return to the source" of African tradition, he also notes that the very nature of armed struggle effectively serves as a critique of that very call. This is particularly the case for the African petite bourgeoisie, which, Cabral argues, must come to identify with the people through joint struggle but can only accomplish this successfully to the extent that the masses retain their own essentially anticolonial identity. The role of culture, then, is to preserve African identity in the face of the psychological and material ravages of colonialism, but at the same time Cabral notes that traditional cultural forms must not be used by the African bourgeoisie to consolidate their class privilege.

If Senghor sees the notion of negritude as completing the one-sided rationality of European culture by bringing to it distinctively African cultural capacities for feeling and intuition, the Nobel Prize–winning author Wole Soyinka sees the theory of negritude as once again playing into the hands of precisely the one-sided logic that it is meant to replace. Soyinka is in strong agreement with the general principle of race retrieval underlying the negritude movement, but he argues with particular force that Senghor and other theorists of negritude make the fateful error of accepting a stereotypically European analysis of both humankind and society, thereby paving the way ironically for a negritude-based justification for colonialism. For Soyinka, race retrieval must be accomplished on African terms, and African civilization must stand as a full-fledged partner with Europe in Senghor's civilization of the universal.

In "Feminism and Revolution," Awa Thiam puts comparatively little emphasis on traditional worldviews of African societies; rather, she is particularly concerned to register the impact of European slavery and colonialism on colonial and postcolonial African social structures. Arguing that African women have suffered from "a double domination, a double enslavement," Thiam stresses that patriarchal social structures—whether or not they are of traditional African origin—are simply incompatible with egalitarian ideals of community, and she calls for a revolution to achieve women's economic and political independence, an independence that would win for women an identity and dignity independent of the acts of men.

Our selection of texts from Africa ends with a speech given by Nelson Mandela, the leader of the African National Congress, just two weeks after his highly publicized release from a prison stay of more than a quarter of a century. Echoing many of the texts included here, Mandela explores a number of dimensions of the theme that the self is inseparable from its community. For him, the key political and social implication of this theme is the goal of a nonracial society for all, a society built on fundamentally democratic structures. Emphasizing the unity and interdependence of a number of different groups in the historical struggle within South Africa, Mandela argues that no particular group should be considered the enemy; oppression is the enemy. At the same time, Mandela urges his audience to maintain a critical perspective on the practices and trappings of traditional culture: in the spirit of Nkrumah and Cabral, he warns of the ways in which traditional modes of thought can be used to generate and perpetuate "neocolonial" (to borrow Nkrumah's term) versions of the very structures of colonial oppression in the new world of postcolonial Africa.

In short, each of these ten texts contributes to a tradition of African thought that posits the question of the relationship between the individual and her/his community as one central to the philosophical enterprise. The indispensability of community for self-realization, the centrality of an ethics that reaches beyond individual satisfaction, and the encompassing framework of a relational worldview are all themes that resonate through these texts. We suggest that these texts offer an eloquent and incisive critique of the fragmentation and alienation of European modernism. The texts from the twentieth century develop a variety of reconfigurations, in the face of the spiritual and material decimation of colonialism, of the African tradition that "I am because we are."

The Declarations of Innocence (ca. 1500 B.C.E.)

Plate XXXI

(1) Ani saith: "Hail, thou whose strides are long, who comest forth from Annu, I have not done iniquity."

(2) "Hail, thou who art embraced by flame, who comest forth from Kher-āba, I have not robbed with violence."

(3) "Hail, Fenṭiu, who comest forth from Khemennu, I have not stolen."

(4) "Hail, Devourer of the Shade, who comest forth from Qernet, I have done no murder; I have done no harm."

(5) "Hail, Nehau, who comest forth from Re-stau, I have not defrauded offerings."

(6) "Hail, god in the form of two lions, who comest forth from heaven, I have not minished oblations."

(7) "Hail, thou whose eyes are of fire, who comest forth from Saut, I have not plundered the god."

(8) "Hail, thou Flame, which comest and goest, I have spoken no lies."

(9) "Hail, Crusher of bones, who comest forth from Suten-ḥenen, I have not snatched away food."

(10) "Hail, thou who shootest forth the Flame, who comest forth from Het-Ptaḥ-ka, I have not caused pain."

(11) "Hail, Qerer, who comest forth from Amentet, I have not committed fornication."

(12) "Hail, thou whose face is turned back, who comest forth from thy hiding place, I have not caused shedding of tears."

(13) "Hail, Bast, who comest forth from the secret place, I have not dealt deceitfully."

(14) "Hail, thou whose legs are of fire, who comest forth out of the darkness, I have not transgressed."

Reprinted from *The Book of the Dead: The Papyrus of Ani in the British Museum,* Egyptian text with interlinear transliteration, translation, introduction, and notes by E. A. Wallis Budge (London: Trustees of the British Museum, 1895), 347–49.

(15) "Hail, Devourer of Blood, who comest forth from the block of slaughter, I have not acted guilefully."

(16) "Hail, Devourer of the inward parts, who comest forth from Mābet, I have not laid waste the ploughed land."

(17) "Hail, Lord of Right and Truth, who comest forth from the city of Right and Truth, I have not been an eavesdropper."

(18) "Hail, thou who dost stride backwards, who comest forth from the city of Bast, I have not set my lips in motion [against any man]."

(19) "Hail, Sertiu, who comest forth from Annu, I have not been angry and wrathful except for a just cause."

(20) "Hail, thou being of two-fold wickedness, who comest forth from Ati(?), I have not defiled the wife of any man."

(21) "Hail, thou two-headed serpent, who comest forth from the torture chamber, I have not defiled the wife of any man."

(22) "Hail, thou who dost regard what is brought unto thee, who comest forth from Pa-Amsu, I have not polluted myself."

(23) "Hail, thou Chief of the mighty, who comest forth from Amentet, I have not caused terror."

(24) "Hail, thou Destroyer, who comest forth from Ḳesiu, I have not transgressed."

(25) "Hail, thou who orderest speech, who comest forth from Urit, I have not burned with rage."

(26) "Hail, thou Babe, who comest forth from Uab, I have not stopped my ears against the words of Right and Truth."

(27) "Hail, Kenemti, who comest forth from Kenemet, I have not worked grief."

(28) "Hail, thou who bringest thy offering, I have not acted with insolence."

(29) "Hail, thou who orderest speech, who comest forth from Unaseṭ, I have not stirred up strife."

(30) "Hail, Lord of faces, who comest forth from Netchfet, I have not judged hastily."

(31) "Hail, Sekheriu, who comest forth from Utten, I have not been an eavesdropper."

(32) "Hail, Lord of the two horns, who comest forth from Saïs, I have not multiplied words exceedingly."

(33) "Hail, Nefer-Tmu, who comest forth from Het-Ptaḥ-ka, I have done neither harm nor ill."

Plate XXXII

(34) "Hail, Tmu in thine hour, who comest forth from Tattu, I have never cursed the king."

(35) "Hail, thou who workest with thy will, who comest forth from Tebu, I have never fouled the water."

(36) "Hail, thou bearer of the sistrum, who comest forth from Nu, I have not spoken scornfully."

(37) "Hail, thou who makest mankind to flourish, who comest forth from Saïs, I have never cursed God."

(38) "Hail, Neheb-ka, who comest forth from thy hiding place, I have not stolen."

(39) "Hail, Neheb-nefert, who comest forth from thy hiding place, I have not defrauded the offerings of the gods."

(40) "Hail, thou who dost set in order the head, who comest forth from thy shrine, I have not plundered the offerings to the blessed dead."

(41) "Hail, thou who bringest thy arm, who comest forth from the city of Maāti, I have not filched the food of the infant, neither have I sinned against the God of my native town."

(42) "Hail, thou whose teeth are white, who comest forth from Ta-she, I have not slaughtered with evil intent the cattle of the god."

✿ The Teachings of Ptahhotep
(ca. 2400 B.C.E.)

These are instructions by the Mayor of the City, who is also the Vizier. His name is Ptahhotep and he serves under Pharoah Assa, who lives for all eternity. The Mayor of the City, Vizier Ptahhotep, addressed the Supreme Divinity, the Deity, as follows:

> God upon the two crocodiles (reference to Heru, who is sometimes shown standing on two crocodiles). My God, the process of aging brings senility. My mind decays and forgetfulness of the things of yesterday has already begun. Feebleness has come and weakness grows. Childlike, one sleeps all day. The eyes are dim and the ears are becoming deaf. The strength is being sapped. The mouth has grown silent and does not speak. The bones ache through and through. Good things now seem evil. The taste is gone. What old age does to people in evil is everything. The nose is clogged and does not breathe. It is painful even to stand or to sit. May your servant be authorized to use the status that old age affords, to teach the hearers, so as to tell them the words of those who have listened to the ways of our ancestors, and of those who have listened to the Gods. May I do this for you, so that strife may be banned from among our people, and so that the Two Shores may serve you?

Then the majesty of the Deity said to Ptahhotep, go ahead and instruct him in the Ancient Wisdom. May he become a model for the children of the great. May obedience enter into him, and may he be devoted to the one who speaks to him. No one is born wise.

And so begins the formulation of Mdw Nfr, *good speech*, to be spoken by the Prince, the Count, God's beloved, the eldest son of the Pharoah, the son of his body, Mayor of the City and Vizier, Ptahhotep, who instructs the ignorant in the knowledge and in the standards of *good speech*. It will profit those who hear. It will be a loss to those who transgress. Ptahhotep began to speak to "Pharoah's son" (to posterity).

Reprinted from Asa G. Hilliard III, Larry Williams, and Nia Damali, eds., *The Teachings of Ptahhotep: The Oldest Book in the World* (Atlanta: Blackwood Press, 1987), 16–37. Reprinted by permission of Asa G. Hilliard III.

1. Do not be proud and arrogant with your knowledge. Consult and converse with the ignorant and the wise, for the limits of art are not reached. No artist ever possesses that perfection to which he should aspire. *Good speech* is more hidden than green stone (emeralds), yet it may be found among maids at the grindstones.

2. If you meet a disputant in the heat of action, one who is more powerful than you, simply fold your arms and bend your back. To confront him will not make him agree with you. Pay no attention to his *evil speech*. If you do not confront him while he is raging, people will call him an ignoramus. Your self-control will be the match for his evil utterances.

3. If you meet a disputant in action, one who is your equal, one who is on your level, you will overcome him by being silent while he is speaking evilly. There will be much talk among those who hear, and your name will be held in high regard among the great.

4. If you meet a disputant in action who is a poor man and who is not your equal, do not attack him because he is weak. Leave him alone. He will confound himself. Do not answer him just so that you can relieve your own heart. Do not vent yourself against your opponent. Wretched is he who injures a poor man. If you ignore him, listeners will wish to do what you want. You will beat him through their reproof.

5. If you are a man who leads, a man who controls the affairs of many, then seek the most perfect way of performing your responsibility so that your conduct will be blameless. Great is Maat (truth, justice, and righteousness). It is everlasting. Maat has been unchanged since the time of Asar. To create obstacles to the following of laws is to open a way to a condition of violence. The transgressor of laws is punished, although the greedy person overlooks this. Baseness may obtain riches, yet crime never lands its wares on the shore. In the end only Maat lasts. Man says, "Maat is my father's ground."

6. Do not scheme against people. God will punish accordingly; If a man says, "I shall live by scheming," he will lack bread for his mouth. If a man says, "I will be rich," he will have to say, "My cleverness has trapped me." If he says, "I will trap for myself," he will not be able to say, "I trapped for my profit." If a man says, "I will rob someone," he will end by being given to a stranger. People's schemes do not prevail. God's command is what prevails. Therefore, live in the midst of peace. What God gives comes by itself.

7. If you are one among guests at the table of a person who is more powerful than you, take what that person gives just as it is set before you. Look at what is before you. Don't stare at your host. Don't speak to him until he asks. One does not know what may displease him. Speak when he has spoken to you. Then your words will please the heart. The man who has plenty of the means of existence acts as his *Ka* (vital force) commands. He will give food to those who he favors. It is the Ka that makes his hand stretch out. The great man gives to the chosen man; thus, eating is under the direction of God. It is a fool who complains about it.

8. If you are a person of trust sent by one great person to another great person, be careful to stick to the essence of the message that you were

asked to transmit. Give the message exactly as he gave it to you. Guard against provocative speech, which makes one great person angry with another. Just keep to the truth. Do not exceed it. However, even though there may have been an outburst in the message, you should not repeat it. Do not malign anyone, great or small; the Ka abhors it.

9. If you plow and if there is growth in your field and God lets it prosper in your hand, don't boast to your neighbor. One has great respect for the silent person. A person of character is a person of wealth. If that person robs, he or she is like a crocodile in the middle of the waters. If God gives you children, don't impose on one who has no children. Neither should you decry or brag about having your own children, for there is many a father who has grief and many a mother with children who is less content than another. It is the lonely whom God nurtures while the family man prays for a follower.

10. If you are poor, then serve a person of worth so that your conduct may be well with God. Do not bring up the fact that he was once poor. Do not be arrogant towards him just because you know about his former state. Respect him now for his position of authority. As for fortune, it obeys its own law and that is her will. It is God's gift. It is God who makes him worthy and who protects him while he sleeps, or who can turn away from him.

11. Follow your heart as long as you live. Do no more than is required. Do not shorten the time of "follow the heart," since that offends the Ka. Don't waste time on daily cares over and beyond providing for your household. When wealth finally comes, then follow your heart. Wealth does no good if you are glum.

12. If you are a wise man, train up a son who will be pleasing to God. If he is straight and takes after you, take good care of him. Do everything that is good for him. He is your son; your Ka begot him. Don't withdraw your heart from him. But an offspring can make trouble. If your son strays and neglects your council and disobeys all that is said, with his mouth spouting evil speech, then punish him for all his talk. God will hate him who crosses you. His guilt was determined in the womb. He who God makes boatless cannot cross the water.

13. If you are a guard in the storehouse, stand or sit rather than leave your post and trespass into someone else's place. Follow this rule from the first. Never leave your post, even when fatigued. Keen is the face to him who enters announced, and spacious is the seat of him who has been asked to come in. The storehouse has fixed rules. All behavior is strictly by the rule. Only a God can penetrate the secure warehouse where the rules are followed even by privileged persons.

14. If you are among the people, then gain your supporters by building trust. The trusted man is one who does not speak the first thing that comes to mind; and he will become a leader. A man of means has a good name, and his face is benign. People will praise him even without his knowledge. On the other hand, he whose heart obeys his belly asks for contempt of himself in the place of love. His heart is naked. His body is unanointed. The great-hearted is a gift of God. He who is ruled by his appetite belongs to the enemy.

15. Report the thing that you were commissioned to report without error. Give your advice in the high council. If you are fluent in your speech, it will not be hard for you to report. Nor will anyone say of you, "Who is he to know this?" As to the authorities, their affairs will fail if they punish you for speaking truth. They should be silent upon hearing the report that you have rendered as you have been told.

16. If you are a man who leads, a man whose authority reaches widely, then you should do perfect things, those which posterity will remember. Don't listen to the words of flatterers or to words that puff you up with pride and vanity.

17. If you are a person who judges, listen carefully to the speech of one who pleads. Don't stop the person from telling you everything that they had planned to tell you. A person in distress wants to pour out his or her heart, even more than they want their case to be won. If you are one who stops a person who is pleading, that person will say, "Why does he reject my plea?" Of course not all that one pleads for can be granted, but a good hearing soothes the heart. The means for getting a true and clear explanation is to listen with kindness.

18. If you want friendship to endure in the house that you enter, the house of a master, of a brother, or of a friend, then in whatever place you enter, beware of approaching the women there. Unhappy is the place where this is done. Unwelcome is he who intrudes on them. A thousand men are turned away from their good because of a short moment that is like a dream, and then that moment is followed by death that comes from having known that dream. Anyone who encourages you to take advantage of the situation gives you poor advice. When you go to do it, your heart says no. If you are one who fails through the lust of women, then no affair of yours can prosper.

19. If you want to have perfect conduct, to be free from every evil, then above all guard against the vice of greed. Greed is a grievous sickness that has no cure. There is no treatment for it. It embroils fathers, mothers, and the brothers of the mother. It parts the wife from the husband. Greed is a compound of all the evils. It is a bundle of all hateful things. That person endures whose rule is rightness, who walks a straight line, for that person will leave a legacy by such behavior. On the other hand, the greedy has no tomb.

20. Do not be greedy in the division of things. Do not covet more than your share. Don't be greedy towards your relatives. A mild person has a greater claim than the harsh one. Poor is the person who forgets his relatives. He is deprived of their company. Even a little bit of what is wanted will turn a quarreler into a friendly person.

21. When you prosper and establish your home, love your wife with ardor. Then fill her belly and clothe her back. Caress her. Give her ointments to soothe her body. Fulfill her wishes for as long as you live. She is a fertile field for her husband. Do not be brutal. Good manners will influence her better than force. Do not contend with her in the courts. Keep her from the need to resort to outside powers. Her eye is her storm when she gazes. It is by such treatment that she will be compelled to stay in your house.

22. Help your friends with things that you have, for you have these things by the grace of God. If you fail to help your friends, one will say you have a selfish Ka. One plans for tomorrow, but you do not know what tomorrow will bring. The right soul is the soul by which one is sustained. If you do praiseworthy deeds, your friends will say "welcome" in your time of need.

23. Don't repeat slander, nor should you even listen to it. It is the spouting of the hot-bellied. Just report a thing that has been observed, not something that has been heard secondhand. If it is something negligible, don't even say anything. He who is standing before you will recognize your worth. Slander is like a terrible dream against which one covers the face.

24. If you are a man of worth who sits at the council of a leader, concentrate on being excellent. Your silence is much better than boasting. Speak when you know that you have a solution. It is the skilled person who should speak when in council. Speaking is harder than all other work. The one who understands this makes speech a servant.

25. If you are mighty and powerful then gain respect through knowledge and through your gentleness of speech. Don't order things except as it is fitting. The one who provokes others gets into trouble. Don't be haughty lest you be humbled. But also don't be mute lest you be chided. When you answer one who is fuming, turn your face and control yourself. The flame of the hot-hearted sweeps across everything. But he who steps gently, his path is a paved road. He who is agitated all day has no happy moments, but he who amuses himself all day can't keep his fortune.

26. Do not disturb a great man or distract his attention when he is occupied, trying to understand his task. When he is thus occupied, he strips his body through the love of what he does. Love for the work they do brings men closer to God. These are the people who succeed in what they do.

27. Teach the great what is useful to them. Be an aid to the great before the people. If you let your knowledge impress your leader, your sustenance from him will then come from his soul. As his favorite's belly is filled, so will your back be clothed, and his help will be there to sustain you. For your leader whom you love and who lives by useful knowledge in turn will give you good support. Thus will the love of you endure in his belly. He is a soul who loves to listen.

28. If you are an official of high standing, and you are commissioned to satisfy the many, then hold to a straight line. When you speak, don't lean to one side or to the other. Beware lest someone complain, saying to the judges, "He has distorted things," and then your very deeds will turn into a judgment of you.

29. If you are angered by a misdeed, then lean toward a man on account of his rightness. Pass over the misdeed and don't remember it, since God was silent to you on the first day of your misdeed.

30. If you are great after having been humble, if you have gained your wealth after having been poor and then go to a town that you know and that knows your former condition, don't put your trust in your newly acquired wealth, which has come to you as a gift of God. If you do, one day someone there who is poor may very well overtake you.

31. Accept the authority of your leaders; then your house will endure in its wealth. Your rewards will come from the right place. Wretched is he who opposes his leader. One lives as long as he is mild. Baring your arm does not hurt it. Do not plunder your neighbor's house or steal the goods of one who is near you, lest he denounce you before you are even heard. One who is argumentative is a mindless person. If he is also known as an aggressor, then that hostile man will have trouble in the neighborhood.

32. Be circumspect in matters of sexual relations.

33. If you examine the character of a friend, don't ask other people; approach your friend. Deal with him alone, so as not to suffer from his anger. You may argue with him after a little while. You may test his heart in conversation. If what he has seen escapes him, if he does something that annoys you, stay friendly with him and do not attack. Be restrained and don't answer him with hostility. Do not leave him and do not attack him. His time will not fail to come. He cannot escape his fate.

34. Be generous as long as you live. What leaves the storehouse does not return. It is the food in the storehouse that one must share that is coveted. One whose belly is empty becomes an accuser. One who is deprived becomes an opponent. Therefore, do not have an accuser or an opponent as a neighbor. Your kindness to your neighbors will be a memorial to you for years after you satisfy their needs.

35. Know your friends and then you prosper. Don't be mean towards your friends. They are like a watered field and greater than any material riches you may have, for what belongs to one belongs to another. The character of one who is well-born should be a profit to him. Good nature is a memorial.

36. Punish firmly and chastise soundly; then repression of crime becomes an example. But punishment except for crime will turn the complainer into an enemy.

37. If you take for a wife a good-time woman who is joyful and who is well-known in the town, if she is fickle and seems to live for the moment, do not reject her. Let her eat. The joyful person brings happiness.

If you listen to my sayings, all of your affairs will go forward. Their value resides in their truth. The memory of these sayings goes on in the speech of men and women because of the worth of their precepts. If every word is carried on, they will not perish in this land. If advice is given for the good, the great will speak accordingly. This is a matter of teaching a person to speak to posterity. He or she who hears it becomes a master hearer. It is good to speak to posterity. Posterity will listen.

If an example is set by him or her who leads, he or she will be beneficent forever, his wisdom lasting for all time. The wise person feeds the Ka with what endures, so that it is happy with that person on earth. The wise is known by his or her wisdom. The great is known by his or her good actions. The heart of the wise matches his or her tongue and his or her lips are straight when he or she speaks. The wise have eyes that are made to see and ears that are made to hear what will profit the offspring. The wise person who acts with Maat is free of falsehood and disorder.

Useful is hearing to a son who hears. If hearing enters the hearer, then the hearer becomes a listener. Hearing well is speaking well. Useful is hearing to one who hears. Hearing is better than everything else. It creates good will. How good it is for a son to understand his father's words. That son will reach old age through those words.

He who hears is beloved of God. He whom God hates does not hear. The heart makes of its owner a hearer or a non-hearer. Man's heart is his life, prosperity, and health. The hearer is one who hears what is said. He who loves to hear is one who acts on what is said. How good it is for a son to listen to his father. How happy is he to whom it is said, "Your son is a master of hearing." The hearer of whom this is said is well-endowed indeed and is honored by his father. That hearer's remembrance is in the mouth of the living, those who are on earth and those who will be.

If a man's son accepts his father's words, then no plan of his will go wrong. So teach your son to be a hearer, one who will be valued by the officials, one who will guide his speech by what he has been told, one who is regarded as a hearer. This son will excel and his deeds will stand out, while failure will follow those who do not hear. The wise wakes up early, to his lasting gain, while the fool is hard-pressed.

The fool who does not hear, he can do nothing at all. He looks at ignorance and sees knowledge. He looks at harmfulness and sees usefulness. He does everything that one detests and is blamed for it every day. He lives on the things by which one dies. His food is evil speech. His sort is known to the officials who say, "There goes a living death every day." One ignores the things that he does because of his many daily troubles.

A son who hears is a follower of Heru. It will go well with him when he has heard. When he is old and has reached the period where he is venerated, then he will speak likewise to his own children, renewing then the teachings of his father.

Every man teaches as he acts. He will speak to the children so that they will speak to their children. He will set an example and not give offense. So if justice stands firm, your children will live. As to the first child who gets into trouble, when people see it, they will say about the child, "That is just like him," and they will also say when they even hear a rumor about the child, "That is just like him, too."

To see everyone is to satisfy the many. Any riches that you have are useless without the many. Don't say something and then take it back. Don't put one thing in place of another. Beware of releasing the restraints in you, lest the wise man say, "Listen, if you want to endure in the mouth of the hearers, speak after you have mastered the craft." If you speak to good purpose, all your affairs will be in place.

Conceal your heart. Control your mouth. Then you will be known among the officials. Be quite exact before your leader. Act so that no one will say to him, "He is the son of that one."

Be deliberate when you speak so as to say things that count. Then the officials who listen will say, "How good is the thing that comes from his mouth." Act so that your leader will say of you, "How good is he whom his father has taught. When he came forth from his body, he told him all that was in his mind, and he does even more than he was told."

The good son is the gift of God and exceeds what is told him by his leader. He will do right when his heart is straight. As you succeed me, sound in body, a Pharoah, content with all that was done, may you obtain many years of life.

The things that I did on earth were not small. I have had 110 years of life. As a gift of the Pharoah, I have had honors exceeding those of the ancestors, by doing Maat until the state of veneration.

It is done, from its beginning to its end, as it was found in the writings of the ancestors and Deity.

PAUL MBUYA AKOKO (1891–1981)

An Interview with H. Odera Oruka
(ca. late 1970s)

The Luo Concept of Time

Q. Did the Luo speak of things which happened, say, one hundred years ago?

A. In *Dholuo*, "Luo Language," time is known as *kinde*. The Luo have always had quite a lot to say about those things which happened long ago by using specific events to mark out or pinpoint the location of such events on the time-continuum. Ex hypothesi, a person may refer to a famine which had taken place as a result of drought. That would be quite a story. Another example which could be given is the case of a man who defended the tribe during wars, e.g., legendary Luanda Magere from Kano. Herein lie some examples of references made to past occurrences which could be, as indeed they are, used as points of reference on the time-continuum. These are then related to events which are meant to be dated.

This method of dating events is necessarily approximate, since those events used as paradigms are located in period blocks. We may call this the psychological method of dating events as opposed to the modern mechanical method, in which people rely on the use of mechanical devices such as clocks, watches, and so forth. The "Dholuo" word for a past event is *chon*, which in Kiswahili is *zamani*. For present, current events, the Dholuo word is *tinde* and the Kiswahili word is *sasa*.

Q. Did people also speak of things which will take place, say, twenty years hence, which events the English call future?

A. Now, with respect to the word future, the Luo speak of *gi ma nobi*, for I think there is no one single word which exactly corresponds to the English "future." This future may be definite, where people might have some idea when they expect an event to take place. On the other hand, it may be

Reprinted from *Sage Philosophy: Indigenous Thinkers and Modern Debate on African Philosophy*, edited by H. Odera Oruka (Leiden: E. J. Brill, 1990), 135–48, with permission of E. J. Brill.

indefinite, as may be illustrated with the activities of prophets and what-
nots foretelling events which they expect to take place in a future which it
is not possible to ascertain at the time of prophecy.

Prophets, *Johulo* in Dholuo, for example, prophesied the coming of Europeans to Luo land long before the time of my own generation and even
before our own fathers were born. These diviners also foresaw a famine
which they claimed, *before the event,* would force people to eat animal
skins. This caused quite a stir at the time because animal skin was used
only for decoration and also as items for clothing. The history of the Luo
confirms the coming to pass of this event. Now the Luo word *chieng* is
neutral, for it is not restricted to any particular tense. Therefore, it can be
used to refer to a past or future event depending upon the context of its use
in a sentence. There has quite often arisen a confusion in its use when it is
taken as synonymous with the phrase "*gi ma nobi,*" which means *future*
or, more fully, that event which will come to pass at a future date. Clearly,
therefore, the word and the phrase cognitively mean and so are used to
stand for different situations: whereas gi ma nobi means future, chieng
could properly be taken to illustrate an event which has occurred (past) or
one which is yet to take place (future).

Religion and the Concept of God

Q. What do you think God is? What is religion, and why do you think people
believe in God?

A. Long ago, there were no denominations or factions in matters of religion.
The Luo regarded *Nyasaye* (God) as omnipresent. People turned to Him for
help in all manner of ways. For example, the person going to war would
appeal to Nyasaye to help defeat his enemy. Where he was victorious, he
concluded that it was all due to the favorable disposition of Nyasaye. The
interesting thing here is that the vanquished also expected the help of the
same Nyasaye. Now when a patient recovered from his illness, he acknowledged the help of Nyasaye. He believed also that there was, in addition, an
element of luck, but that it was Nyasaye who brought luck his way.

People acknowledged Nyasaye and so when they rose in the morning
they looked at *wang chieng'* (the face of the sun), for God was thought to
reside there as one might expect [of] an occupant of a house. The sun was
therefore believed to be capable of acting the role of an intermediary
between people and God. Thus, people showed the palms of their hands
to the face of the sun in supplication. Now as the sun set in the west,
people would look directly at it, saying, "Set well so that no evil thing
befalls us." During this period, religion was not fragmented and so there

were no denominations or factions. People recognized one Nyasaye, which in my opinion is the correct attitude.

Q. The Europeans brought the concept of *dini* (denominations). Do you think that God and Luo God is the same God?

A. It was the coming of the European missionaries which introduced the element of fragmentation into religion. Notwithstanding, the European concept of God and our own concept is basically the same, for there is only one God if there is God, and there is God. Although the Luo recognized one Nyasaye, they were wrong to think that their God (Nyasaye) is different from the God of the Europeans. Thus we had, as a result of this incoherent thinking among the Luo, a situation in which other tribes thought that they too had their own God. This is totally mistaken. I can demonstrate this quite simply by pointing at the rather pedestrian fact that *nature is uniform*. The existence of many gods would have resulted in pulling the universe in different directions: this takes care of any possibility of there existing a pantheon of gods.

Q. Is it correct that the *jodolo* used witchcraft to kill people?

A. Now there were the jodolo, who were the people responsible for offering sacrifices. These holy people were thought to know where God dwelt. However, some wrongly thought that the jodolo also practiced witchcraft. They were in fact God-fearing people who offered sacrifice and prayers on behalf of supplicants. For example, if rain failed, then the jodolo would be invited to offer prayers and sacrifice to Nyasaye so that there would be rain. Among the Luo of long ago, those who recognized and feared God were good people. However, there were the *jojuog* [night runners], who did evil things. Those who feared God and obeyed the elders prospered. The fear of God and the respect of elders were linked, since elders in the earthly hierarchy represented God, who was thought to be at the head of the heavenly hierarchy. From this point of view of morality, belief in God served a purpose, a good positive end.

Q. But were the jojuog truly powerful?

A. I think not. They got their reputation, and so their power, from the fact of the death of their enemies, who may have died from fear when threatened with death. The jojuog used this psychological ploy to get rid of their enemies. So in some cases, where the death of a person may well have been due to disease of some sort or other, the *jajuok* [singular of jojuog] would say, "I told him he would see when he offended me." So people come to fear the jajuok.

However, I do not think that they had real power. It was only fear which killed those who died as a result of the threats from the jajuok. Now if a person who it was thought had power to kill people wagged his finger at you, is it surprising that his reputation would help to instill a psychological fear in you? But I do not think they had real power. Unless somebody manages to poison his enemy, there ought not be any fear of death. Poisoning or physical attack are the only ways by which a person could be killed. Clearly, therefore, some people die through being instilled with the fear of death.

The Education of Young People

Q. How were the young people educated before the Europeans arrived here in Kenya?

A. There are two types of education: formal and informal. Education has always been considered a very important aspect of the upbringing of a child by the Luo. This teaching and tests were extremely rigorous. These were conducted and supervised by elders considered wise by the community. The boys were usually divided into groups. One group may be given instructions on the art of fighting. Here, such skills as the use of spear and shield might be imparted. There were different other types of training. It is important to note that the people in charge of these exercises were men and women who had made their mark on the community. They were usually the wisest, the best in the village. It is not unlike the situation today, when only the people formally trained are allowed to handle the education of the youth.

The only difference lies in the fact that whereas in modern times teachers are required to go to a place specifically appointed for the purpose of passing instructions or teaching (school), in the old days, it was not so. There would be, for example, a wise man living in South Nyanza, and all the young people in his area as well as neighboring communities would be required to go to him for instructions.

It was a distinct quality in these elders that they were often very ready to acknowledge their limitations. So whenever they felt unable to help or cope, they would suggest the name of another wise person to whom they were willing to defer.

Unfortunately, these men and women of quality are now very few remaining. They are dying off. And the people of the younger generation are showing interest only in such things as stories and the history of Europeans in Africa and other such things, instead of looking for the roots of their culture. So the traditional wisdom is not, or at any rate does not seem to be, continuing. The younger people, the youth of today in their ignorance, seem to look down upon the traditions of their fathers. I think something ought to be done to rekindle interest in the study of the traditional life of our people.

Q. We hear so much about people who were great because they fought in wars; are people remembered for their intelligence?

A. Now as to greatness, it is wrong, I believe, to think that the famous Luo people attained their greatness only because they fought in wars. In this context, one always hears of a name like Luanda Magere, and justly. But there are also those who are remembered for their intelligence and erudition.

There were people like Gor, a very clever man, as well as Maina son of Mbuya. Gor was a very famous man who even had a football club named after him. He certainly knew the ways of the world. He was very clever. It was believed that he had the capacity to change himself into many things. But people were wrong, because Gor himself told me that he never changed into anything. When he was going into enemy territory, he would paint himself liberally with dust. He thus looked like a madman. He was very clever. He was a master of disguise and this, in my opinion, explains why he was able to roam freely in enemy territory without being recognized. Sometimes, of course, he would carry many odd things about his person. He was no doubt a very versatile individual.

Q. Do you think you are one of today's wise men? Are you a wise man?

A. People have often asked, "Mzee Mbuya, are you a wise man?" to which I always answer, "No." I do not think I am wise, for there are many people who are wiser than I am. It is only that I do not know them. But I see young people coming to me. One man may come to me saying, "I have some problems because I married without a go-between." Young women also come seeking my advice. One may say, "I am in difficulty because I married the wrong man. What am I to do?" On the whole, I have in this respect found women more intelligent than men, for they are more inclined to follow useful advice.

Man and Woman: Both Have Equally Important Roles in Society

Q. Do you think that man and woman should be considered equals?

A. There is a popular Luo belief that the man is the owner and master of the homestead, the whole homestead, but I think this belief is wrong. For when we come to the house, the woman is in control there. In the house, the man can only ask for things. He cannot do as he pleases without any restraint. However, the woman too cannot do anything without asking her husband. Thus, husband and wife help each other. Where peace is desired, each person tries not to overstep the boundary which common sense determines in relationships.

However, on the question of equality of the sexes in political and social terms, I personally think that unnecessary problems may be created if [this is] not carefully handled. For women still need many more years before reaching the level of their menfolk. It is only after many more years of education and orientation that this equality will come. It ought not to be forced. But if people take it hastily, the result will be problems, avoidable problems. Education will in time help to redress this imbalance, since men and women are inherently equal. It is opportunity or lack of it which causes inequality.

So given the view that man and woman are inherently equal, we see that a woman can be more intelligent than a man, just as a man can also be more intelligent than a woman.

Of course, there is a tradition in which women are portrayed and indeed come to see themselves as inferior. This in my opinion is due to nothing other than laziness on the part of women. This type of woman goes about with a chip on her shoulder, saying, "I am only a woman, why are you not treating me gently and favorably?" That a person happens to be a woman is not by itself a justification for her getting favorable treatment.

On the other hand, men generally do not like betraying the fact, at any rate in public, that there are times when their women do surpass them in matters with respect to the knowledge of certain things. However, when the husband and wife are in the privacy of their home, one may at times find the woman not only matching but exceeding her husband's prowess in many ways. This is neither unusual nor extraordinary.

On the Idea of Communalism

Q. What do you think of the old Luo idea of communalism?

A. Now the sense in which we may justly say that the Luo in the traditional setting practiced communalism is not one in which people generously shared property or wealth. Their idea of communalism is, I think, of a cooperative nature. For example, where one person had cattle, everybody ipso facto had cattle. For the owner of the cattle would distribute his cattle among people who did not have cattle, so that the less well-off people may take care of them. However, the cattle was never completely given away. The poor were only given temporary charge of these animals by their better-off neighbors. For example, the cattle owner may give one poor man four cows, another five cows, and so on, to look after. The result is that everybody had cows to look after and so milk to drink.

Where a person wants to get married but did not have such things as cows, etc., other people would chip in. One person might contribute a calf, another a bull, and so forth. Thus with the cooperative help of neighbors and relatives, a man who otherwise would have been in difficulty became able to cope with the expenses of getting married. And when this person who himself was helped became able, he too felt obliged to help others. Help is thus spread throughout the community and everybody felt a sense of belonging. This is different from the political communism we hear so much about these days.

In a famine situation, no one was allowed or left to starve. Here the communal spirit comes into its own. A wealthy man would give to the poor. He may feel able to give a basket of grains to one man, two baskets to another, according to the needs of these individuals. Thus everyone had something to eat. It was considered antisocial if anyone kept things to himself alone. But then there was also the extended family system, which made people generally feel that they all belonged to one family; it turned mere neighbors into relations of a sort.

A person who brews beer would be happier when there are others to share it with him. On the other hand, a person may prepare food and invite others to share it with him. That is what used to happen. No person was allowed to become destitute. Where in a village, and this was extremely rare, a person died of hunger, the people of the village were made a laughing stock by people of the neighboring villages, because it was considered shameful for a person to be left to starve to death.

Q. Do you think this spirit exists today?

A. This communal spirit is sadly being allowed to die out through the importation of foreign ideas and processes of modernization. A means ought to be found whereby what is good in our past is accommodated in things new and modern.

Q. Given the nature of things today, do you think that communalism can go on?

A. As I have tried to explain, the introduction of the modern way of life is gradually bringing to an end this communal spirit. It is much to be regretted that everybody is now so obsessed with his person that he does not show much interest in what else is going on around him. The order of the day is now one in which individuals say, "I want a car, a large house, and so forth: therefore, in order to be able to afford all these things, I must concentrate all my efforts only upon my own person." Thus the very laudable communal spirit is gradually giving way to the modern aggressive individualism. But are we tending or at any rate likely to become like the Europeans? I do not know.

Q. Do you think that all peoples are born equal, or are there some races born with less intelligence?

A. Now it must be understood that people are born with certain differences, which must be acknowledged. Even in a communist society, there are still people who have more strength than others. There are those who may, for example, have enough strength to be capable of fighting an animal as strong as a lion. There are those who can have so much food by sheer hard work. Others still are good only at rearing animals, and so forth. Thus we see that people are not equal in every respect.

However, it is my opinion that because a person is born with superior powers, [there] is all the more reason why that person ought to place his extra or superior powers at the service of his less well-off neighbors. Given his superior powers, he can produce more food to feed others so that all may live together in happiness. Otherwise the people may develop jealousy of or even hatred for the more fortunate.

Q. What is the nature of the equality which existed in the communal environment?

A. The fact that I have expressed the view that people ought to continue to live together, helping one another as in the old days, is not to be taken to entail the possible conclusion that there still will not be those who, for example, have more power and wealth. Even if all lived equally, but there still will exist that man, I mean the more enterprising one, who would have a lot of animals. Those animals are his and must remain his. The fact that he helps to feed other people only reinforces this position. To say that there was *equality* in the communal environment simply because no one was allowed to become destitute is totally unwarranted. It is in fact false. As I explained above, equality is not the reason for communalism in Africa.

Man Is Superior to Animals

Q. What are the main differences between man and animals?

A. When we consider man in relation to animals, we find that there are differences: man is superior to the animal. For although both have life in thought and behavior, man provides for the future, whereas the animal does not. We also find that man is not really afraid of animals, even though some animals can be very fierce. This is because man has intellect, which animals lack. And if an animal gets the scent of man, it must run away. Again, man is both a thinking (rational) and a social being. This he manifests through the use of his intellect.

There Is a Cleavage between Freedom and Happiness

Q. What do you think is the significance of *thuolo* (freedom)?

A. Thuolo means simply to be able to act as one pleases. For example, a person who is bonded, as a slave is, may be released from the bondage. Upon release, that person becomes a free man. He is free. Or say a person fought a battle or did other things to liberate himself; if he is successful, then he becomes a free man. He becomes free to will whatever he wishes. This is thuolo.

Secondly, an unmarried girl living at home with her parents is not in the thuolo sense free because there are a number of things which she cannot do. For example, she is forbidden from looking into her mother's pot or entering her parents' bedroom, and so forth. However, when she is married and has her own home, then she can do as she pleases. She is free. But this thuolo is limited because she still has her husband, etc. Long ago, before the Europeans first came to Kenya, people thought that we were free. But I do not think that we were a free people. Even now that we have our independence, this nominal independence, how free are we really?

If we consider the matter carefully, we find that we do not have freedom. Are we still not as we were under the Europeans? Government of the pre-independence period hindered people from doing as they pleased, and government today still hinders people from attaining freedom to do as they please. People are forcibly restrained from doing so many things which they otherwise would have liked to do. When people harvest their grains, the government does not allow them to do as they please with it.

Q. Do people generally lack freedom, or do you think there are only a few who enjoy freedom?

A. Some people do have more freedom, relatively than others. People who are leaders in government, for example, the President, have more freedom. But again, when one thinks carefully about the matter, one finds that even the President, as powerful as he is, is himself not free to do those things the cabinet would not have him do. He too is therefore restricted in a sense. Thus there is no person who can be said to be completely free such that he could do anything without any restraint. Therefore, there is no complete freedom. All our actions are, at any rate to some extent, the wishes of other people. And I mean this in a general, universal sense.

Now let us consider this question: "Is the man who is happy not happy on the account that nobody interferes with him in his actions?" The answer to this question is no, for there is a clear distinction between *freedom* and *happiness*.

Q. What ought a person do who wants freedom?

A. If a person works hard and acquires a lot of animals and wealth generally so that he does not depend upon anybody, then the person is free. A person cannot be free if he works for and so depends upon another person. Neither can a person be free merely by the fact that he is wealthy, for he still needs and depends upon the activities of others (for example, his workers) in the production of his wealth. And we have not mentioned the constraint placed upon all individuals by governments. So then, even if a person has a lot of wealth, if this person is restrained or affected in his actions by the will of others, then the best he is entitled to claim is happiness, not freedom. Therefore no one has complete freedom.

On Law and Punishment

Q. Did the Luo have their own system of law and punishment long ago?

A. Before the coming of Europeans, the Luo had their own system of law and punishment. Thus, there were law courts of a sort. A court was described as *Kar ng'ado bura* (a place of passing judgment). Here elders sat in judgment, but only those elders who were known to be the wisest, not just anybody.

Now where a person was convicted of an offense, he was punished, but not executed, however serious the offense, even in cases of murder. The Luo did not approve of killing people except in war. This explains why those found guilty of a capital offense were never sentenced to death. It was considered also not proper that a grown-up man should be whipped. However, any wrongdoer who had committed a serious offense was banished from the community. In such circumstances he was exiled to a place which is far away from his home. This was considered a drastic enough punishment, reserved only for very serious offenses. A man who had transgressed might be cursed as a punishment. This class of offenders was allowed to remain within the community, having been reduced to the level of feeble-minded idiots. Another type of punishment was that of administration of a drug which made such offenders become very stupid. The drug could also make a person very ill for a considerably long period of time. This would give the elders the opportunity of reforming such an offender and, if reformed, an antidote was administered so that the person became his normal self again.

Q. What of the confiscation of an offender's property?

A. Now where a person committed murder, his property was confiscated as punishment. The confiscated property was then turned over to the family of the murdered person in compensation. If, for example, the murdered person was a married man, and his wife was to decide to remarry and bear a child in the name of the deceased husband, then ten cows were confiscated. In the alternative, the murderer was made to pay whatever dowry was necessary.

People of Different Races and Tribes Must Learn to Live Together in Peace

Q. Do you think the world would have been better if there were only one race?

A. There are different types of people in the world and so there are different races, on the macro-level, and tribes, on the micro-level. This is undoubtedly a fact. Any tribe or race which attempts to wipe out other tribes or races such that only one tribe or race remains is embarking upon an exercise in futility. The Luo used to think, albeit wrongly, that they could wipe out other tribes or at any rate subjugate them because they believed in the supremacy of their tribe. Clearly, this is a recipe for trouble. The Luo should therefore learn to understand the other tribes so that all live together in harmony. For it is not possible, I think, for the Luo, Kisii, Kikuyu, Kamba, and other tribes each to do away with their traditions. The differences will remain and so must be accommodated.

Q. What do you think accounts for the fighting among people of different tribes and races?

A. There is fighting and bad feelings among people of different tribes and even among peoples of different races. This situation is likely to continue until people turn their attention to the elimination of the causes of war rather than the effects, as is all too often the case at present. Wars are caused by the avarice and greed of men for both wealth and power.

Q. What do you think brings about this bad feeling?

A. Now a race or tribe might consider itself so strong that other races or tribes cannot equal it. Such a race or tribe would therefore not tolerate any act which it considers a disrespect from an "inferior" race or tribe. This is the germ of the dangerous idea that weaker races or tribes are ripe for plunder. My own view is that this idea has an affinity with the belief that might is right, i.e., the right is always subordinate to might. Such are the germs which cause wars.

Q. It has been claimed that some races have superior intellectual powers. Do you think there is any justification for this claim?

A. When a race is wealthy, there is an almost invariable tendency for it to claim superiority. However, I do not think that any particular people or race or tribe was created by God to be superior. Wealth can be acquired by any people. Thus all races have, inherently, equal power. This power is nevertheless put to use in different ways and hence manifests differences in development. The intelligence which the Europeans present is the intelligence God prophesied would come into the world in the present phase of world history. However, this intelligence is not the property of any one people. God said intelligence would come into the world. The Europeans themselves gained some of their knowledge or intelligence from other races, as we are now gaining much knowledge from them. We are, in time, likely to equal the Europeans in achievement. We may even surpass them. They were not born with more intelligence than other people. Even today, there are people in Europe who lack the intelligence we see in some Europeans. Let us therefore define an intelligent race as a race which has used its acquired intelligence wisely. In this sense, knowledge has an affinity with intelligence.

Of course the foregoing are my own views, which are not representative of the general Luo belief system. Long ago, the Luo believed no other tribe was superior to it. They thought they were the greatest. They used to boast in this way. They claimed that the Luo were second only to the Europeans and therefore were the *wazungu wa Kisumu*, i.e., the Europeans of Kisumu, the town which they affectionately described as their London and the Luoland they termed U.K. They were crazy.

In those days, the Luo were not only warriors and fighters, but also very learned and intelligent people. They were thus able to work on European farms and also serve as the servants of the Europeans. They were to be found everywhere. The Luo were in ascendancy mainly, I think, because the other tribes did not think of engaging in these multifarious activities. As a result, the Luo wrongly thought they were superior to others.

On the Relationship between Life and Death

—Without death, life would have
little or no significance, and yet
death is not the *antithesis* of life,
but its climax—

Q. What are your own views about life and death?

A. The question of life and death is fundamentally a puzzling one. It is therefore a matter which is not easy to understand. Life was given by God. After that, there is death. At death, life is lost. And yet the Luo did not accept the idea that a dead man was lost. Their belief was that a dead person was only asleep and was alive in another place. Thus the deceased was sent on an errand to other person(s) who had preceded him to the great beyond. The Luo believed that a dead man, because he had shed his earthly body, had thereby acquired the capacity to see and communicate with others in the world of spirits. Thus if a person who was a good person died, people were happy on account of the fact that the deceased had the capacity to affect the spirit world for good.

Q. How does making the spirit world better affect the living world?

A. This happiness on the occasion of the death of a good person stems from the belief that the deceased would join in the struggle against those evil spirits thought to be waging a terrorizing and haunting war against the living from the spirit world. Where the haunting went on unabated, further appeals were made to the deceased for more help. For the Luo, therefore, upon death, the spirit went to another place. Thus those still alive could not see him. Only the body, which when alive accommodated the departed spirit, was buried. It was thought that bodies became empty shells upon death.

Q. Did people believe the dead could hear them?

A. The Luo believe the deceased could hear their cries for help. I think the Luo were right here because the dead heard their supplication. An appeal to the dead person was usually made from his graveside.

It appears the Christian Europeans as well as the Jews believed in the power of the spirit of the dead to affect [us] here on earth. I strongly believe the Luo lived with the Jews a long time ago. The Luo and the Jews did live together. For the type and mode of Luo sacrifices are not unlike those of the Jews. Even the Luo practice of segregating cooking utensils is similar to the Jewish practice.

Q. What are your own views about all this?

A. I do accept the Luo beliefs regarding the relationship between life and death. I also believe that God has hidden the secret of death and, as a result, no living person can have the knowledge of the spirit world, which clearly exists since only the body is buried at death.

LÉOPOLD SÉDAR SENGHOR (1906–)

Negritude: A Humanism of the Twentieth Century (1966)

During the last thirty or so years that we have been proclaiming negritude, it has become customary, especially among English-speaking critics, to accuse us of *racialism*. This is probably because the word is not of English origin. But, in the language of Shakespeare, is it not in good company with the words humanism and socialism? Mphahleles[1] have been sent about the world saying, "Negritude is an inferiority complex"; but the same word cannot mean both racialism and inferiority complex without contradiction. The most recent attack comes from Ghana, where the government has commissioned a poem entitled "I Hate Negritude"—as if one could hate oneself, hate one's being, without ceasing to be.

No, negritude is none of these things. It is neither racialism nor self-negation. Yet it is not just affirmation; it is rooting oneself in oneself, and self-confirmation; confirmation of one's *being*. Negritude is nothing more or less than what some English-speaking Africans have called the *African personality*. It is no different from the "black personality" discovered and proclaimed by the American New Negro movement. As the American Negro poet Langston Hughes wrote after the First World War: "We, the creators of the new generation, want to give expression to our *black personality* without shame or fear . . . We know we are handsome. Ugly as well. The drums weep and the drums laugh." Perhaps our only originality, since it was the West Indian poet Aimé Césaire who coined the word negritude, is to have attempted to define the concept a little more closely; to have developed it as a weapon, as an instrument of liberation and as a contribution to the humanism of the twentieth century.

But, once again, what is negritude? Ethnologists and sociologists today speak of different civilizations. It is obvious that peoples differ in their ideas and their languages, in their philosophies and their religions, in their customs and their institutions, in their literature and their art. Who would deny

Reprinted from *The Africa Reader,* edited by Wilfred Cartey and Martin Kilson, 2 vols. (New York: Random House, 1970), vol. 2, 179–92.

that Africans, too, have a certain way of conceiving life and of living it? A certain way of speaking, singing, and dancing; of painting and sculpturing, and even of laughing and crying? Nobody, probably; for otherwise we would not have been talking about "Negro art" for the last sixty years, and Africa would be the only continent today without its ethnologists and sociologists. What, then, is negritude? It is—as you can guess from what precedes—*the sum of the cultural values of the black world;* that is, a certain active presence in the world, or better, in the universe. It is, as John Reed and Clive Wake call it, a certain "way of relating oneself to the world and to others."[2] Yes, it is essentially relations with others, an opening out to the world, contact and participation with others. Because of what it is, negritude is necessary in the world today: it is a humanism of the twentieth century.

The Revolution of 1889

But let us go back to 1885 and the morrow of the Berlin Conference. The European nations had just finished, with Africa, their division of the planet. Including the United States of America, they were five or six at the height of their power who dominated the world. Without any complexes, they were proud of their material strength; prouder even of their science, and paradoxically, of their *race*. It is true that at that time this was not a paradox. Gobineau, the nineteenth-century philosopher of racial supremacy, had, by a process of osmosis, even influenced Marx,[3] and Disraeli was the great theoretician of that "*English race*, proud, tenacious, confident in itself, that no climate, no change can undermine." (The italics are mine.) Leo Frobenius, the German ethnologist, one of the first to apprehend the rich complexity of African culture, writes in *The Destiny of Civilizations:* "Each of the great nations that considers itself personally responsible for the 'destiny of the world' believes it possesses the key to the understanding of the whole and the other nations. It is an attitude raised from the past."[4]

In fact, this attitude "raised from the past" had begun to be discredited toward the end of the nineteenth century by books like Bergson's *Time and Free Will,* which was published in 1889.[5] Since the Renaissance, the values of European civilization had rested essentially on discursive reason and facts, on logic and matter. Bergson, with an eminently dialectical subtlety, answered the expectation of a public weary of scientism and naturalism. He showed that facts and matter, which are the objects of discursive reason, were only the outer surface that had to be transcended by *intuition* in order to achieve a *vision in depth of reality.*

But the Revolution of 1889—as we shall call it—did not only affect art and literature, it completely upset the sciences. In 1880, only a year before the invention of the word electron, a distinction was still being drawn between matter and energy. The former was inert and unchangeable, the latter was not. But what characterized both of them was their permanence and their continuity. They were both subject to a strict mechanical determinism. Matter and energy had, so to speak, existed from the beginning of time; they could change their shape, but not their substance. All we lacked in order to know them objectively in space and time were sufficiently accurate instruments of investigation and measurement.

Well, in less than fifty years, all these principles were to be outmoded and even rejected. Thirty years ago already, the new discoveries of science—quanta, relativity, wave mechanics, the uncertainty principle, electron spin—had upset the nineteenth-century notion of determinism, which denied man's free will, along with the concepts of matter and energy. The French physicist Broglie revealed to us the duality of matter and energy, or the wave-particle principle that underlies things; the German physicist Heisenberg showed us that objectivity was an illusion and that we could not observe facts without modifying them; others showed that, on the scale of the infinitely small as on that of the immensely great, particles act on one another. Since then, the physico-chemical laws, like matter itself, could no longer appear unchangeable. Even in the field and on the scale where they were valid, they were only rough approximations, no more than probabilities. It was enough to scrape the surface of things and of facts to realize just how much instability there is, defying our measuring instruments, probably because they are only mechanical: *material.*

It was on the basis of these discoveries, through a combination of logical coherence and amazing intuition of scientific experiment and inner experience, that Pierre Teilhard de Chardin was able to transcend the traditional dichotomies with a new dialectic, to reveal to us the living, throbbing unity of the universe. On the basis, then, of the new scientific discoveries, Teilhard de Chardin transcends the old dualism of the philosophers and the scientists, which Marx and Engels had perpetuated by giving matter precedence over the spirit. He advanced the theory that the stuff of the universe is not composed of two realities, but of a single reality in the shape of two phenomena; that there is not matter and energy, not even matter and spirit, but spirit-matter, just as there is space-time. Matter and spirit become a "network of relations," as the French philosopher Bachelard called it: energy, defined as a network of forces. In matter-spirit there is, therefore, only one energy, which has two aspects. The first, *tangential energy,* which is external, is material and quantitative. It links together the corpuscles, or particles, that make up matter. The other, *radial energy,* which is internal, is psychic and qualitative. It is centripetal force. It organizes into a complex the center-to-center relations of the internal particles of a corpuscle. Since energy is force, it follows that radial energy is the creative force, the "primary stuff of things," and tangential energy is only a residual product "caused by the interreactions of the elementary 'centers' of the consciousness, imperceptible where life has not yet occurred, but clearly apprehensible by our experience at a sufficiently advanced stage in the development of matter" (Teilhard de Chardin).[6] It follows that where life has not yet occurred the physico-chemical laws remain valid within the limitations we have defined above, while in the living world, as we rise from plant to animal and from animal to man, the psyche increases in consciousness until it makes and expresses itself in freedom. "Makes itself": that is, *realizes* itself, by means of—yet by transcending—material well-being through an increase of spiritual life. Realizes itself: by that I mean it develops in harmonious fashion the two complementary elements of the soul: the heart and the mind.

The Philosophy of Being

The paradox is only apparent when I say that negritude, by its ontology (that is, its philosophy of being), its moral law and its aesthetic, is a response to the modern humanism that European philosophers and scientists have been preparing since the end of the nineteenth century and as Teilhard de Chardin and the writers and artists of the mid-twentieth century present it.

Firstly, African ontology. Far back as one may go into his past, from the northern Sudanese to the southern Bantu, the African has always and everywhere presented a concept of the world which is diametrically opposed to the traditional philosophy of Europe. The latter is essentially *static, objective, dichotomic*; it is in fact, dualistic, in that it makes an absolute distinction between body and soul, matter and spirit. It is founded on separation and opposition: on analysis and conflict. The African, on the other hand, conceives the world, beyond the diversity of its forms, as a fundamentally mobile, yet unique, reality that seeks synthesis. This needs development.

It is significant that in Wolof, the main language of Senegal, there are at least three words to translate the word "spirit," *xel, sago,* or *degal,* whereas images have to be used for the word "matter": *lef* (thing) or *yaram* (body). The African is, of course, sensitive to the external world, to the material aspect of beings and things. It is precisely because he is more so than the white European, because he is sensitive to the tangible qualities of things—shape, color, smell, weight, etc.—that the African considers these things merely as signs that have to be interpreted and transcended in order to reach the reality of human beings. Like others, more than others, he distinguishes the pebble from the plant, the plant from the animal, the animal from man; but, once again, the accidents and appearances that differentiate these kingdoms only illustrate different aspects of the same reality. This reality is *being* in the ontological sense of the word, and it is life force. For the African, matter in the sense the Europeans understand it is only a system of signs which translates the single reality of the universe: being, which is spirit, which is life force. Thus the whole universe appears as an infinitely small, and at the same time an infinitely large, network of life forces which emanate from God and end in God, who is the source of all life forces. It is He who vitalizes and devitalizes all other beings, all the other life forces.

I have not wandered as far as might be thought from modern ontology. European ethnologists, Africanists, and artists use the same words and the same expressions to designate the ultimate reality of the universe they are trying to know and to express: spider's web, network of forces, communicating vessels, system of canals, etc. This is not very different, either, from what the scientists and chemists say. As far as African ontology is concerned, too, there is no such thing as dead matter: every being, every thing—be it only a grain of sand—radiates a life force, a sort of wave-particle; and sages, priests, kings, doctors, and artists all use it to help bring the universe to its fulfillment.

For the African, contrary to popular belief, is not passive in face of the order—or disorder—of the world. His attitude is fundamentally ethical. If the moral law of the African has remained unknown for so long, it is because it derives, naturally, from his conception of the world: from his ontology—so naturally that both have remained unknown, denied even, by Europeans, because they have not been brought to their attention by being re-examined by each new generation of Africans.

So God tired of all the possibilities that remained confined within Him, unexpressed, dormant, and as if dead. And God opened His mouth, and he spoke at length a word that was harmonious and rhythmical. All these possibilities expressed by the mouth of God *existed* and had the vocation *to live:* to express God in their turn by establishing the link with God and all the forces deriving from Him.

In order to explain this *morality in action* of negritude, I must go back a little. Each of the identifiable life forces of the universe—from the grain of sand to the ancestor[7]—is, itself and in its turn, a network of life forces—as modern physical chemistry confirms: a network of elements that are contradictory in appearance but really *complementary.* Thus, for the African, man is composed, of course, of matter and spirit, of body and soul; but at the same time he is also composed of a virile and a feminine element: indeed, of several "souls." Man is therefore a composition of mobile life forces which interlock: a world of solidarities that seek to knit themselves together. Because he exists, he is at once end and beginning: end of the three orders of the mineral, the vegetable, and the animal, but beginning of the human order.

Let us ignore for the moment the first three orders and examine the human order. Above man and based on him lies this fourth world of concentric circles, bigger and bigger, higher and higher, until they reach God along with the whole of the universe. Each circle—family, village, province, nation, humanity—is, in the image of man and by vocation, a close-knit society.

So, for the African, living according to the moral law means living according to his nature, composed as it is of contradictory elements but complementary life forces. Thus he gives stuff to the stuff of the universe and tightens the threads of the tissue of life. Thus he transcends the contradictions of the elements and works toward making the life forces complementary to one another: in himself first of all, as man, but also in the whole of human society. It is by bringing the complementary life forces together in this way that man reinforces them in their movement towards God and, in reinforcing them, he reinforces himself; that is, he passes from *existing* to *being*. He cannot reach the highest form of being, for in fact only God has this quality; and He has it all the more fully as creation, and all that exists, fulfil themselves and express themselves in Him.

Dialogue

Ethnologists have often praised the unity, the balance, and the harmony of African civilization, of black society, which was based both on the *community* and on the *person,* and in which, because it was founded on dialogue and reciprocity, the group had priority over the individual without crushing him, but allowing him to blossom as a person. I would like to emphasize at this point how much these characteristics of negritude enable it to find its place in contemporary humanism, thereby permitting black Africa to make its contribution to the "Civilization of the Universal" which is so necessary in our divided but interdependent world of the second half of the twentieth century. A contribution, first of all, to international cooperation, which must be and which shall be the cornerstone of that civilization. It is through these virtues of negritude that decolonization has been accomplished without too much bloodshed or hatred and that a positive form of cooperation based on dialogue and reciprocity has been established between former colonizers and colonized. It is through these virtues that there has been a new spirit at the United Nations, where the "no" and the bang of the fist on the table are no longer signs of strength. It is through these virtues that peace through cooperation could extend to South Africa, Rhodesia, and the Portuguese colonies, if only the dualistic spirit of the whites would open itself to dialogue.

In fact, the contribution of negritude to the Civilization of the Universal is not of recent origin. In the fields of literature and art, it is contemporary with the Revolution of 1889. The French poet Arthur Rimbaud (1854–1891) had already associated himself with negritude. But in this article I want to concentrate on the "Negro revolution"—the expression belongs to Emmanuel Berl—which helped to stir European plastic art at the beginning of this century.

Art, like literature, is always the expression of a certain conception of the world and of life; the expression of a certain philosophy and, above all, of a certain ontology. Corresponding to the philosophical and scientific movement of 1889 there was not only a literary evolution—symbolism, then surrealism—but another revolution, or rather revolutions, in art, which were called, taking only the plastic arts, nabism, expressionism, fauvism, and cubism. A world of life forces that have to be *tamed* is substituted for a closed world of permanent and continuous substances that have to be *reproduced*.

Since the Greek *kouroi* (the term used for the statues of young men in classical Greek sculpture), the art of the European West had always been based on realism; the work of art had always been an imitation of the object: a *physeôs mimêsis*, to use Aristotle's expression: a corrected imitation, "improved," "idealized" by the requirements of rationality, but imitation all the same. The interlude of the Christian Middle Ages is significant insofar as Christianity is itself of Asian origin and strongly influenced by the African, Saint Augustine. To what will the artist then give expression? No longer to purely objective matter, but to his spiritual self; that is, to his inner self, his spirituality, and beyond himself to the spirituality of his age and of mankind. No longer by means of perspective, relief, and chiaroscuro, but, as the French painter Bazaine writes, "by the most hidden workings of instinct and the sensibility." Another French painter, André Masson, makes it more explicit when he writes: "By a simple interplay of shapes and colors legibly ordered." This interplay of shapes and colors is that of the life forces, which has been illustrated in particular by a painter like Soulages.

"Interplay of life forces": and so we come back to—negritude. As the French painter Soulages, in fact, once told me, the African aesthetic is "that of contemporary art." I find indirect proof of this in the fact that, while the consecration and spread of the new aesthetic revolution have occurred in France, the majority of its promoters were of Slav and Germanic origin; people who, like the Africans, belong to the mystical civilizations of the senses. Of course, without the discovery of African art, the revolution would still have taken place, but probably without such vigor and assurance and such a deepening of the knowledge of man. The fact that an art of the subject and of the spirit should have germinated outside Europe, in Africa—to which ethnologists had not yet given its true place in world culture—was proof of the human value of the message of the new European art.

Over and above its aesthetic lesson—to which we shall return later—what Picasso, Braque, and the other artists and early explorers of African art were seeking was, in the first place, just this: its human value. For in black Africa art is not a separate activity, in itself or for itself: it is a social activity, a technique of living, a handicraft in fact. But it is a major activity that brings all other activities to their fulfilment, like prayer in the Christian Middle Ages: birth and education, marriage and death, sport, even war. All human activities down to the least daily act must be integrated into the subtle inter-play of life forces—family, tribal, national, world, and universal forces. This harmonious interplay of life forces must be helped by *subordinating* the lower forces—mineral, vegetable, and animal—to their relations with man, and the forces of human society to its relations with the divine being through the intermediary of the ancestral beings.

A year or two ago I attended, on the cliffs of Bandiagara in the Mali Repub-lic, an entertainment which was a microcosm of Dogon art.[8] Even though it was but a pale reflection of the splendors of the past, this "play-concert" was an extremely significant expression of the Dogon vision of the universe. It was declaimed, sung, and danced, sculptured and presented in costume. The whole of the Dogon universe was portrayed in this symbiosis of the arts, as is the custom in black Africa. The universe—heaven and earth—was there-fore *represented* through the intermediary of man, whose ideogram is the same as that of the universe. Then the world was *re-presented* by means of masks, each of which portrayed, at one and the same time, a totemic animal, an ancestor, and a spirit. Others portrayed the foreign peoples: nomadic Fulani[9] and white Europeans. The aim of the entertainment was, by means of the symbiosis of the arts—poetry, song, dance, sculpture, and painting, used as techniques of integration—to *recreate* the universe and the contemporary world, but in a more harmonious way by making use of African humor, which corrects distortions at the expense of the foreign Fulani and the white conquerors. But this ontological vision was an entertainment—that is, an artistic demonstration—as well: a joy for the soul because a joy for the eyes and ears.

It was perhaps—indeed, it was certainly—this last aspect of the African aesthetic lesson that first attracted Picasso and Braque when, toward 1906, they discovered African art and were inspired by it. For my part, what struck me from the start of the Dogon play-concert, even before I tried to under-stand its meaning, was the harmony of form and movement, of color and rhythm, that characterized it. It is this harmony by which, as a spectator, I was moved; which, in the recreation of reality, acts on the invisible forces whose appearances are only signs, subordinates them in a complementary fashion to one another, and establishes the link between them and God through the intermediary of Man. By appearances I mean the attributes of matter that strike our senses: shape and color, timbre and tone, movement and rhythm.

I have said that these appearances are signs. They are more than that: they are meaningful signs, the "lines of force" of the life forces, insofar as they are used in their pure state, with only their characteristics of shape, color, sound, movement, and rhythm. Recently M. Lods, who teaches at the National School of Art of Senegal, was showing me the pictures his students intend exhibiting at the projected Festival of African Arts. I was immediately struck by the noble and elegant interplay of shape and color. When I discovered that the pictures were not completely abstract, that they portrayed ladies, princes, and noble animals, I was almost disappointed. There was no need for me to be: the very interplay of colored shapes perfectly expressed that elegant nobility that characterizes the art of the northern Sudan.

This, then, is Africa's lesson in aesthetics: art does not consist in photographing nature but in taming it, like the hunter when he reproduces the call of the hunted animal, like a separated couple, or two lovers, calling to each other in their desire to be reunited. The call is not the simple reproduction of the cry of the Other; it is a call of complementarity, a *song:* a call of harmony to the harmony of union that enriches by increasing *being.* We call it pure harmony. Once more, Africa teaches that art is not photography; if there are images, they are rhythmical. I can suggest or create anything— a man, a moon, a fruit, a smile, a tear—simply by assembling shapes and colors (painting/sculpture), shapes and movements (dance), timbre and tones (music), provided that this assembling is not an aggregation, but that it is ordered and, in short, rhythmical. For it is rhythm—the main virtue, in fact, of negritude—that gives the work of art its beauty. Rhythm is simply the movement of attraction or repulsion that expresses the life of the cosmic forces; symmetry and asymmetry, repetition or opposition: in short, the lines of force that link the meaningful signs that shapes and colors, timbre and tones, are.

Before concluding, I should like to pause for a moment on the apparent contradiction that must have been noticed between contemporary European art (which places the emphasis on the subject) and African art (which places it on the object). This is because the Revolution of 1889 began by reacting, of necessity, against the superstition of the *object;* and the existentialist ontology of the African, while it is based on the being-subject, has God as its pole-object; God who is the fullness of being. What was noticed, then, was simply a nuance. For the contemporary European, and the African, the work of art, like the act of knowing, expresses the confrontation, the embrace, of subject and object: "That penetration," wrote Bazaine, "that great common structure, that deep resemblance between Man and the world, without which there is no living form."

We have seen what constitutes for the African the "deep resemblance between Man and the world." For him, then, the act of restoring the order of the world by recreating it through art is the reinforcement of the life forces in the universe and, consequently, of God, the source of all life forces—or, in other words, the being of the universe. In this way, we reinforce ourselves at the same time, both as interdependent forces and as beings whose being consists in revitalizing ourselves in the recreation of art.

[1]The South African writer Ezekiel Mphahlele, author of *The African Image* (New York: Praeger, 1962), strongly disagrees with the concept of negritude.

[2]Léopold Sédar Senghor, *Selected Poems*, trans. with introduction by John Reed and Clive Wake (New York: Atheneum, 1964). See also Senghor, *Prose and Poetry*, selected and trans. by John Reed and Clive Wake (London: Oxford University Press, 1965).

[3]Arthur Comte de Gobineau, *The Inequality of Human Races*, trans. Adrian Collins, introduction by Oscar Levy (New York: H. Fertig, 1967).

[4]Leo Frobenius, *Le destin des civilisations*, traduit par N. Guterman (Paris: Gallimard, 1940).

[5]Henri Bergson, *Time and Free Will: An Essay on the Immediate Data of Consciousness*, trans. R. L. Pogson (New York: Macmillan, 1913).

[6]See Pierre Teilhard de Chardin, *Human Energy*, trans. J. M. Cohen (New York: Harcourt Brace Jovanovich, 1969), especially 113–62.

[7]In African religion, the ancestors are the essential link between the living and God. This is why they are surrounded by a complex ritual so as to ensure the maintenance of this link.

[8]The Dogon are a West African tribe among whom wood sculpture has achieved a very remarkable degree of excellence.

[9]The Fulani are a nomadic, pastoral people found throughout West Africa.

KWAME NKRUMAH (1909–1972)

🏵 Consciencism (1964)

Practice without thought is blind; thought without practice is empty. The three segments of African society which I specified in the last chapter, the traditional, the Western, and the Islamic, coexist uneasily; the principles animating them are often in conflict with one another. I have in illustration tried to show how the principles which inform capitalism are in conflict with the socialist egalitarianism of the traditional African society.

What is to be done, then? I have stressed that the two other segments, in order to be rightly seen, must be accommodated only as experiences of the traditional African society. If we fail to do this, our society will be racked by the most malignant schizophrenia.

Our attitude to the Western and the Islamic experience must be purposeful. It must also be guided by thought, for practice without thought is blind. What is called for as a first step is a body of connected thought which will determine the general nature of our action in unifying the society which we have inherited, this unification to take account, at all times, of the elevated ideals underlying the traditional African society. Social revolution must therefore have, standing firmly behind it, an intellectual revolution, a revolution in which our thinking and philosophy are directed towards the redemption of our society. Our philosophy must find its weapons in the environment and living conditions of the African people. It is from those conditions that the intellectual content of our philosophy must be created. The emancipation of the African continent is the emancipation of man. This requires two aims: first, the restitution of the egalitarianism of human society, and, second, the logistic mobilization of all our resources towards the attainment of that restitution.

The philosophy that must stand behind this social revolution is that which I have once referred to as philosophical consciencism; consciencism is the map in intellectual terms of the disposition of forces which will enable African society to digest the Western and the Islamic and the Euro-Christian ele-

Reprinted from *Consciencism*, by Kwame Nkrumah (New York: Monthly Review, 1964), 78–79, 95–105. © 1964 by Monthly Review Press. Reprinted by permission of Monthly Review Foundation.

ments in Africa, and develop them in such a way that they fit into the African personality. The African personality is itself defined by the cluster of humanist principles which underlie the traditional African society. Philosophical consciencism is that philosophical standpoint which, taking its start from the present content of the African conscience, indicates the way in which progress is forged out of the conflict in that conscience.

Its basis is in materialism. The minimum assertion of materialism is the absolute and independent existence of matter. Matter, however, is also a plenum of forces which are in antithesis to one another. The philosophical point of saying this is that matter is thus endowed with powers of self-motion. . . .

According to philosophical consciencism, ethical rules are not permanent but depend on the stage reached in the historical evolution of a society, so, however, that cardinal principles of egalitarianism are conserved.

A society does not change its ethics by merely changing its rules. To alter its ethics, its principles must be different. Thus, if a capitalist society can become a socialist society, then a capitalist society will have changed its ethics. Any change of ethics constitutes a revolutionary change.

Nevertheless, many times moral rules have changed so startlingly as to give the impression of a revolution in ethics. For example, one can take that profound change in our attitude to offenders for which modern psychology is responsible. Modern psychology brings to our notice relevant facts of whose existence we have no inkling in our dreams. When these new facts change our attitude, moral rules have not necessarily changed. But application of them is withheld, for the new considerations provoke a reclassification of the act involved, and, possibly, bring it under a different ethical rule. In that case, a different moral attitude could become relevant.

Investigations into the psychology of delinquency are a case in point. Such investigations tend by their results to attenuate the acrimony of our moral attitude to delinquents, by compelling us, not admittedly to waive moral rules, but to reclassify delinquent acts.

The cardinal ethical principle of philosophical consciencism is to treat each man as an end in himself and not merely as a means. This is fundamental to all socialist or humanist conceptions of man. It is true that Immanuel Kant also identified this as a cardinal principle of ethics, but whereas he regarded it as an immediate command of reason, we derive it from a materialist viewpoint.

This derivation can be made by way of that egalitarianism which, we have seen, is the social reflection of materialism. Egalitarianism is based on the monistic thesis of materialism. Matter is one even in its different manifestations. If matter is one, it follows that there is a route connecting any two manifestations of matter. This does not mean that between any two manifestations of matter there is a route which does not pass through any third form; the route need not be direct, for it may take one back to the primary form of matter. Dialectical processes are not unilinear, they do not follow just one line, but are ramified. There is a route from any twig of a tree to any other twig, such that the route never leaves the tree. But this does not mean that the twigs all have some one point in common, for it may be necessary to pass to the trunk and join another branch in order to pass from one twig to another. Nevertheless there is this route. The different manifestations of matter are all results of dialectical processes unfolding according to objective laws. There is a determinate process through which every manifestation is derived.

In saying, however, that there is a route between any two forms of matter, I do not attach the implication that any one form of matter can in fact be derived from any other form, for this may involve the reversal of a process which is irreversible. The upshot of what I mean is the continuity of nature: though the dialectical evolution of matter may lead to culs-de-sac (like the vanished plants and animals of prehistoric days), dialectical evolution contains no hiatuses.

It is the basic unity of matter, despite its varying manifestations, which gives rise to egalitarianism. Basically, man is one, for all men have the same basis and arise from the same evolution according to materialism. This is the objective ground of egalitarianism.

David Hume raised the question that ethical philosophies begin with statements of fact and suddenly seek to base statements of appraisal thereon, without explaining the legitimacy of their inference. If man is basically one, then if action is objectively attentive to this fact, it must be guided by principles. The guiding principles can be stated with such generality that they become autonomous. That is to say, first, that if action is to conform to the objectivity of human unity, then it must be guided by general principles which always keep this objectivity in view, principles which would prevent action from proceeding as if men were basically different. Second, these principles, because they relate to fact, can be stated boldly, as though they were autonomous, like the principle that an individual should not be treated by another merely as a means but always as an end.

If ethical principles are founded on egalitarianism, they must be objective. If ethical principles arise from an egalitarian idea of the nature of man, they must be generalizable, for according to such an idea man is basically one, in the sense defined. It is to this nondifferential generalization that expression is given in the command to treat each man as an end in himself, and not merely as a means. That is, philosophical consciencism, though it has the same cardinal principle of ethics as Kant, differs from Kant in founding ethics on a philosophical idea of the nature of man. This is what Kant describes as ethics based on anthropology. By anthropology Kant means any study of the nature of man, and he forbids ethics to be based on such a study.

It is precisely this that philosophical consciencism does. It also agrees with the traditional African outlook on many points, and thus fulfils one of the conditions which it sets for itself. In particular, it agrees with the traditional African idea of the absolute and independent existence of matter, the idea of its powers of self-motion in the sense explained, the idea of categorial convertibility, and the idea of the grounding of cardinal principles of ethics in the nature of man.

The traditional African standpoint, of course, accepts the absolute and independent idea of matter. If one takes the philosophy of the African, one finds that in it the absolute and independent existence of matter is accepted. Further, matter is not just dead weight, but alive with forces in tension. Indeed, for the African, everything that exists, exists as a complex of forces in tension. In holding force in tension to be essential to whatever exists, he is, like Thales and like philosophical consciencists, endowing matter with an original power of self-motion; they were endowing it with what matter would need to initiate qualitative and substantial changes.

When a plurality of men exists in society, and it is accepted that each man needs to be treated as an end in himself, not merely as a means, there transpires a transition from ethics to politics. Politics become actual, for institutions need to be created to regulate the behaviour and actions of the plurality of men in society in such a way as to conserve the fundamental ethical principle of the initial worthiness of each individual. Philosophical consciencism consequently adumbrates a political theory and a social-political practice which together seek to ensure that the cardinal principles of ethics are effective.

The social-political practice is directed at preventing the emergence or the solidifying of classes, for in the Marxist conception of class structure, there is exploitation and the subjection of class to class. Exploitation and class subjection are alike contrary to consciencism. By reason of its egalitarian tenet, philosophical consciencism seeks to promote individual development, but in such a way that the conditions for the development of all become the conditions for the development of each; that is, in such a way that the individual development does not introduce such diversities as to destroy the egalitarian basis. The social-political practice also seeks to coordinate social forces in such a way as to mobilize them logistically for the maximum development of society along true egalitarian lines. For this, planned development is essential.

In its political aspect, philosophical consciencism is faced with the realities of colonialism, imperialism, disunity, and lack of development. Singly

and collectively these four militate against the realization of a social justice
based on ideas of true equality.

The first step is to liquidate colonialism wherever it is. In *Towards Colonial
Freedom* I stated that it is the aim of colonial governments to treat their
colonies as producers of raw materials, and at the same time as the dumping
ground of the manufactured goods of foreign industrialists and foreign capitalists.[1] I have always believed that the basis of colonialism is economic, but
the solution of the colonial problem lies in political action, in a fierce and
constant struggle for emancipation as an indispensable first step toward
securing economic independence and integrity.

I said earlier on that consciencism regards matter as a plenum of forces in
tension, and that in its dialectical aspect, it holds categorial conversion to be
possible by a critical disposition of matter. This gives us a clue how to analyze
the fact of colonialism, not only in Africa, but indeed everywhere. It also
gives us a clue how to defeat it.

In a colonial situation, there are forces which tend to promote colonialism,
to promote those political ties by means of which a colonialist country binds
its colonies to itself with the primary object of furthering her economic advantages. Colonialism requires exertion, and much of that exertion is taken
up by the combat of progressive forces, forces which seek to negate this
oppressive enterprise of greedy individuals and classes by means of which
an egotistical imposition of the strong is made upon the weak.

Just as the placid appearance of matter only disguises the tension of forces
underlying that appearance, like the bow of Heraclitus, so in a colonial territory, an opposition of reactionary and revolutionary forces can nevertheless
give an impression of final and acquiescent subjugation. But just as a quality
can be changed by quantitative (measurable) changes of a critical nature in
matter, so this acquiescent impression can be obliterated by a change in the
relation of the social forces. These opposing sets of forces are dynamic, in the
sense that they seek and tend to establish some social condition. One may
therefore refer to them by the name of action in order to make their dynamic
nature explicit. In that case, one may say that, in a colonial situation, positive
action and negative action can be discerned. Positive action will represent
the sum of those forces seeking social justice in terms of the destruction
of oligarchic exploitation and oppression. Negative action will correspondingly represent the sum of those forces tending to prolong colonial subjugation and exploitation. Positive action is revolutionary and negative action is
reactionary.

It ought to be recognized at the outset that the introduced terms of positive and negative action are abstractions. But the ground for them is in social
reality. It is quite possible by means of statistical analysis to discover the ways
in which positive action and negative action are related in any given society.

The statistical analysis will be of such facts as production, distribution, income, etc. Any such analysis must reveal one of three possible situations. Positive action may exceed negative action, or negative action may exceed positive action, or they may form an unstable equilibrium.

In a colonial situation, negative action undoubtedly outweighs positive action. In order that true independence should be won, it is necessary that positive action should come to overwhelm negative action. Admittedly, a semblance of true independence is possible without this specific relation. When this happens, we say that neocolonialism has set in, for neocolonialism is a guise adopted by negative action in order to give the impression that it has been overcome by positive action. Neocolonialism is negative action playing possum.

In order to forestall this, it is necessary for positive action to be backed by a mass party, and qualitatively to improve this mass so that, by education and an increase in its degree of consciousness, its aptitude for positive action becomes heightened. We can therefore say that, in a colonial territory, positive action must be backed by a mass party, complete with its instruments of education. This was why the Convention People's Party of Ghana developed from an early stage its education wing, workers' wing, farmers' wing, youth wing, women's wing, etc. In this way, the people received constant political education, their self-awareness was increased, and such a self-image was formed as ruthlessly excluded colonialism in all its guises. It is also in the backing of millions of members and supporters, united by a common radical purpose, that the revolutionary character of the Convention People's Party consists, and not merely in the piquancy of its programmes. Its mass and national support made it possible to think in realistic terms of instituting changes of a fundamental nature in the social hotch-potch bequeathed by colonialism.

A people's parliamentary democracy with a one-party system is better able to express and satisfy the common aspirations of a nation as a whole than a multiple-party parliamentary system, which is in fact only a ruse for perpetuating and covers up the inherent struggle between the haves and the have-nots.

In order that a territory should acquire the nominal attributes of independence, it is of course not necessary that positive action should exceed negative action. When a colonialist country sees the advance of positive action, it unfailingly develops a policy of containment, a policy whereby it seeks to check this advance and limit it. This policy often takes the form of conferences and protracted constitutional reforms.

Containment is, however, accepted by the colonialist country only as a second best. What it would really like to do is to roll back positive action. It is when it is assured of the impossibility of rolling back the billows of history that it applies the policy of containment, that it tries to limit the achievement of progress by devising frivolous reforms. The colonialist country seeks to divert positive action into channels which are harmless to it.

To do this it resorts to diverse, subtle means. Having abandoned direct violence, the colonialist country imparts a deceptive orientation to the negative forces in its subject territory. These negative forces become the political wolf masquerading in sheep's clothing; they join the clamour for independence and are accepted in good faith by the people. It is then that, like a wasting disease, they seek from the inside to infest, corrupt, pervert, and thwart the aspirations of the people.

The people, the body and the soul of the nation, the final sanction of political decisions and the inheritors of sovereignty, cannot be fooled for long. Quick on the scent, they ferret out these Janus-faced politicians who run with the hare and hunt with the hounds. They turn away from them. Once this colonialist subterfuge is exposed and the minion accomplices discredited, the colonial power has no option but to acknowledge the independence of the people. By its very next act, however, it seeks without grace to neutralize this same independence by fomenting discontent and disunity; and, finally, by arrant ingratiation and wheedling, it attempts to disinherit the people and constitute itself their conscience and their will, if not their voice and their arm. Political decisions, just as they were before independence was won, lose their reference to the welfare of the people, and serve once again the well-being and security of the erstwhile colonial power and the clique of self-centered politicians.

Any oblique attempt of a foreign power to thwart, balk, corrupt, or otherwise pervert the true independence of a sovereign people is neocolonialist. It is neocolonialist because it seeks, notwithstanding the acknowledged sovereignty of a people, to subordinate their interests to those of a foreign power.

A colonialist country can in fact offer independence to a people, not with the intention which such an act might be thought to imply, but in the hope that, the positive and progressive forces thus appeased and quietened, the people might be exploited with greater serenity and comfort.

Neocolonialism is a greater danger to independent countries than is colonialism. Colonialism is crude, essentially overt, and apt to be overcome by a purposeful concert of national effort. In neocolonialism, however, the people are divided from their leaders and, instead of providing true leadership and guidance, which is informed at every point by the ideal of the general welfare, leaders come to neglect the very people who put them in power and incautiously become instruments of suppression on behalf of the neocolonialists.

It is far easier for the proverbial camel to pass through the needle's eye, hump and all, than for an erstwhile colonial administration to give sound and honest counsel of a *political* nature to its liberated territory. To allow a foreign country, especially one which is loaded with economic interests in our continent, to tell us what *political* decisions to take, what *political* courses to follow, is indeed for us to hand back our independence to the oppressor on a silver platter.

Likewise, since the motivation of colonialism, whatever protean forms it may take, is well and truly economic, colonialism itself being but the institution of political bonds fastening colonies to a colonialist country, with the primary object of the metropolitan economic advantages, it is essential that a liberated territory should not bind her economy to that of the ousted rulers. The liberation of a people institutes principles which enjoin the recognition and destruction of imperialistic domination, whether it is political, economic, social, or cultural. To destroy imperialistic domination in these forms, political, economic, social, and cultural action must always have reference to the needs and nature of the liberated territory, and it is from these needs and nature that the action must derive authenticity. Unless this self-reference is religiously maintained, a liberated territory will welcome with open arms the very foe which it has sought to destroy at cost of terrible suffering.

The true welfare of a people does not admit of compromise. If we compromise on the true interest of our people, the people must one day judge us, for it is with their effort and their sacrifice, with their forbearance and their denial, that independence is won. Independence once won, it is possible to rule against the erstwhile colonial power, but it is not really possible to rule against the wish and interest of the people.

The people are the backbone of positive action. It is by the people's effort that colonialism is routed; it is by the sweat of the people's brow that nations are built. The people are the reality of national greatness. It is the people who suffer the depredations and indignities of colonialism, and the people must not be insulted by dangerous flirtations with neocolonialism.

There is a fundamental law of the evolution of matter to higher forms. This evolution is dialectical. And it is also the fundamental law of society. It is out of tension that being is born. Becoming is a tension, and being is the child of that tension of opposed forces and tendencies.

Just as in the physical universe, since the moving object is always impressed upon by external forces, any motion is in fact a resultant, so in society every development, every progressive motion, is a resultant of unharmonious forces, a resultant, a triumph, of positive action over negative action.

This triumph must be accompanied by knowledge. For in the way that the process of natural evolution can be aided by human intervention based upon knowledge, so social evolution can be helped along by political intervention based upon knowledge of the laws of social development. Political action aimed at speeding up social evolution is of the nature of a catalyst.

The need for such a catalyst is created by the fact that natural evolution is always wasteful. It takes place at the cost of massive loss of life and at the cost of extreme anguish. Evolution speeded by scientific knowledge is prompter, and represents an economy of material. In the same way, the catalysis which political action introduces into social evolution represents an economy of time, life, and talent.

Without positive action, a colonial territory cannot be truly liberated. It is doomed to creep in its petty pace from day to day towards the attainment of a sham independence that turns to dust, independence which is shot through and through with the supreme interest of an alien power. To achieve true liberation, positive action must begin with an objective analysis of the situation which it seeks to change. Such an analysis I attempted in *Towards Colonial Freedom*. Positive action must, furthermore, seek an alignment of all the forces of progress and, by marshalling them, confront the negative forces. It must at the same time anticipate and contain its own inner contradictions, for though positive action unites those forces of a situation which are in regard to a specific purpose progressive, many of these forces will contain tendencies which are in other respects reactionary.

Hence, when positive action resorts to an alignment of forces, it creates in itself seams at which this alignment might fall apart. It is essential that positive action should in its dialectical evolution anticipate this seminal disintegration and discover a way of containing the future schismatic tendencies, a way of nipping fragmentation in the bud as colonialism begins to reel and totter under the frontal onslaught of positive action.

But even with colonialism worsted, positive action cannot relent, for it is at about this time that the schismatic tendencies referred to ripen. Besides, political independence, though worthwhile in itself, is still only a means to the fuller redemption and realization of a people. When independence has been gained, positive action requires a new orientation away from the sheer destruction of colonialism and towards national reconstruction.

It is indeed in this address to national reconstruction that positive action faces its gravest dangers. The cajolement, the wheedlings, the seductions, and the Trojan horses of neocolonialism must be stoutly resisted, for neocolonialism is a latter-day harpy, a monster which entices its victims with sweet music.

In order to be able to carry out this resistance to neocolonialism at every point, positive action requires to be armed with an ideology, an ideology which, vitalizing it and operating through a mass party, shall equip it with a regenerative concept of the world and life, forge for it a strong continuing link with our past, and offer to it an assured bond with our future. Under the searchlight of an ideology, every fact affecting the life of a people can be assessed and judged, and neocolonialism's detrimental aspirations and sleights of hand will constantly stand exposed.

In order that this ideology should be comprehensive, in order that it should light up every aspect of the life of our people, in order that it should affect the total interest of our society, establishing a continuity with our past, it must be socialist in form and in content and be embraced by a mass party.

And yet socialism in Africa today tends to lose its objective content in favor of a distracting terminology and in favor of a general confusion. Discussion centers more on the various conceivable types of socialism than upon the need for socialist development. More is surely required than a mere reaction against a policy of domination. Independence is of the people; it is won by the people for the people. That independence is of the people is admitted by every enlightened theory of sovereignty. That it is won by the people is to be seen in the success of mass movements everywhere. That it is won for the people follows from their ownership of sovereignty. The people have not mastered their independence until it has been given a national and social content and purpose that will generate their well-being and uplift.

The socialism of a liberated territory is subject to a number of principles if independence is not to be alienated from the people. When socialism is true to its purpose, it seeks a connection with the egalitarian and humanist past of the people before their social evolution was ravaged by colonialism; it seeks from the results of colonialism those elements (like new methods of industrial production and economic organization) which can be adapted to serve the interest of the people; it seeks to contain and prevent the spread of those anomalies and domineering interests created by the capitalist habit of colonialism; it reclaims the psychology of the people, erasing the "colonial mentality" from it; and it resolutely defends the independence and security of the people. In short, socialism recognizes dialectic, the possibility of creation from forces which are opposed to one another; it recognizes the creativity of struggle, and, indeed, the necessity of the operation of [oppositional] forces to any change. It also embraces materialism and translates this into social terms of equality. Hence philosophical consciencism.

¹Kwame Nkrumah, *Towards Colonial Freedom: Africa in the Struggle Against World Imperialism* (London: Heinemann, 1962).

JULIUS K. NYERERE (1922–)

 Ujamaa—The Basis of African Socialism (1962)

Socialism, like democracy, is an attitude of mind. In a socialist society it is the socialist attitude of mind, and not the rigid adherence to a standard political pattern, which is needed to ensure that the people care for each other's welfare.

The purpose of this paper is to examine that attitude. It is not intended to define the institutions which may be required to embody it in a modern society.

In the individual, as in the society, it is an attitude of mind which distinguishes the socialist from the nonsocialist. It has nothing to do with the possession or nonpossession of wealth. Destitute people can be potential capitalists—exploiters of their fellow human beings. A millionaire can equally well be a socialist; he may value his wealth only because it can be used in the service of his fellow men. But the man who uses wealth for the purpose of dominating any of his fellows is a capitalist. So is the man who would if he could!

I have said that a millionaire can be a good socialist. But a socialist millionaire is a rare phenomenon. Indeed, he is almost a contradiction in terms. The appearance of millionaires in any society is no proof of its affluence; they can be produced by very poor countries like Tanganyika just as well as by rich countries like the United States of America. For it is not efficiency of production nor the amount of wealth in a country which makes millionaires; it is the uneven distribution of what is produced. The basic difference between a socialist society and a capitalist society does not lie in their methods of producing wealth, but in the way that wealth is distributed. While, therefore, a millionaire could be a good socialist, he could hardly be the product of a socialist society.

Since the appearance of millionaires in a society does not depend on its affluence, sociologists may find it interesting to try and find out why our

Reprinted from *Freedom and Unity,* by Julius K. Nyerere (New York: Oxford University Press, 1968), 162–71, with permission of author.

societies in Africa did not, in fact, produce any millionaires—for we certainly had enough wealth to create a few. I think they would discover that it was because the organization of traditional African society—its distribution of the wealth it produced—was such that there was hardly any room for parasitism. They might also say, of course, that as a result of this, Africa could not produce a leisured class of landowners, and therefore there was nobody to produce the works of art or science [of] which capitalist societies can boast. But the works of art and the achievements of science are products of the intellect—which, like land, is one of God's gifts to man. And I cannot believe that God is so careless as to have made the use of one of His gifts depend on the misuse of another!

Defenders of capitalism claim that the millionaire's wealth is the just reward for his ability or enterprise. But this claim is not borne out by the facts. The wealth of the millionaire depends as little on the enterprise or abilities of the millionaire himself as the power of a feudal monarch depended on his own efforts, enterprise, or brain. Both are users, exploiters, of the abilities and enterprise of other people. Even when you have an exceptionally intelligent and hardworking millionaire, the difference between his intelligence, his enterprise, his hard work, and those of other members of society, cannot possibly be proportionate to the difference between their "rewards." There must be something wrong in a society where one man, however hardworking or clever he may be, can acquire as great a reward as a thousand of his fellows can acquire between them.

Acquisitiveness for the purpose of gaining power and prestige is unsocialist. In an acquisitive society, wealth tends to corrupt those who possess it. It tends to breed in them a desire to live more comfortably than their fellows, to dress better, and in every way to outdo them. They begin to feel they must climb as far above their neighbors as they can. The visible contrast between their own comfort and the comparative discomfort of the rest of society becomes almost essential to the enjoyment of their wealth, and this sets off the spiral of personal competition—which is then antisocial.

Apart from the antisocial effects of the accumulation of personal wealth, the very desire to accumulate it must be interpreted as a vote of no confidence in the social system. For when a society is so organized that it cares about its individuals, then, provided he is willing to work, no individual within that society should worry about what will happen to him tomorrow if he does not hoard wealth today. Society itself should look after him, or his widow, or his orphans. This is exactly what traditional African society succeeded in doing. Both the "rich" and the "poor" individual were completely secure in African society. Natural catastrophe brought famine, but it brought famine to everybody—poor or rich. Nobody starved, either of food or of human dignity, because he lacked personal wealth; he could depend on the wealth possessed by the community of which he was a member. That was socialism. That is socialism. There can be no such thing as acquisitive socialism, for that would be another contradiction in terms. Socialism is essentially distributive. Its concern is to see that those who sow reap a fair share of what they sow.

The production of wealth, whether by primitive or modern methods, requires three things. First, land. God has given us the land, and it is from the land that we get the raw materials which we reshape to meet our needs. Secondly, tools. We have found by simple experience that tools do help! So we make the hoe, the axe, or the modern factory or tractor, to help us to produce wealth—the goods we need. And, thirdly, human exertion—or labour. We don't need to read Karl Marx or Adam Smith to find out that neither the land nor the hoe actually produces wealth. And we don't need to take degrees in economics to know that neither the worker nor the landlord produces land. Land is God's gift to man—it is always there. But we do know, still without degrees in economics, that the axe and the plough were produced by the laborer. Some of our more sophisticated friends apparently have to undergo the most rigorous intellectual training simply in order to discover that stone axes were produced by that ancient gentleman "early man" to make it easier for him to skin the impala he had just killed with a club, which he had also made for himself!

In traditional African society, everybody was a worker. There was no other way of earning a living for the community. Even the elder, who appeared to be enjoying himself without doing any work and for whom everybody else appeared to be working, had in fact worked hard all his younger days. The wealth he now appeared to possess was not his personally; it was only "his" as the elder of the group which had produced it. He was its guardian. The wealth itself gave him neither power nor prestige. The respect paid to him by the young was his because he was older than they, and had served his community longer; and the "poor" elder enjoyed as much respect in our society as the "rich" elder.

When I say that in traditional African society everybody was a worker, I do not use the word worker simply as opposed to employer but also as opposed to loiterer or idler. One of the most socialist achievements of our society was the sense of security it gave to its members, and the universal hospitality on which they could rely. But it is too often forgotten, nowadays, that the basis of this great socialistic achievement was this: that it was taken for granted that every member of society—barring only the children and the infirm—contributed his fair share of effort towards the production of its wealth. Not only was the capitalist, or the landed exploiter, unknown to traditional African society, but we did not have that other form of modern parasite—the loiterer, or idler, who accepts the hospitality of society as his right but gives nothing in return! Capitalistic exploitation was impossible. Loitering was an unthinkable disgrace.

Those of us who talk about the African way of life and quite rightly take a pride in maintaining the tradition of hospitality which is so great a part of it might do well to remember the Swahili saying: "*Mgeni siku mbili; siku ya tatu mpe jembe*"—or, in English, "Treat your guest as a guest for two days; on the third day, give him a hoe!" In actual fact, the guest was likely to ask for the hoe even before his host had to give him one—for he knew what was expected of him, and would have been ashamed to remain idle any longer. Thus, working was part and parcel, was indeed the very basis and justification, of this socialist achievement of which we are so justly proud.

There is no such thing as socialism without work. A society which fails to give its individuals the means to work, or, having given them the means to work, prevents them from getting a fair share of the products of their own sweat and toil, needs putting right. Similarly, an individual who can work—and is provided by society with the means to work—but does not do so is equally wrong. He has no right to expect anything from society because he contributes nothing to society.

The other use of the word worker, in its specialized sense of employee as opposed to employer, reflects a capitalist attitude of mind which was introduced into Africa with the coming of colonialism and is totally foreign to our own way of thinking. In the old days the African had never aspired to the possession of personal wealth for the purpose of dominating any of his fellows. He had never had labourers or "factory hands" to do his work for him. But then came the foreign capitalists. They were wealthy. They were powerful. And the African naturally started wanting to be wealthy, too. There is nothing wrong in our wanting to be wealthy; nor is it a bad thing for us to want to acquire the power which wealth brings with it. But it most certainly is wrong if we want the wealth and the power so that we can dominate somebody else. Unfortunately there are some of us who have already learnt to covet wealth for that purpose, and who would like to use the methods which the capitalist uses in acquiring it. That is to say, some of us would like to use, or exploit, our brothers for the purpose of building up our own personal power and prestige. This is completely foreign to us, and it is incompatible with the socialist society we want to build here.

Our first step, therefore, must be to re-educate ourselves; to regain our former attitude of mind. In our traditional African society we were individuals within a community. We took care of the community, and the community took care of us. We neither needed nor wished to exploit our fellow men.

And in rejecting the capitalist attitude of mind which colonialism brought into Africa, we must reject also the capitalist methods which go with it. One of these is the individual ownership of land. To us in Africa, land was always recognized as belonging to the community. Each individual within our society had a right to the use of land, because otherwise he could not earn his living, and one cannot have the right to life without also having the right to some means of maintaining life. But the African's right to land was simply the right to use it: he had no other right to it, nor did it occur to him to try and claim one.

The foreigner introduced a completely different concept, the concept of land as a marketable commodity. According to this system, a person could claim a piece of land as his own private property whether he intended to use it or not. I could take a few square miles of land, call them "mine," and then go off to the moon. All I had to do to gain a living from "my" land was to charge a rent to the people who wanted to use it. If this piece of land was in an urban area, I had no need to develop it at all; I could leave it to the fools who were prepared to develop all the other pieces of land surrounding "my" piece, and in doing so automatically to raise the market value of mine. Then I could come down from the moon and demand that these fools pay me through their noses for the high value of "my" land, a value which they themselves had created for me while I was enjoying myself on the moon! Such a system is not only foreign to us, it is completely wrong. Landlords, in a society which recognizes individual ownership of land, can be and usually are in the same class as the loiterers I was talking about: the class of parasites.

We must not allow the growth of parasites here in Tanganyika. The TANU Government must go back to the traditional African custom of land holding. That is to say, a member of society will be entitled to a piece of land on condition that he uses it. Unconditional, or "freehold," ownership of land (which leads to speculation and parasitism) must be abolished. We must, as I have said, regain our former attitude of mind—our traditional African socialism—and apply it to the new societies we are building today. TANU has pledged itself to make socialism the basis of its policy in every field. The people of Tanganyika have given us their mandate to carry out that policy by electing a TANU government to lead them. So the Government can be relied upon to introduce only legislation which is in harmony with socialist principles.

But, as I said at the beginning, true socialism is an attitude of mind. It is therefore up to the people of Tanganyika—the peasants, the wage-earners, the students, the leaders, all of us—to make sure that this socialist attitude of mind is not lost through the temptations to personal gain (or to the abuse of positions of authority) which may come our way as individuals, or through the temptation to look on the good of the whole community as of secondary importance to the interests of our own particular group.

Just as the elder, in our former society, was respected for his age and his service to the community, so in our modern society this respect for age and service will be preserved. And in the same way as the rich elder's apparent wealth was really only held by him in trust for his people, so today the apparent extra wealth which certain positions of leadership may bring to the individuals who fill them can be theirs only in so far as it is a necessary aid to the carrying out of their duties. It is a tool entrusted to them for the benefit of the people they serve. It is not theirs personally; and they may not use any part of it as a means of accumulating more for their own benefit, nor as an insurance against the day when they no longer hold the same positions. That would be to betray the people who entrusted it to them. If they serve the community while they can, the community must look after them when they are no longer able to do so.

In tribal society, the individuals or the families within a tribe were rich or poor according to whether the whole tribe was rich or poor. If the tribe prospered, all the members of the tribe shared in its prosperity. Tanganyika today is a poor country. The standard of living of the masses of our people is shamefully low. But if every man and woman in the country takes up the challenge and works to the limit of his or her ability for the good of the whole society, Tanganyika will prosper; and that prosperity will be shared by all her people.

But it must be shared. The true socialist may not exploit his fellows. So that if the members of any group within our society are going to argue that, because they happen to be contributing more to the national income than some other groups, they must therefore take for themselves a greater share of the profits of their own industry than they actually need, and if they insist on this in spite of the fact that it would mean reducing their group's contribution to the general income and thus slowing down the rate at which the whole community can benefit, then that group is exploiting (or trying to exploit) its fellow human beings. It is displaying a capitalist attitude of mind.

There are bound to be certain groups which, by virtue of the market value of their particular industry's products, will contribute more to the nation's income than others. But the others may actually be producing goods or services which are of equal or greater intrinsic value, although they do not happen to command such a high artificial value. For example, the food produced by the peasant farmer is of greater social value than the diamonds mined at Mwadui. But the mine-workers of Mwadui could claim, quite correctly, that their labour was yielding greater financial profits to the community than that of the farmers. If, however, they went on to demand that they should therefore be given most of that extra profit for themselves, and that no share of it should be spent on helping the farmers, they would be potential capitalists!

This is exactly where the attitude of mind comes in. It is one of the purposes of trade unions to ensure for the workers a fair share of the profits of their labour. But a fair share must be fair in relation to the whole society. If it is greater than the country can afford without having to penalize some other section of society, then it is not a fair share. Trade union leaders and their followers, as long as they are true socialists, will not need to be coerced by the government into keeping their demands within the limits imposed by the needs of society as a whole. Only if there are potential capitalists amongst them will the socialist government have to step in and prevent them from putting their capitalist ideas into practice!

As with groups, so with individuals. There are certain skills, certain qualifications, which for good reasons command a higher rate of salary for their possessors than others. But here again the true socialist will demand only that return for his skilled work which he knows to be a fair one in proportion to the wealth or poverty of the whole society to which he belongs. He will not, unless he is a would-be capitalist attempt to blackmail the community by demanding a salary equal to that paid to his counterpart in some far wealthier society.

European socialism was born of the agrarian revolution and the industrial revolution which followed it. The former created the landed and the landless classes in society; the latter produced the modern capitalist and the industrial proletariat.

These two revolutions planted the seeds of conflict within society, and not only was European socialism born of that conflict, but its apostles sanctified the conflict itself into a philosophy. Civil war was no longer looked upon as something evil, or something unfortunate, but as something good and necessary. As prayer is to Christianity or to Islam, so civil war (which they call class war) is to the European version of socialism—a means inseparable from the end. Each becomes the basis of a whole way of life. The European socialist cannot think of his socialism without its father—capitalism!

Brought up in tribal socialism, I must say I find this contradiction quite intolerable. It gives capitalism a philosophical status which capitalism neither claims nor deserves. For it virtually says, "Without capitalism, and the conflict which capitalism creates within society, there can be no socialism!" This glorification of capitalism by the doctrinaire European socialists, I repeat, I find intolerable.

African socialism, on the other hand, did not have the "benefit" of the agrarian revolution or the industrial revolution. It did not start from the existence of conflicting classes in society. Indeed I doubt if the equivalent for the word class exists in any indigenous African language; for language describes the ideas of those who speak it, and the idea of class or caste was nonexistent in African society.

The foundation and the objective of African socialism is the extended family. The true African socialist does not look on one class of men as his brethren and another as his natural enemies. He does not form an alliance with the "brethren" for the extermination of the "non-brethren." He rather regards all men as his brethren—as members of his ever extending family. That is why the first article of TANU's creed is *"Binadamu wote ni ndugu zangu, na Afrika ni moja."* If this had been originally put in English, it could have been "I believe in human brotherhood and the unity of Africa."

Ujamaa, then, or "familyhood," describes our socialism. It is opposed to capitalism, which seeks to build a happy society on the basis of the exploitation of man by man; and it is equally opposed to doctrinaire socialism, which seeks to build its happy society on a philosophy of inevitable conflict between man and man.

We in Africa have no more need of being converted to socialism than we have of being taught democracy. Both are rooted in our own past—in the traditional society which produced us. Modern African socialism can draw from its traditional heritage the recognition of "society" as an extension of the basic family unit. But it can no longer confine the idea of the social family within the limits of the tribe, nor, indeed, of the nation. For no true African socialist can look at a line drawn on a map and say, "The people on this side of that line are my brothers, but those who happen to live on the other side of it can have no claim on me"; every individual on this continent is his brother.

It was in the struggle to break the grip of colonialism that we learned the need for unity. We came to recognize that the same socialist attitude of mind which, in the tribal days, gave to every individual the security that comes of belonging to a widely extended family must be preserved within the still wider society of the nation. But we should not stop there. Our recognition of the family to which we all belong must be extended yet further—beyond the tribe, the community, the nation, or even the continent—to embrace the whole society of mankind. This is the only logical conclusion for true socialism.

AMILCAR CABRAL (1921–1973)

✸ Identity and Dignity in the Context of the National Liberation Struggle (1972)

Introduction

The people's struggle for national liberation and independence from imperialist rule has become a driving force of progress for humanity and undoubtedly constitutes one of the essential characteristics of contemporary history.

An objective analysis of imperialism insofar as it is a fact or a "natural" historical phenomenon, indeed "necessary" in the context of the type of economic political evolution of an important part of humanity, reveals that imperialist rule, with all its train of wretchedness, of pillage, of crime and of destruction of human and cultural values, was not just a negative reality. The vast accumulation of capital in half-a-dozen countries of the northern hemisphere, which was the result of piracy, of the confiscation of the property of other peoples and of the ruthless exploitation of the work of these peoples, will not only lead to the monopolization of colonies, but to the division of the world and more imperialist rule.

In the rich countries, imperialist capital, constantly seeking to enlarge itself, increased the creative capacity of man and brought about a total transformation of the means of production, thanks to the rapid progress of science, of techniques, and of technology. This accentuated the pooling of labor and brought about the ascension of huge areas of population. In the colonized countries, where colonization on the whole blocked the historical process of the development of the subjected peoples or else eliminated them radically or progressively, imperialist capital imposed new types of relationships on indigenous society, the structure of which became more complex, and it stirred up, fomented, poisoned, or resolved contradictions and social conflicts; it introduced, together with money and the development of internal and external markets, new elements in the economy; it brought about

Reprinted from *Return to the Source*, by Amilcar Cabral (New York: Monthly Review Press, 1973), 9–25. © 1973 by PAIGC. Reprinted by permission of Monthly Review Foundation.

the birth of new nations from human groups or from peoples who were at different stages of historical development.

It is not to defend imperialist domination to recognize that it gave new nations to the world, the dimensions of which it reduced, and that it revealed new stages of development in human societies; and in spite of or because of the prejudices, the discrimination, and the crimes which it occasioned, it contributed to a deeper knowledge of humanity as a moving whole, as a unity in the complex diversity of the characteristics of its development.

Imperialist rule on many continents favored a multilateral and progressive (sometimes abrupt) confirmation not only between different men but also between different societies. The practice of imperialist rule—its affirmation or its negation—demanded (and still demands) a more or less accurate knowledge of the society it rules and of the historical reality (economic, social, and cultural) in the middle of which it exists. This knowledge is necessarily exposed in terms of comparison with the dominating subject and with its own historical reality. Such a knowledge is a vital necessity in the practice of imperialist rule, which results in the confrontation, mostly violent, between two identities which are totally dissimilar in their historical elements and contradictory in their different functions. The search for such a knowledge contributed to a general enrichment of human and social knowledge in spite of the fact that it was one-sided, subjective, and very often unjust.

In fact, man has never shown as much interest in knowing other men and other societies as during this century of imperialist domination. An unprecedented mass of information, of hypotheses and theories, has been built up, notably in the fields of history, ethnology, ethnography, sociology, and culture, concerning people or groups brought under imperialist domination. The concepts of race, caste, ethnicity, tribe, nation, culture, identity, dignity, and many others, have become the object of increasing attention from those who study men and the societies described as primitive or evolving.

More recently, with the rise of liberation movements, the need has arisen to analyze the character of these societies in the light of the struggle they are waging, and to decide the factors which launch or hold back this struggle. The researchers are generally agreed that, in this context, culture shows special significance. So one can argue that any attempt to clarify the true role of culture in the development of the (pre-independence) liberation movement can make a useful contribution to the broad struggle of the people against imperialist domination.

In this short lecture, we consider particularly the problems of the "return to the source," and of identity and dignity in the context of the national liberation movement.

Part I

The fact that independence movements are generally marked, even in their early stages, by an upsurge of cultural activity has led to the view that such movements are preceded by a "cultural renaissance" of the subject people. Some go as far as to suggest that culture is one means of collecting together a group, even a *weapon* in the struggle for independence.

From the experience of our own struggle and one might say that of the whole of Africa, we consider that there is a too-limited, even mistaken idea of the vital role of culture in the development of the liberation movement. In our view, this arises from a fake generalization of a phenomenon which is real but limited, which is at a particular level in the vertical structure of colonized societies—at the level of the *elite* or the colonial *diasporas*. This generalization is unaware of or ignores the vital element of the problem: the indestructible character of the cultural resistance of the masses of the people when confronted with foreign domination.

Certainly imperialist domination calls for cultural oppression and attempts either directly or indirectly to do away with the most important elements of the culture of the subject people. But the people are only able to create and develop the liberation movement because they keep their culture alive despite continual and organized repression of their cultural life and because they continue to resist culturally, even when their politico-military resistance is destroyed. And it is cultural resistance which, at a given moment, can take on new forms, i.e., political, economic, armed to fight foreign domination.

With certain exceptions, *the period of colonization* was not long enough, at least in Africa, for there to be a significant degree of destruction or damage of the most important facets of the culture and traditions of the subject people. Colonial experience of imperialist domination in Africa (genocide, racial segregation, and apartheid excepted) shows that the only so-called positive solution which the colonial power put forward to repudiate the subject people's cultural resistance was *assimilation*. But the complete failure of the policy of "progressive assimilation" of native populations is the living proof both of the falsehood of this theory and of the capacity of the subject people to resist. As far as the Portuguese colonies are concerned, the maximum number of people assimilated was 0.3 percent of the total population (in Guinea), and this was after five hundred years of civilizing influence and half a century of "colonial peace."

On the other hand, even in the settlements where the overwhelming majority of the population are indigenous peoples, the area occupied by the colonial power and especially the area of *cultural influence* is usually restricted to coastal strips and to a few limited parts in the interior. Outside the boundaries of the capital and other urban centers, the influence of the colonial power's culture is almost nil. It only leaves its mark at the very top of the colonial social pyramid—which created colonialism itself—and particularly it influences what one might call the indigenous lower middle class and a very small number of workers in urban areas.

It can thus be seen that the masses in the rural areas, like a large section of the urban population, say, in all, over 99 percent of the indigenous population, are untouched or almost untouched by the culture of the colonial power. This situation is partly the result of the necessarily obscurantist character of the imperialist domination which, while it despises and suppresses indigenous culture, takes no interest in promoting culture for the masses, who are their pool for forced labor and the main object of exploitation. It is also the result of the effectiveness of cultural resistance of the people, who when they are subjected to political domination and economic exploitation find that their own culture acts as a bulwark in preserving their *identity.* Where the indigenous society has a vertical structure, this defense of their cultural heritage is further strengthened by the colonial power's interest in protecting and backing the cultural influence of the ruling classes, their allies.

The above argument implies that generally speaking there is not any marked destruction or damage to culture or tradition, neither for the masses in the subject country nor for the indigenous ruling classes (traditional chief, noble families, religious authorities). Repressed, persecuted, humiliated, betrayed by certain social groups who have compromised with the foreign power, culture took refuge in the villages, in the forests, and in the spirit of the victims of domination. Culture survives all these challenges and, through the struggle for liberation, blossoms forth again. Thus the question of a return to the source or of a cultural renaissance does not arise and could not arise for the masses of these people, for it is they who are the repository of the culture and at the same time the only social sector who can preserve and build it up and *make history.*

Thus, in Africa at least, for a true idea of the real role which culture plays in the development of the liberation movement, a distinction must be made between the situation of the masses, who preserve their culture, and that of the social groups who are assimilated or partially so, who are cut off and culturally alienated. Even though the indigenous colonial elite who emerged during the process of colonization still continues to pass on some element of indigenous culture, yet they live both materially and spiritually according to the foreign colonial culture. They seek to identify themselves increasingly with this culture, both in their social behaviors and in their appreciation of its values.

In the course of two or three generations of colonization, a social class arises made up of civil servants; people who are employed in various branches of the economy, especially commerce; professional people; and a few urban and agricultural landowners. This indigenous petite bourgeoisie, which emerged out of foreign domination and is indispensable to the system of colonial exploitation, stands midway between the masses of the working class in town and country and the small number of local representatives of the foreign ruling class. Although they may have quite strong links with the masses and with the traditional chiefs, generally speaking they aspire to a way of life which is similar if not identical with that of the foreign minority. At the same time, while they restrict their dealings with the masses, they try to become integrated into this minority, often at the cost of family or ethnic ties and always at great personal cost. Yet despite the apparent exceptions, they do not succeed in getting past the barriers thrown up by the system. They are prisoners of the cultural and social contradictions of their lives. They cannot escape from their role as a marginal class, or a "marginalized" class.

The marginal character or the "marginality" of this class both in their own country and in the diasporas established in the territory of the colonial power is responsible for the sociocultural conflicts of the colonial elite or the indigenous petite bourgeoisie, played out very much according to their material circumstances and level of acculturation but always at the individual level, never collectively.

It is within the framework of this daily drama, against the backcloth of the usually violent confrontation between the mass of the people and the ruling colonial class, that a feeling of bitterness or a *frustration complex* is bred and develops among the indigenous petite bourgeoisie. At the same time, they are becoming more and more conscious of a compelling need to question their marginal status and to rediscover an identity.

Thus they turn to the people around them, the people at the other extreme of the sociocultural conflict—the native masses. For this reason arises the problem of "return to the source," which seems to be even more pressing the greater the isolation of the petite bourgeoisie (or native elites) and their acute feelings of frustration, as in the case of African diasporas living in the colonial or racist metropolis. It comes as no surprise that the theories or "movements" such as Pan-Africanism or Negritude (two pertinent expressions arising mainly from the assumption that all black Africans have a cultural identity) were propounded outside black Africa. More recently, the black Americans' claim to an African identity is another proof, possibly rather a desperate one, of the need for a return to the source, although clearly it is influenced by a new situation: the fact that the great majority of African people are now independent.

But the return to the source is not and cannot in itself be an *act of struggle* against foreign domination (colonialist and racist), and it no longer necessarily means a return to traditions. It is the denial by the petite bourgeoisie of the pretended supremacy of the culture of the dominant power over that of the dominated people with which it must identify itself. The return to the source is therefore not a voluntary step, but the only possible reply to the demand of concrete need, historically determined and enforced by the inescapable contradiction between the colonized society and the colonial power, the mass of the people exploited and the foreign exploitive class, a contradiction in the light of which each social stratum or indigenous class must define its position.

When the return to the source goes beyond the individual and is expressed through groups or movements, the contradiction is transformed into struggle (secret or overt), and is a prelude to the pre-independence movement or of the struggle for liberation from the foreign yoke. So the return to the source is of no historical importance unless it brings not only real involvement in the struggle for independence, but also complete and absolute identification with the hopes of the mass of the people, who contest not only the foreign culture but also the foreign domination as a whole. Otherwise, the "return to the source" is nothing more than an attempt to find short-term benefits—knowingly or unknowingly, a kind of political opportunism.

One must point out that the return to the source, apparent or real, does not develop at one time and in the same way in the heart of the indigenous petite bourgeoisie. It is a slow process, broken up and uneven, whose development depends on the degree of acculturation of each individual, of the material circumstances of his life, on the forming of his ideas, and on his experience as a social being. This unevenness is the basis of the split of the indigenous petite bourgeoisie into three groups when confronted with the liberation movement: a) a minority which, even if it wants to see an end to foreign domination, clings to the dominant colonialist class and openly opposes the movement to protect its social position; b) a majority of people who are hesitant and indecisive; c) another minority of people who share in the building and leadership of the liberation movement.

But the latter group, which plays a decisive role in the development of the pre-independence movement, does not truly identify with the mass of the people (with their culture and hopes) except through struggle, the scale of this identification depending on the kind or methods of struggle, on the ideological basis of the movement, and on the level of moral and political awareness of each individual.

Part II

Identification of a section of the indigenous petite bourgeoisie with the mass of the people has an essential prerequisite: *that, in the face of destructive action by imperialist domination, the masses retain their identity,* separate and distinct from that of the colonial power. It is worthwhile therefore to decide in what circumstances this retention is possible; why, when, and at what levels of the dominated society is raised the problem of the loss or absence of identity; and in consequence it becomes necessary to assert or reassert in the framework of the pre-independence movement a separate and distinct identity from that of the colonial power.

The identity of an individual or a particular group of people is a bio-sociological factor outside the will of that individual or group, but which is meaningful only when it is expressed in relation to other individuals or other groups. The dialectical character of identity lies in the fact that an individual (or a group) is only similar to certain individuals (or groups) if it is also different to other individuals (or groups).

The definition of an identity, individual or collective, is at the same time the affirmation and denial of a certain number of characteristics which define the individuals or groups, through *historical* (biological and sociological) factors at a moment of their development. In fact, identity is not a constant, precisely because the biological and sociological factors which define it are in constant change. Biologically and sociologically, there are no two beings (individual or collective) completely the same or completely different, for it is always possible to find in them common or distinguishing characteristics. Therefore the identity of a being is always a relative quality, even circumstantial, for defining it demands a selection, more or less rigid and strict, of the biological and sociological characteristics of the being in question. One must point out that in the fundamental binomial in the definition of identity, the sociological factors are more determining than the biological. In fact, if it is correct that the biological element (inherited genetic patrimony) is the inescapable physical basis of the existence and continuing growth of identity, it is no less correct that the sociological element is the factor which gives it objective substance by giving content and form and allowing confrontation and comparison between individuals and between groups. To make a total definition of identity, the inclusion of the biological element is indispensable, but does not imply a sociological similarity, whereas two beings who are sociologically exactly the same must necessarily have similar biological identities.

This shows on the one hand the supremacy of the social over the individual condition, for society (human, for example) is a higher form of life. It shows, on the other hand, the need not to confuse the *original identity*, of which the biological element is the main determinant, and the *actual identity*, of which the main determinant is the sociological element. Clearly, the identity of which one must take account at a given moment of the growth of a being (individual or collective) is the actual identity, and awareness of that being reached only on the basis of his original identity is incomplete, partial and false, for it leaves out or does not comprehend the decisive influence of social conditions on the content and form of identity.

In the formation and development of individual or collective identity, the social condition is an objective agent, arising from economic, political, social, and cultural aspects which are characteristic of the growth and history of the society in question. If one argues that the economic aspect is fundamental, one can assert that identity is in a certain sense the expression of an economic reality. This reality, whatever the geographical context and the path of development of the society, is defined by the level of productive forces (the relationship between man and nature) and by the means of production (the relations between men and between classes within this society). But if one accepts that culture is a dynamic synthesis of the material and spiritual conditions of the society and expresses relationships both between man and nature and between the different classes within a society, one can assert that identity is, at the individual and collective level and beyond the economic condition, the expression of culture. This is why to attribute, recognize, or declare the identity of an individual or group is above all to place that individual or group in the framework of a culture. Now as we all know, the main prop of culture in any society is the social structure. One can therefore draw the conclusion that the possibility of a movement group keeping (or losing) its identity in the face of foreign domination depends on the extent of the destruction of its social structure under the stresses of that domination.

As for the effects of imperialist domination on the social structure of the dominated people, one must look here at the case of classic colonialism, against which the pre-independence movement is contending. In that case, whatever the stage of historical development of the dominated society, the social structure can be subjected to the following experiences: a) *total destruction,* mixed with immediate or gradual liquidation of the indigenous people and replacement by a foreign people; b) *partial destruction,* with the settling of a more or less numerous foreign population; c) *ostensible preservation,* brought about by the restriction of the indigenous people in geographical areas or special reserves usually without means of living, and the massive influx of a foreign population.

The fundamentally horizontal character of the social structure of African people, due to the profusion of ethnic groups, means that the cultural resistance and degree of retention of identity are not uniform. So even where ethnic groups have broadly succeeded in keeping their identity, we observe that the most *resistant* groups are those which have had the most violent battles with the colonial power during the period of effective occupation or those who because of their geographical location have had least contact with the foreign presence.

One must point out that the attitude of the colonial power towards the ethnic groups creates an insoluble contradiction: on the one hand it must divide or keep divisions in order to rule, and for that reason favors separation if not conflict between ethnic groups; on the other hand, to try to keep the permanency of its domination, it needs to destroy the social structure, culture, and by implication identity, of these groups. Moreover, it must protect the ruling class of those groups (like, for example, the Fula tribe or nation in our country) which have given decisive support during the colonial conquest—a policy which favors the preservation of the identity of these groups.

As has already been said, there are not usually important changes in respect of culture in the upright shape of the indigenous social pyramids (groups or societies with a state). Each level or class keeps its identity, linked with that of the group but separate from that of other social classes. Conversely, in the urban centers as in some of the interior regions of the country where the cultural influence of the colonial power is felt, the problem of identity is more complicated. While the bottom and the top of the social pyramid (that is, the mass of the working class drawn from different ethnic groups and the foreign dominant class) keep their identities, the middle level of this pyramid (the indigenous petite bourgeoise), culturally uprooted, alienated, or more or less assimilated, engages in a sociological battle in search of its identity. One must also point out that though united by a new identity—granted by the colonial power—the foreign dominant class can not free itself from the contradictions of its own society, which it brings to the colonized country.

When at the initiative of a minority of the indigenous petite bourgeoisie allied with the indigenous masses the pre-independence movement is launched, the masses have no need to assert or reassert their identity, which they have never confused nor would have known how to confuse with that of the colonial power. This need is felt only by the indigenous petite bourgeoisie, which finds itself obliged to take up a position in the struggle which opposes the masses to the colonial power. However, the reassertion of identity distinct from that of the colonial power is not always achieved by all the petite bourgeoisie. It is only a minority who do this, while another minority asserts, often in a noisy manner, the identity of the foreign dominant class, while the silent majority is trapped in indecision.

Moreover, even when there is a reassertion of an identity distinct from that of the colonial power, therefore the same as that of the masses, it does not show itself in the same way everywhere. One part of the middle-class minority engaged in the pre-independence movement, uses the foreign cultural norms, calling on literature and art, to express the discovery of its identity rather than to express the hopes and sufferings of the masses. And precisely because he uses the language and speech of the minority colonial power, he only occasionally manages to influence the masses, generally illiterate and familiar with other forms of artistic expression. This does not, however, remove the value of the contribution of the development of the struggle made by this petite bourgeoise minority, for it can at the same time influence a sector of the uprooted or those who are late-comers to its own class and an important sector of public opinion in the colonial metropolis, notably the class of intellectuals.

The other part of the lower middle class which from the start joins in the pre-independence movement finds, in its prompt share in the liberation struggle and in integration with the masses, the best means of expression of identity distinct from that of the colonial power.

That is why identification with the masses and reassertion of identity can be temporary or definitive, apparent or real, in the light of the daily efforts and sacrifices demanded by the struggle itself. A struggle which, while being the organized political expression of a culture, is also and necessarily a proof not only of identity but also of dignity.

In the course of the process of colonialist domination, the masses, whatever the characteristic of the social structure of the group to which they belong, do not stop resisting the colonial power. In a first phase—that of conquest, cynically called pacification—they resist, gun in hand, foreign occupation. In a second phase—that of the golden age of triumphant colonialism—they offer the foreign domination passive resistance, almost silent, but blazoned with many revolts, usually individual and once in a while collective. The revolt is particularly in the field of work and taxes, even in social contacts with the representatives, foreign or indigenous, of the colonial power. In a third phase—that of the liberation struggle—it is the masses who provide the main strength which employs political or armed resistance to challenge and to destroy foreign domination. Such a prolonged and varied resistance is possible only because, while keeping their culture and identity, the masses keep intact the sense of their individual and collective dignity, despite the worries, humiliations, and brutalities to which they are often subjected.

The assertion or reassertion by the indigenous petite bourgeoisie of identity distinct from that of the colonial power does not and could not bring about restoration of a sense of dignity to that class alone. In this context, we see that the sense of dignity of the petite bourgeoisie class depends on the objective moral and social feeling of each individual, on his subjective attitude towards the two poles of the colonial conflict, between which he is forced to live out the daily drama of colonization. This drama is the more shattering to the extent to which the petite bourgeoisie, in fulfilling its role, is made to live alongside both the foreign dominating class and the masses. On one side, the petite bourgeoisie is the victim of frequent if not daily humiliation by the foreigner, and on the other side it is aware of the injustice to which the masses are subjected and of their resistance and spirit of rebellion. Hence arises the apparent paradox of colonial domination: it is from within the indigenous petite bourgeoisie, a social class which grows from colonialism itself, that arise the first important steps towards mobilizing and organizing the masses for the struggle against the colonial power.

The struggle, in the face of all kinds of obstacles and in a variety of forms, reflects the awareness or grasp of a complete identity, generalizes and consolidates the sense of dignity strengthened by the development of political awareness, and derives from the culture or cultures of the masses in revolt one of its principal strengths.

WOLE SOYINKA (1934–   )

🏵 from *Myth, Literature, and the African World* (1976)

The question must now be confronted: How comes it then that, despite the extolled self-apprehending virtues of these and other works, it is possible to entertain a hostile attitude towards the programmatic summation in the secular vision of negritude? There is none of these works whose ideals may not be interpreted as the realization of the principles of race-retrieval which are embodied in the concept of negritude, yet negritude continues to arouse more than a mere semantic impatience among the later generation of African writers and intellectuals, in addition to—let this be remembered—serious qualifications of or tactical withdrawal from the full conception of negritude by a number of writers who assisted at its origin.

The vision of negritude should never be underestimated or belittled. What went wrong with it is contained in what I earlier expressed as the contrivance of a creative ideology and its falsified basis of identification with the social vision. This vision in itself was that of restitution and re-engineering of a racial psyche, the establishment of a distinct human entity and the glorification of its long-suppressed attributes. (On an even longer-term basis, as universal alliance with the world's dispossessed.) In attempting to achieve this laudable goal, however, negritude proceeded along the route of oversimplification. Its re-entrenchment of black values was not preceded by any profound effort to enter into this African system of values. It extolled the apparent. Its reference points took far too much colouring from European ideas, even while its messiahs pronounced themselves fanatically African. In attempting to refute the evaluation to which black reality had been subjected, negritude adopted the Manichean tradition of European thought and inflicted it on a culture which is most radically anti-Manichean. It not only accepted the dialectical structure of European ideological confrontations, but borrowed from the very components of its racist syllogism.

By way of elaboration, let us extend Sartre's grading of negritude as "the minor term of a dialectical progression." The "theoretical and practical assertion of the supremacy of the white man is its thesis; the position of negritude as an antithetical value is the bottom of negativity."[1] This was the position in which negritude found itself; we will now pose a pair of syllogisms from the racist philosophy that provoked it into being:

(*a*) Analytical thought is a mark of high human development.
The European employs analytical thought.
Therefore the European is highly developed.
(*b*) Analytical thought is a mark of high human development.
The African is incapable of analytical thought.
Therefore the African is not highly developed.

(For "analytical thought" substitute scientific inventiveness, etc.)

The dialectic progression in history of these two syllogisms need not be dwelt upon: the European is highly developed, the African is not, therefore, etc. Slavery and colonialism took their basic justification from such palpably false premises. But the temper of the times (both the liberal conscience of Europe and the new assertiveness of the victims of Eurocentric dialectics) required a rephrasing of premises and conclusions—preferably of course, even for liberal Europe, the conclusions only. Negritude strangely lent approval to this partial methodology, accepting in full the premises of both syllogisms and the conclusion of (*a*), justifying Sartre's commentary that the theoretical and practical assertion of the supremacy of the white man was the tacitly adopted thesis, and failing utterly to demolish it. The conclusion of (*a*) was never challenged, though attempts were made to give new definitions to what constitutes high development. The method there was to reconstruct (*b*) altogether, while leaving (*a*) intact. This was the initial error. Negritude did not bother to free the black races from the burden of its acceptance. Even the second premise of (*a*), "The European employs analytical thought," is falsely posed, for it already implies a racial separatism which provides the main argument. Is the entire exercise not rendered futile if we substituted for this, "Man is capable of analytical thought"? The negritudinists did not; they accepted the battleground of Eurocentric prejudices and racial chauvinism, and moved to replace syllogism (*b*) with an amended version:

(*c*) Intuitive understanding is *also* a mark of human development.
The African employs intuitive understanding.
Therefore the African is highly developed.

(For "intuitive understanding" substitute the dance, rhythm, etc.)

The dialectic progression which moved, logically enough, from this amendment, positing the attractive universality of negritude, was based on (*a*) and (*c*), resulting in a symbiotic human culture—the black leaven in the white metallic loaf. How could the mistake ever have been made that the new propositions in (c) wiped away the inherent insult of (b), which was merely a development of the racist assumptions of (a)? They said, oh yes, the Gobineaus of the world are right; Africans neither think nor construct, but it doesn't matter because—voila!—they intuit! And so they moved to construct a romantic edifice, confident that its rhythmic echoes would drown the repugnant conclusion of proposition (b), which of course simply refused to go away. How could it, when its premises were constantly reinforced by affirmations such as this: "Emotive sensitivity. Emotion is completely Negro as reason is Greek. Water rippled by every breeze? Unsheltered soul blown by every wind, whose fruit often drops before it is ripe? Yes, in one way, *The Negro is richer in gifts than in works.*"[2]

This is not, judging by the literature and the tracts which emerged from negritude, an unfair extract. Negritude trapped itself in what was primarily a defensive role, even though its accents were strident, its syntax hyperbolic and its strategy aggressive. It accepted one of the most commonplace blasphemies of racism, that the black man has nothing between his ears, and proceeded to subvert the power of poetry to glorify this fabricated justification of European cultural domination. Suddenly, we were exhorted to give a cheer for those who never invented anything, a cheer for those who never explored the oceans. The truth, however, is that there isn't any such creature. An even more distressing deduction which escaped the euphoricists of such negativism is that they, poets, had turned themselves into laudators of creative truncation. They suggest something which is indeed alien to the African worldview: that there are watertight categories of the creative spirit, that creativity is not one smooth-flowing source of human regeneration. The very idea of separating the manifestations of the human genius is foreign to the African worldview. Self-subjugation to the actual artifacts which man has himself created is of course something else, and is equally alien to the African creative spirit, but the negritudinists were not referring to that. Their propaganda for creative separatism went much deeper. And one of its unfortunate byproducts was a mounting narcissism which involved contemplation of the contrived self in the supposed tragic grandeur of the cultural dilemma. Thus, admittedly at the bottom regions of such poetry, we encountered:

> Here we stand
> infants overblown
> poised between two civilisations
> finding the balance irksome
> itching for something to happen
> to tip us one way or the other
> groping in the dark for a helping hand

and finding none.
I'm tired, O my God, I'm tired,
I'm tired of hanging in the middle way—
but where can I go?[3]

Some critics, through taking this kind of versification more seriously than could be warranted by language or composition, try to see in it a certain phase of development to which negritude gave the decisive answer. Adrian Roscoe makes this suggestion in his *Mother is Gold*.[4] I disagree. This kind of poetry was of course a product of negritude, but not of its practitioners. The dilemma is self-conscious. The question at the tail end of the poem sounds rhetorical, as if the writer has no real interest in the answer. It was part of a totally artificial angst fabricated by a handful of writers *after* negritude revealed to them the very seductive notion that they had to commence a search for their Africanness. Until then, they were never even aware that it was missing. The opportunity to create a lot of mileage out of this potentially tragic loss was too great to miss; unfortunately, as in the above example, it was not always matched by the poetic talent.

This was one of the unfortunate byproducts of negritude, the abysmal angst of low achievement. By contrast there were exquisite nuggets of lyric celebration in these excavations of the vanishing racial psyche, such as the following familiar lines of Birago Diop. They are some of the best to have come from the negritudinist movement because the conviction they carry is self-evident. The poem is not a manifesto in verse form, nor does it pretend to be the summation of the cosmogonic view which gave rise to it. It may occasionally sound proselytizing, as indeed most of the poetry of this movement does, but it is the quiet enthusiasm of the initiate, the sharing instinct of the votive who has experienced immersion in a particular dimension of reality and calls out from within his spiritual repletion. Because of its unusual lyrical possession by an integral reality of the African world, I shall quote it in full.

                    Breath
Listen more to things
Than to words that are said.
The water's voice sings
And the flame cries
And the wind that brings
The woods to sighs
Is the breathing of the dead.
Those who are dead have never gone away.
They are in the shadows darkening around,
They are in the shadows fading into day,
The dead are not under the ground.

They are in the trees that quiver,
They are in the woods that weep,
They are in the waters of the rivers,
They are in the waters that sleep.
They are in the crowds, they are in the homestead.
The dead are never dead.

Listen more to things
Than to words that are said.
The water's voice sings
And the flame cries
And the wind that brings
The woods to sighs
Is the breathing of the dead.
Who have not gone away
Who are not under the ground
Who are never dead.

Those who are dead have never gone away.
They are at the breast of the wife.
They are in the child's cry of dismay
And the firebrand bursting into life.
The dead are not under the ground.
They are in the fire that burns low
They are in the grass with tears to shed,
In the rock where whining winds blow
They are in the forest, they are in the homestead.
The dead are never dead.

Listen more to things
Than to words that are said.
The water's voice sings
And the flame cries
And the wind that brings
The woods to sighs
Is the breathing of the dead.

And repeats each day
The Covenant where it is said
That our fate is bound to the law,
And the fated of the dead who are not dead
To the spirits of breath who are stronger than they.
We are bound to Life by this harsh law
And by this Covenant we are bound
To the deeds of the breathings that die
Along the bed and the banks of the river,
To the deeds of the breaths that quiver

In the rock that whines and the grasses that cry
To the deeds of the breathings that lie
In the shadow that lightens and grows deep
In the tree that shudders, in the woods that weep,
In the waters that flow and the waters that sleep,
To the spirits of breath which are stronger than they
That have taken the breath of the deathless dead
Of the dead who have never gone away
Of the dead who are not now under the ground.

Listen more to things
Than to words that are said.
The water's voice sings
And the flame cries
And the wind that brings
The woods to sighs
Is the breathing of the dead.[5]

Now such a poem conveys an important, even fundamental aspect of the worldview of traditional Africa and remains within this mandate. Diop does not suggest here that the African could not manufacture tools to help him dig a grave to inter the body of this undead dead, nor that every medical effort is not made to keep the body alive until it is too late, nor that the sickness and the treatment are determined by intuition rather than through long-evolved systems of medical research and practice, herbal, surgical, and psychiatric. Unfortunately the bulk of negritudinist poets were not content to confine their redefinition of society in this way.

It should not surprise us that the most dogmatic statements about the potential vision of negritude were made by European intellectuals. And such statements are an ideological stab in the back. There was a kind of poetic justice in this. Negritude, having laid its cornerstone on a European intellectual tradition, however bravely it tried to reverse its concepts (leaving its tenets untouched), was a foundling deserving to be drawn into, nay, even considered a case for benign adoption by European ideological interests. That it was something which should exist in its own right, which deserved to be considered a product and a vindication of a separate earth and civilization, did not occur to Jean-Paul Sartre who, proposing the toast of negritude, proceeded literally to drink it under the table. It was not difficult. Negritude was already intoxicated by its own presumptions.

Negritude is the low ebb in a dialectical progression. The theoretical and practical assertion of white supremacy is the thesis; negritude's role as an antithetical value is the negative stage. But this negative stage will not satisfy the Negroes who are using it, and they are well aware of this. They know that they are aiming for human synthesis or fulfilment in a raceless society. Negritude is destined to destroy itself; it is the path and the goal, the means but not the end.[6]

As Fanon cried out in anguish: "And so, it is not I who make a meaning for myself, but it is the meaning that was already there, preexisting, waiting for me."[7]

And what is this end which Sartre envisages? The transcendence over racial concepts and alignment with the proletarian struggle. Like all ideologues who ignore the existence or pretend the nonexistence of factors which do not fit into the framework of an ideological projection, Sartre ignores the important fact that Negritude was a creation by and for a small elite. The search for a racial identity was conducted by and for a minuscule minority of uprooted individuals, not merely in Paris but in the metropolis of the French colonies. At the same time as this historical phenomenon was taking place, a drive through the real Africa, among the real populace of the African world, would have revealed that these millions had never at any time had cause to question the existence of their—negritude. This is why, even in a country like Senegal where negritude is the official ideology of the régime, it remains a curiosity for the bulk of the population and an increasingly shopworn and dissociated expression even among the younger intellectuals and litterateurs.

As for the pipe dream of Sartre that it would pass through stages of development and merge itself within the context of the proletarian fight, one would have thought that it was obvious enough that negritude was the property of a bourgeois intellectual elite, and that there was therefore far greater likelihood that it would become little more than a diversionary weapon in the eventual emergence of a national revolutionary struggle wherever the flag-bearers of negritude represent the power-holding elite. Sartre was not being naive, however. He had merely, as would any confident ideologue, classified this colonial movement as springing from the intellectual conditioning of the mother culture; he rightly assumed that any movement founded on an antithesis which responded to the Cartesian "I think, therefore I am" with "I feel, therefore I am" must be subject to a dialectical determinism which made all those who "are" obedient to laws formulated on the European historical experience. How was he to know, if the proponents of the universal vision of negritude themselves did not, that the African world did not and need not share the history of civilizations trapped in political Manicheisms? The principle of definition in the African world system is far more circumspect, and constantly avoids the substitution of the temporal or partial function or quality for the essence of an active or inert sociopolitical totality. The fundamental error was one of procedure: negritude stayed within a preset system of Eurocentric intellectual analysis both of man and society and tried to redefine the African and his society in those externalized terms. In the end, even the poetry of celebration for this supposed self-retrieval became indistinguishable from the mainstream of French poetry. The autumn of the flowers of evil had, through a shared tradition of excessive self-regarding, become confused with the spring of African rebirth. Fanon's warning went unheeded: "To us, the man who adores the Negro is as 'sick' as the man who abominates him."[8]

But this problem does not apply to the negritudinists alone. African intellectualism in general, and therefore African attitudes to race and culture, have failed to come to grips with the very foundations of Eurocentric epistemology. Let us take this simple but basic example of the syllogistic method of inquiry, one which is applied as readily to mathematical or scientific propositions as to supposed verities ranging from the origin of the universe to the fluctuating prices of oil on the market. The basis of this European intellectual tradition necessarily admits the unprovable or the outright falsity, a fact demonstrated in considerable measure by Europe's analysis and conclusion about other cultures and civilizations. This process of intellection requires the propagandist knack of turning the unprovable into an authoritative concept, indoctrinating society into the acceptance of a single, simple criterion as governing any number of human acts and habits, evaluations, and even habits of understanding.[9] (Freudianism is one of the most notorious modern examples.) The criterion proliferates, creates its own special language and its microworld of hierarchic subconcepts in an internally cohering pattern. The European intellectual temperament appears to be historically conducive to the infiltration of such mono-criteria. It is the responsibility of today's African intellectual not only to question these criteria, but to avoid the conditioning of the social being by the mono-criterion methodology of Europe.

Sartre, for instance, anxious to prove that the idea of race can mingle with that of class, writes, "the first [race] is concrete and particular, the second is universal and abstract; the one stems from what Jaspers calls understanding and the other from intellection; the first is the result of a psychological syncretism and the second is a methodical construction based on experience."[10] From this he concludes that negritude is destined to prepare the "synthesis or realization of the human in a society without races." Now let us, from an Afrocentric bias of concepts, examine the contrasting relations posed above. Does the racial self-conception of the African really exclude the process of intellection? More critically, is the reality of African social structure—from which "class" alone can obtain concrete definition—not a thorough fusion of individual functional relations with society, one that cannot be distinguished from a "psychological syncretism" of self and community, from a mode of self-conceiving that is identical with that of racial belonging? The contrary is not only unprovable but *inconceivable* in the traditional African view of man, and the question then remains whether this conceptual totalism cannot be rescued from European compartmentalist intellect or must be subsumed by the more assertive culture in the "realization of the human in a society without races." The answer, for the negritudinist, latterly became yes to the second option, predictably. For negritude, having yielded to the seduction of synthetic European intellectualism, accepted the consequences that befall the junior relation in all dialectic progressions. Possessed, they tried to constrict the protean universalism of the African experience into the obverse monothetical appendage (Sartre calls it antithesis, naturally) of a particularized, unprovable, and even irrelevant European criterion.

Let us respond, very simply, as I imagine our mythical brother innocent would respond in his virginal village, pursuing his innocent sports, suddenly confronted by the figure of Descartes in his pith helmet, engaged in the mission of piercing the jungle of the black prelogical mentality with his intellectual canoe. As our Cartesian ghost introduces himself by scribbling on our black brother's—naturally—tabula rasa the famous proposition, "I think, therefore I am," we should not respond, as the negritudinists did, with "I feel, therefore I am," for that is to accept the arrogance of a philosophical certitude that has no foundation in the provable, one which reduces the cosmic logic of being to a functional particularism of being. I cannot imagine that our "authentic black innocent" would ever have permitted himself to be manipulated into the false position of countering one pernicious Manicheism with another. He would sooner, I suspect, reduce our white explorer to syntactical proportions by responding: "You think, therefore you are a thinker. You are one-who-thinks, white-creature-in-pith-helmet-in-African-jungle-who-thinks and, finally, white-man-who-has-problems-believing-in-his-own-existence." And I cannot believe that he would arrive at that observation solely by intuition.

[1]This and other quotations from Sartre are from his essay "Orphée noir," preface to Léopold Senghor, ed., *Anthologie de la nouvelle poésie nègre et malagache de langue française* (Presses universitaires de France, 1948). For an English translation, see Jean-Paul Sartre, *Black Orpheus*, trans. Arthur Gilette (New York: University Place Book Shop, 1963).

[2]Italics and exclamation mark mine, the rest Senghor's, from "Ce que l'homme noir apporte," in Senghor, *Liberté I: Négritude et humanisme* (Paris: Editions du Seuil, 1964), 24.

[3]Mabel Segun in Frances Ademola, ed., *Reflections* (Lagos: African Universities Press, 1962), 65.

[4]Roscoe, *Mother is Gold* (Cambridge University Press, 1971).

[5]*French African Verse*, trans. John Reed and Clive Wake (Heinemann, 1964), 25. The poem *Souffles* ("Breath") appears in Birago Diop's *Leurres et lueurs* (Paris: Présence Africaine, 1960).

[6]Sartre, *Orphée noir*, in Senghor, *Anthologie*, xli.

[7]Frantz Fanon, *Black Skin, White Masks,* trans. Charles Lam Markmann (New York: Grove Press, 1967), 134.

[8]Ibid, 8.

[9]Notes made some years ago, parts of which are lost, suggest that this sentence was actually copied in confirmation of my observations, from a book I was reading at the time, but do not indicate which book.

[10]Sartre, xli.

AWA THÍAM

Feminism and Revolution (1978)

While women from industrialized countries are focusing their attention on the problem of creating a typically female language, the daughters of black Africa are still at the stage of seeking their own dignity, for the recognition of their own specificity as human beings. This specificity has always been refused them by white colonialists or neocolonialists and by their own black males. One only needs to glance briefly at history to realize this. Africa in the fifteenth and sixteenth centuries was the source of human merchandise, the "black gold" of the time: slaves to be scattered all over America and the Caribbean.

It's not a matter of saying, "Black sisters, look out! The struggle of women from industrialized countries is not our struggle," but simply of reminding ourselves—although some black women are aware of this—that our own struggle, the black women's struggle, has not yet reached the same point as that of European women. Our primary, fundamental demands are not the same. Institutionalized polygamy flourishes in black Africa; sexual mutilatory practices flourish, forced marriages, child brides . . . But on the other hand, black women have to combat the same scourges as their European sisters. Nevertheless, we must distinguish between two levels of exploitation and oppression of women: the first, where women who are oppressed and exploited do not understand the situation, and remain in thrall, as passive victims—this is the case with a good many black women, whether traditionalists or not; the second, where exploitation and oppression are partially understood and give rise to theorizing, sometimes leading to movements for the liberation of women, as in the United States and Europe.

But it is essential to clarify certain issues. European feminists have often compared the exploitation of women to that of the black people of the United States or Africa. Thus, in the message sent by Kate Millett to the organizers of "Ten Hours against Rape," held by the MLF (Mouvement pour la Libération des Femmes) at the Mutualité in Paris in June 1976, we read: "Rape is to women what lynching is to blacks." As if it were possible to make

Reprinted from *Speak Out, Black Sisters: Feminism and Oppression in Black Africa*, by Awa Thíam (London: Pluto, 1987), 113–28, with permission of Pluto Press.

the equation: women equal blacks (insofar as both are oppressed); therefore, rape equals lynching. This is a false argument. Let us compare comparable things. A textual equivalence between "woman" and "black" cannot be justified. One can be of the female sex and of the black race. If rape is to women what lynching is to blacks, then what do we make of the rape of black women by black men? To get rid of the ambiguity inherent in Kate Millett's words, we must make it clear that she is referring to white women, which she does not do. In which case, the above equation still stands, but still cannot be justified. What, in all this, is the position of the black woman? European feminists do not seem to know: they continue to satisfy themselves with the false comparison between the situation of blacks and that of women—by which we must understand white women, even if they don't say so explicitly. Others tell us, "Women are the blacks of the human race." Can they tell us then what or who are black women? The blacks of the blacks of the human race?

You would think that black women did not exist. In fact, they find themselves denied, in this way, by the very women who claim to be fighting for the liberation of all women.

What emerges from the interviews here is the extent of oppression, exploitation, and frustration that is the lot of black African women. With the exception of a middle-class minority (in this case, a few intellectuals), the black African woman, be she town-dweller or villager, married, divorced or single, has a deplorable life.

During the colonial period the African woman suffered a double domination, a double enslavement. She was not only subjected to the colonial, but she was also subjected to the colonized African male. After this period, she faced ever-greater problems: the aftermath of colonization (decolonization appearing only superficially); the tendency to acculturation. She is still under the yoke of males: father, brother, husband; she is the object of sexual satisfaction on the part of the male and forms part of the proof of his prosperity. In a word, she is both an ornamental symbol and a maid-of-all-work.

Let us return to the colonial period. Surely the true status of black African women was identical to that of the Afro-American or Caribbean woman in the days of slavery. She, like them, had to comply with the sexual whims of her white master who, having appropriated her lands, had become omnipotent in her very home.

We are not concerned here with the problem of the liberation of black women in terms of priorities, because two aspects of the black African woman's struggle are closely linked: the struggle for effective economic and political independence and the struggle for the recognition of and respect for the rights and duties of men and women of all races.

The one must not exclude the other. Ideally both struggles should be waged simultaneously. "That doesn't seem possible" would be the reply of sexists and racists. To which we shall retort: we are in Africa, with all that this entails (a colonial or neocolonial society, patriarchy, feudalism). In Algeria, Guinea-Bissau, and many other countries which have fought wars for national liberation genuinely aiming to free their people, including women, we find that there has been no liberation for the latter. In Algeria, women still wear the veil and are confined to the traditional tasks of servant, childbearer, and housekeeper. On top of these, she has the not-inconsiderable role of preserving traditions and customs, which are either too rigid for change or have not yet been adapted to our times.

Women must certainly achieve total independence, but they will have to fight for it, they will have to wrest it from society. They will have to call men's bluff and prove their independence; they will have to reject the alienating influences which have cast a shadow over their lives in the past, and still do to this day.

They have not only to wage a class war but also a sex war. The American Shulamith Firestone has fully understood the complexity and diverse nature of women's struggles. "We shall need a sexual revolution," she states, "much larger than—inclusive of—a socialist one to truly eradicate all class systems."[1]

Black African Women

In the former colonies, be they French, Belgian, or other, the situation of the black woman today is the same as that of her sisters in Zimbabwe or Latin America. Like her black brother, she suffers from the damaging aftermath of colonialism and the crimes of the colonials. But her sufferings are greater than those of men, for she is not only faced with white racism, the exploitation of her race by the colonial, but also the domination that men, black as well as white, exercise over her by virtue of the patriarchal system in which both live.

Because she is a colonized person, she is obliged to work for the colonial, just as the black male is. She is exploited as a unit of production. What is more, she is the cheapest form of labor for the colonial, by virtue of both her color and her sex. Badly paid by the colonial, she is also underpaid in comparison with men. Therefore she is exploited not only as a black but also because she is a woman. But which of these comes first? The fact of being black, without regard to her sex, makes her the slave of the colonial, who simply regards her as a beast of burden in the same way as her black brother. But the difference between them is soon established. It is possible that it was present before the colonial arrived, but it is just as likely that he introduced it to the land that he "confiscated," seeing that this arrangement characterizes his own society, where women are also undervalued.

Both colonial and patriarchal systems decree that the black woman's work is worth less than that of the black male. This is translated into concrete terms in the wage structure, in the importance attached to her, as well as in every other field. Her value as a commodity only goes up for the colonialist when he sees her as an object of sexual satisfaction. (And how!)

It is as well to remember that the submissiveness of the Black female lies behind these communities of half-castes which developed in the colonies. As long as she—the female—is under the domination of the colonial—the male—her relationship to him will always be that of victim to victimizer. He is invested with the power to commit psychological and actual rape on the colonized group.

By virtue of her sexual role, the black woman is sometimes regarded by the white man as a woman. In other words, she is considered to be a woman without being essentially human. Difficult to conceive! We are not far from the old Catholic concept according to which women have no souls.

Wherever the colonials have passed through they have left their mark, not only at the political level but also economically and in society generally: the institution of colonial and neocolonial régimes; the imposition of monocultures, as in Senegal, where the majority of agricultural land is given over to the cultivation of groundnuts, to the detriment of other food crops. This is an evil which Aimé Césaire denounces so eloquently when anyone speaks to him of the progress achieved by the colonial: "They talk to me of progress, of 'achievements,' diseases cured, improved standards of living. *I* am talking about societies drained of their essence, cultures trampled underfoot, institutions undermined, lands confiscated, religions smashed, magnificent artistic creations destroyed, extraordinary *possibilities* wiped out."[2] In addition to this, we should remember the emergence of a half-caste population, however small. Raped by the colonial, or seduced thanks to some trickery, the black woman is reduced to the degrading status of an object of pleasure. With her essence denied, what remains of her self? *There is nothing of her left,* or rather, she is reduced to the state of an instrument. In such a context can there be any love between the colonial and the colonized woman? Or can any human relationship be possible?

The object of this discussion is not to state whether this relationship is possible, but to expose the different forms of oppression and exploitation suffered by the black woman at the hands of the male colonialist. We have finally to consider the relationship of the black woman to the black male: if the latter is the slave of the colonialist, she is the slave of a slave.

The situation of the black woman in an African colonized state is not identical to that of her coloured sister in Latin America. The point where they differ is in their relationship to the whites. In the African colony, the white man is an intruder, an invader; although he is numerically in the minority, he is nevertheless in a position of strength. In Latin America, the black woman has been transplanted, and here she is in the minority. She belongs to the slave race, imported from black Africa and herded into the plantations as labor in the cultivation of cocoa and coffee. The blacks of Latin America are not only outnumbered but also outbalanced in military strength. They are unarmed, therefore more effectively controlled by the whites. And this makes the black woman, belonging as she does to the most deprived social and racial group, the victim of a double oppression.

To sum up: she is exploited by virtue of her sex; her wages even undercut the low wage of the Latin American black male. Moreover, outside her own community she has no contact with other social classes, unless she marries a white man or goes in for prostitution. In this respect, the situation of the black women of Latin America is similar to that described by Frantz Fanon in *Black Skin, White Masks*.[3]

How should the colonial or neocolonial context in which the black African woman lives affect our understanding of a feminist movement aiming to challenge her status in society? Challenging the status of women amounts to challenging the structures of an entire society when this society is patriarchal in nature. All the problems of society—political, cultural, economic—are inextricably linked to the problem of women. The problem of women belongs in a general context.

Where the European woman complains of being doubly oppressed, the black woman of Africa suffers a threefold oppression: by virtue of her sex, she is dominated by man in a patriarchal society; by virtue of her class she is at the mercy of capitalist exploitation; by virtue of her race she suffers from the appropriation of her country by colonial or neocolonial powers. Sexism, racism, class division: three plagues! In order to succeed, the black African feminist movement must set its sights on eradicating these three plagues from society. In other words, the black African women's struggle cannot find a place in any scheme which denies the specificity of women's problems and which only sees their solution in a struggle for national liberation, like that of Algeria. We cannot repeat often enough: Algerian women participated in Algeria's struggle for national liberation. But Algerian women have not been liberated!

Who can guarantee that a war of liberation in a black African country would in fact lead to the suppression of clitoridectomy, of infibulation? Black African women can—and must—no longer allow men to decide for them and to manipulate their lives.

No system of social life has ever, on any level, been able to function without the effective participation of women. They are relied on to bring up children and look after the home, and to perform all the attendant soul-destroying, thankless, and repetitive tasks. As for the man, the job that he appropriates, earning the daily bread, is far and away more profitable than the woman's tasks. His place in the bosom of society is much more interesting. It gives him access to the world at large, the opportunity to develop his intellectual and physical faculties in a range of experiences.

The image of the woman as object is found in all societies at all levels. In industrialized societies, the immigrant—man or woman—is made aware of this state of affairs by observing both public and private life, notably the nuclear family.

According to phallocratic logic the situation is quite natural, so the question whether all that is posited as "feminine" really is so never arises. What is more normal in a society where the male reigns supreme? Whether they come from colonized countries or not, phallocrats are all alike and exercise the same oppression over women. How can we put an end to such a situation?

Women are beginning to realize the need to fight against a system which denies women an authentic existence—that system which is patriarchal and phallocratic. Traditionalism and revolution clash against each other: there is an endless succession of advances and retreats, of rebellions and repression, of short-lived victories and temporary setbacks.

Sometimes the workers triumph, but their triumph is brief. The real outcome of their struggles is less the immediate success than the growing solidarity of the workers. To struggle means to fight with resolution and faith in the certainty of victory, in the promise of future happiness for ourselves or for others; to fight with the firm conviction that positive success will ensue—whether we live to see it or not. We must fight on.

Colonized or neocolonized peoples are living in a dilemma: whether to revolt against a system which exploits them or passively to accept slavery. Either way, the colonized people "get it in the neck." In the first place, the indigenous population suffers the intrusive, oppressive presence of the "settlers"—a presence which they experience as aggression. These settlers subject them to a savage exploitation which is underlined by an attempt to dehumanize them. The circumstances of the indigenous people are inevitably affected: customs are disrupted, lives upset, social structures shattered. The colonized native may not and cannot behave as a free person; he or she must live and act according to the disposition of the settler. This state of affairs dehumanizes the inhabitants. Their liberty is alienated; they are reduced to the state of an instrument. The settler makes use of them, and when they no longer serve a useful purpose or when, in the colonial context, they become a nuisance, the settler disposes of them. This "nuisance" may well indicate an attempt to stand up to the settler, a refusal to obey which unleashes the forces of repression. The rebel is struck down like a mad dog.

That is not an infrequent occurrence: let us not forget Algeria, Vietnam—and it is still going on in South Africa.

Early in 1976, French television offered us the shameful spectacle of a white South African family amusing themselves at the expense of a group of unarmed blacks walking past carrying bundles on their heads. The white man shot at them, causing his wife and children to laugh hysterically. They laughed and laughed at this mock assassination of blacks. They laughed till they cried at the sight of the victims of this cruel sport making off as fast as their legs could carry them. But we'll see who has the last laugh. An alternative strategy lies open to the colonized: while some are sunk in passive submission, others revolt. They take up arms; slave confronts master. The television program to which we have just referred ended with the announcement of the death of the sadistic, murderous settler. He stepped on a landmine. History is rich in examples of similar violent retribution: Dien bien Phu, Algeria, and more recently, Guinea-Bissau, Vietnam, and Angola are outstanding examples.

Man, the Enemy of Woman?

Some women tend to equate man with society and by inference see men as their principal enemy. We do not feel that, as far as black Africa is concerned, men are the enemy. It is certainly true that in any patriarchal system institutions are set up by men, and this might reinforce the arguments given by "sexist" feminists; but we should ask ourselves whether or not men are alienated as well. Doesn't the very fact of having devised a system of values which disadvantage women offer clear proof of men's alienation? The oppression to which he subjects women, and which he perceives as something quite natural, is justified according to an idea of "complementarity." In a patriarchal society, man himself is alienated, so he is not free either. The sex which oppresses the other is not a free sex. A society made up of nonalienated individuals would be an egalitarian society, in which there would be neither master nor slave, neither tyrant nor tyrannized, neither colonial nor colonized, neither chief nor subordinate.

Such a society does not exist. Up until now there have only been attempts to create it. It is now our task to do so. To succeed in this, sexism must be excluded from our praxis, from the praxis of every woman enlisted in the struggle.

A Tribute to Our Mothers

What can we say about customs, civilization, culture? How do we stand in respect of these? Is it our responsibility to ensure their survival? Or should we condemn them as decadent? There is no doubt that they are the defining characteristics of a race. But no culture is static, any more than a civilization is; so customs too must change for better or for worse.

Do black Africans follow Europeans in considering their customs barbarous? How are they preserved? How were they established? A relationship exists between the myths and customs of black Africa. Does this mean that they determine each other? It is difficult to find the answers to these questions, owing to the paucity of unbiased documentation. Most of the available information comes from colonials, who were often eager to document the different ethnic groups with whom they came into contact. We hear from ethnologists, anthropologists, sociologists, or simply civil servants. The last were not concerned with recording African customs objectively and indeed did not take the trouble to understand their real significance within the indigenous societies. Unbiased studies on black Africa, written by whites in the colonial period, are few and far between.

Colonial logic aimed at undermining the structure of traditional black African societies and the destruction of the black identity. Their civilization was, if not destroyed, at least seriously damaged by colonization. This is what Jean-Paul Sartre is referring to when he says,

> The command goes out to relegate the inhabitants of the annexed territory to the level of the ape, to justify the settler in treating them like beasts of burden. Colonial violence not only aims to keep these subjected people at arm's length, but it also seeks to dehumanize them. No effort will be spared to break up their traditions, to substitute our language for theirs, to *destroy their cultures* [author's italics] without offering them our own; they will be stupefied by work.[4]

However, some things have survived in spite of this, especially in ritual and cultural matters. The crimes committed by Europeans did not succeed in wiping out the entire black African civilization, for certain typically African customs have survived. This was no accident, but the result of continual resistance to their erosion, as for example in the matter of initiation rites, which have remained virtually unchanged for centuries in black Africa, right up to the present day. What is the reason for this? Capitulation on the part of black Africans features in practically every field during the colonial period. But it was women in particular who took it upon themselves to preserve certain customs. We should pay them tribute. It is because our mothers, our elders, had the charge of children that they were—and remain—responsible for training them, for transmitting certain myths and beliefs, and instilling in them a spirit of submission to customs. In refusing to allow black African civilization to be destroyed, our mothers were revolutionary. Yet some people describe this attitude as conservative. These women felt the need to preserve something that was precious to them—their cultural heritage. They became aware of something urgent that needed to be done; something had to be saved—that something which was indispensable to the preservation of the black African as such: the black African civilization. This was their aim, and in this they succeeded by dint of insisting on maintaining ancestral practices. Although they did not challenge their state of bondage to men, we nevertheless pay tribute to these women.

BLACK WOMAN
The black woman is not simply
COLOUR
The black woman is not simply
FLESH
The black woman is not simply
MOTHER
The black woman is not simply
LOVER
The black woman is not simply
MUSE
The black woman is not simply . . .
Praised in song as lover, loving-flesh,
praised in song as mother, "mother-protection"
praised in song as color, "color-affirmation"
the songs about the black woman
do not say
who IS
the black woman.
These songs say little
of her afflictions,
pain or pleasure,
heartbreaks, hopes,
. . . her LIFE
The black woman
"That thing lives"
The black woman,
Woman, "that thing" lives woman
"That thing" lives that thing
with battles
    setbacks
    victories
Woman, black woman, Productive force, Matrix, Fighter.
"That thing" IS
The black woman IS

Negro-African Women, Women of the Third World, Women of the Industrialized Countries, The Same Fight!

The emancipation of women
must go hand in hand with men's
relinquishing of a feudal and
bourgeois way of thinking. As for
women themselves, they would
be wrong to wait for government
and party directives to bring
them freedom; they would do
better to count on no-one but
themselves and to fight.

(Ho Chi Minh)

Women, there is a common denominator in your lives: phallocratic violence. It is this violence which makes you think that you don't amount to
anything on your own, without the other, the one who has got "something
between his legs," the one with the phallus. It is this violence which tries by
every possible means to make you play second fiddle. It is this violence of
expression which sometimes robs you of your self-possession, only to bring
you face to face with your true self, however debilitated and battered by male ·
phallocratic behaviour: your noble, dignified, true self that men seek to al-
ienate or destroy. This insidious, misogynous violence can, like a monster,
present itself in different disguises. It can take on a deceptive appearance to
beguile you, to throw dust in your eyes; then may come your violent awakening, or you may be harassed or even murdered in your blind, charmed sleep.
This violence is the daily lot of all oppressed women throughout the world,
whatever they may do. Illiterate or intellectual, none of them escape. It is not
a metaphysical violence; it is real and concrete. It can be not only brutal but
also subtle. However, this male violence remains, as distinct from revolutionary violence, the violence of a system of slavery, which desires the domination of the other, the woman. In this sense, it can be considered a form of
terrorism.

Whatever form it may take, this violence results in the destruction of the
human being. It has a name: phallocratic fascism. As such it must be totally
eliminated from every society, from every social class.

Nevertheless, many people have doubts about the common nature of the
struggles waged by black African women, women of the third world, and
women from Europe. How could these struggles be identical, in view of the
different industrial development, different material and cultural conditions?

What are the specific problems faced by European women? In spite of the level of development reached by their societies, they still feel oppressed and exploited by men. Is this oppression of European women identical to that of the workers? We maintain that there is no common measure between the exploitation of the worker and that suffered by women.

Let us explain. The working woman suffers from the same oppression and exploitation by the capitalist system as the male worker, but to a greater degree since the woman's work is often underrated. Irrespective of this, the woman, compared with the man—her husband, partner, brother, or father— suffers from another form of exploitation which stems from her subjection to the patriarchal system.

How do the problems faced by women in black Africa compare, and how have women there responded to them? In particular, what is their position regarding feminist movements?

Black African women, whether feminist or not, have participated in the national struggles waged on their own soil, thus proving themselves well aware of the problems faced by their countries and their societies. At the present time, we see an increase in the number of women involved in the liberation movements of their countries. Even if black women were not the instigators of these struggles (and that still remains to be proved), whenever it has been a question of fighting to free their countries from a colonial or neocolonial yoke, they have hastened to throw in their lot with the men. Then and only then do we see any sort of equality between men and women. They fight together, literally bearing arms for a common ideal: the liberation of their country. On the field of battle, women run the same risks as men. Whether they belong to an underground resistance movement or not, the colonial perceives them as a target just as much as he does the man. Such a situation puts them on an equal footing: mother fighting side by side with father, girl with boy. The man is forced to recognize the equal status of woman. It is no longer a question of asking whether she is not too weak or too stupid to know how to pull a trigger or throw a hand grenade at the right moment, or hide something or other in the right place. A woman is just as capable of assimilating the techniques of guerrilla warfare as a man. Tasks on the battlefield are shared without distinction according to sex.

But what is the position as soon as the war is over, the victory obtained? This is a logical, legitimate question to ask, since the world has seen the end of several wars of liberation in recent years. Once these wars are over, "things return to normal." In other words, men resume their former occupations, and so do women. The latter have not managed to eliminate certain contradictions inherent in the patriarchal society to which they belong, nor to rise above them. They have not succeeded in getting rid of customs which have no strategic value (tattooing, wearing the veil, etc.). We must refute the claim that the preservation of those customs today is our way of resisting the ever-increasing power of neocolonialism or imperialism.

Guinea

Guinea obtained its independence in 1958, as a consequence of its rejection of de Gaulle's proposed new constitution. A socialist republic was immediately declared. This choice was to have important repercussions for the Guinean masses, imposing gigantic pressures on them. But what happened to the Guinean woman? Where does she now stand in the new order?

We get the impression that, in its daily life—as was reflected in the collective interview reported in an earlier chapter—Guinea is in a state of evolution, while still bearing the deep imprint of its cultural past. Ancestral values die hard. And in certain places and some circles they hold sway. However, it must be emphasized that Guinea is one of the countries that included the integration of women in its political program. It is one of the first states to promote a policy of integration *and* emancipation of women.

When it was necessary to oppose the reactionary forces which sought to keep Guinea under colonial domination, the women of Guinea armed themselves and took their place in the forefront of the fight against the enemy. We can quote the example of the heroic M'Balia Camara, who was assassinated on 9 February 1955, disemboweled while she was carrying the child of the colonials' puppet of that period, David Sylla. The date of her death is celebrated as the National Day of Guinean Women. Guinea also has the highest rate of female participation in government of any African state. By way of comparison, in 1977 Algeria had eight women deputies out of a total of 261, while in Guinea 22 of its 72 deputies were women. Similarly, a woman, Mme. Mafory Bangoura, who had never attended a French school, was appointed Minister for Social Affairs and leader of the women's section of the PDG (Parti Démocratique de Guinée). It is also noteworthy that Guinea's representative at the United Nations is a woman. Women are to be found in every sector of public life. They are engineers, pharmaceutical chemists, secondary and university teachers, regional governors, heads of ministerial cabinets, directors of business concerns. This shows concern for women's progress—but it's not the only sign of this concern.

A genuine desire for change is perceptible among the people of Guinea. This is why we must try to understand (though not to justify or excuse) some of the fundamental consequences of this desire. Change, if it does not come about as a result of long-term reforms, is of necessity sudden and brutal; it is change through revolution. We must recognize this before evaluating what is being and has been achieved by the present Guinean regime.

There has been a great deal of talk of "fabricated" plots and assassinations in Guinea. Some people claim that it has a dictatorial regime. Not being in a position to judge it objectively, we do not intend to indict the internal politics of the country. We must however admit that the condition of women there is far superior to that of any other African state.

The first president of the Republic of Guinea, Ahmed Sékou Touré, seemed to give priority to the task of raising the consciousness of the masses and giving them an education relevant to their needs and social structures, before worrying about other problems. He must have been among those who say, "He who forms youth is master of the future."

What is more, having rejected colonization and all forms of imperialism, Guinea was increasingly cut off from industrialized countries, although relations have recently been re-established. Is Guinea a progressive country? Its motto seems to be "Dignity in poverty rather than slavery with opulence." But is it blinkered to look only at the positive aspects of this country? In spite of claiming to be progressive, is it not in many respects archaic? We are thinking primarily of the continued practice of excision, to which 85 percent of our Guinean sisters are subjected. To quote the following statistics from P. Hanry's *Erotisme africain:*

> 84 percent of the girls are excised, with only 8 percent stating that they are not. Only a very small percentage of women protest against their fate: 12 percent deplore their own excision and 35 percent declare that they do not intend to have their daughters excised. This last figure, higher than the preceding one, certainly implies a protest, but we must compare it with the 44 percent who will have their daughters excised and the 21 percent who have no opinion at present but who risk giving way to the call of tradition when the time arises.[5]

Are we saying then that various political considerations and analyses have deliberately disregarded women's problems? Or were those responsible unaware of their existence? An objective historical analysis would show these practices up for what they are—an attack on women themselves—and not disguise them, or support them on the pretext that they form a part of the traditional cultural past, which is to be held sacred.

Polygamy, too, is among the conditions which restrict the lives of Guinean women—although the country is ahead of other West African states on this count; a struggle against it has been under way since 1968. Indeed, on 16 February 1974 Sékou Touré declared, "We must create a hatred of polygamy among the rising generation."

[1]Shulamith Firestone, *The Dialectic of Sex: The Case for Feminist Revolution,* rev. ed. (New York: Bantam Books, 1971), 12.

[2]Aimé Césaire, *Discourse on Colonialism* (New York: Monthly Review, 1972), 21.

[3]Frantz Fanon, *Black Skin, White Masks,* trans. Charles Lam Markmann (New York: Grove Press, 1967).

[4]Jean-Paul Sartre, *Situations V: Colonialisme et néo-colonialisme* (Paris: Gallimard, 1964), 176. This passage is from Sartre's appreciation of Frantz Fanon's *The Wretched of the Earth,* published as the preface to Fanon, *The Wretched of the Earth,* trans. Constance Farrington (New York: Grove Press, 1968), 15.

[5]P. Hanry, *Erotisme africain* (Paris: Payot, 1970), 47–48.

NELSON MANDELA (1918–   )

✹ We Are Committed to Building a Single Nation in Our Country: Speech at Rally in Durban, February 25, 1990

Mandela amplified various points in the Zulu language: the translations are printed inside chevrons (‹ ›).

Friends, comrades, and the people of Natal, I greet you all. I do so in the name of *peace,* the peace that is so desperately and urgently needed in this region.

In Natal, apartheid is a deadly cancer in our midst, setting house against house and eating away at the precious ties that bind us together. This strife amongst ourselves wastes our energy and destroys our unity. My message to those of you involved in this battle of brother against brother is this: Take your guns, your knives, and your *pangas* [machetes], and throw them into the sea. Close down the death factories. *End this war now!*

We also come together today to renew the ties that make us one people, and to reaffirm a single united strand against the oppression of apartheid. ‹We have gathered here to find a way of building even greater unity than we already have. Unity is the pillar and foundation of our struggle to end the misery which is caused by the oppression which is our greatest enemy. This repression and the violence it creates cannot be ended if we fight and attack each other.›

The people of Natal have fought a long and hard struggle against oppression. The victory of the army of King Cetshwayo kaMpande at the Battle of Isandlwana in 1879 has been an inspiration for those of us engaged in the struggle for justice and freedom in South Africa. At Isandlwana, disciplined Zulu regiments, armed only with shields and spears but filled with courage and determination, thrust back the guns and cannons of the British imperialists.

When the British finally managed to defeat the Zulu kingdom, they divided it up into thirteen new chiefdoms. Later, they annexed the area and gave the land to white farmers. In 1906, in the reign of Dinizulu kaCetshwayo, the colonialists introduced the poll tax and other regulations designed to force Africans to work for wages on white farms. The Zulu people, led by Chief Bambata, refused to bow their proud heads and a powerful spirit of resistance developed which, like the battle of Isandlwana, inspired generations of South Africans.

The ANC [African National Congress] pays tribute to these heroic struggles of the Zulu people to combat oppression. And we are very proud that from the ranks of the Zulu people have emerged outstanding cadres of the ANC and national leaders like Dube, Seme, and Luthuli. We remember another son of Natal, the young and talented Communist Party organizer, Johannes Nkosi, who with three others was brutally murdered in 1930 when he led a march into Durban to protest the hated pass laws.

Another strand in the struggle against oppression began with the formation, right here in Natal, of the first black political organization in Africa. The Natal Indian Congress, founded in 1894, began a tradition of extraparliamentary protest that continues into the present. The next decade saw the increasing radicalization of Indian politics under the leadership of Mahatma Gandhi.

‹In 1906, at the time when Bambata led sections of Africans in a war to destroy the poll tax, our brothers who originated from India, led by Mahatma Gandhi, fought against the oppression of the British government. In 1913, we see Indian workers striking in the sugarcane plantations and in the coal mines. These actions show the oppressed of South Africa waging a struggle to end exploitation and oppression, mounting an important challenge to the repressive British rule.›

In the passive resistance campaign of 1946, over two thousand Indians went to jail, many for occupying land reserved for whites. The campaign made clear the common nature of Indian and African oppression, and the necessity of united resistance. In 1947 this led to the Xuma-Naicker-Dadoo Pact, and to the joint action of Africans and Indians in the Defiance Campaign of 1952. We remind the people of Natal of this long and proud tradition of cooperation between Africans and Indians against racial discrimination and other forms of injustice and oppression. Our unity is our defense, and the unmaking of our oppressors. We are extremely disturbed by recent acts of violence against our Indian compatriots. The perpetrators of these acts are enemies of the liberation movement.

The other great struggle in Natal has been that of the workers. In 1926 the Durban branch of the ICU [Industrial and Commercial Union] powerfully voiced the grievances of migrant workers on the docks, railways, and local industries. In the 1970s Durban workers led the country in a movement to organize and fight for workers' rights. In January 1973, two thousand workers at the Coronation Brick and Tile Factory in Durban came out on strike. They were followed by workers all over Durban.

Out of these strikes grew a host of new unions, new union federations, and eventually COSATU [Congress of South Africa Trade Unions], the biggest and most powerful labor organization in our history. We recognize that battles won in industrial disputes can never be permanently secure without the necessary political changes. Our Defiance Campaign has succeeded in forcing the government to scrap discriminatory laws, and has brought us to the point where we are beginning to glimpse the outlines of a new South Africa. The MDM [Mass Democratic Movement] stands as testimony to the powerful alliance of workers and progressive political organizations.

Whites, too, have made a contribution to the struggle in Natal. It began with the lonely voices of Bishop Colenso and his daughters, who denounced imperialist injustices against the Zulu people and who campaigned vigorously for the freedom of their leaders. The Natal Liberal Party waged a steadfast campaign against removals, and its work has been continued into the present by people like Peter Brown. Whites also contributed significantly to the resurgence of labor struggles in the 1970s through the Wages Commission and the Trade Unions Advisory and Coordinating Council. Our struggle has won the participation of every language and color, every stripe and hue in this country. These four strands of resistance and organization have inspired all South Africans and provide the foundations of our struggle today. We salute your proud and courageous history. ‹No people can boast more proudly of having plowed a significant field in the struggle than the people of Natal.›

The past is a rich resource on which we can draw in order to make decisions for the future, but it does not dictate our choices. We should look back at the past and select what is good, and leave behind what is bad. The issue of chiefship is one such question. Not only in Natal but all through the country there have been chiefs who have been good and honest leaders, who have piloted their people through the dark days of our oppression with skill. These are the chiefs who have looked after the interests of their people, and who enjoy the support of their people. We salute these traditional leaders.

But there have been many bad chiefs who have profited from apartheid and who have increased the burden on their people. We denounce this misuse of office in the strongest terms. There are also chiefs who collaborated with the system, but who have since seen the error of their ways. We commend their change of heart. Chiefly office is not something that history has given to certain individuals to use or abuse as they see fit. Like all forms of leadership, it places specific responsibilities on its holders. As Luthuli, himself a chief, put it, "A chief is primarily a servant of the people. He is the voice of his people."

The Zulu royal house continues today to enjoy the respect of its subjects. It has a glorious history. We are confident that its members will act in ways that will promote the well-being of all South Africans.

The ANC offers a home to all who ascribe to the principles of a free, democratic, nonracial, and united South Africa. We are committed to building a single nation in our country. Our new nation will include blacks and whites, Zulus and Afrikaners, and speakers of every other language. ANC president-general Chief Luthuli said, "I personally believe that here in South Africa, with all of our diversities of color and race, we will show the world a new pattern for democracy." He said, "I think that there is a challenge to us in South Africa, to set a new example for the world." This is the challenge we face today.

To do this we must eliminate all forms of factionalism and regionalism. We praise all organizations which have fought to retain the dignity of our people. Although there are fundamental differences between us, we commend In-katha for their demand over the years for the unbanning of the ANC and the release of political prisoners, as well as for their stand of refusing to partici-pate in a negotiated settlement without the creation of the necessary cli-mate. This stand of Inkatha has contributed in no small measure to making it difficult for the regime to implement successive schemes designed to per-petuate minority rule.

The 1986 Indaba solution proposed for Natal broke new ground insofar as it addressed the question of the exclusion from political power of the African population of Natal and sought to make regional change pioneer national change. But we are now on the threshold of a very different scenario for national change. We are on the edge of a much greater step forward, for *all* our people throughout South Africa. There can be no separate solution for Natal under these conditions, nor can it be argued any longer that there is a need. We believe that Inkatha and all the people of Natal would genuinely welcome a unitary, nonracial, democratic South Africa, the goal of millions throughout the country. Our call is "one nation, one country." ‹We must be one people across the whole of South Africa.›

Yet even now as we stand together on the threshold of a new South Africa, Natal is in flames. Brother is fighting brother in wars of vengeance and re-taliation. Every family has lost dear ones in this strife. In the last few years of my imprisonment, my greatest burden, my deepest suffering, was caused by the reports which reached me of the terrible things which were happening to you people here in Natal. ‹All of us are bereft of loved ones. All of us are aggrieved. Your tears are mine. What has happened has happened and must be accepted by you.› I extend my condolences to all of you who have lost your loved ones in this conflict. Let us take a moment now to remember the thousands who have died in Natal.

It is my duty to remind you now, in the middle of your great sufferings, of the responsibility which we bear today. If we do not bring a halt to this conflict, we will be in grave danger of corrupting the proud legacy of our struggle. We endanger the peace process in the whole of the country.

Apartheid is not yet dead. Equality and democracy continue to elude us. We do not have access to political power. We need to intensify our struggle to achieve our goals. But we cannot do this as long as the conflict amongst ourselves continues. Vigilantes, thugs, and gangs like the notorious Sinyoras have taken advantage of the hardships experienced by our people to profit and gain for themselves. We can stop them, and the descent into lawlessness and violence, only by ceasing our feuds.

Doubts about the role of the police in the conflict continue to jeopardize the finding of a solution. There is an onus on the police to convince the public of their impartiality. The killers of Griffiths and Victoria Mxenge must be brought to book. If there are renegade elements operating within the security forces, they must be exposed and stopped. Justice must not only be done, it must be *seen* to be done.

We recognize that in order to bring war to an end, the two sides must talk. We are pleased to inform you that we are presently preparing for a meeting in the near future between ourselves and the present Zulu monarch, King Zwelithini Goodwill kaBhekuzulu. It is my earnest wish that the meeting will establish a basis on which we can build a real peace.

Repeating the call made by Comrade Walter Sisulu at the Conference for a Democratic Future, we extend the hand of peace to Inkatha and hope that it might one day be possible for us to share a platform with its leader, Chief Mangosuthu Gatsha Buthelezi. We recognize the right of all organizations which are not racist to participate in political life. We commend the actions of those who have involved themselves actively in the search for peace in Natal. We commend the joint UDF/COSATU team. We also commend Dr. Dhlomo, Dr. Mdlalose, and Messrs. Nkheli, Ndlovu, and Zondi from Inkatha, as well as the churches in Natal, and certain business sectors, notably the Pietermaritzburg Chamber of Commerce. Our search for peace is a search for strength.

As a result of our historic struggles, we in the Mass Democratic Movement and in the ANC are the premier political force in the country. This preeminence confers on us responsibilities over and above the concerns of power politics. We have a duty to look beyond our own ranks and our immediate concerns. We must strive more earnestly to unite all the people of our country, and to nurture that unity into a common nationhood. Wherever divisions occur, such as in the strife here in Natal, it is a reflection against us and our greater societal goals. We need to look critically and candidly at aspects of our own practices which may not be acceptable or wise. We need to be rigorous in identifying our own contribution to the escalation of violence wherever it may occur. We have a greater purpose than the defeat of rival oppressed groups. It is the creation of a healthy and vibrant society.

We condemn, in the strongest possible terms, the use of violence as a way of settling differences amongst our people. ‹Great anger and violence can never build a nation. The apartheid regime uses this strife as a pretext for further oppression.›

We would like to see in members of all seasoned political organizations the total absence of intolerance towards those who differ from us on questions of strategy and tactics. Those who approach problems with intolerant attitudes are no credit to the struggle; they actively endanger our future.

The youth have been the shock troops of our struggle. We salute them for the ground which they have gained. Only through commitment have these victories been won; only through discipline can they be consolidated and made to last. ‹The youth must be like the warriors who fought under Shaka, the son of Senzangakhona, fighting with great bravery and skill. These heroes obeyed the commands of their commanders and their leaders. Today the community says, the world says, and I say: End this violence. Let us not be ruled by anger.› Our youth must be ready to demonstrate the same perfect discipline as the armies of King Shaka. If they do not, we will lose the ground which we have gained at such great cost.

The parties to the conflict in Natal have disagreed about a great deal. We have reached a stage where none of the parties can be regarded as right or wrong. Each carries a painful legacy of the past few years. But both sides share a common enemy: the enemy is that of inadequate housing, forced removals, lack of resources as basic as that of water, and rising unemployment. The Freedom Charter asserts that there should be houses, security, and comfort for all. We demand that the government provide these basic necessities of life. ‹The shortage of housing, water, and work opportunities, the forced removal of people, and the destruction of their houses: these are our problems. They must not make us enemies. We must take lessons from what happened in Lamontville; when they said *Asinamali*—We have no money!—they were expressing collectively the problems of the whole community.›

It is thus vital that we end the conflict in Natal, and end it now. Everyone must commit themselves to peace. Women of Natal, in the past and at crucial moments, you have shown greater wisdom than your menfolk. It was you who, in 1929 and again in 1959, identified and struck out at one of the roots of our oppression. You launched powerful campaigns around beer halls. ‹Women such as Dorothy Nyembe, Gladys Manzi, and Ruth Shabane showed sharpness of mind by closing down the beer halls when the men were rendered useless by alcohol and families were being broken up. I hope that the women will again stand up and put their shoulders to the wheel together with the community to end the strife and violence.› More recently the women of Chesterville arranged all-night vigils to protect their children. Mothers, sisters, and daughters of Natal, it falls on you once again to intervene decisively.

I call on the women of Natal. ‹Each and every one of you must play your part!› I charge you with a special responsibility here today. It is you, in your wisdom now, who must begin the work of bringing peace to Natal. Tell your sons, your brothers, and your husbands that you want peace and security. It is you who must show them the real enemy. ‹All women know of mass poverty and homelessness, of children dying from diseases caused by hunger, poverty, and repression. We must therefore end the strife and the fighting and the misunderstanding in the community so that we defeat our common enemy, the apartheid regime.› Open the cooking pots and ask them why there is so little food inside. When the rains come into your homes, place the hands of your men in the pools on the floor, and ask them: "Why?" When your child ails, and you have no money to take it to a doctor, ask them: "Why?" There is only one answer, and that answer is our common deprivation. Go out and meet the women of the other side. Their story is the same. Then take your men with you.

I want to hear from you. From each and every community, I want a report. I want to hear the story of how you made the peace. We place our trust in you.

Viva our mothers!

Viva our sisters!

Viva the women of our land!

I call on the people of Inanda, join hands! All of you from Clermont, join hands; Hambanathi, Hammarsdale, Chesterville, and Mpophomeni, join hands. People of Ashdown, Esikhaweni, Mbali, and Trustfeed, join hands. Those of you who are from Maphumulo's area, you too. Residents of Durban and Pietermaritzburg, it is your turn. Those from strife-torn Umlazi and tragic KwaMashu, join hands also. I know each one of these names from my time in prison. I know each as an explosion of conflict. And those of you whose homes I have not named, you too should join hands. We are many thousands gathered here in this stadium today. Let us now pledge ourselves to peace and to unity. Join hands all of you and raise them up for all to see.

A great deal of energy has been wasted by our people in violent actions across the towns and villages of this province. If we could channel this energy towards the real enemy of the people—apartheid—we could be free within days.

We have already waited for our freedom for far too long. We can wait no longer. Join forces, Indians, coloreds, Africans, and freedom-loving whites, to give apartheid its final blow. In the process, let us develop active democracy. Democratic structures which serve the people must be established in every school, township, village, factory, and farm.

Since my release, I have become more convinced than ever that the real makers of history are the ordinary men and women of our country. Their participation in every decision about the future is the only guarantee of true democracy and freedom. Undue reliance should not be placed on the good-will of the government. It is still a white minority regime concerned to protect white minority rights as far as it can. Nor should our reliance be placed on the abilities of the statesmen amongst us and our political leaders to negotiate an acceptable settlement. It is only the united action of you, the people, that will ensure that freedom is finally achieved. I call, therefore, for an all-round intensification of our struggle. ‹Together we shall conquer!›

Mayibuye i-Afrika! Amandla!

THE   CARIBBEAN

In the texts from the Caribbean included here, the generative themes of African philosophy find expression in the context of the black diaspora forced by the Atlantic slave trade. The ontological emphasis on a relational conception of reality plays a particularly important role in helping define the black community as something distinct from the European community of slaveholders. In turn, the Caribbean philosophical tradition presented here devotes much attention to the issues of constructing notions both of identity and self-determination and of culture and ethos within the framework of the black community. Thus the relational humanism so characteristic of the African tradition finds a new key in the Caribbean, where it is articulated as an explicit response to the tendencies towards dehumanization left in the wake of slavery.

Edward Blyden—born in Saint Thomas but educated in the United States—gives a distinctively religious dimension to the relationship between self and community, while echoing in some ways the contempt for Africa found in his essentially European religious education. Calling for those of African descent to return to their homeland for the purpose of Christianizing the continent, Blyden—who spent most of his adult life in Liberia—nevertheless avoids a simple condemnation of African people for their non-Christian beliefs. Rather, he sees this missionary work as part of helping to build a truly black nation in Africa, a nation in which black people throughout Africa and the diaspora can take pride in the glory of the black race.

The Jamaican Marcus Garvey echoes Blyden's insistence on the indispensability of an African nation for winning respect for black people, but he goes further in insisting that there is little chance for black dignity or self-determination in the Caribbean or the United States. He insists that black colonization in Africa will not repeat the oppression of the indigenous people so characteristic of white colonization, and he grounds this claim in the recognizably African notion that status in the community depends upon loyalty and service to the community. Moreover, Garvey suggests that this new aristocracy of service will create a framework within which people of African descent may once again recognize the special achievements of precolonial African history and culture.

In the work of Haitian Jean Price-Mars, ethnography comes to the aid of philosophy and grounds a new conception of Haitian identity in the extensive survivals of African culture in twentieth century Haiti. Critiquing the "collective bovaryism" that leads the Haitian to misrecognize him / herself as a cultural heir to France, Price-Mars argues for a reclamation of African identity in the diasporan context. What this means in practice is that he calls for his fellow citizens (and, by extension, all people of African descent) to take more seriously their folk traditions, precisely because these traditions constitute the community's mode of resistance to the continuing pressures of European ideology and institutions.

C. L. R. James, perhaps best known for his radical history of the Haitian revolution, *The Black Jacobins*, complements Price-Mars's call for a reclamation of racial identity in the Caribbean with a stinging analysis of the effects of slavery and colonial exploitation on the middle classes in particular. Arguing that the middle classes believe they benefit significantly from imperialist economic structures, the Trinidadian James graphically describes a people torn from their traditional roots of community identification. What replaces an identity grounded in values of community is an objectification reinforced by considerations of material gain, and James suggests that this leads the middle classes to identify unwittingly with the values of the slave-owners of the eighteenth and nineteenth centuries.

In his explosive *Discourse on Colonialism*, the Martinican poet and statesman Aimé Césaire effectively deconstructs the Western notion of civilization somewhat ambivalently upheld even by Blyden and Garvey. Arguing that the Christian civilization brought by colonialism is a lie—that it is neither civil nor a source of significant cultural gifts—Césaire makes a case for the moral preferability of traditional African and diasporan society and culture. Where "colonization equals 'thingification,' " Césaire maintains that non-European civilizations open up the full potential of all human beings insofar as they in no way pretend to be universal. Thus Césaire—one of the most visible proponents of the ideology of negritude—here echoes Senghor's call for a new conception of humanism grounded in the ideals of traditional African communities.

Frantz Fanon, like Césaire a native of Martinique, uses his work as a psychiatrist in Algeria and as a theoretician for the Algerian revolution to explore the complex links between the identity of colonized peoples and their traditional cultures. Fanon argues that racism is a singularly important consequence of colonial rule, a result of the "shameless exploitation" of one group by another, and he shows how getting away from the notion that racism is just "a psychological flaw" is crucial to seeing the ways in which racism contributes to the inferiorization of the colonized. At the same time, Fanon maintains that the rediscovery and reclaiming of traditional culture marks the pivotal moment around which the possibility of decolonization turns.

The Guyanese Walter Rodney—himself the victim of a politically motivated assassination—disagrees with Fanon, arguing that modern history can only be understood properly if the concept of race is used as the cornerstone of analysis. Race remains in Rodney's analysis a mark of power—"power is kept pure milky white"—and he maintains that the crucial political challenge facing all nonwhite people is the recognition of the power that can come from racial identification. One way to bring about this recognition of black power, according to Rodney, is the use of justified violence to attempt to right wrongs that have not been successfully addressed in other, nonviolent ways.

In "The Shadow of the Whip," Merle Hodge brings our selection of texts from the Caribbean to a close with an impassioned indictment of the continuing brutality and violence directed against women in contemporary Caribbean society. Hodge, a novelist and writer originally from Trinidad, analyzes this domestic violence—along with other forms of abuse common in the Caribbean—as a manifestation of the black man's sense of personal inferiority, itself a product of centuries of slavery and colonization. Calling for a "revaluation of black womanhood," Hodge suggests that decolonization ultimately demands a radical transformation of relations between men and women.

These eight thinkers from the Caribbean add to the African philosophical tradition highlighted in the first part of this volume a special concern for the distinctive ways in which the history of slavery and colonization in the region has contributed to dehumanization. This concern goes hand in hand with an explicit interest in reclaiming a black—African—tradition of community and identity, and in this way the African theme of relational humanism is brought to the forefront of the struggle for Caribbean decolonization.

EDWARD W. BLYDEN (1832–1912)

 The Call of Providence to the Descendants
of Africa in America (1862)

> Behold, the Lord thy God hath
> set the land before thee: go up
> and possess it, as the Lord God of
> thy fathers hath said unto thee;
> fear not, neither be discouraged.
>
> —Deut. 1:21

Among the descendants of Africa in this country, the persuasion seems to prevail, though not now to the same extent as formerly, that they owe no special duty to the land of their forefathers; that, their ancestors having been brought to this country against their will and themselves having been born in the land, they are in duty bound to remain here and give their attention exclusively to the acquiring for themselves, and perpetuating to their posterity, social and political rights, notwithstanding the urgency of the call which their fatherland, by its forlorn and degraded moral condition, makes upon them for their assistance.

All other people feel a pride in their ancestral land, and do everything in their power to create for it, if it has not already, an honorable name. But many of the descendants of Africa, on the contrary, speak disparagingly of their country, are ashamed to acknowledge any connection with that land, and would turn indignantly upon any who would bid them go up and take possession of the land of their fathers.

It is a sad feature in the residence of Africans in this country that it has begotten in them a forgetfulness of Africa—a want of sympathy with her in her moral and intellectual desolation, and a clinging to the land which for centuries has been the scene of their thralldom. A shrewd European observer of American society says of the Negro in this country that he "makes a thousand fruitless efforts to insinuate himself among men who repulse him; he conforms to the taste of his oppressors, adopts their opinions, and hopes

Reprinted from Edward W. Blyden, *Liberia's Offering* (New York: John A. Gray, 1862), 67–91.

by imitating them to form a part of their community. Having been told from infancy that his race is naturally inferior to that of the whites, he assents to the proposition, and is ashamed of his own nature. In each of his features he discovers a trace of slavery, and, if it were in his power, he would willingly rid himself of everything that makes him what he is."[1]

It cannot be denied that some very important advantages have accrued to the black man from his deportation to this land, but it has been at the expense of his manhood. Our nature in this country is not the same as it appears among the lordly natives of the interior of Africa, who have never felt the trammels of a foreign yoke. We have been dragged into depths of degradation. We have been taught a cringing servility. We have been drilled into contentment with the most undignified circumstances. Our finer sensibilities have been blunted. There has been an almost utter extinction of all that delicacy of feeling and sentiment which adorns character. The temperament of our souls has become harder or coarser, so that we can walk forth here, in this land of indignities, in ease and in complacency, while our complexion furnishes ground for every species of social insult which an intolerant prejudice may choose to inflict.

But a change is coming over us. The tendency of events is directing the attention of the colored people to some other scene, and Africa is beginning to receive the attention which has so long been turned away from her; and as she throws open her portals and shows the inexhaustible means of comfort and independence within, the black man begins to feel dissatisfied with the annoyances by which he is here surrounded, and looks with longing eyes to his fatherland. I venture to predict that, within a very brief period, that downtrodden land instead of being regarded with prejudice and distaste, will largely attract the attention and engage the warmest interest of every man of color. A few have always sympathized with Africa, but it has been an indolent and unmeaning sympathy—a sympathy which put forth no effort, made no sacrifices, endured no self-denial, braved no obloquy for the sake of advancing African interests. But the scale is turning, and Africa is becoming the all-absorbing topic.

It is my desire on the present occasion to endeavor to set before you the work which, it is becoming more and more apparent, devolves upon the black men of the United States; and to guide my thoughts, I have chosen the words of the text: "Behold, the Lord thy God hath set the land before thee: go up and possess it, as the Lord God of thy fathers hath said unto thee; fear not, neither be discouraged."

You will at once perceive that I do not believe that the work to be done by black men is in this country. I believe that their field of operation is in some other and distant scene. Their work is far nobler and loftier than that which they are now doing in this country. It is theirs to betake themselves to injured

Africa, and bless those outraged shores, and quiet those distracted families with the blessings of Christianity and civilization. It is theirs to bear with them to that land the arts of industry and peace, and counteract the influence of those horrid abominations which an inhuman avarice has introduced—to roll back the appalling cloud of ignorance and superstition which overspreads the land, and to rear on those shores an asylum of liberty for the downtrodden sons of Africa wherever found. This is the work to which Providence is obviously calling the black men of this country.

I am aware that some, against all experience, are hoping for the day when they will enjoy equal social and political rights in this land. We do not blame them for so believing and trusting. But we would remind them that there is a faith against reason, against experience, which consists in believing or pretending to believe very important propositions upon very slender proofs, and in maintaining opinions without any proper grounds. It ought to be clear to every thinking and impartial mind that there can never occur in this country an equality, social or political, between whites and blacks. The whites have for a long time had the advantage. All the affairs of the country are in their hands. They make and administer the laws; they teach the schools; here, in the North, they ply all the trades, they own all the stores, they have possession of all the banks, they own all the ships and navigate them; they are the printers, proprietors, and editors of the leading newspapers, and they shape public opinion. Having always had the lead, they have acquired an ascendancy they will ever maintain. The blacks have very few or no agencies in operation to counteract the ascendant influence of the Europeans. And instead of employing what little they have by a unity of effort to alleviate their condition, they turn all their power against themselves by their endless jealousies, and rivalries, and competition, everyone who is able to "pass" being emulous of a place among Europeans or Indians. This is the effect of their circumstances. It is the influence of the dominant class upon them. It argues no essential inferiority in them—no more than the disadvantages of the Israelites in Egypt argued their essential inferiority to the Egyptians. They are the weaker class overshadowed and depressed by the stronger. They are the feeble oak dwarfed by the overspreadings of a large tree, having not the advantage of rain, and sunshine, and fertilizing dews.

Before the weaker people God has set the land of their forefathers, and bids them go up and possess it without fear or discouragement. Before the tender plant he sets an open field, where in the unobstructed air and sunshine it may grow and flourish in all its native luxuriance.

There are two ways in which God speaks to men: one is by his word and the other by his providence. He has not sent any Moses, with signs and wonders, to cause an exodus of the descendants of Africa to their fatherland, yet he has loudly spoken to them as to their duty in the matter. He has spoken by his providence. First, by suffering them to be brought here and placed in circumstances where they could receive a training fitting them for the work of civilizing and evangelizing the land whence they were torn, and by preserving them under the severest trials and afflictions. Secondly, by allowing them, notwithstanding all the services they have rendered to this country, to be treated as strangers and aliens, so as to cause them to have anguish of spirit, as was the case with the Jews in Egypt, and to make them long for some refuge from their social and civil deprivations. Thirdly, by bearing a portion of them across the tempestuous seas back to Africa, by preserving them through the process of acclimation, and by establishing them in the land, despite the attempts of misguided men to drive them away. Fourthly, by keeping their fatherland in reserve for them in their absence.

The manner in which Africa has been kept from invasion is truly astounding. Known for ages, it is yet unknown. For centuries its inhabitants have been the victims of the cupidity of foreigners. The country has been rifled of its population. It has been left in some portions almost wholly unoccupied, but it has remained unmolested by foreigners. It has been very near the crowded countries of the world, yet none has relieved itself to any great extent of its overflowing population by seizing upon its domains. Europe, from the North, looks wishfully and with longing eyes across the narrow straits of Gilbraltar. Asia, with its teeming millions, is connected with us by an isthmus wide enough to admit of her throwing thousands into the country. But notwithstanding the known wealth of the resources of the land, of which the report has gone into all the earth, there is still a terrible veil between us and our neighbors, the all-conquering Europeans, which they are only now essaying to lift; while the teeming millions of Asia have not even attempted to leave their boundaries to penetrate our borders. Neither alluring visions of glorious conquests nor brilliant hopes of rapid enrichment could induce them to invade the country. It has been preserved alike from the boastful civilization of Europe and the effete and barbarous institutions of Asia. We call it, then, a Providential interposition that while the owners of the soil have been abroad, passing through the fearful ordeal of a most grinding oppression, the land, though entirely unprotected, has lain uninvaded. We regard it as a providential call to Africans everywhere, to "go up and possess the land"; so that in a sense that is not merely constructive and figurative but truly literal, God says to the black men of this country, with reference to Africa: "Behold, I set the land before you, go up and possess it."

Of course it cannot be expected that this subject of the duty of colored men to go up and take possession of their fatherland will be at once clear to every mind. Men look at objects from different points of view, and form their opinions according to the points from which they look, and are guided in their actions according to the opinions they form. As I have already said, the majority of exiled Africans do not seem to appreciate the great privilege of going and taking possession of the land. They seem to have lost all interest in that land, and to prefer living in subordinate and inferior positions in a strange land among oppressors, to encountering the risks involved in emigrating to a distant country. As I walk the streets of these cities, visit the hotels, go on board the steamboats, I am grieved to notice how much intelligence, how much strength and energy is frittered away in those trifling employments, which, if thrown into Africa, might elevate the millions of that land from their degradation, tribes at a time, and create an African power which would command the respect of the world and place in the possession of Africans, its rightful owners, the wealth which is now diverted to other quarters. Most of the wealth that could be drawn from that land, during the last six centuries, has passed into the hands of Europeans, while many of Africa's own sons, sufficiently intelligent to control those immense resources, are sitting down in poverty and dependence in the land of strangers—exiles when they have so rich a domain from which they have never been expatriated, but which is willing, nay, anxious to welcome them home again.

We need some African power, some great center of the race where our physical, pecuniary, and intellectual strength may be collected. We need some spot whence such an influence may go forth in behalf of the race as shall be felt by the nations. We are now so scattered and divided that we can do nothing. The imposition begun last year by a foreign power upon Haiti and which is still persisted in fills every black man who has heard of it with indignation, but we are not strong enough to speak out effectually for that land. When the same power attempted an outrage upon the Liberians, there was no African power strong enough to interpose. So long as we remain thus divided, we may expect impositions. So long as we live simply by the sufferance of the nations, we must expect to be subject to their caprices.

Among the free portion of the descendants of Africa, numbering about four or five millions, there is enough talent, wealth, and enterprise to form a respectable nationality on the continent of Africa. For nigh three hundred years their skill and industry have been expended in building up the southern countries of the New World, the poor, frail constitution of the Caucasian not allowing him to endure the fatigue and toil involved in such labors. Africans and their descendants have been the laborers, and the mechanics, and the artisans in the greater portion of this hemisphere. By the results of their labor the European countries have been sustained and enriched. All the cotton, coffee, indigo, sugar, tobacco, etc., which have formed the most important articles of European commerce, have been raised and prepared for market by the labor of the black man. Dr. Palmer of New Orleans bears the same testimony.[2] And all this labor they have done, for the most part not only without compensation but with abuse, and contempt, and insult as their reward.

Now, while Europeans are looking to our fatherland with such eagerness of desire and are hastening to explore and take away its riches, ought not Africans in the Western hemisphere to turn their regards thither also? We need to collect the scattered forces of the race, and there is no rallying-ground more favorable than Africa. There,

> No pent-up Utica contracts our powers,
> The whole boundless continent is ours.

Ours as a gift from the Almighty when he drove asunder the nations and assigned them their boundaries; and ours by peculiar physical adaptation.

An African nationality is our great need, and God tells us by his providence that he has set the land before us, and bids us go up and possess it. We shall never receive the respect of other races until we establish a powerful nationality. We should not content ourselves with living among other races, simply by their permission or their endurance, as Africans live in this country. We must build up Negro states; we must establish and maintain the various institutions; we must make and administer laws, erect and preserve churches, and support the worship of God; we must have governments; we must have legislation of our own; we must build ships and navigate them; we must ply the trades, instruct the schools, control the press, and thus aid in shaping the opinions and guiding the destinies of mankind. Nationality is an ordinance of nature. The heart of every true Negro yearns after a distinct and separate nationality.

Impoverished, feeble, and alone, Liberia is striving to establish and build up such a nationality in the home of the race. Can any descendant of Africa turn contemptuously upon a scene where such efforts are making? Would not every right-thinking Negro rather lift up his voice and direct the attention of his brethren to that land? Liberia, with outstretched arms, earnestly invites all to come. We call them forth out of all nations; we bid them take up their all and leave the countries of their exile, as of old the Israelites went forth from Egypt, taking with them their trades and their treasures, their intelligence, their mastery of arts, their knowledge of the sciences, their practical wisdom, and everything that will render them useful in building up a nationality. We summon them from these States, from the Canadas, from the East and West Indies, from South America, from everywhere, to come and take part with us in our great work.

But those whom we call are under the influence of various opinions, having different and conflicting views of their relations and duty to Africa, according to the different standpoints they occupy. So it was with another people who, like ourselves, were suffering from the effects of protracted thralldom, when on the borders of the land to which God was leading them. When Moses sent out spies to search the land of Canaan, every man, on his return, seemed to be influenced in his report by his peculiar temperament, previous habits of thought, by the degree of his physical courage, or by something peculiar in his point of observation. All agreed, indeed, that it was an exceedingly rich land, "flowing with milk and honey," for they carried with them on their return a proof of its amazing fertility. But a part, and a larger part, too, saw only giants and walled towns, and barbarians and cannibals. "Surely," said they, "it floweth with milk and honey. Nevertheless the people be strong that dwell in the land, and the cities are walled, and very great; and moreover we saw the children of Anak there. The land through which we have gone to search it, is a land that eateth up the inhabitants thereof; and all the people that we saw in it are men of a great stature. And there we saw the giants, the sons of Anak, which come of the giants; and we were in our own sight as grasshoppers, and so we were in their sight." It was only a small minority of that company that saw things in a more favorable light. "Caleb stilled the people before Moses, and said, Let us go up at once and possess it; for we be well able to overcome it" (Num. 13).

In like manner there is division among the colored people of this country with regard to Africa, that land which the providence of God is bidding them go up and possess. Spies sent from different sections of this country by the colored people—and many a spy not commissioned—have gone to that land, and have returned and reported. Like the Hebrew spies, they have put forth diverse views. Most believe Africa to be a fertile and rich country, and an African nationality a desirable thing. But some affirm that the land is not fit to dwell in, for "it is a land that eateth up the inhabitants thereof," notwithstanding the millions of strong and vigorous aborigines who throng all parts of the country, and the thousands of colonists who are settled along the coast; some see in the inhabitants incorrigible barbarism, degradation, and superstition, and insuperable hostility to civilization; others suggest that the dangers and risks to be encountered, and the self-denial to be endured, are too great for the slender advantages which, as it appears to them, will accrue from immigration. A few only report that the land is open to us on every hand—that "every prospect pleases," and that the natives are so tractable that it would be a comparatively easy matter for civilized and Christianized black men to secure all the land to Christian law, liberty, and civilization.

I come today to defend the report of the minority. The thousands of our own race, emigrants from this country, settled for more than forty years in that land, agree with the minority report. Dr. Barth and other travelers to the east and southeast of Liberia endorse the sentiment of the minority, and testify to the beauty, and healthfulness, and productiveness of the country, and to the mildness and hospitality of its inhabitants. In Liberia we hear from natives, who are constantly coming to our settlements from the far interior, of land exuberantly fertile, of large, numerous, and wealthy tribes, athletic and industrious; not the descendants of Europeans—according to Bowen's insane theory—but *black* men, pure Negroes, who live in large towns, cultivate the soil, and carry on extensive traffic, maintaining amicable relations with each other and with men from a distance.

The ideas that formerly prevailed of the interior of Africa, which suited the purposes of poetry and sensation writing, have been proved entirely erroneous. Poets may no longer sing with impunity of Africa:

> A region of drought, where no river glides,
> Nor rippling brook with osiered sides;
> Where sedgy pool, nor bubbling fount,
> Nor tree, nor cloud, nor misty mount,
> Appears to refresh the aching eye,
> But barren earth and the burning sky,
> And the blank horizon round and round.

No; missionary and scientific enterprises have disproved such fallacies. The land possesses every possible inducement. That extensive and beauteous domain which God has given us appeals to us and to black men everywhere by its many blissful and benignant aspects; by its flowery landscapes, its beautiful rivers, its serene and peaceful skies; by all that attractive and perennial verdure which overspreads the hills and valleys; by its every prospect lighted up by delightful sunshine; by all its natural charms, it calls upon us to rescue it from the grasp of remorseless superstition, and introduce the blessings of the Gospel.

But there are some among the intelligent colored people of this country who, while they profess to have great love for Africa and tell us that their souls are kindled when they hear of their fatherland, yet object to going themselves because, as they affirm, the black man has a work to accomplish in this land—he has a destiny to fulfill. He, the representative of Africa, like the representatives from various parts of Europe, must act his part in building up this great composite nation. It is not difficult to see what the work of the black man is in this land. The most inexperienced observer may at once read his destiny. Look at the various departments of society here in the *free* North; look at the different branches of industry, and see how the black man is aiding to build up this nation. Look at the hotels, the saloons, the steamboats, the barbershops, and see how successfully he is carrying out his destiny! And there is an extreme likelihood that such are forever to be the exploits which he is destined to achieve in this country until he merges his African peculiarities in the Caucasian.

Others object to the *climate* of Africa, first, that it is unhealthy, and sec-

ondly, that it is not favorable to intellectual progress. To the first, we reply
that it is not more insalubrious than other new countries. Persons going to
Africa who have not been broken down as to their constitutions in this country stand as fair a chance of successful acclimation as in any other country of
large, unbroken forests and extensively uncleared lands. In all new countries
there are sufferings and privations. All those countries which have grown up
during the last two centuries, in this hemisphere, have had as a foundation
the groans, and tears, and blood of the pioneers. But what are the sufferings
of pioneers, compared with the greatness of the results they accomplish for
succeeding generations? Scarcely any great step in human progress is made
without multitudes of victims. Every revolution that has been effected, every
nationality that has been established, every country that has been rescued
from the abominations of savagism, every colony that has been planted, has
involved perplexities and sufferings to the generation who undertook it. In
the evangelization of Africa, in the erection of African nationalities, we can
expect no exception. The man, then, who is not able to suffer and to die for
his fellows when necessity requires it is not fit to be a pioneer in this great
work.

We believe, as we have said, that the establishment of an African nationality in Africa is the great need of the African race; and the men who have
gone or may hereafter go to assist in laying the foundations of empire, so far
from being dupes, or cowards, or traitors, as some have ignorantly called
them, are the truest heroes of the race. They are the soldiers rushing first into
the breach—physicians who at the risk of their own lives are first to explore
an infectious disease. How much more nobly do they act than those who
have held for years that it is nobler to sit here and patiently suffer with our
brethren! Such sentimental inactivity finds no respect in these days of rapid
movement. The world sees no merit in mere innocence. The man who contents himself to sit down and exemplify the virtue of patience and endurance
will find no sympathy from the busy, restless crowd that rush by him. Even
the "sick man" must get out of the way when he hears the tramp of the
approaching host, or be crushed by the heedless and massive car of progress.
Blind Bartimeuses are silenced by the crowd. The world requires active service; it respects only productive workers. The days of hermits and monks
have passed away. Action—work, work—is the order of the day. Heroes in the
strife and struggle of humanity are the demand of the age. "They who would
be free, *themselves* must *strike* the blow."[3]

With regard to the objection founded upon the unfavorableness of the
climate to intellectual progress, I have only to say that proper moral agencies, when set in operation, cannot be overborne by physical causes. "We
continually behold lower laws held in restraint by higher; mechanic by dynamic; chemical by vital; physical by moral."[4] It has not yet been proved that

with the proper influences, the tropics will not produce men of "cerebral activity." Those races which have degenerated by a removal from the North to the tropics did not possess the proper moral power. They had in themselves the seed of degeneracy, and would have degenerated anywhere. It was not Anglo-Saxon blood, nor a temperate climate, that kept the first emigrants to this land from falling into the same indolence and inefficiency which have overtaken the European settlers in South America, but the Anglo-Saxon Bible—the principles contained in that book, are the great conservative and elevating power. Man is the same, and the human mind is the same, whether existing beneath African suns or Arctic frosts. I can conceive of no difference. It is the moral influences brought to bear upon the man that make the difference in his progress.

"High degrees of moral sentiment," says a distinguished American writer,[5] "control the unfavorable influences of climate; and some of our grandest examples of men and of races come from the equatorial regions." Man is elevated by taking hold of that which is higher than himself. Unless this is done, climate, color, race, will avail nothing.

> —unless above himself he can
> Erect himself, how poor a thing is man![6]

For my own part, I believe that the brilliant world of the tropics, with its marvels of nature, must of necessity give to mankind a new career of letters, and new forms in the various arts, whenever the millions of men at present uncultivated shall enjoy the advantages of civilization.

Africa will furnish a development of civilization which the world has never yet witnessed. Its great peculiarity will be its moral element. The Gospel is to achieve some of its most beautiful triumphs in that land. "God shall enlarge Japheth, and he shall dwell in the tents of Shem," was the blessing upon the European and Asiatic races (Gen. 9:27). Wonderfully have these predictions been fulfilled. The all-conquering descendants of Japheth have gone to every clime, and have planted themselves on almost every shore. By means fair and unfair, they have spread themselves, have grown wealthy and powerful. They have been truly "enlarged." God has "dwelt in the tents of Shem," for so some understand the passage. The Messiah—God manifest in the flesh—was of the tribe of Judah. He was born and dwelt in the tents of Shem. The promise to Ethiopia, or Ham, is like that to Shem, of a spiritual kind. It refers not to physical strength, not to large and extensive domains, not to foreign conquests, not to widespread domination, but to the possession of spiritual qualities, to the elevation of the soul heavenward, to spiritual aspirations and divine communications. "Ethiopia shall stretch forth her hands unto God" (Ps. 68:31). Blessed, glorious promise! Our trust is not to be in chariots or horses, not in our own skill or power, but our help is to be in the name of the

Lord. And surely, in reviewing our history as a people, whether we consider our preservation in the lands of our exile, or the preservation of our fatherland from invasion, we are compelled to exclaim: "Hitherto hath the Lord helped us!" Let us, then, fear not the influences of climate. Let us go forth stretching out our hands to God, and if it be as hot as Nebuchadnezzar's furnace, there will be one in the midst like unto the Son of God, counteracting its deleterious influences.

Behold, then, the Lord our God has set the land before us, with its burning climate, with its privations, with its moral, intellectual, and political needs, and by his providence he bids us go up and possess it without fear or discouragement. Shall we go up at his bidding? If the black men of this country, through unbelief or indolence or for any other cause, fail to lay hold of the blessings which God is proffering to them, and neglect to accomplish the work which devolves upon them, the work will be done, but others will be brought in to do it and to take possession of the country.

For while the colored people here are tossed about by various and conflicting opinions as to their duty to that land, men are going thither from other quarters of the globe. They are entering the land from various quarters with various motives and designs, and may eventually so preoccupy the land as to cut us off from the fair inheritance which lies before us, unless we go forth without further delay and establish ourselves.

The enterprise and energy manifested by white men who, with uncongenial constitutions, go from a distance to endeavor to open up that land to the world are far from creditable to the civilized and enlightened colored men of the United States, when contrasted with their indifference in the matter. A noble army of self-expatriated evangelists have gone to that land from Europe and America; and, while anxious to extend the blessings of true religion, they have in no slight degree promoted the cause of science and commerce. Many have fallen, either from the effects of the climate or by the hands of violence; still the interest in the land is by no means diminished. The enamored worshiper of science and the Christian philanthropist are still laboring to solve the problem of African geography and to elevate its benighted tribes. They are not only disclosing to the world the mysteries of regions hitherto unexplored, but tribes whose very existence had not before been known to the civilized world have been brought, through their instrumentality, into contact with civilization and Christianity. They have discovered in the distant portions of that land countries as productive as any in Europe and America. They have informed the world of bold and lofty mountains, extensive lakes, noble rivers, falls rivaling Niagara, so that, as a result of their arduous, difficult, and philanthropic labors of exploration, the cause of Christianity, ethnology, geography, and commerce has been, in a very important degree, subserved.

Dr. Livingstone, the indefatigable African explorer who, it is estimated, has passed over not less than eleven thousand miles of African ground, speaking of the motives which led him to those shores and still keep him there in spite of privations and severe afflictions says:

> I expect to find for myself no large fortune in that country; nor do I expect to explore any large portions of a new country; but I do hope to find a pathway, by means of the river Zambesi, which may lead to highlands, where Europeans may form a settlement, and where, by opening up communication and establishing commercial intercourse with the natives of Africa, they may slowly, but not the less surely, impart to the people of that country the knowledge and inestimable blessings of Christianity.[7]

The recently formed Oxford, Cambridge, and Dublin Missionary Society state their object to be to spread Christianity among the untaught people of Central Africa, "so to operate among them as by mere teaching and influence to help *to build up native Christian states.*" The idea of building up "native Christian states" is a very important one, and is exactly such an idea as would be carried out if there were a large influx of civilized blacks from abroad.

I am sorry to find that among some in this country the opinion prevails that in Liberia a distinction is maintained between the colonists and the aborigines, so that the latter are shut out from the social and political privileges of the former. No candid person who has read the laws of Liberia or who has visited that country can affirm or believe such a thing. The idea no doubt arises from the fact that the aborigines of a country generally suffer from the settling of colonists among them. But the work of Liberia is somewhat different from that of other colonies which have been planted on foreign shores. The work achieved by other emigrants has usually been the enhancement of their own immediate interests; the increase of their physical comforts and conveniences; the enlargement of their borders by the most speedy and available methods, without regard to the effect such a course might have upon the aborigines. Their interests sometimes coming into direct contact with those of the owners of the soil, they have not unfrequently, by their superior skill and power, reduced the poor native to servitude or complete annihilation. The Israelites could live in peace in the land of Canaan only by exterminating the indigenous inhabitants. The colony that went out from Phoenicia and that laid the foundations of empire on the northern shores of Africa at first paid a yearly tax to the natives; with the increasing wealth and power of Carthage, however, the respective conditions of the Carthaginians and the natives were changed, and the Phoenician adventurers assumed and maintained a dominion over the Libyans. The colonies from Europe which landed at Plymouth Rock, at Boston, and at Jamestown—which took possession of the West India islands and of Mexico—

treated the aborigines in the same manner. The natives of India, Australia, and New Zealand are experiencing a similar treatment under the overpowering and domineering rule of the Anglo-Saxons. Eagerness for gain and the passion for territorial aggrandisement have appeared to the colonists necessary to their growth and progress.

The work of Liberia, as I have said, is different and far nobler. We, on the borders of our fatherland, cannot, as the framers of our Constitution wisely intimated, allow ourselves to be influenced by "avaricious speculations," or by desires for "territorial aggrandisement." Our work there is moral and intellectual as well as physical. We have to work upon the *people* as well as upon the *land*—upon *mind* as well as upon *matter.* Our prosperity depends as much upon the wholesome and elevating influence we exert upon the native population as upon the progress we make in agriculture, commerce, and manufacture. Indeed the conviction prevails in Liberia among the thinking people that we can make no important progress in these things without the cooperation of the aborigines. We believe that no policy can be more suicidal in Liberia than that which would keep aloof from the natives around us. We believe that our life and strength will be to elevate and incorporate them among us as speedily as possible.

And, then, the aborigines are not a race alien from the colonists. We are a part of them. When alien and hostile races have come together, as we have just seen, one has had to succumb to the other; but when different peoples of the same family have been brought together, there has invariably been a fusion, and the result has been an improved and powerful class. When three branches of the great Teutonic family met on the soil of England, they united. It is true that at first there was a distinction of caste among them in consequence of the superiority in every respect of the great Norman people; but, as the others came up to their level, the distinctions were quietly effaced, and Norman, Saxon, and Dane easily amalgamated. Thus, "a people inferior to none existing in the world was formed by the mixture of three branches of the great Teutonic family with each other and the aboriginal Britons."[8]

In America we see how readily persons from all parts of Europe assimilate; but what great difficulty the Negro, the Chinese, and the Indian experience! We find here representatives from all the nations of Europe easily blending with each other. But we find elements that will not assimilate. The Negro, the Indian, and the Chinese, who do not belong to the same family, repel each other, and are repelled by the Europeans. "The antagonistic elements are in contact, but refuse to unite, and as yet no agent has been found sufficiently potent to reduce them to unity."

But the case with Americo-Liberians and the aborigines is quite different. We are all descendants of Africa. In Liberia there may be found persons of almost every tribe in West Africa, from Senegal to Congo. And not only do we and the natives belong to the same race, but we are also of the same family. The two peoples can no more be kept from assimilating and blending than water can be kept from mingling with its kindred elements. The policy of Liberia is to diffuse among them as rapidly as possible the principles of Christianity and civilization, to prepare them to take an active part in the duties of the nationality which we are endeavoring to erect. Whence, then, comes the slander which represents Liberians as "maintaining a distance from the aborigines—a constant and uniform separation"?

To take part in the noble work in which they are engaged on that coast, the government and people of Liberia earnestly invite the descendants of Africa in this country.[9] In all our feebleness, we have already accomplished something; but very little in comparison of what has to be done. A beginning has been made, however—a great deal of preparatory work accomplished. And if the intelligent and enterprising colored people of this country would emigrate in large numbers, an important work would be done in a short time. And we know exactly the kind of work that would be done. We know that where now stand unbroken forests would spring up towns and villages, with their schools and churches—that the natives would be taught the arts of civilization—that their energies would be properly directed—that their prejudices would disappear—that there would be a rapid and important revulsion from the practices of heathenism, and a radical change in their social condition—that the glorious principles of a Christian civilization would diffuse themselves throughout those benighted communities. Oh! that our people would take this matter into serious consideration, and think of the great privilege of kindling in the depths of the moral and spiritual gloom of Africa a glorious light—of causing the wilderness and the solitary place to be glad— the desert to bloom and blossom as the rose—and the whole land to be converted into a garden of the Lord.

Liberia, then, appeals to the colored men of this country for assistance in the noble work which she has begun. She appeals to those who believe that the descendants of Africa live in the serious neglect of their duty if they fail to help to raise the land of their forefathers from her degradation. She appeals to those who believe that a well-established African nationality is the most direct and efficient means of securing respectability and independence for the African race. She appeals to those who believe that a rich and fertile country like Africa, which has lain so long under the cheerless gloom of ignorance, should not be left any longer without the influence of Christian civilization—to those who deem it a far more glorious work to save extensive tracts of country from barbarism and continued degradation than to amass for themselves the means of individual comfort and aggrandisement—to those who believe that there was a providence in the deportation of our forefathers from the land of their birth, and that that same providence now points to a work in Africa to be done by us, their descendants. Finally, Liberia appeals to all African patriots and Christians—to all lovers of order and refinement—to lovers of industry and enterprise—of peace, comfort, and happiness—to those who, having felt the power of the Gospel in opening up to them life and immortality, are desirous that their benighted kindred should share in the same blessings. "Behold, the Lord thy God hath set the land before thee: go up and possess it, as the Lord God of thy fathers hath said unto thee; fear not, neither be discouraged."

[1]See Alexis DeTocqueville, *Democracy in America*, eds. J. P. Mayer and Max Lerner, new trans. by George Lawrence (New York: Harper & Row, 1966), 312–33.

[2]In the famous sermon of this distinguished divine on *Slavery: A Divine Trust*, he says: "The enriching commerce which has built the splendid cities and marble palaces of England as well as of America, has been largely established upon the products of Southern soil; and the blooms upon Southern fields, gathered by black hands, have fed the spindles and looms of Manchester and Birmingham not less than of Lawrence and Lowell." Benjamin Morgan Palmer, *Slavery: A Divine Trust—Thanksgiving Sermon, Delivered at the First Presbyterian Church, New Orleans, on Thursday, December 29, 1860* (New York: G. F. Nesbitt, 1861).

[3]George Gordon, Lord Byron, *Childe Harold's Pilgrimage*, Canto 2, Stanza 76.

[4]Dean Trench, quoted by Baden Powell, "On the Study of the Evidences of Christianity," in *Essays and Reviews*, 5th ed. (London: Longman, Green, Longman, and Roberts, 1861).

[5]Ralph Waldo Emerson, "American Civilization," in *The Works of Ralph Waldo Emerson* (New York: Tudor Publishing, [nd]), III: 230.

[6]Samuel Daniel, "To the Lady Margaret, Countess of Cumberland," lines 98–99.

[7]For an elaboration of similar ideas, see David Livingstone, *Missionary Travels in South Africa, Including a Sketch of Sixteen Years' Residence in the Interior of Africa* (New York: Harper, 1858), 718–25.

[8]Thomas Babington Macaulay, *The History of England from the Accession of James II*, 5 vols. (Philadelphia: Porter and Coates, 1007), 1:27.

[9]The Legislature of Liberia, at its last session, 1861–62, passed an act authorizing the appointment of Commissioners to "itinerate among and lecture to the people of color in the United States of North-America, to present to them the claims of Liberia, and its superior advantages as a desirable home for persons of African descent." The President appointed for this work Professors Crummell and Blyden and J. D. Johnson, Esq.

MARCUS GARVEY (1887–1940)

✿ Africa for the Africans (1919)

For five years the Universal Negro Improvement Association has been advocating the cause of Africa for the Africans—that is, that the Negro peoples of the world should concentrate upon the object of building up for themselves a great nation in Africa.

When we started our propaganda toward this end several of the so-called intellectual Negroes who have been bamboozling the race for over half a century said that we were crazy, that the Negro peoples of the Western world were not interested in Africa and could not live in Africa. One editor and leader went so far as to say at his so-called Pan-African Congress that American Negroes could not live in Africa, because the climate was too hot. All kinds of arguments have been adduced by these Negro intellectuals against the colonization of Africa by the black race. Some said that the black man would ultimately work out his existence alongside of the white man in countries founded and established by the latter. Therefore, it was not necessary for Negroes to seek an independent nationality of their own. The old-time stories of "African fever," "African bad climate," "African mosquitos," "African savages," have been repeated by these "brainless intellectuals" of ours as a scare against our people in America and the West Indies taking a kindly interest in the new program of building a racial empire of our own in our motherland. Now that years have rolled by and the Universal Negro Improvement Association has made the circuit of the world with its propaganda, we find eminent statesmen and leaders of the white race coming out boldly advocating the cause of colonizing Africa with the Negroes of the western world. A year ago Senator McCullum of the Mississippi Legislature introduced a resolution in the House for the purpose of petitioning the Congress of the United States of America and the President to use their good influence in securing from the Allies sufficient territory in Africa in liquidation of the war debt, which territory should be used for the establishing of an independent nation for American Negroes. About the same time Senator France of Maryland gave expression to a similar desire in the Senate of the

Reprinted from *Philosophy and Opinions of Marcus Garvey,* by Marcus Garvey, edited by Amy Jacques-Garvey, 2 vols. (New York: Universal Publishing, 1923–1925), 1:68–72.

United States. During a speech on the "Soldiers' Bonus," he said: "We owe a big debt to Africa and one which we have too long ignored. I need not enlarge upon our peculiar interest in the obligation to the people of Africa. Thousands of Americans have for years been contributing to the missionary work which has been carried out by the noble men and women who have been sent out in that field by the churches of America."

Germany to the Front

This reveals a real change on the part of prominent statesmen in their attitude on the African question. Then comes another suggestion from Germany, for which Dr. Heinrich Schnee, a former governor of German East Africa, is author. This German statesman suggests in an interview given out in Berlin and published in New York that America take over the mandatories of Great Britain and France in Africa for the colonization of American Negroes. Speaking on the matter, he says, "As regards the attempt to colonize Africa with the surplus American colored population, this would in a long way settle the vexed problem, and under the plan such as Senator France has outlined, might enable France and Great Britain to discharge their duties to the United States, and simultaneously ease the burden of German reparations which is paralyzing economic life."

With expressions as above quoted from prominent world statesmen, and from the demands made by such men as Senators France and McCullum, it is clear that the question of African nationality is not a far-fetched one, but is as reasonable and feasible as was the idea of an American nationality.

A "Program" at Last

I trust that the Negro peoples of the world are now convinced that the work of the Universal Negro Improvement Association is not a visionary one, but very practical, and that it is not so far-fetched, but can be realized in a short while if the entire race will only cooperate and work toward the desired end. Now that the work of our organization has started to bear fruit we find that some of these "doubting Thomases" of three and four years ago are endeavoring to mix themselves up with the popular idea of rehabilitating Africa in the interest of the Negro. They are now advancing spurious "programs" and in a short while will endeavor to force themselves upon the public as advocates and leaders of the African idea.

It is felt that those who have followed the career of the Universal Negro Improvement Association will not allow themselves to be deceived by these Negro opportunists who have always sought to live off the ideas of other people.

The Dream of a Negro Empire

It is only a question of a few more years when Africa will be completely colonized by Negroes, as Europe is by the white race. What we want is an independent African nationality, and if America is to help the Negro peoples of the world establish such a nationality, then we welcome the assistance.

It is hoped that when the time comes for American and West Indian Negroes to settle in Africa, they will realize their responsibility and their duty. It will not be to go to Africa for the purpose of exercising an over-lordship over the natives, but it shall be the purpose of the Universal Negro Improvement Association to have established in Africa that brotherly cooperation which will make the interests of the African native and the American and West Indian Negro one and the same, that is to say, we shall enter into a common partnership to build up Africa in the interests of our race.

Oneness of Interests

Everybody knows that there is absolutely no difference between the native African and the American and West Indian Negroes, in that we are descendants from one common family stock. It is only a matter of accident that we have been divided and kept apart for over three hundred years, but it is felt that when the time has come for us to get back together, we shall do so in the spirit of brotherly love, and any Negro who expects that he will be assisted here, there, or anywhere by the Universal Negro Improvement Association to exercise a haughty superiority over the fellows of his own race makes a tremenduous mistake. Such men had better remain where they are and not attempt to become in any way interested in the higher development of Africa.

The Negro has had enough of the vaunted practice of race superiority as inflicted upon him by others; therefore, he is not prepared to tolerate a similar assumption on the part of his own people. In America and the West Indies, we have Negroes who believe themselves so much above their fellows as to cause them to think that any readjustment in the affairs of the race should be placed in their hands for them to exercise a kind of an autocratic and despotic control, as others have done to us for centuries. Again I say, it would be advisable for such Negroes to take their hands and minds off the now-popular idea of colonizing Africa in the interest of the Negro race, because their being identified with this new program will not in any way help us because of the existing feeling among Negroes everywhere not to tolerate the infliction of race or class superiority upon them, as is the desire of the self-appointed and self-created race leadership that we have been having for the last fifty years.

The Basis of an African Aristocracy

The masses of Negroes in America, the West Indies, South and Central America are in sympathetic accord with the aspirations of the native Africans. We desire to help them build up Africa as a Negro empire, where every black man, whether he was born in Africa or in the Western world, will have the opportunity to develop on his own lines under the protection of the most favorable democratic institutions.

It will be useless, as before stated, for bombastic Negroes to leave America and the West Indies to go to Africa, thinking that they will have privileged positions to inflict upon the race that bastard aristocracy that they have tried to maintain in this Western world at the expense of the masses. Africa shall develop an aristocracy of its own, but it shall be based upon service and loyalty to race. Let all Negroes work toward that end. I feel that it is only a question of a few more years before our program will be accepted, not only by the few statesmen of America who are now interested in it, but by the strong statesmen of the world, as the only solution to the great race problem. There is no other way to avoid the threatening war of the races that is bound to engulf all mankind, which has been prophesied by the world's greatest thinkers; there is no better method than by apportioning every race to its own habitat.

The time has really come for the Asiatics to govern themselves in Asia, as the Europeans are in Europe and the Western world, so also is it wise for the Africans to govern themselves at home, and thereby bring peace and satisfaction to the entire human family.

MARCUS GARVEY (1887–1940)

🏵 The Future as I See It (1919)

It comes to the individual, the race, the nation once in a lifetime to decide upon the course to be pursued as a career. The hour has now struck for the individual Negro as well as the entire race to decide the course that will be pursued in the interest of our own liberty.

We who make up the Universal Negro Improvement Association have decided that we shall go forward, upward, and onward toward the great goal of human liberty. We have determined among ourselves that all barriers placed in the way of our progress must be removed, must be cleared away, for we desire to see the light of a brighter day.

The Negro Is Ready

The Universal Negro Improvement Association for five years has been proclaiming to the world the readiness of the Negro to carve out a pathway for himself in the course of life. Men of other races and nations have become alarmed at this attitude of the Negro in his desire to do things for himself and by himself. This alarm has become so universal that organizations have been brought into being here, there, and everywhere for the purpose of deterring and obstructing this forward move of our race. Propaganda has been waged here, and there, and everywhere for the purpose of misinterpreting the intention of this organization; some have said that this organization seeks to create discord and discontent among the races; some say we are organized for the purpose of hating other people. Every sensible, sane, and honest-minded person knows that the Universal Negro Improvement Association has no such intention. We are organized for the absolute purpose of bettering our condition, industrially, commercially, socially, religiously, and politically. We are organized not to hate other men, but to lift ourselves and to demand respect of all humanity. We have a program that we believe to be righteous; we believe it to be just, and we have made up our minds to lay down ourselves on the altar of sacrifice for the realization of this great hope

Reprinted from *Philosophy and Opinions of Marcus Garvey,* by Marcus Garvey, edited by Amy Jacques-Garvey, 2 vols. (New York: Universal Publishing, 1923–1925), 1:73–78.

of ours, based upon the foundation of righteousness. We declare to the world that Africa must be free, that the entire Negro race must be emancipated from industrial bondage, peonage, and serfdom; we make no compromise, we make no apology in this our declaration. We do not desire to create offense on the part of other races, but we are determined that we shall be heard, that we shall be given the rights to which we are entitled.

The Propaganda of Our Enemies

For the purpose of creating doubts about the work of the Universal Negro Improvement Association, many attempts have been made to cast shadow and gloom over our work. They have even written the most uncharitable things about our organization; they have spoken so unkindly of our effort, but what do we care? They spoke unkindly and uncharitably about all the reform movements that have helped in the betterment of humanity. They maligned the great movement of the Christian religion; they maligned the great liberation movements of America, of France, of England, of Russia; can we expect, then, to escape being maligned in this, our desire for the liberation of Africa and the freedom of four hundred million Negroes of the world?

We have unscrupulous men and organizations working in opposition to us. Some [are] trying to capitalize on the new spirit that has come to the Negro to make profit out of it to their own selfish benefit; some are trying to set back the Negro from seeing the hope of his own liberty, and thereby poisoning our people's mind against the motives of our organization; but every sensible, farseeing Negro in this enlightened age knows what propaganda means. It is the medium of discrediting that which you are opposed to, so that the propaganda of our enemies will be of little avail as soon as we are rendered able to carry to our peoples scattered throughout the world the true message of our great organization.

"Crocodiles" as Friends

Men of the Negro race, let me say to you that a greater future is in store for us; we have no cause to lose hope, to become fainthearted. We must realize that upon ourselves depend our destiny, our future; we must carve out that future, that destiny, and we who make up the Universal Negro Improvement Association have pledged ourselves that nothing in the world shall stand in our way, nothing in the world shall discourage us, but opposition shall make us work harder, shall bring us closer together so that as one man the millions of us will march on toward that goal that we have set for ourselves. The new Negro shall not be deceived. The new Negro refuses to take advice from anyone who has not felt with him, and suffered with him. We have suffered for three hundred years; therefore, we feel that the time has come when only those who have suffered with us can interpret our feelings and our spirit. It takes the slave to interpret the feelings of the slave; it takes the unfortunate man to interpret the spirit of his unfortunate brother; and so it takes the suffering Negro to interpret the spirit of his comrade. It is strange that so many people are interested in the Negro now, willing to advise him how to act and what organizations he should join, yet nobody was interested in the Negro to the extent of not making him a slave for two hundred and fifty years, reducing him to industrial peonage and serfdom after he was freed; it is strange that the same people can be so interested in the Negro now as to tell him what organization he should follow and what leader he should support.

Whilst we are bordering on a future of brighter things, we are also at our danger period, when we must either accept the right philosophy or go down by following deceptive propaganda which has hemmed us in for many centuries.

Deceiving the People

There is many a leader of our race who tells us that everything is well, and that all things will work out themselves, and that a better day is coming. Yes, all of us know that a better day is coming; we all know that one day we will go home to Paradise, but whilst we are hoping by our Christian virtues to have an entry into Paradise we also realize that we are living on earth, and that the things that are practised in Paradise are not practiced here. You have to treat this world as the world treats you; we are living in a temporal, material age, an age of activity, an age of racial, national selfishness. What else can you expect but to give back to the world what the world gives to you, and we are calling upon the four hundred million Negroes of the world to take a decided stand, a determined stand, that we shall occupy a firm position; that position shall be an emancipated race and a free nation of our own. We are determined that we shall have a free country; we are determined that we shall have a flag; we are determined that we shall have a government second to none in the world.

An Eye for an Eye

Men may spurn the idea, they may scoff at it; the metropolitan press of this country may deride us; yes, white men may laugh at the idea of Negroes talking about government; but let me tell you there is going to be a government, and let me say to you also that whatsoever you give, in like measure it shall be returned to you. The world is sinful, and therefore man believes in the doctrine of an eye for an eye, a tooth for a tooth. Everybody believes that revenge is God's, but at the same time we are men, and revenge sometimes springs up, even in the most Christian heart.

Why should man write down a history that will react against him? Why should man perpetrate deeds of wickedness upon his brother which will return to him in like measure? Yes, the Germans maltreated the French in the Franco-Prussian war of 1870, but the French got even with the Germans in 1918. It is history, and history will repeat itself. Beat the Negro, brutalize the Negro, kill the Negro, burn the Negro, imprison the Negro, scoff at the Negro, deride the Negro, it may come back to you one of these fine days, because the supreme destiny of man is in the hands of God. God is no respecter of persons, whether that person be white, yellow, or black. Today the one race is up, tomorrow it has fallen; today the Negro seems to be the footstool of the other races and nations of the world; tomorrow the Negro may occupy the highest rung of the great human ladder.

But when we come to consider the history of man, was not the Negro a power, was he not great once? Yes, honest students of history can recall the day when Egypt, Ethiopia, and Timbuktu towered in their civilizations, towered above Europe, towered above Asia. When Europe was inhabited by a race of cannibals, a race of savages, naked men, heathens, and pagans, Africa was peopled with a race of cultured black men, who were masters in art, science, and literature; men who were cultured and refined; men who, it was said, were like the gods. Even the great poets of old sang in beautiful sonnets of the delight it afforded the gods to be in companionship with the Ethiopians. Why, then, should we lose hope? Black men, you were once great; you shall be great again. Lose not courage, lose not faith, go forward. The thing to do is to get organized; keep separated and you will be exploited, you will be robbed, you will be killed. Get organized, and you will compel the world to respect you. If the world fails to give you consideration, because you are black men, because you are Negroes, four hundred millions of you shall, through organization, shake the pillars of the universe and bring down creation, even as Samson brought down the temple upon his head and upon the heads of the Philistines.

An Inspiring Vision

So Negroes, I say, through the Universal Negro Improvement Association, that there is much to live for. I have a vision of the future, and I see before me a picture of a redeemed Africa, with her dotted cities, with her beautiful civilization, with her millions of happy children going to and fro. Why should I lose hope, why should I give up and take a back place in this age of progress? Remember that you are men, that God created you Lords of this creation. Lift up yourselves, men, take yourselves out of the mire and hitch your hopes to the stars; yes, rise as high as the very stars themselves. Let no man pull you down, let no man destroy your ambition, because man is but your companion, your equal; man is your brother; he is not your lord; he is not your sovereign master.

We of the Universal Negro Improvement Association feel happy; we are cheerful. Let them connive to destroy us; let them organize to destroy us; we shall fight the more. Ask me personally the cause of my success, and I say opposition; oppose me, and I fight the more, and if you want to find out the sterling worth of the Negro, oppose him, and under the leadership of the Universal Negro Improvement Association he shall fight his way to victory, and in the days to come, and I believe not far distant, Africa shall reflect a splendid demonstration of the worth of the Negro, of the determination of the Negro, to set himself free and to establish a government of his own.

JEAN PRICE-MARS (1876–1969)

From *So Uncle Said* (1929)

The Haitian people have manifested a scarcely disguised discomfort, even something bordering on abhorrence, whenever their distant past is spoken of; a disconcerting paradox, for they have one of the most engaging and moving, if not one of the most beautiful, histories of the world—that of the transplantation of a human race to alien soil in the severest of biological conditions. This condition has resulted from the fact that those people, who because—armed with force and science—they were able to be the artisans of black servitude for over four hundred years, have distorted the Haitian historical adventure by stating that Negroes were the outcasts of humanity, without a history, without morality, without religion, and had to be infused by whatever means available with new moral values, outfitted with a new humanity. When as a result of the crises of change precipitated by the French Revolution the community of slaves in San Domingo rose up and demanded rights which no one had previously dreamed of granting them, the success of their claims proved to be both a difficulty and a surprise to them: the difficulty of choosing a social discipline, the surprise at the adaptation of a heterogeneous herd of people to the stable life of free labor. Obviously the simplest way out for the revolutionaries, in a state of national disunity, was to copy the only model offered to their minds. Thus, for better and for worse, they inserted the new social grouping into the dislocated framework of a scattered white society. It was in this manner that the Negro community of Haiti donned the cast-off attire of Western civilization after 1804. From then on, with a persistency that no setback, sarcasm, or upheaval could hope to deflect, the Haitian community strove to realize what it believed to be its higher destiny by modelling its thoughts and sentiments on an approximation of France, by attempting to resemble that country and by identifying with it. An absurd and grandiose task! A difficult task if ever there was one!

But this is an example of that curious occurrence which, in the metaphysics of M. Gaultier, is called a collective bovaryism, that is, the quality by which a society is able to conceive of itself in terms other than it is. A strik-

Reprinted from *The Ideology of Blackness*, selection translated by Raymond F. Betts, editor (Lexington, MA: D. C. Heath, 1971), 88–94, with permission of Raymond F. Betts.

ingly rich attitude, if the society in question has the means for a creative activity which would lead to an improvement over its present condition. In this event, the quality of imagining itself other than it is becomes an incentive, a powerful force which drives it on to overcome the obstacles found in its forward-directing and ascending path. However, such is a singularly dangerous attitude if the society is weighted down with impedimentia, stuck in the ruts of routine and servile imitation, because then the society seems to make no contribution to the complex play of human progress and will, sooner or later, provide the surest pretext for being wiped off the map by those nations impatient for territorial expansion and ambitious to establish their hegemony. Despite some effort toward alteration and some occasional perception of the situation, it was by the application of the second point of the previously described dilemma that Haiti found its place among the world's peoples. There was, of course, the possibility that the effort would be considered without interest and originality. But, by an irresistible logic, the more we forced ourselves to believe that we were "colored" Frenchmen, the more we simply forgot to be Haitian, which is to say, men born in historically determined conditions, having acquired in our souls, as have all human groups, a psychological complex which gave to the Haitian community its specific form. At that point, everything which was authentically indigenous— language, mores, sentiments, beliefs—became suspect, tarnished with bad taste in the eyes of the elites seized with nostalgia for the lost mother country. As this process occurred, the word "negro," formerly a generic term, acquired a pejorative meaning. As for that of "African," it always has been and is the most humiliating term by which a Haitian can be addressed. Strictly speaking, the most distinguished person in this country would rather that someone found a resemblance between him and an Eskimo or a Samoan or a Tongan rather than to recall his Guinean or Sudanese origins. One should see with what pride several of our most representative personalities suggest the actual existence of some bastard line of descent. All the baseness of colonial promiscuities, the anonymous disgraces of accidental encounters, the brief coupling of two paroxysms, have become the titles of consideration and of glory. What can be the future, what can be the value of a society where such aberrations of judgment, such mistakes of orientation are formed into basic opinions. A very difficult problem for those who are reflective and who have the task of meditating on the social conditions of our environment!

But, one might say, what is the purpose of so much bother over such minute problems, which interest but a very small minority of men living on a very small part of the terrestrial surface?

Perhaps this question is sound.

However, we will allow ourselves the objection that neither the smallness of our territory nor the numerical weakness of our people is sufficient reason for the dismissal by the rest of humanity of those problems which affect the behavior of a group of people. Moreover, our presence on a point of this American archipelago that we have "humanized," the breach we have made in the historical process in order to grasp our place among men, our method of employing the laws of imitation in order to give us an imitative spirit, the pathological deviation that we have imposed on group bovaryism by conceiving ourselves as other than we are, the tragic uncertainty that such a step marks on our evolution at the time when all sorts of imperialisms are disguising their exploitations with the veil of philanthropy—all of that gives a certain relief to the existence of the Haitian community and, before night falls, it is not without purpose to collect the facts of our social life, to determine the deeds and the attitudes of our people, no matter how humble they may be, and to compare them with those of other peoples, to scrutinize their origins, and to situate them in the general existence of man on this planet. These are all factors whose significance cannot be negligible in any judgment of the worth of one part of the human race.

But, in fact, what is the origin of the greater part of the customs that we have spoken about? Are they derived from the local scene or did they really come to us from overseas?

About this matter one can well conjecture. None of them is altogether a local creation, but also none has come to us without alteration. They are like our personality itself, all charged with reminiscences and impressed by the successive mutations which mark the complexity of our ethnic origins. Since our evolution as a people occurred in divergent directions, such that a small number among us has acquired an intellectual and social culture which makes it a world apart—very proud and vain in its ivory tower and having only a distant and formal contact with the rest of the population lost in misery and ignorance—it is among the multitude that we will have the best chance of again finding the thread of oral traditions derived from overseas. When one submits these traditions to a comparative examination, they immediately reveal that Africa, for the most part, is their land of origin.

But just as the beliefs from which they derive . . . divide Africa into distinct zones, so the map of related mores and customs covers the greater part of the Western portion of the Old Continent.

Would you like to be present, comparatively speaking, at the founding of a family in some part of the Congo, the Sudan, or Dahomey?

Ah! I know what repugnance I will encounter in daring to speak to you of Africa and African matters! The subject seems unelegant and completely devoid of interest to you, doesn't it?

Be careful, my friends, that such attitudes do not derive from scandalous ignorance. We live on ideas gone stale by the prodigious absurdity of a poorly arranged culture, and our childish vanity is only satisfied when we recite phrases written by others or when we glorify the notion that "the Gauls were our ancestors."

Well, we only will have the opportunity of being ourselves if we do not repudiate any part of our ancestral heritage. Now, this heritage is eight-tenths a gift of Africa. Moreover, on this small planet which is only an infinitesimal point in space, men have been so mixed for thousands of years that no true intellectual, not even in the United States of America, could uphold the theory of pure races without laughing. If I understand the real science of Sir Harry Johnston, there is not a single Negro whatsoever in the heart of Africa who does not have some drops of Caucasoid blood in his veins and perhaps not a single white man, even the proudest in the United Kingdom, in France, in Spain, or elsewhere, who does not have some drops of Negro or yellow blood in his veins. Such is the truth found in the verse of the poet: "All men are man."

Our ancestors? But why should I be embarrassed to know from whence they came, if I carry my sign of human dignity on my forehead like a radiant star and if in my upward movement toward more understanding I am lightened by the sacred wound of the ideal?

Our ancestors? They are first the dead whose earthly sufferings, courage, intelligence, and sensitivity were blended in the crucible of San Domingo in order to make us what we are: free men. Our ancestors? They are the dead, with combined virtues and vices, who speak softly in our wretched hearts or to our heroic and noble conscience.

Our ancestors? They are those who slowly lifted themselves from primitive animalism to lead toward the transitory beings that we now are, still trembling before the unknown which surrounds us, but heirs to the unfading glory of being men. It is because our ancestors were men who suffered, who loved and who hoped, that we, we also can aspire to the full dignity of being men despite the brutal insolence of all kinds of imperialism.

Whites, blacks, mulattos, *griffes,* octoroons, quatroons, marabouts, *sacatras:* of what significance are these labels from the rejected colonial situation if we believe ourselves to be men resolved to play fully our role as men on this small part of the global scene which is our Haitian society?

Therefore, accept the ancestral patrimony as a block. Walk around it, weigh it, examine it with intelligence and circumspection, and you will see, as if in a broken mirror, that it reflects a reduced image of all of mankind. Yes, the same causes have produced the same effects on the entire surface of the planet. Love, hunger, fear have engendered the same tales in the passionate imagination of men, whether they lived in the all-encircling bush of the Sudan, whether they formerly appeared on the hills where the Acropolis arose or on the banks of the Tiber where the city of the Seven Hills was erected. And this is why the African today provides the sociologist with the elements from which he is able to establish the psychology of primitive man. The constitution of the family is above all for him an act of faith, a religious ceremony of initiation. Such it was in ancient Greece and Rome, and so it is in certain tribes in the Sudan, Dahomey, the Congo—except for the inevitable variations created by the circumstance and necessities of the physical surroundings.

By way of conclusion it remains for us to draw some lessons from the ethnographic comparisons we have made. First, there exists in the marriage ceremony some striking analogies between the customs of classical Greece and Rome and those which are still observed in certain parts of Africa. In addition, our peasant populations on this side of the Atlantic are imbued with these customs also. On all sides one observes the same symbolism which makes the union of man and wife an eminently religious act. One finds almost the same ritual and propitiary sacrifice which obligates the young couple to the gods of the family, the village, and the tribe; nearly the same symbolism which leads to the choice of the white veil and crown, the white loin cloth, powder, and clay as exterior signs of the new life. Just as today in our world the white veil, the orange flower crown, and the white robe are emblems of purity and innocence of the virgin who desires to begin the marital life. Dare I say, gentlemen, that your white ties and gloves are perhaps also outer signs of your purity, of intentions that you bring to the hearth?

In all cases, in Greece, in Rome, and in Africa, man is the master consecrated by ancient custom.

Head of the family, having the responsibility to group around him the gods and ancestors, it is he alone who can authorize who will be allowed to approach the altar where the sacrifice to the titular divinity is made. Whether this thought be more formalized there than here, none of it is absent even if it exists only in a state of survival. It seems to me that a very important social fact derives from these various remarks: if the marriage ceremony is cloaked in such a quality of religious solemnity here as there, it likewise implies the idea of the gravity attached to it, and it implies that the constitution of the family is in close alliance with the continuity of the religious cult and the well-being of the village or the tribe. From this mysterious quality derives the solidity of family ties. Certainly this is true in certain of the regions of Africa about which we have spoken, where a small community is protected by the eldest male who is the natural chief; he is the elder. The union of these communities in a given space forms the village, ruled by a chief chosen among the elders and whose wisdom and experience are appreciated. Can you imagine in these conditions the power of family ties formed in such a conjuncture? Such a condition has constantly been pointed out by Africologists. They state how much the young Negro is attached to his village, to his family group, and particularly to that person who is the living incarnation of it: his mother.

Do you know why the godmother in San Domingo has nearly replaced the mother in the child's affection? It is because most often the hardly weaned child is snatched from this mother whose services are needed for economic exploitation. He henceforth hardly knows anyone but his godmother, while he too awaits the moment when he will become another number in the labor workshop. The deep reason for such a cruel disorder is found in the destructive action exercised by slavery on the social economy of the black, such that this monstrous system has been perpetuated for four centuries by the white race on the black race. Ah, my friends, my heart is not large enough to contain all the love I feel for mankind. I therefore have no room for hatred. But I cannot check myself from the horror of the thought of the carnage and destruction pursued here and on the old continent with an implacable method by those who pride themselves on being a superior humanity, and who now dare reproach the black race for its savagery and institutional instability.

Yes, for four hundred years, the white race, without pity or mercy, aroused internecine war in Africa, pitting Negro against Negro, chasing them without respite or mercy, in order to satisfy this ignoble traffic in human flesh and, in so doing, destroying all native civilization and culture. Then, for another two centuries, the white sailed his boats loaded with human cattle to the shores of this island already bloody from the extermination of the Indian; and during these two centuries of outrageous promiscuity, corruption, and degeneracy, the white soiled the ancient chastity of the Negress and imposed on her the brutal law of concubinage. It is thus that the organization of Negro life was ripped, destroyed, and annihilated by the saddest abomination which has ever stained the face of the earth. The truth of this fact is shown following upon 1804. Then our fathers, in adopting without the slightest concern a legal and religious statute which was so different from their old social concepts, surrendered themselves without thinking about it to the most formidable experience which men have ever endeavored.

For over a hundred years what has been the result? You can see it in this confusion of mores, beliefs, and customs from which slowly emerged a new social order. Perhaps it is now only a chrysalid which causes indignation, mockery, or embarrassment for the impatient, the myopic, and the ignorant, but which philosophers and men of spirit watch attentively and with interest. What will it become in one, two, or five hundred years? I certainly do not know. But what were those nations and people who today have become

rotten from pompous display, prejudices, and hatred, when for over nineteen centuries a magnificent civilization flourished on the banks of the Nile?
What were they? Miserable barbarians, history answers.

Men pass by; it is perhaps good that they are not eternal.

This is why those among us who make a profession of investigating the
historical and ethnic origins of Haitian people are captivated by the dazzling
intuition that its past will reply to its future. But for heaven's sake, my friends,
do not scorn our ancestral patrimony. Love it, consider it as an intangible
whole. Rather, repeat the proud statement that the ancient bard placed in
the mouth of an inhabitant of Mount Olympus: "There is nothing ugly in my
father's house."

C. L. R. JAMES (1901–1989)

The West Indian Middle Classes (1961)

The middle classes in the West Indies, colored peoples, constitute one of the most peculiar classes in the world, peculiar in the sense of their unusual historical development and the awkward and difficult situation they occupy in what constitutes the West Indian nation, or, nowadays, some section of it.

Let me get one thing out of the way. They are not a defective set of people. In intellectual capacity, i.e., ability to learn, to familiarize themselves with the general scholastic requirements of Western civilization, they are and for some time have been unequalled in the colonial world. If you take percentages of scholastic achievement in relation to population among the under-developed, formerly colonial, colored countries, West Indians would probably be at the head and, I believe, not by a small margin either. What they lack, and they lack plenty, is not due to any inherent West Indian deficiency. If that were so we would be in a bad way indeed. I set out to show that the blunders and deficiencies of which they are guilty are historically caused and therefore can be historically corrected. Otherwise we are left with the demoralizing result: "That is the way West Indians are," and closely allied to this: "The man or men who have brought us into this mess are bad men. Let us search for some good men." As long as you remain on that level, you understand nothing and your apparently "good" men turn rapidly into men who are no good. That is why I shall keep as far away from individuals as I can and stick to the class. I am not fighting to win an election.

For something like twenty years we have been establishing the premises of a modern democratic society: parliamentary government, democratic rights, party politics, etc. The mere existence of these is totally inadequate— the smash-up of the Federation has proved that. We now have to move on to a more advanced stage. To think that what I say is the last word in political wisdom is to make me into just another West Indian politician. I am posing certain profound, certain fundamental questions. Their urgency lies in the fact that our political pundits and those who circulate around them consistently ignore them, try to pretend that they do not exist.

Reprinted from *Party Politics in the West Indies,* by C. L. R. James (Trinidad: Vedic Enterprises, 1962), 130–39.

Who and what are our middle classes? What passes my comprehension is that their situation is never analyzed in writing, or even mentioned in public discussion. That type of ignorance, abstinence, shame, or fear simply does not take place in a country like Britain. There must be some reason for this stolid silence about themselves, some deep, underlying compulsion. We shall see.

Our West Indian middle classes are for the most part colored people of some education in a formerly slave society. That means that for racial and historical reasons they are today excluded from those circles which are in control of big industry, commerce, and finance. They are almost as much excluded from large-scale agriculture, sugar for example. That is point number one. Thus they as a class of people have no knowledge or experience of the productive forces of the country. That stands out painfully in everything they do and everything they do not do. Mr. Nehru talks about India's new steel mills, President Nasser talked about his dam which caused a war, President Nkrumah talked and preached about his Volta Dam for ten years before he got it. A West Indian politician talks about how much money he will get from the British government or from the United States. It is because the class from which he comes had and has no experience whatever in matters of production. It is the same in agriculture. They have never had anything to do with the big sugar estates. Banking is out of their hands and always has been. There is no prospect that by social intermixing, intermarriage, etc., they will ever get into those circles. They have been out, are out, and from all appearances will remain out. That is a dreadful position from which to have to govern a country. In Britain, France, Australia, you have capitalist parties, men who represent and are closely associated with big capital, big agriculture, finance. You have also labor parties. In Britain a hundred members in the House of Commons are placed there by the union movement. The Labour Party members are the heads or connected with the heads of the union movement, of the Labour Party, of the cooperative movement; thus, apart from Parliament, they have a social base. In the West Indies some of the politicians have or have had posts in the labor or union movement. But as a class they have no base anywhere. They are professional men, clerical assistants, here and there a small business man, and of late years administrators, civil servants, and professional politicians, and, as usual, a few adventurers. Most of the political types who come from this class live by politics. All personal distinction and even in some cases the actual means of life and the means of improving the material circumstances of life spring from participation, direct or indirect, in the government, or circles sympathetic to or willing to play ball with the government. Thus the politicians carry into politics all the weaknesses of the class from which they come.

They have no trace of political tradition. Until twenty years ago they had no experience of political parties or of government. Their last foray in that sphere was a hundred and thirty years ago, when they threatened the planters with rebellion of themselves *and the slaves* if they were not permitted to exercise the rights of citizens. Since then they have been quiet as mice. On rare occasions they would make a protest and, the ultimate pitch of rebellion, go to the Colonial Office. They did not do any more because all they aimed at was being admitted to the ruling circle of expatriates and local whites. More than that they did not aspire to. It is most significant that the father of the antiimperialist democratic movement is a white man, A. A. Cipriani, and the biggest names are Alexander Bustamante, who spent a lot of his life in Spain, Cuba, and the United States, and Uriah Butler, a working man: not one of them is a member of the ordinary middle class. Sir Grantley Adams may appear to be one. He most certainly is not. After being educated abroad, he came back to Barbados, which alone of the West Indian islands had an elected House of Representatives. He neglected what would have been a brilliant and lucrative profession at the bar to plunge himself into politics. Middle-class West Indians do not do that.

Knowledge of production, of political struggles, of the democratic tradition, they have had none. Their ignorance and disregard of economic development is profound and deeply rooted in their past and present situation. They do not even seem to be aware of it. For several generations they have been confined to getting salaries or fees, money for services rendered. That is still their outlook.

For generations their sole aim in life was to be admitted to the positions to which their talents and education entitled them, and from which they were unjustly excluded. On rare occasions an unexpected and difficult situation opened a way for an exceptional individual, but for the most part they developed political skill only in crawling or worming their way into recognition by government or big business. When they did get into the charmed government circles or government itself, they either did their best to show that they could be as good servants of the Colonial Office as any, or when they rose to become elected members in the legislature, some of them maintained a loud (but safe) attack on the government. They actually did little. They were not responsible for anything, so they achieved a cheap popularity without any danger to themselves.

Thus the class has been and is excluded from the centers of economic life, they have no actual political experience, they have no political tradition. The democracy and West Indianization was won by mass revolt. Even this revolt was led by men who were not typically middle class. When, after 1937–38, the democratic movement started, it was a labor movement. Gradually, however, the British government felt itself compelled to make the civil service

West Indian, i.e., middle class. By degrees the middle class took over the political parties. The Colonial Office carefully what-it-called educated them to govern, with the result that the Federation is broken up and every territory is in a political mess.

Let us stick to the class, the class from which most of our politicians come, and from which they get most of their views on life and society.

All this politicians' excitement about independence is not to be trusted. In recent years the middle classes have not been concerned about independence. They were quite satisfied with the lives they lived. I never saw or heard one of them around the politicians who was actively for independence. Their political representation faithfully reproduced this attitude. I can say and dare not be challenged that in 1959 one man and one only was for independence, Dr. Williams. I do not know one single West Indian politician who supported him except with some noncommittal phrases. You cannot speak with too much certainty of a class unless you have made or have at your disposal a careful examination. But of the politicians I am absolutely certain. Independence was not an integral part of their politics. The evidence for this is overwhelming and at the slightest provocation I shall make it public. The drive for independence now is to cover up the failure of the Federation.

If you watch the social connections of the politicians and the life they live, you will see why their politics is what it is. I do not know any social class which lives so completely without ideas of any kind. They live entirely on the material plane. In a published address Sir Robert Kirkwood quotes Vidia Naipaul, who has said of them that they seem to aim at nothing more than being second-rate American citizens. It is much more than that. They aim at nothing. Government jobs and the opportunities which association with the government gives allow them the possibility of accumulating material goods. That is all.

Read their speeches about the society in which they live. They have nothing to say. Not one of them. They promise more jobs and tell the population that everybody will have a chance to get a better job. They could not say what federation meant. They are unable to say what independence means. Apart from the constitution and the fact that now they will govern without Colonial Office intervention, they have nothing to say. They are dying to find some communists against whom they can thunder and so make an easier road to American pockets. What kind of society they hope to build they do not say because they do not know.

Their own struggle for posts and pay, their ceaseless promising of jobs, their sole idea of a national development as one where everybody can aim at getting something more, the gross and vulgar materialism, the absence of any ideas or elementary originality of thought; the tiresome repetition of commonplaces aimed chiefly at impressing the British, this is the outstanding characteristic of the West Indian middle class. The politicians they produce only reproduce politically the thin substance of the class.

Let us stay here for a while. These people have to know what they are. Nobody except our novelists is telling them.

We live in a world in the throes of a vast reorganization of itself. The religious question is back on the order of discussion. Two world wars and a third in the offing, Nazism, Stalinism, have made people ask: where is humanity going? Some say that we are now reaching the climax of that preoccupation with science and democracy, which well over a hundred and fifty years ago substituted itself for religion as the guiding principle of mankind. Some believe we have to go back to religion. Others that mankind has never made genuine democracy the guiding light for society. Freud and Jung have opened depths of uncertainty and doubt of the rationality of human intelligence. Where the West Indian middle class (with all its degrees) stands on this, who is for, who is against, who even thinks of such matters, nobody knows. They think they can live and avoid such questions. You can live, but in 1962 you cannot govern that way.

Are they capitalists, i.e., do they believe in capitalism, socialism, communism, anarchism, anything? Nobody knows. They keep as far as they can from committing themselves to anything. This is a vitally practical matter. Are you going to plan your economy? To what degree is that possible, and compatible with democracy? To West Indian politicians a development program is the last word in economic development. They never discuss the plan, what it means, what it can be. If they feel any pressure they forthwith baptize their development program as "planning."

Where does personality, literature, art, the drama stand today in relation to a national development? What is the relation between the claims of individuality and the claims of the state? What does education aim at? To make citizens capable of raising the productivity of labor, or to give them a conception of life? West Indian intellectuals who are interested in or move around politics avoid these questions as if they were the plague.

Some readers may remember seeing the movie of the night of the independence of Ghana, and hearing Nkrumah choose at that time to talk about the African personality. This was to be the aim of the Ghanaian people with independence. Is there a West Indian personality? Is there a West Indian nation? What is it? What does it lack? What must it have? The West Indian middle classes keep far from these questions. The job, the car, the fridge, the trip abroad, preferably under government auspices and at government expense, these seem to be the beginning and end of their preoccupations. What foreign forces, social classes, ideas do they feel themselves allied with or attached to? Nothing. What in their own history do they look back to as a beginning of which they are the continuation? I listen to them, I read their speeches and their writings. "Massa day done" seems to be the extreme limit of their imaginative concepts of West Indian nationalism. Today nationalism is under fire and every people has to consider to what extent its nationalism has to be mitigated by international considerations. Of this as of so much else the West Indian middle class is innocent. What happens after independence? For all you can hear from them, independence is a dead end. Apart from the extended opportunities of jobs with government, independence is as great an abstraction as was federation. We achieve independence and they continue to govern.

It has been pointed out to me, in a solid and very brilliant manuscript, that the accommodation of the middle class to what is in reality an impossible position is primarily due to the fact that, contrary to the general belief, it is in essence a position they have been in for many years. They or their most distinguished representatives have always been in the situation where the first necessity of advance or new status was to curry favor with the British authorities. The easiest way to continued acceptance was to train yourself to be able to make an impact as British and as submissive as possible. Now they have political power their attitude is the same only more so. Where formerly they had to accommodate themselves to the Governor and all such small fry, today they deal directly with the British Colonial Secretary and British cabinet ministers, with foreign business interests themselves instead of only their representatives abroad. The strenuous need and desire to accommodate, the acceptance of a British code of manners, morals, and economic and political procedures, that is what they have always done, especially the upper civil servants. They have had to live that way because it was the only way they could live. That new combination of a West Indianized civil service and a West Indianized political grouping are a little further along the road, but it is the same road on which they have always travelled. The man who has worked out something usually finds the aptest illustration of it. In conversation with me the author of this really superb piece of insight and analysis has said: "If they had had to deal with, for instance, Japanese or even German businessmen, they would act differently. They would have been conscious of a sharp change. With the British they are not conscious of any break with the past. Accustomed for generations to hang around the British and search diligently for ways and means to gain an advantage, they now do of their own free will what they formerly had to do."

Having lived, as a class, by receiving money for services rendered, they transfer their age-old habits to government. But as this recent analysis shows, the very objective circumstances of their new political positions in office have merely fortified their experiences out of office.

It is such a class of people which has the government of the West Indies in its hands. In all essential matters they are, as far as the public is concerned, devoid of any ideas whatever. This enormous statement I can make with the greatest confidence, for no one can show any speech, any document, any report on which any of these matters—and the list is long—are treated with any serious application to the West Indian situation. These are the people from whom come the political leaders of the West Indies. The politicians are what they are not by chance.

What is the cause of this? A list of causes will be pure empiricism allowing for an infinite amount of "on the one hand" and "on the other hand." The cause is not in any individual and not in any inherent national weakness. The cause is in their half-and-half position between the economic masters of the country and the black masses. They are not an ordinary middle class with strong personal ties with the upper class and mobility to rise among them and form social ties with them. From that they are cut off completely. And (this is hard for the outsiders to grasp, but it is a commonplace in the West Indies) for centuries they have had it as an unshakeable principle that they are in status, education, morals, and manners separate and distinct from the masses of the people. The role of education in the West Indies has had a powerful influence here. The children of an aristocracy or of a big bourgeoisie take education in their stride. Their status is not derived from it. But where your grandfather or even your father had some uncertain job or was even an agricultural laborer, a good education is a form of social differentiation. It puts you in a different class. Twenty years is too short a time to overcome the colonial structure which they inherit, the still powerful influence of the local whites, still backed by the Colonial Office. The civil service open to them fortifies this sentiment. It is not that no progress has been made. Writing in 1932 and analyzing the political representatives of the colored people, I had this to say:

> Despising black men, these intermediates, in the Legislative Council and out of it, are forever climbing up the climbing wave, governed by one dominating motive—acceptance by white society. It would be unseemly to lower the tone of this book by detailing with whom, when, and how Colonial Secretaries and Attorneys-General distribute the nod distant, the bow cordial, the shake-hand friendly, or the cut direct as may seem fitting to their exalted highnesses; the transports of joy into which men, rich, powerful and able, are thrown by a few words from the Colonial Secretary's wife or a smile from the Chief Justice's daughter. These are legitimate game, yet suit a lighter hand and less strenuous atmosphere than this. But political independence and social aspirations cannot run between the same shafts; sycophancy soon learns to call itself moderation; and invitations to dinner or visions of a knighthood form the strongest barriers to the wishes of the people.

All this is and has been common knowledge in Trinidad for many years. The situation shows little signs of changing. The constitution is calculated to encourage rather than to suppress the tendency.

That has been overcome. A black man of ability and influence can make his way. In personal relations, in strictly personal relations, the political types meet the white economic masters with a confidence and certainty far removed from the strange quirks of thirty years ago. But their ancestry (as described above) is bad. They are political nouveaux-riches. And all such lack assurance (or are very rude in unimportant matters). This middle class with political power minus any economic power are still politically paralyzed before their former masters, who are still masters. The only way of changing the structure of the economy and setting it on to new paths is by mobilizing the mass against all who will stand in the way. Not one of them, even the professed communist Jagan, dares to take any such step. They tinker with the economy, they wear themselves out seeking grants, loans, and foreign investments which they encourage by granting fabulous advantages dignified by the name of pioneer status. (It is impossible to conceive any people more unlike the pioneers who extended the American nation than these investors of little money with large possibilities.) Here is the hurdle against which the Federation broke its back. Sitting uneasily on the fence between these two classes, so changed now from their former status, the middle classes and the middle-class politicians they produce saw federation as everything else but a definitive change in the economic life and the social relations which rested upon it. The economy lives for the most part on a sugar quota granted by the British government. In a society where new political relations are clamped upon old economic relations, the acceptance of the quota system appears to give an impregnable position to the old sugar plantation owners. This reinforces the age-old position of the classes and fortifies the timidity of the middle classes. They therefore are frantic in building more roads, more schools, a hospital; except where, as in Jamaica, it cannot be hidden, they turn a blind eye to the spectres of unemployment and underemployment, in fact do everything to maintain things essentially as they were. It is no wonder, therefore, that they discuss nothing, express no opinions (except to the Americans that they are anticommunist), keep themselves removed from all the problems of the day, take no steps to see that the population is made aware of the real problems which face it, and indeed show energy and determination only to keep away or discredit any attempts to have the population informed on any of the great problems which are now disturbing mankind. They know very well what they are doing. Any such discussion can upset the precarious balance which they maintain. Any topic which may enlarge the conception of democracy is particularly dangerous because it may affect the attitude of the mass of the population. How deeply ingrained is this sentiment is proved by the fact that nowhere in the islands has the middle class found it necessary to establish a daily paper devoted to the national interest. In fact in Trinidad when it became obvious that this was not only possible but everyone expected it, the political leadership was indifferent when it was not actively hostile. After twenty years nowhere have they felt it necessary to have a daily paper of their own. The obvious reason for that is that they have nothing to say. They want to win the election and touch nothing fundamental.

It is obvious to all observers that this situation cannot continue indefinitely. The populations of the islands are daily growing more restless and dissatisfied. The middle classes point to parliamentary democracy, trade unions, party politics, and all the elements of democracy. But these are not things in themselves. They must serve a social purpose and here the middle classes are near the end of their tether. Some of them are preparing for troubles, trouble with the masses. Come what may, they are going to keep them in order. Some are hoping for help from the Americans, from the Organisation of American States.

Without a firm social base, they are not a stable grouping. Some are playing with the idea of dictatorship, a benevolent dictatorship. But different groupings are appearing among them. Those educated abroad are the most reactionary, convinced as they are of their own superiority. The lower middle class locally educated are to a large degree ready for political advances—they are socially very close to the mass. There are also groupings according to age. Those over fifty have grown up with an innate respect for British ideals. They welcome in the new regime positions of status from which they were formerly excluded, but they accommodate themselves easily to authority. But the younger generation has grown up with no respect for any authority whatever; even some from abroad who have gone into good government jobs bring with them from Europe and the New World the skepticism prevailing there of any particular doctrine or social morality. Independence will compel the posing of some definite social discipline. The old order is gone. No new order has appeared. The middle classes have their work cut out for them. Their brief period of merely enjoying new privileges after three hundred years of being excluded is about over.

The West Indian middle classes have a high standard of formal education. They are uneducated and will have to educate themselves in the stern realities of West Indian economic and social life. Independence will place them face to face with the immense messes the imperialists are leaving behind. The economic mess is the greatest mess of all, and the other messes draw sustenance from it. It is not insoluble. Far from it. Economic development on the grand scale is first of all people, and history has endowed us with the potentially most powerful and receptive masses in all the underdeveloped countries. The effects of slavery and colonialism are like a miasma all around choking us. One hundred and fifty years ago, when the Nonconformists told the slave-owners, "You cannot continue to keep human beings in this condition," all the slave-owners could reply was, "You will ruin the economy, and further what can you expect from people like these?" When you try to tell the middle classes of today, "Why not place responsibility for the economy on the people?" their reply is the same as that of the old slave-owners: "You will ruin the economy, and further what can you expect from people like these?" The ordinary people of the West Indies who have borne the burden for centuries are very tired of it. They do not want to substitute new masters for old. They want no masters at all. Unfortunately they do not know much. Under imperialism they had had little opportunity to learn anything. History will take its course, only too often a bloody one.

AIMÉ CÉSAIRE (1913–   )

from *Discourse on Colonialism* (1955)

A civilization that proves incapable of solving the problems it creates is a decadent civilization.

A civilization that chooses to close its eyes to its most crucial problems is a stricken civilization.

A civilization that uses its principles for trickery and deceit is a dying civilization.

The fact is that the so-called European civilization—"Western" civilization—as it has been shaped by two centuries of bourgeois rule, is incapable of solving the two major problems to which its existence has given rise: the problem of the proletariat and the colonial problem; that Europe is unable to justify itself either before the bar of "reason" or before the bar of "conscience"; and that, increasingly, it takes refuge in a hypocrisy which is all the more odious because it is less and less likely to deceive.

Europe is indefensible.

Apparently that is what the American strategists are whispering to each other.

That in itself is not serious.

What is serious is that "Europe" is morally, spiritually indefensible.

And today the indictment is brought against it not by the European masses alone, but on a world scale, by tens and tens of millions of men who, from the depths of slavery, set themselves up as judges.

The colonialists may kill in Indochina, torture in Madagascar, imprison in black Africa, crack down in the West Indies. Henceforth the colonized know that they have an advantage over them. They know that their temporary "masters" are lying.

Therefore that their masters are weak.

And since I have been asked to speak about colonization and civilization, let us go straight to the principal lie which is the source of all the others.

Colonization and civilization?

Reprinted from *Discourse on Colonialism*, by Aimé Césaire, translated by Joan Pinkham (New York: Monthly Review, 1972), 9–25. © 1972 by Monthly Review Press. Reprinted by permission of Monthly Review Foundation.

In dealing with this subject, the commonest curse is to be the dupe in good faith of a collective hypocrisy that cleverly misrepresents problems, the better to legitimize the hateful solutions provided for them.

In other words, the essential thing here is to see clearly, to think clearly—that is, dangerously—and to answer clearly the innocent first question: what, fundamentally, is colonization? To agree on what it is not: neither evangelization, nor a philanthropic enterprise, nor a desire to push back the frontiers of ignorance, disease, and tyranny, nor a project undertaken for the greater glory of God, nor an attempt to extend the rule of law. To admit once for all, without flinching at the consequences, that the decisive actors here are the adventurer and the pirate, the wholesale grocer and the shipowner, the gold digger and the merchant, appetite and force, and behind them, the baleful projected shadow of a form of civilization which, at a certain point in its history, finds itself obliged, for internal reasons, to extend to a world scale the competition of its antagonistic economies.

Pursuing my analysis, I find that hypocrisy is of recent date; that neither Cortez discovering Mexico from the top of the great teocalli nor Pizzaro before Cuzco (much less Marco Polo before Cambaluc) claims that he is the harbinger of a superior order; that they kill; that they plunder; that they have helmets, lances, cupidities; that the slavering apologists came later; that the chief culprit in this domain is Christian pedantry, which laid down the dishonest equations *Christianity equals civilization, paganism equals savagery,* from which there could not but ensue abominable colonialist and racist consequences, whose victims were to be the Indians, the yellow peoples, and the Negroes.

That being settled, I admit that it is a good thing to place different civilizations in contact with each other; that it is an excellent thing to blend different worlds; that whatever its own particular genius may be, a civilization that withdraws into itself atrophies; that for civilizations, exchange is oxygen; that the great good fortune of Europe is to have been a crossroads, and that because it was the locus of all ideas, the receptacle of all philosophies, the meeting place of all sentiments, it was the best center for the redistribution of energy.

But then I ask the following question: has colonization really *placed civilizations in contact?* Or, if you prefer, of all the ways of *establishing contact,* was it the best?

I answer *no.*

And I say that between *colonization* and *civilization* there is an infinite distance; that out of all the colonial expeditions that have been undertaken, out of all the colonial statutes that have been drawn up, out of all the memoranda that have been despatched by all the ministries; there could not come a single human value.

First we must study how colonization works to *decivilize* the colonizer, to *brutalize* him in the true sense of the word, to degrade him, to awaken him to buried instincts, to covetousness, violence, race hatred, and moral relativism; and we must show that each time a head is cut off or an eye put out in Vietnam, and in France they accept the fact, each time a little girl is raped, and in France they accept the fact, each time a Madagascan is tortured and in France they accept the fact, civilization acquires another dead weight; a universal regression takes place, a gangrene sets in, a center of infection begins to spread; and that at the end of all these treaties that have been violated, all these lies that have been propagated, all these punitive expeditions that have been tolerated, all these prisoners who have been tied up and "interrogated," all these patriots who have been tortured, at the end of all the racial pride that has been encouraged, all the boastfulness that has been displayed, a poison has been instilled into the veins of Europe and, slowly but surely, the continent proceeds toward *savagery.*

And then one fine day the bourgeoisie is awakened by a terrific reverse shock: the gestapos are busy, the prisons fill up, the torturers around the racks invent, refine, discuss.

People are surprised, they become indignant. They say: "How strange! But never mind—it's Nazism, it will pass!" And they wait, and they hope; and they hide the truth from themselves, that it is barbarism, but the supreme barbarism, the crowning barbarism that sums up all the daily barbarisms; that it is Nazism, yes, but that before they were its victims, they were its accomplices; that they tolerated that Nazism before it was inflicted on them, that they absolved it, shut their eyes to it, legitimized it, because, until then, it had been applied only to non-European peoples; that they have cultivated that Nazism, that they are responsible for it, and that before engulfing the whole of Western, Christian civilization in its reddened waters, it oozes, seeps, and trickles from every crack.

Yes, it would be worthwhile to study clinically, in detail, the steps taken by Hitler and Hitlerism and to reveal to the very distinguished, very humanistic, very Christian bourgeois of the twentieth century that without his being aware of it, he has a Hitler inside him, that Hitler *inhabits* him, that Hitler is his *demon,* that if he rails against him, he is being inconsistent and that, at bottom, what he cannot forgive Hitler for is not *crime* in itself, *the crime against man,* it is not *the humiliation of man as such,* it is the crime against the white man, the humiliation of the white man, and the fact that he applied to Europe colonialist procedures, which until then had been reserved exclusively for the Arabs of Algeria, the coolies of India, and the blacks of Africa.

And that is the great thing I hold against pseudohumanism: that for too long it has diminished the rights of man, that its concept of those rights has been—and still is—narrow and fragmentary, incomplete and biased and, all things considered, sordidly racist.

I have talked a good deal about Hitler. Because he deserves it: he makes it possible to see things on a large scale and to grasp the fact that capitalist society, at its present stage, is incapable of establishing a concept of the rights of all men, just as it has proved incapable of establishing a system of individual ethics. Whether one likes it or not, at the end of the blind alley that is Europe, I mean the Europe of Adenauer, Schuman, Bidault, and a few others, there is Hitler. At the end of capitalism, which is eager to outlive its day, there is Hitler. At the end of formal humanism and philosophic renunciation, there is Hitler.

And this being so, I cannot help thinking of one of his statements: "We aspire not to equality but to domination. The country of a foreign race must become once again a country of serfs, of agricultural laborers, or industrial workers. It is not a question of eliminating the inequalities among men but of widening them and making them into a law."

That rings clear, haughty, and brutal and plants us squarely in the middle of howling savagery. But let us come down a step.

Who is speaking? I am ashamed to say it: it is the Western *humanist*, the "idealist" philosopher. That his name is Renan is an accident. That the passage is taken from a book entitled *La Réforme intellectuelle et morale*, that it was written in France just after a war which France had represented as a war of right against might, tells us a great deal about bourgeois morals.

> The regeneration of the inferior or degenerate races by the superior races is part of the providential order of things for humanity. With us, the common man is nearly always a déclassé nobleman, his heavy hand is better suited to handling the sword than the menial tool. Rather than work, he chooses to fight, that is, he returns to his first estate. *Regere imperio populos*, that is our vocation. Pour forth this all-consuming activity onto countries which, like China, are crying aloud for foreign conquest. Turn the adventurers who disturb European society into a *ver sacrum*, a horde like those of the Franks, the Lombards, or the Normans, and every man will be in his right role. Nature has made a race of workers, the Chinese race, who have wonderful manual dexterity and almost no sense of honor; govern them with justice, levying from them, in return for the blessing of such a government, an ample allowance for the conquering race, and they will be satisfied; a race of tillers of the soil, the Negro; treat him with kindness and humanity, and all will be as it should; a race of masters and soldiers, the European race. Reduce this noble race to working in the *ergastulum* like Negroes and Chinese, and they rebel. In Europe, every rebel is, more or less, a soldier who has missed his calling, a creature made for the heroic life, before whom you are setting *a task that is contrary to his race*—a poor worker, too good a soldier. But the life at which our workers rebel would make a Chinese or a fellah happy, as they are not military creatures in the least. *Let each one do what he is made for, and all will be well.*[1]

Hitler? Rosenberg? No, Renan.

But let us come down one step further. And it is the long-winded politician. Who protests? No one, so far as I know, when M. Albert Sarraut, the former governor-general of Indochina, holding forth to the students at the Ecole Coloniale, teaches them that it would be puerile to object to the European colonial enterprises in the name of "an alleged right to possess the land one occupies, and some sort of right to remain in fierce isolation, which would leave unutilized resources to lie forever idle in the hands of incompetents."

And who is roused to indignation when a certain Reverend Barde assures us that if the goods of this world "remained divided up indefinitely, as they would be without colonization, they would answer neither the purposes of God nor the just demands of the human collectivity"?

Since, as his fellow Christian, the Reverend Muller, declares: "Humanity must not, cannot allow the incompetence, negligence, and laziness of the uncivilized peoples to leave idle indefinitely the wealth which God has confided to them, charging them to make it serve the good of all."

No one.

I mean not one established writer, not one academician, not one preacher, not one crusader for the right and for religion, not one "defender of the human person."

And yet, through the mouths of the Sarrauts and the Bardes, the Mullers and the Renans, through the mouths of all those who considered—and consider—it lawful to apply to non-European peoples "a kind of expropriation for public purposes" for the benefit of nations that were stronger and better equipped, it was already Hitler speaking!

What am I driving at? At this idea: that no one colonizes innocently, that no one colonizes with impunity either; that a nation which colonizes, that a civilization which justifies colonization—and therefore force—is already a sick civilization, a civilization that is morally diseased, that irresistibly, progressing from one consequence to another, one repudiation to another, calls for its Hitler, I mean its punishment.

Colonization: bridgehead in a campaign to civilize barbarism, from which there may emerge at any moment the negation of civilization, pure and simple.

Elsewhere I have cited at length a few incidents culled from the history of colonial expeditions.

Unfortunately, this did not find favor with everyone. It seems that I was pulling old skeletons out of the closet. Indeed!

Was there no point in quoting Colonel de Montagnac, one of the conquerors of Algeria: "In order to banish the thoughts that sometimes besiege me, I have some heads cut off, not the heads of artichokes but the heads of men."

Would it have been more advisable to refuse the floor to Count d'Hérisson: "It is true that we are bringing back a whole barrelful of ears collected, pair by pair, from prisoners, friendly or enemy."

Should I have refused Saint-Arnaud the right to profess his barbarous faith: "We lay waste, we burn, we plunder, we destroy the houses and the trees."

Should I have prevented Marshal Bugeaud from systematizing all that in a daring theory and invoking the precedent of famous ancestors: "We must have a great invasion of Africa, like the invasions of the Franks and the Goths."

Lastly, should I have cast back into the shadows of oblivion the memorable feat of arms of General Gérard and kept silent about the capture of Ambike, a city which, to tell the truth, had never dreamed of defending itself: "The native riflemen had orders to kill only the men, but no one restrained them; intoxicated by the smell of blood, they spared not one woman, not one child. . . . At the end of the afternoon, the heat caused a light mist to arise: it was the blood of the five thousand victims, the ghost of the city, evaporating in the setting sun."

Yes or no, are these things true? And the sadistic pleasures, the nameless delights that send voluptuous shivers and quivers through Loti's carcass when he focuses his field glasses on a good massacre of the Annamese? True or not true?[2] And if these things are true, as no one can deny, will it be said, in order to minimize them, that these corpses don't prove anything?

For my part, if I have recalled a few details of these hideous butcheries, it is by no means because I take a morbid delight in them, but because I think that these heads of men, these collections of ears, these burned houses, these Gothic invasions, this steaming blood, these cities that evaporate at the edge of the sword, are not to be so easily disposed of. They prove that colonization, I repeat, dehumanizes even the most civilized man; that colonial activity, colonial enterprise, colonial conquest, which is based on contempt for the native and justified by that contempt, inevitably tends to change him who undertakes it; that the colonizer, who in order to ease his conscience gets into the habit of seeing the other man as *an animal*, accustoms himself to treating him like an animal, and tends objectively to transform *himself* into an animal. It is this result, this boomerang effect of colonization, that I wanted to point out.

Unfair? No. There was a time when these same facts were a source of pride, and when, sure of the morrow, people did not mince words. One last quotation; it is from a certain Carl Siger, author of an *Essai sur la colonisation:*

The new countries offer a vast field for individual, violent activities which, in the metropolitan countries, would run up against certain prejudices, against a sober and orderly conception of life, and which, in the colonies, have greater freedom to develop and, consequently, to affirm their worth. Thus to a certain extent the colonies can serve as a safety valve for modern society. Even if this were their only value, it would be immense.[3]

Truly, there are stains that it is beyond the power of man to wipe out and that can never be fully expiated.

But let us speak about the colonized.

I see clearly what colonization has destroyed: the wonderful Indian civilizations—and neither Deterding nor Royal Dutch nor Standard Oil will ever console me for the Aztecs and the Incas.

I see clearly the civilizations, condemned to perish at a future date, into which it has introduced a principle of ruin: the South Sea islands, Nigeria, Nyasaland. I see less clearly the contributions it has made.

Security? Culture? The rule of law? In the meantime, I look around and wherever there are colonizers and colonized face to face, I see force, brutality, cruelty, sadism, conflict, and, in a parody of education, the hasty manufacture of a few thousand subordinate functionaries, "boys," artisans, office clerks, and interpreters necessary for the smooth operation of business.

I spoke of contact.

Between colonizer and colonized there is room only for forced labor, intimidation, pressure, the police, taxation, theft, rape, compulsory crops, contempt, mistrust, arrogance, self-complacency, swinishness, brainless elites, degraded masses.

No human contact, but relations of domination and submission which turn the colonizing man into a classroom monitor, an army sergeant, a prison guard, a slave driver, and the indigenous man into an instrument of production.

My turn to state an equation: colonization equals "thingification."

I hear the storm. They talk to me about progress, about "achievements," diseases cured, improved standards of living.

I am talking about societies drained of their essence, cultures trampled underfoot, institutions undermined, lands confiscated, religions smashed, magnificent artistic creations destroyed, extraordinary *possibilities* wiped out.

They throw facts at my head, statistics, mileages of roads, canals, and railroad tracks.

I am talking about thousands of men sacrificed to the Congo-Océan.[4] I am talking about those who, as I write this, are digging the harbor of Abidjan by hand. I am talking about millions of men torn from their gods, their land, their habits, their life—from life, from the dance, from wisdom.

I am talking about millions of men in whom fear has been cunningly instilled, who have been taught to have an inferiority complex, to tremble, kneel, despair, and behave like flunkeys.

They dazzle me with the tonnage of cotton or cocoa that has been exported, the acreage that has been planted with olive trees or grapevines.

I am talking about natural *economies* that have been disrupted—harmonious and viable economies adapted to the indigenous population—about food crops destroyed, malnutrition permanently introduced, agricultural development oriented solely toward the benefit of the metropolitan countries, about the looting of products, the looting of raw materials.

They pride themselves on abuses eliminated.

I too talk about abuses, but what I say is that on the old ones—very real—they have superimposed others—very detestable. They talk to me about local tyrants brought to reason; but I note that in general the old tyrants get on very well with the new ones, and that there has been established between them, to the detriment of the people, a circuit of mutual services and complicity.

They talk to me about civilization, I talk about proletarianization and mystification.

For my part, I make a systematic defense of the non-European civilizations.

Every day that passes, every denial of justice, every beating by the police, every demand of the workers that is drowned in blood, every scandal that is hushed up, every punitive expedition, every police van, every gendarme and every militiaman, brings home to us the value of our old societies.

They were communal societies, never societies of the many for the few.

They were societies that were not only antecapitalist, as has been said, but also *anticapitalist.*

They were democratic societies, always.

They were cooperative societies, fraternal societies.

I make a systematic defense of the societies destroyed by imperialism.

They were the fact, they did not pretend to be the idea; despite their faults, they were neither to be hated nor condemned. They were content to be. In them, neither the word *failure* nor the word *avatar* had any meaning. They kept hope intact.

Whereas those are the only words that can, in all honesty, be applied to the European enterprises outside Europe. My only consolation is that periods of colonization pass, that nations sleep only for a time, and that peoples remain.

This being said, it seems that in certain circles they pretend to have discovered in me an "enemy of Europe" and a prophet of the return to the ante-European past.

For my part, I search in vain for the place where I could have expressed such views; where I ever underestimated the importance of Europe in the history of human thought; where I ever preached a *return* of any kind; where I ever claimed that there could be a return.

The truth is that I have said something very different: to wit, that the great historical tragedy of Africa has been not so much that it was too late in making contact with the rest of the world, as the manner in which that contact was brought about; that Europe began to "propagate" at a time when it had fallen into the hands of the most unscrupulous financiers and captains of industry; that it was our misfortune to encounter that particular Europe on our path, and that Europe is responsible before the human community for the highest heap of corpses in history.

In another connection, in judging colonization, I have added that Europe has gotten on very well indeed with all the local feudal lords who agreed to serve, woven a villainous complicity with them, rendered their tyranny more effective and more efficient, and that it has actually tended to prolong artificially the survival of local pasts in their most pernicious aspects.

I have said—and this is something very different—that colonialist Europe has grafted modern abuse onto ancient injustice, hateful racism onto old inequality.

That if I am attacked on the grounds of intent, I maintain that colonialist Europe is dishonest in trying to justify its colonizing activity a posteriori by the obvious material progress that has been achieved in certain fields under the colonial regime—since *sudden change* is always possible, in history as elsewhere; since no one knows at what stage of material development these same countries would have been if Europe had not intervened; since the technical outfitting of Africa and Asia, their administrative reorganization, in a word, their "Europeanization," was (as is proved by the example of Japan) in no way tied to the European *occupation;* since the Europeanization of the non-European continents could have been accomplished otherwise than under the heel of Europe; since this movement of Europeanization *was in progress;* since it was even slowed down; since in any case it was distorted by the European takeover.

The proof is that at present it is the indigenous peoples of Africa and Asia who are demanding schools, and colonialist Europe which refuses them; that it is the African who is asking for ports and roads, and colonialist Europe which is niggardly on this score; that it is the colonized man who wants to move forward, and the colonizer who holds things back.

[1]Ernest Renan, *La réforme intellectuelle et morale* (Paris: Calmann-Lévy, 1929).

[2]This is a reference to the account of the taking of Thuan-An which appeared in *Le Figaro* in September 1883 and is quoted in Nicholas Serban's book, *Pierre Loti, sa vie et son oeuvre*, préface de Louis Barthou (Paris: Les presses françaises, 1924). "Then the

great slaughter had begun. They had fired in double-salvos! and it was a pleasure to see these sprays of bullets, that were so easy to aim, come down on them twice a minute, surely and methodically, on command. . . . We saw some who were quite mad and stood up seized with a dizzy desire to run. . . . They zigzagged, running every which way in this race with death, holding their garments up around their waists in a comical way . . . and then we amused ourselves counting the dead, etc."

[3]Carl Siger, *Essai sur la colonisation* (Paris: Société du Mercure de France, 1907).

[4]A railroad line connecting Brazzaville with the port of Pointe-Noire. *Trans.*

FRANTZ FANON (1925–1961)

✺ Racism and Culture (1956)

The unilaterally decreed normative value of certain cultures deserves our careful attention. One of the paradoxes immediately encountered is the rebound of egocentric, sociocentric definitions.

There is first affirmed the existence of human groups having no culture; then of a hierarchy of cultures; and finally, the concept of cultural relativity.

We have here the whole range from overall negation to singular and specific recognition. It is precisely this fragmented and bloody history that we must sketch on the level of cultural anthropology.

There are, we may say, certain constellations of institutions, established by particular men in the framework of precise geographical areas, which at a given moment have undergone a direct and sudden assault of different cultural patterns. The technical, generally advanced development of the social group that has thus appeared enables it to set up an organized domination. The enterprise of deculturation turns out to be the negative of a more gigantic work of economic and even biological enslavement.

The doctrine of cultural hierarchy is thus but one aspect of a systematized hierarchization implacably pursued.

The modern theory of the absence of cortical integration of colonial peoples is the anatomic-physiological counterpart of this doctrine. The apparition of racism is not fundamentally determining. Racism is not the whole but the most visible, the most day-to-day and, not to mince matters, the crudest element of a given structure.

To study the relations of racism and culture is to raise the question of their reciprocal action. If culture is the combination of motor and mental behavior patterns arising from the encounters of man with nature and with his fellow man, it can be said that racism is indeed a cultural element. There are thus cultures with racism and cultures without racism.

This precise cultural element, however, has not become encysted. Racism has not managed to harden. It has had to renew itself, to adapt itself, to change its appearance. It has had to undergo the fate of the cultural whole that informed it.

The vulgar, primitive, oversimple racism purported to find in biology—the Scriptures having proved insufficient—the material basis of the doctrine. It would be tedious to recall the efforts then undertaken: the comparative form of the skulls, the quantity and the configuration of the folds of the brain, the characteristics of the cell layers of the cortex, the dimensions of the vertebrae, the microscopic appearance of the epiderm, etc. . . .

Intellectual and emotional primitivism appeared as a banal consequence, a recognition of existence.

Such affirmations, crude and massive, give way to a more refined argument. Here and there, however, an occasional relapse is to be noted. Thus the "emotional instability of the Negro," the "subcritical integration of the Arab," the "quasi-generic culpability of the Jew" are data that one comes upon among a few contemporary writers. The monograph by J. Carothers, for example, sponsored by the World Health Organization, invokes "scientific arguments" in support of a physiological lobotomy of the African Negro.

These old-fashioned positions tend in any case to disappear. This racism that aspires to be rational, individual, genotypically and phenotypically determined, becomes transformed into cultural racism. The object of racism is no longer the individual man but a certain form of existing. At the extreme, such terms as "message" and "cultural style" are resorted to. "Occidental values" oddly blend with the already famous appeal to the fight of the "cross against the crescent."

The morphological equation, to be sure, has not totally disappeared, but events of the past thirty years have shaken the most solidly anchored convictions, upset the checkerboard, restructured a great number of relationships.

The memory of Nazism, the common wretchedness of different men, the common enslavement of extensive social groups, the apparition of "European colonies," in other words the institution of a colonial system in the very heart of Europe, the growing awareness of workers in the colonizing and racist countries, the evolution of techniques, all this has deeply modified the problem and the manner of approaching it.

We must look for the consequences of this racism on the cultural level.

Racism, as we have seen, is only one element of a vaster whole: that of the systematized oppression of a people. How does an oppressing people behave? Here we rediscover constants.

We witness the destruction of cultural values, of ways of life. Language, dress, techniques are devalorized. How can one account for this constant? Psychologists, who tend to explain everything by movements of the psyche, claim to discover in behavior on the level of contacts between individuals the criticism of an original hat, of a way of speaking, of walking . . .

Such attempts deliberately leave out of account the special character of the colonial situation. In reality the nations that undertake a colonial war have no concern for the confrontation of cultures. War is a gigantic business and every approach must be governed by this datum. The enslavement, in the strictest sense, of the native population is the prime necessity.

For this its systems of reference have to be broken. Expropriation, spoliation, raids, objective murder are matched by the sacking of cultural patterns, or at least condition such sacking. The social panorama is destructured; values are flaunted, crushed, emptied.

The lines of force, having crumbled, no longer give direction. In their stead a new system of values is imposed, not proposed but affirmed, by the heavy weight of cannons and sabers.

The setting up of the colonial system does not of itself bring about the death of the native culture. Historic observation reveals, on the contrary, that the aim sought is rather a continued agony than a total disappearance of the pre-existing culture. This culture, once living and open to the future, becomes closed, fixed in the colonial status, caught in the yoke of oppression. Both present and mummified, it testifies against its members. It defines them in fact without appeal. The cultural mummification leads to a mummification of individual thinking. The apathy so universally noted among colonial peoples is but the logical consequence of this operation. The reproach of inertia constantly directed at "the native" is utterly dishonest. As though it were possible for a man to evolve otherwise than within the framework of a culture that recognizes him and that he decides to assume.

Thus we witness the setting up of archaic, inert institutions, functioning under the oppressor's supervision and patterned like a caricature of formerly fertile institutions . . .

These bodies appear to embody respect for the tradition, the cultural specificities, the personality of the subjugated people. This pseudorespect in fact is tantamount to the most utter contempt, to the most elaborate sadism. The characteristic of a culture is to be open, permeated by spontaneous, generous, fertile lines of force. The appointment of "reliable men" to execute certain gestures is a deception that deceives no one. Thus the Kabyle *dje-maas* named by the French authority are not recognized by the natives. They are matched by another djemaa democratically elected. And naturally the second as a rule dictates to the first what his conduct should be.

The constantly affirmed concern with "respecting the culture of the native populations" accordingly does not signify taking into consideration the values borne by the culture, incarnated by men. Rather, this behavior betrays a determination to objectify, to confine, to imprison, to harden. Phrases such as "I know them," "that's the way they are," show this maximum objectification successfully achieved. I can think of gestures and thoughts that define these men.

Exoticism is one of the forms of this simplification. It allows no cultural confrontation. There is on the one hand a culture in which qualities of dynamism, of growth, of depth can be recognized. As against this, we find characteristics, curiosities, things, never a structure.

Thus in an initial phase the occupant establishes his domination, massively affirms his superiority. The social group, militarily and economically subjugated, is dehumanized in accordance with a polydimensional method.

Exploitation, tortures, raids, racism, collective liquidations, rational oppression take turns at different levels in order literally to make of the native an object in the hands of the occupying nation.

This object man, without means of existing, without a raison d'être, is broken in the very depth of his substance. The desire to live, to continue, becomes more and more indecisive, more and more phantomlike. It is at this stage that the well-known guilt complex appears. In his first novels, Wright gives a very detailed description of it.

Progressively, however, the evolution of techniques of production, the industrialization, limited though it is, of the subjugated countries, the increasingly necessary existence of collaborators, impose a new attitude upon the occupant. The complexity of the means of production, the evolution of economic relations inevitably involving the evolution of ideologies, unbalance the system. Vulgar racism in its biological form corresponds to the period of crude exploitation of man's arms and legs. The perfecting of the means of production inevitably brings about the camouflage of the techniques by which man is exploited, hence of the forms of racism.

It is therefore not as a result of the evolution of people's minds that racism loses its virulence. No inner revolution can explain this necessity for racism to seek more subtle forms, to evolve. On all sides men become free, putting an end to the lethargy to which oppression and racism had condemned them.

In the very heart of the "civilized nations" the workers finally discover that the exploitation of man, at the root of a system, assumes different faces. At this stage racism no longer dares appear without disguise. It is unsure of itself. In an ever greater number of circumstances the racist takes to cover. He who claimed to "sense," to "see through" those others, finds himself to be a target, looked at, judged. The racist's purpose has become a purpose haunted by bad conscience. He can find salvation only in a passion-driven commitment such as is found in certain psychoses. And having defined the symptomatology of such passion-charged deliria is not the least of Professor Baruk's merits.

Racism is never a super-added element discovered by chance in the

course of the investigation of the cultural data of a group. The social constellation, the cultural whole, are deeply modified by the existence of racism.

It is a common saying nowadays that racism is a plague of humanity. But
we must not content ourselves with such a phrase. We must tirelessly look for
the repercussions of racism at all levels of sociability. The importance of the
racist problem in contemporary American literature is significant. The Negro
in motion pictures, the Negro and folklore, the Jew and children's stories, the
Jew in the café are inexhaustible themes.

Racism, to come back to America, haunts and vitiates American culture.
And this dialectical gangrene is exacerbated by the coming to awareness and
the determination of millions of Negroes and Jews to fight this racism by
which they are victimized.

This passion-charged, irrational, groundless phase, when one examines it,
reveals a frightful visage. The movement of groups, the liberation in certain
parts of the world of men previously kept down, make for a more and more
precarious equilibrium. Rather unexpectedly, the racist group points accus-
ingly to a manifestation of racism among the oppressed. The "intellectual
primitivism" of the period of exploitation gives way to the "medieval, in fact
prehistoric fanaticism" of the period of the liberation.

For a time it looked as though racism had disappeared. This soul-soothing,
unreal impression was simply the consequence of the evolution of forms
of exploitation. Psychologists spoke of a prejudice having become unconscious. The truth is that the rigor of the system made the daily affirmation of
a superiority superfluous. The need to appeal to various degrees of approval
and support, to the native's cooperation, modified relations in a less crude,
more subtle, more "cultivated" direction. It was not rare, in fact, to see a
"democratic and humane" ideology at this stage. The commercial undertak-
ing of enslavement, of cultural destruction, progressively gave way to a verbal mystification.

The interesting thing about this evolution is that racism was taken as a
topic of meditation, sometimes even as a publicity technique.

Thus the blues—"the black slave lament"—was offered up for the admiration of the oppressors. This modicum of stylized oppression is the exploiter's
and the racist's rightful due. Without oppression and without racism you
have no blues. The end of racism would sound the knell of great Negro
music . . .

As the all-too-famous Toynbee might say, the blues are the slave's response
to the challenge of oppression.

Still today, for many men, even colored, Armstrong's music has a real
meaning only in this perspective.

Racism bloats and disfigures the face of the culture that practices it. Literature, the plastic arts, songs for shopgirls, proverbs, habits, patterns, whether

they set out to attack it or to vulgarize it, restore racism. This means that a social group, a country, a civilization cannot be unconsciously racist.

We say once again that racism is not an accidental discovery. It is not a hidden, dissimulated element. No superhuman efforts are needed to bring it out.

Racism stares one in the face, for it so happens that it belongs in a characteristic whole: that of the shameless exploitation of one group of men by another which has reached a higher stage of technical development. This is why military and economic oppression generally precedes, makes possible, and legitimizes racism.

The habit of considering racism as a mental quirk, as a psychological flaw, must be abandoned.

But the men who are a prey to racism, the enslaved, exploited, weakened social group—how do they behave? What are their defense mechanisms?

What attitudes do we discover here?

In an initial phase we have seen the occupying power legitimizing its domination by scientific arguments, the "inferior race" being denied on the basis of race. Because no other solution is left it, the racialized social group tries to imitate the oppressor and thereby to deracialize itself. The "inferior race" denies itself as a different race. It shares with the "superior race" the convictions, doctrines, and other attitudes concerning it.

Having witnessed the liquidation of its systems of reference, the collapse of its cultural patterns, the native can only recognize with the occupant that "God is not on his side." The oppressor, through the inclusive and frightening character of his authority, manages to impose on the native new ways of seeing, and in particular a pejorative judgment with respect to his original forms of existing.

This event, which is commonly designated as alienation, is naturally very important. It is found in the official texts under the name of assimilation.

Now this alienation is never wholly successful. Whether or not it is because the oppressor quantitatively and qualitatively limits the evolution, unforeseen, disparate phenomena manifest themselves.

The inferiorized group had admitted, since the force of reasoning was implacable, that its misfortunes resulted directly from its racial and cultural characteristics.

Guilt and inferiority are the usual consequences of this dialectic. The oppressed then tries to escape these, on the one hand by proclaiming his total and unconditional adoption of the new cultural models, and on the other by pronouncing an irreversible condemnation of his own cultural style.[1]

Yet the necessity that the oppressor encounters at a given point to dissimulate the forms of exploitation does not lead to the disappearance of this exploitation. The more elaborate, less crude economic relations require a daily coating, but the alienation at this level remains frightful.

Having judged, condemned, abandoned his cultural forms, his language, his food habits, his sexual behavior, his way of sitting down, of resting, of laughing, of enjoying himself, the oppressed *flings himself* upon the imposed culture with the desperation of a drowning man.

Developing his technical knowledge in contact with more and more perfected machines, entering into the dynamic circuit of industrial production, meeting men from remote regions in the framework of the concentration of capital, that is to say, on the job, discovering the assembly line, the team, production "time," in other words yield per hour, the oppressed is shocked to find that he continues to be the object of racism and contempt.

It is at this level that racism is treated as a question of persons. "There are a few hopeless racists, but you must admit that on the whole the population likes . . ."

With time all this will disappear.

This is the country where there is the least amount of race prejudice . . .

. At the United Nations there is a commission to fight race prejudice.

Films on race prejudice, poems on race prejudice, messages on race prejudice . . .

Spectacular and futile condemnations of race prejudice. In reality, a colonial country is a racist country. If in England, in Belgium, or in France, despite the democratic principles affirmed by these respective nations, there are still racists, it is these racists who, in their opposition to the country as a whole, are logically consistent.

It is not possible to enslave men without logically making them inferior through and through. And racism is only the emotional, affective, sometimes intellectual explanation of this inferiorization.

The racist in a culture with racism is therefore normal. He has achieved a perfect harmony of economic relations and ideology. The idea that one forms of man, to be sure, is never totally dependent on economic relations, in other words—and this must not be forgotten—on relations existing historically and geographically among men and groups. An ever greater number of members belonging to racist societies are taking a position. They are dedicating themselves to a world in which racism would be impossible. But everyone is not up to this kind of objectivity, this abstraction, this solemn commitment. One cannot with impunity require of a man that he be against "the prejudices of his group."

And, we repeat, every colonialist group is racist.

"Acculturized" and deculturized at one and the same time, the oppressed continues to come up against racism. He finds this sequel illogical, what he has left behind him inexplicable, without motive, incorrect. His knowledge, the appropriation of precise and complicated techniques, sometimes his intellectual superiority as compared to a great number of racists, lead him to qualify the racist world as passion-charged. He perceives that the racist atmosphere impregnates all the elements of the social life. The sense of an overwhelming injustice is correspondingly very strong. Forgetting racism as a consequence, one concentrates on racism as cause. Campaigns of deintoxication are launched. Appeal is made to the sense of humanity, to love, to respect for the supreme values ...

Race prejudice in fact obeys a flawless logic. A country that lives, draws its substance from the exploitation of other peoples, makes those peoples inferior. Race prejudice applied to those peoples is normal.

Racism is therefore not a constant of the human spirit.

It is, as we have seen, a disposition fitting into a well-defined system. And anti-Jewish prejudice is no different from anti-Negro prejudice. A society has race prejudice or it has not. There are no degrees of prejudice. One cannot say that a given country is racist but that lynchings or extermination camps are not to be found there. The truth is that all that and still other things exist on the horizon. These virtualities, these latencies circulate, carried by the lifestream of psycho-affective, economic relations ...

Discovering the futility of his alienation, his progressive deprivation, the inferiorized individual, after this phase of deculturation, of extraneousness, comes back to his original positions.

This culture, abandoned, sloughed off, rejected, despised, becomes for the inferiorized an object of passionate attachment. There is a very marked kind of overvaluation that is psychologically closely linked to the craving for forgiveness.

But behind this simplifying analysis there is indeed the intuition experienced by the inferiorized of having discovered a spontaneous truth. This is a psychological datum that is part of the texture of history and of truth.

Because the inferiorized rediscovers a style that had once been devalorized, what he does is in fact to cultivate culture. Such a caricature of cultural existence would indicate, if it were necessary, that culture must be lived, and cannot be fragmented. It cannot be had piecemeal.

Yet the oppressed goes into ecstasies over each rediscovery. The wonder is permanent. Having formerly emigrated from his culture, the native today explores it with ardor. It is a continual honeymoon. Formerly inferiorized, he is now in a state of grace.

Not with impunity, however, does one undergo domination. The culture of the enslaved people is sclerosed, dying. No life any longer circulates in it. Or more precisely, the only existing life is dissimulated. The population that normally assumes here and there a few fragments of life, which continues to attach dynamic meanings to institutions, is an anonymous population. In a colonial system these are the traditionalists.

The former emigré, by the sudden ambiguity of his behavior, causes consternation. To the anonymity of the traditionalist he opposes a vehement and aggressive exhibitionism.

The state of grace and aggressiveness are the two constants found at this stage, aggressiveness being the passion-charged mechanism making it possible to escape the sting of paradox.

Because the former emigré is in possession of precise techniques, because his level of action is in the framework of relations that are already complex, these rediscoveries assume an irrational aspect. There is an hiatus, a discrepancy between intellectual development, technical appropriation, highly differentiated modes of thinking and of logic, on the one hand, and a "simple, pure" emotional basis on the other . . .

Rediscovering tradition, living it as a defense mechanism, as a symbol of purity, of salvation, the decultured individual leaves the impression that the mediation takes vengeance by substantializing itself. This falling back on archaic positions having no relation to technical development is paradoxical. The institutions thus valorized no longer correspond to the elaborate methods of action already mastered.

The culture put into capsules, which has vegetated since the foreign domination, is revalorized. It is not reconceived, grasped anew, dynamized from within. It is shouted. And this headlong, unstructured, verbal revalorization conceals paradoxical attitudes.

It is at this point that the incorrigible character of the inferiorized is brought out for mention. Arab doctors sleep on the ground, spit all over the place, etc. . . .

Negro intellectuals consult a sorcerer before making a decision, etc. . . .

"Collaborating" intellectuals try to justify their new attitude. The customs, traditions, beliefs formerly denied and passed over in silence are violently valorized and affirmed.

Tradition is no longer scoffed at by the group. The group no longer runs away from itself. The sense of the past is rediscovered, the worship of ancestors resumed . . .

The past, becoming henceforth a constellation of values, becomes identified with the Truth.

This rediscovery, this absolute valorization almost in defiance of reality, objectively indefensible, assumes an incomparable and subjective importance. On emerging from these passionate espousals, the native will have decided, "with full knowledge of what is involved," to fight all forms of exploitation and of alienation of man. At this same time, the occupant, on the other hand, multiplies appeals to assimilation, then to integration, to community.

The native's hand-to-hand struggle with his culture is too solemn, too abrupt an operation to tolerate the slightest slip-up. No neologism can mask the new certainty: the plunge into the chasm of the past is the condition and the source of freedom.

The logical end of this will to struggle is the total liberation of the national territory. In order to achieve this liberation, the inferiorized man brings all his resources into play, all his acquisitions, the old and the new, his own and those of the occupant.

The struggle is at once total, absolute. But then race prejudice is hardly found to appear.

At the time of imposing his domination, in order to justify slavery, the oppressor had invoked scientific argument. There is nothing of the kind here.

A people that undertakes a struggle for liberation rarely legitimizes race prejudice. Even in the course of acute periods of insurrectional armed struggle one never witnesses the recourse to biological justifications.

The struggle of the inferiorized is situated on a markedly more human level. The perspectives are radically new. The opposition is the henceforth classical one of the struggles of conquest and of liberation.

In the course of struggle the dominating nation tries to revive racist arguments but the elaboration of racism proves more and more ineffective. There is talk of fanaticism, of primitive attitudes in the face of death, but once again the now-crumbling mechanism no longer responds. Those who were once unbudgeable, the constitutional cowards, the timid, the eternally inferiorized, stiffen and emerge bristling.

The occupant is bewildered.

The end of race prejudice begins with a sudden incomprehension.

The occupant's spasmed and rigid culture, now liberated, opens at last to the culture of people who have really become brothers. The two cultures can affront each other, enrich each other.

In conclusion, universality resides in this decision to recognize and accept the reciprocal relativism of different cultures, once the colonial status is irreversibly excluded.

[1]A little-studied phenomenon sometimes appears at this stage. Intellectuals, students, belonging to the dominant group, make "scientific" studies of the dominated society, its art, its ethical universe.

In the universities the rare colonized intellectuals find their own cultural system being revealed to them. It even happens that scholars of the colonizing countries grow enthusiastic over this or that specific feature. The concepts of purity, naiveté, innocence appear. The native intellectual's vigilance must here be doubly on the alert.

WALTER RODNEY (1942–1980)

Black Power, a Basic Understanding (1969)

Black Power is a doctrine about black people, for black people, preached by black people. I'm putting it to my black brothers and sisters that the color of our skins is the most fundamental thing about us. I could have chosen to talk about people of the same island, or the same religion, or the same class—but instead I have chosen skin color as essentially the most binding factor in our world. In so doing, I am not saying that is the way things ought to be. I am simply recognizing the real world—that is the way things are. Under different circumstances, it would have been nice to be color blind, to choose my friends solely because their social interests coincided with mine—but no conscious black man can allow himself such luxuries in the contemporary world.

Let me emphasize that the situation is not of our making. To begin with, the white world defines who is white and who is black. In the United States if one is not white, then one is black; in Britain, if one is not white then one is colored; in South Africa, one can be white, colored, or black depending upon how white people classify you. There was a South African boxer who was white all his life, until the other whites decided that he was really colored. Even the fact of whether you are black or not is to be decided by white people—by White Power. If a Jamaican black man tried to get a room from a landlady in London, who said "No Coloreds," it would not impress her if he said he was West Indian, quite apart from the fact that she would already have closed the door in his black face. When a Pakistani goes to the Midlands he is as colored as a Nigerian. The Indonesian is the same as a Surinamer in Holland; the Chinese and New Guineans have as little chance of becoming residents and citizens in Australia as do you and I. The definition which is most widely used the world over is that once you are not obviously white then you are black, and are excluded from power—power is kept pure milky white.

Reprinted from *The Groundings with My Brothers*, by Walter Rodney (London: Bogle L'Ouverture, 1969), 16–23, with permission of Bogle L'Ouverture Press Ltd.

The black people of whom I speak, therefore, are nonwhites—the hundreds of millions of people whose homelands are in Asia and Africa, with another few millions in the Americas. A further subdivision can be made with reference to all people of African descent whose position is clearly more acute than that of most nonwhite groups. It must be noted that once a person is said to be black by the white world, then that is usually the most important thing about him; fat or thin, intelligent or stupid, criminal or sportsman—these things pale into insignificance. Actually I've found out that a lot of whites literally cannot tell one black from another. Partly this may be due to the fact that they do not personally know many black people, but it reflects a psychological tendency to deny our individuality by refusing to consider us as individual human beings.

Having said a few things about black and white, I will try to point out the power relations between them. By the outbreak of the First World War in 1914, the capitalist division of the world was complete. It was a division which made capitalists dominant over workers and white people dominant over black. At that point, everywhere in the world, white people held power in all its aspects—political, economic, military, and even cultural. In Europe, the whites held power—this goes without saying. In the Americas the whites had committed mass murder as far as many "Red Indian" tribes were concerned, and they herded the rest into reservations like animals or forced them into the disadvantageous positions, geographically and economically, in Central and South America. In Australia and New Zealand, a similar thing had occurred on a much smaller scale. In Africa, European power reigned supreme except in a few isolated spots like Ethiopia; and where whites were actually settled, the Africans were reduced to the status of second-class citizens in their own country. All this was following upon a historical experience of 400 years of slavery, which had transferred millions of Africans to work and die in the New World. In Asia, Europe's power was felt everywhere except in Japan and areas controlled by Japan. The essence of White Power is that it is exercised over black peoples—whether or not they are minority or majority, whether it was a country belonging originally to whites or to blacks. It is exercised in such a way that black people have no share in that power and are, therefore, denied any say in their own destinies.

Since 1911, White Power has been slowly reduced. The Russian Revolution put an end to Russian imperialism in the Far East, and the Chinese Revolution by 1949 had emancipated the world's largest single ethnic group from the white power complex. The rest of Asia, Africa, and Latin America (with minor exceptions such as North Korea, North Vietnam, and Cuba) have remained within the white power network to this day. We live in the section of the world under white domination—the imperialist world. The Russians are white and have power but they are not a colonial power oppressing black peoples. The white power which is our enemy is that which is exercised over black peoples, irrespective of which group is in the majority and irrespective of whether the particular country belonged originally to whites or blacks.

We need to look very carefully at the nature of the relationships between color and power in the imperialist world. There are two basic sections in the imperialist world—one that is dominated and one that is dominant. Every country in the dominant metropolitan area has a large majority of whites— the U.S., Britain, France, etc. Every country in the dominated colonial areas has an overwhelming majority of nonwhites, as in most of Asia, Africa, and the West Indies. Power, therefore, resides in the white countries and is exercised over blacks. There is the mistaken belief that black people achieved power with independence, e.g., Malaya, Jamaica, and Kenya, but a black man ruling a dependent state within the imperialist system has no power. He is simply an agent of the whites in the metropolis, with an army and a police force designed to maintain the imperialist way of things in that particular colonial area.

When Britain announced recently that it was withdrawing troops from East of Suez, the American Secretary of State remarked that something would have to be done to fill the "power vacuum." This involved Saudi Arabia, India, Pakistan, Ceylon, and Malaysia. The white world in their own way were saying that all these blacks amounted to nothing; for power was white and when white power is withdrawn, a vacuum is created, which could only be filled by another white power.

By being made into colonials, black people lost the power which we previously had of governing our own affairs, and the aim of the white imperialist world is to see that we never regain this power. The Congo provides an example of this situation. There was a large and well-developed Congolese empire before the white man reached Africa. The large Congolese empire of the fifteenth century was torn apart by Portuguese slave traders and what remained of the Congo came to be regarded as one of the darkest spots in dark Africa. After regaining political independence the Congolese people settled down to reorganize their lives, but white power intervened, set up the black stooge Tshombe, and murdered both Lumumba and the aspirations of the Congolese people. Since then, paid white mercenaries have harassed the Congo. Late last year, 130 of these hired white killers where chased out of the Congo and cornered in the neighboring African state of Burundi. The white world intervened and they have all been set free. These are men who for months were murdering, raping, pillaging, disrupting economic production, and making a mockery of black life and black society. Yet white power said not a hair on their heads was to be touched. They did not even have to stand trial or reveal their names. Conscious blacks cannot possibly fail to realize that in our own homelands we have no power, abroad we are discriminated against, and everywhere the black masses suffer from poverty. You can put together in your own mind a picture of the whole world, with the white imperialist beast crouched over miserable blacks. And don't forget to label us poor. There is nothing with which poverty coincides so absolutely as with the color black—small or large population, hot or cold climates, rich or poor in natural resouces—poverty cuts across all of these factors in order to find black people.

That association of wealth with whites and poverty with blacks is not accidental. It is the nature of the imperialist relationship that enriches the metropolis at the expense of the colony, i.e., it makes the whites richer and the blacks poorer.

The Spaniards went to Central and South America, and robbed thousands of tons of silver and gold from Indians. The whole of Europe developed on the basis of that wealth, while millions of Indian lives were lost and the societies and cultures of Central and South America were seriously dislocated. Europeans used their guns in Asia to force Asians to trade at huge profits to Europe, and in India the British grew fat while at the same time destroying Indian irrigation. Africa and Africans suffered from the greatest crimes at the hands of Europeans through the slave trade and slavery in the West Indies and the Americas. In all those centuries of exploitation, Europeans have climbed higher on our backs and pushed us down into the dirt. White power has, therefore, used black people to make whites stronger and richer and to make blacks relatively, and sometimes absolutely, weaker and poorer.

Black Power as a movement has been most clearly defined in the U.S.A. Slavery in the U.S. helped create the capital for the development of the U.S. as the foremost capitalist power, and the blacks have subsequently been the most exploited sector of labor. Many blacks live in that supposedly great society at a level of existence comparable to blacks in the poorest section of the colonial world. The blacks in the U.S. have no power. They have achieved prominence in a number of ways—they can sing, they can run, they can box, play baseball, etc., but they have no power. Even in the fields where they excel, they are straws in the hands of whites. The entertainment world, the record-manufacturing business, sport as a commercial enterprise are all controlled by whites—blacks simply perform. They have no power in the areas where they are overwhelming majorities, such as the city slums and certain parts of the southern United States, for the local governments and law-enforcement agencies are all white controlled. This was not always so. For one brief period after the Civil War in the 1860s, blacks in the U.S. held power. In that period (from 1865 to 1875) slavery had just ended, and the blacks were entitled to the vote as free citizens. Being in the majority in several parts of the southern United States, they elected a majority of their own black representatives and helped to rebuild the South, introducing advanced ideas such as education for all (blacks as well as whites, rich and poor). The blacks did not rule the United States, but they were able to put forward their own viewpoints and to impose their will over the white racist minority in several states. This is a concrete historical example of Black Power in the United States, but the whites changed all that, and they have seen to it that such progress was never again achieved by blacks. With massive white immigration, the blacks became a smaller minority within the United States as a whole and even in the south, so that a feeling of hopelessness grew up.

The present Black Power movement in the United States is a rejection of hopelessness and the policy of doing nothing to halt the oppression of blacks by whites. It recognizes the absence of black power, but is confident of the potential of black power on this globe. Marcus Garvey was one of the first advocates of Black Power, and is still today the greatest spokesman ever to have been produced by the movement of black consciousness. "A race without power and authority is a race without respect," wrote Garvey. He spoke to all Africans on the earth, whether they lived in Africa, South America, the West Indies, or North America, and he made blacks aware of their strength when united. The U.S. was his main field of operation, after he had been chased out of Jamaica by the sort of people who today pretend to have made him a hero. All of the black leaders who have advanced the cause in the U.S. since Garvey's time have recognized the international nature of the struggle against White Power. Malcolm X, our martyred brother, became the greatest threat to White Power in the U.S. because he began to seek a broader basis for his efforts in Africa and Asia, and he was probably the first individual who was prepared to bring the race question in the U.S. up before the United Nations as an issue of international importance. The Student Nonviolent Coordinating Committee (S.N.C.C.), the important Black Power organization, developed along the same lines; and at about the same time that the slogan Black Power came into existence a few years ago, S.N.C.C. was setting up a foreign affairs department, headed by James Foreman, who afterwards travelled widely in Africa. Stokely Carmichael has held serious discussions in Vietnam, Cuba, and the progressive African countries, such as Tanzania and Guinea. These are all steps to tap the vast potential of power among the hundreds of millions of oppressed black peoples.

Meanwhile, one significant change had occurred since Garvey. The emphasis within the U.S. is that black people there have a stake in that land, which they have watered with their sweat, tears, and blood, and black leadership is aware of the necessity and the desirability of fighting white power simultaneously at home and abroad. Certain issues are not yet clear about the final shape of society in America. Some form of coexistence with whites is the desired goal of virtually all black leaders, but it must be a society which blacks have a hand in shaping, and blacks should have power commensurate with their numbers and contribution to U.S. development. To get that, they have to fight.

Black Power as a slogan is new, but it is really an ideology and a movement of historical depth. The one feature that is new about it as it is currently exercised in the U.S. is the advocacy of violence. Previously, black people prayed, we were on our best behavior, we asked the whites "please," we smiled so that our white teeth illuminated our black faces. Now it is time to show our teeth in a snarl rather than a smile. The death of Martin Luther King gave several hypocritical persons the opportunity to make stupid remarks about the virtues of nonviolence. Some of the statements made in the Jamaica press and on the radio and TV were made by individuals who probably think that the Jamaican black man is completely daft. We were told that violence in itself is evil, and that, whatever the cause, it is unjustified morally. By what standard of morality can the violence used by a slave to break his chains be considered the same as the violence of a slave master? By what standards can we equate the violence of blacks who have been oppressed, suppressed, depressed, and repressed for four centuries with the violence of white fascists? Violence aimed at the recovery of human dignity and at equality cannot be judged by the same yardstick as violence aimed at maintenance of discrimination and oppression.

White Americans would certainly argue the moral and practical necessity of their participation in the First and particularly the Second World War. What is curious is that thousands of black people fought and died in these wars entirely in the interest of the white man. Colonialism is the opposite of freedom and democracy and yet black colonials fought for this against the fascism of Hitler—it was purely in the interests of the white "Mother Countries." Slaves fought for American independence and for the North in the American Civil War. Black, oppressed Americans went in thousands to fight for justice in the world wars, in Korea and in Vietnam. We have fought heroically in the white men's cause. It is time to fight in our own.

Violence in the American situation is inescapable. White society is violent, white American society is particularly violent, and white American society is especially violent towards blacks.

Slavery was founded and maintained by violence, and in the 100 years since the "Emancipation" of slaves in the U.S. the society has continued to do black people violence by denying them any power or influence (except for the occasional individual). Their interests are therefore ignored, so that thousands of black babies die each year because of lack of proper food, shelter, and medicine, while hundreds of thousands are destroyed emotionally and intellectually because of conditions of poverty and discrimination. This is the worst sort of violence, and it is accompanied by many acts of individual violence carried out by white citizens, police, and sheriffs against blacks. Most incidents of rioting in recent years arose spontaneously out of self-defense and out of anger against brutality. When black Americans react to meet force with force this should surprise nobody, because even the most harmless animal will finally turn in desperation against its hunters. It is useful to know that this is the conclusion arrived at not only by Black Power leaders, but also by the official committee of the U.S. Senate which was appointed to investigate the racial situation.

Apart from local violent protest (riots), U.S. society faces the possibility of large-scale racial war. The book *Black Power,* written by Stokely Carmichael and Charles Hamilton (and now banned by "White Power" Jamaican government), stresses that its aim was to present an opportunity to work out the racial question without resort to force, but if that opportunity was missed the society was moving towards destructive racial war.[1] In such a war, black people would undoubtedly suffer because of their minority position, but as an organized group they could wreck untold damage on the whites. The white racists and warmongers cannot drop their bombs on black people *within the U.S.A.,* and whatever damage is done to property means damage to white property. We have nothing to lose for they are the capitalists. Black people could not hope to, nor do they want to, dominate the whites, but large sections of the black youth realize that they cannot shrink from fighting to demonstrate the hard way that a ten percent minority of 22 million cannot be treated as though they did not exist. Already the limited violence of the past few years has caused more notice to be taken of the legitimate social, economic, political, and cultural demands of black people than has been the case for the previous one hundred years. The goal is still a long way off, for it is not only in a crisis that the blacks must be considered. When decisions are taken in the normal day-to-day life of the U.S.A., the interests of the blacks must be taken into account *out of respect for their power*—power that can be used destructively if it is not allowed to express itself constructively. This is what Black Power means in the particular conditions of the U.S.A.

[1]Stokely Carmichael and Charles V. Hamilton, *Black Power: The Politics of Liberation in America* (New York: Vintage, 1967).

MERLE HODGE (1944–   )

✿ The Shadow of the Whip: A Comment on Male-Female Relations in the Caribbean (1972)

The man-woman relationship is nowhere a straightforward, uncomplicated one—it is always perhaps the most vulnerable, the most brittle of human relationships. And in the Caribbean this relationship has been adversely affected by certain factors of our historical development, notably, I think, by the legacy of violence and disruption with which our society has never adequately come to terms.

Caribbean society was born out of brutality, destructiveness, rape; the destruction of the Amerindian peoples, the assault on Africa, the forced uprooting and enslavement of the African; the gun, the whip, the authority of force. Yet the Caribbean area today is not particularly noted for any large-scale, organized violence. Caribbean governments sit securely and complacently, with or without popular support.

But the violence of our history has not evaporated. It is still there. It is there in the relations between adult and child, between black and white, between man and woman. It has been internalized, it has seeped down into our personal lives. Drastic brutality—physical and verbal—upon children is an accepted part of child-rearing in the Caribbean. "Gavin," threatens Laura of *Miguel Street* to one of her children, "Gavin, if you don't come here this minute, I make you fart fire, you hear." And C. L. R. James in his novel *Minty Alley* describes a hair-raising scene of violence upon a child which contains not an inch of exaggeration.[1]

Our capacity for verbal violence is limitless. Teasing and heckling are taken to lengths which would shock in another society. For example, we award nicknames on the basis of hopeless physical deformities—"Hop-and-Drop," for example, for a polio victim who walks with a pathetic limp. Our expres-

Reprinted from *Is Massa Day Dead?*, edited by Orde Coombs (Garden City: Anchor, 1974), 177–81. © 1974 by Doubleday, a division of Bantam Doubleday Dell Publishing Group, Inc. Used by permission of Doubleday.

sions of abuse would fill catalogs. Quarreling is a national pastime—quarrels are spectacular: a great deal of energy and artistry are applied to body movements, the ingenuity of insults, the graphic recitation of the antagonist's crimes; a good quarrel will provide a morning's dramatic diversion for a whole neighborhood, for quarrels often emerge onto the street as if in search of an adequate stage.

And the fact that a physical fight between a man and a woman—or more accurately, a woman-beating—may erupt into the open air and rage for hours without any serious alarm on the part of onlookers for the safety of the woman, without attracting the intervention of the law, is a strong comment on our attitudes: "Never never put yu mouth / In husband-and-wife business," runs the refrain of one calypso, a word of warning to the sentimental, to those who may be naive enough to think that a woman minds being beaten by her man. It is the message of many a calypso. Another song recounts with mock disapproval a public "licking." The thinly veiled sexual imagery is a stock device of calypso, but here it illustrates effectively the idea of violence being part and parcel of the normal relations between man and woman: a policemen who would intervene is rebuffed by none other than the "victim" of the licking:

> Constable have a care
> This is my man licking me here
> And if he feel to lick me
> He could lick me,
> Dammit, don't interfere.

Of course, calypsonians are mainly men, and men are largely responsible for perpetuating the myth of women thriving on violence from their men:

> Every now and then cuff them down,
> They'll love you long and they'll love you strong.
> Black-up their eye
> Bruise-up their knee
> And they will love you eternally.

The idea is not far removed from the maxim coined in the era of slavery: "*Battre un nègre, c'est le nourrir*"—a beating is food to a nigger.

But of course, violence in its narrowest definition, namely, physical violence, is only a visible manifestation of a wider disruption, a basic breakdown of respect. For violence to women includes the whole range of mental cruelty which is part and parcel of women's experience in the Caribbean.

Every now and then our attention is drawn to this existing situation when a woman, known to her neighbors as a devoted, hard-working, self-sacrificing mother, of no particular wickedness, appears trembling and speechless before a judge for having killed her man.

And the familiar, almost humdrum details roll out again—a history of intolerable ill-treatment by the man both upon her and upon her children: neglect, desertion, humiliation, tyranny, unreasonableness, lack of consideration . . . the last straw falls and the woman runs at him with a kitchen knife.

It would seem that the precedents of this case stretch far enough back into our history to have entered our folklore—there is the folk song about Betsy Thomas, who killed her husband stone cold dead in the market and had no doubt that she would be absolved of crime: "I ain't kill nobody but me husband." In fact, our society implicitly acknowledges the permanent situation out of which husband killings arise, in the leniency the court generally affords to a woman who has been driven to this act. Of course, killing your man is an extreme measure, but, again, it is a crisis which is but the visible tip of the iceberg or, to bring our imagery home, the eruption of a volcano that all along has been silently cooking.

The black man in the role of dispenser of violence is very likely a descendant of the white slave-overseer asserting an almost bottomless authority over the whipped. But there is one fundamental difference, for whereas the overseer beat and tortured his victim because he had power over him, the black man ill-treating his woman is expressing his desire for power, is betraying a dire insecurity vis-à-vis the female.

In the Caribbean the "war of the sexes" takes on a very special character. It is not a straight fight between handicapped woman on the one hand and omnipotent man on the other. From the very beginning of West Indian history the black woman has had a de facto "equality" thrust upon her—the equality of cattle in a herd. We became "equal" from the moment African men and women were bundled together onto galleys, men and women clamped to the floor alongside each other for the horrifying middle passage. A slave was a slave—male or female—a head of livestock, a unit of the power that drove the plantation. The women worked equally hard out in the fields with the men, were equally subject to torture and brutality. The black woman in the Caribbean has never been a delicate flower locked away in a glass case and "protected" from responsibility. Of course, the African woman in Africa is no delicate flower either, wielding a tremendous physical force in her daily chores of pounding, planting, etc., all the while carrying around her latest child upon her back.

From the very beginning of our history on this side of the Atlantic, woman has been mobilized in the society's work force. But there was, of course, some division of labor or functions, and this is where the male-female trouble began.

In the first place, the whole humiliation of slavery meant an utter devaluation of the manhood of the race; the male was powerless to carry out his traditional role of protector of the tribe, he was unable to defend either himself or his women and children from capture and transportation, from daily mishandling. His manhood was reduced to his brawn for the labor he could do for his master and to his reproductive function.

And the function of fatherhood was limited to fertilizing the female. Gone was the status of head of the family, for there was no family, no living in a unit with wife and children. A man might not even know who his children were, and at any rate they did not belong to him in any sense; he was unable to provide for them—their owner performed the function of provider. The black man had no authority over his children, but the woman did. The children's mothers, or female child-rearers, were responsible for the upbringing of the race. Women became mother and father to the race.

And it is this concentration of moral authority in the person of the woman that has influenced relations between men and women of African descent in the Caribbean. For today the average Afro-West Indian is still reared more or less singlehandedly by a mother, or aunt, or big sister, or godmother—the men have still not returned to the functions of fatherhood. Fathers are either physically absent—the prevalent pattern of concubinage and male mobility results in a man not necessarily staying put in one household until the children he has deposited there have grown up—or, even when the father is present in the home, his part in the bringing up of the children is a limited one. His role is not clearly defined and not binding. One of the roles he may play is that of punisher, administering beatings at the request of the mother; but the strongest influence in the home is usually female.

The society may be called a matriarchal one—many of our ancestors were in fact brought from West African societies which were matriarchal in structure, although there this by no means implied an abdication of responsibility on the part of the males. But this meant that our women had precedents of matriarchy upon which to draw in the new situation of male defection.

The Caribbean, and indeed black America on the whole, has produced the new black matriarch, the strong female figure who is responsible not only for the propagation of the race but by whose strength our humanity has been preserved.

Most Afro-West Indians have grown up "fatherless" in one way or another; most have been reared under almost exclusive female influence. So in the society moral authority is female, an authority that may sometimes be harsh and driven to extremes by the situation of stress in which a Caribbean mother often finds herself—often ill-feeling against a deserting man is vented upon the children he has left in her lap.

Caribbean writing teems with the strong woman type. Many of Samuel Selvon's immigrants are our feckless, happy-go-lucky men now and then marshaled into responsibility by brisk, matter-of-fact women. The female figures of James's *Minty Alley:* the dignified, almost statuesque Mrs. Rouse;

Maisie the wraith, invincible in any situation. The women of *Miguel Street*, bawling out, battering (as well as being battered by) or working to support their unstable men. And I have discovered that my own book, *Crick Crack, Monkey*, is full of strong woman figures and that men are, like Auntie Beatrice's husband, "either absent or unnoticeable"—even the heroine's succession of "uncles" do not constitute any solid presence.[2] And I had once intended to give the children a grandfather—Ma's husband—but I had conceived of him as an invalid in a rocking chair, ably looked after by Ma!

Caribbean woman has developed a strong moral fiber to compensate for the weakening of the male. Hence the desire of the man to do her down, to put her in her place, to safeguard his manhood threatened by the authority of the female upstart.

The black man in the Caribbean is capable of deep respect for his mother and for older women in general. The worst insult in our language is to curse a man's mother. An "obscenity" flung in the heat of quarrel is, quite simply, "Yu mother!" Authority is female; a man will have instinctive qualms about disrespecting his mother or, by extension, her contemporaries, but he will take his revenge on the black female by seeking to degrade women within reach of his disrespect.

Young men at a loose end (usually unemployed—the devaluation of black manhood is perpetuated in economic frustration) will position themselves on a culvert, at a street corner, on a pavement, and vie with each other in the ingenuity of their comments to embarrass women going by. The embarrassment of woman is part of the national ethos, stemming, I am convinced, from a deep-seated resentment against the strength of women.

In Trinidad the calypsonian, the folk poet, is assured of heartfelt, howling approval when he devotes his talent to the degradation of woman:

> Clarabelle,
> She could chase the Devil from Hell
> With the kind of way she does smell
> Anytime she pass yu could tell.

Our folk poet is rarely given to flattering and extolling the qualities of womanhood—woman and her sexual attributes are almost only a stock dirty joke in his repertoire. And the calypsonian mirrors collective attitudes—he is the product of his society and sings to please his audience.

There has, however, been one major development in our contemporary history which promises to have a salutary effect upon relations between black men and women in the Caribbean. This is the advent of black power ideology.

An important element of the history of male-female relations in the Caribbean has been the imposition of European standards of physical beauty—the tendency of the man to measure the desirability of women by these standards, and the corresponding struggle of black women to alter their appearance as far as possible in the direction of European requirements for beauty but of course still falling short of these requirements. A large part of male disrespect for the black woman was an expression of his dissatisfaction with her, "inferior" as she was to the accepted white ideal of womanhood.

This bred a great deal of destructive dishonesty, a canker eating away at the roots of our self-respect. For these attitudes were especially destructive as they were to a large extent disavowed or even entirely subconscious. A man would vehemently deny that he could be the victim of this mesmerism. His cousin, yes, damn fool who went to England to study and could find nothing else to get married to but a white woman—but *he* would never be found putting milk in his coffee, unthinkable, *he* had a healthy attitude toward these white people.

It was indeed a difficult burden to bear—his very deep-seated resentment of whitedom and this hopeless involvement with them.

Today's ideology has begun to liberate us from this particular dishonesty. It has forced into the open, and at a popular level (a success not achieved by the literary movements of the first half of the century), the discussion of our polarization toward whiteness, and it has effectively set about revising our concepts of physical beauty. The progressive abolition of hair-straightening in the Caribbean is a momentous revolution. It is part of the revaluation of the black woman.

And the revaluation of black womanhood inevitably also implies a restoration of black manhood, when the black man no longer forcibly evaluates his women by the standards of a man who once held the whip hand over him. It is one stage of his liberation from the whip hand.

And it is only when our lives cease to be governed by the shadow of the whip that we can begin to heal the grave disruption of relations between men and women that we have suffered in the Caribbean.

[1] V. S. Naipaul, *Miguel Street* (Harmondsworth: Penguin, 1959) and C. L. R. James, *Minty Alley*, introduction by Kenneth Ramchand (London: New Beacon, 1971).

[2] Merle Hodge, *Crick Crack, Monkey*, introduction by Roy Narinesingh (London: Heinemann, 1981).

N O R T H   A M E R I C A

The black experience in North America shares important historical roots with that in the Caribbean: in both regions, slavery assaulted the black community while reinforcing the need for this community, and strategies of dehumanization were integral to the dominant group's maintenance of its domination. Thus, as in the Caribbean, black philosophy in North America— at least that North American tradition we highlight here—works with the generative themes of the African philosophical tradition in ways that stress the importance of community in preserving and refiguring identity. However, where Caribbean philosophy announces itself as a fundamental player in the struggle for decolonization, black philosophy in North America situates itself more typically on the side of radical reform of the social, political, and economic institutions of the United States. Given the enormous power of the nation, both international and internal, dehumanizing assaults on African-American identity have tended to go hand in hand with attempts to socialize blacks into various forms of assimilation to majority cultural expectations. One result of this is that the relational humanism so characteristic of Africa and the Caribbean is inflected in a somewhat more individualistic direction in the United States, bringing African-American thought closer to the majority norm of American individualism. One important consequence of this is that black philosophy in the United States attains a high degree of visibility by the middle of the nineteenth century, as free blacks begin to articulate a philosophical critique of American slavery, paving the way for later reformist programs of various sorts.

Frederick Douglass, perhaps best known for his slavery autobiographies and for his deep commitment to abolitionism, opens our selection of texts with a stinging indictment of the absence of community between blacks and whites in the America of the 1850s. Speaking to a largely white audience, Douglass argues that the Fourth of July "is *yours*, not *mine*," but he goes on to make a powerful case for the possibility of a truly integrated community in the United States. He does this, in part, by appealing to the principles which guided the country's founders, suggesting that—despite their own commitment to slavery and other systems of oppression—the founders developed the framework for a genuine political community. Douglass goes on to stress that Christianity too carries within it principles for the nurturing of a nonoppressive community, and he closes by urging Americans to live up to the high ideals of their political and religious heritage.

Alexander Crummell, born free and educated formally, focuses his attention on the rupture of community between African Americans and Africans. Addressing blacks in the United States, Crummell argues (with more than a little paternalism) that they have a moral and spiritual duty to return to Africa to civilize and Christianize their kin, while engaging in commerce for the benefit of both Africans and African Americans. Crummell's special emphasis here is on the ways in which the bonds of kinship ground this duty, and he argues that the act of restoring community is essentially an act of self-determination. The Pan-Africanist thrust of Crummell's argument issues in a vision of the future in which the high civilization of a new, Christianized Africa will effectively call into question all racist accounts of differences of color.

Anna Julia Cooper, a free, educated, and middle-class black woman, turns her attention back to the plight of African Americans, arguing that a precondition for genuine interracial community is that black women be accorded basic rights. Herself apparently affected by the contumely regarding Africa described by (and appropriated by) Crummell, Cooper argues for social regeneration in much the way that Crummell argues for racial redemption. Although one might read her analysis as relegating black women to the home, Cooper clearly goes beyond this to stress the centrality of strong families to the progress of the race.

In his address to the Atlanta Exposition, Booker T. Washington—himself born into slavery—argues that the key to the health of the Southern community, both black and white, depends on respect for the dignity of work. It is productive work that will forge a new interracial community in the South, a community based on mutual economic progress. At the same time, Washington suggests that whites recognize that blacks have always been a major part of the life of the South and that the loyalty of African Americans to their slave masters in the past reflects the deep interest in community shared by blacks across the South. In this respect, at least, Washington seems to anticipate a future in which the interracial community will be grounded in mutual respect and inclusive civil rights.

The work of W. E. B. Du Bois marks the crucial transition from the nineteenth century to the twentieth century in African-American thought, and in the course of his remarkable eighty-year career Du Bois made innumerable contributions to a variety of key subjects. Our three selections from his vast body of writings highlight ways in which Du Bois's views about race, in particular, open up broad issues of identity and community and point the way towards a full articulation of a relational humanism with recognizably African foundations. Early in his philosophical development—in an oft-reprinted essay, "The Conservation of Races"—Du Bois had defended an essentialist position that each different race had a distinctive essence, the preservation of which was necessary to world civilization. However, in the essays included here, we see Du Bois developing a critique of precisely such an essentialism, arguing instead that race is fundamentally a social construction, but a social construction with horribly real implications for those individuals designated by the categories of race. While Du Bois would go on in the final decades of his life to emphasize class analysis more strongly—both intraracial and interracial—the suggestions about the meaning and meanness of race found in these texts from Du Bois's middle period raise issues constantly negotiated and reexamined by later twentieth century African-American philosophers.

In "Does Race Antipathy Serve Any Good Purpose?" Du Bois emphasizes that "race is a vague, unknown term," and he devotes most of his essay to accounting for the persistence of racism and to deconstructing the rationalizations used to support racist ideas and policies. At bottom, his position here is that the concept of race is used to divide the single species of humanity and to justify unjust and inhumane treatment that cannot be defended in any other way.

In his essay "On Being Ashamed of Oneself"—written nearly twenty years later—Du Bois turns to issues of race pride and race suicide, stressing that there are enormous dangers at the heart of black people's uncritical assimilation to ideals of the dominant culture. In particular, the possibility of black community is shattered by the intraracial class divisions furthered by the norms of white American society. These class divisions, Du Bois argues, lead to shame or fear of being identified as black, and this shame in turn undermines the possibility of larger communities, both intraracial and interracial. The solution to these problems lies, Du Bois insists, in group action by which blacks of different class and national backgrounds come together to work for the material, political, and social betterment of all black people.

In the excerpt included here from his fairly late autobiography, *Dusk of Dawn*, Du Bois details the white representations of race he encountered in his early years and elaborates the ways in which learning the connections between race, economics, status, and culture led to his feeling an authentic part of the black community. Social heritage thus becomes the basis of racial kinship, and Du Bois goes on to explore ways of reclaiming an essentially African tradition of community and identity within community, seeing in this tradition humankind's finest hope for social well-being.

In his preface to the influential anthology *The New Negro*, Alain Locke situates the intellectual and artistic flowering of the Harlem Renaissance at the threshold of "medieval" and "modern" America, arguing that the Harlem of the 1920s and 1930s is paving the way for "a new democracy." This growth of a new democracy is itself grounded in a new psychology, according to Locke, one in which the bond among blacks in the U.S. is recognized to be a "common consciousness" rather than a "common condition." It is in the arts that this common consciousness is most fully expressed, and Locke sees the Harlem Renaissance as the fundamental force behind the growing sense of Pan-Africanism that will ultimately transform the condition and status of black people throughout the world.

From the Harlem Renaissance our selections jump to the 1960s with the work of Malcolm X, Martin Luther King, Jr., and Angela Davis, three of the most significant black voices in philosophy to speak up in the first twenty-five years following the 1954 Supreme Court decision in the case of Brown v. Board of Education of Topeka. During this period, at least five distinct intellectual and social movements complicated the question of community in black America: the civil rights movement, Black Power, Pan-Africanism, feminism, and socialism. The civil rights movement brought new emphasis on and hope for a genuine interracial community, while Black Power was in significant part a response to white resistance to that notion of community. The resurgence of Pan-Africanism in the wake of drives for national independence in the Africa of the 1960s represented not only a logical extension of the Black Power strategy but a newly concrete form of identification for black Americans with the struggles of African blacks. Finally, black feminism emerged in part as a critique of patriarchal structures in the civil rights movement, Black Power, and Pan-Africanism, while the turn to socialism was largely a critique of the procapitalist sympathies of the other four movements.

In Malcolm X's "Speech on 'Black Revolution,'" delivered to a predominantly white audience in 1964, he sketches the basis of the Black Power movement. Arguing that African Americans are victims of internal colonialism, Malcolm X proposes that black nationalism is a natural response to this colonialism in order to effect positive change. He calls on the black community to shift its emphasis from civil rights to human rights, but he goes beyond this to stress the need for black people to come together politically, economically, and psychologically so as to reclaim their own destiny. Malcolm X's vision of community, however, is not limited to blacks or other people of color. Despite the complicity of white liberals in the dehumanization of blacks, he suggests that a bloodless revolution is still possible if structures of black political and economic power are developed and nurtured.

Indeed, Malcolm X argues that it is ultimately in the interest of whites to foster such a community, given the shifting balance of power away from Europeans at the international level.

Throughout the speeches, sermons, and writings of Martin Luther King, Jr., we see him revising but never abandoning his fundamental belief in the moral rightness and imperative of "the beloved community" of all humankind. In the excerpt included here from King's last book, he addresses the complexities of the relationship between Black Power and community. From his perspective, the call for Black Power stems from an historical and contemporary absence of authentic interracial community in the United States. It is a strong reaction to the insistence on white privilege and the white devaluation of black life. King argues that the failure of white power and conscience has been the major factor leading to black economic and political powerlessness and thus to various assaults on the black psyche. From this it follows that Black Power is necessary to economic security, political influence, and psychological health within the black community. King spells out his vision of Black Power by insisting that black self-help must be encouraged in grappling with poverty, that limited political action must be combined with activity at the level of larger coalitions to increase political strength, and that assertive selfhood must replace the shame spawned by the cultural genocide of United States history. Nonetheless, King remains skeptical about what appear to be the nihilism, violence, and separatism inherent in the Black Power movement. Although he understands the sources of despair that eventuate in nihilism and recognizes the suspicion generated by betrayals of coalition, King sees no way for blacks to develop a viable future based on these negative principles.

Angela Davis—an icon of late 1960s black socialist feminism—emphasizes in her 1987 article the importance of empowering the community of the dispossessed. Hearkening back to the vision of the late nineteenth century black women's club movement with its motto of "lifting as we climb," Davis criticizes the white women's movement for its racism and classism. Arguing that the roots of sexism and other forms of oppression are to be found in the same economic and political institutions responsible for racism, Davis insists that the agenda for women's empowerment must challenge monopoly capitalism. The long-range goal, for Davis, is the transformation of the socioeconomic conditions consequent to capitalism by means of socialism.

The concluding selections bring us to the late 1980s and early 1990s, where leading black philosophers continually struggle to make sense of what they see as the worsening conditions of black America, twenty-five years after the apparent triumphs of the civil rights movement. Often these thinkers focus on the role of philosophy as an academic discipline in the critique and restructuring of contemporary society, and again we see a number of variations on the general theme of relational humanism.

Lucius Outlaw's essay explores relationships between philosophical discourse and race and ethnicity; he suggests that considerations of race and ethnicity play a critical role at this historical moment in the revisioning of possibilities for the flourishing of both self and community. Outlaw argues that the depriviteging of such considerations by most European philosophers reflects the racism, sexism, and class bias inherent in the enterprise of philosophy. He insists that philosophy itself must be reevaluated so as to identify these biases, expand the "universals" of philosophy to include the formerly excluded, and allow space within the discipline to properly appreciate group-based particularities. Such a renewed valorization of racial and ethnic diversity would enable us, Outlaw argues, to draw on each other's cultural strengths and thereby discover new bases for democratic practices.

In important ways, bell hooks's essay echoes and extends the central argument made by Davis: sexism is interlocked with racism and classism, and thus feminism must work to free all who want to be free of white male privilege and sexism. Moreover, hooks stresses that women must begin by focusing on their own social identity and recognizing the ways in which women—although dominated in general by men—are also quite capable of dominating others in turn. The feminist revolution that hooks projects is one of women as subjects loving themselves while men come to understand and love their own masculinity enough to resist the diverse modes by which masculinity can promote dehumanization.

Molefi Kete Asante—the leading advocate of Afrocentrism—explicitly posits self-love as a necessary dimension of the opposition to dehumanization. He focuses on education as the pivotal institutional agent in effecting the dehumanization of black people in the United States, and thus he stresses that reflection on modes of education is central to the development of a black critical consciousness. Arguing that self-identity is essentially a matter of cultural identity, Asante emphasizes the linkages between individual mental health and that of the community, noting ways in which educational institutions can promote each sort of mental health.

In both selections included here from the work of Cornel West, issues of racial identity and community are framed within a concern for the role of intellectual discourse and the academic disciplines in the struggle for a better world. In "Learning to Talk of Race," West argues that public discourse about race in the United States contributes to the conservation of racist systems of oppression. Thus the common assumption that blacks constitute a "problem" in the United States—a problem that might be handled in either politically liberal or conservative ways—both reinscribes the traditional hierarchy of domination between blacks and whites and effectively shifts the focus of attention away from fundamental moral and spiritual flaws in American society. West goes on to show how an authentic multiracial community is possible only by means of a transformation of values away from the "hedonistic self-indulgence and narcissistic self-regard" that characterize America's market-oriented society.

Similar themes appear in "The Black Underclass and Black Philosophers," a talk given to a meeting of black philosophers. Here West explicitly faces the question of the relevance of philosophy as a discipline to the plight of the black underclass. Extending the argument of his first essay, West details ways in which the commodification at the basis of American society has directly and effectively destroyed what was once a relatively harmonious black community. Issues of class and gender divide black people, and the culture of consumption has led to an unparallelled level of black self-destruction. The task that black intellectuals face, according to West, is that of building new institutions and ultimately a new community that might begin to call into question the assumptions, values, and practices of the dominant society. To do this, he argues, black philosophers must never lose sight in their work of their origins.

Leonard Harris brings our anthology to a close with a stinging indictment of postmodernism's social and political implications. While this general move is fairly common in other critiques of postmodernism, Harris's argument is notable in showing how the logic internal to postmodernism paradoxically rearticulates a vision of the present as a kind of utopia, thus effectively marginalizing both human suffering and coherent resistance to that suffering. Crucial to Harris's critique is the idea that postmodern attempts to rethink the human subject in a decentered way collapse notions of composite self-identity, notions of how human beings constitute themselves and are constituted by the (multiple) communities within which they live and work. In destroying the possibility for an identity rooted in community, postmodern theorists, according to Harris, decisively undermine the possibility of authentic moral agency.

The texts of these fourteen African-American thinkers, then, offer a variety of suggestions for the reform of social, economic, and political institutions in the United States. Common to all is the claim—which we have seen to have clear roots in ancient African thought—that human community is indispensable for the sustenance of human selves. Community depends upon values that go beyond the consumerist value of personal satisfaction; in this respect each of these thinkers subscribes to a relational view of the human condition. It is this view of the human condition—what we have termed "relational humanism" and have seen articulated in philosophical texts from Africa and the Caribbean as well as from North America—that provides the basis for these philosophers to construct new visions of American society. And it is these diverse visions of what Martin Luther King, Jr., called "the beloved community" that give a new and specifically American content to the African tradition that "I am because we are."

FREDERICK DOUGLASS (1817–1895)

🏵 Oration, Delivered in Corinthian Hall, Rochester, July 5, 1852

Mr. President, Friends, and Fellow Citizens:

He who could address this audience without a quailing sensation has stronger nerves than I have. I do not remember ever to have appeared as a speaker before any assembly more shrinkingly, nor with greater distrust of my ability, than I do this day. A feeling has crept over me, quite unfavorable to the exercise of my limited powers of speech. The task before me is one which requires much previous thought and study for its proper performance. I know that apologies of this sort are generally considered flat and unmeaning. I trust, however, that mine will not be so considered. Should I seem at ease, my appearance would much misrepresent me. The little experience I have had in addressing public meetings, in country school houses, avails me nothing on the present occasion.

The papers and placards say that I am to deliver a Fourth July oration. This certainly sounds large and out of the common way for me. It is true that I have often had the privilege to speak in this beautiful hall, and to address many who now honor me with their presence. But neither their familiar faces nor the perfect gauge I think I have of Corinthian Hall seems to free me from embarrassment.

That fact is, ladies and gentlemen, the distance between this platform and the slave plantation from which I escaped is considerable—and the difficulties to be overcome in getting from the latter to the former are by no means slight. That I am here today, is, to me, a matter of astonishment as well as of gratitude. You will not, therefore, be surprised if in what I have to say I evince no elaborate preparation, nor grace my speech with any high-sounding exordium. With little experience and with less learning, I have been able to throw my thoughts hastily and imperfectly together; and trusting to your patient and generous indulgence, I will proceed to lay them before you.

Reprinted from Frederick Douglass, *Oration, Delivered in Corinthian Hall, Rochester, July 5th, 1852* (Rochester: Lee, Mann, 1852).

This, for the purpose of this celebration, is the Fourth of July. It is the birthday of your national independence and of your political freedom. This, to you, is what the Passover was to the emancipated people of God. It carries your minds back to the day and the act of your great deliverance, and to the signs and to the wonders associated with that act and that day. This celebration also marks the beginning of another year of your national life and reminds you that the Republic of America is now seventy-six years old. I am glad, fellow citizens, that your nation is so young. Seventy-six years, though a good old age for a man, is but a mere speck in the life of a nation. Three score years and ten is the allotted time for individual men; but nations number their years by thousands. According to this fact, you are even now only in the beginning of your national career, still lingering in the period of childhood. I repeat, I am glad this is so. There is hope in the thought, and hope is much needed, under the dark clouds which lower above the horizon. The eye of the reformer is met with angry flashes, portending disastrous times; but his heart may well beat lighter at the thought that America is young, and that she is still in the impressible stage of her existence. May he not hope that high lessons of wisdom, of justice, and of truth will yet give direction to her destiny? Were the nation older, the patriot's heart might be sadder, and the reformer's brow heavier. Its future might be shrouded in gloom, and the hope of its prophets go out in sorrow. There is consolation in the thought that America is young. Great streams are not easily turned from channels, worn deep in the course of ages. They may sometimes rise in quiet and stately majesty and inundate the land, refreshing and fertilizing the earth with their mysterious properties. They may also rise in wrath and fury, and bear away, on their angry waves, the accumulated wealth of years of toil and hardship. They, however, gradually flow back to the same old channel, and flow on as serenely as ever. But while the river may not be turned aside, it may dry up, and leave nothing behind but the withered branch and the unsightly rock to howl in the abyss-sweeping wind the sad tale of departed glory. As with rivers, so with nations.

Fellow citizens, I shall not presume to dwell at length on the associations that cluster about this day. The simple story of it is that, seventy-six years ago, the people of this country were British subjects. The style and title of your "sovereign people" (in which you now glory) was not then born. You were under the British Crown. Your fathers esteemed the English government as the home government, and England as the fatherland. This home government, you know, although a considerable distance from your home, did, in the exercise of its parental prerogatives, impose upon its colonial children such restraints, burdens, and limitations as, in its mature judgment, it deemed wise, right, and proper.

But your fathers, who had not adopted the fashionable idea of this day of the infallibility of government and the absolute character of its acts, presumed to differ from the home government in respect to the wisdom and the justice of some of those burdens and restraints. They went so far in their excitement as to pronounce the measures of government unjust, unreasonable, and oppressive, and altogether such as ought not to be quietly submitted to. I scarcely need say, fellow citizens, that my opinion of those measures fully accords with that of your fathers. Such a declaration of agreement on my part would not be worth much to anybody. It would certainly prove nothing as to what part I might have taken, had I lived during the great controversy of 1776. To say *now* that America was right and England wrong is exceedingly easy. Everybody can say it; the dastard, not less than the noble brave, can flippantly discant of the tyranny of England towards the American colonies. It is fashionable to do so; but there was a time when to pronounce against England and in favor of the cause of the colonies tried men's souls. They who did so were accounted in their day plotters of mischief, agitators and rebels, dangerous men. To side with the right, against the wrong, with the weak against the strong, and with the oppressed against the oppressor! *here* lies the merit, and the one which, of all others, seems unfashionable in our day. The cause of liberty may be stabbed by the men who glory in the deeds of your fathers. But, to proceed.

Feeling themselves harshly and unjustly treated by the home government, your fathers, like men of honesty and men of spirit, earnestly sought redress. They petitioned and remonstrated; they did so in a decorous, respectful, and loyal manner. Their conduct was wholly unexceptionable. This, however, did not answer the purpose. They saw themselves treated with sovereign indifference, coldness and scorn. Yet they persevered. They were not the men to look back.

As the sheet anchor takes a firmer hold, when the ship is tossed by the storm, so did the cause of your fathers grow stronger as it breasted the chilling blasts of kingly displeasure. The greatest and best of British statesmen admitted its justice, and the loftiest eloquence of the British Senate came to its support. But with the blindness which seems to be the unvarying characteristic of tyrants since Pharaoh and his hosts were drowned in the Red Sea, the British government persisted in the exactions complained of.

The madness of this course, we believe, is admitted now, even by England; but we fear the lesson is wholly lost on our present rulers.

Oppression makes a wise man mad. Your fathers were wise men, and if they did not go mad, they became restive under this treatment. They felt themselves the victims of grievous wrongs, wholly incurable in their colonial capacity. With brave men there is always a remedy for oppression. Just here, the idea of a total separation of the colonies from the crown was born! It was a startling idea, much more so than we at this distance of time regard it. The timid and the prudent (as has been intimated) of that day were of course shocked and alarmed by it.

Such people lived then, had lived before, and will probably ever have a place on this planet; and their course, in respect to any great change (no matter how great the good to be attained, or the wrong to be redressed by it) may be calculated with as much precision as can be the course of the stars. They hate all changes but silver, gold, and copper change! Of this sort of change they are always strongly in favor.

These people were called tories in the days of your fathers; and the appellation probably conveyed the same idea that is meant by a more modern though a somewhat less euphonious term, which we often find in our papers applied to some of our old politicians.

Their opposition to the then-dangerous thought was earnest and powerful; but amid all their terror and affrighted vociferations against it, the alarming and revolutionary idea moved on, and the country with it.

On the second of July, 1776, the old Continental Congress, to the dismay of the lovers of ease and the worshippers of property, clothed that dreadful idea with all the authority of national sanction. They did so in the form of a resolution; and as we seldom hit upon resolutions, drawn up in our day, whose transparency is at all equal to this, it may refresh your minds and help my story if I read it: "Resolved. That these united colonies *are,* and of right, ought to be free and Independent States; that they are absolved from all allegiance to the British Crown; and that all political connection between them and the State of Great Britain *is,* and ought to be, dissolved."

Citizens, your fathers made good that resolution. They succeeded; and today you reap the fruits of their success. The freedom gained is yours; and you, therefore, may properly celebrate this anniversary. The Fourth of July is the first great fact in your nation's history—the very ring-bolt in the chain of your yet undeveloped destiny.

Pride and patriotism, not less than gratitude, prompt you to celebrate and to hold it in perpetual remembrance. I have said that the Declaration of Independence is the *ringbolt* to the chain of your nation's destiny; so indeed I regard it. The principles contained in that instrument are saving principles. Stand by those principles, be true to them on all occasions, in all places, against all foes, and at whatever cost.

From the round top of your ship of state, dark and threatening clouds may be seen. Heavy billows, like mountains in the distance, disclose to the leeward huge forms of flinty rocks! That *bolt* drawn, that *chain* broken, and all is lost. *Cling to this day—cling to it,* and to its principles, with the grasp of a storm-tossed mariner to a spar at midnight.

The coming into being of a nation in any circumstances is an interesting event. But besides general considerations, there were peculiar circumstances which make the advent of this republic an event of special attractiveness.

The whole scene, as I look back to it, was simple, dignified, and sublime.

The population of the country, at the time, stood at the insignificant number of three millions. The country was poor in the munitions of war. The population was weak and scattered, and the country a wilderness unsubdued. There were then no means of concert and combination such as exist now. Neither steam nor lightning had then been reduced to order and discipline. From the Potomac to the Delaware was a journey of many days. Under these and innumerable other disadvantages, your fathers declared for liberty and independence and triumphed.

Fellow citizens, I am not wanting in respect for the fathers of this republic. The signers of the Declaration of Independence were brave men. They were great men, too—great enough to give fame to a great age. It does not often happen to a nation to raise, at one time, such a number of truly great men. The point from which I am compelled to view them is not certainly the most favorable; and yet I cannot contemplate their great deeds with less than admiration. They were statesmen, patriots, and heroes, and for the good they did, and the principles they contended for, I will unite with you to honor their memory.

They loved their country better than their own private interests; and though this is not the highest form of human excellence, all will concede that it is a rare virtue, and that when it is exhibited, it ought to command respect. He who will intelligently lay down his life for his country is a man whom it is not in human nature to despise. Your fathers staked their lives, their fortunes, and their sacred honor on the cause of their country. In their admiration of liberty, they lost sight of all other interests.

They were peace men; but they preferred revolution to peaceful submission to bondage. They were quiet men; but they did not shrink from agitating against oppression. They showed forbearance; but they knew its limits. They believed in order; but not in the order of tyranny. With them, nothing was *settled* that was not right. With them, justice, liberty, and humanity were *final;* not slavery and oppression. You may well cherish the memory of such men. They were great in their day and generation. Their solid manhood stands out the more as we contrast it with these degenerate times.

How circumspect, exact, and proportionate were all their movements! How unlike the politicians of an hour! Their statesmanship looked beyond the passing moment, and stretched away in strength into the distant future. They seized upon eternal principles, and set a glorious example in their defense. Mark them!

Fully appreciating the hardships to be encountered, firmly believing in the right of their cause, honorably inviting the scrutiny of an onlooking world, reverently appealing to heaven to attest their sincerity, soundly comprehending the solemn responsibility they were about to assume, wisely measuring the terrible odds against them, your fathers, the fathers of this republic, did most deliberately, under the inspiration of a glorious patriotism and with a sublime faith in the great principles of justice and freedom, lay deep the cornerstone of the national superstructure, which has risen and still rises in grandeur around you.

Of this fundamental work, this day is the anniversary. Our eyes are met with demonstrations of joyous enthusiasm. Banners and pennants wave exultingly on the breeze. The din of business, too, is hushed. Even mammon seems to have quitted his grasp on this day. The ear-piercing fife and the stirring drum unite their accents with the ascending peal of a thousand church bells. Prayers are made, hymns are sung, and sermons are preached in honor of this day; while the quick martial tramp of a great and multitudinous nation, echoed back by all the hills, valleys, and mountains of a vast continent, bespeak the occasion one of thrilling and universal interest—a nation's jubilee.

Friends and citizens, I need not enter further into the causes which led to this anniversary. Many of you understand them better than I do. You could instruct me in regard to them. That is a branch of knowledge in which you feel, perhaps, a much deeper interest than your speaker. The causes which led to the separation of the colonies from the British crown have never lacked for a tongue. They have all been taught in your common schools, narrated at your firesides, unfolded from your pulpits, and thundered from your legislative halls, and are as familiar to you as household words. They form the staple of your national poetry and eloquence.

I remember also that, as a people, Americans are remarkably familiar with all facts which make in their own favor. This is esteemed by some as a national trait—perhaps a national weakness. It is a fact that whatever makes for the wealth or for the reputation of Americans and can be had *cheap!* will be found by Americans. I shall not be charged with slandering Americans if I say I think the American side of any question may be safely left in American hands.

I leave, therefore, the great deeds of your fathers to other gentlemen whose claim to have been regularly descended will be less likely to be disputed than mine!

The Present

My business, if I have any here today, is with the present. The accepted time with God and his cause is the ever-living now.

> Trust no future, however pleasant,
>   Let the dead past bury its dead;
> Act, act in the living present,
>   Heart within, and God overhead.

We have to do with the past only as we can make it useful to the present and to the future. To all inspiring motives, to noble deeds which can be gained from the past, we are welcome. But now is the time, the important time. Your fathers have lived, died, and have done their work, and have done much of it well. You live and must die, and you must do your work. You have no right to enjoy a child's share in the labor of your fathers, unless your children are to be blest by your labors. You have no right to wear out and waste the hard-earned fame of your fathers to cover your indolence. Sydney Smith tells us that men seldom eulogize the wisdom and virtues of their fathers, but to excuse some folly or wickedness of their own. This truth is not a doubtful one. There are illustrations of it near and remote, ancient and modern. It was fashionable, hundreds of years ago, for the children of Jacob to boast, we have "Abraham to our father," when they had long lost Abraham's faith and spirit. That people contented themselves under the shadow of Abraham's great name, while they repudiated the deeds which made his name great. Need I remind you that a similar thing is being done all over this country today? Need I tell you that the Jews are not the only people who built the tombs of the prophets, and garnished the sepulchres of the righteous? Washington could not die till he had broken the chains of his slaves. Yet his monument is built up by the price of human blood, and the traders in the bodies and souls of men shout—"We have Washington to '*our father.*' "—Alas! that it should be so; yet so it is.

> The evil that men do, lives after them,
> The good is oft' interred with their bones.

Fellow citizens, pardon me, allow me to ask, why am I called upon to speak here today? What have I, or those I represent, to do with your national independence? Are the great principles of political freedom and of natural justice, embodied in that Declaration of Independence, extended to us? and am I, therefore, called upon to bring our humble offering to the national altar, and to confess the benefits and express devout gratitude for the blessings resulting from your independence to us?

Would to God, both for your sakes and ours, that an affirmative answer could be truthfully returned to these questions! Then would my task be light, and my burden easy and delightful. For *who* is there so cold that a nation's sympathy could not warm him? Who so obdurate and dead to the claims of gratitude that would not thankfully acknowledge such priceless benefits? Who so stolid and selfish that would not give his voice to swell the hallelujahs of a nation's jubilee, when the chains of servitude had been torn from his limbs? I am not that man. In a case like that, the dumb might eloquently speak, and the "lame man leap as an hart."

But such is not the state of the case. I say it with a sad sense of the disparity between us. I am not included within the pale of this glorious anniversary! Your high independence only reveals the immeasurable distance between us. The blessings in which you, this day, rejoice, are not enjoyed in common.—The rich inheritance of justice, liberty, prosperity, and independence bequeathed by your fathers is shared by you, not by me. The sunlight that brought life and healing to you has brought stripes and death to me. This Fourth July is *yours*, not *mine. You* may rejoice, *I* must mourn. To drag a man in fetters into the grand illuminated temple of liberty, and call upon him to join you in joyous anthems, were inhuman mockery and sacrilegious irony. Do you mean, citizens, to mock me, by asking me to speak today? If so, there is a parallel to your conduct. And let me warn you that it is dangerous to copy the example of a nation whose crimes, towering up to heaven, were thrown down by the breath of the Almighty, burying that nation in irrecoverable ruin! I can today take up the plaintive lament of a peeled and woe-smitten people!

"By the rivers of Babylon, there we sat down. Yea! we wept when we remembered Zion. We hanged our harps upon the willows in the midst thereof. For there, they that carried us away captive, required of us a song; and they who wasted us required of us mirth, saying, Sing us one of the songs of Zion. How can we sing the Lord's song in a strange land? If I forget thee, O Jerusalem, let my right hand forget her cunning. If I do not remember thee, let my tongue cleave to the roof of my mouth" (Ps. 137: 1–6).

Fellow citizens; above your national, tumultuous joy, I hear the mournful wail of millions! whose chains, heavy and grievous yesterday, are today rendered more intolerable by the jubilee shouts that reach them. If I do forget, if I do not faithfully remember those bleeding children of sorrow this day, "may my right hand forget her cunning, and may my tongue cleave to the roof of my mouth!" To forget them, to pass lightly over their wrongs, and to chime in with the popular theme, would be treason most scandalous and shocking, and would make me a reproach before God and the world. My subject, then, fellow citizens, is AMERICAN SLAVERY. I shall see this day and its popular characteristics from the slave's point of view. Standing there, identified with the American bondman, making his wrongs mine, I do not hesitate to declare with all my soul that the character and conduct of this nation never looked blacker to me than on this Fourth of July! Whether we turn to the declarations of the past or to the professions of the present, the conduct of the nation seems equally hideous and revolting. America is false to the past, false to the present, and solemnly binds herself to be false to the future. Standing with God and the crushed and bleeding slave on this occasion, I will, in the name of humanity which is outraged, in the name of liberty which is fettered, in the name of the constitution and the Bible, which are disregarded and trampled upon, dare to call in question and to denounce, with all the emphasis I can command, everything that serves to perpetuate slavery—the great sin and shame of America! "I will not equivocate; I will not excuse"; I will use the severest language I can command; and yet not one word shall escape me that any man, whose judgment is not blinded by prejudice or who is not at heart a slaveholder, shall not confess to be right and just.

But I fancy I hear some one of my audience say, it is just in this circumstance that you and your brother abolitionists fail to make a favorable impression on the public mind. Would you argue more, and denounce less, would you persuade more, and rebuke less, your cause would be much more likely to succeed. But, I submit, where all is plain there is nothing to be argued. What point in the antislavery creed would you have me argue? On what branch of the subject do the people of this country need light? Must I undertake to prove that the slave is a man? That point is conceded already. Nobody doubts it. The slaveholders themselves acknowledge it in the enactment of laws for their government. They acknowledge it when they punish disobedience on the part of the slave. There are seventy-two crimes in the state of Virginia which if committed by a black man (no matter how ignorant he be) subject him to the punishment of death; while only two of the same crimes will subject a white man to the like punishment.—What is this but the acknowledgement that the slave is a moral, intellectual, and responsible being. The manhood of the slave is conceded. It is admitted in the fact that southern statute books are covered with enactments forbidding, under severe fines and penalties, the teaching of the slave to read or to write.—When you can point to any such laws, in reference to the beasts of the field, then I may consent to argue the manhood of the slave. When the dogs in your streets, when the fowls of the air, when the cattle on your hills, when the fish of the sea, and the reptiles that crawl, shall be unable to distinguish the slave from a brute, *then* will I argue with you that the slave is a man!

For the present, it is enough to affirm the equal manhood of the Negro race. Is it not astonishing that, while we are ploughing, planting, and reaping, using all kinds of mechanical tools, erecting houses, constructing bridges, building ships, working in metals of brass, iron, copper, silver, and gold; that, while we are reading, writing and ciphering, acting as clerks, merchants, and secretaries, having among us lawyers, doctors, ministers, poets, authors, editors, orators, and teachers; that, while we are engaged in all manner of enterprises common to other men, digging gold in California, capturing the whale in the Pacific, feeding sheep and cattle on the hillside, living, moving, acting, thinking, planning, living in families as husbands, wives and children, and, above all, confessing and worshipping the Christian's God, and looking hopefully for life and immortality beyond the grave, we are called upon to prove that we are men!

Would you have me argue that man is entitled to liberty? that he is the rightful owner of his own body? You have already declared it. Must I argue the wrongfulness of slavery? Is that a question for Republicans? Is it to be settled by the rules of logic and argumentation, as a matter beset with great difficulty, involving a doubtful application of the principle of justice, hard to be understood? How should I look today, in the presence of Americans, dividing and subdividing a discourse to show that men have a natural right to freedom? speaking of it relatively, and positively, negatively, and affirmatively. To do so would be to make myself ridiculous, and to offer an insult to your understanding.—There is not a man beneath the canopy of heaven that does not know that slavery is wrong *for him.*

What, am I to argue that it is wrong to make men brutes, to rob them of their liberty, to work them without wages, to keep them ignorant of their relations to their fellow men, to beat them with sticks, to flay their flesh with the lash, to load their limbs with irons, to hunt them with dogs, to sell them at auction, to sunder their families, to knock out their teeth, to burn their flesh, to starve them into obedience and submission to their masters? Must I argue that a system thus marked with blood and stained with pollution is *wrong?* No! I will not. I have better employment for my time and strength than such arguments would imply.

What, then, remains to be argued? Is it that slavery is not divine; that God did not establish it; that our doctors of divinity are mistaken? There is blasphemy in the thought. That which is inhuman cannot be divine! *Who* can reason on such a proposition? They that can, may; I cannot. The time for such argument is past.

At a time like this, scorching irony, not convincing argument, is needed. O! had I the ability, and could I reach the nation's ear, I would today pour out a fiery stream of biting ridicule, blasting reproach, withering sarcasm, and stern rebuke. For it is not light that is needed, but fire; it is not the gentle shower, but thunder. We need the storm, the whirlwind, and the earthquake. The feeling of the nation must be quickened; the conscience of the nation must be roused; the propriety of the nation must be startled; the hypocrisy of the nation must be exposed; and its crimes against God and man must be proclaimed and denounced.

What, to the American slave, is your Fourth of July? I answer; a day that reveals to him, more than all other days in the year, the gross injustice and cruelty to which he is the constant victim. To him, your celebration is a sham; your boasted liberty, an unholy license; your national greatness, swelling vanity; your sounds of rejoicing are empty and heartless; your denunciations of tyrants, brass-fronted impudence; your shouts of liberty and equality, hollow mockery; your prayers and hymns, your sermons and thanksgivings, with all your religious parade and solemnity, are to him mere bombast, fraud, deception, impiety, and hypocrisy—a thin veil to cover up crimes which would disgrace a nation of savages. There is not a nation on the earth guilty of practices more shocking and bloody than are the people of these United States, at this very hour.

Go where you may, search where you will, roam through all the monarchies and despotisms of the old world, travel through South America, search out every abuse, and when you have found the last, lay your facts by the side of the everyday practices of this nation, and you will say with me that, for revolting barbarity and shameless hypocrisy, America reigns without a rival. . . .

Religious Liberty

I take this law [the Fugitive Slave Law] to be one of the grossest infringements of Christian liberty, and if the churches and ministers of our country were not stupidly blind or most wickedly indifferent, they too would so regard it.

At the very moment that they are thanking God for the enjoyment of civil and religious liberty, and for the right to worship God according to the dictates of their own consciences, they are utterly silent in respect to a law which robs religion of its chief significance, and makes it utterly worthless to a world lying in wickedness. Did this law concern the "*mint, anise* and *cummin*"—abridge the right to sing psalms, to partake of the sacrament, or to engage in any of the ceremonies of religion—it would be smitten by the thunder of a thousand pulpits. A general shout would go up from the church, demanding *repeal, repeal, instant repeal!*—And it would go hard with that politician who presumed to solicit the votes of the people without inscribing this motto on his banner. Further, if this demand were not complied with, another Scotland would be added to the history of religious liberty, and the stern old covenanters would be thrown into the shade. A John Knox would be seen at every church door, and heard from every pulpit, and Fillmore would have no more quarter than was shown by Knox to the beautiful but treacherous Queen Mary of Scotland.—The fact that the church of our country (with fractional exceptions) does not esteem the Fugitive Slave Law as a declaration of war against religious liberty implies that that church regards religion simply as a form of worship, an empty ceremony, and *not* a vital principle, requiring active benevolence, justice, love and good will towards man. It esteems sacrifice above mercy; psalm-singing above right doing; solemn meetings above practical righteousness. A worship that can be conducted by persons who refuse to give shelter to the houseless, to give bread to the hungry, clothing to the naked, and who enjoin obedience to a law forbidding these acts of mercy, is a curse, not a blessing to mankind. The Bible addresses all such persons as "scribes, pharisees, hypocrites, who pay tithe of *mint, anise,* and *cummin,* and have omitted the weightier matters of the law, judgment, mercy and faith" (Matt. 23:23).

The Church Responsible

But the church of this country is not only indifferent to the wrongs of the slave, it actually takes sides with the oppressors. It has made itself the bulwark of American slavery, and the shield of American slave-hunters. Many of its most eloquent Divines, who stand as the very lights of the church, have shamelessly given the sanction of religion and the Bible to the whole slave system.—They have taught that man may, properly, be a slave; that the relation of master and slave is ordained of God; that to send back an escaped bondman to his master is clearly the duty of all the followers of the Lord Jesus Christ; and this horrible blasphemy is palmed off upon the world for Christianity.

For my part, I would say, welcome infidelity! welcome atheism! welcome anything! in preference to the gospel, *as preached by those Divines!* They convert the very name of religion into an engine of tyranny and barbarous cruelty, and serve to confirm more infidels, in this age, than all the infidel writings of Thomas Paine, Voltaire, and Bolingbroke put together have done. These ministers make religion a cold and flinty-hearted thing, having neither principles of right action nor bowels of compassion. They strip the love of God of its beauty, and leave the throne of religion a huge, horrible, repulsive form. It is a religion for oppressors, tyrants, man-stealers, and *thugs.* It is not that "*pure and undefiled religion*" which is from above, and which is "*first pure, then peaceable, easy to be entreated,* full of mercy and good fruits, *without partiality, and without hypocrisy.*" But a religion which favors the rich against the poor; which exalts the proud above the humble; which divides mankind into two classes, tyrants and slaves; which says to the man in chains, *stay there;* and to the oppressor, *oppress on;* it is a religion which may be professed and enjoyed by all the robbers and enslavers of mankind; it makes God a respecter of persons, denies his fatherhood of the race, and tramples in the dust the great truth of the brotherhood of man. All this we affirm to be true of the popular church, and the popular worship of our land and nation—a religion, a church, and a worship which, on the authority of inspired wisdom, we pronounce to be an abomination in the sight of God. In the language of Isaiah, the American church might be well addressed. "Bring no more vain oblations; incense is an abomination unto me: the new moons and Sabbaths, the calling of assemblies, I cannot away with; it is iniquity, even the solemn meeting. Your new moons, and your appointed feasts my soul hateth. They are a trouble to me; I am weary to bear them; and when ye spread forth your hands I will hide mine eyes from you. Yea! when ye make many prayers, I will not hear. YOUR HANDS ARE FULL OF BLOOD; cease to do evil, learn to do well; seek judgment; relieve the oppressed; judge for the fatherless; plead for the widow."

The American church is guilty, when viewed in connection with what it is doing to uphold slavery; but it is superlatively guilty when viewed in connection with its ability to abolish slavery.

The sin of which it is guilty is one of omission as well as of commission. Albert Barnes but uttered what the common sense of every man at all observant of the actual state of the case will receive as truth, when he declared that "there is no power out of the church that could sustain slavery an hour, if it were not sustained in it."

Let the religious press, the pulpit, the Sunday school, the conference meeting, the great ecclesiastical, missionary, bible, and tract associations of the land array their immense powers against slavery, and slaveholding; and the whole system of crime and blood would be scattered to the winds, and that they do not do this involves them in the most awful responsibility of which the mind can conceive.

In prosecuting the antislavery enterprise, we have been asked to spare the church, to spare the ministry; but *how*, we ask, could such a thing be done? We are met on the threshold of our efforts for the redemption of the slave, by the church and ministry of the country, in battle arrayed against us; and we are compelled to fight or flee. From *what* quarter, I beg to know, has proceeded a fire so deadly upon our ranks, during the last two years, as from the northern pulpit? As the champions of oppressors, the chosen men of American theology have appeared—men, honored for their so-called piety and their real learning. The LORDS of Buffalo, the SPRINGS of New York, the LATHROPS of Auburn, the COXES and SPENCERS of Brooklyn, the GANNETS and SHARPS of Boston, the DEWEYS of Washington, and other great religious lights of the land have, in utter denial of the authority of *Him* by whom they professed to be called to the ministry, deliberately taught us, against the example of the Hebrews, and against the remonstrance of the Apostles, they teach *that we ought to obey man's law before the law of God.*

My spirit wearies of such blasphemy; and how such men can be supported as the "standing types and representative of Jesus Christ" is a mystery which I leave others to penetrate. In speaking of the American church, however, let it be distinctly understood that I mean the *great mass* of the religious organizations of our land. There are exceptions, and I thank God that there are. Noble men may be found, scattered all over these northern states, of whom Henry Ward Beecher of Brooklyn, Samuel J. May of Syracuse, and my esteemed friend on the platform [Reverend R. R. Raymond] are shining examples; and let me say further that upon these men lies the duty to inspire our ranks with high religious faith and zeal, and to cheer us on in the great mission of the slave's redemption from his chains.

Religion in England and Religion in America

One is struck with the difference between the attitude of the American church towards the antislavery movement and that occupied by the churches in England towards a similar movement in that country. There, the church, true to its mission of ameliorating, elevating, and improving the condition of mankind, came forward promptly, bound up the wounds of the West Indian slave, and restored him to his liberty. There, the question of emancipation was a high religious question. It was demanded in the name of humanity and according to the law of the living God. The Sharps, the Clarksons, the Wilberforces, the Buxtons, the Burchells, and the Knibbs were alike famous for their piety and for their philanthropy. The antislavery movement *there* was not an antichurch movement, for the reason that the church took its full share in prosecuting that movement: and the antislavery movement in this country will cease to be an antichurch movement when the church of this country shall assume a favorable instead of a hostile position towards that movement.

Americans! your republican politics, not less than your republican religion, are flagrantly inconsistent. You boast of your love of liberty, your superior civilization, and your pure Christianity, while the whole political power of the nation (as embodied in the two great political parties) is solemnly pledged to support and perpetuate the enslavement of three millions of your countrymen. You hurl your anathemas at the crowned-headed tyrants of Russia and Austria, and pride yourselves on your democratic institutions, while you yourselves consent to be the mere *tools* and *bodyguards* of the tyrants of Virginia and Carolina. You invite to your shores fugitives of oppression from abroad, honor them with banquets, greet them with ovations, cheer them, toast them, salute them, protect them, and pour out your money to them like water; but the fugitives from your own land you advertise, hunt, arrest, shoot, and kill. You glory in your refinement, and your universal education; yet you maintain a system as barbarous and dreadful as ever stained the character of a nation—a system begun in avarice, supported in pride, and perpetuated in cruelty. You shed tears over fallen Hungary, and make the sad story of her wrongs the theme of your poets, statesmen, and orators, till your gallant sons are ready to fly to arms to vindicate her cause against her oppressors; but, in regard to the ten thousand wrongs of the American slave, you would enforce the strictest silence, and would hail him as an enemy of the nation who dares to make those wrongs the subject of

public discourse! You are all on fire at the mention of lib
Ireland, but are as cold as an iceberg at the thought of libe
of America.—You discourse eloquently on the dignity of l
tain a system which, in its very essence, casts a stigma upo
bare your bosom to the storm of British artillery, to throw o
tax on tea; and yet wring the last hard-earned farthing from t
black laborers of your country. You profess to believe "that, of o
made all nations of men to dwell on the face of all the eartl   ..u nath
commanded all men everywhere to love one another; yet you notoriously
hate (and glory in your hatred) all men whose skins are not colored like your
own. You declare before the world and are understood by the world to declare that you *"hold these truths to be self evident, that all men are created
equal; and are endowed by their Creator with certain inalienable rights; and
that, among these are, life, liberty, and the pursuit of happiness"*; and yet you
hold securely, in a bondage which according to your own Thomas Jefferson
*"is worse than ages of that which your fathers rose in rebellion to oppose," a
seventh part* of the inhabitants of your country.

Fellow citizens! I will not enlarge further on your national inconsistencies.
The existence of slavery in this country brands your republicanism as a
sham, your humanity as a base pretense, and your Christianity as a lie. It
destroys your moral power abroad; it corrupts your politicians at home. It
saps the foundation of religion; it makes your name a hissing, and a byword
to a mocking earth. It is the antagonistic force in your government, the only
thing that seriously disturbs and endangers your *union*. It fetters your progress; it is the enemy of improvement, the deadly foe of education; it fosters
pride; it breeds insolence; it promotes vice; it shelters crime; it is a curse to
the earth that supports it; and yet you cling to it, as if it were the sheet anchor
of all your hopes. Oh! be warned! be warned! a horrible reptile is coiled up in
your nation's bosom; the venomous creature is nursing at the tender breast
of your youthful republic; *for the love of God, tear away,* and fling from you
the hideous monster, and *let the weight of twenty millions crush and destroy
it forever.* . . .

Allow me to say, in conclusion, notwithstanding the dark picture I have
this day presented of the state of the nation, I do not despair of this country.
There are forces in operation which must inevitably work the downfall of
slavery. *"The arm of the Lord is not shortened"* (Isa. 59:1), and the doom of
slavery is certain. I therefore leave off where I began, with *hope*. While drawing encouragement from the Declaration of Independence, the great principles it contains, and the genius of American institutions, my spirit is also
cheered by the obvious tendencies of the age. Nations do not now stand in
the same relation to each other that they did ages ago. No nation can now
shut itself up, from the surrounding world, and trot round in the same old

of its fathers without interference. The time *was* when such could be done. Long-established customs of hurtful character could formerly fence themselves in, and do their evil work with social impunity. Knowledge was then confined and enjoyed by the privileged few, and the multitude walked on in mental darkness. But a change has now come over the affairs of mankind. Walled cities and empires have become unfashionable. The arm of commerce has borne away the gates of the strong city. Intelligence is penetrating the darkest corners of the globe. It makes its pathway over and under the sea, as well as on the earth. Wind, steam, and lightning are its chartered agents. Oceans no longer divide, but link nations together. From Boston to London is now a holiday excursion. Space is comparatively annihilated.— Thoughts expressed on one side of the Atlantic are distinctly heard on the other.

The far off and almost fabulous Pacific rolls in grandeur at our feet. The celestial empire, the mystery of ages, is being solved. The fiat of the Almighty, *Let there be Light,* has not yet spent its force. No abuse, no outrage whether in taste, sport, or avarice, can now hide itself from the all-pervading light. The iron shoe and crippled foot of China must be seen, in contrast with nature. *Africa must rise and put on her yet-unwoven garment. "Ethiopia shall stretch out her hand unto God"* (Ps. 68:31).

ALEXANDER CRUMMELL (1819–1898)

The Relations and Duties of Free Colored Men in America to Africa

A Letter to Charles B. Dunbar, 1861

High School, Mount Vaughan, Cape Palmas, Liberia, 1st September, 1860

My Dear Sir,—It is now many months since I received a letter from you, just as you were about sailing from our shores for your home. In that note you requested me to address you a letter setting forth my views concerning Liberia, suggesting at the same time that such a letter might prove interesting to many of our old friends and schoolmates in New York. I have not forgotten your request, although I have not heretofore complied with it. Though convinced of the need and possible usefulness of such a letter as you asked from me, I have shrunk from a compliance with your request. Not to mention other grounds of reluctance, let me say here that I have felt it a venturesome thing to address four-hundred thousand men; albeit it be indirectly through you. Neither my name, position, nor any personal qualities give me authority thus to do. The only excuse I have is the depth and solemnity of all questions connected with Africa. I see that no one else of our race has done it; perhaps I may be pardoned for assuming so great a task.

I may add here that I address the free colored men of America because I am identified with them, and not because I feel that *they* especially and above all the other sons of Africa in distant lands are called upon for zeal and interest in her behalf. It is the exaggeration of the relation of *American* black men to Africa which has turned the hearts of many of her own children from her. Your duties in this respect are no greater than those of our West Indian, Haitian, and eventually our Brazilian brethren. Whatever in this letter applies to our brethren in the United States applies in an equal degree to them. But I am not the man to address them. I fear I *presume*, even in writing this letter to American black men, and have only just now concluded to do so

Reprinted from Alexander Crummell, *The Future of Africa: Being Addresses, Sermons, etc., Delivered in the Republic of Liberia* (New York: Charles Scribner, 1862).

by the encouragement I have received in two pleasant interviews with Mr. Campbell and Dr. Delany.

And even now it is with doubt and diffidence that I conclude to send you this communication. My reluctancy has arisen chiefly from a consideration of the claim put forth by leading colored men in the United States, to the effect that it is unjust to disturb their residence in the land of their birth, by a continual call to go to Africa. This claim is, in my opinion, a most just one. Three centuries' residence in a country seems clearly to give any people a right to their nationality therein, without disturbance. Our brethren in America have other claims besides this; they have made large contributions to the clearing of their country; they have contributed by sweat and toil to the wealth thereof; and by their prowess and their blood, they have participated in the achievement of its liberties. But their master right lies in the fact that they are Christians; and one will have to find some new page and appendage to the Bible to get the warrant for Christians to repel and expatriate Christians on account of blood, or race, or color. In fact, it seems to me a most serious thing to wantonly trench upon rights thus solemnly and providentially guaranteed a people, that is, by a constant, ceaseless, fretting iteration of a repelling sentiment.

Of course I do not intend anything akin to this in my letter. I need not insult the intellect and conscience of any colored man who thinks it his duty to labor for his race on American soil by telling him that it is his duty to come to Africa. If he is educated up to the ideas of responsibility and obligation, he knows his duty better than I do. And indeed, generally, it is best to leave individuals to themselves as to the *details* of obligation and responsibility.

"The primal duties shine aloft like stars"; and it is only when men *will* not see them, we are bound to repeat and re-utter them, until the souls of men are aroused, and they are moved to moral resolution and to noble actions. But as to the *mode, form,* and *manner* of meeting their duties, let the common sense of every man decide it for himself.

My object in writing this letter is not to vex any of our brethren by the iteration of the falsehood that America is not their home, nor by the misty theory that they will all yet have to come to Liberia. I do not even intend to invite anyone to Liberia; glad as I would be to see around me many of the wise and sterling men I know in the United States, who would be real acquisitions to this nation, and as much as I covet their society, I am not putting in a plea for colonization. My object is quite different; in fact it is not a strict compliance with the terms of your letter, for I shall have but little to say about Liberia. But believing that *all* men hold some relation to the land of their fathers, I wish to call the attention of the sons of Africa in America to their relations and duty to the land of their fathers.

And even on such a theme I know I must prepare myself for the rebuff from many—"Why talk to *us* of fatherland? What have we to do with Africa? We are not Africans; we are Americans. You ask no peculiar interest on the part of Germans, Englishmen, the Scotch, the Irish, the Dutch, in the land of their fathers; why then do you ask it of us?"

Alas for us, as a race! so deeply harmed have we been by oppression that we have lost the force of strong, native principles and prime natural affections. Because exaggerated contempt has been poured upon us, we too become apt pupils in the school of scorn and contumely. Because repudiation of the black man has been for centuries the wont of civilized nations, black men themselves get shame at their origin and shrink from the terms which indicate it.

Sad as this is, it is not to be wondered at. Oppression not only makes a wise man mad, it robs him also of his self-respect. And this is our loss; but having emerged from slavery, it is our duty to cast off its grave-clothes and resist its deadly influences.

Our ancestors were unfortunate, miserable, and benighted; but nothing more. Their history was a history not of ignominy and disgrace but of heathenism and benightedness. And even in that state they exhibited a nobleness of native character, they cherished such virtues and manifested so much manliness and bravery, that the civilized world is now magnanimous enough to recognize such traits; and its greatest men are free to render their warm eulogies.[1]

When these colored men question the duty of interest in Africa because they are not Africans, I beg to remind them of the kindred duty of self-respect. And my reply to such queries as I have mentioned above is this: First, that there is no need of asking the interest of Englishmen, Germans, Dutchmen, and others in the land of their fathers, because they have this interest, and are always proud to cherish it. And second, I remark that the abject state of Africa is a most real and touching appeal to *any* heart for sympathy and aid. It is an appeal, however, which comes with a double force to every civilized man who has Negro blood flowing in his veins.

Africa lies low and is wretched. She is the maimed and crippled arm of humanity. Her great powers are wasted. Dislocation and anguish have reached every joint. Her condition in every point calls for succor: moral, social, domestic, political, commercial, intellectual. Whence shall flow aid, mercy, advantage to her? Here arises the call of duty and obligation to colored men. Other people may, if they choose, forget the homes of their sires; for almost every European nation is now reaping the fruits of a thousand years' civilization. Every one of them can spare thousands and even millions of their sons to build up civilization in Australia, Canada, New Zealand, South Africa, or

Victoria. But Africa is the victim of her heterogeneous idolatries. Africa is wasting away beneath the accretions of civil and moral miseries. Darkness covers the land and gross darkness the people. Great social evils universally prevail. Confidence and security are destroyed. Licentiousness abounds everywhere. Moloch rules and reigns throughout the whole continent; and by the ordeal of Sassy-wood, fetishes, human sacrifices, and devil worship is devouring men, women, and little children. They have not the Gospel. They are living without God. The cross has never met their gaze; and its consolations have never entered their hearts, nor its everlasting truths cheered their deaths.

And all this only epitomizes the miseries of Africa, for it would take a volume to detail and enumerate them. But this is sufficient to convince any son of Africa that the land of our fathers is in great spiritual need, and that those of her sons who haply have ability to aid in her restoration, will show mercy to her, and perform an act of filial love and tenderness which is but their "reasonable service."

I have two objects in view in addressing you this letter: *one* relates to the temporal, material interests of adventurous, enterprising, colored men; and the *other* pertains to the best and most abiding interests of the million masses of heathen on this continent—I mean their evangelization.

First, I am to speak with reference to the temporal and material interests of adventurous, enterprising, and aspiring men in the United States of America. I wish to bring before such persons reasons why they should feel interest in Africa. These reasons are not, I am free to confess, directly and distinctively philanthropic; although I do, indeed, aim at human well-being through their force and influence. But I appeal now more especially to the hopes, desires, ambition, and aspirations of such men. I am referring to that sentiment of self-regard which prompts to noble exertions for support and superiority. I am aiming at that principle of self-love which spurs men on to a self-advantage and self-aggrandizement, a principle which, in its normal state and in its due degree, to use the words of Butler, "is as just and morally good as any affection whatever." In fine, I address myself to all that class of sentiments in the human heart which creates a thirst for wealth, position, honor, and power. I desire the auxiliary aid of this class of persons, and this class of motives, for it is such influences and agencies which are calculated to advance the material growth of Africa. She needs skill, enterprise, energy, *worldly* talent, to raise her; and these applied here to her needs and circumstances will prove the handmaid of religion and will serve the great purposes of civilization and enlightenment through all her borders.

There seems to me to be a natural call upon the children of Africa in foreign lands to come and participate in opening the treasures of the land of their fathers. Though these treasures are the manifest gift of God to the Negro race, yet that race reaps but the most partial measure of their good and advantage. It has always been thus in the past, and now as the resources of Africa are being more and more developed, the extent of *our* interest therein is becoming more and more diminutive. The slave trade is interdicted throughout Christendom; the chief powers of earth have put a lien upon the system of slavery; interest and research in Africa have reached a state of intensity; mystery has been banished from some of her most secret quarters; sunlight, after ages of darkness, has burst in upon the charmed regions of her wealth and value; and yet the negro, on his native soil, is but "a hewer of wood and drawer of water"; and the sons of Africa in foreign lands, inane and blinded, suffer the adventurous foreigner, with greed and glut, to jostle him aside, and to seize, with skill and effect, upon their own rightful inheritance. . . .

And now perhaps you ask, "How shall the children of Africa, sojourning in foreign lands, avail themselves of the treasures of this continent?" I answer briefly, "In the same way white men do." *They* have pointed out the way; let us follow in the same track and in the use of the like (legitimate) agencies by which trade is facilitated and money is made by them.

Perhaps this is too general; let me therefore attempt something more specific and distinctive.

First, then, I remark that if individuals are unable to enter upon a trading system, they can form associations. If *one* has not sufficient capital, four or six united can make a good beginning. If a few persons cannot make the venture, then a company can be formed. It was in this way the first attempts at trading were made by the Dutch and the English, both in India and Africa. A few men associated themselves together, and sent out their agent or agents, and started a factory. And from such humble beginnings, in the seventeenth century, has arisen that magnificent Indian Empire, which has helped to swell the vast wealth and the cumbrous capital of England, from whose arena have come forth such splendid and colossal characters as Clive, and Washington, and Metcalf, and the Laurences, and Havelock, and which has furnished the church of Christ a field on which to display the Apostolic virtues and the primitive self-sacrifice of Middleton, and Heber, and Wilson, of Henry Martyn, of Fox and Ragland.

Without doubt God designs as great things as these for Africa, and among the means and agencies He will employ, commercial enterprise is most certainly one. To this end, however, high souls and lofty resolves are necessary, as in any other vocation of life. Of course the timid, the overcautious, the fearful, men in whose constitution Faith is a needed quality, are not fitted for this service. If ever the epoch of Negro civilization is brought about in Africa;

whatever *external* influences may be brought to bear upon this end; whatever foreign agencies and aids, black men themselves are without doubt to be the chief instruments. But they are to be men of force and energy; men who will not suffer themselves to be outrivaled in enterprise and vigor; men who are prepared for pains, and want, and suffering; men of such invincible courage that the spirit cannot be tamed by transient failures, incidental misadventure, or even glaring miscalculations; men who can exaggerate the feeblest resources into potent agencies and fruitful capital. Moreover these men are to have strong moral proclivities, equal to the deep penetration and the unyielding tenacity of their minds. No greater curse could be entailed upon Africa than the sudden appearance upon her shores of a mighty host of heartless black buccaneers (for such indeed they would prove themselves);— men sharpened up by letters and training; filled with feverish greed; with hearts utterly alien from moral good and human wellbeing; and only regarding Africa as a convenient goldfield from which to extract emolument and treasure to carry off to foreign quarters.

Such men would only reproduce the worst evils of the last three sad centuries of Africa's history, and quickly and inevitably so soil their character that the *just* imputation would be fastened upon them of that malignant lie which has recently been spread abroad through Europe and America against us; that is, of complicity with the slave trade.[2]

Happily for Africa, most of the yearnings of her sons towards her are gentle, humane, and generous. When the commercial one shall show itself, it will not differ, I feel assured, from all the others her children have showed. God grant that it may soon burst from many warm and ardent and energetic hearts, for the rescue of a continent!

Second, I proceed to show that the whole coast offers facilities for adventurous traders. There are few if any localities but where they can set up their factories and commence business. If there are exceptions they are rare; and even then, not really such, but cases where at some previous time the natives have been so basely and knavishly treated that they themselves have learned to practice the same upon some hapless, unsuspecting captain and his crew. As a general thing, however, native African chiefs court and invite the residence of a trader in their neighborhood, will give him protection, and will strive to secure his permanent stay. On our Liberian coast we see the proof of this in the many factories in existence at divers points. I have myself seen mere boys—young Englishmen not of age—who have come out to this country seeking their fortunes, living on the coast in native towns, without any civilized companionship, and carrying on a thriving trade. The chiefs have an interest in these men, and therefore make their residence safe and comfortable. The traders' presence and barter give the king or head man importance, increase his wealth, augment his influence in the neighborhood, swell the population of his town, and thus make it the center or capital of the surrounding region. But even if it were not thus, the security of traders is ensured by the felt power of the three great nations of the civilized world. Such, and so great is the naval force of England, France, and America on this coast that the coast may be regarded as protected. The native chiefs, for many hundred miles, have been taught to fear the destructive instruments of war they carry with them, and nowadays but seldom give occasion for their use.

But aside from all this, I may remark here, first, that of all rude and uncivilized men, the native African is the mildest and most gentle; and second, that no people in the world are so given to trade and barter as the negroes of the western coast of Africa.

Thirdly, let me refer to the means and facilities colored men have for an entrance upon African commerce. And first, I would point out the large amount of capital which is lying in their hands dead and unproductive. There is, as you are doubtless aware, no small amount of wealth possessed by the free colored population of the United States, both North and South. Notwithstanding the multitudinous difficulties which beset them in the pathway of improvement, our brethren have shown capacity, perseverance, oftentimes thrift and acquisitiveness. As a consequence they are, all over the Union, owners of houses, farms, homesteads, and divers other kinds of property; and stored away in safe quarters, they have large amounts of gold and silver; deep down in large stockings, in the corners of old chests, in dark and undiscoverable nooks and crannies; besides larger sums invested in banks, and locked up in the safes of city savings banks.

I have no statistics by me of the population and property of the colored people of Cincinnati, but I am told that their wealth exceeds that of the same class, in any other city in the American Union—that is, according to their numbers. Nashville, Tennessee, Charleston, South Carolina, St. Louis, Missouri, Mobile, and New Orleans, stand in nearly the same category. Baltimore holds a respectable position. In the "Weekly Anglo-African" (September 1859) I find that the church property of the colored population in Philadelphia is put down at $231,484. Doubtless their personal real estate must be worth millions. And the same must be true of New York City.

The greater portion of their wealth, however, is unproductive. As a people we have been victimized in a pecuniary point of view, as well as morally and politically; and as a consequence there is an almost universal dread of entrusting our monies in the hands of capitalists, and trading companies, and stock; though in the great cities large sums are put in savings banks. There are few, however, who have the courage to take shares in railroad and similar companies, and in many places it could not be done. . . .

These are some of the *material* influences which would result from this movement. The moral and philanthropic results would be equally if not more notable. The kings and tradesmen of Africa, having the *demonstration* of Negro capacity before them, would hail the presence of their black kinsmen from America,[3] and would be stimulated to a generous emulation. To the farthest interior, leagues and combinations would be formed with the men of commerce, and thus civilization, enlightenment, and Christianity would be carried to every state, and town, and village of interior Africa. The galling remembrances of the slave trade on the coast and of slavery in America would quicken the blood and the brain of both parties; and every wretch of a slave trader who might visit the coast would have to atone for his temerity by submitting to the rigid code framed for piracy. And when *this* disturbing and destructive hindrance to African progress was once put down, noble cities, vast agricultural establishments, the seeds of universities, and groundwork of church organizations would spring up all along the banks, and up the valley of the Niger.[4]

There is one certain commercial result—to return to my subject—that would surely grow out of this movement; I mean the flow of large amounts of capital from the monied men of America, that is, if black men showed skill, energy, and practicability. Philanthropy would come forward with largesse for colored men, thus developing the resources of Africa. Religion would open a large and generous hand in order to hasten the redemption of a continent alien from Christ and His church. And capital would hasten forward, not only for its wonted reduplication, but also to exemplify the vitality and fruitfulness which it always scatters from golden hands in its open pathway. And when you consider the fact of kinship, on our part, with Africa, the less liability to fever, the incentive to gain, the magnificent objects before us, and the magnificent field on which to develop them, and the probable early power of intelligent black men to penetrate, scatheless, any neighborhood where they might reside, you can see the likelihood of an early repossession of Africa, in trade, commerce, and moral power, by her now scattered children, in distant lands. . . .

I turn now to the *religious* aspect of this subject. In speaking of the religious needs of Africa, it is not necessary I should attempt a picture of her miserable condition, nor enter into the details of her wretchedness. Her very name is suggestive of uttermost spiritual need; of abounding moral desolation; of the deepest, darkest ignorance; of wild and sanguinary superstitions. This whole continent, with its million masses of heathen, presents one broad, almost unbroken, unmitigated view of moral desolation and spiritual ruin. And this fact creates the demand upon the Christian world for ministers and teachers, for the purpose of her evangelization. "The field is the world," and the church is to occupy it; and she will occupy it.

As members of the church of Christ, the sons of Africa in foreign lands are called upon to bear their part in the vast and sacred work of her evangelization. I might press this point on the grounds of piety, of compassion, or sympathy, but I choose a higher principle. For next to the grand ideas which pertain to the Infinite, His attributes and perfections, there is none loftier and grander than that of duty—"Stern daughter of the voice of God." It is the duty of black men to feel and labor for the salvation of the mighty millions of their kin all through this continent. I know that there is a class of her children who repudiate any close and peculiar connection with Africa. They and their fathers have been absent from this soil for centuries. In the course of time their blood has been mingled somewhat with that of other peoples and races. They have been brought up and habituated to customs entirely diverse from those of their ancestors in this land. And while the race here are in barbarism, they, on the other hand, are civilized and enlightened.

But notwithstanding these pleas there are other great facts which grapple hold of these men and bind them to this darkened, wretched Negro race by indissoluble bonds. There is the fact of kinship, which a lofty manhood and a proud generosity keeps them now and ever will keep them from disclaiming. There are the strong currents of kindred blood which neither time nor circumstance can ever entirely wash out. There are the bitter memories of ancestral wrongs, of hereditary servitude, which cannot be forgotten till "the last syllable of recorded time." There is the bitter pressure of legal proscription, and of inveterate caste, which will crowd closer and closer their ranks, deepening brotherhood and sympathy, and preserving, vital, the deep consciousness of distinctive race. There still remains the low imputation of Negro inferiority, necessitating a protracted and an earnest battle, creative of a generous pride to vindicate the race, and inciting to noble endeavor to illustrate its virtues and its genius.

How then can these men ever forget Africa? How cut the links which bind them to the land of their fathers? I affirm therefore that it is the duty of black men, in foreign lands, to live and to labor for the evangelization of the land of their fathers: first, on the ground of humanity; second, because they themselves are Negroes, or the descendants of Negroes, and are measurably responsible to God for the salvation of their heathen kin; and thirdly, I press the consideration of duty on the ground that they are Christians. In the good providence of God they have been enabled to pass out of the spiritual benightedness of their fathers, into the high table lands and the divine atmosphere of Christian truth and Christian conviction. . . .

For near three centuries the Negro race in exile and servitude has been groveling in lowly places, in deep degradation. Circumstance and position alike have divorced us from the pursuits which give nobleness and grandeur to life. In our time of trial we have shown, it is true, a matchless patience, and a quenchless hope; the one prophetic of victory, and the other the germ of a high Christian character, now developing. These better qualities, however, have been disproportioned, and the life of the race in general has been alien from ennobling and aspiring effort.

But the days of passivity should now come to an end. The active, creative, and saving powers of the race should begin to show themselves. The power of the Negro, if he has such power, to tell upon human interests, and to help shape human destinies, should at an early day make full demonstration of itself. We owe it to ourselves, to our race, and to our generous defenders and benefactors, both in Europe and America, to show that we are capable "of receiving the seed of present history into a kindly yet a vigorous soil, and [that we can] reproduce it, the same, and yet new, for a future period"[5] in all the homes of this traduced yet vital and progressive race.

Surely the work herein suggested is fitted to just such ends, and is fully worthy the noblest faculties and the highest ambition. If I were aiming but to startle the fancy, to kindle the imagination, and thereby to incite to brave and gallant deeds, I know no theme equal to this in interest and commanding influence. And just this *is* the influence it is now exerting upon passionate and romantic minds, in England and the United States, in France and Germany, in Austria and Sardinia. These civilized states are sending out their adventurous travelers to question, on the spot, the mysterious spell which seems to shut out Africa from the world and its civilization. These enterprising spirits are entering every possible avenue to the heart of Africa, anxious to assure the inner tribes of the continent that the enlightened populations of Europe would fain salute them as brethren and share with them the culture and enlightenment which, during the ages, have raised *them* from rudeness and degradation, if they can only induce them to throw aside the exclusiveness of paganism and the repulsiveness of barbarism.

But the enlightened sons of Africa in distant lands are called to a far higher work than even this, a work which as much transcends mere civilization as the abiding interests of eternity outvie the transient concerns of time. To wrest a continent from ruin; to bless and animate millions of torpid and benighted souls; to destroy the power of the devil in his strongholds, and to usher therein light, knowledge, blessedness, inspiring hope, holy faith, and abiding glory, is without doubt a work which not only commands the powers of the noblest men, but is worthy the presence and the zeal of angels. It is just this work which now claims and calls for the interest and the activity of the sons of Africa. Its plainest statement and its simplest aspect are sufficient, it seems to me, to move these men in every quarter of the world to profound sensibility, to deep resolve, to burning ardor. Such a grand and awful neces-

sity, covering a vast continent, touching the best hopes, and the endless
destiny of millions of men, ought I think to stir the souls of many a self-
sacrificing spirit and quicken him to lofty purposes and noble deeds. And
when one considers that never before in human history has such a grand and
noble work been laid out in the Divine Providence before the Negro race,
and that it rises up before them in its full magnitude now, at the very time
when they are best fitted for its needs and requirements, it seems difficult to
doubt that many a generous and godly soul will hasten to find his proper
place in this great work of God and man, whether it be by the personal and
painful endeavors of a laborer in the field of duty, or by the generous bene-
factions and the cheering incitements which serve to sustain and stimulate
distant and tried workers in their toils and trials. "A benefaction of this kind
seems to enlarge the very being of a man, extending it to distant places and
to future times, inasmuch as unseen countries and after ages may feel the
effects of his bounty, while he himself reaps the reward in the blessed society
of all those who, having turned many to righteousness, shine as the stars
forever and ever."[6]

[1]For a most able and discriminating article upon this topic, see *Westminster Review,*
Jan. 7, 1842, article by Dr. Arnold. Also, those humane and truthful essays of Mr. Heaps
in *Friends in Council,* vol. 2.

[2]Nothing can be more judicious than the following words of Commander Foote—
"Let then the black man be judged fairly, and not presumed to have become all at
once and by miracle, of a higher order than old historic nations, through many generations of whom the political organization of the world has been slowly developing
itself. There will be among them men who are covetous, or men who are tyrannical, or
men who would sacrifice public interests, or any others to their own; men who would
now go into the slave trade if they could, or rob hen roosts, or intrigue for office, or
pick pockets, rather than trouble their heads or their hands with more honorable
occupations. It should be remembered by visitors that such things will be found in
Liberia; *not because men are black, but because men are men." Africa and the American Flag* (New York: D. Appleton, 1854), 206.

It is most encouraging to find ever and anon a writer who in speaking of colored
men avoids the exaggeration of them either into demi-gods or monkeys. Even Commander Foote well nigh loses his balance, on the *same* page whence the above just
sentence is taken. In the paragraph which immediately follows this extract, he gives
expression to opinions sweepingly disparaging to the Negro race, and not of *certain*
historical accuracy. Commander Foote says—"*No negro has done anything to lighten
or brighten the links of human policy.*" Such a broad assertion implies that the writer
has cleared up all the mysteries of past history, but upon the point, that is, "the
relation of Egypt to the negro race," though still a disputed question; yet with such
authorities on our side as Dr. Pitchard, Cardinal Wiseman, and that ripe scholar, the
late Alexander H. Everett, one would have supposed Commander Foote would have
been a little less venturesome. Moreover, I beg to say that Touissant L'Ouverture *is* an
historical character. Goodwin in his lectures on colonial slavery says: "Can the West
India Islands, since their first discovery by Columbus, boast a single name which

deserves comparison with that of Touissant L'Ouverture?" Read Harriet Martineau's "Hour and the Man"; Wordsworth's fine sonnet addressed to "Touissant in Prison"; and the noble poem of John G. Whittier, on the same theme; and then compare the opinions of these high names with Commander Foote's broad assertions.

[3]Just this has been the experience of Dr. Delany, as I hear from valued friends there, at Lagos, and other places.

[4]The great hindrance to African evangelization at the present time is the slave trade. Missionaries feel this all along the coast, from Cape Palmas to Congo.

[5]Dr. Arnold. Inaugural Lecture.

[6]George Berkeley, "A Proposal for the Better Supplying of Churches in Our Foreign Plantations, and for Converting the Savage Americans to Christianity, by a College to be Erected in the Summer Islands, Otherwise Called the Isles of Bermuda" (1725), in Alexander Campbell Fraser, ed., *The Works of George Berkeley, D.D.,* 4 vols. (Oxford: Clarendon Press, 1871), 3:213–31, 230.

ANNA JULIA COOPER (1858–1964)

🏵 Womanhood: A Vital Element in the Regeneration and Progress of a Race (1886)

The two sources from which, perhaps, modern civilization has derived its noble and ennobling ideal of woman are Christianity and the feudal system. . . .

Here was the confluence of the two streams we have been tracing, which, united now, stretch before us as a broad majestic river. In regard to woman it was the meeting of two noble and ennobling forces, two kindred ideas, the resultant of which, we doubt not, is destined to be a potent force in the betterment of the world.

Now after our appeal to history comparing nations destitute of this force and so destitute also of the principle of progress with other nations among whom the influence of woman is prominent coupled with a brisk, progressive, satisfying civilization—if in addition we find this strong presumptive evidence corroborated by reason and experience, we may conclude that these two equally varying concomitants are linked as cause and effect; in other words, that the position of woman in society determines the vital elements of its regeneration and progress.

Now that this is so on a priori grounds all must admit. And this not because woman is better or stronger or wiser than man, but from the nature of the case, because it is she who must first form the man by directing the earliest impulses of his character.

Byron and Wordsworth were both geniuses and would have stamped themselves on the thought of their age under any circumstances; and yet we find the one a savor of life unto life, the other of death unto death. "Byron, like a rocket, shot his way upward with scorn and repulsion, flamed out in wild, explosive, brilliant excesses and disappeared in darkness made all the more palpable."[1]

Wordsworth lent of his gifts to reinforce that "power in the Universe which

Reprinted from *A Voice from the South,* by Anna Julia Cooper (Xenia, OH: Aldine Printing House, 1892), 19–47.

makes for righteousness" by taking the harp handed him from heaven and using it to swell the strains of angelic choirs. Two locomotives equally mighty stand facing opposite tracks; the one to rush headlong to destruction with all its precious freight, the other to toil grandly and gloriously up the steep embattlements to heaven and to God. Who—who can say what a world of consequences hung on the first placing and starting of these enormous forces!

Woman, mother—your responsibility is one that might make angels tremble and fear to take hold! To trifle with it, to ignore or misuse it, is to treat lightly the most sacred and solemn trust ever confided by God to humankind. The training of children is a task on which an infinity of weal or woe depends. Who does not covet it? Yet who does not stand awestruck before its momentous issues! It is a matter of small moment, it seems to me, whether that lovely girl in whose accomplishments you take such pride and delight can enter the gay and crowded salon with the ease and elegance of this or that French or English gentlewoman, compared with the decision as to whether her individuality is going to reinforce the good or the evil elements of the world. The lace and the diamonds, the dance and the theater, gain a new significance when scanned in their bearings on such issues. Their influence on the individual personality, and through her on the society and civilization which she vitalizes and inspires—all this and more must be weighed in the balance before the jury can return a just and intelligent verdict as to the innocence or banefulness of these apparently simple amusements.

Now the fact of woman's influence on society being granted, what are its practical bearings on the work which brought together this conference of colored clergy and laymen in Washington? We come not here to talk. Life is too busy, too pregnant with meaning and far-reaching consequences to allow you to come this far for mere intellectual entertainment.

The vital agency of womanhood in the regeneration and progress of a race, as a general question, is conceded almost before it is fairly stated. I confess one of the difficulties for me in the subject assigned lay in its obviousness. The plea is taken away by the opposite attorney's granting the whole question.

Woman's influence on social progress—who in Christendom doubts or questions it? One may as well be called on to prove that the sun is the source of light and heat and energy to this many-sided little world.

Nor, on the other hand, could it have been intended that I should apply the position when taken and proven to the needs and responsibilities of the women of our race in the South. For is it not written, "Cursed is he that cometh after the king?" And has not the king already preceded me in "The Black Woman of the South"?[2]

They have had both Moses and the prophets in Dr. Crummell and if they hear not him, neither would they be persuaded though one came up from the South.

I would beg, however, with the Doctor's permission, to add my plea for the *colored girls* of the South—that large, bright, promising, fatally beautiful class that stands shivering like a delicate plantlet before the fury of tempestuous elements, so full of promise and possibilities, yet so sure of destruction; often without a father to whom they dare apply the loving term, often without a stronger brother to espouse their cause and defend their honor with his life's blood; in the midst of pitfalls and snares, waylaid by the lower classes of white men, with no shelter, no protection nearer than the great blue vault above, which half conceals and half reveals the one caretaker they know so little of. Oh, save them, help them, shield, train, develop, teach, inspire them! Snatch them, in God's name, as brands from the burning! There is material in them well worth your while, the hope in germ of a staunch, helpful, re-generating womanhood on which primarily rests the foundation stones of our future as a race.

It is absurd to quote statistics showing the Negro's bank account and rent rolls, to point to the hundreds of newspapers edited by colored men and lists of lawyers, doctors, professors, D. D.'s, LL. D.'s, etcetera, etcetera, etcetera, while the source from which the life-blood of the race is to flow is subject to taint and corruption in the enemy's camp.

True progress is never made by spasms. Real progress is growth. It must begin in the seed. Then, first the blade, then the ear, after that the full corn in the ear. There is something to encourage and inspire us in the advancement of individuals since their emancipation from slavery. It at least proves that there is nothing irretrievably wrong in the shape of the black man's skull, and that under given circumstances his development, downward or upward, will be similar to that of other average human beings.

But there is no time to be wasted in mere felicitation. That the Negro has his niche in the infinite purposes of the eternal, no one who has studied the history of the last fifty years in America will deny. That much depends on his own right comprehension of his responsibility and rising to the demands of the hour, it will be good for him to see; and how best to use his present so that the structure of the future shall be stronger and higher and brighter and nobler and holier than that of the past is a question to be decided each day by every one of us.

The race is just twenty-one years removed from the conception and expe-rience of a chattel, just at the age of ruddy manhood. It is well enough to pause a moment for retrospection, introspection, and prospection. We look back, not to become inflated with conceit because of the depths from which we have arisen, but that we may learn wisdom from experience. We look within that we may gather together once more our forces and, by improved and more practical methods, address ourselves to the tasks before us. We look forward with hope and trust that the same God whose guiding hand led our fathers through and out of the gall and bitterness of oppression will still lead and direct their children to the honor of His name and for their ultimate salvation.

But this survey of the failures or achievements of the past, the difficulties and embarrassments of the present, and the mingled hopes and fears for the future, must not degenerate into mere dreaming nor consume the time which belongs to the practical and effective handling of the crucial questions of the hour; and there can be no issue more vital and momentous than this of the womanhood of the race.

Here is the vulnerable point, not in the heel, but at the heart of the young Achilles; and here must the defenses be strengthened and the watch re-doubled.

We are the heirs of a past which was not our fathers' moulding. "Every man the arbiter of his own destiny" was not true for the American Negro of the past: and it is no fault of his that he finds himself today the inheritor of a manhood and womanhood impoverished and debased by two centuries and more of compression and degradation.

But weaknesses and malformations, which today are attributable to a vicious schoolmaster and a pernicious system, will a century hence be rightly regarded as proofs of innate corruptness and radical incurability.

Now the fundamental agency under God in the regeneration, the retraining of the race, as well as the groundwork and starting point of its progress upward, must be the *black woman.*

With all the wrongs and neglects of her past, with all the weakness, the debasement, the moral thralldom of her present, the black woman of today stands mute and wondering at the Herculean task devolving upon her. But the cycles wait for her. No other hand can move the lever. She must be loosed from her bands and set to work.

Our meager and superficial results from past efforts prove their futility; and every attempt to elevate the Negro, whether undertaken by himself or through the philanthropy of others, cannot but prove abortive unless so directed as to utilize the indispensable agency of an elevated and trained womanhood.

A race cannot be purified from without. Preachers and teachers are helps, and stimulants and conditions as necessary as the gracious rain and sunshine are to plant growth. But what are rain and dew and sunshine and cloud if there be no life in the plant germ? We must go to the root and see that that is sound and healthy and vigorous, and not deceive ourselves with waxen flowers and painted leaves of mock chlorophyll.

We too often mistake individuals' honor for race development and so are ready to substitute pretty accomplishments for sound sense and earnest purpose.

A stream cannot rise higher than its source. The atmosphere of homes is no rarer and purer and sweeter than are the mothers in those homes. A race is but a total of families. The nation is the aggregate of its homes. As the whole is sum of all its parts, so the character of the parts will determine the characteristics of the whole. These are all axioms and so evident that it seems gratuitous to remark it; and yet, unless I am greatly mistaken, most of the unsatisfaction from our past results arises from just such a radical and palpable error, as much almost on our own part as on that of our benevolent white friends.

The Negro is constitutionally hopeful and proverbially irrepressible, and naturally stands in danger of being dazzled by the shimmer and tinsel of superficials. We often mistake foliage for fruit and overestimate or wrongly estimate brilliant results.

The late Martin R. Delany, who was an unadulterated black man, used to say when honors of state fell upon him that when he entered the council of kings the black race entered with him; meaning, I suppose, that there was no discounting his race identity and attributing his achievements to some admixture of Saxon blood. But our present record of eminent men, when placed beside the actual status of the race in America today, proves that no man can represent the race. Whatever the attainments of the individual may be, unless his home has moved on pari passu, he can never be regarded as identical with or representative of the whole.

Not by pointing to sunbathed mountaintops do we prove that Phœbus warms the valleys. We must point to homes, average homes, homes of the rank and file of horny-handed toiling men and women of the South (where the masses are), lighted and cheered by the good, the beautiful, and the true—then and not till then will the whole plateau be lifted into the sunlight.

Only the black woman can say, "When and where I enter, in the quiet, undisputed dignity of my womanhood, without violence and without suing or special patronage, then and there the whole *Negro race enters with me.*" Is it not evident then that as individual workers for this race we must address ourselves with no halfhearted zeal to this feature of our mission. The need is felt and must be recognized by all. There is a call for workers, for missionaries, for men and women with the double consecration of a fundamental love of humanity and a desire for its melioration through the Gospel; but superadded to this we demand an intelligent and sympathetic comprehension of the interests and special needs of the Negro.

I see not why there should not be an organized effort for the protection and elevation of our girls such as the White Cross League in England. English women are strengthened and protected by more than twelve centuries of Christian influences, freedom, and civilization; English girls are dispirited and crushed down by no such all-levelling prejudice as that supercilious caste spirit in America which cynically assumes a Negro woman cannot be a lady. English womanhood is beset by no such snares and traps as betray the unprotected, untrained colored girl of the South, whose only crime and dire destruction often is her unconscious and marvelous beauty. Surely then if English indignation is aroused and English manhood thrilled under the leadership of a bishop of the English church to build up bulwarks around their wronged sisters, Negro sentiment cannot remain callous and Negro effort nerveless in view of the imminent peril of the mothers of the next generation. "*I am my sister's keeper!*" should be the hearty response of every man and woman of the race, and this conviction should purify and exalt the narrow, selfish, and petty personal aims of life into a noble and sacred purpose.

We need men who can let their interest and gallantry extend outside the circle of their aesthetic appreciation, men who can be a father, a brother, a friend to every weak, struggling, unshielded girl. We need women who are so sure of their own social footing that they need not fear leaning to lend a hand to a fallen or falling sister. We need men and women who do not exhaust their genius splitting hairs on aristocratic distinctions and thanking God they are not as others, but earnest, unselfish souls, who can go into the highways and byways, lifting up and leading, advising and encouraging with the truly catholic benevolence of the Gospel of Christ.

As Church workers we must confess our path of duty is less obvious; or rather our ability to adapt our machinery to our conception of the peculiar exigencies of this work as taught by experience and our own consciousness of the needs of the Negro is as yet not demonstrable. Flexibility and aggressiveness are not such strong characteristics of the Church today as in the Dark Ages.

As a mission field for the Church the southern Negro is in some aspects most promising; in others, perplexing. Aliens neither in language and customs nor in associations and sympathies, naturally of deeply rooted religious instincts and taking most readily and kindly to the worship and teachings of the Church, surely the task of proselytizing the American Negro is infinitely less formidable than that which confronted the Church in the barbarians of Europe. Besides, this people already look to the Church as the hope of their race. Thinking colored men almost uniformly admit that the Protestant Episcopal Church with its quiet, chaste dignity and decorous solemnity, its instructive and elevating ritual, its bright chanting and joyous hymning, is eminently fitted to correct the peculiar faults of worship—the rank exuberance and often ludicrous demonstrativeness of their people. Yet, strange to say, the Church, claiming to be missionary and catholic, urging that schism is sin and denominationalism inexcusable, has made in all these years almost no inroads upon this semicivilized religionism.

Harvests from this overripe field of home missions have been gathered in by Methodists, Baptists, and not least by Congregationalists, who were unknown to the freedmen before their emancipation.

Our clergy numbers less than two dozen priests of Negro blood and we have hardly more than one self-supporting colored congregation in the entire Southland, while the organization known as the A. M. E. Church has 14,063 ministers, itinerant and local; 4,069 self-supporting churches; 4,275 Sunday-schools, with property valued at $7,772,284, raising yearly for church purposes $1,427,000.

Stranger and more significant than all, the leading men of this race (I do not mean demagogues and politicians, but men of intellect, heart, and race devotion, men to whom the elevation of their people means more than personal ambition and sordid gain—and the men of that stamp have not all died yet), the Christian workers for the race, of younger and more cultured growth, are noticeably drifting into sectarian churches, many of them declaring all the time that they acknowledge the historic claims of the Church, believe her apostolicity, and would experience greater personal comfort, spiritual and intellectual, in her revered communion. It is a fact which any one may verify for himself that representative colored men, professing that in their heart of hearts they are Episcopalians, are actually working in Methodist and Baptist pulpits; while the ranks of the Episcopal clergy are left to be filled largely by men who certainly suggest the propriety of a *"perpetual diaconate"* if they cannot be said to have created the necessity for it.

Now where is the trouble? Something must be wrong. What is it?

A certain Southern bishop of our Church reviewing the situation, whether in Godly anxiety or in Gothic antipathy I know not, deprecates the fact that the colored people do not seem *drawn* to the Episcopal Church, and comes to the sage conclusion that the Church is not adapted to the rude, untutored minds of the freedmen, and that they may be left to go to the Methodists and Baptists whither their racial proclivities undeniably tend. How the good bishop can agree that all-foreseeing wisdom and catholic love would have framed his Church as typified in his seamless garment and unbroken body, and yet not leave it broad enough and deep enough and loving enough to seek and save and hold seven millions of God's poor, I cannot see.

But the doctors, while discussing their scientifically conclusive diagnosis of the disease, will perhaps not think it presumptuous in the patient if he dares to suggest where at least the pain is. If this be allowed, a *Black woman of the South* would beg to point out two possible oversights in this southern work which may indicate in part both a cause and a remedy for some failure. The first is *not calculating for the black man's personality;* not having respect, if I may so express it, to his manhood or deferring at all to his conceptions of the needs of his people. When colored persons have been employed it was too often as machines or as manikins. There has been no disposition, generally, to get the black man's ideal or to let his individuality work by its own gravity, as it were. A conference of earnest Christian men have met at regular intervals for some years past to discuss the best methods of promoting the welfare and development of colored people in this country. Yet, strange as it may seem, they have never invited a colored man or even intimated that one would be welcome to take part in their deliberations. Their remedial contrivances are purely theoretical or empirical, therefore, and the whole machinery devoid of soul.

The second important oversight in my judgment is closely allied to this and probably grows out of it, and that is not developing Negro womanhood as an essential fundamental for the elevation of the race, and utilizing this agency in extending the work of the Church.

Of the first I have possibly already presumed to say too much since it does not strictly come within the province of my subject. However, Macaulay somewhere criticizes the Church of England as not knowing how to use fanatics, and declares that had Ignatius Loyola been in the Anglican instead of the Roman communion, the Jesuits would have been schismatics instead of Catholics; and if the religious awakenings of the Wesleys had been in Rome, she would have shaven their heads, tied ropes around their waists, and sent them out under her own banner and blessing. Whether this be true or not, there is certainly a vast amount of force potential for Negro evangelization rendered latent, or worse, antagonistic by the halting, uncertain, I had almost said *trimming* policy of the Church in the South. This may sound both presumptuous and ungrateful. It is mortifying, I know, to benevolent wisdom, after having spent itself in the execution of well-conned theories for the ideal development of a particular work, to hear perhaps the weakest and humblest element of that work asking, "What doest thou?"

Yet so it will be in life. The "thus far and no farther" pattern cannot be fitted to any growth in God's kingdom. The universal law of development is onward and upward. It is God-given and inviolable. From the unfolding of the germ in the acorn to reach the sturdy oak, to the growth of a human soul into the full knowledge and likeness of its Creator, the breadth and scope of the movement in each and all are too grand, too mysterious, too like God himself, to be encompassed and locked down in human molds.

After all the southern slave owners were right: either the very alphabet of intellectual growth must be forbidden and the Negro dealt with absolutely as a chattel having neither rights nor sensibilities, or else the clamps and irons of mental and moral as well as civil compression must be riven asunder and the truly enfranchised soul led to the entrance of that boundless vista through which it is to toil upwards to its beckoning God as the buried seed germ to meet the sun.

A perpetual colored diaconate, carefully and kindly superintended by the white clergy; congregations of shiny-faced peasants with their clean white aprons and sunbonnets catechised at regular intervals and taught to recite the creed, the Lord's prayer, and the ten commandments—duty towards God and duty towards neighbor; surely such well-tended sheep ought to be grateful to their shepherds and content in that station of life to which it pleased God to call them. True, like the old professor lecturing to his solitary student, we make no provision here for irregularities. Questions must be kept till after class, or dispensed with altogether. That some do ask questions and insist on answers, in class too, must be both impertinent and annoying. Let not our spiritual pastors and masters however be grieved at such self-assertion as merely signifies we have a destiny to fulfill and as men and women we must *be about our Father's business.*

It is a mistake to suppose that the Negro is prejudiced against a white ministry. Naturally there is not a more kindly and implicit follower of a white man's guidance than the average colored peasant. What would to others be an ordinary act of friendly or pastoral interest he would be more inclined to regard gratefully as a condescension. And he never forgets such kindness. Could the Negro be brought near to his white priest or bishop, he is not suspicious. He is not only willing but often longs to unburden his soul to this intelligent guide. There are no reservations when he is convinced that you are his friend. It is a saddening satire on American history and manners that it takes something to convince him.

That our people are not drawn to a church whose chief dignitaries they see only in the chancel, and whom they reverence as they would a painting or an angel, whose life never comes down to and touches theirs with the inspiration of an objective reality, may be perplexing truly (American caste and American Christianity both being facts) but it need not be surprising. There must be something of human nature in it, the same as that which brought about that the Word was made flesh and dwelt among us, that He might draw us towards God.

Men are not drawn by abstractions. Only sympathy and love can draw, and until our Church in America realizes this and provides a clergy that can come in touch with our life and have a fellow feeling for our woes, without being imbedded and frozen up in their Gothic antipathies, the good bishops are likely to continue perplexed by the sparsity of colored Episcopalians.

A colored priest of my acquaintance recently related to me, with tears in his eyes, how his reverend Father in God, the bishop who had ordained him, had met him on the cars on his way to the diocesan convention and warned him, not unkindly, not to take a seat in the body of the convention with the white clergy. To avoid disturbance of their godly placidity he would of course please sit back and somewhat apart. I do not imagine that that clergyman had very much heart for the Christly (!) deliberations of that convention.

To return, however, it is not on this broader view of Church work, which I mentioned as a primary cause of its halting progress with the colored people, that I am to speak. My proper theme is the second oversight of which in my judgment our Christian propagandists have been guilty: or, the necessity of church training, protecting and uplifting our colored womanhood as indispensable to the evangelization of the race.

Apelles did not disdain even that criticism of his lofty art which came from an uncouth cobbler; and may I not hope that the writer's oneness with her subject both in feeling and in being may palliate undue obtrusiveness of opinions here. That the race cannot be effectually lifted up till its women are truly elevated we take as proven. It is not for us to dwell on the needs, the neglects, and the ways of succor, pertaining to the black woman of the South. The ground has been ably discussed and an admirable and practical plan proposed by the oldest Negro priest in America, advising and urging that special organizations such as Church sisterhoods and industrial schools be devised to meet her pressing needs in the Southland. That some such movements are vital to the life of this people and the extension of the Church among them is not hard to see. Yet the pamphlet fell stillborn from the press. So far as I am informed the Church has made no motion towards carrying out Dr. Crummell's suggestion.

The denomination which comes next our own in opposing the proverbial emotionalism of Negro worship in the South, and which in consequence like ours receives the cold shoulder from the old heads, resting as we do under the charge of not having religion and not believing in conversion—the Congregationalists—have quietly gone to work on the young, have established industrial and training schools, and now almost every community in the South is yearly enriched by a fresh infusion of vigorous young hearts, cultivated heads, and helpful hands that have been trained at Fisk, at Hampton, in Atlanta University, and in Tuskegee, Alabama.

These young people are missionaries actual or virtual both here and in Africa. They have learned to love the methods and doctrines of the Church which trained and educated them; and so Congregationalism surely and steadily progresses.

Need I compare these well-known facts with results shown by the Church in the same field and during the same or even a longer time?

The institution of the Church in the South, to which she mainly looks for the training of her colored clergy and for the help of the black woman and colored girl of the South, has graduated since the year 1868, when the school was founded, *five young women*; and while yearly numerous young men have been kept and trained for the ministry by the charities of the Church, the number of indigent females who have here been supported, sheltered, and trained is phenomenally small. Indeed, to my mind, the attitude of the Church toward this feature of her work is as if the solution of the problem of Negro missions depended solely on sending a quota of deacons and priests into the field, girls being a sort of tertium quid whose development may be promoted if they can pay their way and fall in with the plans mapped out for the training of the other sex. Now I would ask in all earnestness, does not this force potential deserve by education and stimulus to be made dynamic? Is it not a solemn duty incumbent on all colored churchmen to make it so? Will not the aid of the Church be given to prepare our girls in head, heart, and hand for the duties and responsibilities that await the intelligent wife, the Christian mother, the earnest, virtuous, helpful woman, at once both the lever and the fulcrum for uplifting the race?

As Negroes and churchmen we cannot be indifferent to these questions. They touch us most vitally on both sides. We believe in the Holy Catholic Church. We believe that, however gigantic and apparently remote the consummation, the Church will go on conquering and to conquer till the kingdoms of this world, not excepting the black man and the black woman of the South, shall have become the kingdoms of the Lord and of his Christ.

That past work in this direction has been unsatisfactory we must admit. That without a change of policy results in the future will be as meagre, we greatly fear. Our life as a race is at stake. The dearest interests of our hearts are in the scales. We must either break away from dear old landmarks and plunge out in any line and every line that enables us to meet the pressing need of our people, or we must ask the Church to allow and help us, untrammelled by the prejudices and theories of individuals, to work aggressively under her direction as we alone can, with God's help, for the salvation of our people.

The time is ripe for action. Self-seeking and ambition must be laid on the altar. The battle is one of sacrifice and hardship, but our duty is plain. We have been recipients of missionary bounty in some sort for twenty-one years. Not even the senseless vegetable is content to be a mere reservoir. Receiving without giving is an anomaly in nature. Nature's cells are all little workshops for manufacturing sunbeams, the product to be *given out* to earth's inhabitants in warmth, energy, thought, action. Inanimate creation always pays back an equivalent.

Now, *How much owest thou my Lord?* Will his account be overdrawn if he call for singleness of purpose and self-sacrificing labor for your brethren? Having passed through your drill school, will you refuse a general's commission even if it entail responsibility, risk, and anxiety, with possibly some adverse criticism? Is it too much to ask you to step forward and direct the work for your race along those lines which you know to be of first and vital importance?

Will you allow these words of Ralph Waldo Emerson? "In ordinary," says he, "we have a snappish criticism which watches and contradicts the opposite party. We want the will which advances and dictates [acts]. Nature has made up her mind that what cannot defend itself, shall not be defended. Complaining never so loud and with never so much reason, is of no use. What cannot stand must fall; *and the measure of our sincerity and therefore of the respect of men is the amount of health and wealth we will hazard in the defense of our right.*"

[1]Henry Bidleman Bascom, *Bascom's Works,* vol. 3, *Lectures on Mental and Moral Philosophy, on Natural Theology, and on the History and Philosophy of Letters* (Nashville: Southern Methodist Publishing House, 1881).

[2]Alexander Crummell, "The Black Woman of the South: Her Neglects and Her Needs," in Alexander Crummell, *Destiny and Race: Selected Writings, 1840–1898,* ed. with introduction by Wilson Jeremiah Moses (Amherst: University of Massachusetts Press, 1992), 211–23.

BOOKER T. WASHINGTON (1856–1915)

The Atlanta Exposition Address (1895)

Mr. President and Gentlemen of the Board of Directors and Citizens.

One-third of the population of the South is of the Negro race. No enterprise seeking the material, civil, or moral welfare of this section can disregard this element of our population and reach the highest success. I but convey to you, Mr. President and Directors, the sentiment of the masses of my race when I say that in no way have the value and manhood of the American Negro been more fittingly and generously recognized than by the managers of this magnificent Exposition at every stage of its progress. It is a recognition that will do more to cement the friendship of the two races than any occurrence since the dawn of our freedom.

Not only this, but the opportunity here afforded will awaken among us a new era of industrial progress. Ignorant and inexperienced, it is not strange that in the first years of our new life we began at the top instead of at the bottom; that a seat in Congress or the state legislature was more sought than real estate or industrial skill; that the political convention or stump speaking had more attractions than starting a dairy farm or truck garden.

A ship lost at sea for many days suddenly sighted a friendly vessel. From the mast of the unfortunate vessel was seen a signal, "Water, water; we die of thirst!" The answer from the friendly vessel at once came back, "Cast down your bucket where you are." A second time the signal, "Water, water; send us water!" ran up from the distressed vessel, and was answered, "Cast down your bucket where you are." And a third and fourth signal for water was answered, "Cast down your bucket where you are." The captain of the distressed vessel, at last heeding the injunction, cast down his bucket, and it came up full of fresh, sparkling water from the mouth of the Amazon river. To those of my race who depend on bettering their condition in a foreign land or who underestimate the importance of cultivating friendly relations with the southern white man, who is their next-door neighbour, I would say:

Reprinted from *Up From Slavery: An Autobiography,* by Booker T. Washington (New York: Doubleday, Page, 1901).

"Cast down your bucket where you are"—cast it down in making friends in every manly way of the people of all races by whom we are surrounded.

Cast it down in agriculture, mechanics, in commerce, in domestic service, and in the professions. And in this connection it is well to bear in mind that whatever other sins the South may be called to bear, when it comes to business, pure and simple, it is in the South that the Negro is given a man's chance in the commercial world, and in nothing is this Exposition more eloquent than in emphasizing this chance. Our greatest danger is that in the great leap from slavery to freedom we may overlook the fact that the masses of us are to live by the productions of our hands, and fail to keep in mind that we shall prosper in proportion as we learn to dignify and glorify common labor and put brains and skill into the common occupations of life; shall prosper in proportion as we learn to draw the line between the superficial and the substantial, the ornamental gewgaws of life and the useful. No race can prosper till it learns that there is as much dignity in tilling a field as in writing a poem. It is at the bottom of life we must begin, and not at the top. Nor should we permit our grievances to overshadow our opportunities.

To those of the white race who look to the incoming of those of foreign birth and strange tongue and habits for the prosperity of the South, were I permitted I would repeat what I say to my own race, "Cast down your bucket where you are." Cast it down among the eight millions of Negroes whose habits you know, whose fidelity and love you have tested in days when to have proved treacherous meant the ruin of your firesides. Cast down your bucket among these people who have, without strikes and labor wars, tilled your fields, cleared your forests, builded your railroads and cities, and brought forth treasures from the bowels of the earth, and helped make possible this magnificent representation of the progress of the South. Casting down your bucket among my people, helping and encouraging them as you are doing on these grounds, and to education of head, hand, and heart, you will find that they will buy your surplus land, make blossom the waste places in your fields, and run your factories. While doing this, you can be sure in the future, as in the past, that you and your families will be surrounded by the most patient, faithful, law-abiding, and unresentful people that the world has seen. As we have proved our loyalty to you in the past, in nursing your children, watching by the sick-bed of your mothers and fathers, and often following them with tear-dimmed eyes to their graves, so in the future, in our humble way, we shall stand by you with a devotion that no foreigner can approach, ready to lay down our lives, if need be, in defense of yours, interlacing our industrial, commercial, civil, and religious life with yours in a way that shall make the interests of both races one. In all things that are purely social we can be as separate as the fingers, yet one as the hand in all things essential to mutual progress.

There is no defense or security for any of us except in the highest intelligence and development of all. If anywhere there are efforts tending to curtail the fullest growth of the Negro, let these efforts be turned into stimulating, encouraging, and making him the most useful and intelligent citizen. Effort or means so invested will pay a thousand percent interest. These efforts will be twice blessed—"blessing him that gives and him that takes."

There is no escape through law of man or God from the inevitable:

> The laws of changeless justice bind
>   Oppressor with oppressed;
> And close as sin and suffering joined
>   We march to fate abreast.

Nearly sixteen millions of hands will aid you in pulling the load upward, or they will pull against you the load downward. We shall constitute one-third and more of the ignorance and crime of the South, or one-third its intelligence and progress; we shall contribute one-third to the business and industrial prosperity of the South, or we shall prove a veritable body of death, stagnating, depressing, retarding every effort to advance the body politic.

Gentlemen of the Exposition, as we present to you our humble effort at an exhibition of our progress, you must not expect overmuch. Starting thirty years ago with ownership here and there in a few quilts and pumpkins and chickens (gathered from miscellaneous sources), remember the path that has led from these to the inventions and production of agricultural implements, buggies, steam engines, newspapers, books, statuary, carving, paintings, the management of drug stores and banks, has not been trodden without contact with thorns and thistles. While we take pride in what we exhibit as a result of our independent efforts, we do not for a moment forget that our part in this exhibition would fall far short of your expectations but for the constant help that has come to our educational life, not only from the southern states, but especially from northern philanthropists, who have made their gifts a constant stream of blessing and encouragement.

The wisest among my race understand that the agitation of questions of social equality is the extremest folly, and that progress in the enjoyment of all the privileges that will come to us must be the result of severe and constant struggle rather than of artificial forcing. No race that has anything to contribute to the markets of the world is long in any degree ostracized. It is important and right that all privileges of the law be ours, but it is vastly more important that we be prepared for the exercises of these privileges. The opportunity to earn a dollar in a factory just now is worth infinitely more than the opportunity to spend a dollar in an opera house.

In conclusion, may I repeat that nothing in thirty years has given us more hope and encouragement, and drawn us so near to you of the white race, as this opportunity offered by the Exposition; and here bending, as it were, over the altar that represents the results of the struggles of your race and mine, both starting practically empty-handed three decades ago, I pledge that in your effort to work out the great and intricate problem which God has laid at the doors of the South, you shall have at all times the patient, sympathetic help of my race; only let this be constantly in mind, that while from representations in these buildings of the product of field, of forest, of mine, of factory, letters, and art much good will come, yet far above and beyond material benefits will be that higher good that, let us pray God, will come, in a blotting out of sectional differences and racial animosities and suspicions, in a determination to administer absolute justice, in a willing obedience among all classes to the mandates of law. This, this, coupled with our material prosperity, will bring into our beloved South a new heaven and a new earth.

W. E. B. DU BOIS (1868–1963)

 # Does Race Antipathy Serve Any Good Purpose? (1914)

There are four classes of reasons usually given in defense of race antagonism.

1. It is an instinctive repulsion from something harmful and is, therefore, a subtle condition of ultimate survival.

The difficulty with this theory is that it does not square with the facts: race antipathy is not instinctive but a matter of careful education. Black and white children play together gladly and know no prejudice until it is implanted precept upon precept and by strong social pressure; and when it is so implanted it is just as strong in cases where there is no physical difference as it is where physical differences are striking. The racial repulsion in the Balkans among peoples of practically the same blood is today greater than it was between whites and blacks on the Virginia plantations.

2. Racial antagonism, whether instinctive or not, is a reasonable measure of self-defense against undesirable racial traits.

This second proposition is the one which usually follows careful examination of the first. After all, it is admitted "instinct" is an unimportant fact. Instincts are simply accumulated reasons in the individual or in the race. The reasons for antagonizing inferior races are clear and may be summed up as follows:

> Poor health and stamina.
> Low ability.
> Harmful ideals of life.

We are now on surer ground because we can now appeal to facts. But no sooner do we make this appeal than we are astonished to find that there are surprising little data. Is it true that the Negro as a physical animal is inferior to the white man or is he superior? Is the high death rate of the Indian a proof of his poor physique or is it proof of wretched conditions of life which would long ago have killed off a weaker people? And, again, is spiritual superiority always in direct proportion to physical strength in races any more than in

Reprinted from the *Boston Globe*, 19 July 1914.

individuals? Connected with this matter of health comes the question of physical beauty, but surely, if beauty were to become a standard of survival how small our world population would be!

It is argued, however, that it may be granted that the physical stamina of all races is probably approximately the same and that physical comeliness is rather a matter of taste and selection than of absolute racial difference. However, when it comes to intellectual ability the races differ so enormously that superior races must in self-defense repel the inferior sternly, even brutally. Two things, however, must be said in answer to this: First, the prejudice against the Jews, age-long and worldwide, is surely not based on inferior ability. We have only to name Jeremiah, D'Israeli, and Jesus Christ to set our minds at rest on that point. Moreover, if we compare the intellectual ability of Teuton and Chinese, which is inferior? Or, if we take Englishman and Bantu, is the difference a difference of native ability or of training and environment? The answer to this is simple: We do not know. But arguing from all known facts and analogies we must certainly admit, in the words of the secretary of the First International Races Congress, that "an impartial investigator would be inclined to look upon the various important peoples of the world as, to all intents and purposes, essentially equals in intellect, enterprise, morality and physique."[1]

3. Racial antipathy is a method of race development.

We may admit so far as physique and native ability go that, as Ratzel says, "There is only one species of man; the variations are numerous, but do not go deep."[2] At the same time it is plain that Europe has outstripped China in civilization, and China has outstripped Africa. Here at least are plain facts. Is not racial antipathy a method of maintaining the European level of culture? But is it necessary for the runner to hate and despise the man he is outdistancing? Can we only maintain culture in one race by increasing barbarism in others? Does it enhance the "superiority" of white men to allow them to steal from yellow men and enslave black men and reduce colored women to concubinage and prostitution? Surely not. Admitting that in the world's history again and again this or that race has outstripped another in culture, it is impossible to prove that inherent racial superiority was the cause or that the level of culture has been permanently raised in one race by keeping other races down.

4. Race antipathy is a method of group specialization.

This argument admits the essential equality of races but insists on the difference in gifts and argues that antipathy between races allows each to develop its own peculiar gifts and aptitudes. Does it? That depends on the antipathy. If antipathy means the enslaving of the African, the exploitation of the Chinese, the peonage of Mexicans, and the denial of schools to American

Negroes, then it is hard to see where the encouragement comes in. If it means the generous encouragement of all men according to their gifts and ability then why speak of race antipathy or encourage it? Let us call it human uplift and universal brotherhood and be done with it.

Such are the arguments. Most persons use all four at once and skillfully skip from one to the other. Each argument has in other days been applied to individuals and social classes, but we have outgrown that. We apply it today to races because race is a vague, unknown term which may be made to cover a multitude of sins. After all, what is a Race? and how many races are there? Von Luschan, one of the greatest of modern anthropologists, says, "The question of the number of human races has quite lost its raison d' etre, and has become a subject rather of philosophic speculation than of scientific research."[3] What we have on earth is men. Shall we help them or hinder them? Shall we hate and kill them or love and preserve and uplift them? Which method will do us most good? This is the real question of race antipathy.

[1]See Du Bois's account of Gustav Spiller's remarks in W. E. B. Du Bois, "The First Universal Races Congress," in Herbert Aptheker, ed., *Writings by W. E. B. Du Bois in Periodicals Edited by Others*, 4 vols. (Millwood, NY: Kraus-Thomson, 1982), 2:50.

[2]Friedrich Ratzel, *The History of Mankind*, trans. from 2d German ed. by A. J. Butler, introduction by E. B. Tylor, 3 vols. (New York: Macmillan, 1896), 1:9.

[3]Felix von Luschan, quoted in Du Bois, "The First Universal Races Congress," 2:49.

W. E. B. DU BOIS (1868–1963)

On Being Ashamed of Oneself: An Essay on Race Pride (1933)

My grandfather left a passage in his diary expressing his indignation at receiving an invitation to a Negro picnic. Alexander DuBois, born in the Bahamas, son of Dr. James DuBois of the well-known DuBois family of Poughkeepsie, N. Y., had been trained as a gentleman in the Cheshire School of Connecticut, and the implications of a Negro picnic were anathema to his fastidious soul. It meant close association with poverty, ignorance, and suppressed and disadvantaged people, dirty and with bad manners.

This was in 1856. Seventy years later, Marcus Garvey discovered that a black skin was in itself a sort of patent to nobility, and that Negroes ought to be proud of themselves and their ancestors, for the same or analogous reasons that made white folk feel superior.

Thus, within the space of three-fourths of a century, the pendulum has swung between race pride and race suicide, between attempts to build up a racial ethos and attempts to escape from ourselves. In the years between emancipation and 1900, the theory of escape was dominant. We were, by birth, law, and training, American citizens. We were going to escape into the mass of Americans in the same way that the Irish and Scandinavians and even the Italians were beginning to disappear. The process was going to be slower on account of the badge of color; but then, after all, it was not so much the matter of physical assimilation as of spiritual and psychic amalgamation with the American people.

For this reason, we must oppose all segregation and all racial patriotism; we must salute the American flag and sing "Our Country 'Tis of Thee" with devotion and fervor, and we must fight for our rights with long and carefully planned campaign, uniting for this purpose with all sympathetic people, colored and white.

This is still the dominant philosophy of most American Negroes and it is back of the objection to even using a special designation like Negro or even Afro-American or any such term.

Reprinted from *The Crisis* 40 (September 1933): 199–200.

But there are certain practical difficulties connected with this program which are becoming more and more clear today. First of all comes the fact that we are still ashamed of ourselves and are thus stopped from valid objection when white folks are ashamed to call us human. The reasons of course are not as emphatic as they were in the case of my grandfather. I remember a colored man, now expatriate, who made this discovery in my company, some twenty-five years ago. He was a handsome, burning brown, tall, straight, and well-educated, and he occupied a position which he had won, across and in spite of the color line. He did not believe in Negroes, for himself or his family, and he planned elaborately to escape the trammels of race. Yet he had responded to a call for a meeting of colored folk which touched his interests, and he came. He found men of his own caliber and training; he found men charming and companionable. He was thoroughly delighted. I know that never before, or I doubt if ever since, he had been in such congenial company. He could not help mentioning his joy continually and reiterating it.

All colored folk had gone through the same experience, for more and more largely in the last twenty-five years, colored America has discovered itself; has discovered groups of people, association with whom is a poignant joy, and despite their ideal of American assimilation, in more and more cases and with more and more determined object, they seek each other.

That involves, however, a drawing of class lines inside the Negro race, and it means the emergence of a certain social aristocracy, who by reasons of looks and income, education and contact, form the sort of upper social group which the world has long known and helped to manufacture and preserve. The early basis of this Negro group was simply color and a bald imitation of the white environment. Later, it tended more and more to be based on wealth and still more recently on education and social position.

This leaves a mass of untrained and uncultured colored folk and even of trained but ill-mannered people and groups of impoverished workers of whom this upper class of colored Americans are ashamed. They are ashamed both directly and indirectly, just as any richer or better sustained group in a nation is ashamed of those less fortunate and withdraws its skirts from touching them. But more than that, because the upper colored group is desperately afraid of being represented before American whites by this lower group, or being mistaken for them, or being treated as though they were part of it, they are pushed to the extreme of effort to avoid contact with the poorest classes of Negroes. This exaggerates, at once, the secret shame of being identified with such people and the anomaly of insisting that the physical characteristics of these folk which the upper class shares are not the stigmata of degradation.

When, therefore, in offense or defense, the leading group of Negroes must make common cause with the masses of their own race, the embarrassment or hesitation becomes apparent. They are embarrassed and indignant because an educated man should be treated as a Negro, and that no Negroes receive credit for social standing. They are ashamed and embarrassed because of the compulsion of being classed with a mass of people over whom they have no real control and whose action they can influence only with difficulty and compromise and with every risk of defeat.

Especially is all natural control over this group difficult—I mean control of law and police, of economic power, of guiding standards and ideals, of news propaganda. On this comes even greater difficulty because of the incompatibility of any action which looks toward racial integrity and race action with previous ideals. What are we really aiming at? The building of a new nation or the integration of a new group into an old nation? The latter has long been our ideal. Must it be changed? Should it be changed? If we seek new group loyalty, new pride of race, new racial integrity—how, where, and by what method shall these things be attained? A new plan must be built up. It cannot be the mere rhodomontade and fatuous propaganda on which Garveyism was based. It has got to be farsighted planning. It will involve increased segregation and perhaps migration. It will be pounced upon and aided and encouraged by every "nigger-hater" in the land.

Moreover, in further comment on all this, it may be pointed out that this is not the day for the experiment of new nations or the emphasis of racial lines. This is, or at least we thought it was, the day of the inter-nation, of humanity, and the disappearance of "race" from our vocabulary. Are we American Negroes seeking to move against or into the face of this fine philosophy? Here then is the real problem, the real new dilemma between rights of American citizens and racial pride, which faces American Negroes today and which is not always or often clearly faced.

The situation is this: America, in denying equality of rights, of employment and social recognition to American Negroes, has said in the past that the Negro was so far below the average nation in social position that he could not be recognized until he had developed further. In the answer to this, the Negro has eliminated five-sixths of his illiteracy according to official figures, and greatly increased the number of colored persons who have received education of the higher sort. They still are poor with a large number of delinquents and dependents. Nevertheless, their average situation in this respect has been greatly improved and, on the other hand, the emergence and accomplishment of colored men of ability has been undoubted. Notwithstanding this, the Negro is still a group apart, with almost no social recognition, subject to insult and discrimination, with income and wage far below the average of the nation and the most deliberately exploited industrial class in America. Even trained Negroes have increasing difficulty in making a living sufficient to sustain a civilized standard of life. Particularly in the recent vast economic changes, color discrimination as it now goes on is going to make it increasingly difficult for the Negro to remain an integral part of the industrial machine or to increase his participation in accordance with his ability.

The integration of industry is making it more and more possible for executives to exercise their judgment in choosing for key positions persons who can guide the industrial machine, and the exclusion of persons from such positions merely on the basis of race and color or even Negro descent is a widely recognized and easily defended prerogative. All that is necessary for any Christian American gentleman of high position and wide power to say in denying place and promotion to an eligible candidate is: "He is of Negro descent." The answer and excuse is final and all but universally accepted. For this reason, the Negro's opportunity in state-directed industry and his opportunity in the great private organization of industry, if not actually growing less, is certainly much smaller than his growth in education and ability. Either the industry of the nation in the future is to be conducted by private trusts or by government control. There seems in both to be little or no chance of advancement for the Negro worker, the educated artisan, and the educated leader.

On the other hand, organized labor is giving Negroes less recognition today than ever. It has practically excluded them from all the higher lines of skilled work, on railroads, in machine shops, in manufacture, and in the basic industries. In agriculture, where the Negro has theoretically the largest opportunity, he is excluded from successful participation not only by conditions common to all farmers, but by special conditions due to lynching, lawlessness, disfranchisement, and social degradation.

Facing these indisputable facts, there is on the part of the leaders of public opinion in America no effective response to our agitation or organized propaganda. Our advance in the last quarter century has been in segregated, racially integrated institutions and efforts, and not in effective entrance into American national life. In Negro churches, Negro schools, Negro colleges, Negro business, and Negro art and literature, our advance has been determined and inspiring; but in industry, general professional careers, and national life, we have fought battle after battle and lost more often than we have won. There seems no hope that America in our day will yield in its color or race hatred any substantial ground, and we have no physical nor economic power, nor any alliance with other social or economic classes that will force compliance with decent civilized ideals in church, state, industry, or art.

The next step, then, is certainly one on the part of the Negro and it involves group action. It involves the organization of intelligent and earnest people of Negro descent for their preservation and advancement in America, in the West

Indies, and in Africa; and no sentimental distaste for racial or national unity can be allowed to hold them back from a step which sheer necessity demands.

A new organized group action along economic lines, guided by intelligence and with the express object of making it possible for Negroes to earn a better living and, therefore, more effectively to support agencies for social uplift, is without the slightest doubt the next step. It will involve no opposition from white America because they do not believe we can accomplish it. They expect always to be able to crush, insult, ignore, and exploit twelve million individual Negroes without intelligent organized opposition. This organization is going to involve deliberate propaganda for race pride. That is, it is going to start out by convincing American Negroes that there is no reason for their being ashamed of themselves; that their record is one which should make them proud; that their history in Africa and the world is a history of effort, success, and trial, comparable with that of any other people.

Such measured statements can and will be exaggerated. There will be those who will want to say that the black race is the first and greatest of races, that its accomplishments are most extraordinary, that its desert is most obvious and its mistakes negligible. This is the kind of talk we hear from people with the superiority complex among the white and the yellow race.

We cannot entirely escape it, since it is just as true and just as false as such statements among other races; but we can use intelligence in modifying and restraining it. We can refuse deliberately to lie about our history, while at the same time taking just pride in Nefertari, Askia, Moshesh, Toussaint, and Frederick Douglass, and testing and encouraging belief in our own ability by organized economic and social action.

There is no other way; let us not be deceived. American Negroes will be beaten into submission and degradation if they merely wait unorganized to find some place voluntarily given them in the new reconstruction of the economic world. They must themselves force their race into the new economic set-up and bring with them the millions of West Indians and Africans by peaceful organization for normative action or else drift into greater poverty, greater crime, greater helplessness, until there is no resort but the last red alternative of revolt, revenge and war.

W. E. B. DU BOIS (1868–1963)

The Concept of Race (1940)

I do not know how I came first to form my theories of race. The process was probably largely unconscious. The differences of personal appearance between me and my fellows, I must have been conscious of when quite young. Whatever distinctions came because of that did not irritate me; they rather exalted me because, on the whole, while I was still a youth, they gave me exceptional position and a chance to excel rather than handicapping me.

Then of course, when I went South to Fisk, I became a member of a closed racial group with rites and loyalties, with a history and a corporate future, with an art and philosophy. I received these eagerly and expanded them so that when I came to Harvard the theory of race separation was quite in my blood. I did not seek contact with my white fellow students. On the whole I rather avoided them. I took it for granted that we were training ourselves for different careers in worlds largely different. There was not the slightest idea of the permanent subordination and inequality of my world. Nor again was there any idea of racial amalgamation. I resented the assumption that we desired it. I frankly refused the possibility while in Germany and even in America gave up courtship with one "colored" girl because she looked quite white, and I should resent the inference on the street that I had married outside my race.

All this theory, however, was disturbed by certain facts in America, and by my European experience. Despite everything, race lines were not fixed and fast. Within the Negro group especially there were people of all colors. Then too, there were plenty of my colored friends who resented my ultra "race" loyalty and ridiculed it. They pointed out that I was not a "Negro," but a mulatto; that I was not a Southerner but a Northerner, and my object was to be an American and not a Negro; that race distinctions must go. I agreed with this in part and as an ideal, but I saw it leading to inner racial distinction in the colored group. I resented the defensive mechanism of avoiding too-dark companions in order to escape notice and discrimination in public. As a

Reprinted from *Dusk of Dawn*, by W. E. B. Du Bois (New York: Harcourt, Brace and World, 1940), 100–102, 103–4, 114–15, 116–17, 128–33. © Harcourt Brace 1940. Reprinted with permission of Harcourt Brace and David Du Bois.

sheer matter of taste, I wanted the color of my group to be visible. I hotly championed the inclusion of two black schoolmates whose names were not usually on the invitation list to our social affairs. In Europe my friendships and close contact with white folk made my own ideas waver. The eternal walls between races did not seem so stern and exclusive. I began to emphasize the cultural aspects of race. . . .

I early began to take a direct interest in my own family as a group and became curious as to that physical descent which so long I had taken for granted quite unquestioningly. But I did not at first think of any but my Negro ancestors. I knew little and cared less of the white forebears of my father. But this chauvinism gradually changed. There is, of course, nothing more fascinating than the question of the various types of mankind and their intermixture. The whole question of heredity and human gift depends upon such knowledge; but ever since the African slave trade and before the rise of modern biology and sociology, we have been afraid in America that scientific study in this direction might lead to conclusions with which we were loath to agree; and this fear was in reality because the economic foundation of the modern world was based on the recognition and preservation of so-called racial distinctions. In accordance with this, not only Negro slavery could be justified, but the Asiatic coolie profitably used and the labor classes in white countries kept in their places by low wage.

It is not singular then that here in America and in the West Indies, where we have had the most astonishing modern mixture of human types, scientific study of the results and circumstances of this mixture has not only lagged but been almost nonexistent. We have not only not studied race and race mixture in America, but we have tried almost by legal process to stop such study. It is for this reason that it has occurred to me just here to illustrate the way in which Africa and Europe have been united in my family. There is nothing unusual about this interracial history. It has been duplicated thousands of times; but on the one hand, the white folk have bitterly resented even a hint of the facts of this intermingling; while black folk have recoiled in natural hesitation and affected disdain in admitting what they know. . . .

This, then, was my racial history and as such it was curiously complicated. With Africa I had only one direct cultural connection and that was the African melody which my great-grandmother Violet used to sing. Where she learned it, I do not know. Perhaps she herself was born in Africa or had it of a mother or father stolen and transported. But at any rate, as I wrote years ago in the "Souls of Black Folk," "coming to the valleys of the Hudson and Housatonic, black, little, and lithe, she shivered and shrank in the harsh north winds, looked longingly at the hills, and often crooned a heathen melody to the child between her knees, thus:

Do bana coba, gene me, gene me!
Do bana coba, gene me, gene me!
Ben d' nuli, nuli, nuli, nuli, ben d' le.

The child sang it to his children and they to their children's children, and so two hundred years it has traveled down to us and we sing it to our children, knowing as little as our fathers what its words may mean, but knowing well the meaning of its music."

Living with my mother's people I absorbed their culture patterns, and these were not African so much as Dutch and New England. The speech was an idiomatic New England tongue with no African dialect; the family customs were New England, and the sex mores. My African racial feeling was then purely a matter of my own later learning and reaction; my recoil from the assumptions of the whites; my experience in the South at Fisk. But it was nonetheless real and a large determinant of my life and character. I felt myself African by "race" and by that token was African and an integral member of the group of dark Americans who were called Negroes. . . .

What is Africa to me? Once I should have answered the question simply: I should have said "fatherland" or perhaps better "motherland" because I was born in the century when the walls of race were clear and straight; when the world consisted of mutually exclusive races; and even though the edges might be blurred, there was no question of exact definition and understanding of the meaning of the word. One of the first pamphlets that I wrote in 1897 was on "The Conservation of Races," wherein I set down as the first article of a proposed racial creed: "We believe that the Negro people as a race have a contribution to make to civilization and humanity which no other race can make."

Since then the concept of race has so changed and presented so much of contradiction that as I face Africa I ask myself: what is it between us that constitutes a tie which I can feel better than I can explain? Africa is, of course, my fatherland. Yet neither my father nor my father's father ever saw Africa or knew its meaning or cared overmuch for it. My mother's folk were closer and yet their direct connection, in culture and race, became tenuous; still, my tie to Africa is strong. On this vast continent were born and lived a large portion of my direct ancestors going back a thousand years or more. The mark of their heritage is upon me in color and hair. These are obvious things, but of little meaning in themselves, only important as they stand for real and more subtle differences from other men. Whether they do or not, I do not know nor does science know today.

But one thing is sure and that is the fact that since the fifteenth century these ancestors of mine and their other descendants have had a common history, have suffered a common disaster, and have one long memory. The actual ties of heritage between the individuals of this group vary with the ancestors that they have in common and many others: Europeans and Semites, perhaps Mongolians, certainly American Indians. But the physical bond is least and the badge of color relatively unimportant save as a badge; the real essence of this kinship is its social heritage of slavery, the discrimination and insult; and this heritage binds together not simply the children of Africa, but extends through yellow Asia and into the South Seas. It is this unity that draws me to Africa. . . .

The one great lack in Africa is communication—communication as represented by human contact, movement of goods, dissemination of knowledge. All these things we have—we have in such crushing abundance that they have mastered us and defeated their real good. We meet human beings in such throngs that we cannot know or even understand them—they become to us inhuman, mechanical, hateful. We are choked and suffocated, tempted and killed by goods accumulated from the ends of the earth; our newspapers and magazines so overwhelm us with knowledge—knowledge of all sorts and kinds from particulars as to our neighbors' underwear to Einstein's mathematics—that one of the great and glorious joys of the African bush is to escape from "news."

On the other hand, African life with its isolation has deeper knowledge of human souls. The village life, the forest ways, the teeming markets, bring in intimate human knowledge that the West misses, sinking the individual in the social. Africans know fewer folk, but know them infinitely better. Their intertwined communal souls, therefore, brook no poverty nor prostitution—these things are to them un-understandable. On the other hand, they are vastly ignorant of what the world is doing and thinking, and of what is known of its physical forces. They suffer terribly from preventable disease, from unnecessary hunger, from the freaks of the weather.

Here, then, is something for Africa and Europe both to learn; and Africa is eager, breathless, to learn—while Europe? Europe laughs with loud guffaws. Learn of Africa? Nonsense. Poverty cannot be abolished. Democracy and firm government are incompatible. Prostitution is world-old and inevitable. And Europe proceeds to use Africa as a means and not as an end, as a hired tool and welter of raw materials and not as a land of human beings.

I think it was in Africa that I came more clearly to see the close connection between race and wealth. The fact that, even in the minds of the most dogmatic supporters of race theories and believers in the inferiority of colored folk to white, there was a conscious or unconscious determination to increase their incomes by taking full advantage of this belief. And then gradually this thought was metamorphosed into a realization that the income-bearing value of race prejudice was the cause and not the result of theories of race inferiority; that particularly in the United States the income of the Cotton Kingdom based on black slavery caused the passionate belief in Negro inferiority and the determination to enforce it even by arms.

I have wandered afield from miscegenation in the West Indies to race blending and segregation in America and to a glimpse of present Africa. Now to return to the American concept of race. It was in my boyhood, as I have intimated, an adventure. In my youth, it became the vision of a glorious crusade where I and my fellows were to match our mettle against white folk and show them what black folk could do. But as I grew older the matter became more serious and less capable of jaunty settlement. I not only met plenty of persons equal in ability to myself but often with greater ability and nearly always with greater opportunity. Racial identity presented itself as a matter of trammels and impediments, as "tightening bonds about my feet." As I looked out into my racial world the whole thing verged on tragedy. My "way was cloudy" and the approach to its high goals by no means straight and clear. I saw the race problem was not as I conceived, a matter of clear, fair competition, for which I was ready and eager. It was rather a matter of segregation, of hindrance and inhibitions, and my struggles against this and resentment at it began to have serious repercussions upon my inner life.

It is difficult to let others see the full psychological meaning of caste segregation. It is as though one, looking out from a dark cave in a side of an impending mountain, sees the world passing and speaks to it; speaks courteously and persuasively, showing them how these entombed souls are hindered in their natural movement, expression, and development; and how their loosening from prison would be a matter not simply of courtesy, sympathy, and help to them, but aid to all the world. One talks on evenly and logically in this way, but notices that the passing throng does not even turn its head, or if it does, glances curiously and walks on. It gradually penetrates the minds of the prisoners that the people passing do not hear; that some thick sheet of invisible but horribly tangible plate glass is between them and the world. They get excited; they talk louder; they gesticulate. Some of the passing world stop in curiosity; these gesticulations seem so pointless; they laugh and pass on. They still either do not hear at all or hear but dimly, and even what they hear, they do not understand. Then the people within may become hysterical. They may scream and hurl themselves against the barriers, hardly realizing in their bewilderment that they are screaming in a vacuum unheard and that their antics may actually seem funny to those outside looking in. They may even, here and there, break through in blood and disfigurement, and find themselves faced by a horrified, implacable, and quite overwhelming mob of people frightened for their own very existence.

It is hard under such circumstances to be philosophical and calm, and to think through a method of approach and accommodation between castes. The entombed find themselves not simply trying to make the outer world understand their essential and common humanity, but even more, as they become inured to their experience, they have to keep reminding themselves that the great and oppressing world outside is also real and human and in its essence honest. All my life I have had continually to haul my soul back and say, "All white folk are not scoundrels nor murderers. They are, even as I am, painfully human."

One development continually recurs: any person outside of this wall of glass can speak to his own fellows, can assume a facile championship of the entombed, and gain the enthusiastic and even gushing thanks of the victims. But this method is subject to two difficulties: first of all, not being possibly among the entombed or capable of sharing their inner thought and experience, this outside leadership will continually misinterpret and compromise and complicate matters, even with the best of will. And secondly, of course, no matter how successful the outside advocacy is, it remains impotent and unsuccessful until it actually succeeds in freeing and making articulate the submerged caste.

Practically, this group imprisonment within a group has various effects upon the prisoner. He becomes provincial and centered upon the problems of his particular group. He tends to neglect the wider aspects of national life and human existence. On the one hand he is unselfish, so far as his inner group is concerned. He thinks of himself not as an individual but as a group man, a "race" man. His loyalty to this group idea tends to be almost unending and balks at almost no sacrifice. On the other hand, his attitude toward the environing race congeals into a matter of unreasoning resentment and even hatred, deep disbelief in them and refusal to conceive honesty and rational thought on their part. This attitude adds to the difficulties of conversation, intercourse, understanding between groups.

This was the race concept which has dominated my life, and the history of which I have attempted to make the leading theme of this book. It had as I have tried to show all sorts of illogical trends and irreconcilable tendencies. Perhaps it is wrong to speak of it at all as a concept rather than as a group of contradictory forces, facts, and tendencies. At any rate I hope I have made its meaning to me clear. It was for me, as I have written, first a matter of dawning realization, then of study and science; then a matter of inquiry into the diverse strands of my own family; and finally consideration of my connection, physical and spiritual, with Africa and the Negro race in its homeland. All this led to an attempt to rationalize the racial concept and its place in the modern world.

ALAIN LOCKE (1886–1954)

✸ The New Negro (1925)

In the last decade something beyond the watch and guard of statistics has happened in the life of the American Negro, and the three Norns who have traditionally presided over the Negro problem have a changeling in their laps. The sociologist, the philanthropist, the race leader are not unaware of the New Negro, but they are at a loss to account for him. He simply cannot be swathed in their formulae. For the younger generation is vibrant with a new psychology; the new spirit is awake in the masses, and under the very eyes of the professional observers is transforming what has been a perennial problem into the progressive phases of contemporary Negro life.

Could such a metamorphosis have taken place as suddenly as it has appeared to? The answer is no; not because the New Negro is not here, but because the Old Negro had long become more of a myth than a man. The Old Negro, we must remember, was a creature of moral debate and historical controversy. His has been a stock figure perpetuated as an historical fiction, partly in innocent sentimentalism, partly in deliberate reactionism. The Negro himself has contributed his share to this through a sort of protective social mimicry forced upon him by the adverse circumstances of dependence. So for generations in the mind of America, the Negro has been more of a formula than a human being—a something to be argued about, condemned or defended, to be "kept down," or "in his place," or "helped up," to be worried with or worried over, harassed or patronized, a social bogey or a social burden. The thinking Negro even has been induced to share this same general attitude, to focus his attention on controversial issues, to see himself in the distorted perspective of a social problem. His shadow, so to speak, has been more real to him than his personality. Through having had to appeal from the unjust stereotypes of his oppressors and traducers to those of his liberators, friends, and benefactors he has had to subscribe to the traditional positions from which his case has been viewed. Little true social or self-understanding has or could come from such a situation.

But while the minds of most of us, black and white, have thus burrowed in

Reprinted from *The New Negro: An Interpretation*, edited by Alain Locke (New York: Albert and Charles Boni, 1925), 3–16.

the trenches of the Civil War and Reconstruction, the actual march of development has simply flanked these positions, necessitating a sudden reorientation of view. We have not been watching in the right direction; set North and South on a sectional axis, we have not noticed the East till the sun has us blinking.

Recall how suddenly the Negro spirituals revealed themselves; suppressed for generations under the stereotypes of Wesleyan hymn harmony, secretive, half-ashamed, until the courage of being natural brought them out—and behold, there was folk music. Similarly the mind of the Negro seems suddenly to have slipped from under the tyranny of social intimidation and to be shaking off the psychology of imitation and implied inferiority. By shedding the old chrysalis of the Negro problem we are achieving something like a spiritual emancipation. Until recently, lacking self-understanding, we have been almost as much of a problem to ourselves as we still are to others. But the decade that found us with a problem has left us with only a task. The multitude perhaps feels as yet only a strange relief and a new vague urge, but the thinking few know that in the reaction the vital inner grip of prejudice has been broken.

With this renewed self-respect and self-dependence, the life of the Negro community is bound to enter a new dynamic phase, the buoyancy from within compensating for whatever pressure there may be of conditions from without. The migrant masses, shifting from countryside to city, hurdle several generations of experience at a leap, but more important, the same thing happens spiritually in the life attitudes and self-expression of the Young Negro, in his poetry, his art, his education, and his new outlook, with the additional advantage, of course, of the poise and greater certainty of knowing what it is all about. From this comes the promise and warrant of a new leadership. As one of them has discerningly put it:

> We have tomorrow
> Bright before us
> Like a flame.
>
> Yesterday, a night-gone thing
> A sun-down name.
>
> And dawn today
> Broad arch above the road we came.
> We march![1]

This is what, even more than any "most creditable record of fifty years of freedom," requires that the Negro of today be seen through other than the dusty spectacles of past controversy. The day of aunties, uncles, and mammies is equally gone. Uncle Tom and Sambo have passed on, and even the

Colonel and George play barnstorm roles from which they escape with relief when the public spotlight is off. The popular melodrama has about played itself out, and it is time to scrap the fictions, garret the bogeys, and settle down to a realistic facing of facts.

First we must observe some of the changes which since the traditional lines of opinion were drawn have rendered these quite obsolete. A main change has been, of course, that shifting of the Negro population which has made the Negro problem no longer exclusively or even predominantly Southern. Why should our minds remain sectionalized, when the problem itself no longer is? Then the trend of migration has not only been toward the North and the central Midwest, but city-ward and to the great centers of industry—the problems of adjustment are new, practical, local, and not peculiarly racial. Rather they are an integral part of the large industrial and social problems of our present-day democracy. And finally, with the Negro rapidly in process of class differentiation, if it ever was warrantable to regard and treat the Negro en masse it is becoming with every day less possible, more unjust, and more ridiculous.

In the very process of being transplanted, the Negro is becoming transformed.

The tide of Negro migration, northward and city-ward, is not to be fully explained as a blind flood started by the demands of war industry coupled with the shutting off of foreign migration, or by the pressure of poor crops coupled with increased social terrorism in certain sections of the South and Southwest. Neither labor demand, the boll weevil, nor the Ku Klux Klan is a basic factor, however contributory any or all of them may have been. The wash and rush of this human tide on the beach line of the northern city centers is to be explained primarily in terms of a new vision of opportunity, of social and economic freedom, of a spirit to seize, even in the face of an extortionate and heavy toll, a chance for the improvement of conditions. With each successive wave of it, the movement of the Negro becomes more and more a mass movement toward the larger and the more democratic chance—in the Negro's case a deliberate flight not only from countryside to city, but from medieval America to modern.

Take Harlem as an instance of this. Here in Manhattan is not merely the largest Negro community in the world, but the first concentration in history of so many diverse elements of Negro life. It has attracted the African, the West Indian, the Negro American; has brought together the Negro of the North and the Negro of the South; the man from the city and the man from the town and village; the peasant, the student, the business man, the professional man, artist, poet, musician, adventurer and worker, preacher and criminal, exploiter and social outcast. Each group has come with its own separate motives and for its own special ends, but their greatest experience has been the finding of one another. Proscription and prejudice have thrown these dissimilar elements into a common area of contact and interaction. Within this area, race sympathy and unity have determined a further fusing of sentiment and experience. So what began in terms of segregation becomes more and more, as its elements mix and react, the laboratory of a great race-welding. Hitherto, it must be admitted that American Negroes have been a race more in name than in fact, or to be exact, more in sentiment than in experience. The chief bond between them has been that of a common condition rather than a common consciousness, a problem in common rather than a life in common. In Harlem, Negro life is seizing upon its first chances for group expression and self-determination. It is—or promises at least to be—a race capital. That is why our comparison is taken with those nascent centers of folk expression and self-determination which are playing a creative part in the world today. Without pretense to their political significance, Harlem has the same role to play for the New Negro as Dublin has had for the New Ireland or Prague for the New Czechoslovakia.

Harlem, I grant you, isn't typical—but it is significant, it is prophetic. No sane observer, however sympathetic to the new trend, would contend that the great masses are articulate as yet, but they stir, they move, they are more than physically restless. The challenge of the new intellectuals among them is clear enough—the "race radicals" and realists who have broken with the old epoch of philanthropic guidance, sentimental appeal, and protest. But are we after all only reading into the stirrings of a sleeping giant the dreams of an agitator? The answer is in the migrating peasant. It is the man farthest down who is most active in getting up. One of the most characteristic symptoms of this is the professional man, himself migrating to recapture his constituency after a vain effort to maintain in some southern corner what for years back seemed an established living and clientele. The clergyman following his errant flock, the physician or lawyer trailing his clients, supply the true clues. In a real sense it is the rank and file who are leading, and the leaders who are following. A transformed and transforming psychology permeates the masses.

When the racial leaders of twenty years ago spoke of developing race pride and stimulating race consciousness, and of the desirability of race solidarity, they could not in any accurate degree have anticipated the abrupt feeling that has surged up and now pervades the awakened centers. Some of the recognized Negro leaders and a powerful section of white opinion identified with "race work" of the older order have indeed attempted to discount this feeling as a passing phase, an attack of race nerves, so to speak, an aftermath of the war, and the like. It has not abated, however, if we are to gauge by the present tone and temper of the Negro press, or by the shift in popular support from the officially recognized and orthodox spokesmen to those of the independent, popular, and often radical type who are unmistakable symptoms of a new order. It is a social disservice to blunt the fact that the Negro of the northern centers has reached a stage where tutelage, even of the most interested and well-intentioned sort, must give place to new relationships, where positive self-direction must be reckoned with in ever-increasing measure. The American mind must reckon with a fundamentally changed Negro.

The Negro too, for his part, has idols of the tribe to smash. If on the one hand the white man has erred in making the Negro appear to be that which would excuse or extenuate his treatment of him, the Negro, in turn, has too often unnecessarily excused himself because of the way he has been treated. The intelligent Negro of today is resolved not to make discrimination an extenuation for his shortcomings in performance, individual or collective; he is trying to hold himself at par, neither inflated by sentimental allowances nor depreciated by current social discounts. For this he must know himself and be known for precisely what he is, and for that reason he welcomes the new scientific rather than the old sentimental interest. Sentimental interest in the Negro has ebbed. We used to lament this as the falling off of our friends; now we rejoice and pray to be delivered both from self-pity and condescension. The mind of each racial group has had a bitter weaning, apathy or hatred on one side matching disillusionment or resentment on the other; but they face each other today with the possibility at least of entirely new mutual attitudes.

It does not follow that if the Negro were better known, he would be better liked or better treated. But mutual understanding is basic for any subsequent cooperation and adjustment. The effort toward this will at least have the effect of remedying in large part what has been the most unsatisfactory feature of our present stage of race relationships in America, namely the fact that the more intelligent and representative elements of the two race groups have at so many points got quite out of vital touch with one another.

The fiction is that the life of the races is separate, and increasingly so. The fact is that they have touched too closely at the unfavorable and too lightly at the favorable levels.

While interracial councils have sprung up in the South, drawing on forward elements of both races, in the northern cities manual laborers may brush elbows in their everyday work, but the community and business leaders have experienced no such interplay or far too little of it. These segments must achieve contact or the race situation in America becomes desperate. Fortunately this is happening. There is a growing realization that in social effort the cooperative basis must supplant long-distance philanthropy, and that the only safeguard for mass relations in the future must be provided in the carefully maintained contacts of the enlightened minorities of both race groups. In the intellectual realm a renewed and keen curiosity is replacing the recent apathy; the Negro is being carefully studied, not just talked about and discussed. In art and letters, instead of being wholly caricatured, he is being seriously portrayed and painted.

To all of this the New Negro is keenly responsive as an augury of a new democracy in American culture. He is contributing his share to the new social understanding. But the desire to be understood would never in itself have been sufficient to have opened so completely the protectively closed portals of the thinking Negro's mind. There is still too much possibility of being snubbed or patronized for that. It was rather the necessity for fuller, truer self-expression, the realization of the unwisdom of allowing social discrimination to segregate him mentally, and a counter-attitude to cramp and fetter his own living—and so the spite-wall that the intellectuals built over the color line has happily been taken down. Much of this reopening of intellectual contacts has centered in New York and has been richly fruitful, not merely in the enlarging of personal experience, but in the definite enrichment of American art and letters and in the clarifying of our common vision of the social tasks ahead.

The particular significance in the re-establishment of contact between the more advanced and representative classes is that it promises to offset some of the unfavorable reactions of the past, or at least to resurface race contacts somewhat for the future. Subtly the conditions that are molding a New Negro are molding a new American attitude.

However, this new phase of things is delicate; it will call for less charity but more justice; less help, but infinitely closer understanding. This is indeed a critical stage of race relationships because of the likelihood, if the new temper is not understood, of engendering sharp group antagonism and a second crop of more calculated prejudice. In some quarters, it has already done so. Having weaned the Negro, public opinion cannot continue to paternalize. The Negro today is inevitably moving forward under the control largely of his own objectives. What are these objectives? Those of his outer life are happily already well and finally formulated, for they are none other than the ideals of American institutions and democracy. Those of his inner life are yet in process of formation, for the new psychology at present is more of a consensus of feeling than of opinion, of attitude rather than of program. Still some points seem to have crystallized.

Up to the present one may adequately describe the Negro's inner objectives as an attempt to repair a damaged group psychology and reshape a warped social perspective. Their realization has required a new mentality for the American Negro. And as it matures we begin to see its effects; at first, negative, iconoclastic, and then positive and constructive. In this new group psychology we note the lapse of sentimental appeal, then the development of a more positive self-respect and self-reliance; the repudiation of social dependence, and then the gradual recovery from hypersensitiveness and "touchy" nerves, the repudiation of the double standard of judgment with its special philanthropic allowances and then the sturdier desire for objective and scientific appraisal; and finally the rise from social disillusionment to race pride, from the sense of social debt to the responsibilities of social contribution, and offsetting the necessary working and commonsense acceptance of restricted conditions, the belief in ultimate esteem and recognition. Therefore the Negro today wishes to be known for what he is, even in his faults and shortcomings, and scorns a craven and precarious survival at the price of seeming to be what he is not. He resents being spoken of as a social ward or minor, even by his own, and to being regarded a chronic patient for the sociological clinic, the sick man of American democracy. For the same reasons, he himself is through with those social nostrums and panaceas, the so-called solutions of his problem, with which he and the country have been so liberally dosed in the past. Religion, freedom, education, money—in turn, he has ardently hoped for and peculiarly trusted these things; he still believes in them, but not in blind trust that they alone will solve his life problem.

Each generation, however, will have its creed, and that of the present is the belief in the efficacy of collective effort, in race cooperation. This deep feeling of race is at present the mainspring of Negro life. It seems to be the outcome of the reaction to proscription and prejudice; an attempt, fairly successful on the whole, to convert a defensive into an offensive position, a handicap into an incentive. It is radical in tone, but not in purpose, and only the most stupid forms of opposition, misunderstanding, or persecution could make it otherwise. Of course, the thinking Negro has shifted a little toward the left with the world trend, and there is an increasing group who affiliate with radical and liberal movements. But fundamentally for the present the Negro is radical on race matters, conservative on others, in other words a forced radical, a social protestant rather than a genuine radical. Yet under further pressure and injustice, iconoclastic thought and motives will inevitably increase. Harlem's quixotic radicalisms call for their ounce of democracy today lest tomorrow they be beyond cure.

The Negro mind reaches out as yet to nothing but American wants, American ideas. But this forced attempt to build his Americanism on race values is a unique social experiment, and its ultimate success is impossible except through the fullest sharing of American culture and institutions. There should be no delusion about this. American nerves in sections unstrung with race hysteria are often fed the opiate that the trend of Negro advance is wholly separatist, and that the effect of its operation will be to encyst the Negro as a benign foreign body in the body politic. This cannot be—even if it were desirable. The racialism of the Negro is no limitation or reservation with respect to American life; it is only a constructive effort to build the obstructions in the stream of his progress into an efficient dam of social energy and power. Democracy itself is obstructed and stagnated to the extent that any of its channels are closed. Indeed they cannot be selectively closed. So the choice is not between one way for the Negro and another way for the rest, but between American institutions frustrated on the one hand and American ideals progressively fulfilled and realized on the other.

There is, of course, a warrantably comfortable feeling in being on the right side of the country's professed ideals. We realize that we cannot be undone without America's undoing. It is within the gamut of this attitude that the thinking Negro faces America, but with variations of mood that are if anything more significant than the attitude itself. Sometimes we have it taken with the defiant ironic challenge of McKay:

> Mine is the future grinding down to-day
> Like a great landslip moving to the sea,
> Bearing its freight of débris far away
> Where the green hungry waters restlessly
> Heave mammoth pyramids, and break and roar
> Their eerie challenge to the crumbling shore.

Sometimes, perhaps more frequently as yet, it is taken in the fervent and almost filial appeal and counsel of Weldon Johnson's:

> O Southland, dear Southland!
> Then why do you still cling
> To an idle age and a musty page,
> To a dead and useless thing?

But between defiance and appeal, midway almost between cynicism and hope, the prevailing mind stands in the mood of the same author's *To America*, an attitude of sober query and stoical challenge:

> How would you have us, as we are?
>   Or sinking 'neath the load we bear,
> Our eyes fixed forward on a star,
>   Or gazing empty at despair?

> Rising or falling? Men or things?
>   With dragging pace or footsteps fleet?
> Strong, willing sinews in your wings,
>   Or tightening chains about your feet?

More and more, however, an intelligent realization of the great discrepancy between the American social creed and the American social practice forces upon the Negro the taking of the moral advantage that is his. Only the steadying and sobering effect of a truly characteristic gentleness of spirit prevents the rapid rise of a definite cynicism and counter-hate and a defiant superiority feeling. Human as this reaction would be, the majority still deprecate its advent, and would gladly see it forestalled by the speedy amelioration of its causes. We wish our race pride to be a healthier, more positive achievement than a feeling based upon a realization of the shortcomings of others. But all paths toward the attainment of a sound social attitude have been difficult; only a relatively few enlightened minds have been able, as the phrase puts it, to rise above prejudice. The ordinary man has had until recently only a hard choice between the alternatives of supine and humiliating submission and stimulating but hurtful counter-prejudice. Fortunately from some inner, desperate resourcefulness has recently sprung up the simple expedient of fighting prejudice by mental passive resistance, in other words, by trying to ignore it. For the few, this manna may perhaps be effective, but the masses cannot thrive upon it.

Fortunately there are constructive channels opening out into which the balked social feelings of the American Negro can flow freely.

Without them there would be much more pressure and danger than there is. These compensating interests are racial, but in a new and enlarged way. One is the consciousness of acting as the advance guard of the African peoples in their contact with twentieth century civilization; the other, the sense of a mission of rehabilitating the race in world esteem from that loss of prestige for which the fate and conditions of slavery have so largely been responsible. Harlem, as we shall see, is the center of both these movements; she is the home of the Negro's "Zionism." The pulse of the Negro world has begun to beat in Harlem. A Negro newspaper carrying news material in English, French, and Spanish, gathered from all quarters of America, the West Indies, and Africa, has maintained itself in Harlem for over five years. Two important magazines, both edited from New York, maintain their news and circulation consistently on a cosmopolitan scale. Under American auspices and backing, three pan–African congresses have been held abroad for the discussion of common interests, colonial questions, and the future cooperative development of Africa. In terms of the race question as a world problem, the Negro mind has leapt, so to speak, upon the parapets of prejudice and extended its cramped horizons. In so doing it has linked up with the growing group consciousness of the dark peoples and is gradually learning their common interests. As one of our writers has recently put it: "It is imperative that we understand the white world in its relations to the non-white world." As with the Jew, persecution is making the Negro international.

As a world phenomenon this wider race consciousness is a different thing from the much-asserted rising tide of color. Its inevitable causes are not of our making. The consequences are not necessarily damaging to the best interests of civilization. Whether it actually brings into being new armadas of conflict or argosies of cultural exchange and enlightenment can only be decided by the attitude of the dominant races in an era of critical change. With the American Negro, his new internationalism is primarily an effort to recapture contact with the scattered peoples of African derivation. Garveyism may be a transient, if spectacular, phenomenon, but the possible role of the American Negro in the future development of Africa is one of the most constructive and universally helpful missions that any modern people can lay claim to.

Constructive participation in such causes cannot help giving the Negro valuable group incentives, as well as increased prestige at home and abroad. Our greatest rehabilitation may possibly come through such channels, but for the present, more immediate hope rests in the revaluation by white and black alike of the Negro in terms of his artistic endowments and cultural contributions, past and prospective. It must be increasingly recognized that the Negro has already made very substantial contributions, not only in his folk art, music especially, which has always found appreciation, but in larger, though humbler and less acknowledged ways. For generations the Negro has been the peasant matrix of that section of America which has most under-valued him, and here he has contributed not only materially in labor and in social patience, but spiritually as well. The South has unconsciously absorbed the gift of his folk temperament. In less than half a generation it will be easier to recognize this, but the fact remains that a leaven of humor, sentiment, imagination, and tropic nonchalance has gone into the making of the South from a humble, unacknowledged source. A second crop of the Negro's gifts promises still more largely. He now becomes a conscious contributor and lays aside the status of a beneficiary and ward for that of a collaborator and participant in American civilization. The great social gain in this is the releasing of our talented group from the arid fields of controversy and debate to the productive fields of creative expression. The especially cultural recognition they win should in turn prove the key to that revaluation of the Negro which must precede or accompany any considerable further betterment of race relationships. But whatever the general effect, the present generation will have added the motives of self-expression and spiritual development to the old and still unfinished task of making material headway and progress. No one who understandingly faces the situation with its substantial accomplishment or views the new scene with its still more abundant promise can be entirely without hope. And certainly, if in our lifetime the

Negro should not be able to celebrate his full initiation into American democracy, he can at least, on the warrant of these things, celebrate the attainment of a significant and satisfying new phase of group development, and with it a spiritual coming of age.

[1]Langston Hughes, "Youth," in *The New Negro: An Interpretation,* Alain Locke, ed. (New York: Albert and Charles Boni, 1925), 142.

MALCOLM X (1925–1965)

✸ Speech on "Black Revolution" (New York, April 8, 1964)

Friends and enemies, tonight I hope that we can have a little fireside chat with as few sparks as possible being tossed round, especially because of the very explosive condition that the world is in today. Sometimes, when a person's house is on fire and someone comes in yelling fire, instead of the person who is awakened by the yell being thankful, he makes the mistake of charging the one who awakened him with having set the fire. I hope that this little conversation tonight about the Black revolution won't cause many of you to accuse us of igniting it when you find it at your doorstep.

I'm still a Muslim, that is, my religion is still Islam. I still believe that there is no god but Allah and that Muhammad is the apostle of Allah. That just happens to be my personal religion. But in the capacity which I am functioning in today, I have no intention of mixing my religion with the problems of 22 million Black people in this country. Just as it's possible for a great man whom I greatly respect, Ben Bella, to be a Muslim and still be a nationalist, and another one whom I greatly respect, Gamal Nasser, to be a Muslim and still be a nationalist, and Sukarno of Indonesia to be a Muslim and still be a nationalist, it was nationalism which enabled them to gain freedom for their people.

I'm still a Muslim but I'm also a nationalist, meaning that my political philosophy is Black nationalism, my economic philosophy is Black nationalism, my social philosophy is Black nationalism. And when I say that this philosophy is Black nationalism, to me this means that the political philosophy of Black nationalism is that which is designed to encourage our people, the Black people, to gain complete control over the politics and the politicians of our own community.

Our economic philosophy is that we should gain economic control over the economy of our own community, the businesses and the other things which create employment so that we can provide jobs for our own people instead of having to picket and boycott and beg someone else for a job.

And, in short, our social philosophy means that we feel that it is time to get together among our own kind and eliminate the evils that are destroying the moral fiber of our society, like drug addiction, drunkenness, adultery that leads to an abundance of bastard children, welfare problems. We believe that we should lift the level or the standard of our own society to a higher level wherein we will be satisfied and then not inclined toward pushing ourselves into other societies where we are not wanted.

All that aside, tonight we are dealing with the Black Revolution. During recent years there has been much talk about a population explosion, and whenever they are speaking of the population explosion, in my opinion they are referring primarily to the people in Asia or in Africa—the black, brown, red, and yellow people. It is seen by people of the West that as soon as the standard of living is raised in Africa and Asia, automatically the people begin to reproduce abundantly. And there has been a great deal of fear engendered by this in the minds of the people of the West, who happen to be, on this earth, a very small minority.

In fact, in most of the thinking and planning of whites in the West today, it's easy to see the fear in their minds, conscious minds and subconscious minds, that the masses of dark people in the West, in the East rather, who already outnumber them, will continue to increase and multiply and grow until they eventually overrun the people of the West like a human sea, a human tide, a human flood. And the fear of this can be seen in the minds, in the actions, of most of the people here in the West in practically everything that they do. It governs political views and it governs their economic views and it governs most of their attitudes toward the present society.

I was listening to Dirksen, the senator from Illinois, in Washington, D.C., filibustering the civil rights bill, and one thing that he kept stressing over and over and over was that if this bill is passed it will change the social structure of America. Well, I know what he's getting at, and I think that most other people today, and especially our people, know what is meant when these whites who filibuster these bills and express fears of changes in the social structure—our people are beginning to realize what they mean.

Just as we can see that all over the world one of the main problems facing the West is race, likewise here in America today, most of your Negro leaders as well as the whites agree that 1964 itself appears to be one of the most explosive years yet in the history of America on the racial front, on the racial scene. Not only is this racial explosion probably to take place in America, but all of the ingredients for this racial explosion in America to blossom into a worldwide racial explosion present themselves right here in front of us.

America's racial powder keg, in short, can actually fuse or ignite a worldwide powder keg.

And whites in this country who are still complacent when they see the possibilities of racial strife getting out of hand—and you are complacent simply because you think you outnumber the racial minority in this country; what you have to bear in mind is wherein you might outnumber us in this country, you don't outnumber us all over the earth.

And any kind of racial explosion that takes place in this country today, in 1964, is not a racial explosion that can be confined to the shores of America. It is a racial explosion that can ignite the racial powder keg that exists all over the planet that we call earth. Now I think that nobody would disagree that the dark masses of Africa and Asia and Latin America are already seething with bitterness, animosity, hostility, unrest, and impatience with the racial intolerance that they themselves have experienced at the hands of the white West.

And just as they themselves have the ingredients of hostility toward the West in general, here we also have 22 million African Americans, Black, brown, red, and yellow people in this country who are also seething with bitterness and impatience and hostility and animosity at the racial intolerance not only of the white West but of white America in particular.

And by the hundreds of thousands today we find our own people have become impatient, turning away from your white nationalism, which you call democracy, toward the militant uncompromising policy of Black nationalism. I point out right here that as soon as we announced we were going to start a Black nationalist party in this country, we received mail from coast to coast, especially from young people at the college level, the university level, who expressed complete sympathy and support and a desire to take an active part in any kind of political action based on Black nationalism, designed to correct or eliminate immediately evils that our people have suffered here for four hundred years.

The Black nationalists to many of you may represent only a minority in the community. And therefore you might have a tendency to classify them as something insignificant. But just as the fuse is the smallest part or the smallest piece in the powder keg, it is yet that little fuse that ignites the entire powder keg. The Black nationalists to you may represent a small minority in the so-called Negro community. But they just happen to be composed of the type of ingredient necessary to fuse or ignite the entire Black community. And this is one thing that whites—whether you call yourselves liberals or conservatives or racists or whatever else you might choose to be—one thing that you have to realize is, where the Black community is concerned, although there the large majority you come in contact with may impress you as being moderate and patient and loving and long-suffering and all that kind of stuff, the minority who you consider to be Muslims or nationalists happen to be made of the type of ingredient that can easily spark the Black community. This should be understood. Because to me a powder keg is nothing without a fuse.

Nineteen sixty-four will be America's hottest year; her hottest year yet; a year of much racial violence and much racial bloodshed. But it won't be blood that's going to flow only on one side. The new generation of Black people that have grown up in this country during recent years are already forming the opinion—and it's just an opinion—that if there is to be bleeding, it should be reciprocal—bleeding on both sides.

It should also be understood that the racial sparks that are ignited here in America today could easily turn into a flaming fire abroad, which only means it could engulf all the people of this earth into a giant race war. You cannot confine it to one little neighborhood, or one little community, or one little country. What happens to a Black man in America today happens to the black man in Africa. What happens to a Black man in America and Africa happens to the black man in Asia and to the man down in Latin America. What happens to one of us today happens to all of us. And when this is realized I think that the whites—who are intelligent even if they aren't moral or aren't just or aren't impressed by legalities—those who are intelligent will realize that when they touch this one, they are touching all of them, and this in itself will have a tendency to be a checking factor.

The seriousness of this situation must be faced up to. I was in Cleveland last night—Cleveland, Ohio. In fact I was there Friday, Saturday, and yesterday. Last Friday the warning was given that this is a year of bloodshed, that the Black man has ceased to turn the other cheek, that he has ceased to be nonviolent, that he has ceased to feel that he must be confined to all these restraints that are put upon him by white society in struggling for what white society says he was supposed to have had a hundred years ago.

So today, when the Black man starts reaching out for what America says are his rights, the Black man feels that he is within his rights—when he becomes the victim of brutality by those who are depriving him of his rights—to do whatever is necessary to protect himself. And an example of this was taking place last night at this same time in Cleveland, where the police were putting water hoses on our people there and also throwing tear gas at them and they met a hail of stones, a hail of rocks, a hail of bricks. Couple weeks ago in Jacksonville, Florida, a young teenage Negro was throwing Molotov cocktails.

Well, Negroes didn't do this ten years ago. But what you should learn from this is that they are waking up. It was stones yesterday, Molotov cocktails today; it will be hand grenades tomorrow and whatever else is available the next day. The seriousness of this situation must be faced up to. You should not feel that I am inciting someone to violence. I'm only warning of a powder-keg situation. You can take it or leave it. If you take the warning perhaps you can still save yourself. But if you ignore it or ridicule it, well, death is already at your doorstep. There are 22 million African Americans who are ready to fight for independence right here. When I say fight for independence right here, I don't mean any nonviolent fight, or turn-the-other-cheek fight. Those days are gone. Those days are over.

If George Washington didn't get independence for this country nonviolently, and if Patrick Henry didn't come up with a nonviolent statement, and you taught me to look upon them as patriots and heroes, then it's time for you to realize that I have studied your books well.

Our people, 22 million African Americans, are fed up with America's hypocritical democracy, and today we care nothing about the odds that are against us. Every time a Black man gets ready to defend himself, some Uncle Tom tries to tell us, how can you win? That's Tom talking. Don't listen to him. This is the first thing we hear: the odds are against you. You're dealing with Black people who don't care anything about odds. We care nothing about odds.

Again I go right back to the people who founded and secured the independence of this country from the colonial power of England. When George Washington and the others got ready to declare or come up with the Declaration of Independence, they didn't care anything about the odds of the British Empire. They were fed up with taxation without representation. And you've got 22 million Black people in this country today, 1964, who are fed up with taxation without representation and will do the same thing, who are ready, willing, and justified to do the same thing today to bring about independence for our people that your forefathers did to bring about independence for your people.

And I say your people because I certainly couldn't include myself among those for whom independence was fought in 1776. How in the world can a Negro talk about the Declaration of Independence when he is still singing "We Shall Overcome"? Our people are increasingly developing the opinion that we just have nothing to lose but the chains of segregation and the chains of second-class citizenship.

So 1964 will see the Negro revolt evolve and merge into the worldwide black revolution that has been taking place on this earth since 1945. The so-called revolt will become a real black revolution. Now the black revolution has been taking place in Africa and Asia and in Latin America. Now when I say black, I mean nonwhite. Black, brown, red, or yellow. Our brothers and sisters in Asia, who were colonized by the Europeans, our brothers and sisters in Africa, who were colonized by the Europeans, and in Latin America, the peasants, who were colonized by the Europeans, have been involved in a struggle since 1945 to get the colonists, or the colonizing powers, the Europeans, off their land, out of their country.

This is a real revolution. Revolution is always based on land. Revolution is never based on begging somebody for an integrated cup of coffee. Revolutions are never fought by turning the other cheek. Revolutions are never based upon love your enemy and pray for those who spitefully use you. And revolutions are never waged singing "We Shall Overcome." Revolutions are based upon bloodshed. Revolutions are never compromising. Revolutions are never based upon negotiations. Revolutions are never based upon any kind of tokenism whatsoever. Revolutions are never even based upon that which is begging a corrupt society or a corrupt system to accept us into it. Revolutions overturn systems, and there is no system on this earth which has proven itself more corrupt, more criminal, than this system that in 1964 still colonizes 22 million African Americans, still enslaves 22 million Afro-Americans.

There is no system more corrupt than a system that represents itself as the example of freedom, the example of democracy, and can go all over this earth telling other people how to straighten out their house, and you have citizens of this country who have to use bullets if they want to cast a ballot. The greatest weapon the colonial powers have used in the past against our people has always been divide and conquer.

America is a colonial power. She has colonized 22 million Afro-Americans by depriving us of first-class citizenship, by depriving us of civil rights, actually by depriving us of human rights. She has not only deprived us of the right to be a citizen, she has deprived us of the right to be human beings, the right to be recognized and respected as men and women. And in this country the Black can be fifty years old and he is still a "boy."

I grew up with white people. I was integrated before they even invented the word and I have never met white people yet—if you are around them long enough—who won't refer to you as a boy or a gal, no matter how old you are or what school you came out of, no matter what your intellectual or professional level is. In this society we remain boys.

So America's strategy is the same strategy as that which was used in the past by the colonial powers: divide and conquer. She plays one Negro leader against the other. She plays one Negro organization against the other. She makes us think we have different objectives, different goals. As soon as one Negro says something, she runs to this Negro and asks him, "What do you think about what he said?" Why, anybody can see through that today—except some of the Negro leaders.

All of our people have the same goals. The same objective. That objective is freedom, justice, equality. All of us want recognition and respect as human beings. We don't want to be integrationists. Nor do we want to be separationists. We want to be human beings. Integration is only a method that is used by some groups to obtain freedom, justice, equality, and respect as human beings. Separation is only a method that is used by other groups to obtain freedom, justice, equality, or human dignity.

So our people have made the mistake of confusing the methods with the objectives. As long as we agree on objectives, we should never fall out with each other just because we believe in different methods or tactics or strategy to reach a common objective.

We have to keep in mind at all times that we are not fighting for integration, nor are we fighting for separation. We are fighting for recognition as human beings. We are fighting for the right to live as free humans in this society. In fact, we are actually fighting for rights that are even greater than civil rights and that is human rights.

We are fighting for human rights in 1964. This is a shame. The civil rights struggle has failed to produce concrete results because it has kept us barking up the wrong tree. It has made us put the cart ahead of the horse. We must have human rights before we can secure civil rights. We must be respected as humans before we can be recognized as citizens.

Among the so-called Negroes in this country, as a rule the civil rights groups, those who believe in civil rights, they spend most of their time trying to prove they are Americans. Their thinking is usually domestic, confined to the boundaries of America, and they always look upon themselves as a minority. When they look upon themselves upon the American stage, the American stage is a white stage. So a Black man standing on that stage in America automatically is in the minority. He is the underdog, and in his struggle he always uses an approach that is a begging, hat-in-hand, compromising approach.

Whereas the other segment or section in America, known as the nationalist, Black nationalists, are more interested in human rights than they are in civil rights. And they place more stress on human rights than they do on civil rights. The difference between the thinking and the scope of the Negroes who are involved in the human rights struggle and those who are involved in the civil rights struggle—those so-called Negroes involved in the human rights struggle don't look upon themselves as Americans.

They look upon themselves as a part of dark mankind. They see the whole struggle not within the confines of the American stage, but they look upon the struggle on the world stage. And, in the world context, they see that the dark man outnumbers the white man. On the world stage the white man is just a microscopic minority.

So in this country you find two different types of Afro-Americans, the type who looks upon himself as a minority and you as the majority, because his scope is limited to the American scene; and then you have the type who looks upon himself as part of the majority and you as part of a microscopic minority. And this one uses a different approach in trying to struggle for his rights. He doesn't beg. He doesn't thank you for what you give him, because you are only giving him what he should have had a hundred years ago. He doesn't think you are doing him any favors.

He doesn't see any progress that he has made since the Civil War. He sees not one iota of progress because, number one, if the Civil War had freed him, he wouldn't need civil rights legislation today. If the Emancipation Proclamation, issued by that great shining liberal called Lincoln, had freed him, he wouldn't be singing "We Shall Overcome" today. If the amendments to the Constitution had solved his problem, still his problem wouldn't be here today. And even if the Supreme Court desegregation decision of 1954 was genuinely and sincerely designed to solve his problem, his problem wouldn't be with us today.

So this kind of Black man is thinking, he can see where every maneuver that America has made—supposedly to solve this problem—has been nothing but political trickery and treachery of the worst order. So today he doesn't have any confidence in these so-called liberals. Now I know that you all that have come in here tonight don't call yourselves liberals. Because that's a nasty name today. It represents hypocrisy. So these two different types of Black people exist in the so-called Negro community and they are beginning to wake up and their awakening is producing a very dangerous situation.

So you have whites in the community who express sincerity when they say they want to help. Well, how can they help? How can a white person help the Black man solve his problem? Number one: you can't solve it for him. You can help him solve it, but you can't solve it for him today. One of the best ways that you can solve it—or to help him solve it—is to let the so-called Negro, who has been involved in the civil rights struggle, see that the civil rights struggle must be expanded beyond the level of civil rights to human rights. Once it is expanded beyond the level of civil rights to the level of human rights, it opens the door for all of our brothers and sisters in Africa and Asia, who have their independence, to come to our rescue.

Why, when you go to Washington, D.C., expecting those crooks down there to pass some kind—and that's what they are—to pass some kind of civil rights legislation to correct a very criminal situation, what you are doing is encouraging the Black man, who is the victim, to take his case into the court that's controlled by the criminal that made him the victim. It will never be solved in that way. Just like running from the wolf to the fox. The civil rights struggle involves the Black man taking his case to the white man's court. But when he fights it at the human rights level, it is a different situation. It opens the door to take Uncle Sam to the world court. The Black man doesn't have to go to court to be free. Uncle Sam should be taken to court and made to tell why the Black man is not free in a so-called free society. Uncle Sam should be taken into the United Nations and charged with violating the UN charter on human rights.

You can forget civil rights. How are you going to get civil rights with men like Eastland and men like Dirksen and men like Johnson? It has to be taken out of their hands and taken into the hands of those whose power and authority exceed theirs. Washington has become too corrupt. Uncle Sam's conscience—Uncle Sam has become bankrupt when it comes to a conscience—it is impossible for Uncle Sam to solve the problem of 22 million Black people in this country. It is absolutely impossible to do it in Uncle Sam's courts—whether it is the Supreme Court or any other kind of court that comes under Uncle Sam's jurisdiction.

The only alternative that the Black man has in America today is to take it out of Senator Dirksen's and Senator Eastland's and President Johnson's jurisdiction and take it downtown on the East River and place it before that body of men who represent international law and let them know that the human rights of Black people are being violated in a country that professes to be the moral leader of the free world.

Any time you have a filibuster in America, in the Senate, in 1964 over the rights of 22 million Black people, over the citizenship of 22 million Black people or that will affect the freedom and justice and equality of 22 million Black people, it's time for that government itself to be taken before a world court. How can you condemn South Africa? There are only 11 million of our people in South Africa; there are 22 million of them here. And we are receiving an injustice which is just as criminal as that which is being done to the black people of South Africa.

So today those whites who profess to be liberals—and as far as I am concerned it's just lip profession—you understand why our people don't have civil rights. You're white. You can go and hang out with another white liberal and see how hypocritical they are. While a lot of you sitting right here know that you've seen whites up in a Negro's face with flowery words and as soon as that Negro walks away you listen to how your white friend talks. We have Black people who can pass as white. We know how you talk.

We can see that it is nothing but a governmental conspiracy to continue to deprive the Black people in this country of their rights. And the only way we will get these rights restored is by taking it out of Uncle Sam's hands. Take him to court and charge him with genocide, the mass murder of millions of Black people in this country—political murder, economic murder, social murder, mental murder. This is the crime that this government has committed, and if you yourself don't do something about it in time, you are going to open the doors for something to be done about it from outside forces.

I read in the paper yesterday where one of the Supreme Court justices, Goldberg, was crying about the violation of human rights of 3 million Jews in the Soviet Union. Imagine this. I haven't got anything against Jews, but that's their problem. How in the world are you going to cry about problems on the other side of the world when you haven't got the problems straightened out here? How can the plight of 3 million Jews in Russia be qualified to be taken to the United Nations by a man who is a justice in this Supreme Court and is supposed to be a liberal, supposed to be a friend of Black people, and hasn't opened up his mouth one time about taking the plight of Black people down here to the United Nations?

Our people are becoming more politically mature. Their eyes are coming open. They are beginning to see the trend in all of the American politics today. They notice that every time there is an election it is so close among whites that they have to count the votes over again. This happened in Massachusetts when they were running for governor, this happened in Rhode Island, it happened in Minnesota, and many other places, and it happened in the election between Kennedy and Nixon. Things are so close that any minority that has a bloc vote can swing it either way.

And I think that most students of political science agree that it was the 80 percent support that Kennedy got from the Black man in this country that enabled him to sit in the White House. Sat down there four years and the Negro was still in the doghouse. The same ones that we put in the White House have continued to keep us in the doghouse. The Negro can see that he holds the balance of power in this country politically.

It is he who puts in office the one who gets in office. Yet when the Negro helps that person get in office the Negro gets nothing in return. All he gets is a few appointments. A few handpicked, Uncle Tom, handkerchief-head Negroes are given big jobs in Washington, D.C. And then those Negroes come back and try and make us think that the administration is going to lead us to the promised land of integration. And the only ones whose problems have been solved have been those handpicked Negroes. A few big Negroes got jobs who didn't even need the jobs. They already were working. But the masses of Black people are still unemployed.

The present administration, the Democratic administration, has been down there for four years. Yet no meaningful legislation has been passed by them that proposes to benefit Black people in this country, despite the fact that in the House they have 257 Democrats and only 177 are Republicans.

They control two-thirds of the House. In the Senate there are 67 Democrats and only 33 Republicans. The Democrats control two-thirds of the government and it is the Negroes who put them in a position to control the government. Yet they give the Negroes nothing in return but a few handouts in the form of appointments that are only used as window dressing to make it appear that the problem is being solved.

No, something is wrong. And when these Black people wake up and find out for real the trickery and the treachery that has been heaped upon us, you are going to have revolution. And when I say revolution I don't mean that stuff they were talking about last year about "We Shall Overcome." The Democrats get Negro support, yet the Negroes get nothing in return. The Negroes put the Democrats first, yet the Democrats put the Negroes last. And the alibi that the Democrats use—they blame the Dixiecrats.

A Dixiecrat is nothing but a Democrat in disguise. You show me a Dixiecrat and I'll show a Democrat. And chances are, you show me a Democrat and I'll show you a Dixiecrat. Because Dixie in reality means all that territory south of the Canadian border. There are sixteen senatorial committees that run this government. Of the sixteen senatorial committees that run the government, ten of them are controlled by chairmen that are from the South. Of the twenty congressional committees that help run the government, twelve of them are controlled by southern segregationists.

Think of this: ten of the senatorial committees are in the hands of the Dixiecrats, twelve of the twenty congressional committees are in the hands of the Dixiecrats. These committees control the government. And you're going to tell us that the South lost the Civil War? The South controls the government. And they control it because they have seniority. And they have seniority because in the states that they come from, they deny Negroes the right to vote.

If Negroes could vote south of the—yes, if Negroes could vote south of the Canadian border—south South, if Negroes could vote in the southern part of the South, Ellender wouldn't be the head of the Agricultural and Forestry Committee, Richard Russell wouldn't be head of the Armed Services Committee, Robertson of Virginia wouldn't be head of the Banking and Currency Committee. Imagine that, all of the banking and currency of the government is in the hands of a cracker.

In fact, when you see how many of these committee men are from the South, you can see that we have nothing but a cracker government in Washington, D.C. And their head is a cracker president. I said a cracker president. Texas is just as much a cracker state as Mississippi—and even more so. In Texas they lynch you with a Texas accent and in Mississippi they lynch you with a Mississippi accent.

And the first thing this man did when he came in office was invite all the big Negroes down for coffee. James Farmer was one of the first ones—the head of CORE. I have nothing against him. He's all right—Farmer, that is. But could that same president have invited James Farmer to Texas for coffee? And if James Farmer went to Texas, could he have taken his white wife with him to have coffee with the president? Any time you have a man who can't straighten out Texas, how can he straighten out the country? No, you're barking up the wrong tree.

If Negroes in the South could vote, the Dixiecrats would lose power. When the Dixiecrats lost power, the Democrats would lose power. A Dixiecrat lost is a Democrat lost. Therefore the two of them have to conspire with each other to stay in power. The northern Dixiecrat puts all the blame on the southern Dixiecrat. It's a con game, a giant political con game. The job of the northern Democrat is to make the Negro think that he is our friend. He is always smiling and wagging his tail and telling us how much he can do for us if we vote for him. But, at the same time he's out in front telling us what he's going to do, behind the door he's in cahoots with the southern Democrat setting up the machinery to make sure he'll never have to keep his promise.

This is the conspiracy that our people have faced in this country for the past one hundred years. And today you have a new generation of Black people who have come on the scene, who have become disenchanted with the entire system, who have become disillusioned over the system, and who are ready now and willing to do something about it. So in my conclusion in speaking about the Black revolution, America today is at a time or in a day or at an hour where she is the first country on this earth that can actually have a bloodless revolution. In the past, revolutions have been bloody. Historically you just don't have a peaceful revolution. Revolutions are bloody; revolutions are violent; revolutions cause bloodshed and death follows in their paths. America is the only country in history in a position to bring about a revolution without violence and bloodshed. But America is not morally equipped to do so.

Why is America in a position to bring about a bloodless revolution? Because the Negro in this country holds the balance of power and if the Negro in this country were given what the Constitution says he is supposed to have, the added power of the Negro in this country would sweep all of the racists and the segregationists out of office. It would change the entire political structure of the country. It would wipe out the Southern segregationism that now controls America's foreign policy, as well as America's domestic policy.

And the only way without bloodshed that this can be brought about is that the Black man has to be given full use of the ballot in every one of the fifty states. But if the Black man doesn't get the ballot, then you are going to be faced with another man who forgets the ballot and starts using the bullet.

Revolutions are fought to get control of land, to remove the absentee land-lord and gain control of the land and the institutions that flow from that land. The Black man has been in a very low condition because he has had no control whatsoever over any land. He has been a beggar economically, a beggar politically, a beggar socially, a beggar even when it comes to trying to get some education. So that in the past, the type of mentality that was developed in this colonial system among our people, today is being overcome. And as the young ones come up they know what they want. And as they listen to your beautiful preaching about democracy and all those other flowery words, they know what they're supposed to have.

So you have a people today who not only know what they want, but also know what they are supposed to have. And they themselves are creating another generation that is coming up that not only will know what it wants and know what it should have, but also will be ready and willing to do whatever is necessary to see that what they should have materializes immediately. Thank you.

MARTIN LUTHER KING, JR. (1929–1968)

✦ Black Power (1967)

Black Power is now a part of the nomenclature of the national community. To some it is abhorrent, to others dynamic; to some it is repugnant, to others exhilarating; to some it is destructive, to others it is useful. Since Black Power means different things to different people and indeed, being essentially an emotional concept, can mean different things to the same person on differing occasions, it is impossible to attribute its ultimate meaning to any single individual or organization. One must look beyond personal styles, verbal flourishes, and the hysteria of the mass media to assess its values, its assets and liabilities honestly.

First, it is necessary to understand that Black Power is a cry of disappointment. The Black Power slogan did not spring full grown from the head of some philosophical Zeus. It was born from the wounds of despair and disappointment. It is a cry of daily hurt and persistent pain. For centuries the Negro has been caught in the tentacles of white power. Many Negroes have given up faith in the white majority because "white power" with total control has left them empty-handed. So in reality the call for Black Power is a reaction to the failure of white power.

It is no accident that the birth of this slogan in the civil rights movement took place in Mississippi—the state symbolizing the most blatant abuse of white power. In Mississippi the murder of civil rights workers is still a popular pastime. In that state more than forty Negroes and whites have either been lynched or murdered over the last three years, and not a single man has been punished for these crimes. More than fifty Negro churches have been burned or bombed in Mississippi in the last two years, yet the bombers still walk the streets surrounded by the halo of adoration. This is white power in its most brutal, cold-blooded, and vicious form.

Many of the young people proclaiming Black Power today were but yesterday the devotees of black-white cooperation and nonviolent direct action.

Reprinted from *Where Do We Go From Here: Chaos or Community?* by Martin Luther King, Jr. (Boston: Beacon, 1967), 32–39, 40–41, 43–44, 47–54. © Martin Luther King, Jr., 1967. Reprinted by arrangement with The Heirs to the Estate of Martin Luther King, Jr., c/o Joan Daves Agency as agent for the proprietor.

With great sacrifice and dedication and a radiant faith in the future they labored courageously in the rural areas of the South; with idealism they accepted blows without retaliating; with dignity they allowed themselves to be plunged into filthy, stinking jail cells; with a majestic scorn for risk and danger they nonviolently confronted the Jim Clarks and the Bull Connors of the South, and exposed the disease of racism in the body politic. If they are America's angry children today, this anger is not congenital. It is a response to the feeling that a real solution is hopelessly distant because of the inconsistencies, resistance, and faintheartedness of those in power. If Stokely Carmichael now says that nonviolence is irrelevant, it is because he, as a dedicated veteran of many battles, has seen with his own eyes the most brutal white violence against Negroes and white civil rights workers, and he has seen it go unpunished.

Their frustration is further fed by the fact that even when blacks and whites die together in the cause of justice, the death of the white person gets more attention and concern than the death of the black person. Stokely and his colleagues from SNCC were with us in Alabama when Jimmy Lee Jackson, a brave young Negro man, was killed and when James Reeb, a committed Unitarian white minister, was fatally clubbed to the ground. They remembered how President Johnson sent flowers to the gallant Mrs. Reeb, and in his eloquent "We Shall Overcome" speech paused to mention that one person, James Reeb, had already died in the struggle. Somehow the President forgot to mention Jimmy, who died first. The parents and sister of Jimmy received no flowers from the President. The students felt this keenly. Not that they felt that the death of James Reeb was less than tragic, but because they felt that the failure to mention Jimmy Jackson only reinforced the impression that to white America the life of a Negro is insignificant and meaningless.

There is also great disappointment with the federal government and its timidity in implementing the civil rights laws on its statute books. The gap between promise and fulfillment is distressingly wide. Millions of Negroes are frustrated and angered because extravagant promises made little more than a year ago are a mockery today. When the 1965 Voting Rights Law was signed, it was proclaimed as the dawn of freedom and the open door to opportunity. What was minimally required under the law was the appointment of hundreds of registrars and thousands of federal marshals to inhibit southern terror. Instead, fewer than sixty registrars were appointed and not a single federal law officer capable of making arrests was sent into the South. As a consequence the old way of life—economic coercion, terrorism, murder, and inhuman contempt—has continued unabated. This gulf between the laws and their enforcement is one of the basic reasons why Black Power advocates express contempt for the legislative process.

The disappointment mounts as they turn their eyes to the North. In the northern ghettos, unemployment, housing discrimination, and slum schools mock the Negro who tries to hope. There have been accomplishments and some material gain, but these beginnings have revealed how far we have yet to go. The economic plight of the masses of Negroes has worsened. The gap between the wages of the Negro worker and those of the white worker has widened. Slums are worse and Negroes attend more thoroughly segregated schools today than in 1954.

The Black Power advocates are disenchanted with the inconsistencies in the militaristic posture of our government. Over the last decade they have seen America applauding nonviolence whenever the Negroes have practiced it. They have watched it being praised in the sit-in movements of 1960, in the Freedom Rides of 1961, in the Albany movement of 1962, in the Birmingham movement of 1963, and in the Selma movement of 1965. But then these same black young men and women have watched as America sends black young men to burn Vietnamese with napalm, to slaughter men, women, and children; and they wonder what kind of nation it is that applauds nonviolence whenever Negroes face white people in the streets of the United States but then applauds violence and burning and death when these same Negroes are sent to the field of Vietnam.

All of this represents disappointment lifted to astronomical proportions. It is disappointment with timid white moderates who feel that they can set the timetable for the Negro's freedom. It is disappointment with a federal administration that seems to be more concerned about winning an ill-considered war in Vietnam than about winning the war against poverty here at home. It is disappointment with white legislators who pass laws in behalf of Negro rights that they never intended to implement. It is disappointment with the Christian church that appears to be more white than Christian, and with many white clergymen who prefer to remain silent behind the security of stained-glass windows. It is disappointment with some Negro clergymen who are more concerned about the size of the wheel base on their automobiles than about the quality of their service to the Negro community. It is disappointment with the Negro middle class that has sailed or struggled out of the muddy ponds into the relatively fresh-flowing waters of the mainstream, and in the process has forgotten the stench of the backwaters where their brothers are still drowning.

Second, Black Power, in its broad and positive meaning, is a call to black people to amass the political and economic strength to achieve their legitimate goals. No one can deny that the Negro is in dire need of this kind of legitimate power. Indeed, one of the great problems that the Negro confronts is his lack of power. From the old plantations of the South to the newer ghettos of the North, the Negro has been confined to a life of voicelessness and powerlessness. Stripped of the right to make decisions concerning his life and destiny, he has been subject to the authoritarian and sometimes whimsical decisions of the white power structure. The plantation and the ghetto were created by those who had power both to confine those who had no power and to perpetuate their powerlessness. The problem of transforming the ghetto is, therefore, a problem of power—a confrontation between the forces of power demanding change and the forces of power dedicated to preserving the status quo.

Power, properly understood, is the ability to achieve purpose. It is the strength required to bring about social, political, or economic changes. In this sense power is not only desirable but necessary in order to implement the demands of love and justice. One of the greatest problems of history is that the concepts of love and power are usually contrasted as polar opposites. Love is identified with a resignation of power and power with a denial of love. It was this misinterpretation that caused Nietzsche, the philosopher of the "will to power," to reject the Christian concept of love. It was this same misinterpretation which induced Christian theologians to reject Nietzsche's philosophy of the "will to power" in the name of the Christian idea of love. What is needed is a realization that power without love is reckless and abusive and that love without power is sentimental and anemic. Power at its best is love implementing the demands of justice. Justice at its best is love correcting everything that stands against love.

There is nothing essentially wrong with power. The problem is that in America power is unequally distributed. This has led Negro Americans in the past to seek their goals through love and moral suasion devoid of power and white Americans to seek their goals through power devoid of love and conscience. It is leading a few extremists today to advocate for Negroes the same destructive and conscienceless power that they have justly abhorred in whites. It is precisely this collision of immoral power with powerless morality which constitutes the major crisis of our times.

In his struggle for racial justice, the Negro must seek to transform his condition of powerlessness into creative and positive power. One of the most obvious sources of this power is political. In *Why We Can't Wait* I wrote at length of the need for Negroes to unite for political action in order to compel the majority to listen. I urged the development of political awareness and strength in the Negro community, the election of blacks to key positions, and the use of the bloc vote to liberalize the political climate and achieve our just aspirations for freedom and human dignity. To the extent that Black Power advocates these goals, it is a positive and legitimate call to action that we in the civil rights movement have sought to follow all along and which we must intensify in the future.

Black Power is also a call for the pooling of black financial resources to achieve economic security. While the ultimate answer to the Negroes' economic dilemma will be found in a massive federal program for all the poor along the lines of A. Philip Randolph's Freedom Budget, a kind of Marshall Plan for the disadvantaged, there is something that the Negro himself can do to throw off the shackles of poverty. Although the Negro is still at the bottom of the economic ladder, his collective annual income is upwards of $30 billion. This gives him a considerable buying power that can make the difference between profit and loss in many businesses.

Through the pooling of such resources and the development of habits of thrift and techniques of wise investment, the Negro will be doing his share to grapple with his problem of economic deprivation. If Black Power means the development of this kind of strength within the Negro community, then it is a quest for basic, necessary, legitimate power.

Finally, Black Power is a psychological call to manhood. For years the Negro has been taught that he is nobody, that his color is a sign of his biological depravity, that his being has been stamped with an indelible imprint of inferiority, that his whole history has been soiled with the filth of worthlessness. All too few people realize how slavery and racial segregation have scarred the soul and wounded the spirit of the black man. The whole dirty business of slavery was based on the premise that the Negro was a thing to be used, not a person to be respected. . . .

Out of the soil of slavery came the psychological roots of the Black Power cry. Anyone familiar with the Black Power movement recognizes that defiance of white authority and white power is a constant theme; the defiance almost becomes a kind of taunt. Underneath it, however, there is a legitimate concern that the Negro break away from "unconditional submission" and thereby assert his own selfhood.

Another obvious reaction of Black Power to the American system of slavery is the determination to glory in blackness and to resurrect joyously the African past. In response to the emphasis on their masters' "enormous power," Black Power advocates contend that the Negro must develop his own sense of strength. No longer are "fear, awe and obedience" to rule. This accounts for, though it does not justify, some Black Power advocates who encourage contempt and even uncivil disobedience as alternatives to the old patterns of slavery. Black Power assumes that Negroes will be slaves unless there is a new power to counter the force of the men who are still determined to be masters rather than brothers.

It is in the context of the slave tradition that some of the ideologues of the Black Power movement call for the need to develop new and indigenous codes of justice for the ghettos, so that blacks may move entirely away from their former masters' "standards of good conduct." Those in the Black Power movement who contend that blacks should cut themselves off from every level of dependence upon whites for advice, money, or other help are obviously reacting against the slave pattern of "perfect dependence" upon the masters.

Black Power is a psychological reaction to the psychological indoctrination that led to the creation of the perfect slave. While this reaction has often led to negative and unrealistic responses and has frequently brought about intemperate words and actions, one must not overlook the positive value in calling the Negro to a new sense of manhood, to a deep feeling of racial pride, and to an audacious appreciation of his heritage. The Negro must be grasped by a new realization of his dignity and worth. He must stand up amid a system that still oppresses him and develop an unassailable and majestic sense of his own value. He must no longer be ashamed of being black.

The job of arousing manhood within a people that have been taught for so many centuries that they are nobody is not easy. Even semantics have conspired to make that which is black seem ugly and degrading. In Roget's Thesaurus there are some 120 synonyms for "blackness" and at least sixty of them are offensive—such words as "blot," "soot," "grime," "devil," and "foul." There are some 134 synonyms for "whiteness," and all are favorable, expressed in such words as "purity," "cleanliness," "chastity," and "innocence." A white lie is better than a black lie. The most degenerate member of a family is the "black sheep," not the "white sheep." Ossie Davis has suggested that maybe the English language should be "reconstructed" so that teachers will not be forced to teach the Negro child sixty ways to despise himself and thereby perpetuate his false sense of inferiority and the white child 134 ways to adore himself and thereby perpetuate his false sense of superiority.

The history books, which have almost completely ignored the contribution of the Negro in American history, have only served to intensify the Negroes' sense of worthlessness and to augment the anachronistic doctrine of white supremacy. . . .

The tendency to ignore the Negro's contribution to American life and strip him of his personhood is as old as the earliest history books and as contemporary as the morning's newspaper. To offset this cultural homicide, the Negro must rise up with an affirmation of his own Olympian manhood. Any movement for the Negro's freedom that overlooks this necessity is only waiting to be buried. As long as the mind is enslaved the body can never be free. Psychological freedom, a firm sense of self-esteem, is the most powerful weapon against the long night of physical slavery. No Lincolnian Emancipation Proclamation or Kennedyan or Johnsonian civil rights bill can totally bring this kind of freedom. The Negro will only be truly free when he reaches down to the inner depths of his own being and signs with the pen and ink of assertive selfhood his own emancipation proclamation. With a spirit straining toward true self-esteem, the Negro must boldly throw off the manacles of self-abnegation and say to himself and the world: "I am somebody. I am a person. I am a man with dignity and honor. I have a rich and noble history, however painful and exploited that history has been. I am black *and* comely." This self-affirmation is the black man's need made compelling by the white man's crimes against him. This is positive and necessary power for black people.

Nevertheless, in spite of the positive aspects of Black Power, which are compatible with what we have sought to do in the civil rights movement all along without the slogan, its negative values, I believe, prevent it from having the substance and program to become the basic strategy for the civil rights movement in the days ahead.

Beneath all the satisfaction of a gratifying slogan, Black Power is a nihilistic philosophy born out of the conviction that the Negro can't win. It is, at bottom, the view that American society is so hopelessly corrupt and enmeshed in evil that there is no possibility of salvation from within. Although this thinking is understandable as a response to a white power structure that never completely committed itself to true equality for the Negro, and a diehard mentality that sought to shut all windows and doors against the winds of change, it nonetheless carries the seeds of its own doom. . . .

The Black Power movement of today, like the Garvey "Back to Africa" movement of the 1920s, represents a dashing of hope, a conviction of the inability of the Negro to win, and a belief in the infinitude of the ghetto. While there is much grounding in past experience for all these feelings, a revolution cannot succumb to any of them. Today's despair is a poor chisel to carve out tomorrow's justice.

Black Power is an implicit and often explicit belief in black separatism. Notice that I do not call it black racism. It is inaccurate to refer to Black Power as racism in reverse, as some have recently done. Racism is a doctrine of the congenital inferiority and worthlessness of a people. While a few angry proponents of Black Power have, in moments of bitterness, made wild statements that come close to this kind of racism, the major proponents of Black Power have never contended that the white man is innately worthless.

Yet behind Black Power's legitimate and necessary concern for group unity and black identity lies the belief that there can be a separate black road to power and fulfillment. Few ideas are more unrealistic. There is no salvation for the Negro through isolation.

One of the chief affirmations of Black Power is the call for the mobilization of political strength for black people. But we do not have to look far to see that effective political power for Negroes cannot come through separatism. Granted that there are cities and counties in the country where the Negro is in a majority, they are so few that concentration on them alone would still leave the vast majority of Negroes outside the mainstream of American political life.

Out of the eighty-odd counties in Alabama, the state where SNCC sought to develop an all-black party, only nine have a majority of Negroes. Even if blacks could control each of these counties, they would have little influence in overall state politics and could do little to improve conditions in the major Negro population centers of Birmingham, Mobile, and Montgomery. There are still relatively few Congressional districts in the South that have such large black majorities that Negro candidates could be elected without the aid of whites. Is it a sounder program to concentrate on the election of two or three Negro Congressmen from predominantly Negro districts or to concentrate on the election of fifteen or twenty Negro Congressmen from southern districts where a coalition of Negro and white moderate voters is possible?

Moreover, any program that elects all black candidates simply because they are black and rejects all white candidates simply because they are white is politically unsound and morally unjustifiable. It is true that in many areas of the South Negroes still must elect Negroes in order to be effectively represented. SNCC staff members are eminently correct when they point out that in Lowndes County, Alabama, there are no white liberals or moderates and no possibility for cooperation between the races at the present time. But the Lowndes County experience cannot be made a measuring rod for the whole of America. The basic thing in determining the best candidate is not his color but his integrity.

Black Power alone is no more insurance against social injustice than white power. Negro politicians can be as opportunistic as their white counterparts if there is not an informed and determined constituency demanding social reform. What is most needed is a coalition of Negroes and liberal whites that will work to make both major parties truly responsive to the needs of the poor. Black Power does not envision or desire such a program.

Just as the Negro cannot achieve political power in isolation, neither can he gain economic power through separatism. While there must be a continued emphasis on the need for blacks to pool their economic resources and withdraw consumer support from discriminating firms, we must not be oblivious to the fact that the larger economic problems confronting the Negro community will only be solved by federal programs involving billions of dollars. One unfortunate thing about Black Power is that it gives priority to race precisely at a time when the impact of automation and other forces have made the economic question fundamental for blacks and whites alike. In this context a slogan "Power for Poor People" would be much more appropriate than the slogan "Black Power."

However much we pool our resources and "buy black," this cannot create the multiplicity of new jobs and provide the number of low-cost houses that will lift the Negro out of the economic depression caused by centuries of deprivation. Neither can our resources supply quality integrated education. All of this requires billions of dollars which only an alliance of liberal-labor-civil-rights forces can stimulate. In short, the Negroes' problem cannot be solved unless the whole of American society takes a new turn toward greater economic justice.

In a multiracial society no group can make it alone. It is a myth to believe that the Irish, the Italians, and the Jews—the ethnic groups that Black Power advocates cite as justification for their views—rose to power through separatism. It is true that they stuck together. But their group unity was always enlarged by joining in alliances with other groups such as political machines and trade unions. To succeed in a pluralistic society, and an often hostile one at that, the Negro obviously needs organized strength, but that strength will only be effective when it is consolidated through constructive alliances with the majority group.

Those proponents of Black Power who have urged Negroes to shun alliances with whites argue that whites as a group cannot have a genuine concern for Negro progress. Therefore, they claim, the white man's main interest in collaborative effort is to diminish Negro militancy and deflect it from constructive goals.

Undeniably there are white elements that cannot be trusted, and no militant movement can afford to relax its vigilance against halfhearted associates or conscious betrayers. Every alliance must be considered on its own merits. Negroes may embrace some and walk out on others where their interests are imperiled. Occasional betrayals, however, do not justify the rejection of the principle of Negro-white alliance.

The oppression of Negroes by whites has left an understandable residue of suspicion. Some of this suspicion is a healthy and appropriate safeguard. An excess of skepticism, however, becomes a fetter. It denies that there can be reliable white allies, even though some whites have died heroically at the side of Negroes in our struggle and others have risked economic and political peril to support our cause.

The history of the movement reveals that Negro-white alliances have played a powerfully constructive role, especially in recent years. While Negro initiative, courage, and imagination precipitated the Birmingham and Selma confrontations and revealed the harrowing injustice of segregated life, the organized strength of Negroes alone would have been insufficient to move Congress and the administration without the weight of the aroused conscience of white America. In the period ahead Negroes will continue to need this support. Ten percent of the population cannot by tensions alone induce 90 percent to change a way of life.

Within the white majority there exists a substantial group who cherish democratic principles above privilege and who have demonstrated a will to fight side by side with the Negro against injustice. Another and more substantial group is composed of those having common needs with the Negro and who will benefit equally with him in the achievement of social progress. There are, in fact, more poor white Americans than there are Negro. Their need for a war on poverty is no less desperate than the Negro's. In the South they have been deluded by race prejudice and largely remained aloof from common action. Ironically, with this posture they were fighting not only the Negro but themselves. Yet there are already signs of change. Without formal alliances, Negroes and whites have supported the same candidates in many de facto electoral coalitions in the South because each sufficiently served his own needs.

The ability of Negroes to enter alliances is a mark of our growing strength, not of our weakness. In entering an alliance, the Negro is not relying on white leadership or ideology; he is taking his place as an equal partner in a common endeavor. His organized strength and his new independence pave the way for alliances. Far from losing independence in an alliance, he is using it for constructive and multiplied gains.

Negroes must shun the very narrow-mindedness that in others has so long been the source of our own afflictions. We have reached the stage of organized strength and independence to work securely in alliances. History has demonstrated with major victories the effectiveness, wisdom, and moral soundness of Negro-white alliance. The cooperation of Negro and white based on the solid ground of honest conscience and proper self-interest can continue to grow in scope and influence. It can attain the strength to alter basic institutions by democratic means. Negro isolation can never approach this goal.

In the final analysis the weakness of Black Power is its failure to see that the black man needs the white man and the white man needs the black man. However much we may try to romanticize the slogan, there is no separate black path to power and fulfillment that does not intersect white paths, and there is no separate white path to power and fulfillment, short of social disaster, that does not share that power with black aspirations for freedom and human dignity. We are bound together in a single garment of destiny. The language, the cultural patterns, the music, the material prosperity, and even the food of America are an amalgam of black and white.

James Baldwin once related how he returned home from school and his mother asked him whether his teacher was colored or white. After a pause he answered: "She is a little bit colored and a little bit white." This is the dilemma of being a Negro in America. In physical as well as cultural terms every Negro is a little bit colored and a little bit white. In our search for identity we must recognize this dilemma.

Every man must ultimately confront the question, "Who am I?" and seek to answer it honestly. One of the first principles of personal adjustment is the principle of self-acceptance. The Negro's greatest dilemma is that in order to be healthy he must accept his ambivalence. The Negro is the child of two cultures—Africa and America. The problem is that in the search for wholeness all too many Negroes seek to embrace only one side of their natures. Some, seeking to reject their heritage, are ashamed of their color, ashamed of black art and music, and determine what is beautiful and good by the standards of white society. They end up frustrated and without cultural roots. Others seek to reject everything American and to identify totally with Africa, even to the point of wearing African clothes. But this approach leads also to frustration because the American Negro is not an African. The old Hegelian synthesis still offers the best answer to many of life's dilemmas. The American Negro is neither totally African nor totally Western. He is Afro-American, a true hybrid, a combination of two cultures.

Who are we? We are the descendants of slaves. We are the offspring of noble men and women who were kidnapped from their native land and chained in ships like beasts. We are the heirs of a great and exploited continent known as Africa. We are the heirs of a past of rope, fire, and murder. I for one am not ashamed of this past. My shame is for those who became so inhuman that they could inflict this torture upon us.

But we are also Americans. Abused and scorned though we may be, our destiny is tied up with the destiny of America. In spite of the psychological appeals of identification with Africa, the Negro must face the fact that America is now his home, a home that he helped to build through blood, sweat, and tears. Since we are Americans the solution to our problem will not come through seeking to build a separate black nation within a nation, but by finding that creative minority of the concerned from the ofttimes apathetic majority, and together moving toward that colorless power that we all need for security and justice.

In the first century B.C., Cicero said: "Freedom is participation in power." Negroes should never want all power because they would deprive others of their freedom. By the same token, Negroes can never be content without participation in power. America must be a nation in which its multiracial people are partners in power. This is the essence of democracy toward which all Negro struggles have been directed since the distant past when he was transplanted here in chains. . . .

ANGELA Y. DAVIS (1944–   )

🏵 Radical Perspectives on the Empowerment of Afro-American Women: Lessons for the 1980s (1987)

The concept of empowerment is hardly new to Afro-American women. For almost a century, we have been organized in bodies that have sought collectively to develop strategies that illuminate the way to economic and political power for ourselves and our communities. In the last decade of the nineteenth century, after having been repeatedly shunned by the racially homogeneous women's rights movement, black women organized their own club movement. In 1895—five years after the founding of the General Federation of Women's Clubs, which consolidated a club movement reflecting concerns of middle-class white women—one hundred black women from ten states met in the city of Boston, under the leadership of Josephine St. Pierre Ruffin, to discuss the creation of a national organization of black women's clubs. As compared to their white counterparts, the Afro-American women issuing the call for this national club movement articulated principles that were more openly political in nature. They defined the primary function of their clubs as an ideological as well as an activist defense of black women—and men—from the ravages of racism. When the meeting was convened, its participants emphatically declared that, unlike their white sisters, whose organizational policies were seriously tainted by racism, they envisioned their movement as one open to all women:

> Our woman's movement is woman's movement in that it is led and directed by women for the good of women and men, for the benefit of *all* humanity, which is more than any one branch or section of it. We want, we ask the active interest of our men, and, too, we are not drawing the color line; we are women, American women, as intensely interested in all that pertains to us as such as all other American women; we are not alienating or withdrawing, we are only coming to the front, willing to join any others in the same work and cordially inviting and welcoming any others to join us.[1]

Reprinted from the *Harvard Educational Review* 58, no. 3 (August 1988): 348–53. Reprinted by permission of the *Harvard Educational Review*.

The following year, the formation of the National Association of Colored Women's Clubs was announced. The motto chosen by the Association was "Lifting as We Climb."[2]

The nineteenth-century women's movement was also plagued by classism. Susan B. Anthony wondered why her outreach to working-class women on the issue of the ballot was so frequently met with indifference. She wondered why these women seemed to be much more concerned with improving their economic situation than with achieving the right to vote.[3] As essential as political equality may have been to the larger campaign for women's rights, in the eyes of Afro-American and white working-class women it was not synonymous with emancipation. That the conceptualization of strategies for struggle was based on the peculiar condition of white women of the privileged classes rendered those strategies discordant with working-class women's perceptions of empowerment. It is not surprising that many of them told Ms. Anthony, "Women want bread, not the Ballot."[4] Eventually, of course, working-class white women, and Afro-American women as well, reconceptualized this struggle, defining the vote not as an end in itself—not as the panacea that would cure all the ills related to gender-based discrimination—but rather as an important weapon in the continuing fight for higher wages, better working conditions, and an end to the omnipresent menace of the lynch mob.

Today, as we reflect on the process of empowering Afro-American women, our most efficacious strategies remain those that are guided by the principle used by black women in the club movement. We must strive to "lift as we climb." In other words, we must climb in such a way as to guarantee that all of our sisters, regardless of social class, and indeed all of our brothers, climb with us. This must be the essential dynamic of our quest for power—a principle that must not only determine our struggles as Afro-American women, but also govern all authentic struggles of dispossessed people. Indeed, the overall battle for equality can be profoundly enhanced by embracing this principle.

Afro-American women bring to the women's movement a strong tradition of struggle around issues that politically link women to the most crucial progressive causes. This is the meaning of the motto, "Lifting as We Climb." This approach reflects the often unspoken interests and aspirations of masses of women of all racial backgrounds. Millions of women today are concerned about jobs, working conditions, higher wages, and racist violence. They are concerned about plant closings, homelessness, and repressive immigration legislation. Women are concerned about homophobia, ageism, and discrimination against the physically challenged. We are concerned about Nicaragua and South Africa, and we share our children's dreams that tomorrow's world will be delivered from the threat of nuclear omnicide. These are some of the issues that should be made a part of the overall struggle for women's rights, if there is to be a serious commitment to the empowerment of women who, throughout history, have been rendered invisible. These are some of the issues we should consider if we wish to lift as we climb.

During this decade we have witnessed an exciting resurgence of the women's movement. If the first wave of the movement appeared in the 1840s, and the second wave in the 1960s, then we are approaching the crest of a third wave in the final days of the 1980s. When the feminist historians of the twenty-first century attempt to recapitulate the third wave, will they ignore the momentous contributions of Afro-American women, who have been leaders and activists in movements often confined to women of color, but whose accomplishments have invariably advanced the cause of white women as well? Will the exclusionary policies of the mainstream women's movement—from its inception to the present—which have often compelled Afro-American women to conduct their struggle for equality outside the ranks of that movement, continue to result in the systematic omission of our names from the roster of prominent leaders and activists of the women's movement? Will there continue to be two distinct continua of the women's movement, one visible and another invisible? One publicly acknowledged and another ignored except by the conscious progeny of the working-class women—black, Latina, Native American, Asian, and white—who forged that hidden continuum? If this question is answered in the affirmative, it will mean that women's quest for equality will continue to be gravely deficient. The revolutionary potential of the women's movement still will not have been realized. The racist-inspired flaws of the first and second waves of the women's movement will have become the inherited flaws of the third wave.

How can we guarantee that this historical pattern is broken? As advocates of and activists for women's rights in the later 1980s, we must begin to merge that double legacy and create a single continuum, one that solidly represents the aspirations of all women in our society. We must begin to create a revolutionary, multiracial women's movement that seriously addresses the main issues affecting poor and working-class women. In order to tap the potential for such a movement, we must further develop those sectors of the movement that are addressing seriously issues affecting poor and working-class women, such as jobs, pay equity, paid maternity leave, federally subsidized child care, protection from sterilization abuse, and subsidized abortions. Women of all racial and class backgrounds will benefit greatly from such an approach.

Creating a revolutionary women's movement will not be simple. For decades, white women activists have repeated the complaint that women of color frequently fail to respond to their appeals: "We invited them to our meetings, but they didn't come; We asked them to participate in our demonstration, but they didn't show; They just don't seem to be interested in women's studies." The process cannot be initiated merely by intensified efforts to attract Latina or Afro-American or Asian or Native American women into the existing organizations dominated by white women of the more privileged economic strata. The particular concerns of women of color must be included in the agenda.

An issue of special concern to Afro-American women is unemployment. Indeed, the most fundamental prerequisite for empowerment is the ability to earn an adequate living. The Reagan administration boasts that unemployment has leveled off, leaving only (!) 7.5 million people unemployed. However, black people in general are twice as likely to be unemployed as white people, and black teenagers are almost three times as likely to be unemployed as white teenagers.[5] We must remember that these figures do not include the millions who hold part-time jobs, although they want and need full-time employment. A disproportionate number of these underemployed individuals are women. Neither do the figures reflect those who, out of utter frustration, have ceased to search for employment, nor those whose unemployment insurance has run out, nor those who have never had a job. Women on welfare are among those who are not counted as unemployed.

The AFL-CIO estimates that there are 18 million people of working age without jobs. These still critical levels of unemployment, distorted and misrepresented by the Reagan administration, are fundamentally responsible for the impoverished status of Afro-American women, the most glaring evidence of which resides in the fact that women, together with their dependent children, constitute the fastest growing sector of the population of 4 million homeless in the United States. There can be no serious discussion of empowerment today if we do not embrace the plight of the homeless with an enthusiasm as passionate as that with which we embrace issues more immediately related to our own lives.

The United Nations declared 1987 to be the Year of Shelter for the Homeless, although only the developing countries were the initial focus of this resolution. Eventually, it became clear that the United States is an "undeveloping country." Two-thirds of the 4 million homeless in this country are families, and 40 percent of them are Afro-American.[6] In some urban areas, as many as 70 percent of the homeless are black. In New York City, for example, 60 percent of the homeless population is black, 20 percent Latino, and 20 percent white.[7] Presently, under New York's Work Incentive Program, homeless women and men are employed to clean toilets, wash graffiti from subway trains, and clean parks at wages of sixty-two cents an hour, a mere fraction of the minimum wage.[8] In other words, the homeless are being compelled to provide slave labor for the government if they wish to receive assistance.

Black women scholars and professionals cannot afford to ignore the straits of those of our sisters who are acquainted with the immediacy of oppression in a way many of us are not. The process of empowerment cannot be simplistically defined in accordance with our own particular class interests. We must learn to lift as we climb.

If we are to elevate the status of our entire community as we scale the heights of empowerment, we must be willing to offer organized resistance to the proliferating manifestations of racist violence across the country. A virtual race riot took place on the campus of one of the most liberal educational institutions in this country some months ago. In the aftermath of the 1986 World Series, white students at the University of Massachusetts, Amherst, who were purportedly fans of the losing Boston Red Sox, vented their wrath on black students, whom they perceived as surrogates for the winning team, the New York Mets, because of the predominance of black players on the New York team. When individuals in the crowd yelled "black bitch" at a black woman student, a black man who hastened to defend her was seriously wounded and was rushed, unconscious, to the hospital. Another one of the many dramatic instances of racist harassment to occur on college campuses during this period was the burning of a cross in front of the Black Students Cultural Center at Purdue University.[9] In December 1986, Michael Griffith, a young black man, lost his life in what amounted to a virtual lynching by a mob of white youths in the Howard Beach, Queens, section of New York City. Not far from Atlanta, civil rights marchers were attacked on Dr. Martin Luther King's birthday by a mob led by the Ku Klux Klan. An especially outrageous instance in which racist violence was officially condoned was the acquittal of Bernhard Goetz, who, on his own admission, attempted to kill four black youths because he *felt* threatened by them on a New York subway.

Black women have organized before to oppose racist violence. The birth of the Black Women's Club Movement at the end of the nineteenth century was in large part a response to the epidemic of lynching during that era. Leaders like Ida B. Wells and Mary Church Terrell recognized that black women could not move toward empowerment if they did not radically challenge the reign of lynch law in the land. Today, in the late 1980s, Afro-American women must actively take the lead in the movement against racist violence, as did our sister-ancestors almost a century ago. We must lift as we climb. As our ancestors organized for the passage of a federal anti-lynch law—and indeed involved themselves in the women's suffrage movement for the purpose of securing that legislation—we must today become activists in the effort to secure legislation declaring racism and anti-Semitism crimes. As extensive as publicized instances of racist violence may be at this time, many more racist-inspired crimes go unnoticed as a consequence of the failure of law enforcement to classify them specifically as such. A person scrawling swastikas or "KKK" on an apartment building may simply be charged—if criminal charges are brought at all—with defacing property or malicious mischief. Recently, a Ku Klux Klansman who burned a cross in front of a black family's home was charged with "burning without a permit." We need federal and local laws against acts of racist and anti-Semitic violence. We must organize, lobby, march, and demonstrate in order to guarantee their passage.

As we organize, lobby, march, and demonstrate against racist violence, we who are women of color must be willing to appeal for multiracial unity in the spirit of our sister-ancestors. Like them we must proclaim: We do not draw the color line. The only line we draw is one based on our political principles. We know that empowerment for the masses of women in our country will never be achieved as long as we do not succeed in pushing back the tide of racism. It is not a coincidence that sexist-inspired violence—and, in particular, terrorist attacks on abortion clinics—has reached a peak during the same period in which racist violence has proliferated dramatically. Violent attacks on women's reproductive rights are nourished by these explosions of racism. The vicious anti-lesbian and anti-gay attacks are a part of the same menacing process. The roots of sexism and homophobia are found in the same economic and political institutions that serve as the foundation of racism in this country, and, more often than not, the same extremist circles that inflict violence on people of color are responsible for the eruptions of violence inspired by sexist and homophobic biases. Our political activism must clearly manifest our understanding of these connections.

We must always attempt to lift as we climb. Another urgent point on our political agenda—that of Afro-American as well as all progressive women—must be the repeal of the Simpson–Rodino Act: a racist law that spells repression for vast numbers of women and men who are undocumented immigrants in this country. Camouflaged as an amnesty program, the eligibility restrictions are so numerous that hundreds of thousands of people stand to be prosecuted and deported under its provisions. Amnesty is provided in a restricted way only for those who came to this country before 1982. Thus, vast numbers of Mexicans, who have recently crossed the border in an attempt to flee impoverishment generated by the unrestricted immigration of U.S. corporations into their country, are not eligible for citizenship. Salvadorans and other Central Americans who have escaped political persecution in their respective countries over the last few years will not be offered amnesty. We must organize, lobby, march, and demonstrate for a repeal of the Simpson–Rodino Act. We must lift as we climb.

When we as Afro-American women, when we as women of color, proceed to ascend toward empowerment, we lift up with us our brothers of color, our white sisters and brothers in the working class, and indeed all women who experience the effects of sexist oppression. Our activist agenda must encompass a wide range of demands. We must call for jobs and for the unionization of unorganized women workers, and, indeed, unions must be compelled to take on such issues as affirmative action, pay equity, sexual harassment on the job, and paid maternity leave. Black and Latina women are AIDS victims in disproportionately large numbers. We therefore have an urgent need to demand emergency funding for AIDS research. We must also oppose all instances of repressive mandatory AIDS testing and quarantining, as well as homophobic manipulations of the AIDS crisis. Effective strategies for the reduction of teenage pregnancy are needed, but we must beware of succumbing to propagandistic attempts to relegate to young single mothers the responsibility for our community's impoverishment.

In this unfortunate era of Reaganism, it should be clear that there are forces in our society that reap enormous benefits from the persistent, deepening oppression of women. Members of the Reagan administration include advocates for the most racist, sexist, and anti–working-class circles of contemporary monopoly capitalism. These corporations prop up apartheid in South Africa and profit from the spiraling arms race, while they propose the most vulgar and irrational forms of anti-Sovietism—invoking, for example, the "evil empire" image popularized by Ronald Reagan—as justifications for their omnicidal ventures. If we are not afraid to adopt a revolutionary stance, if, indeed, we wish to be radical in our quest for change, then we must get to the root of our oppression. After all, "radical" simply means grasping things at the root. Our agenda for women's empowerment must thus be unequivocal in its challenge to monopoly capitalism as a major obstacle to the achievement of equality.

I want to suggest, as I conclude, that we link our grassroots organizing, our essential involvement in electoral politics, and our involvement as activists in mass struggles with the long-range aim of fundamentally transforming the socioeconomic conditions that generate and persistently nourish the various forms of oppression we suffer. Let us learn from the strategies of our sisters in South Africa and Nicaragua. As Afro-American women, as women of color in general, as progressive women of all racial backgrounds, let us join our sisters *and* brothers across the globe who are attempting to forge a new socialist order—an order which will reestablish socioeconomic priorities so that the quest for monetary profit will never be permitted to take precedence over the real interests of human beings. This is not to say that our problems will magically dissipate with the advent of socialism. Rather, such a social order should provide us with the real opportunity to extend further our struggles, with the assurance that one day we will be able to redefine the basic elements of our oppression as useless refuse of the past.

[1]Gerda Lerner, *Black Women in White America* (New York: Pantheon Books, 1972), 443.

[2]These clubs proliferated in the progressive political scene during this era. By 1916—twenty years later—50,000 women in 28 federations and over 1,000 clubs were members of the National Association of Colored Women's Clubs. See Paula Giddings's discussion of the origins and evolution of the Black Women's Club Movement in *When and Where I Enter* (New York: William Morrow, 1984), chaps. 4–6.

[3]Miriam Schneir, ed., *Feminism: The Essential Historical Writings* (New York: Vintage, 1972), 138–42.

[4]Schneir, *Feminism.*

[5]Children's Defense Fund, *Black and White Children in America: Key Facts* (Washington, DC: Author, 1985), 21–22.

[6]*WREE-VIEW* 12, nos. 1 & 2 (January–April 1987).

[7]*WREE-VIEW.*

[8]*WREE-VIEW.*

[9]The incidence of racial violence on college campuses has increased significantly since this speech was delivered in the summer of 1987. "Reports of racist acts at U.S. colleges and universities have been piling up at an increased pace for several years, and now, fresh incidents and controversies seem to arise almost daily" ("Racism, A Stain on Ivory Towers," *The Boston Sunday Globe,* 28 February 1988, 1). In response to these incidents, students have organized themselves to improve the racial climate on their campuses. For example, in March 1988, a coalition of multiracial domestic and international students at Hampshire College in Amherst, Massachusetts, demonstrated the seriousness of their concerns by staging a building take-over and demanding specific correctives.

LUCIUS OUTLAW (1944–)

🏵 Philosophy, Ethnicity, and Race (1988)

Introduction

Millions of us throughout the world are living during very problematic and challenging times. The reasons are numerous and quite complex, made more so by much of what we might otherwise celebrate as milestones of human achievement in many areas: artistic creativity, material and agricultural productivity, science and technology, medicine, transportation and communication, the magnitude and velocity of knowledge and information accumulation and dispersal, and political transformations, to mention a few. A complete litany of the problems and challenges we face is unnecessary. (Nor am I capable of providing one, or would be disposed to do so if I could . . .) No doubt we all can supply examples from personal and shared experiences, elaborated by teachings from our homes, churches, synagogues, mosques, temples, and other critical institutions; by claimants to knowledge on our t.v.s, radios, CDs, etc.; by learnings from our classes and seminars; and, most assuredly, from speakers at our high school graduations and the ceremonies yet to come at Quinnipiac.

If we are to survive and flourish, we will, of course, have to find ways to meet the challenges and resolve the problems. However, since much of what confronts us today is made more complex and challenging by its relative uniqueness, we find ourselves without reservoirs of experience and knowledge that are directly and immediately applicable to the difficulties we encounter (for example: managing the now constant threat of conflict leading to thermonuclear warfare and the real possibility of the elimination of virtually all of humanity). Consequently, we are compelled to forge new approaches—intellectual, moral/practical, institutional, or cultural in the larger sense—with all of the fear and trepidation, all of the risk, that such pioneering efforts embody. (Need I add, however, that such situations of challenge also provide possibilities for the deepest experiences of our finitude, our mortality, and of the joys of prevailing against the odds?) And in the

Reprinted from Lucius Outlaw, *Philosophy, Ethnicity, and Race*, The Alfred P. Stiernotte Lectures in Philosophy (Hamden, CT: Quinnipiac College, 1989). Reprinted with permission of Quinnipiac College.

face of great challenges, often a near compelling strategy that is most readily available is to seek comfort in what seems to be the wisdom of sedimented knowledge and experience already at work in what we do at present. Yet doing so may well be to succumb to the inertia of the familiar but inappropriate.

Of course, we philosophers can tell the difference, can we not? For isn't this our calling: to achieve the foundational knowledge—the *wisdom*—that will make it possible for us to distinguish the *real* from the apparent, the *true* from the false, *appropriate* from inappropriate, knowledge that, in its timelessness and universality, is secure from the vagaries of historical changes? Or so we (philosophers) have said, and some of us continue to say. On this characterization of philosophy I should be able, if I am a *real* philosopher, to set forth the principles, and strategies based on them, for meeting the challenges we face.

But I will not do so. First, because I am concerned only with a particular subset of challenges which are pointed to by the title of this lecture: namely, those of "race" and "ethnicity" in relation to "philosophy." I think these matters are sufficiently compelling to require at least some of our best effort, as I hope to make clear. Thus, I invite you to join me in wrestling with them. Second, precisely because I want to question this construal of philosophy as the chief executive of a timeless wisdom, particularly as it relates to the matters of race and ethnicity. The contribution of philosophy and philosophers to the successful resolution of challenges and problems is, I think, more limited, but potentially more valuable nonetheless, than keeping timeless wisdom.

Why race and ethnicity in relation to philosophy? In short, because I am convinced that we are living through a period in which race and ethnicity are so challenging to the prospect of our enjoying a future in which we can and will flourish that we are compelled to undertake a fundamental revision of some of our basic convictions regarding who we are, what our lives should be about, and how we will achieve our goals, both individually and collectively. Since such concerns have provided the motivating core for much of Western philosophy (and its sibling fields of inquiry) for more than two thousand years, and philosophy, in various incarnations, has contributed substantially to the accumulated store of knowledge that passes for wisdom with regard to these concerns, this review and revision calls, as well, for a re-evaluation of philosophy itself.

Finally, there is the deeply personal dimension to my focusing on these issues, for they all come together in a poignant way to constitute my very being and to inform my daily life, and, thereby, to condition the lives of all who interact with me: I am a philosopher; I teach portions of the history of the discipline; but I do so as a person of a racial/ethnic group whose existence in America and throughout the world is marked by the holocaust of enslavement and other forms of oppression which have been rationalized by some of the "best" minds in the pantheon of Western philosophers. Thus, not only in practical living must I contend with constricting factors having to do with the politics of race and ethnicity, I must do battle, as well, inside the very citadel of reason where enlightenment leading to enhanced living is supposed to have its wellspring: in the practices and achievements of philosophy. As a person of African descent participating in the enterprise of philosophy, I have committed myself to confronting this seedy aspect of its underside and to the clearing of intellectual and social spaces in which we might come together to work and dwell in peace and harmony with justice. To this extent I take seriously the long-standing commitment of philosophy to radical critique leading to enhanced living, and seek to use this commitment against the discipline in the interest of the latter's refinement.

From "Universality" to "Particularity": The Politics of "Difference"

The challenge that is the focus of my concern is part of a much larger complex of practical and intellectual struggles, spanning many years, that recently have been grouped under the heading "the politics of difference." Examples include efforts to include persons from once excluded groups in educational, social, and occupational settings through the targeting practices of affirmative action programs; various struggles emerging from the contemporary women's movement; and, in general, the use of racial, ethnic, gender, and sexual lifestyle identifiers as the organization focus for politics and the bases for fashioning terms of justice.

What is shared by this wide range of endeavors is the attempt to revise both social-political life and intellectual domains and practices in order to facilitate the legitimate "play of differences," where difference is prized over forced homogenization—or the hegemony of one group and its values and practices over all others while masking this dominance in liberal, democratic dress. Central to this effort are two basic beliefs. First, that a full appreciation of what it means to be human requires that we take proper note of human groupings, the definitive characteristics of which (combining historically mediated physical, psychological, and cultural factors) are constitutive, in varying degrees, of the persons in the group. Second, that the principles on which we would base both the organization of sociopolitical life and those intellectual enterprises whose objects are living human beings take explicit account of these constitutive differences. Doing so, we proponents say, can and ought to lead to the acknowledged and promoted substantial enrichment of our collective life, given the wealth of messages, ideals, and practices contributed by various groups comprising our multidimensional social wholes (i.e., local, national, international . . .). Not doing so results not only in our collective impoverishment, but, particularly when there is active opposition to those who are "different," this failure contributes directly to distortions of the cultural spaces we all occupy and to the deformation and self-deformation of members of those groups. Among the groups for whom these matters continue to be pressing issues are those constituted, at least in part, by factors termed racial and / or ethnic.

There are many aspects to the challenge posed by the advocacy of forms of political, social, cultural, and intellectual life in which the play of differences is a normative, nurtured feature. For this occasion I wish to focus primarily on what doing so requires of our basic conceptions of ourselves as individual persons and as ordered associates in sociopolitical structures and practices. And here, promoting the play of differences runs counter to some of the most basic tendencies of liberal democratic political thought and practices, and of modern Enlightenment philosophy on which it is based: namely, to look beyond what are often regarded as accidental differences, including race and ethnicity to the "substantial core" or *essence,* which, ontologically, is the definitive constitutive factor of the human species, and thus is shared by all humans. For a long time now, that essence has been identified as *reason.* Knowing and exercising this essence has been thought central to securing "universality" in epistemological matters as a foundation for unity and order in sociopolitical praxis.

For opponents of the project to give freer rein to the play of differences, emphasis on *particularity* subverts these quests and, in practical terms, threatens the always tenuous achievements of cognitive and political normativity thought to be secured by the universality of reason. The achievement and perpetuation of knowledge (in science and philosophy, for example) become exposed to the acidic effects of "relativism"; and the freedom, peace, and prosperity of political stability won through liberal (or, in today's terms, "conservative") politics are jeopardized by possibilities of drift, chaos, or, at worst, anarchy.

Such possibilities are real. Whether they are *probable* depends on a number of factors. But it is neither logically, socially, or historically *necessary* that such consequences follow from a greater play of differences. Achieving that increased play while preserving and enhancing social and intellectual life is precisely what I see as the challenge to be met in an appropriate valorization of race and ethnicity.

The Challenge to Philosophy

The challenge confronts philosophy directly. As I have noted, one of the central endeavors of Western philosophy continues to be that of attempting to provide the definitive characterization of what it is to be human (of what it is to be "man"). And, in general, the terms in which the characterizations have been and are articulated are void of any explicit references to race and ethnicity. Certainly the Enlightenment was a triumph of precisely this mode of characterizing humans. It was a triumph that made possible substantive progressive achievements in human history, won against some forces that, had they triumphed instead, would have given us a world not much to the liking of many of us, myself included.

But the victory was not without costs. At the very least, in focusing on what is shared in pursuit of unity and universality, the unique, the dissimilar, the individual, the particular is disregarded. And in doing so, a tension is created at the core of Enlightenment philosophy's view of man: between its specification of the shared and universal in the characterization of the human species that makes us all "the same" and its emphasis on the free, rational *individual*. Further, the aspirations of universalist philosophy notwithstanding, where *generally* race, ethnicity, gender, etc., were irrelevant to the formulations of key notions, the full truth of the matter discloses the ethnocentricism and racism, sexism, and class biases at the very heart of the enterprise: whether invoked in the Greek-barbarian distinction, the enslavement of non-Greeks and constraining of women when fifth and fourth century Greece was at its zenith, or in the continued oppression of women and the enslavement and oppression of African peoples during and after the modern Enlightenment.

Of course, one might argue that where we find racism, ethnocentricism, class bias, or sexism in philosophy it is due to the failure of particular thinkers to live up to the terms of humanism called for by the universalist notions of humans as rational beings—for some, created in the image of God—who are rightly worthy of respect, and that a correction of such situations requires only that the guilty parties come to be governed by the logic of these notions. Consequently, no revision of the central notions about man is required. I disagree. Not only is it necessary to extend the privileged notions to groups of persons previously excluded from coverage (e.g., women, Africans and people of African descent, other peoples of color), I hope to make a credible case that these notions, while substantive in many ways in contributing to our sense of ourselves, and thus to the organization of our individual and collective life, are also insufficient in ways that can only be corrected by revising them to include space for an appreciation of group-based particularities. We must rethink "*man*" if some of the challenges to practical life are to be overcome.

Will doing so constitute a retreat from the achievements of ancient and modern Western Enlightenments? It could, depending on how one proceeds. But it also opens us to challenging possibilities for social learning that may provide us with bases for enhanced living, for realizing futures which we otherwise might not live due to our failure to evolve. This is the possibility that I hold out to those who disagree with me and solicit, with thanks, your patience and attention as I present my case.

I shall do so by briefly rehearsing (from my perspective, of course . . .) certain legacies of the enterprise of philosophy involving constructing and trusteeing the image of "man." My focus will be on the central roles of reason in these endeavors, particularly as they relate to the development of political strategies deployed in the organization and management of social life. I shall argue that at critical historical junctures reason is made a whore in service to politics when it is prostituted by fashioning and manipulating the "white mythology" of assimilated universalism through "melted" particularities as a masking apology for domination. But when those who would be melted refuse—or the politics of the situation in reality repudiate, in blatant self-contradiction, their entry into the pot for the meltdown, even when they are willing to do so—we have conditions like those we are presently living through, in which the different and "unmeltable" force reconsiderations of the social project and of the understanding and the wisdom which would ground it. I will offer a modest proposal for that reconsideration.

Enlightenment through Philosophy: From Diversity to "Unity"

Philosophy: Architect and Custodian of "Man"

Certainly the narratives of Greek life and thought that have dominated philosophical discourses and provided much of the enterprise with a self-image and agenda have presented the fulfillment of the quest for wisdom as knowledge of what *is* beyond the merely apparent once it becomes clear that what *appears* to be the case may not always be so. Certainly sensory experiences cannot provide us with definitive knowledge of what is. Nor can history and tradition, or other modes of experience by way of the emotions, imagination, or spirit, provide assured guidance in practical life, across time, in a way that guarantees stability and insures that what is appropriate will always be chosen as the thing to do. The conviction of Heraclitus that all is change does not win out as the dominant philosophical orientation. Instead, it is replaced by a strategy that presumes that there is something more than the apparent, that change is a feature of some*thing* which undergoes changes, and that the goal of "true" knowledge is the uncovering or "illumination" of that something and the articulation of its character.

This strategy gives rise to other moves, one of which is particularly relevant to this discussion: namely, the gradual elaboration of a repertoire of hierarchical oppositions thought to be necessary for getting at the definitive structure of what *is* at its most fundamental level, with reason providing the means for distinguishing between them. Thus the distinctions between true/false, real/apparent, essential/accidental. Further, early in the game, a way of reading experience led to the conclusion that although there was change, all was not chaos: change, in most cases, was ordered (day/night; the seasons; the natural order of birth, development, decline, and death—and rebirth?).

The task of understanding man as a being subject to time was conditioned by this complex of intellectual strategies. From Homer onwards, speech and thinking—both referred to by the term *logos,* complemented by *nous* or "reason"—were thought by some Greek thinkers to be what distinguish humans from other animals. These terms became integral parts of the philosophical self-image. Through these concepts and others ("truth," "goodness," "virtue," etc.), a fundamental, orienting, and *grounding* linkage was made between the microcosm of human existence and the macrocosm of the cosmos, between the divine mind and/or the governing principles and processes of the universe and the mind as the *essence* of the human. Logos was thought to be the code of being; the task of understanding (i.e., the proper and successful exercise of human logos or nous that resulted in the acquisition of knowledge) was then to grasp and decipher this code and to organize and direct human praxis, guided by the wisdom derived from the deciphering, or from the continued exercise and achievement of understanding.

Further, logos and nous were thought to be attributes that all humans share. Implied in this is the idea that humans are alike, thus are "unified" in and through logos and nous.

While this was not a generally shared notion at the time, it emerged in the thought of various persons across the years. More prevalent was the distinction between Greeks and barbarians, though the notion of a unified species that was nurtured by influential figures contributed to undermining it.[1] Among the contributors were Thucydides and the medical writers, who conceived mankind as a single species requiring rational study and did so via a biological approach which maintained humankind's unity but admitted its diversity while seeking a *reasoned* explanation for it in place of accounts supplied by tradition and prejudice. A major contributor, it turns out, was Socrates, who emerged in the period of ferment between the fifth and fourth centuries during which a number of key ideas appeared that were elaborated later:

the notion of a single universal and permanent "human nature"; the belief that certain physical attributes are common to all men; the concept of a human unity made up of diverse elements; the rejection of traditional divisions between men as artificial and relative, not natural or absolute; the picture of "civilised man" as the human norm.[2]

Plato is perhaps the most familiar developer of these ideas in their full implications without, however, having worked out a particular treatise on the unity of mankind. Such a notion, instead, must be pulled together from his writings on the soul and other matters for which initial approaches were articulated by Socrates: namely, that the soul (*psyche*) is the vital part of us, the primary feature of which is logos, i.e., reason and articulate speech. Aristotle continued the exploration, making important contributions in his own right, in part by bringing together two lines of approach: on the one hand, the scientific tradition with its emphasis on the unity of the human species with egalitarian implications contributing to a disregard of accepted divisions among human beings; on the other, the idea of hierarchical gradations among persons based on defective *natures* that made for different possibilities for fulfilling the human *telos*, now identified with "rationality."[3]

Further, the task of determining all of this was assigned to philosophers by both Plato and Aristotle. On the basis of supposed certainty regarding epistemological matters, in conjunction with a particular philosophical anthropology, the Knowers were felt justified in rank-ordering groups of humans on the basis of judgments regarding their *natures*—a complex of generic features shared by the members of particular groups (e.g., females, children, non-Greeks, slaves). Aristotle's formulations in this area provided a powerful rationalization of Hellenistic practices.

"Reason" and Universalism: The Unity of Mankind

The Aristotelian strategy, building on Socrates, Plato, and others, who identified reason as a definitive feature of human animals, proved decisive, particularly in defining human diversity as a function of different natures. It was useful for some church thinkers during the Middle Ages and was put to work during the Enlightenment—the "Age of Reason"—even as the strategy of universalism was elaborated into explicit accounts of human nature that were to contribute to major political transformations that revolutionized Europe and what became America during the seventeenth and eighteenth centuries. A complex historical period, the Enlightenment is distinctive because of the decisive contributions of formal and popularizing thinkers—*philosophes* and philosophers[4]—to the elaboration of the ideas that became fuel for and rationalizations of the political transformations that led to decidedly new social formations. These thinkers help set the terms of and usher in *modernity*, an emergent historical conjunction, in part configured by social, political, economic, and cultural arrangements and developments at the core of which were a cluster of new ideas regarding reason, nature, and progress.[5]

For Enlightenment thinkers reason was a form of common sense enhanced by logical and scientific training. As with all physiological functions, reason, they thought, worked virtually the same way in all humans as products of nature's design. However, for these thinkers eighteenth century environmental conditions in the West—the wider cultural environment including church, state, social and economic class, ignorance, prejudice, superstition, poverty, and vice—had, in most humans, sufficiently corrupted reason to impede its normal and proper functioning.[6] But improvement was possible with the appropriate intervention, particularly through education, even though it might require an extended period of time. Progress—that is, historical development, orchestrated by reason, leading to the amelioration of corrupting, restricting conditions and thus to the fulfillment of human telos—would result from the reformation of social life guided by the "enlightened."

America—with its capitalist, so-called free enterprise economic order, its representative democracy structured by a host of rights, and its protected realm of civic privacy, all three resting on the universalized but privileged Enlightenment notion of man—is a paradigm of one complex form of a near successful Enlightenment project, Thomas Jefferson, a paradigmatic Enlightenment philosopher (and Ronald Reagan and George Bush claimants to trusteeship of the legacy?). Yet both America and Jefferson are also equally paradigmatic of the near self-contradicting tensions inscribed in the core of Enlightenment thought and practice: the universalist implications of the unity of mankind commitment to its philosophical anthropology anchored in its ideas regarding reason, on the one side; its attempt to manage human diversity by elaborating a hierarchy defined in terms of the purity, corruption, level of development of reason—or even the presence or absence of the ability to reason—in particular groups of persons, on the other.

The Whore of Reason: Managing Diversity through Hierarchy

Reason, Power, and the Other

For Jefferson and this nation, the enslavement of Africans was a crucible for the Enlightenment project. The institutionalization of slavery as a legitimate venture meant that a contradiction—between the universalism in the Enlightenment view of man, fueling the rationalization of the revolution and formation of the new republic guided by the principles of reason, and the rationalization of slavery, using hierarchically ranked racial distinctions—was firmly ensconced, practically and intellectually, in the heart of the great experiment called America. The compromise in behalf of solidarity among the colonies—increasingly regionalized by conflicting emerging political economies of neofeudal agricultural capitalism based on slave labor in the South and mercantile capitalism in the North and East—required a retreat from enlightened principles: reason became whore to political expediency. Or, as we might now say, the nexus of power and knowledge, with the latter serving the former, was demonstrated with brutal frankness.

But, as yet another rationalization: that is to say, the deal was done with reason's sanction. Certainly, as noted, Aristotle had worked out a scheme in which the recognition of human diversity in terms of hierarchical ordering was in accord with reason: groups of persons differed as a function of their *natures*, which determined their *end* or *telos*, the most that they were capable of being when fully developed. In his words: "the nature of a thing is its end. For what each thing is when fully developed, we call its nature, whether we are speaking of a man, a horse, or a family. Besides, the final cause and end of a thing is the best . . ."[7] The roles filled by persons of different groups demonstrated the practical truth of this "explanation" in Athens. Thus, it was "rational" to order social relations in such a manner that hierarchy brought the range of natures into functional relationships that were appropriate to those on each level: husband to wife; father to children; master to slave, Greek to barbarian:

> But is there any one thus intended by nature to be a slave, and for whom such a condition is expedient and right, or rather is not all slavery a violation of nature?
>
> There is no difficulty in answering this question, on grounds both of reason and of fact. For that some should rule and others be ruled is a thing not only necessary, but expedient; from the hour of their birth, some are marked out for subjection, others for rule.[8]
>
> [F]or in all things which form a composite whole and which are made up of parts, whether continuous or discrete, a distinction between the ruling and the subject element comes to light. Such a duality exists in living creatures, but not in them only; it originates in the constitution of the universe. . . .[9]

When Europeans encountered African "others," these valorizations were readily deployed in the rationalization of racial / ethnic differences into relations of superordination and subordination. Hegel, certainly one of the major figures of continental European philosophy, was quite explicit about the matter.

Africa must be divided into three parts: one is that which lies south of the desert of Sahara—Africa proper—the Upland almost entirely unknown to us . . .; the second is that to the north of the desert—European Africa (if we may so call it) . . .; the third is the river region of the Nile. . . .

Africa proper, as far as History goes back, has remained—for all purposes of connection with the rest of the World—shut up; it is the Gold-land compressed within itself—the land of childhood, which lying beyond the day of self-conscious history, is enveloped in the dark mantle of Night. . . . The second portion of Africa is the river district of the Nile—Egypt; which was adapted to become a mighty centre of independent civilization, and therefore is as isolated and singular in Africa as Africa itself appears in relation to the other parts of the world. . . . This part was to be—must be attached to Europe. . . .

The peculiarly African character is difficult to comprehend, for the very reason that in reference to it, we must quite give up the principle which naturally accompanies all our ideas—the category of Universality. In Negro life the characteristic point is the fact that consciousness has not yet attained to the realization of any substantial objective existence—as for example, God, or Law—in which the interest of man's volition is involved and in which he realizes his own being. This distinction between himself as an individual and the universality of his essential being, the African in the uniform, undeveloped oneness of his existence has not yet attained; so that the knowledge of an absolute Being, an Other and a Higher than his individual self, is entirely wanting. The Negro, as already observed, exhibits the natural man in his completely wild and untamed state. We must lay aside all thought of reverence and morality—all that we call feeling—if we would rightly comprehend him; there is nothing harmonious with humanity to be found in this type of character. . . .

At this point we leave Africa, not to mention it again. For it is no historical part of the World; it has no movement or development to exhibit. Historical movements in it—that is in its northern part—belong to the Asiatic or European World. Carthage displayed there an important transitory phase of civilization; but, as a Phoenician colony, it belongs to Asia. Egypt will be considered in reference to the passage of the human mind from its Eastern to its Western phase, but it does not belong to the African Spirit. What we properly understand by Africa, is the Unhistorical, Undeveloped Spirit, still involved in the conditions of mere nature, and which had to be presented here only as on the threshold of the World's History.

Having eliminated this introductory element, we find ourselves for the first time on the real theatre of History.[10]

This orientation rode the ships with the Europeans migrating to this land. It was literally made-to-order for the situation of compromise faced by the founders and had long been sanctified by various churches that worked out interpretations of the curse imposed on Adam and his progeny, as recorded in the *Bible,* so that one son was doomed to be forever marked by a dark stain (black skin?). In this historical case, the Other—Africans—had their difference fixed ontologically through reasoning strategies articulated by Aristotle, historically and culturally by Hegel, spiritually and biologically by the *Bible*, to mention just a few participants in this grand conspiracy. And "race" became a principal vehicle for this fixation. Universalism was reason-prepared, by both classical and modern Enlightenments, to handle diversity through reason-privileged hierarchy.

The Careers of "Race" and "Ethnicity"

Constructing Others: "Race" and the Evolutionary "Chain of Being"[11]

There is, of course, nothing more fascinating than the question of the various types of mankind and their intermixture. The whole question of heredity and human gift depends upon such knowledge; but ever since the African slave trade and before the rise of modern biology and sociology, we have been afraid in America that scientific study in this direction might lead to conclusions with which we were loath to agree; and this fear was, in reality, because the economic foundation of the modern world was based on the recognition and preservation of so-called racial distinctions. In accordance with this, not only Negro slavery could be justified, but the Asiatic coolie profitably used and the labor classes in white countries kept in their places by low wage.[12]

Race theory . . . had up until fairly modern times no firm hold on European thought. On the other hand, race theory and race prejudice were by no means unknown at the time when the English colonists came to North America. Undoubtedly, the age of exploration led many to speculate on race differences at a period when neither Europeans nor Englishmen were prepared to make allowances for vast cultural diversities. Even though race theories had not then secured wide acceptance or even sophisticated formulation, the first contacts of the Spanish with the Indians in the Americas can now be recognized as the beginning of a struggle between conceptions of the nature of primitive peoples which has not yet been wholly settled. . . . Although in the seventeenth century race theories had not as yet developed any strong scientific or theological rationale, the contact of the English with Indians, and soon afterward with Negroes, in the New World led to the formation of institutions and relationships which were later justified by appeals to race theories.[13]

For most of us, that there are different races of people is one of the most obvious features of our social worlds. The term *race* is thus a vehicle for beliefs and values deployed in the organization of our life-worlds and to structure our encounters and relations with persons who are significantly different from us in terms of physical features (skin color and other anatomical characteristics) and, combined with these, differences in language, behavior, ideas, and other cultural matters. In the United States especially, race is a constitutive element of our common sense, [and] thus is a key component of our "taken-for-granted valid reference schema" through which we get on in the world.[14] And, as we constantly face the need to resolve difficulties posing varying degrees of danger to the social whole in which race is the hidden or focal point of contention (or serves as a shorthand explanation for the source of contentious differences), we are reinforced in our assumption that race is self-evident. True to the prediction of W. E. B. Du Bois, the twentieth century has indeed been dominated by "the problem of the color line," and is likely to be so for the remainder of the century and well into the next. In particular, we are confronted by the need to face a persistent problem within Western societies, one that, in the U.S. and other European societies in particular, makes for yet another historical conjuncture of crisis proportions: the prospects for—and the concrete configurations of—democracy in the context of historic shifts in the demographics of racial pluralism.

The centripetal, potentially balkanizing forces of racial pluralism have been intensified during the past quarter-century as political mobilization and organization often have been based on heightened racial self-consciousness, a development that displaced the constraining effects of the once dominant paradigm of "ethnicity" and the assimilationist agenda it served.[15] According to the logic of ethnicity as the paradigm for conceptualizing group differences and fashioning social policy to deal with them, the socially divisive effects of "ethnic" differences were to disappear in the social-cultural "melting pot"; or, ethnic identity would be maintained across time but would be mediated by principles of the body politic: all *individuals*, without regard to race, creed, color, or national origin, were to have an equal *opportunity* to achieve success on the basis of demonstrated achievement (i.e., merit). For assimilationists and pluralists, *group* characteristics (ethnicity) were to have no play in the determination of merit; their legitimacy was restricted to the private sphere of "culture." With this the pluralists and assimilationists are explicitly drawing off of the Enlightenment legacy of universalism.

During the past twenty years, however, race and ethnicity have been *primary* vehicles for conceptualizing and organizing around group differences with the demand that social justice be applied to persons *as members of particular groups*, and that justice be measured by *results*, not just by opportunities. With the assimilationist agenda of the ethnic paradigm no longer hegemonic, combined with the rising demographics of the "unmeltable" ethnics in the American population (and the populations of other countries) and the preponderance of "race thinking" infecting political life, race has emerged—yet again—as the focus of social conflict.

The notion of race as a fundamental component of race thinking has had a powerful career in Western history (though such thinking has not been limited to the West). Even a cursory review of this history should do much to dislodge the concept from its place as provider of access to a self-evident, obvious, even ontologically *given* characteristic of humankind. For what comes out of such a review is the recognition that though race is continually with us as an organizing, explanatory concept, what the term refers to—that is, the supposed origin and basis of racial differences—has not remained constant. The use of "race" has virtually always been in service to political agendas, beyond more "disinterested" efforts simply to "understand" the basis of perceptually obvious (and otherwise not obvious, but real nonetheless) differences among human groups.

"Race" and Science

The career of race does not begin in science but predates it and emerges from a general need to account for the unfamiliar or, simply, to classify objects of experience, and thus to organize the life-world. How—or why—it was that race came to play important classifying, organizing roles is not clear:

> The career of the race concept begins in obscurity, for experts dispute whether the word derives from an Arabic, a Latin, or a German source. The first recorded use in English of the word "race" was in a poem by William Dunbar of 1508. . . . During the next three centuries the word was used with growing frequency in a literary sense as denoting simply a class of persons or even things. . . . In the nineteenth, and increasingly in the twentieth century, this loose usage began to give way and the word came to signify groups that were distinguished biologically.[16]

This nineteenth-century development was antedated by others in preceding centuries that apparently generated a more compelling need for classificatory ordering in the social world and, subsequently, the use of race as such a device. First, there were the tensions within Europe arising from encounters among different groups of peoples, particularly "barbarians"— whether defined culturally or, more narrowly, religiously. (And it should be noted that within European thought and elsewhere, the color black was associated with evil and death, with sin in the Christian context. The valorizing power inherent in this was ready-to-hand with Europe's encounter with Africa.) A more basic impetus, intensified by these tensions, came from the need to account for human origins in general, for human diversity in particular. Finally, there were the quite decisive European voyages to America and Africa, and the development of capitalism and the slave trade.[17]

The authority of race as an organizing, classificatory concept was strengthened during the eighteenth century when "evidence from geology, zoology, anatomy and other fields of scientific enquiry was assembled to support a claim that racial classification would help explain many human differences . . ."[18] "Race" contributed to a form of "typological thinking"—a mode of conceptualization that was at the center of the agenda of emerging scientific praxis at the time—that facilitated the classification of human groups. As noted, Plato and Aristotle were precursors of such thinking: the former with his theory of forms; the latter via his classification of things in terms of their nature. In the modern period the science of race began in comparative morphology with its stress on pure types as classificatory vehicles.

A major contributor to this unfolding agenda of classificatory thought was the botanist Linnaeus.[19] Other persons were particularly significant contributors to the development of such thought as it related to theories of racial types. According to Banton and Harwood, Johan Friedrich Blumenbach provided the first systematic racial classification in his *Generis Humani Varietate Nativa Liber* (*On the Natural Variety of Mankind,* 1775). This was followed by the work of James Cowles Prichard (*Generis Humani Varietate,* 1808).[20] Georges Cuvier, a French anatomist, put forth a physical cause theory of races in 1800 in arguing that physical nature determined culture. He classified humans into three major groups, along an implied descending scale: whites, yellows, and blacks. As Banton and Harwood interpreted Cuvier's work, central to his thinking was the notion of type more than that of race: "Underlying the variety of the natural world was a limited number of pure types, and if their nature could be grasped it was possible to interpret the diverse forms which could temporarily appear as a result of hybrid mating."[21] Other important contributions include S. G. Morton's publication of a volume on the skulls of American Indians (1839) and one on Egyptian skulls (1845). His work was extended and made popular by J. C. Nott and G. R. Gliddon in their *Types of Mankind* (1854). Charles Hamilton Smith (*The Natural History of the Human Species,* 1848) developed Cuvier's line of argument in Britain. By Smith's reckoning, according to Banton and Harwood, "The Negro's lowly place in the human order was a consequence of the small volume of his brain."[22] Smith's former student, Robert Knox (*The Races of Men,* 1850), argued likewise. Finally, there was Count Joseph Arthur de Gobineau's four-volume *Essay on the Inequality of Human Races* (1854), in which he argued that, in the words of Banton and Harwood, "the major world civilizations . . . were the creations of different races and that race-mixing was leading to the inevitable deterioration of humanity."[23]

Two significant achievements resulted from these efforts. First, drawing on the rising authority of science as the realization and guardian of systematic, certain knowledge, there was the legitimation of race as a gathering concept for morphological features that were thought to distinguish varieties of homo sapiens supposedly related to one another through the logic of a *natural* hierarchy of groups. Secondly, there was the legitimation of the view that the behavior of a group and its members was determined by their place in this hierarchy.[24] Consequently, science-authorized and legitimated notions about race, when combined with social projects involving the distinguishing and ultimately the control of racially different persons and groups—as in the case of the enslavement of Africans—took root and grew to become part of common sense. Race was now "obvious."

The science of race peaked during the middle of the nineteenth century, according to Banton and Harwood. By the end of the century, however, a variety of racial classifications had brought confusion, in part because "no one was quite sure what races were to be classified *for.* A classification is a tool. The same object may be classified differently for different purposes. No one can tell what is the best classification without knowing what it has to do."[25] The situation was both assisted and complicated by the work of Darwin and Mendel. Social Darwinism emerged as an effort by some (notably Herbert Spencer and Ludwig Gumplowicz) to apply Darwin's principles regarding heredity and natural selection to human groups and endeavors, thereby to provide firmer grounding for the science of race (a move Darwin was reluctant to make). Such moves were particularly useful in justifying the dominance of certain groups over others (British over Irish; Europeans over Africans . . .).

On the other hand, however, Darwin's *Origins* shifted the terrain of scientific discourse from morphology and the stability of pure types to a subsequent genetics-based approach to individual characteristics and the effects on them of processes of change, thus to a focus on the analysis of variety. With the additional contributions of Mendel, this development proved revolutionary:

> A racial type was defined by a number of features which are supposed to go together . . . The racial theorists of the nineteenth century assumed there was a natural law which said that such traits were invariably associated and were transmitted to the next generation as part of a package deal. Gregor Mendel's research showed that this was not necessarily the case. . . . [It] also showed that trait variation *within* a population was just as significant as trait variations *between* populations . . . traits do not form part of a package but can be shuffled like a pack of playing cards.[26]

And since environmental impacts that condition natural selection in addition to factors of heredity and the interplay between dominant and recessive traits are important factors in the "shuffling" of traits, the notion of pure racial types with fixed essential characteristics was displaced: biologically (i.e., genetically) one can only speak of "clines."[27]

The biology of races thus became more a matter of studying diversities within—as well as among—groups, and, of particular interest, of studying the "evolution" of groups across time and space. Joined to these efforts were contributions from the *social* science of race: i.e., understanding members of particular groups as sharing some distinctive biological features—though not thereby constituting the groups as biologically pure types—but with respect to which sociocultural factors are of particular importance, but in ways significantly different from the thinking of the nineteenth century theorists of racial types. For many scientists the old nineteenth century notion of "race" had become useless as a classificatory concept, and hence certainly did not support in any scientifically valid way the political agendas of racists. As noted by Livingstone, "yesterday's science is today's common sense and tomorrow's nonsense."[28] Revolutions within sciences (natural and social) conditioned transformed approaches to race, though the consequences have still not completely supplanted the popular, commonsensical notions of races as pure types, as the programs of the Ku Klux Klan, among others, indicate.

The conceptual terrain for this later, primarily twentieth-century approach to race continues to be, in large part, the notion of evolution, now understood in ways significantly conditioned by the precursive work of Mendel and Darwin, social Darwinists notwithstanding. In the space opened by this revised version of the concept it became possible at least to work at synthesizing insights drawn from natural science (genetics, biochemistry) and social science (anthropology, sociology, psychology, ethology) for a fuller understanding of "geographical races."[29] On the one hand, studies of *organic* evolution focus on changes in the gene pool of a group or groups; studies of *superorganic* evolution, on the other hand, are concerned with changes in the "behavior repertoire" of a group or groups—that is, with their sociocultural development.[30] And a legitimate, continually challenging—though difficult to answer—question is to what extent, if at all, *superorganic* evolution is a function of *organic* evolution, or to what extent, if at all, the two forms of evolution are mutually influential.

But what is a race in the framework of organic evolution and the global social context of the late twentieth century? Certainly not a group of persons who are genetically homogeneous, a situation that is likely only in places where we might find a people who has remained completely isolated from other groups and hence has not been involved in intergroup sexual reproductions. On the contrary, the logics of the capitalist world system have drawn virtually all peoples into the "global village" and facilitated much "crossbreeding." But capitalism notwithstanding, "raciation"—i.e., the development of the distinctive gene pools of various groups which determine the relative frequencies of characteristics shared by their members, but generally not by them alone—has also been a function, in part, of chance. Consequently:

Since populations' genetic compositions vary over time, race classifications can never be permanent; today's classification may be obsolete in one hundred generations. More importantly, modern race classifications attempt to avoid being arbitrary by putting populations *of presumed common evolutionary descent* into the same racial group. Common descent, however, is inferred from similarity in gene frequencies, and here the problem lies. For . . . a population's gene frequencies are determined not only by its ancestry but also by the processes of natural selection and genetic drift. This means that two populations could, in principle, be historically unrelated but genetically quite similar if they had been independently subject to similar evolutionary forces. To place them in the same racial group would, as a step in the study of evolution, be quite misleading. In the absence of historical evidence of descent, therefore, it is difficult to avoid the conclusion that classifying races is merely a convenient but biologically arbitrary way of breaking down the variety of gene frequency data into a manageable number of categories.[31]

When we classify a group as a race, then, at best we refer to generally shared characteristics derived from a "pool" of genes. Social, cultural, and geographical factors, in addition to those of natural selection, all impact on this pool to condition raciation: sometimes to sustain the pool's relative configuration (for example, by isolating the group—culturally or physically—from outbreeding); sometimes to modify it (as when "mulattoes" were produced in the U.S. in significant part through slave masters' of European descent appropriating African women for their—the "masters"—sexual pleasure). It is possible to study the evolution of a particular group over time (a case of *specific* evolution) with some success. The prospects for success are more limited, however, when the context of concern is *general* evolution—that is, the grouping of all of the world's peoples into ordered categories "with the largest and most heterogeneous societies in the top category and the smallest and most homogeneous in the bottom."[32] In either case—general or specific evolution—the concern is with *superorganic* evolution: that is, with changes in behavior repertoires. And such changes are not determined by the *genetic* specificities of races.

But not all persons (or groups) think so. Though evolutionary—as opposed to typological—thinking, in some form, is at present the dominant intellectual framework for systematic reconstructions and explanations of human natural and social history, it, too, has been enlisted in the service of those who would have science pass absolution on their political agendas: to rationalize and legitimate the empowerment of certain groups, certain races, over others. Even if stripped of the more crude elements of social Darwinism's survival of the fittest, there are still those who offer us a science of race that is preoccupied with ordering human groups along an *ascending* scale, with a particular group's placement on the scale being a function of the level of their supposed development (or lack thereof) toward human perfectibility: from "primitive" to "civilized," "undeveloped" or "underdeveloped" to "developed" or "advanced."

Such arguments find fertile soil for nourishment and growth now that "evolution" (organic and superorganic, often without distinction), frequently conceived as linear development along a single path which *all* races have to traverse, is now a basic feature of our "common sense"—Creationists excepted—and as we still face political problems emerging from conflicts among racial groups. Race continues to function as a critical yardstick for the rank-ordering of human groups both "scientifically" and sociopolitically, the latter with support from the former. At bottom, then, "race"—sometimes explicitly, quite often implicitly—continues to be a major fulcrum of struggles over the acquisition and exercise of power and the distribution of social goods.

What is the result of this extended review of the career of "race" in science? We are left with the decisive conclusion, certainly, that race is only partially determined by biology. Biological factors provide boundary conditions and possibilities which, in complex interplay with environmental, cultural, and social factors, affect raciation and the development of geographical races.

Ethnicity

A review of the career of "ethnicity" leads to very similar conclusions, in part because it has often been used as a synonym for "race." With good reason, apparently, for the etymology of "ethnicity" reveals that the root term involved a physiological association that was retained in English: the word "ethnic" derives, via Latin, from the Greek *ethnikos*, the adjectival form of *ethnos*, a nation or race.[33] Later there were shifts from a biological (physiological) context of meaning to one that included cultural characteristics and political structures, though the shifts have been neither consistent nor unidirectional.[34] In short, definitions of "ethnic group" and "ethnicity" have been muddy.[35]

Ethnicity became paradigmatic for conceptualizing groupings of different humans during the 1920s–1930s, having successfully challenged the then prevailing biologistic approach to races which evolved after slavery to "explain" the "racial inferiority" of people of African descent—and, thereby, the "superiority" of the "white race." On one account, the rise of ethnicity to the status of reigning paradigm can be charted in its use in at least three distinct ways. First, prior to the 1930s it was an insurgent approach that challenged the biologistic view of race, an attack that was led by "progressive" scholars, activists, and policymakers for whom what has come to be called the Chicago school of sociology was a decisive institutional site. In this intellectual and social context, race was regarded as a social category and but one of a number of determinants of ethnicity or ethnic group identity. Second, during the decades spanning the 1930s through the mid-1960s, the paradigm served as the liberal / progressive "common sense" of race, a period in which assimilationism and cultural pluralism emerged as themes of discourses devoted to the articulation of strategies to guide the development of America into an "integrated" social whole in which racial / ethnic differences were "melted" away by the rationalist heat of egalitarian principles. This agenda, and the theorizing of ethnicity which was its intellectual articulation, was formed to meet the problems resulting from the migration and "culture contact" of European immigrants, hence the emphasis on—and the intellectual acceptance of the inevitability and desirability of—integration.

But the victory of the ethnicity paradigm in service to integration (that is, assimilation) was to prove hollow, in significant part because the paradigm and agenda were rooted in a framework structured so tightly around European experiences and concerns that there was a serious failure to appreciate the extent to which inequalities conditioned by biologically informed geographical raciations differed from inequalities that could be appropriately understood through the concepts of an ethnicity localized to groups of various lines of European descent. Thus, in the post-1965 period, when the Black Power movement ushered in an agenda decisively distinct from the assimilationism of the civil rights movement—and, in doing so, excited persons comprising other groups to likewise seek social justice in distributive terms referenced to their ethnic identity, not just to their being Americans—ethnicity as paradigm for integration was sharply challenged. The responses of some proponents of its continued dominance defined the paradigm's third agenda of deployment: as a defense of "conservative" egalitarianism against the "radical" assault of proponents of "group rights"—Blacks, women, ethnics who refused to be melted—that has forced a renewed focus on race, ethnicity, and the politics of difference.[36]

Beyond the "White Mythology"

We are thus in the midst of the rise of the unmeltables: that is, of social movements organized around a "new ethnicity"—new relative to the long dominance of the paradigm of assimilation—based on the use of cultural as well as biological characteristics by persons from various groups to identify *themselves* as being part of particular ethnic groups and to formulate their claims for social justice using these identifiers.

One student of this new ethnicity, Michael Novak, shares my reading of the times: this heightened awareness and articulation of ethnicity (he terms it "cultural awareness"), when politicized, makes this a major factor in global affairs, "perhaps even one of the major sources of political energy in our era."[37] Novak identifies a number of important components of the new ethnicity that are worth noting:

- it is "post-tribal," that is to say, it arises in an era when virtually every cultural group has been obliged to become aware of many others;
- it arises in an era of advanced technology that, paradoxically, liberates energies for more intense self-consciousness while simultaneously binding many cultures together in standardized technical infrastructures;
- it arises during a period of intense centripetal and homogenizing forces; and
- in some cases it involves a rebellion against forces of technical power, thus manifests a certain rebellion against the supposed moral superiority of modernity.[38]

In light of all this, combined with similar developments having to do with race, how might the challenges of race and ethnicity be met successfully?

We are in the midst of a historical conjuncture that is relatively new, one highly charged by efforts to achieve democracy in a multiethnic, multiracial society where "group thinking" is a decisive feature of social and political life. I join Novak and others in calling for a serious revision of the liberal tradition flowing out of the modern enlightenment, a tradition that has too often been a cloak for the hegemony of the complex metaphysics, ontology, and philosophical anthology of a "white mythology" which "reassembles and reflects the culture of the West: the white man takes his own mythology, Indo-European mythology, his own logos, that is, the *mythos* of his idiom, for the universal form of that he must still wish to call Reason."[39] This notion of reason, argued for—by philosophy in particular—through the classical and modern Enlightenments, must be revised in favor of a seriously reconstructed concept of universal reason and a revision of the idea of philosophy, as well. In the words of Novak:

> No one would deny that there is a perfectly straightforward sense in which all human beings are members of the same human family; every human being is bound by imperatives of reasoning, justification, and communication across cultural and other boundaries; and each human being is entitled to claims of fundamental human dignity. Still, it is also widely grasped today that reason itself operates in pluralistic modes. It would be regarded as "cultural imperialism" to suggest that only one form of reasoning is valid in all matters. It would be regarded as naïve to believe that the content of human experiencing, imagining, understanding, judging, and deciding were everywhere the same. . . . It seems important for a liberal civilization today to thread its way philosophically between the Scylla of relativity and the Charybdis of too narrow a conception of universal reason.[40]

But philosophy has seldom taken up such a project, having been much too preoccupied with the search for the invariant structures of experience and the invariant operations of human understanding.[41] As important as this quest has been—and it has resulted in significant achievements in thought that have contributed, as well, to our practical life in very positive ways—it is not sufficient. Moreover, when it is allowed to dominate our efforts to give philosophical grounding to our collective and individual life, we sow the seeds that are harvested as the strife of renewed ethnicity and raciation, as millions are unable to locate themselves in satisfying ways or find social justice, in the terms and practices of social ordering predicated on the stifling universalism of the old liberalism.

As in previous Enlightenments, philosophers can make substantial contributions to the project suggested by Novak. But we can do so only after adopting a more critical appreciation of difference, conceived in terms of race and ethnicity, that preserves the progressive achievements of the old Enlightenments while contributing to our moving beyond them. In promoting this development I do not seek refuge in romanticism. Instead, what I desire is a new form of "liberalism," what Novak terms a *cosmopolitan* rather than *universalist* liberalism, which should rest on two pillars: "a firm commitment to the laborious but rewarding enterprise of full, mutual, intellectual understanding; and a respect for differences of nuance and subtlety, particularly in the area of those diversifying 'lived values' that have lain until now, in all cultures, so largely unarticulated."[42] The elaboration of this new liberalism in its possible social-political realizations would be an important contribution from philosophy, something those of us involved in the discipline have not yet worked out as fully as we might.

This elaboration must include insights gained from explorations of the "other side" of race and ethnicity: namely, the lived experiences of persons within racial/ethnic groups for whom their race or ethnicity is a fundamental and *positive* element of their identity, thus of their lifeworld. That race or ethnicity are without scientific bases in biological terms does *not* mean, thereby, that they are without any social value whatsoever, racism notwithstanding. Nor is that value diminished when we accept the view that what race and ethnicity mean is a function of changing historical conditions and agendas. In important cases the agendas are formed by persons who define themselves, in part, in group terms, and do so in ways that are far from detrimental to the social whole. A new liberalism that truly contributes to enlightenment and emancipation must appreciate such endeavors and appropriate the integrity of those who see themselves through the prisms of race and ethnicity, and who change their definitions of themselves. We should not err yet again in thinking that "race thinking" or "ethnic thinking" must be completely eliminated on the way to an emancipated and just society. Further, that elimination is both unlikely and unnecessary. Certainly the socially divisive forms and consequences of race thinking or ethnic thinking ought to be eliminated, to whatever extent possible. But a critical cosmopolitan liberalism which contributes to the learning and social evolution that secure democratic emancipation, in the context of racial and ethnic diversity, would be of no small consequence.

I can provide you no detailed scenario of what our social life would look like were this project completed. As with all living, this proposal is filled with serious risk. But so is status quo. However, I invite you to join me in taking this risk, beginning with a careful review of your own experiences of the challenges and joys of successfully negotiating encounters with persons who were decidedly "different" from you, and where success did not require either of you to cease being who you were entirely. Finally, as down payment on the claim not only that the risk of forging a cosmopolitan liberalism is worth taking but that it can, in fact, be achieved, I offer incontrovertible evidence: I am here before you as an honored lecturer; you are here as honored guests granting me a most respectful hearing. I am who I am without loss; and you continue to be who you are. Furthermore, I have certainly gained from my preparation of this lecture, and from my visit to Quinnipiac College. If my contribution has been worthy of your coming, then we know, through our own direct experiences, what can be achieved, and how philosophy can make a contribution to the achievement of social relations respectful of differences that are, nonetheless, mediated by shared understanding.

¹See H. C. Baldry, *The Unity of Mankind in Greek Thought* (Cambridge, England: Cambridge University Press, 1965).

²Ibid, 52.

³Ibid, 93.

⁴Crane Brinton, "Enlightenment," *The Encyclopedia of Philosophy*, Vol. 2 (New York: Macmillan & Free Press, 1967), 519. Persons in the first group—*philosophes*—were popularizers, propagandists of the Enlightenment, and included men of letters, journalists, salon discussants: Voltaire, Diderot, Condorcet, Holbach; those in the second group were formal philosophers: Hobbes, Locke, Berkeley, Hume, Kant. As with such distinctions, however, this one does not provide for clean separations.

⁵Ibid, 520.

⁶Ibid.

⁷Aristotle, *Politics*, Book 1, chapter 5, 1252B, 30–33.

⁸Ibid, 1254A, 18–24.

⁹Ibid, 1254A, 29–33.

¹⁰G. W. F. Hegel, "Introduction," *The Philosophy of History* (New York: Dover Publications, 1956), 91–99. This work is produced from lectures delivered by Hegel in the winter of 1830–31, though there had been two previous deliveries in 1822–23 and 1824–25. See Charles Hegel's "Preface" to *The Philosophy of History*, xi–xiii. These ideas were expressed more than seventy years prior to the 1895 European cannibalization of Africa by a person who was to become one of Germany's and Europe's most famous philosophers, and helped to nurture a complex of ideas that rationalized European racism.

¹¹The discussions covering this subsection through section IV are taken from my

"Towards a Critical Theory of 'Race' " in *Anatomy of Racism*, David T. Goldberg, editor, Minneapolis: University of Minnesota Press, 1990.

[12]W. E. B. Du Bois, "The Concept of Race," in *Dusk of Dawn: An Essay Toward an Autobiography of a Race Concept* (New York: Schoken Books, 1968 [1940]), 103.

[13]Thomas F. Gossett, *Race: The History of an Idea in America* (Dallas: Southern Methodist University Press, 1963), 16–17.

[14]Alfred Schutz and Thomas Luckmann, *The Structures of the Life-World*, Richard M. Zaner and H. Tristram Engelhardt, Jr., trans. (Evanston: Northwestern University Press, 1973), 8.

[15]"In contrast to biologically oriented approaches, the ethnicity-based paradigm was an insurgent theory which suggested that race was a *social* category. Race was but one of a number of determinants of ethnic group identity or ethnicity. Ethnicity itself was understood as the result of a group formation process based on culture and descent." Michael Omi and Howard Winant, "The dominant paradigm: ethnicity-based theory," in *Racial Formation in the United States* (New York: Routledge & Kegan Paul, 1986), 14–24, 15.

[16]Michael Banton and Jonathan Harwood, *The Race Concept* (New York: Praeger, 1975), 13.

[17]Ibid, 14.

[18]Ibid, 13.

[19]"The eighteenth-century Swedish botanist Linnaeus achieved fame by producing a classification of all known plants which extracted order from natural diversity. Scientists of his generation believed that by finding the categories to which animals, plants and objects belonged they were uncovering new sections of God's plan for the universe. Nineteenth-century race theorists inherited much of this way of looking at things." Ibid, 46.

[20]Ibid, 24–25. Both works were closely studied in Europe and the U.S.

[21]Ibid, 27.

[22]Ibid, 28.

[23]Ibid, 29–30. These authors observe that while Gobineau's volumes were not very influential at the time of their publication, they were later to become so when used by Hitler in support of his claims regarding the supposed superiority of the "Aryan race."

[24]"*Homo sapiens* was presented as a species divided into a number of races of different capacity and temperament. Human affairs could be understood only if individuals were seen as representatives of races for it was there that the driving forces of human history resided." Ibid, 30.

[25]Ibid, 38.

[26]Ibid, 47–49.

[27]"An article by an anthropologist published in 1962 declared in the sharpest terms that the old racial classifications were worse than useless and that a new approach had established its superiority. This article, entitled 'On the Non-existence of Human Races,' by Frank B. Livingstone, did not advance any new findings or concepts, but it brought out more dramatically than previous writers the sort of change that had occurred in scientific thinking. . . . The kernel of Livingstone's argument is contained in his phrase 'there are no races, there are only clines.' A cline is a gradient of change in a measurable genetic character. Skin colour provides an easily noticed example." Ibid, 56–57.

[28]Quoted by Banton and Harwood, 58.

[29]"When we refer to races we have in mind their geographically defined categories which are sometimes called 'geographical races,' to indicate that while they have some distinctive biological characteristics they are not pure types." Ibid, 62.

[30]Ibid, 63. "The main mistake of the early racial theorists was their failure to appreciate the difference between organic and superorganic evolution. They wished to explain all changes in biological terms." Ibid, 66.

[31]Ibid, 72–73, emphasis in the original.

[32]Ibid, 77.

[33]William Petersen, "Concepts of Ethnicity," *Harvard Encyclopedia of American Ethnic Groups* (Cambridge: Harvard University Press, 1980), 234–42, 234.

[34]Ibid, 234.

[35]Omi & Winant, 14.

[36]For a fuller discussion of the career of paradigmatic "ethnicity" see Omi & Winant, 14–16.

[37]Michael Novak, "Pluralism: A Humanistic Perspective," *Harvard Encyclopedia of American Ethnic Groups* (Cambridge: Harvard University Press, 1980), 772–81, 774.

[38]Novak, 774.

[39]Jacques Derrida, "White Mythology: Metaphor in the Text of Philosophy," in *Margins of Philosophy*, Alan Bass, trans. (Chicago: University of Chicago Press, 1982), 207–71, 213.

[40]Novak, 775.

[41]Ibid.

[42]Ibid, 776.

BELL HOOKS (1952–)

 # Feminism: A Transformational Politic
(1989)

We live in a world in crisis—a world governed by politics of domination, one in which the belief in a notion of superior and inferior and its concomitant ideology—that the superior should rule over the inferior—affects the lives of all people everywhere, whether poor or privileged, literate or illiterate. Systematic dehumanization, worldwide famine, ecological devastation, industrial contamination, and the possibility of nuclear destruction are realities which remind us daily that we are in crisis. Contemporary feminist thinkers often cite sexual politics as the origin of this crisis. They point to the insistence on difference as that factor which becomes the occasion for separation and domination and suggest that differentiation of status between females and males globally is an indication that patriarchal domination of the planet is the root of the problem. Such an assumption has fostered the notion that elimination of sexist oppression would necessarily lead to the eradication of all forms of domination. It is an argument that has led influential Western white women to feel that feminist movement should be *the* central political agenda for females globally. Ideologically, thinking in this direction enables Western women, especially privileged white women, to suggest that racism and class exploitation are merely the offspring of the parent system: patriarchy. Within feminist movement in the West, this has led to the assumption that resisting patriarchal domination is a more legitimate feminist action than resisting racism and other forms of domination. Such thinking prevails despite radical critiques made by black women and other women of color who question this proposition. To speculate that an oppositional division between men and women existed in early human communities is to impose on the past, on these nonwhite groups, a world view that fits all too neatly within contemporary feminist paradigms that name man as the enemy and woman as the victim.

Clearly, differentiation between strong and weak, powerful and powerless, has been a central defining aspect of gender globally, carrying with it the assumption that men should have greater authority than women, and should rule over them. As significant and important as this fact is, it should not obscure the reality that women can and do participate in politics of domination, as perpetrators as well as victims—that we dominate, that we are dominated. If focus on patriarchal domination masks this reality or becomes the means by which women deflect attention from the real conditions and circumstances of our lives, then women cooperate in suppressing and promoting false consciousness, inhibiting our capacity to assume responsibility for transforming ourselves and society.

Thinking speculatively about early human social arrangement, about women and men struggling to survive in small communities, it is likely that the parent-child relationship with its very real imposed survival structure of dependency, of strong and weak, of powerful and powerless, was a site for the construction of a paradigm of domination. While this circumstance of dependency is not necessarily one that leads to domination, it lends itself to the enactment of a social drama wherein domination could easily occur as a means of exercising and maintaining control. This speculation does not place women outside the practice of domination, in the exclusive role of victim. It centrally names women as agents of domination, as potential theoreticians and creators of a paradigm for social relationships wherein those groups of individuals designated as strong exercise power both benevolently and coercively over those designated as weak.

Emphasizing paradigms of domination that call attention to woman's capacity to dominate is one way to deconstruct and challenge the simplistic notion that man is the enemy, woman the victim, the notion that men have always been the oppressors. Such thinking enables us to examine our role as women in the perpetuation and maintenance of systems of domination. To understand domination, we must understand that our capacity as women and men to be either dominated or dominating is a point of connection, of commonality. Even though I speak from the particular experience of living as a black woman in the United States, a white-supremacist, capitalist, patriarchal society, where small numbers of white men (and honorary "white men") constitute ruling groups, I understand that in many places in the world oppressed and oppressor share the same color. I understand that right here in this room, oppressed and oppressor share the same gender. Right now as I speak, a man who is himself victimized, wounded, hurt by racism and class exploitation is actively dominating a woman in his life—that even as I speak, women who are ourselves exploited, victimized, are dominating children. It is necessary for us to remember, as we think critically about domination, that we all have the capacity to act in ways that oppress, dominate, wound (whether or not that power is institutionalized). It is necessary to remember that it is first the potential oppressor within that we must resist—the potential victim within that we must rescue—otherwise we cannot hope for an end to domination, for liberation.

This knowledge seems especially important at this historical moment when black women and other women of color have worked to create awareness of the ways in which racism empowers white women to act as exploiters and oppressors. Increasingly this fact is considered a reason we should not support feminist struggle even though sexism and sexist oppression is a real issue in our lives as black women (see, for example, Vivian Gordon's *Black Women, Feminism, and Black Liberation: Which Way?*).[1] It becomes necessary for us to speak continually about the convictions that inform our continued advocacy of feminist struggle. By calling attention to interlocking systems of domination—sex, race, and class—black women and many other groups of women acknowledge the diversity and complexity of female experience, of our relationship to power and domination. The intent is not to dissuade people of color from becoming engaged in feminist movement. Feminist struggle to end patriarchal domination should be of primary importance to women and men globally not because it is the foundation of all other oppressive structures but because it is that form of domination we are most likely to encounter in an ongoing way in everyday life.

Unlike other forms of domination, sexism directly shapes and determines relations of power in our private lives, in familiar social spaces, in that most intimate context—home—and in that most intimate sphere of relations—family. Usually, it is within the family that we witness coercive domination and learn to accept it, whether it be domination of parent over child, or male over female. Even though family relations may be, and most often are, informed by acceptance of a politic of domination, they are simultaneously relations of care and connection. It is this convergence of two contradictory impulses—the urge to promote growth and the urge to inhibit growth—that provides a practical setting for feminist critique, resistance, and transformation.

Growing up in a black, working-class, father-dominated household, I experienced coercive adult male authority as more immediately threatening, as more likely to cause immediate pain, than racist oppression or class exploitation. It was equally clear that experiencing exploitation and oppression in the home made one feel all the more powerless when encountering dominating forces outside the home. This is true for many people. If we are unable to resist and end domination in relations where there is care, it seems totally unimaginable that we can resist and end it in other institutionalized relations of power. If we cannot convince the mothers and / or fathers who care not to humiliate and degrade us, how can we imagine convincing or resisting an employer, a lover, a stranger who systematically humiliates and degrades?

Feminist effort to end patriarchal domination should be of primary concern precisely because it insists on the eradication of exploitation and oppression in the family context and in all other intimate relationships. It is that political movement which most radically addresses the person—the personal—citing the need for transformation of self, of relationships, so that we might be better able to act in a revolutionary manner, challenging and resisting domination, transforming the world outside the self. Strategically, feminist movement should be a central component of all other liberation struggles because it challenges each of us to alter our person, our personal engagement (either as victims or perpetrators or both) in a system of domination.

Feminism, as liberation struggle, must exist apart from and as a part of the larger struggle to eradicate domination in all its forms. We must understand that patriarchal domination shares an ideological foundation with racism and other forms of group oppression, that there is no hope that it can be eradicated while these systems remain intact. This knowledge should consistently inform the direction of feminist theory and practice. Unfortunately, racism and class elitism among women has frequently led to the suppression and distortion of this connection so that it is now necessary for feminist thinkers to critique and revise much feminist theory and the direction of feminist movement. This effort at revision is perhaps most evident in the current widespread acknowledgement that sexism, racism, and class exploitation constitute interlocking systems of domination—that sex, race, and class, and not sex alone, determine the nature of any female's identity, status, and circumstance, the degree to which she will or will not be dominated, the extent to which she will have the power to dominate.

While acknowledgement of the complex nature of woman's status (which has been most impressed upon everyone's consciousness by radical women of color) is a significant corrective, it is only a starting point. It provides a frame of reference which must serve as the basis for thoroughly altering and revising feminist theory and practice. It challenges and calls us to rethink popular assumptions about the nature of feminism that have had the deepest impact on a large majority of women, on mass consciousness. It radically calls into question the notion of a fundamentally common female experience which has been seen as the prerequisite for our coming together, for political unity. Recognition of the interconnectedness of sex, race, and class highlights the diversity of experience, compelling redefinition of the terms for unity. If women do not share "common oppression," what then can serve as a basis for our coming together?

Unlike many feminist comrades, I believe women and men must share a common understanding—a basic knowledge of what feminism is—if it is ever to be a powerful mass-based political movement. In *Feminist Theory: from margin to center*,[2] I suggest that defining feminism broadly as "a movement to end sexism and sexist oppression" would enable us to have a common political goal. We would then have a basis on which to build solidarity. Multiple and contradictory definitions of feminism create confusion and undermine the effort to construct feminist movement so that it addresses everyone. Sharing a common goal does not imply that women and men will not have radically divergent perspectives on how that goal might be reached. Because each individual starts the process of engagement in feminist struggle at a unique level of awareness, very real differences in experience, perspective, and knowledge make developing varied strategies for participation and transformation a necessary agenda.

Feminist thinkers engaged in radically revisioning central tenets of feminist thought must continually emphasize the importance of sex, race, and class as factors which *together* determine the social construction of femaleness, as it has been so deeply ingrained in the consciousness of many women active in feminist movement that gender is the sole factor determining destiny. However, the work of education for critical consciousness (usually called consciousness-raising) cannot end there. Much feminist consciousness-raising has in the past focused on identifying the particular ways men oppress and exploit women. Using the paradigm of sex, race, and class means that the focus does not begin with men and what they do to women, but rather with women working to identify both individually and collectively the specific character of our social identity.

Imagine a group of women from diverse backgrounds coming together to talk about feminism. First they concentrate on working out their status in terms of sex, race, and class using this as the standpoint from which they begin discussing patriarchy or their particular relations with individual men. Within the old frame of reference, a discussion might consist solely of talk about their experiences as victims in relationship to male oppressors. Two women—one poor, the other quite wealthy—might describe the process by which they have suffered physical abuse by male partners and find certain commonalities which might serve as a basis for bonding. Yet if these same two women engaged in a discussion of class, not only would the social construction and expression of femaleness differ, so too would their ideas about how to confront and change their circumstances. Broadening the discussion to include an analysis of race and class would expose many additional differences even as commonalities emerged.

Clearly the process of bonding would be more complex, yet this broader discussion might enable the sharing of perspectives and strategies for change that would enrich rather than diminish our understanding of gender. While feminists have increasingly given lip service to the idea of diversity, we have not developed strategies of communication and inclusion that allow for the successful enactment of this feminist vision.

Small groups are no longer the central place for feminist consciousness-raising. Much feminist education for critical consciousness takes place in women's studies classes or at conferences which focus on gender. Books are a primary source of education, which means that already masses of people who do not read have no access. The separation of grassroots ways of sharing feminist thinking across kitchen tables from the spheres where much of that thinking is generated, the academy, undermines feminist movement. It would further feminist movement if new feminist thinking could be once again shared in small group contexts, integrating critical analysis with discussion of personal experience. It would be useful to promote anew the small group setting as an arena for education for critical consciousness, so that women and men might come together in neighborhoods and communities to discuss feminist concerns.

Small groups remain an important place for education for critical consciousness for several reasons. An especially important aspect of the small group setting is the emphasis on communicating feminist thinking, feminist theory, in a manner that can be easily understood. In small groups, individuals do not need to be equally literate or literate at all because the information is primarily shared through conversation, in dialogue which is necessarily a liberatory expression. (Literacy should be a goal for feminists even as we ensure that it not become a requirement for participation in feminist education.) Reforming small groups would subvert the appropriation of feminist thinking by a select group of academic women and men, usually white, usually from privileged class backgrounds.

Small groups of people coming together to engage in feminist discussion, in dialectical struggle make a space where "the personal is political" as a starting point for education for critical consciousness can be extended to include politicization of the self that focuses on creating understanding of the ways sex, race, and class together determine our individual lot and our collective experience. It would further feminist movement if many well-known feminist thinkers would participate in small groups, critically re-examining ways their works might be changed by incorporating broader perspectives. All efforts at self-transformation challenge us to engage in ongoing, critical self-examination and reflection about feminist practice, about how we live in the world. This individual commitment, when coupled with engagement in collective discussion, provides a space for critical feedback which strengthens our efforts to change and make ourselves new. It is in this commitment to feminist principles in our words and deeds that the hope of feminist revolution lies.

Working collectively to confront difference, to expand our awareness of sex, race, and class as interlocking systems of domination, of the ways we reinforce and perpetuate these structures, is the context in which we learn the true meaning of solidarity. It is this work that must be the foundation of feminist movement. Without it, we cannot effectively resist patriarchal domination; without it, we remain estranged and alienated from one another. Fear of painful confrontation often leads women and men active in feminist movement to avoid rigorous critical encounter, yet if we cannot engage dialectically in a committed, rigorous, humanizing manner, we cannot hope to change the world. True politicization—coming to critical consciousness—is a difficult, "trying" process, one that demands that we give up set ways of thinking and being, that we shift our paradigms, that we open ourselves to the unknown, the unfamiliar. Undergoing this process, we learn what it means to struggle and in this effort we experience the dignity and integrity of being that comes with revolutionary change. If we do not change our consciousness, we cannot change our actions or demand change from others.

Our renewed commitment to a rigorous process of education for critical consciousness will determine the shape and direction of future feminist movement. Until new perspectives are created, we cannot be living symbols of the power of feminist thinking. Given the privileged lot of many leading feminist thinkers, in terms of status, class, and race, it is harder these days to convince women of the primacy of this process of politicization. More and more, we seem to form select interest groups composed of individuals who share similar perspectives. This limits our capacity to engage in critical discussion. It is difficult to involve women in new processes of feminist politicization because so many of us think that identifying men as the enemy, resisting male domination, gaining equal access to power and privilege is the end of feminist movement. Not only is it not the end, it is not even the place we want revitalized feminist movement to begin. We want to begin as women seriously addressing ourselves, not solely in relation to men, but in relation to an entire structure of domination of which patriarchy is one part. While the struggle to eradicate sexism and sexist oppression is and should be the primary thrust of feminist movement, to prepare ourselves politically for this effort we must first learn how to be in solidarity, how to struggle with one another.

Only when we confront the realities of sex, race, and class, the ways they divide us, make us different, stand us in opposition, and work to reconcile and resolve these issues will we be able to participate in the making of feminist revolution, in the transformation of the world. Feminism, as Charlotte Bunch emphasizes again and again in *Passionate Politics,* is a transformational politics, a struggle against domination wherein the effort is to change ourselves as well as structures. Speaking about the struggle to confront difference, Bunch asserts:

> A crucial point of the process is understanding that reality does not look the same from different people's perspective. It is not surprising that one way feminists have come to understand about differences has been through the love of a person from another culture or race. It takes persistence and motivation—which love often engenders—to get beyond one's ethnocentric assumptions and really learn about other perspectives. In this process and while seeking to eliminate oppression, we also discover new possibilities and insights that come from the experience and survival of other peoples.[3]

Embedded in the commitment to feminist revolution is the challenge to love. Love can be and is an important source of empowerment when we struggle to confront issues of sex, race, and class. Working together to identify and face our differences—to face the ways we dominate and are dominated—to change our actions, we need a mediating force that can sustain us so that we are not broken in this process, so that we do not despair.

Not enough feminist work has focused on documenting and sharing ways individuals confront differences constructively and successfully. Women and men need to know what is on the other side of the pain experienced in politicization. We need detailed accounts of the ways our lives are fuller and richer as we change and grow politically, as we learn to live each moment as committed feminists, as comrades working to end domination. In reconceptualizing and reformulating strategies for future feminist movement, we need to concentrate on the politicization of love, not just in the context of talking about victimization in intimate relationships, but in a critical discussion where love can be understood as a powerful force that challenges and resists domination. As we work to be loving, to create a culture that celebrates life, that makes love possible, we move against dehumanization, against domination. In *Pedagogy of the Oppressed,* Paulo Freire evokes this power of love, declaring:

> I am more and more convinced that true revolutionaries must perceive the revolution, because of its creative and liberating nature, as an act of love. For me, the revolution, which is not possible without a theory of revolution—and therefore science—is not irreconcilable with love. . . . The distortion imposed on the word "love" by the capitalist world cannot prevent the revolution from being essentially loving in character, nor can it prevent the revolutionaries from affirming their love of life.[4]

That aspect of feminist revolution that calls women to love womanness, that calls men to resist dehumanizing concepts of masculinity, is an essential part of our struggle. It is the process by which we move from seeing ourselves as objects to acting as subjects. When women and men understand that working to eradicate patriarchal domination is a struggle rooted in the longing to make a world where everyone can live fully and freely, then we know our work to be a gesture of love. Let us draw upon that love to heighten our awareness, deepen our compassion, intensify our courage, and strengthen our commitment.

[1]Vivian Verdell Gordon, *Black Women, Feminism, and Black Liberation: Which Way?* (Chicago: Third World Press, 1985).

[2]bell hooks, *Feminist Theory: from margin to center* (Boston: South End Press, 1984).

[3]Charlotte Bunch, *Passionate Politics: Essays, 1968 to 1986—Feminist Theory in Action* (New York: St. Martin's Press, 1987), 338.

[4]Paulo Freire, *Pedagogy of the Oppressed,* trans. Myra Bergman Ramos (New York: Seabury Press, 1970), 77, n. 4.

MOLEFI KETE ASANTE (1942–   )

 The Afrocentric Idea in Education (1991)

Introduction

Many of the principles that govern the development of the Afrocentric idea in education were first established by Carter G. Woodson in *The Mis-Education of the Negro* (1933). Indeed, Woodson's classic reveals the fundamental problems pertaining to the education of the African person in America. As Woodson contends, African Americans have been educated away from their own culture and traditions and attached to the fringes of European culture: thus dislocated from themselves, Woodson asserts that African Americans often valorize European culture to the detriment of their own heritage (7). Although Woodson does not advocate rejection of American citizenship or nationality, he believed that assuming African Americans hold the same position as European Americans vis-à-vis the realities of America would lead to the psychological and cultural death of the African American population. Furthermore, if education is ever to be substantive and meaningful within the context of American society, Woodson argues, it must first address the African's historical experiences, both in Africa and America (7). That is why he places on education, and particularly on the traditionally African American colleges, the burden of teaching the African American to be responsive to the long traditions and history of Africa as well as America. Woodson's alert recognition, more than fifty years ago, that something is severely wrong with the way African Americans are educated provides the principal impetus for the Afrocentric approach to American education.

In this article I will examine the nature and scope of this approach, establish its necessity, and suggest ways to develop and disseminate it throughout all levels of education. Two propositions stand in the background of the theoretical and philosophical issues I will present. These ideas represent the core presuppositions on which I have based most of my work in the field of education, and they suggest the direction of my own thinking about what

Reprinted from *The Journal of Negro Education* 60, no. 2 (1991): 170–80. © 1991, Howard University. Reprinted with permission of *The Journal of Negro Education* and Molefi Kete Asante.

education is capable of doing to and for an already politically and economically marginalized people—African Americans:

(1) Education is fundamentally a social phenomenon whose ultimate purpose is to socialize the learner; to send a child to school is to prepare that
child to become part of a social group.
(2) Schools are reflective of the societies that develop them (i.e., a white-
supremacist-dominated society will develop a white-supremacist educational system).

Definitions

An alternative framework suggests that other definitional assumptions can
provide a new paradigm for the examination of education within the American society. For example, in education, *centricity* refers to a perspective that
involves locating students within the context of their own cultural references
so that they can relate socially and psychologically to other cultural perspectives. Centricity is a concept that can be applied to any culture. The cen-
trist paradigm is supported by research showing that the most productive
method of teaching any student is to place his or her group within the center of the context of knowledge (Asante 1990). For white students in America
this is easy because almost all the experiences discussed in American classrooms are approached from the standpoint of white perspectives and history. American education, however, is not centric; it is Eurocentric. Consequently, nonwhite students are also made to see themselves and their groups
as the "acted upon." Only rarely do they read or hear of nonwhite people as
active participants in history. This is as true for a discussion of the American
Revolution as it is for a discussion of Dante's *Inferno;* for instance, most classroom discussions of the European slave trade concentrate on the activities of
whites rather than on the resistance efforts of Africans. A person educated in
a truly centric fashion comes to view all groups' contributions as significant
and useful. Even a white person educated in such a system does not assume
superiority based upon racist notions. Thus, a truly centric education is
different from a Eurocentric, racist (that is, white-supremacist) education.

Afrocentricity is a frame of reference wherein phenomena are viewed from
the perspective of the African person. The Afrocentric approach seeks in every situation the appropriate centrality of the African person (Asante 1987).
In education this means that teachers provide students the opportunity to
study the world and its people, concepts, and history from an African world
view. In most classrooms, whatever the subject, whites are located in the
center perspective position. How alien the African-American child must feel,
how like an outsider! The little African-American child who sits in a classroom and is taught to accept as heroes and heroines individuals who de-

famed African people is being actively decentered, dislocated, and made into a nonperson, one whose aim in life might be to one day shed that "badge of inferiority": his or her blackness. In Afrocentric educational settings, however, teachers do not marginalize African-American children by causing them to question their own self-worth because their people's story is seldom told. By seeing themselves as the subjects rather than the objects of education—be the discipline biology, medicine, literature, or social studies—African-American students come to see themselves not merely as seekers of knowledge but as integral participants in it. Because all content areas are adaptable to an Afrocentric approach, African-American students can be made to see themselves as centered in the reality of any discipline.

It must be emphasized that Afrocentricity is *not* a black version of Eurocentricity (Asante 1987). Eurocentricity is based on white-supremacist notions whose purposes are to protect white privilege and advantage in education, economics, politics, and so forth. Unlike Eurocentricity, Afrocentricity does not condone ethnocentric valorization at the expense of degrading the other groups' perspectives. Moreover, Eurocentricity presents the particular historical reality of Europeans as the sum total of the human experience (Asante 1987). It imposes Eurocentric realities as universal; i.e., that which is white is presented as applying to the human condition in general, while that which is nonwhite is viewed as group-specific and therefore not human. This explains why some scholars and artists of African descent rush to deny their blackness; they believe that to exist as a black person is not to exist as a universal human being. They are the individuals Woodson identified as preferring European art, language, and culture over African art, language, and culture; they believe that anything of European origin is inherently better than anything produced by or issuing from their own people. Naturally, the person of African descent should be centered in his or her historical experiences as an African, but Eurocentric curricula produce such aberrations of perspective among persons of color.

Multiculturalism in education is a nonhierarchical approach that respects and celebrates a variety of cultural perspectives on world phenomena (Asante 1991). The multicultural approach holds that although European culture is the majority culture in the United States, that is not sufficient reason for it to be imposed on diverse student populations as universal. Multiculturalists assert that education, to have integrity, must begin with the proposition that all humans have contributed to world development and the flow of knowledge and information, and that most human achievements are the result of mutually interactive, international effort. Without a multicultural education, students remain essentially ignorant of the contributions of a major portion of the world's people. A multicultural education is thus a fundamental necessity for anyone who wishes to achieve competency in almost any subject.

The Afrocentric idea must be the stepping-stone from which the multicultural idea is launched. A truly authentic multicultural education, therefore, must be based upon the Afrocentric initiative. If this step is skipped, multicultural curricula, as they are increasingly being defined by white "resisters" (to be discussed below), will evolve without any substantive infusion of African-American content, and the African-American child will continue to be lost in the Eurocentric framework of education. In other words, the African-American child will neither be confirmed nor affirmed in his or her own cultural information. For the mutual benefit of all Americans, this tragedy, which leads to the psychological and cultural dislocation of African-American children, can and should be avoided.

The Revolutionary Challenge

Because it centers African-American students inside history, culture, science, and so forth rather than outside these subjects, the Afrocentric idea presents the most revolutionary challenge to the ideology of white supremacy in education during the past decade. No other theoretical position stated by African Americans has ever captured the imagination of such a wide range of scholars and students of history, sociology, communications, anthropology, and psychology. The Afrocentric challenge has been posed in three critical ways:

(1) It questions the imposition of the white-supremacist view as universal and/or classical (Asante 1990).
(2) It demonstrates the indefensibility of racist theories that assault multiculturalism and pluralism.
(3) It projects a humanistic and pluralistic viewpoint by articulating Afrocentricity as a valid, nonhegemonic perspective.

Suppression and Distortion: Symbols of Resistance

The forces of resistance to the Afrocentric, multicultural transformation of the curriculum and teaching practices began to assemble their wagons almost as quickly as word got out about the need for equality in education (Ravitch 1990). Recently, the renowned historian Arthur Schlesinger and others formed a group called the Committee for the Defense of History. This is a paradoxical development because only lies, untruths, and inaccurate information need defending. In their arguments against the Afrocentric perspective, these proponents of Eurocentrism often clothe their arguments in false categories and fake terms (i.e., "pluralistic" and "particularistic" multiculturalism) (Keto 1990; Asante 1991). Besides, as the late African scholar Cheikh Anta Diop (1980) maintained: "African history and Africa need no defense." Afrocentric education is not against history. It is *for* history—correct, accurate history—and if it is against anything, it is against the marginalization of African-American, Hispanic-American, Asian-American, Native-American, and other nonwhite children. The Committee for the Defense of History is nothing more than a futile attempt to buttress the crumbling pillars of a white-supremacist system that conceals its true motives behind the cloak of American liberalism. It was created in the same spirit that generated Bloom's *The Closing of the American Mind* (1987) and Hirsch's *Cultural Literacy: What Every American Needs to Know* (1987), both of which were placed at the service of the white hegemony in education, particularly its curricular hegemony. This committee and other evidences of white backlash are a predictable challenge to the contemporary thrust for an Afrocentric, multicultural approach to education.

Naturally, different adherents to a theory will have different views on its meaning. While two discourses presently are circulating about multiculturalism, only one is relevant to the liberation of the minds of African and white people in the United States. That discourse is Afrocentricity: the acceptance of Africa as central to African people. Yet, rather than getting on board with Afrocentrists to fight against white hegemonic education, some whites (and some blacks as well) have opted to plead for a return to the educational plantation. Unfortunately for them, however, those days are gone, and such misinformation can never be packaged as accurate, correct education again.

Ravitch (1990), who argues that there are two kinds of multiculturalism—*pluralist multiculturalism* and *particularist multiculturalism*—is the leader of those professors whom I call resisters or opponents to Afrocentricity and multiculturalism. Indeed, Ravitch advances the imaginary divisions in multicultural perspectives to conceal her true identity as a defender of white supremacy. Her tactics are the tactics of those who prefer Africans and other nonwhites to remain on the mental and psychological plantation of Western civilization. In their arrogance the resisters accuse Afrocentrists and multiculturalists of creating "fantasy history" and "bizarre theories" of nonwhite people's contributions to civilization. What they prove, however, is their own ignorance. Additionally, Ravitch and others (Nicholson 1990) assert that multiculturalism will bring about the "tribalization" of America, but in reality America has always been a nation of ethnic diversity. When one reads their works on multiculturalism, one realizes that they are really advocating the imposition of a white perspective on everybody else's culture. Believing that the Eurocentric position is indisputable, they attempt to resist and impede the progressive transformation of the monoethnic curriculum. Indeed, the closets of bigotry have opened to reveal various attempts by white scholars (joined by some blacks) to defend white privilege in the curriculum in much the same way as it has been so staunchly defended in the larger society. It was perhaps inevitable that the introduction of the Afrocentric idea would open up the discussion of the American school curriculum in a profound way.

Why has Afrocentricity created so much of a controversy in educational circles? The idea that an African-American child is placed in a stronger position to learn if he or she is centered—that is, if the child sees himself or herself within the content of the curriculum rather than at its margins—is not novel (Asante 1980). What is revolutionary is the movement from the idea (conceptual stage) to its implementation in practice, when we begin to teach teachers how to put African-American youth at the center of instruction. In effect, students are shown how to see with new eyes and hear with new ears. African-American children learn to interpret and center phenomena in the context of African heritage, while white students are taught to see that their own centers are not threatened by the presence or contributions of African Americans and others.

The Condition of Eurocentric Education

Institutions such as schools are conditioned by the character of the nation in which they are developed. Just as crime and politics are different in different nations, so, too, is education. In the United States a "whites-only" orientation has predominated in education. This has had a profound impact on the quality of education for children of all races and ethnic groups. The African-American child has suffered disproportionately, but white children are also the victims of monoculturally diseased curricula.

The Tragedy of Ignorance

During the past five years many white students and parents have approached me after presentations with tears in their eyes or expressing their anger about the absence of information about African Americans in the schools. A recent comment from a young white man at a major university in the Northeast was especially striking. As he said to me, "My teacher told us that Martin Luther King was a commie and went on with the class." Because this student's teacher made no effort to discuss King's ideas, the student maliciously had been kept ignorant. The vast majority of white Americans are likewise ignorant about the bountiful reservoirs of African and African-American history, culture, and contributions. For example, few Americans of any color have heard the names of Cheikh Anta Diop, Anna Julia Cooper, C. L. R. James, or J. A. Rogers. All were historians who contributed greatly to our understanding of the African world. Indeed, very few teachers have ever taken a course in African-American studies; therefore, most are unable to provide systematic information about African Americans.

Afrocentricity and History

Most of America's teaching force are victims of the same system that victimizes today's young. Thus, American children are not taught the names of the African ethnic groups from which the majority of the African-American population are derived; few are taught the names of any of the sacred sites in Africa. Few teachers can discuss with their students the significance of the Middle Passage or describe what it meant or means to Africans. Little mention is made in American classrooms of either the brutality of slavery or the ex-slaves' celebration of freedom. American children have little or no understanding of the nature of the capture, transport, and enslavement of Africans. Few have been taught the true horrors of being taken, shipped naked across twenty-five days of ocean, broken by abuse and indignities of all kinds, and dehumanized into a beast of burden, a thing without a name. If our students only knew the truth, if they were taught the Afrocentric perspective on the Great Enslavement, and if they knew the full story about the events since slavery that have served to constantly dislocate African Americans, their behavior would perhaps be different. Among these events are the infamous constitutional compromise of 1787, which decreed that African Americans were, by law, the equivalent of but three-fifths of a person (see Franklin 1974); the 1857 Dred Scott decision in which the Supreme Court avowed that African Americans had no rights whites were obliged to respect (Howard 1857); the complete dismissal and nonenforcement of Section 2 of the Fourteenth Amendment to the Constitution (this amendment, passed in 1868, stipulated as one of its provisions a penalty against any state that denied African Americans the right to vote, and called for the reduction of a state's delegates to the House of Representatives in proportion to the number of disenfranchised African-American males therein); and the much-mentioned, as-yet-unreceived forty acres and a mule, reparation for enslavement, promised to each African-American family after the Civil War by Union General William T. Sherman and Secretary of War Edwin Stanton (Oubre 1978, 18–19, 182–83; see also Smith 1987, 106–7). If the curriculum were enhanced to include readings from the slave narratives, the diaries of slave ship captains, the journals of slaveowners, the abolitionist newspapers, the writings of the freedmen and freedwomen, the accounts of African-American civil rights, civic, and social organizations, and numerous others, African-American children would be different, white children would be different—indeed, America would be a different nation today.

America's classrooms should resound with the story of the barbaric treatment of the Africans, of how their dignity was stolen and their cultures destroyed. The recorded experiences of escaped slaves provide the substance for such learning units. For example, the narrative of Jacob and Ruth Weldon presents a detailed account of the Middle Passage (Feldstein 1971). The Weldons noted that Africans, having been captured and brought onto the slave ships, were chained to the deck, made to bend over, and "branded with a red hot iron in the form of letters or signs dipped in an oily preparation and pressed against the naked flesh till it burnt a deep and ineffaceable scar, to show who was the owner" (33–37). They also recalled that those who screamed were lashed on the face, breast, thighs, and backs with a "cat-o'-nine tails" wielded by white sailors: "Every blow brought the returning lash pieces of grieving flesh" (44). They saw "mothers with babies at their breasts basely branded and lashed, hewed and scarred, till it would seem as if the very heavens must smite the infernal tormentors with the doom they so richly merited" (44). Children and infants were not spared from this terror. The Weldons tell of a nine-month-old baby on board a slave ship being flogged because it would not eat. The ship's captain ordered the child's feet placed in boiling water, which dissolved the skin and nails, then ordered the child whipped again; still the child refused to eat. Eventually the captain killed the baby with his own hands and commanded the child's mother to throw the dead baby overboard. When the mother refused, she, too, was beaten, then forced to the ship's side, where "with her head averted so she might not see it, she dropped the body into the sea" (44). In a similar vein a captain of a ship with 440 Africans on board noted that 132 had to be thrown overboard to save water (47). As another wrote, the "groans and soffocating [sic] cries for air and water coming from below the deck sickened the soul of humanity" (44).

Upon landing in America the situation was often worse. The brutality of the slavocracy is unequalled for the psychological and spiritual destruction it wrought upon African Americans. Slave mothers were often forced to leave their children unattended while they worked in the fields. Unable to nurse their children or to properly care for them, they often returned from work at night to find their children dead (49). The testimony of Henry Bibb also sheds light on the bleakness of the slave experience:

> I was born May 1815, of a slave mother . . . and was claimed as the property of David White, Esq. . . . I was flogged up; for where I should have received moral, mental, and religious instructions, I received stripes without number, the object of which was to degrade and keep me in subordination. I can truly say that I drank deeply of the bitter cup of suffering and woe. I have been dragged down to the lowest depths of human degradation and wretchedness, by slaveholders. (P. 60)

Enslavement was truly a living death. While the ontological onslaught caused some Africans to opt for suicide, the most widespread results were dislocation, disorientation, and misorientation—all of which are the consequences of the African person being actively decentered. The "Jim Crow" period of second-class citizenship, from 1877 to 1954, saw only slight improvement in the lot of African Americans. This era was characterized by the sharecropper system, disenfranchisement, enforced segregation, internal migration, lynchings, unemployment, poor housing conditions, and separate and unequal educational facilities. Inequitable policies and practices veritably plagued the race.

No wonder many persons of African descent attempt to shed their race and become "raceless." One's basic identity is one's self-identity, which is ultimately one's cultural identity; without a strong cultural identity, one is lost. Black children do not know their people's story and white children do not know the story, but remembrance is a vital requisite for understanding and humility. This is why the Jews have campaigned (and rightly so) to have the story of the European Holocaust taught in schools and colleges. Teaching about such a monstrous human brutality should forever remind the world of the ways in which humans have often violated each other. Teaching about the African Holocaust is just as important for many of the same reasons. Additionally, it underscores the enormity of the effects of physical, psychological, and economic dislocation on the African population in America and throughout the African diaspora. Without an understanding of the historical experiences of African people, American children cannot make any real headway in addressing the problems of the present.

Certainly, if African-American children were taught to be fully aware of the struggles of our African forebears, they would find a renewed sense of purpose and vision in their own lives. They would cease acting as if they have no past and no future. For instance, if they were taught about the historical relationship of Africans to the cotton industry—how African-American men, women, and children were forced to pick cotton from "can't see in the morning 'til can't see at night," until the blood ran from the tips of their fingers where they were pricked by the hard boll; or if they were made to visualize their ancestors in the burning sun, bent double with constant stooping, and dragging rough, heavy croaker sacks behind them—or picture them bringing those sacks trembling to the scale, fearful of a sure flogging if they did not pick enough, perhaps our African-American youth would develop a stronger entrepreneurial spirit. If white children were taught the same information rather than that normally fed them about American slavery, they would probably view our society differently and work to transform it into a better place.

Correcting Distorted Information

Hegemonic education can exist only so long as true and accurate information is withheld. Hegemonic Eurocentric education can exist only so long as whites maintain that Africans and other nonwhites have never contributed to world civilization. It is largely upon such false ideas that invidious distinctions are made. The truth, however, gives one insight into the real reasons behind human actions, whether one chooses to follow the paths of others or not. For example, one cannot remain comfortable teaching that art and philosophy originated in Greece if one learns that the Greeks themselves taught that the study of these subjects originated in Africa, specifically ancient Kemet (Herodotus 1987). The first philosophers were the Egyptians Kagemni, Khun-anup, Ptahhotep, Kete, and Seti; but Eurocentric education is so disjointed that students have no way of discovering this and other knowledge of the organic relationship of Africa to the rest of human history. Not only did Africa contribute to human history, African civilizations predate all other civilizations. Indeed, the human species originated on the continent of Africa—this is true whether one looks at either archaeological or biological evidence.

Two other notions must be refuted. There are those who say that African American history should begin with the arrival of Africans as slaves in 1619, but it has been shown that Africans visited and inhabited North and South America long before European settlers "discovered" the "New World" (Van Sertima 1976). Secondly, although America became something of a home for those Africans who survived the horrors of the Middle Passage, their experiences on the slave ships and during slavery resulted in their having an entirely different (and often tainted) perspective about America from that of the Europeans and others who came, for the most part, of their own free will seeking opportunities not available to them in their native lands. Afrocentricity therefore seeks to recognize this divergence in perspective and create centeredness for African-American students.

Conclusion

The reigning initiative for total curricular change is the movement that is being proposed and led by Africans, namely, the Afrocentric idea. When I wrote the first book on Afrocentricity (Asante 1980), now in its fifth printing, I had no idea that in ten years the idea would both shake up and shape discussions in education, art, fashion, and politics. Since the publication of my subsequent works, *The Afrocentric Idea* (1987) and *Kemet, Afrocentricity, and Knowledge* (1990), the debate has been joined in earnest. Still, for many white Americans (and some African Americans) the most unsettling aspect of the discussion about Afrocentricity is that its intellectual source lies in the research and writings of African-American scholars. Whites are accustomed to being in charge of the major ideas circulating in the American academy. Deconstructionism, Gestalt psychology, Marxism, structuralism, Piagetian theory, and so forth have all been developed, articulated, and elaborated upon at length, generally by white scholars. On the other hand, Afrocentricity is the product of scholars such as Nobles (1986), Hilliard (1978), Karenga (1986), Keto (1990), Richards (1991), and Myers (1989). There are also increasing numbers of young, impressively credentialled African-American scholars who have begun to write in the Afrocentric vein (Jean 1991). They, and even some young white scholars, have emerged with ideas about how to change the curriculum Afrocentrically.

Afrocentricity provides all Americans an opportunity to examine the perspective of the African person in this society and the world. The resisters claim that Afrocentricity is antiwhite; yet if Afrocentricity as a theory is against anything it is against racism, ignorance, and monoethnic hegemony in the curriculum. Afrocentricity is not antiwhite; it is, however, pro-human. Further, the aim of the Afrocentric curriculum is not to divide America, it is to make America flourish as it ought to flourish. This nation has long been divided with regard to the educational opportunities afforded to children. By virtue of the protection provided by society and reinforced by the Eurocentric curriculum, the white child is already ahead of the African-American child by first grade. Our efforts thus must concentrate on giving the African-American child greater opportunities for learning at the kindergarten level. However, the kind of assistance the African-American child needs is as much cultural as it is academic. If the proper cultural information is provided, the academic performance will surely follow suit.

When it comes to educating African-American children, the American educational system does not need a tune-up, it needs an overhaul. Black children have been maligned by this system. Black teachers have been maligned. Black history has been maligned. Africa has been maligned. Nonetheless, two truisms can be stated about education in America. First, some teachers *can and do* effectively teach African-American children; secondly, if some teachers can do it, others can, too. We must learn all we can about what makes these teachers' attitudes and approaches successful, and then work diligently to see that their successes are replicated on a broad scale. By raising the same questions that Woodson posed more than fifty years ago, Afrocentric education, along with a significant reorientation of the American educational enterprise, seeks to respond to the African person's psychological and cultural dislocation. By providing philosophical and theoretical guidelines and criteria that are centered in an African perception of reality and by placing the African-American child in his or her proper historical context and setting, Afrocentricity may be just the escape hatch African Americans so desperately need to facilitate academic success and "steal away" from the cycle of miseducation and dislocation.

References

Asante, M. K. *Afrocentricity: The Theory of Social Change*. Buffalo, N.Y.: Amulefi, 1980.

——. *The Afrocentric Idea*. Philadelphia: Temple University Press, 1987.

——. *Kemet, Afrocentricity, and Knowledge*. Trenton, N.J.: Africa World Press, 1990.

Bloom, A. *The Closing of the American Mind*. New York: Simon & Schuster, 1987.

Feldstein, S. *Once a Slave: The Slave's View of Slavery*. New York: William Morrow, 1971.

Franklin, J. H. *From Slavery to Freedom*. New York: Knopf, 1974.

Herodotus. *The History*. Chicago: University of Illinois Press, 1987.

Hilliard, A. G., III. "Anatomy and Dynamics of Oppression." Speech delivered at the National Conference on Human Relations in Education, Minneapolis, Minn., 20 June 1978.

Hirsch, E. D. *Cultural Literacy: What Every American Needs to Know*. New York: Houghton Mifflin, 1987.

Howard, B. C. *Report of the Decision of the Supreme Court of the United States and the Opinions of the Justices Thereof in the Case of Dred Scott versus John F. A. Sandford, December Term, 1856*. New York: D. Appleton, 1857.

Jean, C. *Beyond the Eurocentric Veils*. Amherst: University of Massachusetts Press, 1991.

Karenga, M. R. *Introduction to Black Studies*. Los Angeles: University of Sankore Press, 1986.

Keto, C. T. *Africa-Centered Perspective of History*. Blackwood, N.J.: C. A. Associates, 1990.

Nicholson, D. "Afrocentrism and the Tribalization of America." *The Washington Post*, 23 September 1990, B-1.

Nobles, W. *African Psychology*. Oakland, Calif.: Black Family Institute, 1986.

Oubre, C. F. *Forty Acres and a Mule: The Freedman's Bureau and Black Land Ownership*. Baton Rouge: Louisiana State University Press, 1978.

Ravitch, D. "Multiculturalism: E pluribus plures." *American Scholar* (summer 1990): 337–54.

Richards, D. *Let the Circle Be Unbroken*. Trenton, N.J.: Africa World Press, 1991.

Smith, J. O. *The Politics of Racial Inequality: A Systematic Comparative Macro-Analysis from the Colonial Period to 1970*. New York: Greenwood Press, 1987.

Van Sertima, I. *They Came Before Columbus*. New York: Random House, 1976.

Woodson, C. G. *The Education of the Negro Prior to 1861: A History of the Education of the Colored People of the U.S. from the Beginning of Slavery*. New York: G. P. Putnam's Sons, 1915.

——. *The Mis-Education of the Negro*. Washington, D.C.: Associated, 1933.

——. *African Background Outlined*. Washington, D.C.: Association for the Study of Afro-American Life and History, 1936.

CORNEL WEST (1953–)

Learning to Talk of Race (1992)

What happened in Los Angeles this past April was neither a race riot nor a class rebellion. Rather, this monumental upheaval was a multiracial, trans-class, and largely male display of justified social rage. For all its ugly, xenophobic resentment, its air of adolescent carnival, and its downright barbaric behavior, it signified the sense of powerlessness in American society. Glib attempts to reduce its meaning to the pathologies of the black underclass, the criminal actions of hoodlums, or the political revolt of the oppressed urban masses miss the mark. Of those arrested, only 36 percent were black, more than a third had full-time jobs, and most claimed to shun political affiliation. What we witnessed in Los Angeles was the consequence of a lethal linkage of economic decline, cultural decay, and political lethargy in American life. Race was the visible catalyst, not the underlying cause.

The meaning of the earthshaking events in Los Angeles is difficult to grasp because most of us remain trapped in the narrow framework of the dominant liberal and conservative views of race in America, which with its worn-out vocabulary leaves us intellectually debilitated, morally disempowered, and personally depressed. The astonishing disappearance of the event from public dialogue is testimony to just how painful and distressing a serious engagement with race is. Our truncated public discussions of race suppress the best of who and what we are as a people because they fail to confront the complexity of the issue in a candid and critical manner. The predictable pitting of liberals against conservatives, Great Society Democrats against self-help Republicans, reinforces intellectual parochialism and political paralysis.

The liberal notion that more government programs can solve the problems is simplistic—precisely because it focuses *solely* on the economic dimension. And the conservative idea that what is needed is a change in the moral behavior of poor black urban dwellers (especially poor black men, who, they say, should stay married, support their children, and stop committing so much crime) highlights immoral actions while ignoring public responsibility for the immoral circumstances that haunt our fellow citizens.

The common denominator of these views of race is that each still sees black people as a "problem people," in the words of Dorothy I. Height, president of the National Council of Negro Women, rather than as fellow American citizens with problems. Her words echo the poignant "unasked question" of W. E. B. Du Bois, who wrote: "They approach me in a half-hesitant sort of way, eye me curiously or compassionately, and then instead of saying directly, How does it feel to be a problem? they say, I know an excellent colored man in my town. . . . Do not these Southern outrages make your blood boil? At these I smile, or am interested, or reduce the boiling to a simmer, as the occasion may require. To the real question, How does it feel to be a problem? I answer seldom a word." Nearly a century later, we confine discussions about race in America to the "problems" black people pose for whites rather than considering what this way of viewing black people reveals about us as a nation.

This paralyzing framework encourages liberals to relieve their guilty consciences by supporting public funds directed at "the problems"; but at the same time, reluctant to exercise principled criticism of black people, they deny them the freedom to err. Similarly, conservatives blame the "problems" on black people themselves—and thereby render black social misery invisible or unworthy of public attention.

Hence, for liberals, black people are to be "included" and "integrated" into "our" society and culture, while for conservatives they are to be "well behaved" and "worthy of acceptance" by "our" way of life. Both fail to see that the presence and predicaments of black people are neither additions to nor defections from American life, but rather *constitutive elements of that life.*

To engage in a serious discussion of race in America, we must begin not with the problems of black people but with the flaws of American society—flaws rooted in historic inequalities and longstanding cultural stereotypes. How we set up the terms for discussing racial issues shapes our perception and response to these issues. As long as black people are viewed as a "them," the burden falls on blacks to do all the "cultural" and "moral" work necessary for healthy race relations. The implication is that only certain Americans can define what it means to be American—and the rest must simply "fit in."

The emergence of strong black-nationalist sentiments among blacks, especially young people, is a revolt against this sense of having to fit in. The variety of black-nationalist ideologies, from the moderate views of Supreme Court Justice Clarence Thomas in his youth to those of Louis Farrakhan today, rest upon a fundamental truth: white America has been historically weak-willed in insuring racial justice and has continued to resist accepting fully the humanity of blacks. As long as double standards and differential treatment abound—as long as the rap performer Ice-T is harshly condemned while former Los Angeles Police Chief Daryl F. Gates's antiblack comments are received in polite silence, as long as Dr. Leonard Jeffries's anti-Semitic statements are met with vitriolic outrage while Presidential candidate Patrick J. Buchanan's are received with a genteel response—black nationalisms will thrive.

Afrocentrism, a contemporary species of black nationalism, is a gallant yet misguided attempt to define an African identity in a white society perceived to be hostile. It is gallant because it puts black doings and sufferings, not white anxieties and fears, at the center of discussion. It is misguided because—out of fear of cultural hybridization, silence on the issue of class, retrograde views on black women, homosexuals, and lesbians, and a reluctance to link race to the common good—it reinforces the narrow discussions about race.

To establish a new framework, we need to begin with a frank acknowledgement of the basic humanness and Americanness of each of us. And we must acknowledge that as a people—E Pluribus Unum—we are on a slippery slope toward economic strife, social turmoil, and cultural chaos. If we go down, we go down together. The Los Angeles upheaval forced us to see not only that we are not connected in ways we would like to be but also, in a more profound sense, that this failure to connect binds us even more tightly together. The paradox of race in America is that our common destiny is more pronounced and imperiled precisely when our divisions are deeper. The Civil War and its legacy speak loudly here. Eighty-six percent of white suburban Americans live in neighborhoods that are less than 1 percent black, meaning that the prospects for the country depend largely on how its cities fare in the hands of a suburban electorate. There is no escape from our interracial interdependence, yet enforced racial hierarchy dooms us as a nation to collective paranoia and hysteria—the unmaking of any democratic order.

The verdict that sparked the incidents in Los Angeles was perceived to be wrong by the vast majority of Americans. But whites have often failed to acknowledge the widespread mistreatment of black people, especially black men, by law-enforcement agencies, which helped ignite the spark. The Rodney King verdict was merely the occasion for deep-seated rage to come to the surface. This rage is fed by the "silent" depression ravaging the country—in which real weekly wages of all American workers since 1973 have declined nearly 20 percent, while at the same time wealth has been upwardly distributed.

The exodus of stable industrial jobs from urban centers to cheaper labor markets here and abroad, housing policies that have created "chocolate cities and vanilla suburbs" (to use the popular musical artist George Clinton's memorable phrase), white fear of black crime, and the urban influx of poor Spanish-speaking and Asian immigrants—all have helped erode the tax base of American cities just as the federal government has cut its supports and programs. The result is unemployment, hunger, homelessness, and sickness for millions.

Driving that rage is a culture of hedonistic self-indulgence and narcissistic self-regard. This culture of consumption yields coldhearted and mean-spirited attitudes and actions that turn poor urban neighborhoods into military combat zones and existential wastelands.

And the pervasive spiritual impoverishment grows. The collapse of meaning in life—the eclipse of hope and absence of love of self and others, the breakdown of family and neighborhood bonds—leads to the social deracination and cultural denudement of urban dwellers, especially children. We have created rootless, dangling people with little link to the supportive networks—family, friends, school—that sustain some sense of purpose in life. We have witnessed the collapse of the spiritual communities that help us face despair, disease, and death and that transmit through the generations dignity and decency, excellence and elegance.

The result is lives of what we might call "random nows," of fortuitous and fleeting moments preoccupied with "getting over"—with acquiring pleasure, property, and power by any means necessary. (This is not what Malcolm X meant by this famous phrase.) Postmodern culture is more and more a market culture dominated by gangster mentalities and self-destructive wantonness. This culture engulfs all of us—yet its impact on the disadvantaged is devastating, resulting in extreme violence in everyday life. Sexual violence against women and homicidal assaults by young black men on one another are only the most obvious signs of this empty quest for pleasure, property, and power.

Lastly, this rage is fueled by a political atmosphere in which images, not ideas, dominate, where politicians spend more time raising money than issues. The functions of parties have been displaced by public polls, and politicians behave less as thermostats that determine the climate of opinion than as thermometers registering the public mood. American politics has been rocked by an unleashing of greed among opportunistic public officials—following the lead of their counterparts in the private sphere, where, as of 1989, 1 percent of the population owned 37 percent of the wealth—leading to a profound cynicism and pessimism among the citizenry.

And given the way in which the Republican Party since 1968 has appealed to popular xenophobic images—playing the black, female, and homophobic cards and realigning the electorate along race, sex, and sexual-orientation lines—it is no surprise that the notion that we are all part of one garment of destiny is discredited. Appeals to special interests rather than public interests reinforce this polarization. The Los Angeles upheaval was an expression of utter fragmentation by a powerless citizenry that includes not just the poor but all of us.

What is to be done? How do we capture a new spirit and vision to meet the challenges of the postindustrial city, postmodern culture, and postparty politics?

First, we must admit that the most valuable sources for help, hope, and power consist of ourselves and our common history. As in the ages of Lincoln, Roosevelt, and King, we must look to new frameworks and languages to understand our multilayered crisis and overcome our deep malaise.

Second, we must focus our attention on the public square—the common good that undergirds our national and global destinies. The vitality of any public square ultimately depends on how much we care about the quality of our lives together. The neglect of our public infrastructure, for example—our water and sewage systems, bridges, tunnels, highways, subways, and streets—reflects not only our myopic economic policies, which impede productivity, but also the low priority we place on our common life.

The tragic plight of our children clearly reveals our deep disregard for public well-being. With about one out of five children living in poverty in this country and one out of two black children and two out of five Hispanic children doing so—and with most of our children ill-equipped to live lives of spiritual and cultural quality, neglected by overburdened parents, and bombarded by the market values of profit-hungry corporations—how do we expect ever to constitute a vibrant society?

One essential step is some form of large-scale public intervention to insure access to basic social goods—housing, food, health care, education, child care, and jobs. We must invigorate the common good with a mixture of government, business, and labor that does not follow any existing blueprint. After a period in which the private sphere has been sacralized and the public square gutted, the temptation is to make a fetish of the public square. We need to resist such dogmatic swings.

Last, the major challenge is the need to generate new leadership. The paucity of courageous leaders—so apparent in the response to the events in Los Angeles—requires that we look beyond the same elites and voices that recycle the older frameworks. We need leaders—neither saints nor sparkling television personalities—who can situate themselves within a larger historical narrative of this country and world, who can grasp the complex dynamics of our peoplehood and imagine a future grounded in the best of our past, yet attuned to the frightening obstacles that now perplex us. Our ideals of freedom, democracy, and equality must be invoked to invigorate all of us, especially the landless, propertyless, and luckless. Only a visionary leadership that can motivate "the better angels of our nature," as Lincoln said, and activate possibilities for a freer, more efficient and stable America—only that leadership deserves cultivation and support.

This new leadership must be grounded in grassroots organizing that highlights democratic accountability. Regardless of whether Bill Clinton's cautious neoliberal programs or George Bush's callous conservative policies prevail in November, the challenge to America will be determining whether a genuine multiracial democracy can be created and sustained in an era of global economies and a moment of xenophobic frenzy.

Let us hope and pray that the vast intelligence, imagination, humor, and courage in this country will not fail us. Either we learn a new language of empathy and compassion, or the fire this time will consume us all.

CORNEL WEST (1953–   )

🏵 The Black Underclass and Black Philosophers (1989)

I want to begin by raising the question of what it means to talk about the black underclass from the vantage point of being a black philosopher. It means then that we have to engage in a kind of critical self-inventory, a historical situating and positioning of ourselves as persons who reflect on the situation of those more disadvantaged than us even though we may have relatives and friends in the black underclass. We have to reflect in part on what is our identity as both black intellectuals, as black philosophers, and more broadly as academicians within the professional-managerial class in U.S. advanced-capitalist society. We also must be cognizant of the kind of impact postmodern culture, the culture of this society, is having upon our perceptions, our discourses, our perspectives. Then I'll move to the contemporary discourse on the black underclass. And I'll put forward some theses regarding why I think the black underclass finds itself in the predicament and plight that it is, while highlighting the issue of culture and the way in which culture is linked to institutions and structures. I'll end by saying a few words about what can be done.

Let me begin by raising the issue of the identity of black philosophers. This is an issue that we have been struggling with for over sixteen years when we first came together that lovely evening at Tuskegee Institute in 1973. I want to wax nostalgic about this. It is an issue that all of us have had to come to terms with. What does it mean to be a philosopher of African descent in the American empire? This raises the question of what is our relation to the discipline of philosophy. What is our relation to the dominant paradigms and perspectives in that discipline? Analytic philosophy? Continental modes of philosophizing? To what degree are we willing to transgress these paradigms? What kinds of consequences follow therefrom given the fact that the reward structure of the discipline is such that to transgress means then that we will be

Reprinted from *Prophetic Thought in Postmodern Times*, vol. 2 of *Beyond Eurocentrism and Multiculturalism* (Monroe, Me.: Common Courage Press, 1993), 143–57. Reprinted with permission of Common Courage Press.

marginalized? Now I want to argue that in fact to talk about philosophy in relation to the black underclass means that we have a conception of philosophy that is inexplicably bound to cultural criticism and political engagement. And what I mean by this is that first we begin with a historicist sensibility. And by historicist sensibility I mean that we do things that our colleagues find often times very difficult to do which is to read history seriously and voraciously.

Secondly, it means that we engage in an interdisciplinary or even dedisciplinizing mode of knowledge. And what I mean by this is traversing and cutting across the disciplinary division of knowledge inscribed within the universities and colleges, or to radically call into question the very existence of the disciplines themselves. To dedisciplinize means that you go to wherever you find sources that can help you in constituting your intellectual weaponry. This means it is going to be very difficult to obtain tenure in a philosophy department by doing this kind of thing. And all of us have had to struggle with this. This is a serious issue of how, in fact, we remain engaged in our discipline while also radically calling various aspects of it into question if not the whole thing. And having to deal with the marginal status as if you are not "philosophers," or "serious philosophers," "rigorous philosophers," "precise philosophers." And this is not in any way peculiar to black philosophers. This is true for a number of philosophers who called into question in serious ways the dominant paradigms. But black philosophers, I think especially, have been prone to this kind of perception and treatment. If one begins with a historicist sensibility, if one begins with an interdisciplinary or dedisciplinizing orientation, it means also then that one begins to talk about the *worldliness* of one's philosophical project. Here, I of course borrow a term from Edward Said's work, *The World, the Text and the Critic.*[1] In my worldliness, it means you acknowledge quite explicitly the partisan, partial, engaged character of one's own work. Now of course, the immediate charge is that you engage in politicized forms of knowledge. The more charitable reading is you are simply explicit about your values. You're explicit about your political commitment and yet you believe in a critical dialogue and hope that others will be as explicit and unequivocal as to where they stand in relation to their values and political perspectives. But if we take seriously historicist sensibility with dedisciplinizing modes of knowledge and the worldliness of what one is doing, then I think it no accident that we would find ourselves reflecting on something like the black underclass and thereby using tools that have not been bequeathed to us by philosophy departments. Instead we look to cultural criticism, to sophisticated historical work, and to social theory.

Now when we then make the shift to reflection on the black underclass, we begin by reflecting on where we are and what authorizes the claims that we make about the black underclass. Why? Because we know that we are specially for the most part, and certainly socially, distant from the very object that we are constituting as an object of investigation, namely, brothers and sisters who are locked within the black underclass plight. Now, it means then where are we socially? Where are we in regard to class? Where are we culturally? What has been the impact of the degree to which we have been acculturated and socialized into the culture of critical discourse, or the academic subculture? What kinds of values and sensibilities have shaped our socialization given where we come [from]? Many of us do indeed come from working class origins, some underclass origins, some rural black working class origins, and so forth. And what kind of new animal has been constituted in this black philosopher given these origins and given the acculturation? Now I am not arguing that one has to be autobiographical in this regard. But it seems to me before we even begin to talk about one's identity as a black philosopher, one's agency as a black philosopher, we must ask: Who are we speaking to? Who are we writing to? And who in any way holds us accountable? Is it the profession? In part it must be the profession if we are going to be a part of the profession. But is it solely the profession? And if it is more than the profession, then who else is it? Is it the black intellectual community that cuts across disciplines? So to raise these kinds of questions means that we engage in a kind of critical self-inventory. Where does that take us? I want to put forth three basic claims about this.

First, I want to argue that we find ourselves in many ways marginalized not solely by white philosophers or mainstream philosophers, but we find ourselves marginalized also because we are humanistic intellectuals. And humanistic intellectuals in general are being marginalized in our society. They are being marginalized by the *technical* intellectuals, e.g., physicists, computer scientists, et al., because they receive most of the resources from the huge private enterprises and from the state and from the military-industrial complex that flows from the nation state. Why? Because the products they provide, of course, are quite useful for society as deemed so by their supporters.

Secondly, as humanistic intellectuals we find ourselves marginalized because middlebrow journalists have much more visibility and saliency than we do in the academy. And by middlebrow journalists I mean those who work for *Time,* for *Newsweek,* for *Atlantic Monthly,* for *Harper's,* and others who have a large constituency or at least a large audience. And so the consequence in part is that we find ourselves talking more and more to one another, hoping that this will serve as a way of sustaining our sense of identity as academic humanists who often feel as if we are becoming antiquated and outdated.

Thirdly, I think in addition to this issue of marginalization is the one of demoralization. And by demoralization I mean the crisis of purpose among black intellectuals in general and black philosophers in particular. I think the recent work of Alan Bloom on the right and Russell Jacoby's book, *The Last Intellectuals*,[2] on the left, are quite reflective of this struggle of crisis of purpose among humanistic intellectuals. On the one hand the loss of public intellectuals, the loss of those academicians who can actually intervene into the larger conversation that affects the destiny of large numbers of persons, such as the issue of the black underclass. But on the other hand, it is also reflective of the fact that we find our jobs more and more alienating as we are more and more servicing an upper slice of a labor force that tends to put less and less premium on humanistic studies. So that Pascal begins to displace French as a language—Pascal computer language. So that reading Plato and Aristotle becomes seemingly ornamental and decorative rather than substantive and engaging. It's nice to know a little Plato you can invoke at a cocktail party when you're off relaxing and not making money. But there's no sense that what's at stake might be your very life, as Socrates and many others believed. And this is true at large because while we're in a culture in which the literary is in fact being marginalized vis-à-vis the oral by means of the mass media, by means of film, by means of television, by means of radio, not just the oral but of course it's the audio and the visual that I'm talking about. And for those of us who are still intellectuals of the book, it's nice to run into other people who are reading the same books because there are not that many around anymore. And we might think that John Rawls is really so very, very important, as I think he is. But we also see the degree to which Rawls finds himself as a towering figure, the last liberal political theorist, as someone who has to be translated in broader ways so that the relevance and pertinence of what he has to say is translatable, given the kind of business culture, the business civilization of which we are a part. Now I think this is especially so in the last twenty years, where the hotel civilization—I love that phrase that Henry James invoked, in which you get the fusion of the security of the family and the uncertainty of the market—both profoundly private activities, private institutions often distrustful of the common good and the public interest, but more and more serving as the very model of what our culture looks like. And when we then make the shift to the second moment of my presentation which has to do with this discourse on the underclass, we see in fact that the culture of consumption, which is to say the culture of advanced-capitalist American society, more and more is the culture that evolves around the market, around buying and selling, around a process of commodification that tends to undermine values, structures of meaning, in the name of the expansion of buying and selling, in the name of the procuring profit.

Now this is indeed more than a challenge. I think it is a highly dangerous

situation. Why so? It's dangerous because in a market culture in which commodification holds sway over more and more spheres of human life, one sees
an addiction to stimulation as the requisite for the consumerism which helps
keep the economy going. And therefore it tends to undermine community,
undermine links to history and tradition, undermine neighborhoods, undermine even qualitative relations, since the very notion of commitment becomes more and more contested and bodily stimulation becomes a model
for human relations. We see it in the employment of women's bodies in
dehumanized ways and in the advertising industry. We see it of course in the
sitcoms that tend to evolve around orgiastic intensity. Crack is quite exemplary in this regard. Crack is indeed the postmodern drug because it is the
highest level of stimulation known to the human brain. It is ten times more
[stimulating] than orgasm, an expression of a culture that evolves around the
addiction to stimulation. And stimulation becomes the end and aim much
more so than the means, yet the means is the very sphere in which human
relations, human community, human traditions, are linked to human history, especially traditions of resistance.

Now what has that to do with the black underclass? It has much to do with
the black underclass. Because when we look at the black underclass we see
on the one hand a qualitative fissure in the history of people of African
descent in this country. Now what I mean by this is, that roughly between
1964 and 1967 black neighborhoods underwent qualitative transformation
and the qualitative transformation that they underwent had much to do with
the invasion of a particular kind of commodification, namely the buying and
selling of a particular commodity—drugs. Now whether it's conspiratorial or
not there's no doubt that black communities have fundamentally changed.
For the first time we have the disintegration of the *transclass character* of
black communities in which different classes live together. So the attempt to
sustain the basic institutions of black civil society, family, church, fraternity,
sorority, beauty shop, barber shop, shopkeeper, funeral parlor, that used to
be in place and served as the infrastructures that transmitted the values and
sensibilities to notions of self-respect and self-esteem still had some possibility of distribution across the black community could take place. On the
one hand, it is certainly true that, as was talked about this morning, the
legacy of 244 vicious and pernicious years of slavery still has its impact on
the black psyche. What I mean by this is that the *natal* alienation, the loss
of ties at birth of ascending and descending generations, a loss of ties to
both predecessor and progeny has certainly created an airborne people, a
dangling people, a people who must forever attempt to acquire their self-
identity, and self-image in a positive way as they are bombarded with negative ones.

To live for 244 years with no legal standing, no social status, no public

worth, only economic value means then that the issue of self-identity remains central. Garvey understood this very well. It's still an issue today I want
to suggest. So that the issue of self-doubt, especially among the middle class,
issues of self-contempt among large numbers of black folk, a self-hatred, a
self-affliction, a self-flagellation, all of these still remain crucial issues in
black America, but you can imagine what the legacy of slavery, and the
legacy of *natal* alienation is when it intersects with a culture of consumption
in which addiction to stimulation becomes the only means by which a vitality is preserved by a self in a society which promotes spectatorial passivity
and evasive banality. The culture of consumption generates a passivity by
means of spectatorial enactment and it generates a sense of deadening such
that the self tries to preserve some sense of itself by engaging in some mode
of therapeutic release. We get this in sports, in simulated sexuality, the disco
culture, in music, and so forth. We engage in some ritualistic practice, going
to the Friday night parties, going to church on Sunday, some ritualistic practice for the self to feel as if it is alive, it is vital, it is vibrant. Now you can
imagine, given the legacy of slavery mediated with Jim Crowism, second
class citizenship, urbanization, all the different stages and phases that black
people have been through from 1619 up to the present and then the culture
of consumption that begins to become more and more dominant between
1965 and the present.

What this conjuncture has produced, I want to argue, is the major challenge presented to black America, to black scholars, black intellectuals, and
to black leaders and black people. And the challenge is this: 1) it has produced the highest level of forms of self-destruction known in black history.
And these demons which are at work, the demons of meaninglessness, of
hopelessness, a sense of nothingness conjoined with the institutional and
structural marginalization of large numbers of black people, though not all
(because there is a black working class majority we should not overlook, even
a black prosperity among a selective slice of the black middle class, including
a few of ourselves owing to the struggle of those in the sixties). But, for the
most part, it has produced the highest level of self-destruction known to
black people since we arrived. And the reason why is because for the first
time there are now no longer viable institutions and structures in black
America that can effectively transmit values like hope, virtue, sacrifice, risk,
of putting the needs of others higher or alongside those of oneself. And in the
past, when you've looked at black colleges in which every Sunday they were
forced to sit in those pews and Benjamin Mays would get up and say, "You
must give service to the race," reminding these black, petty bourgeois students that even as they went out into the world they had a cause, they had an
obligation, they had a duty to do something beyond simply that of their own
self-interest. Now what they did may have been narrow, and myopic, and

shortsighted—but they had an institution that was transmitting that value. That's the point. And it's not just the black school—we can talk about the black church, we can talk about fraternities, we can talk about the whole host of other institutions in black civil society. We no longer have this to the degree that we did in the past and they are being eroded slowly but surely. This is what is most frightening. This is why we get the exponential increase in black suicides between 18 and 35, unprecedented in black history. This is why we get escalating black homicides in which you get some of the most coldhearted, mean-spirited dispositions and attitudes displayed by black people against other black people as well as nonblacks. It's a breakdown in the moral fabric. Now, conservatives have made much of this point—Glenn Loury, Thomas Sowell, and a host of others have been saying there's something different about black America now, and they highlight the loss of values. But they understand loss of values as simply choices made by individuals as if they are not shaped by the larger structural institutional realities of the cultural consumption. And of course, these larger structures are affecting America as a whole, not just black America. They are affecting America as a whole, but of course the negative consequences tend to be concentrated among those who have lesser access to financial and emotional resources. Now, given this conjuncture, the question becomes, how then does one generate institutions, infrastructures? What these institutions and infrastructures did was produce certain kinds of people, many morally virtuous people, not perfect people, but persons who are willing to sacrifice and struggle. How do you sustain these institutions and infrastructures that can produce certain kinds of people so that traditions of resistance can be sustained, and if possible, even expanded? So that when the hotter moments of American society emerge—which is to say those moments in which new progressive and prophetic possibilities surface—you have institutions and infrastructures that can come together, take advantage of them. And if black people have learned anything in America, it is that America is a profoundly conservative country, even given all of its commitments to experimentation and improvisation. And by conservative, what I mean is, conservative in terms of its unwillingness to give up its racism, its sexism, its homophobia. And therefore, the question becomes when you have a chance to push the movement forth you have to move quickly because the leaders and organizations will be crushed. The CIA and the FBI will move quickly, and therefore you know it's not going to last that long. But in order to seize that kind of opportunity, you have to have the ability to produce individuals who will sacrifice, who will live and die for the movement. And these are not petty issues. Part of the problem in contemporary black America is that there's not a deep enough care, and therefore not a willingness to sacrifice. Now, it may sound like a moralist claim that I'm making, but I am actually trying to make a systemic claim, because it has to do with the relative paucity of institutions and infra-structures that can produce these kind of people and then for these people to actually sacrifice their time and energy to engage in a kind of struggle, as those who came before us had to do in order to produce us. Now, how do you do that? What has that to do with black philosophy? It has much to do with black philosophy. One is that we do the kind of thing that we have tried to do for the last sixteen years. We engage in institution building. So that we can at least keep each other in part accountable, even if we don't see each other as much as we like. This is very important. It's very small, but it's very impor-tant. It's significant. Because it means, then, not only are we keeping records of what we do, not only are we trying to sustain the vision, trying to hold each other accountable in terms of our sacrifice, and no longer feel as if the issues that once motivated us, issues of freedom, issues of justice, are no longer salient in our own work.

Now I'm not talking about censorship. I'm not talking about indoctrina-tion. I'm talking about accountability. And accountability is mediated by means of discussion and dialogue—respectful discussion and dialogue. But it is accountability, nevertheless. Even as we reflect on the black underclass, we can sustain our institutions to keep the discussion going and then to intervene into the larger discussion about the black underclass. We've talked about the work of William Julius Wilson keeping in mind that there has always been a black underclass since the end of slavery. What is significant now is the size of it, the social gravity of it, and the frightening and terrify-ing responses to it. Again, historical perspective is crucial. What are the ways in which the black underclass's predicament can be enhanced? On the one hand, I think that William Julius Wilson is right; that it is going to be a matter of public policy. That no private institution is either willing and/or able to solve the problem of the black underclass. The only private institu-tions which have the resources to do so, namely multinational corporations, hardly pay their taxes, so you can't expect them to take on a major problem like the black underclass. And the notion of the black middle class—not Wilson's view—as the source of the panacea has to be the biggest hoax ever played on any emerging bourgeoisie in the history of the modern world. No middle class in the modern world has been cast as the source of the resolu-tion of the problems of their ethnic or racial working class and underclass.

First, because they don't have the resources to do it. In addition, we have primarily a *lumpenbourgeoisie*. Which is to say we have no serious economic or business class for the most part. Instead, our businesses tend to be locked within the lower echelons of the entrepreneurial sector of the economy in which the multinational corporate sector is the major controller of resources. So to talk about black business in this way is ridiculous. Mr. Reginald Lewis—the leading black businessman in the country—and Mr. John H. Johnson—

the second leading black businessman in the country—are not a part of the first 500 of *Forbes*. So to look to these folk as the solution is comical.

The focus then becomes the public sphere, the contestation for power within the state, and hence the black participation in politics. But in this very conservative moment it does not look good even at a time when the Democratic Party is undergoing, as we know, a very slow decline itself, especially given its association with black folk. So that it becomes highly problematic as to how one talks creditably about politics and policies. It is very clear that there have to be resources in place to enhance the situation of the black underclass. There's no doubt about it. People don't want to talk about money and resources, but it's the first step—not the only step—but it is the first step.

Without broader employment, without the child care requisite for the women who are the majority of the black underclass nurturing their children, without the manpower and womanpower problems, there can be no serious talk about resolutions of the black underclass. Just a fact. But in addition, as I noted, it's not just a matter of money, it's a matter of values and sensibility, and morally latent ways of life and ways of struggle. There must emerge a new kind of black leadership, a new kind of black organization and association—or set of organizations and associations—that can bring power and pressure to bear on the powers that be. One cannot talk about enhancing the plight of the black underclass without talking about politics, and to talk about politics is to talk about mobilization and organization. And yet to talk about organization and mobilization means to talk about the paucity of institutions and infrastructures.

This is why things become depressing at times. Because when you look around and see what is in place in the black community as it is undergoing this state of siege, you wonder what can be reinvigorated, let alone created, at an institutional level—not just an individual here, not just a book there, just an article there. These are important, but they're limited. One has to talk organizationally, you see. And I would want to argue that, in fact, presently what Professor Lott was talking about in regard to rap music this morning is pertinent here: the degree to which there is institutional articulation of rap music so that power and pressure can be brought to bear as opposed to just the powerful critique mediated through radio. And what kind of institutional translation is taking place? Very little. What are the conditions under which institutional translation can take place? Very difficult issue. And even the Jackson campaign is no answer to this, because there are no serious infrastructures and institutions in the Rainbow Coalition. It's the coming together of persons every four years in a campaign. It's not a deep rooting of institutions and infrastructure in the black and other communities that can be sustained over time and space.

Part of that has to do with Jackson's own institutional impatience. His refusal to engage in serious infrastructure building is part of the problem. And so presently, I would want to argue, that as black intellectuals and as black activists our reflections on the black underclass are significant because the kind of demystification that has taken place today and will take place tomorrow is important at the intellectual level. I want to affirm this and say this quite emphatically, because we live in an anti-intellectual culture and we have to boldly assert our right to engage in intellectual reflection without it having an overnight payoff. It might be linked to a larger project but it may not have overnight payoff but it must be done. If you're thinking as an intellectual who wants to have effectivity and efficacy even further down the road, then you have to think about ways in which the kind of malaise that so much of black America finds itself in can be met. And I would argue that when we look around the black community, what we see is, on the one hand, a set of prophetic churches, and mosques, much of it patriarchal, deeply homophobic, but a link to a black freedom struggle that generates persons who are willing to live and die for struggle. They still produce persons who exude and exemplify what they exult and extol in terms of their values. What else do we see? We see some political organization, some neighborhood blocks or associations. Very important. We see infrastructures in relation to sports, Big Brothers programs, Little Leagues. All these character-building activities that seem minuscule but actually are very important in terms of helping produce certain kinds of persons who are indeed willing to engage in struggle. But that's about it. Even our black colleges, more and more, have been so fundamentally shaped by capitalist values that most of our students are graduating in business and communication. And finding humanistic studies, again, ornamental, decorative, "something I have to take because it's part of a path that old folks used to like but I want to make that money and therefore I'm going to zip through this class and take this business class seriously because I want to get into middle class." That's not just black students, that's students across the board, but it is deeply shaping the values of a whole new generation to whom Malcolm X is Malcolm the Tenth, and Martin Luther King is some kind of cultural icon that has no link whatsoever to everyday lives. What a challenge. That's the impasse and the dilemma that I want to suggest, and I don't have any easy way out other than this institution building, of which this is, in many ways, an instance, given the sixteen-year history of the dialogue of black philosophers. And there are other such institution-building efforts, but I hope that we are on the wave of such an institution-building activity regulated by an all-embracing moral vision, one that talks seriously of class, of gender, of empire, sexual orientation, one that takes seriously social analysis, the historicist sensibility, the dedisciplinizing orientation, and the worldliness. But also one that takes seriously praxis, which is to say, life commitment, which is to say, sacrificial commitment. I'm not calling for martyrdom, I'm just calling for sacrifice. But it's very important because to be a member of the professional managerial class tends to mitigate against this very sense of commitment. Do you have to go against it? And it means then the rewards are less. It means then that the status is indeed less even if you are at a ruling class institution like Princeton. It still means that the status has to have less value because what you are about dwarfs that. In regard to this greater cause we can continue to produce persons who cultivate and build on these traditions of resistance, so that when the hot moment comes—nobody can predict the hot moment—our "December 55 moment" comes. These infrastructures and institutions can begin to come alive quickly before the repression sets in. And the repression will inevitably set in, and the attacks will inevitably set in because this is America. And there is a lot at stake in the prosperity of America. Black people understand that. Yet it can be pushed, and progressive white comrades and feminist comrades will help push. And then we will be pushed back and the next generation will have to engage in their own challenge, and we hope the next generation of black philosophers will reflect on how they're going to deal with those human beings of African descent who are unemployed, underemployed, have inadequate health care, housing, education, and so on. The battle is perennial; yet each of us in our time must fight.

[1]Edward Said, *The World, the Text, and the Critic* (Cambridge: Harvard University Press, 1983).

[2]Russell Jacoby, *The Last Intellectuals: American Culture in the Age of Academe* (New York: Noonday Press, 1987).

LEONARD HARRIS (1948–)

🏵 Postmodernism and Utopia, an Unholy Alliance

The concept of postmodernism is associated with an army of theories about metaphysics, knowledge, descriptive methods, language, culture, the subject, progress, and utopia (Hassan 1987; Koslowski 1987; Levin 1966). Current urban society in the West is considered "postmodern" by Jameson, a Marxist, by Baudrillard, who rejects Marxism, and by Rorty, a pragmatist. The condition of postmodernism has thus been explored by authors from a variety of philosophical bases. There are, I believe, certain indefensible features of descriptions, and theories used to guide descriptions, of postmodern urban centers. I focus on racism within the urban West as a way of exploring these features. I argue that the conception of utopia in the version of the postmodern condition that I consider here is egregious. It is grounded on the indefensible vision of the West as a meta-utopia, a vision which makes invisible the immiserated and renders "the subject" devoid of the traits of agency associated with resisting oppression. My argument does not suggest that all versions of the postmodern condition, or theories used to depict that condition, are conducive to racism. It does, however, critique descriptions and conceptions of utopia in the works of several postmodernists (the implications of my argument for other versions of postmodernism are not considered). By "postmodernists," I mean a specific school of authors with similar views on the nature of the subject and utopia, and who concur, with thinkers from a variety of perspectives, that the condition of life in the urban West is "postmodern."[1]

Postmodernists reject the enlightenment project of seeking universal rules of rationality. The application of such rules was thought by the intellectuals of the enlightenment to lead inextricably to true propositions. Postmodernists believe, however, that propositions do not convey "objective" truth, nor do they correspond to "objective" reality. Universal rules of rationality are,

Reprinted from *Racism, The City and the State*, edited by Malcolm Cross and Michael Keith (London: Routledge, 1993), 31–44. © Routledge, 1993. Reprinted with permission of Routledge.

for postmodernists, subtle norms which help to legitimate the ideological or authoritarian rule of existing discourse, not guides to true propositions. Propositions in science, on Lyotard's account for example, are better understood as performatives—tools which allow us to manipulate our world and ourselves more or less successfully. They do not convey iron laws of nature, but are rather analogous to narratives, e.g., different ways of describing which are more or less useful and interesting. Lyotard defines "*postmodernism* as incredulity toward metanarratives. This incredulity is undoubtedly a product of progress in the sciences: but that progress in turn presupposes it" (Lyotard 1979a/b: xxiv; cf. Sloterdijk 1987).

Postmodernists also reject the enlightenment project of reifying historical subjects. Whether the subject is Hegel's view of consciousness, Kant's view of rational man, or Marx's view of the working class as the agent of history, postmodernists reject the idea that the realization of a suppressed human essence or trait represents the liberation of humanity. The realization of hidden essences is not, for postmodernists, the driving force of history, which is inevitably progressing towards utopia.[2] Rather, the world of decentered, diffractured, and doxical persons with transparent and constantly changing identities both (a) defines personal identity in postmodern culture and (b) represents the traits of what persons are as agents. The existence of ephemeral identities and constantly transvalued personal tastes coalesce to form a sublime, if schizophrenic, urban community. This view of the subject is not a simple juxtaposition of the individual and the social; rather, it is a conception of the subject which defines it in the above terms and perceives its agency in the way that thought, as a stream of often incongruent ideas or a pastiche, is perceived (P. Smith 1988; Hassan 1987). The condition of life in the urban West is thus postmodern in the sense that individuals are without stable identities which they believe represent the realization of some enlightenment concept of human nature. Rather, individuals in the urban West make and remake their identities without foundational commitments; the urban centers of the West are like theaters while their citizens are like actors who frequently change roles; the incongruity of signs and symbols in urban centers defines the existential being of the prototypical postmodern person.

Modernism is associated with the view that science conveys iron laws of nature. Modernity is also associated with the development of material goods such as electricity, public water works, roads, and cars by use of Fordist manufacturing techniques and [by] appeal to one or another "iron law" of management. Following one strand of thought from Thomas Kuhn and Paul Feyerabend, revolutions in science, for postmodernists, occur most often through the rejection of established paradigms by those frequently outside of the science establishment. Science/computers, for Lyotard for example, is revolutionary because it often changes through the rise of new theories to account for anomalies. With free access to knowledge, understood as information held by computer banks, the science / computer bank "could become the 'dream' instrument used to discuss meta-prescriptives rather than used for simply performatives" (Lyotard 1979a/b: 67). For most postmodernists, we should search not for iron laws of nature or indefensible universal rational principles, but unique and interesting descriptions.

Postmodernists favour descriptive discourse. Such descriptions are not intended as "privileged" windows or naked eyes on an objective world, but [as] subversive discourses intended to offer performatives, incredulity or insight, or revealing views about an ephemeral or simulacrum world.

The uniqueness of the postmodern project is neither its naturalization of epistemology, which provides the ground for rejecting the idea that universal rules of thought constitute the core of rationality, nor the rejection of historical subjects. These views, as Rorty, Bernstein, Harvey and others note, have affinity with pragmatist views (R. Bernstein 1985; Rorty 1989; Harvey 1989). What is unique about the postmodern project, in relation to notions of utopia, is the view that the world has come to the end of history. There are two components of the view that the end of history has arrived which are of particular importance to my argument: (a) The belief that the idea of inevitable progress, development towards utopia, or something close to these has been discredited, and (b) the belief that models of the world in which the nature of the subject is realized (models which once masked ideological hegemony) are now delegitimated. Now, in effect, is the postmodern meta-utopia.

A meta-utopia, in Nozick's sense, is an environment or framework in which different utopian visions are permitted (Nozick 1974: 311–12). By "meta-utopia," I will mean this notion. The idea is that a certain condition of social life allows, permits, or makes it possible for individuals or groups to pursue their vision of utopia. From a sort of third person standpoint, these various visions exist under a social umbrella which does not allow any one vision to force its way of life on anyone else. Now is the postmodern meta-utopia: not in the sense that now is the best of all possible worlds because any "best of all possible worlds" would require a totalizing hegemonic language, identity, and corresponding practice, but in the sense that now holds the possibility of heterogeneity of language games, identities, practices, etc. The meta-narrative of postmodernism, I believe, is the notion that the urban West represents just such an environment or framework.

Unlike ecotopias or biotopias in which ecology or biologies are envisioned as a particular loci for universal fulfilment of some human need, trait, or essence, for example in Le Guin's *The Dispossessed,* the postmodernist vision does not suggest that some hidden essence is realizable. Its descriptions of social life correspond to, or represent, what subjects, rationality, and progress are—differentiated, fragmented, ephemeral, and transitory, without determination or teleologies.

The uncovering of meta-narratives is a positive good for such critics of postmodernism as Habermas. However, for Habermas, and arguably early critics of anarchistic forms of pragmatism such as Alain Locke, a focus on difference, fragmentation, ephemeral situations, transitions, irony, and incongruities "discloses a longing for an undefiled, immaculate and stable present" (McCarthy 1984; Rorty 1984; Locke 1989). However, it is this "present" or this "now" which, for postmodernists, is already enthralled as progress and constitutes the end of history.

If we take seriously the view that reason is not an array of universal rules of thought, and a meta-utopia view of the West, it is not too difficult to understand why postmodernists reject the enlightenment concept of historical subjects, i.e., "the idea of a unitary end of history and of a subject" (Lyotard 1979a/b: 73). Conceiving of progress as the unfolding of, or the progressive utility of, universal rules of thought stands contrary to a view that considers concepts of rationality as such inherently imbued with master or meta-narratives functioning as subtle authorities. If this form of authoritarianism is considered to be the principal form of oppression, we have good intuitive grounds, in effect, to draw attention to marginalized modes of thinking, and grounds for conceiving groups as "differentiated subjects," each with their own unique agency. We also have good intuitive grounds to reject concepts of utopia such as those central to the works of Moore, Bellamy, Marx, and Blyden (Moore 1516; Bellamy 1888; Marx and Engels 1848; Blyden 1887; Mudimbe 1988). Their views rested on a background of foundational thinking in terms of universal rules of thought which underlie or guide all humanity, and a unitary end of history for all humanity (Kumar 1987; Geoghegan 1988). We instead have grounds to conceive of life (dropping concepts of utopia all together) in terms of Raban's *Soft City* (1974), Deleuze and Guattari's *Anti-Oedipus* (1977), or Baudrillard's *America* (1989) (cf. Bell 1976).

Evocations of Hyper-Reality

Baudrillard's travelogue *America* scripts: "America is neither dream nor reality. It is hyperreality. It is a hyperreality because it is a utopia which has behaved from the very beginning as though it were already achieved" (Baudrillard 1989: 28). Baudrillard's double entendre is revealing: it means both that America previously behaved as if it were utopia and that it is now Utopia. "It may be that the truth of America can only be seen by a European, since he alone will discover here the perfect simulacrum—that of the immanence and material transcription of all value . . . They are themselves simulation in its most developed state . . ." (Baudrillard 1989: 28–9). The homeless, or those who appear to be homeless, on New York City streets in Baudrillard's description of New York suffer a distress that he describes as analogous to the distress of a diligent jogger.

Invisibility: Shelters for the homeless have increased in New York from 30 in 1981 to 600 in 1989.

Advertisements admonishing society to protect children from abuse are equated with obsessions to save things: children for the future; time and money.

Invisibility: At least 23 percent increase in the homelessness of children and 60 percent increase between 1983 and 1986 in the number of mentally retarded children, most from low income, inner city, African-American communities.

It is arguable that Baudrillard's descriptions erase misery and proffer a morally indefensible association of child neglect, abuse, abduction, and rape with the simulacrum of saving time and money, a simulacrum that's presumed universal and already situated as a meta-utopia. However, there is another feature of Baudrillard's text which reveals not racism in the sense of someone believing in the inferiority or superiority of naturally constituted races, but an amoralism and elliptical hegemonic vision. The concept of postmodernism, I argue, is associated with such a vision—a vision which renders the immiserated irrelevant and blacks, in particular, as ornaments without agencies or resistance.

Baudrillard describes black and Puerto Rican women of New York: "it must be said that black, the pigmentation of the dark races, is like natural make-up that is set off by the artificial kind to produce a beauty which is not sexual, but sublime and animal—a beauty which the pale faces so desperately lack. Whiteness . . . claims all the exotic power of the World, but ultimately will never possess the esoteric and ritual potency of artifice" (Baudrillard 1989: 15–16). He tenders, as a postmodern allowable description of images, one of the oldest stereotypes of racism: black skin as inherently unnatural, pained, exuding animal beauty; white as power, Word, but not artifice / artificial / animal—without substance. Artifice and symbol are real and of great moment: for the benefit of the observer, the observed exist as ornament (Said 1978). As literary devices, his descriptions convey a feeling and imagery which are compatible with images which enliven a chronically racist society (Patterson 1989). And race, itself a social and historical invention, is hardly on the verge of immanent transcription, and is hardly a symbol without substance influencing life changes.

Since narrative has the same status as science's descriptive accuracy, the relevance of blackness as a function of symbolic representation is treated as an accurate presentation of hyper-reality; immiseration is tangential. Baudrillard as a tourist reports, as it turns out, not self-created images and simulacrum, but well-worn stereotypes, impressions, and mythologies. His focus on images is simultaneously a focus on a narrow spectrum of social reality, and that spectrum is taken to represent the very character of social life.

It is arguable that the focus by postmodernists on Western societies, and particular cultural traits of those societies as traits sine qua non with an already constituted mega-utopia, renders their views ethnocentric and colonialist (Hartsock 1987; Parry 1988; Lea 1988). Another approach, however, is that the focus on Western societies not only erases black and oppressed peoples of Western societies, but renders their existence irrelevant; that the conditions taken to be important (such as authoritarian uses of enlightenment meta-narratives and valorizations of historical subjects) allow postmodernists to take the verities of a particular cultural strata and array them as features of the nature of knowledge and reason (Harris 1987; Robinson 1983); that the characteristics that postmodernists believe are important as conduits for liberation from authoritarianism are deleterious for the liberation of the oppressed within Western societies. I focus on the last of these. My approach is that even if the epistemological views identified with the postmodern project are defensible, it does not follow that the inferences drawn from their views support cogent descriptions.

Postmodern Racism and Racialized Identities

The existence of a social identity capable of ready transportation requires, I contend, an already constituted sense of cognitive location. That is, it requires the existence of a composite sense of self-identity—a sense of having a constituted being which is itself over time—in order to be aware of the act of choicemaking and the act of changing preferences. That awareness does not require the existence of a hidden essential reasoning self, but it does require a congruent and memorable mapping of change. By a composite sense of self-identity, I mean the having of intact memories, coherent ranges of experiences over time, particularly experiences of the disenfranchisement of their labor and cultural capital; I mean the existence of an identity which changes, as all identities do, but within a range of similar meanings as distinct from actual schizophrenic personalities; I mean the sort of cognitive memory which allows akratic behaviour whether it is a function of multiple identities, subconscious motivations, inexplicable inclinations, or private meanings (Mele 1988). The identities of woman, African, European, artist, or teacher, for example, have historically transient meanings (Sollors 1989). Within any given historical period, however, if an individual held one or more of these identities, what the identities meant falls within a limited range of possibilities. A background meaning for each, particularly since the enlightenment, involved membership in the moral community of humans.

Exclusion from that community has been a mark or sign used to legitimate suppression and normalize racism. Self-assurance, esteem, and self-respect may be desperately needed by people smouldering under the dehumanizing negation of their being as humans in a racist world, but postmodernists make the possibility of composite senses of self-identity seem either tangential to a future world or already given.

The existence of composite selves, as distinct from an anarchistic, diffractured, or ephemeral self, is denied by postmodernists as a feature definitive of personhood because such notions of identity are often grounded on conceptions of the subject as having some hidden essence. Yet, a composite self—not necessarily one with a hidden essence—is presupposed in depictions by postmodernists of the transient behavior of people in urban centers. What is negated in the concept of the subject by postmodernists is, at the same time, what is required for the subject to be an agent over time.

Imagine a secretary working in a postmodern building. The "world space of multinational capital," as Jameson argued, is crucial to the current world and will probably be crucial in shaping reality in any future world (Jameson 1984; Davis 1985, 1990). The postmodern building and its world allow us to travel through urban space, imaging a community. Discontinuities frame the community. The building adornments may reflect Italian, French, and German influences. Where one is historical, time is diffractured: the slums of Los Angeles sit next to the Bonaventure Hotel; the poverty of working-class communities is encamped on the outside of freeways which nearly encircle, and thereby protect, downtown Atlanta and the Peachtree Hotel (Bayor 1988). A secretary at the Peachtree Hotel can imagine having power, although he may be an underpaid and easily replaceable employee. A sense of community may be engendered in the secretary by open space, flowering plants, cathedral ceilings draped by windows for easy viewing of the outside world, although the secretary is in fact segregated from other workers and alienated from the transient hotel clientele. Neither power nor community constitute the secretary's world, but both are available as imagined reality. As an African-American secretary, his presence is a consequence of long struggles to overcome racial barriers, barriers which have hardly been broken down. There are, for example, more African-American males in American prisons than there are in colleges; the number of African-American males receiving terminal degrees since 1974 has declined. His income is almost certainly lower than that of a white male or female; his job is probably not protected by a union; and he most likely lives in a neighborhood which was historically planned to be segregated and dilapidated. The secretary's situation in a world surrounded by artifice is certainly different from the historical situation of most African-American males, but his position as the least well off is congruent with that history. If the secretary loses his job, he almost assuredly joins the underclass. He thereby joins the legions of persons standing in line at agencies which offer temporary employment; he secures welfare or participates in the underground economy of stolen merchandise or illegal drugs. He may travel north in search of employment, only to join what Baudrillard describes as colourful and exotic break-dancers adorning the streets of New York. His culture does not translate into capital (Wilson 1987; Katz 1986; Williams 1987; Darity 1982). What Baudrillard does not describe, and thereby leaves as irrelevant, is the immiseration of dancers who do so in hopes of payment by passing tourists enjoying the schizophrenia of postmodern urban space. Persons entrapped in the underclass characteristically lack a bank account, credit card, life insurance, and health insurance; they have a thin network of associates and the least number of employed relatives in America; the women are more likely to be raped and abused, and the least likely to receive a salary increase if employed. Experiencing persistent, chronic, and pervasive racism in the various postmodern sites of the urban West engenders a coherent experience of subjugation (Omi and Winant 1986).

Postmodern descriptions allow us to imagine that each racialized neighborhood that we travel through is a normal part of the urban scene. We can, with a sort of schizophrenic taste for food, freely move from one ethnic neighborhood to another, sampling cuisine as we go, imagining membership in each, paying with our credit card in each restaurant, ordering food the same way in each restaurant, using the same language in each, and yet imagining that we have fundamentally travelled to different lands of cuisine in some sense other than having simply tasted different foods. We have touched different cultures. And, as with postmodern anthropology, we are to be self-critical about our role as researchers and avoid making moral judgements (Mascia-Lees et al., 1989; Wagner 1975; Sollors 1989). Moreover, we must imagine as an end state, to be congruent with postmodern vision, urban space dominated by postmodern buildings and peopled by polarized hedonists. That state of affairs must be described without resorting to totalizing theories or master narratives. Each differentiated subject or community of subjects is understood to pursue incremental transformation of capitalism within its own site of experience. Life for postmodernists is totalized as symbolic and simultaneously fragmented. The community of postmodernists is pursued, with the aid of science/computers, sign, symbol, and transient taste, within and through each site.

The West, contrary to the postmodern description, has normalized a form of ghoulish separateness—a form of segregation which exists simultaneously with cosmopolitanism. Persons need not have a sense of owning their neighborhoods, nor be able to identify neatly residential boundaries between one group and another. Segregation, outside of the shanty towns and tenement apartments for the underclass, is enforced by the lack of participation in the cultural and material goods of the dominant society. What actual space people are capable of usurping as a part of their identity becomes a function of resources and options under their control—and those resources or hindrances include racial identity. The apartheid regime of South Africa's active recruitment of whites in the urban centers of Hungary, East Germany, or America, for example, constitutes a part of the options available to whites and an anathema to blacks. Urban space is dependent on the existence of fairly stable racially differentiated communities. They are not tangential to what the West is; they are integral to it. That is, multinationalism (arguably capitalist and socialist) and cosmopolitanism do not exist outside of a racialized world. They could conceivably exist without racial or ethnic disparities, but the forms in which they do exist depend on racialization and immiseration.

The West makes the dominant culture, i.e., the totalized world of credit cards, museums, and transportation, appear color-blind when a good deal of the preconditions for, and requirements of, postmodern culture lie outside the participation of the underclass; the victims of racism are on the bottom of each class strata; each neighborhood is segregated by the lack of empowering tools; and the cuisine of the immiserated generates little capital return except when it is commercialized by multinational corporations, e.g., Cajun cooking and soul food. What is shared, such as the view from the window of the Peachtree Hotel, seems possible in so far as what is separate stays frozen, or new races and ethnic identities become created and are treated as frozen. The urban West stigmatizes and freezes peoples into racial, ethnic, and cultural identities. It does this to the immiserated and powerless, but reserves unto itself the luxury of color-blindness, inter-racial cooperation, cosmopolitanism, and universal freedom for owners and controllers of wealth.

The African-American community, as one among many differentiated subjects, has internal class and status conflicts (Boston 1988; Wilson 1907; Katz 1986). The interest of its middle class is not necessarily congruent with its underclass. The civil rights era ushered in improved conditions for the middle class, and simultaneously an underclass which received few benefits from civil rights legislation. As government agency and social work directors, the middle class lives parasitically astride the underclass. The working class performs personal services, such as secretarial services, but rarely are the services themselves owned or controlled by workers, and their job security is tenuous (Bell 1976). The bifurcation of the African-American community by class separates its interests. Yet, African-American civil servants are less well off than identically situated white civil servants, who are equally dependent on the subjugation of the underclass. Thus, African Americans as a people have an interest over and against the interest of whites. The possibility of African-American liberation from at least the ravages of racism depends, at least in part, on the acquisition of control over resources dictating material outcomes. Capitalism both sets the community apart and compels it to participate conjointly in experiences with other communities. The African-American community consists of networks of common and distinct experiences. What distinguishes it are collective experiences; not artifice, advertisement, and narrative. Whether in Chicago, Illinois or Atlanta, Georgia, whether Los Angeles or New York, the African-American secretary will meet with a common experience. This is so partly because none of the resources that postmodernists believe currently dominate and will shape future worlds are under the control of marginalized peoples, whether they are African Americans sweltering in Chicago's underclass tenement houses, Algerians in France, the Turkish population of Bulgaria, or Indians or West Indians of England. Now is immiseration, not meta-utopia.

The urban American centers most often treated by postmodernists as representative of contemporary redefinitions of time and space, such as Los Angeles, Chicago, Atlanta, and New York, are also centers of the largest black underclass populations and politically disenfranchised white service workers (Boston 1988). The wealth of urban centers depends, in part, on the wealth generated from the proliferation of illegal drugs; the sale of discarded, outdated, and dangerous pharmaceuticals; the sale of foodstuffs to prison systems; and the sale and resale of cheap weapons commonly used in petty crimes. As renters, under-employed service workers, or unemployed, welfare-dependent persons, the underclass does not represent persons who enjoy the architecture which mixes Gregorian columns with mirrored glass windows, or the ease with which persons move from museums with seventeenth-century Italian art to neon light advertisements: it all stands as alien and impenetrable power.

Why suppose that postmodern reality is, or offers a future more than, a world full of dread, decadence, depravity, self-effacing nihilism, and parasitic lifestyles dependent on perpetuating unnecessary misery? Why should a postmodern "meta-prescriptive" necessarily recommend a condemnation of either capitalism or unnecessary misery? Marx believed, for example, that capitalism would universalize itself and find a home in all parts of the world, forcing every society to adapt its mode of production. He also wrongly believed that the working classes of advanced industrial capitalist countries would be the leaders in forging socialist revolutions. When the subject of his attention centred on the "Asian mode of production," he then believed that colonized nations would be the leaders in forging socialist revolutions. The point is that when the subject changes, so too does the perspective of possible futures (Henriques et al. 1984). If the subject is not the Bonaventure

Hotel, the allure of power within multinational corporate headquarters, the transparency, sterility, and indifference of the urban West, but the ghettos which fester in every urban center of the West, the misery of the margin- alized, the racism and genocide of peoples which accompany market expan- sions, and the senses of hope, mission, and beliefs in fairness found among subjugated peoples, then the perspective of now changes. If the totalized world of the urban West, which normalizes segregation, is not considered the basis for cultural pluralism but an anathema against it, then our perspec- tive and evaluation of possible futures also changes.

If postmodern concepts provide an appropriate way of describing the West, then it is not at all clear why the fundamentally parasitic relationship of race is excluded from accounts: the world of race and race relations, I be- lieve, festers in an unholy alliance with the world depicted by postmodern- ists. Exploring that alliance presents strong grounds against postmodern descriptions of social life and, by implications, its notion of the subject and meta-utopia.

Progress and Enlightenment

There is a peculiar alliance between postmodernist views of subjects and progress: epistemological naturalists are not noted for risking their lives for revolutionary causes, nor are revolutions fueled by dystopia or meta-utopia views of possibility. It is arguable that the era of revolution is over, or per- ceived as over, in the postmodern West. However, there are beliefs shared by marxists, pragmatists, and utilitarians which are conspicuously absent from the postmodern conception of subjects and progress: the belief that there is something unnatural, inherently wrong, or morally unjust with the exis- tence of unnecessary misery, and that such wrongs can be corrected through concerted action (Anderson 1984; Harrison and Bluestone 1988). There are also composite traits of personality absent from postmodern depictions of agents—for example, senses of self-esteem, sacrifice, diligence, and dedica- tion to a liberation project. These traits do not connote transient, ephemeral, or fragmented personal identities. The consistency of reasoning required to hold, over time, disdain for unnecessary misery is not suggestive of reason- ing as inherently incongruous.

It has been argued that postmodern concepts of the subject delimit con- ceiving persons as agents of resistance because of the importance that post- modernists place on inherent differences (P. Smith 1988). If, as I argue, the postmodern concept of the subject lacks a viable sense of composite self- identity, not only is it difficult to see how persons enthralled in postmodern culture could be agents of resistance, but how could they have the attitudes associated with the desire to resist? How could they feel morally indignant about personally felt infringements and wrongs, let alone social wrongs?

One way to see this problem is by considering Lyotard's paradigm of revolutionary change and progress—science/computers. If we take the grand theories of the sciences, such as Darwinism, Newtonian physics, or Einstein's theory of relativity, it is arguable that radical changes occur through major paradigm shifts and conceptual breaks which were not achieved through a simple model of routine experimentation and verification, but entailed marginalized modes of thinking and redescriptions. It is also arguable that science/computers is predicted on a concept of progress which includes at least the belief that existing knowledge is inadequate. It holds, in effect, an incredulity towards itself as a condition of its own possibility, and it is through that incredulity of itself that progress, as performativity, and progress of continual redescription and renarration, is possible. The belief that science offers us iron laws of nature is, as Lyotard argues, misguided because what is really revolutionary about science is its incredulity towards nature.

Lyotard's way of defining progress is arguable, however, if, and only if, we make invisible normal science (neither Kuhn nor Feyerabend define progress in general the way Lyotard does). By "normal science," I mean the sort used to manufacture standard supplies and equipment common in the West—for example, telephones, concrete, plastics, or paper products. The sort of science/computer technologies referred to by postmodernists are usually more sophisticated than the sort associated with normal science. Computer banks, for example, rest on industries which produce plastics, wire, and paper. Lyotard's idea of freedom (in terms of everyone having access to the knowledge information in computer banks) as a way of enhancing democratic decision making is meaningless outside of a context of normal science, e.g., outside of a context in which persons have access to, and experience of, telephones and computer terminals. Analogously, the possibility of revolutions within the area of sophisticated science depends on a background of an already existing normal science. Agreed-upon rules, procedures, and tests applied consistently with only incremental change is characteristic of normal science. Changes certainly occur within its range of consistencies, but such changes are incremental and accompanied by rationalist criteria of validity, whether actually applied or only standing as legitimating mythologies. To model progress, in general, on paradigm shifts or the successes of fragmented thinking is to miss an important point: revolutions destroy conditions of coherency and consistency as well as usher in new conditions for normal science; persons who constitute the world of science, whether normal or sophisticated, are characteristically diligent, dedicated, and goal-oriented persons. Placing little to no weight on the importance of these features of science/computers negates the preconditions of science/computer technology and suggests a certain degree of blindness. Analogously, placing little to no weight on the importance of the coherence of experience, ingrained attitudes of self-worth, and consistent moral indignation negates the precondition for the possibility of having the desire to resist.

Utopias traditionally essentialize something that an author believes people hold in common, such as the interest of the working class to transform nature in its own image, the will to freedom, utility maximizing rationality, or transcendental consciousness. Utopia is, then, either considered the realizable outcome of prevailing historical, natural, or evolutionary forces inclined to realize a submerged essence, or it is an impossible world which nonetheless represents what realization would be like. Concepts of utopia have more than once lost their appeal in the face of new social conditions. Moore's *Utopia*, for example, has lost a good deal of appeal because it is so encoded with sixteenth-century aristocratic prejudices; Bellamy's *Looking Backward* idyllic New England egalitarianism lost its power to persuade partially because it offered no solution to America's slavocracy, and few continued to believe that secular science and technology led to strict identity of the individual and the universe, or that democratic egalitarianism is worth the cost of a strictly enforced economic egalitarianism; Marx and Engels's *Communist Manifesto* has lost much of its appeal in contemporary circles because of the importance placed on the leading role of the working class as the agent of universal human liberation when the actual representatives of the working class have been too often autocratic and totalitarian, and the immanent collapse of capitalism is less believable than it once was, and access to consumer goods is no longer considered a bourgeois luxury; Blyden's *Christianity, Islam, and the Negro Race* seems like a conservative's dream of gentle and diligent Africans with Edwardian virtues. In a world which is not convinced by utopias which posit end states which guarantee eternal peace, abundance, equality, the realization of hidden natures, culmination of evolutionary processes, or identity with transcendental or rational essences, utopias as such seem anachronisms.

If utopias are anachronisms, it does not follow that the postmodern description of now is a meta-utopia, i.e., a situation which offers the possibility of pursuing differentiated visions of the good or community grounded on the heterogeneity of identity. The existence of miseries and normalized segregation render considering a postmodern now as something other than a meta-utopia, or an eternal present without hope of radical improvement. The postmodern project is in an unholy alliance with "benign blindness" in the sense that it excludes the reality of immiseration and features of personhood which condition the desire to resist domination.

Conclusion

The postmodern vision of now is an elliptical, hegemonic vision. By this, I mean that the concept of the subject in the postmodernist project under consideration is self-referential, i.e., elliptical—we must presuppose a composite sense of self-identity in order to make sense of a fragmented self which can experience fragmentation; and the referent is hegemonic in the sense that the human as subject is grounded on a valorized model of Western decentered and materially secure whites with access to the resources associated with modernity.

The demise of utopia appeal and ellipse for totalizing concepts of reason, subjects, and progress, the radical increase in schizophrenic environments, diffractured and fragmented subjects, the existence of multiple sites of resistance, and the worldwide domination of multinationalism, all bespeak a world different than that of modernity. Such a world may well be termed "postmodern." Analogously, the demise of racism as the expression of the belief in naturally differentiated kinds of inferior and superior persons, the increase of subjugation through color-blind policies which structure domination, the increase in the world of the homeless, underclass, marginalized, and undocumented person through practices which either destroy their capital in labor and culture or render them useless as tools for self-creativity and flourishing, all bespeak a different world that we may term "postmodern." These new conditions, however, are, by some authors, mistakenly taken to infer the existence of a meta-utopia: a meta-utopia which makes invisible immiseration. The new conditions of postmodernity present new challenges, but negating the preconditions for the possibility of agency and racial change is intuitively an indefensible response.

Imagine that W. E. B. Du Bois was right and "The problem of the twentieth century is the problem of the color line." The postmodern project then makes invisible that line and simultaneously makes tangential immiseration; its meta-narrative erases the existence of composite persons; its descriptions reject the possibility of utopia and simultaneously, through a sort of double entendre or elliptical hegemonic vision, constitute a meta-utopia as an immediate presence described with, and grounded on, benign blindness.

Imagine further that the world is trapped in a vicious twoness of consciousness as a function of two different situations in world space. That twoness is represented by the world of communities which engage in callous calculations of profit and the world of struggle grounded on communion; the hedonistic delight in Salt'n Pepa rap songs and African-American spirituals; the symbolism of the uncommitted single person with a well-paid job living in urban space and the symbol of intact families; the indifference associated with individuals seeking to maximize their individual statuses and the concern and carrying associated with persons diligently risking their freedom to improve the lot of their society; and the world of seemingly endless time requirements to be successful in a career and the equally seemingly endless time requirements involved in sharing affection with children. This twoness of consciousness and its different reasoning modalities is then the labyrinth through which we must tread, not as an end state, not as a meta-utopia, but hopefully as a transient period.

[1]Although they hold many different views, the following authors are associated with the concept of postmodernism that I address: Lyotard, Baudrillard, and Sloterdijk. Less directly, some views of Rorty, Nozick, and Bell are also addressed.

[2]By "utopia," I mean the realization of a world of good, or mostly good, the realization of a hidden nature or potential; the culmination of a process such as evolution or absolute consciousness; an end state of affairs, a state for which incremental changes are possible but radical changes in structure are unlikely and unwarranted; best of all possible worlds; impossible, but best conceivable world upon which this world should be modelled.

References

Anderson, P. "Modernity and Revolution." *New Left Review* 144 (March–April 1984): 96–110.

Baudrillard, J. *America.* New York: Verso, 1989.

Bayor, R. H. "Roads to Racial Segregation: Atlanta in the Twentieth Century." *Journal of Urban History* 15, no. 1 (November 1988): 3–12.

Bell, D. *The Coming of Post-Industrial Society.* New York: Basic Books, 1976.

Bellamy, E. *Looking Backward: 2000–1887.* London: William Reeves, 1888.

Bernstein, R. *Habermas on Modernity.* Oxford: Polity, 1985.

Blyden, E. W. *Christianity, Islam, and the Negro Race.* London: Whittingham, 1887.

Boston, T. D. *Race, Class, and Conservatism.* Boston: Unwin Hyman, 1988.

Darity, W. A., Jr. "The Human Capital Approach to Black-White Earnings Inequality: Some Unsettled Questions." *Journal of Human Resources* 17 (1982): 72–93.

Davis, M. "Urban Renaissance and the Spirit of Postmodernism." *New Left Review* 151 (May–June 1985): 106–12.

———. *City of Quartz: Excavating the Future in Los Angeles.* London: Verso, 1990.

Deleuze, G., and Guattari, F. *Anti-Oedipus: Capitalism and Schizophrenia.* London: Viking Press, 1977.

Geoghegan, V. *Utopianism and Marxism.* New York: Methuen, 1988.

Harris, L. "Historical Subjects and Interest: Race, Class, and Conflict." In *The Year Left,* edited by M. Sprinkler et al., 91–106. New York: Verso, 1987.

Harrison, B., and B. Bluestone. *The Great U-Turn.* New York: Basic Books, 1988.

Hartsock, N. "Rethinking Modernism: Minority vs. Majority Theories." *Cultural Critique* (Fall 1987): 187–206.

Harvey, D. *The Condition of Postmodernity: An Enquiry into the Origins of Cultural Change.* Oxford: Blackwell, 1989.

Hassan, I. *The Postmodern Turn.* Columbus: Ohio State University Press, 1987.

Henriques, J., W. Holloway, C. Urwin, V. Couze, and V. Walkerdine. *Changing the Subject*. London: Methuen, 1984.

Jameson, F. "Postmodernism, or the Cultural Logic of Late Capitalism." *New Left Review* 146 (1984): 53–92.

Katz, M. B. *In the Shadow of the Poorhouse*. New York: Basic Books, 1986.

Koslowski, P. *Die Postmoderne Kultur*. Munich: Beck, 1987.

Kumar, K. *Utopia and Anti-Utopia in Modern Times*. Oxford: Blackwell, 1987.

Le Guin, U. *The Dispossessed*. New York: Avon, 1975.

Lea, K. "In the Most Highly Developed Societies: Lyotard and Postmodernism." *Oxford Literary Review* (1988): 86–104.

Levin, H. *Refractions*. Oxford: Oxford University Press, 1966.

Locke, A. "Values and Imperatives." In *The Philosophy of Alain Locke*, edited by L. Harris, 31–50. Philadelphia: Temple University Press, 1989.

Lyotard, J. F. *The Postmodern Condition: A Report on Knowledge*. Minneapolis: University of Minnesota Press, 1979a.

———. *La condition post-moderne*. Paris: Editions de Minuit, 1979b.

Marx, K., and F. Engels. *Communist Manifesto*. London: Lawrence and Wishart, 1848.

Mascia-Lees, F. E., P. Sharpe, and C. B. Cohen. *Journal of Women in Culture and Society* 15, no. 11 (1989): 7–33.

McCarthy, T. "Reflections on Rationalization in the Theory of Communicative Action." *Praxis International* 4 (2 July 1984).

Mele, A. "Irrationality: A Précis." *Philosophical Psychology* 1, no. 2 (1988): 173–78.

Moore, T. *Utopia* (1516).

Mudimbe, V. Y. *The Invention of Africa*. Bloomington: Indiana University Press, 1988.

Nozick, R. *Anarchy, State, and Utopia*. New York: Basic Books, 1985.

Omi, M., and H. Winant. *Racial Formation in the United States: From the 1960s to the 1980s*. New York: Routledge, 1986.

Parry, B. "Problems in Current Theories of Colonial Discourse." *Oxford Literary Review* (1988): 27–58.

Patterson, O. "Toward a Study of Black America." *Dissent* (fall 1989): 467–86.

Raban, J. *Soft City*. London: E. P. Dutton, 1974.

Robinson, C. J. *Black Marxism*. London: Zed Press, 1983.

Rorty, R. "Habermas and Lyotard on Postmodernity." *Praxis International* 4 (1 April 1984): 32–43.

———. *Contingency, Irony, and Solidarity*. Cambridge: Cambridge University Press, 1989.

Said, E. W. "Zionism from the Standpoint of its Victims." 1978. Reprinted in *Anatomy of Racism*, edited by D. T. Goldberg. Minneapolis: University of Minnesota Press, 1990.

Sloterdijk, P. *Critique of Cynical Reason*. Minneapolis: University of Minnesota Press, 1987.

Smith, P. *Discerning the Subject*. Minneapolis: University of Minnesota Press, 1988.

Sollors, W. *The Invention of Ethnicity*. Oxford: Oxford University Press, 1989.

Wagner, R. *The Invention of Culture*. Chicago: University of Chicago Press, 1975.

Williams, R. "Culture as Human Capital: Methodological and Policy Implications." *Praxis International* 7 (2 July 1987): 152–63.

Wilson, W. J. *The Truly Disadvantaged*. Chicago: University of Chicago Press, 1987.

SELECTED

BIBLIOGRAPHY

Abraham, Willie E. *The Mind of Africa.* Chicago: University of Chicago Press, 1962.

Allen, Norm R., ed. *African-American Humanism: An Anthology.* Buffalo: Prometheus Books, 1991.

American Society of African Culture, ed. *Pan-Africanism Reconsidered.* Westport: Greenwood, 1976.

Ani, Marimba. *Yurugu: An African-Centered Critique of European Cultural Thought and Behavior.* Trenton: Africa World Press, 1994.

Anyanwu, K. C., and Ruch, E. A. *African Philosophy: An Introduction to the Main Philosophical Trends in Contemporary Africa.* Rome: Catholic Book Agency, 1984.

Apostel, Leo. *African Philosophy: Myth or Reality?* Gent: Story-Scientia, 1981.

Appiah, Kwame Anthony. *In My Father's House: Africa in the Philosophy of Culture.* New York: Oxford University Press, 1992.

Asante, Molefi Kete. *The Afrocentric Idea.* Philadelphia: Temple University Press, 1987.

———. *Afrocentricity.* Rev. ed. Trenton: Africa World Press, 1988.

———. *Kemet, Afrocentricity, and Knowledge.* Trenton: Africa World Press, 1990.

———, and Vandi, Abdulai S., eds. *Contemporary Black Thought: Alternative Analyses in Social and Behavioral Science.* Beverly Hills: Sage Publications, 1980.

Azikiwe, Nnamdi. *Renascent Africa.* New York: Humanities Press, 1968.

Betts, Raymond F., ed. *The Ideology of Blackness.* Lexington, Mass.: D. C. Heath, 1971.

Blyden, Edward W. *Christianity, Islam, and the Negro Race.* Baltimore: Black Classic Press, 1994.

Bodunrin, P. O., ed. *Philosophy in Africa: Trends and Perspectives.* Ile-Ife, Nigeria: University of Ile-Ife Press, 1985.

Boxill, Bernard R. *Blacks and Social Justice.* Rev. ed. Lanham, Md.: Rowman and Littlefield, 1992.

Bracey, John H., Jr., August Meier, and Elliott Rudwick, eds. *Black Nationalism in America.* Indianapolis: Bobbs-Merrill, 1970.

Brotz, Howard, ed. *Negro Social and Political Thought, 1850–1920: Representative Texts.* New York: Basic Books, 1966.

Cabral, Amilcar. *Return to the Source: Selected Speeches.* Edited by Africa Information Service. New York: Monthly Review Press, 1973.

———. *Revolution in Guinea: Selected Texts.* Trans. and edited by Richard Handyside. New York: Monthly Review Press, 1969.

Cartey, Wilfred, and Martin Kilson, eds. *The Africa Reader.* 2 vols. New York: Random House, 1970.

Césaire, Aimé. *Discourse on Colonialism.* Trans. Joan Pinkham. New York: Monthly Review Press, 1972.

Chinweizu. *Decolonizing the African Mind.* Lagos: Pero Publishing, 1987.

Chrisman, Robert, and Nathan Hare, eds. *Contemporary Black Thought: The Best from the Black Scholar.* Indianapolis: Bobbs-Merrill, 1973.

Coombs, Orde, ed. *Is Massa Day Dead?: Black Moods in the Caribbean.* Garden City: Anchor, 1974.

Cooper, Anna Julia. *A Voice from the South.* New York: Oxford University Press, 1988.

Crummell, Alexander. *Africa and America: Addresses and Discourses.* New York: Negro Universities Press, 1969.

———. *Destiny and Race: Selected Writings, 1840–1898.* Edited by Wilson J. Moses. Amherst: University of Massachusetts Press, 1992.

———. *The Future of Africa, being Addresses, Sermons, etc., Delivered in the Republic of Liberia.* New York: Negro Universities Press, 1969.

Cruse, Harold. *The Crisis of the Negro Intellectual.* New York: William Morrow, 1967.

Davis, Angela Y. *Women, Culture, and Politics.* New York: Random House, 1989.

———. *Women, Race, and Class.* New York: Random House, 1981.

Diemer, Alwin, ed. *Philosophy in the Present Situation of Africa.* Wiesbaden: Frantz Steiner Verlag, 1981.

Diop, Cheikh Anta. *The African Origin of Civilization: Myth or Reality.* Trans. Mercer Cook. New York: Lawrence Hill, 1974.

———. *Black Africa: The Economic and Cultural Basis for a Federated State.* Trans. Harold Salemson. Westport, Conn.: Lawrence Hill, 1978.

———. *Civilization or Barbarism: An Authentic Anthropology.* Trans. Yaa-Lengi Meema Ngemi. Edited by Harold J. Salemson and Marjolijn de Jager. Brooklyn: Lawrence Hill, 1991.

———. *The Cultural Unity of Black Africa: The Domains of Patriarchy and of Matriarchy in Classical Antiquity.* Introduction by John Henrik Clarke. Afterword by James G. Spady. Chicago: Third World Press, 1978.

Douglass, Frederick. *Frederick Douglass on Women's Rights.* Edited by Phillip S. Foner. New York: Da Capo Press, 1992.

———. *The Life and Writings of Frederick Douglass.* Edited by Phillip S. Foner. 4 vols. New York: International, 1965.

Du Bois, W. E. B. *Against Racism: Unpublished Essays, Papers, Addresses, 1887–1961.* Edited by Herbert Aptheker. Amherst: University of Massachusetts Press, 1985.

———. *Black Reconstruction in America.* Introduction by David Levering Lewis. New York: Atheneum, 1992.

———. *Black Titan: W. E. B. Du Bois.* Edited by John H. Clark, et al. Boston: Beacon Press, 1970.

———. *Darkwater: Voices from Within the Veil.* New introduction by Herbert Aptheker. Millwood, N.Y.: Kraus-Thomson Organization, 1975.

———. *Dusk of Dawn: An Essay toward an Autobiography of a Race Concept.* New introduction by Irene Diggs. New Brunswick, N.J.: Transaction Books, 1992.

———. *Pamphlets and Leaflets.* Compiled and edited by Herbert Aptheker. White Plains, N.Y.: Kraus-Thomson Organization, 1986.

———. *The Seventh Son: The Thought and Writings of W. E. B. Du Bois.* Edited and with an introduction by Julius Lester. 2 vols. New York: Random House, 1971.

——. *The Souls of Black Folk*. Introduction by Arnold Rampersad. New York: Knopf, 1993.

——. *W. E. B. Du Bois Speaks: Speeches and Addresses, 1890–1919*. Edited by Phillip S. Foner. Tribute by Martin Luther King, Jr. New York: Pathfinder Press, 1970.

——. *W. E. B. Du Bois Speaks: Speeches and Addresses, 1920–1963*. Edited by Phillip S. Foner. Tribute by Kwame Nkrumah. New York: Pathfinder Press, 1970.

——. *Writings*. Edited by Nathan Huggins. New York: Library of America, 1986.

——. *Writings in Periodicals Edited by Others*. Compiled and edited by Herbert Aptheker. 4 vols. Millwood, N.Y.: Kraus-Thomson, 1982.

——. *Writings in Periodicals Edited by W. E. B. Du Bois: Selections from* The Crisis. Compiled and edited by Herbert Aptheker. 2 vols. Millwood, N.Y.: Kraus-Thomson, 1983.

Fanon, Frantz. *Black Skin, White Masks*. Trans. Charles Lam Markmann. New York: Grove Press, 1967.

——. *A Dying Colonialism*. Trans. Haakon Chevalier. Introduction by Adolfo Gilly. New York: Grove Press, 1967.

——. *Toward the African Revolution: Political Essays*. Trans. Haakon Chevalier. New York: Grove Press, 1969.

——. *The Wretched of the Earth*. Preface by Jean-Paul Sartre. Trans. Constance Farrington. New York: Grove Press, 1968.

Forsythe, Dennis. *Black Alienation, Black Rebellion*. Washington, D.C.: College and University Press, 1975.

Frye, Charles A., ed. *Level Three: A Black Philosophy Reader*. Lanham, Md.: University Press of America, 1980.

Garvey, Marcus. *Philosophy and Opinions of Marcus Garvey*. Edited by Amy Jacques-Garvey. New preface by Hollis R. Lynch. 2 vols. in 1. New York: Atheneum, 1969.

Gbadegesin, Segun. *African Philosophy: Traditional Yoruba Philosophy and Contemporary African Realities*. New York: P. Lang, 1991.

Gilroy, Paul. *The Black Atlantic: Modernity and Double Consciousness*. Cambridge: Harvard University Press, 1993.

Griaule, Marcel. *Conversations with Ogotemmêli: An Introduction to Dogon Religious Ideas*. New York: Oxford University Press, 1970.

Gyekye, Kwame. *An Essay on African Philosophical Thought: The Akan Conceptual Scheme*. New York: Cambridge University Press, 1987.

Hallen, B., and Sodipo, J. O. *Knowledge, Belief, and Witchcraft: Analytical Experiments in African Philosophy*. Foreword by Dorothy Emmett. London: Ethnographica, 1986.

Harris, Leonard, ed. *Philosophy Born of Struggle: Anthology of Afro-American Philosophy from 1917*. Dubuque: Kendall/Hunt, 1983.

Hickey, Denis. *Contemporary Black Philosophy*. Pasadena: Williams and Williams, 1971.

hooks, bell. *Ain't I a Woman: Black Women and Feminism*. Boston: South End Press, 1981.

——. *Black Looks: Race and Representation*. Boston: South End Press, 1992.

——. *Feminist Theory from Margin to Center*. Boston: South End Press, 1984.

——. *Outlaw Culture: Resisting Representations*. New York: Routledge, 1994.

——. *Sisters of the Yam: Black Women and Self-Recovery*. Boston: South End Press, 1993.

——. *Talking Back: Thinking Feminist, Thinking Black.* Boston: South End Press, 1989.

——. *Teaching to Transgress: Education as the Practice of Freedom.* New York: Routledge, 1994.

——. *Yearning: Race, Gender, and Cultural Politics.* Boston: South End Press, 1990.

——, and Cornel West. *Breaking Bread: Insurgent Black Intellectual Life.* Boston: South End Press, 1991.

Hountondji, Paulin J. *African Philosophy: Myth and Reality.* Trans. Henri Evans with Jonathan Rée. Introduction by Abiola Irele. Bloomington: Indiana University Press, 1983.

James, C. L. R. *American Civilization.* Edited and introduced by Anna Grimshaw and Keith Hart. Afterword by Robert A. Hill. Oxford: Blackwell, 1993.

——. *At the Rendezvous of Victory: Selected Writings.* London: Allison and Busby, 1984.

——. *Beyond a Boundary.* Introduction by Robert Lipsyte. Durham: Duke University Press, 1993.

——. *The Black Jacobins: Toussaint L'Ouverture and the San Domingo Revolution.* 2d ed, rev. New York: Vintage Books, 1989.

——. *C. L. R. James and Revolutionary Marxism: Selected Writings of C. L. R. James, 1939–1949.* Edited by Scott McLemee and Paul Le Blanc. Atlantic Highlands, NJ: Humanities, 1994.

——. *C. L. R. James's 80th Birthday Lectures.* Edited by Margaret Busby and Darcus Howe. London: Race Today Publications, 1984.

——. *The C. L. R. James Reader.* Edited and with an introduction by Anna Grimshaw. Oxford: Blackwell, 1992.

——. *The Future in the Present: Selected Writings.* London: Allison and Busby, 1977.

——. *Notes on Dialectics: Hegel, Marx, Lenin.* London: Allison and Busby, 1980.

——. *Spheres of Existence: Selected Writings.* London: Allison and Busby, 1980.

James, George G. M. *Stolen Legacy: The Greeks were not the authors of Greek Philosophy, but the people of North Africa, commonly called the Egyptians.* New York: Philosophical Library, 1954.

Johnson, James Weldon. *Negro Americans: What Now?* New York: Da Capo Press, 1973.

Karenga, Maulana, and Carruthers, Jacob H., eds. *Kemet and the African Worldview: Research, Rescue, and Restoration—Selected Papers of the Proceedings of the First and Second Conferences of the Association for the Study of Classical African Civilizations.* Los Angeles: University of Sankore Press, 1986.

——, ed. and trans. *The Husia.* Los Angeles: Kawaida, 1984.

King, Martin Luther, Jr. *Strength to Love.* New York: Harper and Row, 1963.

——. *Stride Toward Freedom: The Montgomery Story.* New York: Harper, 1958.

——. *A Testament of Hope: The Essential Writings and Speeches of Martin Luther King, Jr.* Edited by James Melvin Washington. New York: HarperCollins, 1991.

——. *The Trumpet of Conscience.* New York: Harper and Row, 1968.

——. *Where Do We Go From Here: Chaos or Community?* Boston: Beacon Press, 1967.

——. *Why We Can't Wait.* New York: Harper and Row, 1964.

King, Woodie, and Anthony, Earl, eds. *Black Poets and Prophets: The Theory, Practice, and Esthetics of the Pan-Africanist Revolution.* New York: New American Library, 1972.

Kiros, Tedros. *Moral Philosophy and Development: The Human Condition in Africa.* Athens, Oh.: Ohio University, Center for International Studies, 1992.

Lawson, Bill E., ed. *The Underclass Question*. Introduction by Bill E. Lawson. Foreword by William Julius Wilson. Philadelphia: Temple University Press, 1992.

Lichtheim, Miriam, ed. *Ancient Egyptian Literature: A Book of Readings*. 2 vols. Berkeley: University of California Press, n.d.

Littleton, Arthur C., and Mary W. Burger. *Black Viewpoints*. New York: New American Library, 1971.

Locke, Alain, ed. *The New Negro: An Interpretation*. Introduction by Arnold Rampersad. New York: Atheneum, 1992.

———. *The Philosophy of Alain Locke: Harlem Renaissance and Beyond*. Edited by Leonard Harris. Philadelphia: Temple University Press, 1989.

———. *Race Contacts and Interracial Relations: Lectures on the Theory and Practice of Race*. Edited and with an introduction by Jeffrey C. Stewart. Foreword by Michael R. Winston. Preface by Thomas C. Battle. Washington, D.C.: Howard University Press, 1992.

Logan, Rayford W., ed. *What the Negro Wants*. New York: Agathon Press, 1969.

Lowenthal, David, and Lambros Comitas, eds. *Consequences of Class and Color: West Indian Perspectives*. Garden City: Anchor, 1973.

Luthuli, Albert, et al. *Africa's Freedom*. New York: Barnes and Noble, 1964.

Makinde, Moses A. *African Philosophy, Culture, and Traditional Medicine*. Athens, Oh.: Ohio University, Center for International Studies, 1988.

Mandela, Nelson. *I Am Prepared to Die*. London: International Defense and Aid Fund for Southern Africa, 1984.

———. *Nelson Mandela Speaks: Forging a Democratic, Nonracial South Africa*. Edited by Steve Clark. New York: Pathfinder Press, 1993.

———. *No Easy Walk to Freedom*. London: Heinemann, 1990.

———. *The Struggle Is My Life: His Speeches and Writings Brought Together with Historical Documents and Accounts of Mandela in Prison by Fellow Prisoners*. Rev. ed. New York: Pathfinder Press, 1990.

———, and Fidel Castro. *How Far We Slaves Have Come!: South Africa and Cuba in Today's World*. New York: Pathfinder Press, 1991.

Masolo, D. A. *African Philosophy in Search of an Identity*. Bloomington: Indiana University Press, 1994.

McGary, Howard, and Bill E. Lawson. *Between Slavery and Freedom: Philosophy and American Slavery*. Bloomington: Indiana University Press, 1992.

Meier, August, Elliott Rudwick, and Francis L. Broderick, eds. *Black Protest Thought in the Twentieth Century*. 2d ed. New York: Macmillan, 1985.

Minogue, Martin, and Judith Molloy, eds. *African Aims and Attitudes: Selected Documents*. New York: Cambridge University Press, 1974.

Mudimbe, V. Y. *The Idea of Africa*. Bloomington: Indiana University Press, 1994.

———. *The Invention of Africa: Gnosis, Philosophy, and the Order of Knowledge*. Bloomington: Indiana University Press, 1988.

———. *Parables and Fables: Exegesis, Textuality, and Politics in Central Africa*. Madison: University of Wisconsin Press, 1991.

———, ed. *The Surreptitious Speech: Présence Africaine and the Politics of Otherness, 1947–1987*. Chicago: University of Chicago Press, 1992.

Nascimento, Abdias do. *Brazil: Mixture or Massacre?—Essays in the Genocide of a Black People*. Trans. Elisa Larkin Nascimento. 2d rev. ed. Dover, Mass.: Majority Press, 1989.

Nkrumah, Kwame. *Africa Must Unite*. New York: International, 1970.
——. *Challenge of the Congo*. New York: International, 1967.
——. *The Class Struggle in Africa*. New York: International, 1970.
——. *Consciencism: Philosophy and Ideology for Decolonization and Development with Particular Reference to the African Revolution*. New York: Monthly Review Press, 1970.
——. *Handbook of Revolutionary Warfare: A Guide to the Armed Phase of the African Revolution*. New York: International, 1969.
——. *I Speak of Freedom: A Statement of African Ideology*. London: Panaf, 1973.
——. *Neo-Colonialism: The Last Stage of Imperialism*. New York: International, 1976.
——. *Revolutionary Path*. New York: International, 1973.
Nyerere, Julius K. *Freedom and Development: Uhuru na Maendeleo—A Selection from Writings and Speeches, 1968–1973*. New York: Oxford University Press, 1973.
——. *Freedom and Unity: Uhuru na Umoja—A Selection from Writings and Speeches, 1952–1965*. London: Oxford University Press, 1967.
——. *Man and Development: Binadamu na Maendeleo*. London: Oxford University Press, 1974.
——. *Ujamaa: Essays on Socialism*. London: Oxford University Press, 1968.
Okere, Theophilus. *African Philosophy: A Historico-Hermeneutical Investigation of the Conditions of its Possibility*. Lanham, Md.: University Press of America, 1983.
Okolo, Chukwudum B. *Racism: A Philosophic Probe*. Jericho, N.Y.: Exposition Press, 1974.
Olela, Henry. *From Ancient Africa to Ancient Greece: An Introduction to the History of Philosophy*. Edited by Edward F. Collins and Alveda King Beal. Atlanta: Black Heritage, 1981.
Oruka, H. Odera. *The Philosophy of Liberty: An Essay on Political Philosophy*. Nairobi: Standard Textbooks, 1991.
——, ed. *Sage Philosophy: Indigenous Thinkers and Modern Debate on African Philosophy*. Leiden: E. J. Brill, 1990.
——, and D. A. Masolo, eds. *Philosophy and Cultures: Proceedings of the Second Afro-Asian Philosophy Conference*. Nairobi: Bookwise, 1983.
Osei, G. K. *The African Philosophy of Life*. 2d ed. London: African Publication Society, 1971.
Ripley, Peter C., ed. *Witness for Freedom: African American Voices on Race, Slavery, and Emancipation*. Chapel Hill: University of North Carolina Press, 1993.
Rodney, Walter. *The Groundings with My Brothers*. Introduction by Richard Small. London: Bogle L'Ouverture, 1969.
——. *Walter Rodney Speaks: The Making of an African Intellectual*. Introduction by Robert Hill. Foreword by Howard Dodson. Trenton: Africa World Press, 1990.
Senghor, Léopold Sédar. *The Foundations of "Africanité" or "Négritude" and "Arabité."* Trans. Mercer Cook. Paris: Présence Africaine, 1971.
——. *Prose and Poetry*. Selected and trans. by John Reed and Clive Wake. London: Oxford University Press, 1965.
Serequeberhan, Tsenay, ed. *African Philosophy: The Essential Readings*. New York: Paragon House, 1991.
——. *The Hermeneutics of African Philosophy: Horizon and Discourse*. New York: Routledge, 1994.
Soyinka, Wole. *Art, Dialogue, and Outrage: Essays on Literature and Culture*. New York: Pantheon Books, 1993.

——. *Myth, Literature, and the African World*. Cambridge: Cambridge University Press, 1976.

Sumner, Claude. *Classical Ethiopian Philosophy*. Addis Ababa: Commercial Printing Press, 1985.

——. *Ethiopian Philosophy*. 5 vols. Addis Ababa: Central Printing Press, 1974–1982.

Thiam, Awa. *Speak Out, Black Sisters: Feminism and Oppression in Black Africa*. Trans. Dorothy S. Blair. London: Pluto Press, 1986.

Thomas, John Jacob. *Froudacity: West Indian Fables by James Anthony Froude, Explained by John Jacob Thomas*. Philadelphia: Gebbie 1890.

UNESCO. *Teaching and Research in Philosophy: Africa*. Paris: UNESCO, 1984.

Washington, Booker T. *My Larger Education: Being Chapters from My Experience*. Miami: Mnemosyne, 1969.

——, et al. *The Negro Problem: A Series of Articles by Representative Negroes of Today*. New York: AMS Press, 1970.

——. *A New Negro for a New Century*. New York: AMS Press, 1973.

——. *Up From Slavery: An Autobiography*. New York: Gramercy Books, 1993.

——, and Du Bois, W. E. B. *The Negro in the South: His Economic Progress in Relation to his Moral and Religious Development*. New York: Citadel Press, 1970.

Wedderburn, Robert. *The Horrors of Slavery and Other Writings*. Edited with an introduction by Ian McCalman. New York: Markus Weiner, 1991.

West, Cornel. *The American Evasion of Philosophy: A Genealogy of Pragmatism*. Madison: University of Wisconsin Press, 1989.

——. *Beyond Eurocentrism and Multiculturalism*, 2 vols. *Volume One: Prophetic Thought in Postmodern Times; Volume Two: Prophetic Reflections—Notes on Race and Power in America*. Monroe, Me.: Common Courage Press, 1993.

——. *Keeping Faith: Philosophy and Race in America*. New York: Routledge, 1993.

——. *Prophesy Deliverance: An Afro-American Revolutionary Christianity*. Philadelphia: Westminster Press, 1982.

——. *Prophetic Fragments*. Trenton: Africa World Press, 1988.

——. *Race Matters*. Boston: Beacon Press, 1993.

Wiredu, Kwasi. *Philosophy and an African Culture*. New York: Cambridge University Press, 1980.

——, and Kwame Gyekye, eds. *Person and Community: Ghanaian Philosophical Studies I*. Washington, D.C.: Council for Research in Values and Philosophy, 1992.

Wortham, Anne. *The Other Side of Racism: A Philosophical Study of Black Race Consciousness*. Columbus: Ohio State University Press, 1981.

Wright, Richard A., ed. *African Philosophy: An Introduction*. 3d ed. Lanham, Md.: University Press, of America, 1984.

X, Malcolm. *The Autobiography of Malcolm X*. With the assistance of Alex Haley. Introduction by M. S. Handler. Epilogue by Alex Haley. New York: Grove Press, 1965.

——. *By Any Means Necessary*. Edited by George Breitman. 2d ed. New York: Pathfinder Press, 1992.

——. *The End of White World Supremacy: Four Speeches*. Edited and with an introduction by Benjamin Karim. New York: Arcade, 1989.

——. *February, 1965: The Final Speeches*. Edited by Steve Clark. New York: Pathfinder Press, 1992.

——. *Malcolm X: The Last Speeches.* Edited by Bruce Perry. New York: Pathfinder Press, 1989.

——. *Malcolm X Speaks: Selected Speeches and Statements.* Edited with prefatory notes by George Breitman. New York: Grove Weidenfeld, 1990.

——. *The Speeches of Malcolm X at Harvard.* Edited and with an introduction by Archie Epps. New York: William Morrow, 1968.

——. *Two Speeches by Malcolm X.* 2d ed. New York: Pathfinder Press, 1990.

SUDOKU

/

ARCTURUS

This edition published in 2018 by Arcturus Publishing Limited
26/27 Bickels Yard, 151–153 Bermondsey Street,
London SE1 3HA

ISBN: 978-1-78828-213-0
AD005891NT

Printed in China

Contents

How to Solve Sudoku Puzzles

Each sudoku puzzle begins with a grid in which some of the numbers are already in place:

	9	6			8		3	
		1		4	2			
5						8	1	9
4	7	1	2					3
	8	7		6	5			
2			9	4	6			1
8	7	2						5
			3	5		1		
	3		2			4	6	

You need to study the grid in order to decide where other numbers might fit. The numbers used in a sudoku puzzle are 1, 2, 3, 4, 5, 6, 7, 8 and 9 (0 is never used).

For example, in the top left box the number cannot be 9, 6, 8 or 3 (these numbers are already in the top row); nor can it be 5, 4 or 2 (these numbers are already in the far left column); nor can it be 1 (this number is already in the top left box of nine squares), so the number in the top left square is 7, since that is the only possible remaining number.

A completed puzzle is one where every row, every column and every box contains nine different numbers, as shown below:

Column

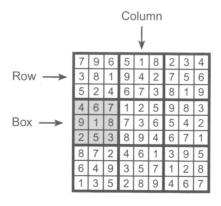

Row

Box

8	7		2		5		1	
1		5		6				3
	6	4	9		1	8	7	
6			3	1	2			4
	5	2		8		1	9	
4			6	5	9			2
	3	6	4		8	5	2	
7				2		9		8
	2		1		6		3	7

1		8	4			3		2
4	3	5			2		7	
			1	6				5
2	5		6	3			1	
7			2		9			4
	8			1	5		6	9
5				7	8			
	7		5			9	4	1
6		2			1	8		7

5		7	3			4		6
8			5		4	7	2	
		3		2	6		9	
7	5	1	4	8				9
		9				3		
3				7	2	5	4	1
	8		6	5		1		
	3	2	8		1			7
1		5			9	6		4

8	5		6		3		4	7
4		9	8			5		2
6				4				8
	6		9	5		8	7	
	9		4		8		2	
	8	3		6	1		5	
3				7				6
7		6			4	1		5
9	1		2		6		3	4

1	8			5			3	2
		2			4	9		
6		5	2	7				8
	2		6		7	8	9	1
	6			2			5	
4	7	1	8		5		2	
3				1	9	2		4
		7	5			6		
9	1			6			7	3

8		2			7		5	1
	9		1		6			8
3	7			5	4		6	
		4	7	3		5		
1		6		8		3		7
		3		4	1	2		
	4		2	7			9	3
2			4		8		7	
5	1		9			8		4

	1		2	4	8		6	
		2	1					7
9	3		5		7		1	4
3				1	2	5		
1	4			8			7	2
		7	6	9				8
5	9		4		1		8	6
8					6	3		
	2		8	7	3		9	

7		5	9			8		4
		8	1	4	2	6		
4	1		8					3
	3		6		4			2
8		4		2		3		1
5			3		1		9	
2					6		5	8
		1	2	3	5	7		
9		7			8	2		6

9				2	7			1
		2				5	3	8
6	4			5	8		7	
4		9	6	1		8		
2			4		3			5
		7		8	9	6		3
	7		5	9			1	4
5	9	1				2		
3			8	6				9

3		9	8	4			1	
6				1		7	8	9
5					7			
	8	6	7		4	1	3	
7	9			3			4	2
	3	5	2		1	9	6	
			6					1
9	6	2		5				8
	5			2	8	6		3

		1		3		6	4	8
6	8	7	4	9				
		5			8			
5	7		2		3		1	6
	6	8		7		2	9	
1	4		8		9		7	3
			1			3		
				2	4	7	6	1
2	1	6		5		4		

	3	5			1			4
			4	8	2		3	
6		8		3			1	7
5	6	2	3				7	
		3	8	1	6	4		
	1				7	6	9	3
4	2			7		8		1
	5		6	9	8			
7			1			3	5	

6		4		3		5		2
7	8			5	2			6
			1				4	
5	9	2			4	8		1
		1	6	8	5	3		
3		8	9			4	5	7
	2				7			
9			8	4			1	3
8		6		1		9		5

7		4		1		6		8
		5	8	2			4	1
1		6	4		7	2		
				3	4		7	9
	1		6		9		2	
5	9		1	8				
		2	9		1	5		4
8	4			5	3	9		
6		9		4		3		7

6		8		9		1		4
	4		5		1		3	
2		3		6		7		5
1		9	4		2	5		6
	2		6	3	7		1	
7		6	1		9	3		2
4		5		1		2		3
	6		2		5		8	
8		2		7		4		1

1			4		9			5
			8	6	3		1	4
4	9	3		7				6
	7		1		2	8		
2		1		3		5		9
		8	7		5		4	
6				5		3	2	8
8	5		3	1	4			
7			2		6			1

	7		8	2		5		
5		8	9			2		4
4			7	1	5			6
		5			8		1	
1	8	6		5		9	4	3
	2		6			7		
8			5	3	6			9
9		3			2	4		7
		1		7	9		6	

8		3		9	1		2	
5				3			1	6
	7		2		4		9	
9		2	4	8				5
		4	5		2	7		
7				1	3	6		2
	5		3		6		7	
6	3			4				8
	9		8	7		3		4

4	6	9	2			3	8	
		7		9		6		
8		1			4	2		7
	2			3	1		5	9
1				7				4
5	7		8	6			2	
3		5	7			9		2
		6		2		5		
	1	2			5	4	3	6

8			7	4		3		2
6	7	2		5		9		
					6	8		
2	9		1		5		3	8
	4	1		3		6	2	
5	3		6		4		7	9
		5	9					
		7		8		2	9	1
9		3		1	7			6

3	2	6			4			
		5	3			1		7
9			6	8			3	
		3		4			7	6
		2	5		8	9		
4	8			3		2		
	6			5	2			8
1		4			7	6		
			1			7	9	4

★ ★

1		2	4	5			6	
			9				1	8
	8	9	2			4		
		1	7				8	3
6			8		2			9
3	7				6	5		
		3			4	7	2	
5	6				7			
	2			1	9	3		4

	3	4		2	5			7
2			8		3			9
		5				8		3
				5	4	7	1	
	2		1		9		4	
	8	1	3	6				
6		8				9		
7			4		1			2
1			6	7		5	3	

	2	8	9			4	7	
		4	1	5	8	6		
1			2				8	
7			6				1	
	6	5				3	9	
	8				2			5
	5				9			6
		2	8	3	6	9		
	3	9			7	1	4	

4			7		8			3
	9			4			2	
3		7	2		6	5		4
	7		4	8	3		6	
5		4				8		1
	6		1	5	7		4	
	8			7			3	
7		6	8		1	2		9
9			5		4			8

6			9		3			4
5		8				7		
9				6	5	2	1	
	8	9		5	1			
	4		7		9		3	
			3	2		6	9	
	1	3	2	4				6
		2				8		1
4			1		8			7

			6	4	8			
2	4			7		3		1
	5	7						6
		3			1	9	2	7
	7		4		2		6	
5	8	2	7			1		
1						5	7	
6		8		1			4	3
			2	9	4			

4	3		6				9	7
	5		4			8		
1			8	3	2			4
		6			8		7	
5	8						4	3
	2		1			5		
9			2	5	7			8
		7			1		2	
2	1				4		6	9

			5	4	2			
8	6			9		4		7
2						3	9	
9	1	7	8				6	
		2	7		4	9		
	8				9	5	7	3
	3	9						8
6		4		8			5	2
			4	1	7			

4		2		5		9		6
	3		1		2		4	
		1		6		2		
6		7	2		9	1		3
	2		5		3		6	
5		3	7		6	8		2
		8		3		5		
	9		6		1		8	
3		4		7		6		9

	5			3	1		9	
6					8			3
2	3	8				6	1	4
	7		3					1
		2	9		6	4		
4					5		8	
9	4	6				1	2	7
5			1					9
	8		2	7			4	

		4			8	2		
7				9	1			3
1	8	9				4	6	7
		8			5			9
	7		6		4		1	
3			2			7		
8	6	7				1	3	5
4			8	5				2
		5	3			6		

4		2		3		1	6	
5	7					3		
			4	8	9			
	3				5	7	9	6
1			9		4			5
9	8	5	3				2	
			6	4	1			
		1					5	7
	2	3		5		9		4

2							4	6
7		4	2	5			3	
	5		4		6		9	
			7	2		1		3
		5	9		1	7		
1		6		8	4			
	3		1		7		5	
	1			3	8	4		2
6	8							9

	2	9			3	5		
3		5		7	1		2	
					9		4	6
5	8		9			7		
1			8		2			4
		6			4		9	5
8	7		1					
	4		3	6		2		7
		3	2			1	8	

2	9	5		6				3
			5	1				7
					9			4
	2	3	8		6	7	4	
8		1				2		9
	6	7	9		1	5	3	
6			3					
7				8	5			
5				4		3	8	2

	3			6			8	
	6	8	9			1	5	
1	4				2		9	3
				5	4	7		6
4								2
7		3	1	8				
5	7		3				6	9
	9	4			7	5	2	
	8			9			7	

		3	4	6		9	1	
	7	5			9			3
1					3			
	5	2			1	8	3	
9				2				6
	6	8	7			2	4	
			8					7
4			5			1	8	
	1	7		3	2	6		

		2	1		7		9	
	9		4			3	7	
	6	4	8	3				
8				6	4			3
1	7						4	6
6			7	8				5
				4	5	2	6	
	3	7			2		8	
	5		9		8	4		

		5	6		9	1		
		9	4	5			2	8
3		4						7
				8	6		9	5
	1		9		7		6	
9	3		2	4				
8						2		3
6	2			1	8	5		
		1	3		2	7		

4	6		1				5	
					4	7	1	6
		5	3	8				2
	9			6		1		5
	3		2		8		7	
6		2		9			3	
7				2	5	9		
9	5	3	6					
	8				9		4	1

		2		9	3	4		5
	4		6					
6		5	7				1	
1		3	4			6		2
	2			3			8	
9		6			5	3		7
	9				8	7		4
					9		5	
5		8	1	2		9		

	8	3	9					1
		5	1				7	
9		1		5	4			6
1	4			8		3		
	2		3		7		8	
		6		2			9	7
3			7	4		9		2
	9				8	4		
6					3	7	5	

	1	7			9			6
8			4				1	5
		2		7	8		4	
			9	6		5	3	1
	4						2	
3	5	9		1	7			
	3		8	5		6		
9	8				2			3
1			6			4	7	

	5	8			2			4
6			9				5	3
		1		8	6		9	
7	3	2		5	8			
	9						1	
			2	4		3	7	5
	7		6	3		4		
2	6				1			7
5			4			9	8	

					3	7		
8	3	1		6		9		
			8	5		4		
4	6		3		5		9	8
5		2				3		1
9	1		2		6		7	4
		4		2	8			
		8		7		1	2	9
		6	9					

		6		4	3			9
2		5			6		8	
	9		1				7	3
9	8	4		6	7			
1								5
			2	8		7	9	4
8	4				5		3	
	6		7			2		8
5			3	2		1		

8			3		2			9
		7		1		8		
9	6		4		8		5	1
		5	7	8	3	1		
4	8						3	2
		3	1	2	4	5		
3	2		5		6		1	7
		6		3		9		
7			8		1			3

5				4	3	6		
9		2			5		7	
	6		8			3	1	
4	7	6		5	1			
		8				9		
			2	7		4	6	1
	4	7			9		3	
	5		1			7		2
		9	3	2				8

	7			2	5	8		1
6	3				9			
		8			1	9	7	
8	9				3	6		
3			4		7			5
		2	9				4	8
	4	5	7			1		
			5				2	4
2		7	1	6			3	

4					9	6		1
		5	2		4			3
7		9		5	3			
	3		6	4			7	
5	7						8	6
	1			7	5		4	
			4	1		5		7
2			8		6	9		
6		1	5					2

			7	2	8		3	
			1		3		6	
7	3	1		5			2	
8			6		5	3		
9	4						1	6
		5	4		9			8
	2			6		4	8	7
	5		2		4			
	8		3	9	7			

7			9					
	2	9	8					6
	1			4	5	2	7	
	5	6	7			1	9	
1				5				3
	9	4			2	8	5	
	3	2	6	1			4	
4					3	7	8	
					4			2

1				6	5			2
5	9	3				8	4	6
		6			4	9		
4					2	3		
	3		1		9		8	
		5	6					7
		1	5			2		
8	5	7				1	9	3
3			8	7				4

		5	4		8	3		
	3			6			7	
6	1			9			4	5
4	9		2		5		8	6
		2	7		6	4		
7	6		9		4		3	2
1	2			7			5	4
	8			4			2	
		6	8		2	1		

9		7	3			8		1
	6		1			5		
1			6	8	4			2
	5		2			4		
8		1				6		5
		9			6		3	
6			4	5	9			7
		4			2		9	
7		3			1	2		4

1	7		6					8
		6	9	2			3	
					5	4	6	9
4				6		2	5	
3			8		2			4
	9	7		5				6
7	5	3	1					
	2			8	4	9		
9					7		1	5

	6			9		4		
3			7		8		5	9
5			2		6		8	
2			4			8	1	
9				7				6
	3	6			5			7
	4		9		1			5
6	1		8		7			4
		5		3			2	

7	9	4		6		5		
			8	1	7	4		
			5		9	2		
	8		6		2			4
6		3				9		1
4			9		1		2	
		6	3		8			
		8	7	5	4			
		5		2		8	3	7

	5	9		7		2		8
			3	4	8			
		7					6	1
5	3	6	1				7	
1			8		3			9
	2				7	1	4	3
6	1					9		
			9	8	5			
8		3		1		7	2	

	7		1		4		6	
		6		2		9		
3	2		5		6		7	8
		3	2	4	5	1		
1	4						5	6
		2	9	6	1	3		
2	9		3		8		1	4
		7		1		8		
	1		6		2		9	

		5					4	6
			5	3	9			
	7	1		4		8		3
8	2	4			1		7	
5			3		8			4
	1		4			6	8	9
3		7		1		5	9	
			8	2	3			
4	6					1		

4	5	8		3				1
			5	6				9
					8			2
	9	3	8		6	1	5	
7	6						4	8
	1	4	7		3	2	9	
3			1					
9				7	5			
5				2		7	1	4

8		1	3					2
		6	2	4				
	4					3	5	7
	2		6	3		7	1	
		4	7		8	5		
	6	8		9	1		3	
6	9	5					4	
				1	3	6		
2					5	8		9

	8	9	7			4	2	
2		5			9	6		3
		3		6		8		
1	6		4	5				
	7						4	
				3	2		1	8
		1		9		3		
5		7	1			9		4
	9	6			8	1	5	

			8	6	9			
3	4			5		8	2	
	5					1		7
2			5			9	1	6
		1	9		8	4		
9	7	3			1			5
1		7					4	
	9	8		1			5	2
			3	8	4			

		1	2		7			
		5	3	9	4			
		2		6		5	4	7
1			7		9		5	
	9	7				8	6	
	5		6		1			3
8	4	3		1		2		
			4	2	5	3		
			8		3	6		

★ ★

	9			8	4	7		
4			7			1		5
	8	1			3			6
2	3	5		1	8			
		7				9		
			3	6		2	5	1
1			6			8	7	
3		4			9			2
		2	4	5			6	

6	1	9		8				2
			1		2			5
			9	7	4			6
		6	7		1		5	
3		8				7		1
	4		5		8	6		
4			6	2	9			
8			4		3			
2				5		9	3	4

★ ★

4			8				5	3
8	3	1			5			
	7		6	2		4		
6				9		7	3	
1			7		2			6
	4	8		3				9
		9		7	4		1	
			3			6	9	4
5	8				9			2

4								7
		6	5		7	9		
	1		4		8		2	
3	7		2		5		4	9
9	8		1		3		5	6
	6		3		4		9	
		2	7		1	5		
1								8

				5	8			
	2	6		4	7	1	8	
4								
6				8		9		
		2	4		3	6		
		9		2				3
								9
	3	7	9	1		2	5	
			5	3				

	6	3	5		8	2	4	
		4	2	3	9	6		
5		2	6		4	1		9
6								2
3		1	8		2	7		4
		5	9	2	3	4		
	7	6	4		5	9	1	

	5		2		3		6	
				6				
2			5		1			8
4	9		7		5		3	2
		2		4		7		
5	7		8		2		9	6
3			1		8			9
				7				
	4		3		9		1	

7			8		6			1
		8	1		4	9		
	3			5			6	
1	2						4	5
		4				3		
3	5						8	7
	1			6			3	
		2	7		3	1		
6			5		9			2

			2		4			
	3	2				1	5	
1		4				7		2
	2		6		1		3	
			8		5			
	6		9		7		4	
8		5				9		3
	4	9				2	7	
			3		8			

			9		8		4	1
					4		3	5
				5		9		
4	8		1		6		7	3
		3				1		
1	9		7		5		8	2
		1		8				
8	6		4					
3	2		6		9			

	7		6		1		3	
4		2				1		6
	8						7	
		9		5		8		
	5		4		8		2	
		4		2		7		
	9						4	
6		3				5		8
	1		3		6		9	

9			4		8			3
	4	8				7	2	
3								6
	6			1			5	
2			6		7			1
	3			2			7	
7								5
	1	6				8	9	
5			8		9			4

8		4	9	1		2		6
	9							
			4	2				
9				3			5	
5			7		2			8
	2			8				9
				4	3			
							7	
1		3		7	6	8		5

5	6						9	4
		3				2		
		8	5		6	3		
3				4				9
		4	2		9	7		
2				7				1
		1	6		8	5		
		9				1		
7	2						6	8

4			6		9			8
8		5				2		6
	9						4	
		9		4		6		
3			7		6			2
		8		1		9		
	7						1	
9		2				4		3
5			9		3			7

		4		8	1			
		9	3					
		6		5		2	1	3
	1							5
	2	3				7	8	
9							6	
7	6	2		9		1		
					6	5		
			1	7		4		

				1	4		6	7
							9	4
		8			5	1		
		9	8					
7				4				1
					3	2		
		7	9			3		
2	9							
6	4		5	7				

1			2		9			8
2		3		4		6		7
8	3						1	6
	9	1				2	7	
6	2						5	4
9		8		6		4		5
5			8		3			2

	6	7			8			4
1						2		5
		3		4			6	
6	1		9					
					6		8	2
	2			9		3		
5		1						7
8			5			1	4	

	8			3			9	
9			1		4			6
		5	7		2	3		
2	9						4	1
		1				5		
5	7						3	8
		3	6		1	9		
4			9		3			5
	2			7			6	

8	9			7			1	3
		6				5		
7			4		8			6
	4			8			3	
			5		6			
	8			1			4	
2			9		4			7
		4				1		
9	6			3			2	4

6								7
	4			3			9	
		8	6		7	4		
8	3		2		9		7	5
			3		8			
2	9		7		1		8	6
		1	9		6	5		
	8			2			1	
5								3

	6	3	8		7			
7				6				
	9	4	3		2			
	2		4		5	8	3	
3								5
	4	8	7		1		2	
			1		3	6	8	
				7				2
			6		9	5	7	

5	3					2		
		9			2	6	4	
	4				7			8
	6		1					
1								4
					8		7	
2			3				8	
	7	6	8			3		
		3					9	5

2					8	3		5
	9	7						2
		8			2		1	
					4	5		
	6						4	
		3	8					
	8		3			6		
1						2	9	
5		6	1					7

					3			1
		2				6		
		7	4	6		3		
				2		7	8	
	2	9	6		8	1	5	
	5	4		1				
		6		3	4	9		
		5				8		
4			2					

	8							6
					1	9		
7	2			5				
		6			9			8
3	5			7			2	9
2			3			4		
				2			8	1
		3	4					
5							7	

	8	2	5		4			
3				1				
	4	1			9			
	1	9	4		3	2	7	
2								3
	5	3	6		7	8	1	
			9			6	2	
				6				5
			1		5	3	9	

		8	4		2	6		
7			8		3			4
				1				
3		7	6		1	9		2
	1			5			4	
8		6	2		9	7		3
				2				
5			1		8			9
		3	9		5	2		

6			8				9	
	9	3	5			7		
		5					1	4
					2		3	
9								2
	8		6					
4	7					1		
		1			6	3	8	
	6				1			5

	2			5	4		6	
	5						9	
		3	2					
				3			4	8
8	3		1		5		7	9
1	6			9				
					9	4		
	1						8	
	7		4	2			5	

1	6						9	5
8								6
	5		4		8		3	
		8	1	7	2	6		
		7	5	3	9	4		
	4		2		6		8	
7								9
3	1						6	4

	4		5	8			7	
					7	9		
	1						8	
3	5			9				
1	2		8		6		9	3
				1			4	6
	3						6	
		5	1					
	8			7	5		2	

6		7	9	8				
9		3						
	8		1				4	
	5		2					
8				9				6
					4		3	
	2				3		6	
						3		5
				6	1	9		7

		6		4				
4	7		2		5			
1	5		9		3			
6			3		4		1	8
		7				9		
9	1		7		8			6
			6		9		8	2
			4		1		9	5
				5		4		

			6		1		3	5
				5		6		
			2		3		7	9
3	1		4		7			2
		4				3		
2			8		6		1	7
1	5		3		8			
		2		6				
6	4		9		5			

		5				3		
6	9						1	4
	1		9		3		5	
3				7				1
	6		8		9		2	
9				5				3
	8		3		2		4	
5	2						3	6
		7				8		

5		7				9		6
2	8			1			3	5
		2	5		7	3		
4								7
		5	4		8	1		
7	2			5			1	9
3		9				4		8

			8				1	
2		5	9	7				
3								
	8		4			1	5	
7				5				6
	5	2			1		3	
								5
				6	5	2		7
	4				9			

	9		1				5	2
3		8					9	
1			9			6		
			4					5
		7				4		
2					1			
		1			2			7
	6					8		9
7	5				6		3	

3		4				8		1
	9						2	
		2	8		4	6		
8				9				5
		1	2		7	4		
7				3				8
		5	7		8	3		
	3						8	
1		7				5		6

		9		2		4	5	7
		1	5					
		3		6	7			
	1							9
4		5				8		6
7							2	
			7	8		3		
					9	2		
9	8	4		1		7		

	9		7		8		1	
		2	5		4	6		
7								4
1		8	3		6	5		9
9		4	8		2	7		3
5								6
		9	4		3	1		
	8		6		7		2	

				5				
		8	2		6	5		
	2		8		9		4	
	7	1	3		8	6	2	
2				7				3
	8	3	4		2	1	5	
	6		9		4		1	
		7	6		1	9		
				3				

	4			8	2	9		
	2	1		9				
			6					8
					8			5
	9			4			2	
7			3					
3					5			
				2		4	1	
		6	1	3			7	

							2	
6			5					
			3	1		7	8	
7		6	9					5
	4			7			1	
2					6	8		7
	1	8		4	7			
					3			9
	7							

	8		2	1				
5							9	1
6			5				3	7
			9				4	
	3	4				5	7	
	6				5			
3	1				9			4
4	2							5
				5	1		2	

	7	4				8	1	
2			4		7			3
3								6
	3			1			8	
1			8		6			9
	6			9			5	
8								5
5			2		4			7
	9	6				4	2	

	6						1	
		3	4		6	8		
9			2		7			5
1	5		6		2		9	8
4	2		3		8		5	7
6			7		1			3
		9	8		4	5		
	7						4	

2	1		4					7
			6	3			8	
3	9							4
					4		7	
	2	4				5	1	
	5		9					
4							6	5
	6			4	3			
5					9		3	1

		9	1	5			8	2
1	4						3	5
				3				
			4			2		6
		2				4		
4		8			6			
				4				
7	2						4	3
5	6			7	3	8		

			9	6	1			
3		6	2		4	1		9
		9				4		
1		5	6		9	8		7
7								6
6		8	5		3	9		1
		3				2		
9		7	4		6	3		8
			7	3	8			

					7	3		
5	9			1				
6							2	
		7			3		1	
1	4			6			3	2
	5		4			8		
	8							5
				2			6	1
		4	9					

5		4	7		2	6		8
7			1	3	8			2
6	1		3		9		2	4
	5						3	
3	7		2		5		8	6
2			8	1	3			5
1		5	9		7	2		3

7								4
1		8		6		9		7
		3	9		7	1		
			6		9			
9								2
			4		1			
		6	2		8	3		
3		4		1		5		9
2								8

8								3
	7	2		6		4	8	
	4		7		8		9	
		8		1		6		
			5		2			
		1		3		8		
	9		8		1		2	
	1	7		9		3	6	
2								5

	1						9	
	2		6		9		8	
4		6		3		7		5
1				7				4
			3		8			
2				9				1
6		9		8		5		2
	3		7		5		4	
	7						1	

			9	6			7	
6	3							4
5	1		4					8
					4		8	
	5	4				2	1	
	2		3					
2					3		6	1
4							9	2
	9			4	6			

	9		3			1	5	
	3					7	6	
		2	4	6				
		9			3			
8		1				5		3
			7			8		
				3	6	4		
	8	4					3	
	1	6			7		8	

			6					2
9	4	6		5				3
				8	4			7
	3					2		
1	8						9	6
		5					4	
7			4	1				
4				2		1	3	9
5					3			

4		9		5		8		3
		7	8		2	1		
	1	4				7	3	
8	9						2	1
	6	5				4	8	
		8	7		3	6		
5		6		4		2		7

4			1		2			6
				3				
		1	9		4	2		
2		5	7		3	6		1
	3			6			5	
1		8	5		9	7		3
		9	4		7	5		
				8				
8			2		5			7

9	5						4	2
7		6		3		8		9
	9		1		6		3	
1								5
	7		9		5		8	
5		7		9		3		4
8	4						1	6

				6				
6	9						8	1
3	5			9	8	2		
	7	5			1			
		1				5		
			7			3	1	
		3	6	4			9	7
1	6						4	5
				1				

		7		2			9	
5					3	6	4	
3	4							8
1		4			2			
			1			5		7
4							7	3
	8	1	5					6
	9			6		1		

	4	1	9		6	7	8	
	8						3	
			7	8	4			
	5	2	1		9	4	7	
		4				9		
	7	9	8		5	2	1	
			2	9	1			
	1						6	
	9	8	6		3	1	2	

5			3		4			6
		4				3		
9		6		8		1		7
			8		9			
		1				4		
			1		5			
3		8		5		2		1
		2				9		
6			2		1			8

		5		7		2	6	9
		3		1	6			
		8	9					
8							5	
	2	9				4	1	
	6							7
					5	7		
			6	4		3		
4	5	2		8		6		

				4	2	7		
	6	7						4	
	9	2			3		6	
			3			6		
6		9				1		4
		5			4			
	5		4			9	1	
	4					3	2	
		8	7	2				

5								8
	4		3		9		7	
6	2						3	4
		7	9	5	2	3		
		5	8	6	1	4		
2	3						8	1
	1		7		4		6	
7								3

	3		1		6		7	
4				7				8
		8	5		4	3		
9	1						8	3
		4				9		
2	5						4	1
		6	8		9	2		
7				1				4
	8		2		7		5	

6	4			5			1	9
3			1		9			4
	1						8	
			4		8			
	9						2	
			9		5			
	2						6	
5			6		2			3
8	3			4			9	7

★ ★ ★

	3			9	4			
	6			8		1	2	4
	7		1					
4						8		
2	1						5	9
		7						6
					6		8	
6	2	5		7			4	
			4	5			3	

	9						6	
		6	3		8	7		
7			5		2			4
	3	5	9		7	4	1	
	7	4	1		5	8	3	
8			2		6			3
		2	4		1	9		
	1						2	

2								1
	8				5			
7			8	3				6
				5		1		4
6		5	1		7	2		9
8		2		9				
4				7	8			3
			3				9	
5								7

6	8	4		1		9		
				8	9	7		
			6			3		
	1							6
4		2				8		5
9							3	
		1			2			
		7	9	5				
		6		3		4	2	9

7		8				5		3
			4		6			
	4	5				9	6	
4			2		1			8
			6		9			
3			5		7			2
	8	7				3	1	
			8		3			
9		1				8		4

2	4	7		6		9		
					4	8		
			2	3		5		
	6							2
3		1				4		7
9							8	
		5		1	2			
		6	9					
		2		8		7	1	9

			1	5			2	6
		7	8					
								1
		9			7	1	4	
6				1				5
	2	1	4			3		
3								
					9	4		
2	1			6	8			

8	5			7			6	9
4			8		9			5
		1				8		
	8			1			2	
			6		3			
	7			2			8	
		3				6		
6			2		8			4
7	1			4			9	2

7	8		3		1			
4	5		7					
		1		5				
3	6		5		2		8	1
		8				4		
2	4		9		8		7	3
				3		8		
					7		3	9
			1		9		4	6

9		4				1		5
8		3	5	9			7	
				4				
					6		3	1
	1						8	
6	8		1					
				1				
	3			2	4	6		9
4		1				8		2

	1						5	
		6	1		9	7		
3			8		4			1
	2		4	1	5		6	
8								9
	6		9	8	2		4	
4			2		1			5
		2	7		6	8		
	3						7	

3			9		6			7
	4						6	
5	7						1	4
		4	1	2	8	6		
		9	7	3	5	2		
4	9						3	1
	5						2	
6			8		4			9

				7	6			
						2		
7	9			3	2		8	6
	2			8		7		
	8		7		5		1	
		1		4			2	
8	1		9	5			3	4
		5						
			4	6				

	3		6		7		5	
	7	5		2		4	6	
1								7
		7		1		8		
			9		4			
		2		8		7		
9								4
	2	1		3		6	8	
	4		7		8		3	

	6				5			
				8		7		3
4			7	6		9		
	9		6					
		1		3		8		
					2		5	
		3		2	8			1
7		8		1				
			4				2	

				5	9			8
8	7	3		4				5
			7					6
		9					8	
1		2				6		7
	4					9		
4					1			
5				6		3	1	9
9			8	2				

3								7
	6	5				8	1	
7			1		8			9
		4		2		3		
2			6		3			5
		6		5		7		
8			9		1			4
	1	9				2	3	
4								6

		6			9			
				4	1		8	3
								1
		5	6			1	7	
3				1				4
	8	1			7	2		
2								
8	1		9	3				
			5			7		

	5	3	4		1	9	2	
		4		2		1		
			6	3	9			
	2						5	
		1				4		
	8						7	
			7	8	2			
		7		6		5		
	6	2	5		4	8	9	

		5	2		7	3		
7			4		6			8
	4						7	
6	1		9		4		3	5
9	3		1		8		4	6
	8						2	
2			5		3			1
		1	7		9	6		

9		5		3				
6				4	9	2		
			7				4	
					4		6	
3				5				1
	7		8					
	8				2			
		1	3	8				5
				1		9		3

3			7		2			9
	1		6		5		3	
		6		9		1		
2		8				3		1
	6						8	
5		4				2		6
		9		2		6		
	7		8		1		4	
1			9		4			5

		8	6		5			
			8				7	
				2			1	6
	3	9	4					
	1			6			2	
					8	3	6	
5	7			1				
	6				7			
			9		6	4		

9	6		5			4		
2				3			7	
		8				5		9
			3			1	9	
	4	7			1			
7		5				9		
	1			6				2
		6			4		1	8

	5		1		4		9	
	9	6		8		1	3	
9	6						8	5
7		5				2		3
2	8						1	4
	7	8		6		4	5	
	1		5		3		2	

2								4
8			5		9			2
	9	5				1	6	
		2		1		6		
1			4		6			3
		4		3		7		
	4	3				8	9	
7			9		8			5
6								7

	5		8	3			9	
	6						3	
					9	7		
				6			5	4
6	1		3		4		7	2
2	8			7				
		8	6					
	2						4	
	3			9	8		1	

6			4		3			7
7	2			5			3	1
2		7				6		5
	6	9				1	8	
5		8				4		3
9	5			2			4	6
3			1		6			8

2	4	9	8	3	1	6	7	5
7	5	6	4	2	9	8	1	3
1	3	8	5	7	6	4	9	2
8	1	3	7	6	5	2	4	9
6	7	5	2	9	4	3	8	1
9	2	4	3	1	8	5	6	7
4	9	2	1	8	3	7	5	6
5	6	7	9	4	2	1	3	8
3	8	1	6	5	7	9	2	4

		4	2		6	7		
	9		1		3		8	
5				7				9
2	4						5	7
		1				4		
9	6						1	3
6				2				8
	3		9		7		4	
		7	8		1	9		

4	2	7	3	1	6	5	9	8
5	9	3	7	2	8	4	1	6
1	6	8	9	4	5	7	3	2
9	1	5	4	6	2	3	8	7
2	8	4	1	3	7	9	6	5
3	7	6	5	8	9	1	2	4
7	5	2	6	9	1	8	4	3
8	3	9	2	5	4	6	7	1
6	4	1	8	7	3	2	5	9

6	5	7	9	2	1	8	4	3
1	3	9	5	8	4	2	7	6
2	4	8	3	7	6	5	1	9
8	7	3	6	5	9	1	2	4
5	6	1	2	4	7	3	9	8
4	9	2	1	3	8	7	6	5
7	2	4	8	9	3	6	5	1
3	1	5	4	6	2	9	8	7
9	8	6	7	1	5	4	3	2

★ ★ ★ ★

1	4	5	6	2	9	8	7	3
7	3	8	4	5	1	9	6	2
2	9	6	3	8	7	5	4	1
6	8	2	9	3	5	4	1	7
9	7	1	2	4	6	3	5	8
3	5	4	7	1	8	6	2	9
8	1	7	5	9	4	2	3	6
4	6	3	8	7	2	1	9	5
5	2	9	1	6	3	7	8	4

6	1	7	5	3	4	9	8	2
4	5	9	2	7	8	1	6	3
2	8	3	1	6	9	4	7	5
7	6	1	3	8	5	2	4	9
9	3	2	7	4	6	5	1	8
5	4	8	9	2	1	6	3	7
8	7	6	4	5	2	3	9	1
1	2	4	8	9	3	7	5	6
3	9	5	6	1	7	8	2	4

★ ★ ★ ★

1	2	6	5	4	3	9	7	8
4	7	3	6	8	9	5	1	2
8	5	9	7	1	2	6	3	4
9	8	1	2	7	4	3	6	5
6	4	5	3	9	1	8	2	7
7	3	2	8	6	5	1	4	9
5	6	7	1	2	8	4	9	3
3	1	4	9	5	7	2	8	6
2	9	8	4	3	6	7	5	1

8	9	5	7	1	2	3	6	4
6	2	7	8	3	4	9	5	1
4	3	1	9	5	6	8	2	7
9	4	6	2	8	7	1	3	5
1	8	3	4	6	5	7	9	2
7	5	2	3	9	1	4	8	6
5	1	9	6	4	8	2	7	3
2	6	8	1	7	3	5	4	9
3	7	4	5	2	9	6	1	8

8	9	1	3	2	6	5	4	7
3	6	5	4	9	7	1	2	8
4	7	2	8	1	5	6	3	9
6	2	3	5	4	8	7	9	1
9	1	4	7	6	2	3	8	5
7	5	8	1	3	9	2	6	4
5	4	7	2	8	3	9	1	6
2	8	6	9	5	1	4	7	3
1	3	9	6	7	4	8	5	2

7	9	1	4	5	2	6	8	3
5	2	4	3	6	8	1	7	9
3	8	6	9	1	7	2	4	5
4	5	2	1	3	9	8	6	7
1	6	7	2	8	5	3	9	4
9	3	8	6	7	4	5	1	2
2	7	5	8	4	6	9	3	1
6	4	3	5	9	1	7	2	8
8	1	9	7	2	3	4	5	6

4	9	6	3	7	2	5	1	8
5	7	2	6	8	1	3	9	4
3	1	8	9	4	5	6	2	7
8	4	5	7	1	9	2	3	6
1	2	7	4	6	3	9	8	5
6	3	9	2	5	8	4	7	1
2	6	1	8	9	4	7	5	3
7	8	3	5	2	6	1	4	9
9	5	4	1	3	7	8	6	2

8	9	2	6	4	7	3	5	1
4	7	3	5	1	8	9	6	2
6	1	5	3	9	2	8	4	7
7	2	1	4	3	9	6	8	5
5	6	4	7	8	1	2	3	9
3	8	9	2	6	5	7	1	4
9	5	8	1	7	6	4	2	3
1	3	7	8	2	4	5	9	6
2	4	6	9	5	3	1	7	8

5	9	8	3	4	6	2	1	7
7	1	6	9	5	2	8	4	3
4	3	2	7	8	1	5	9	6
6	8	9	5	7	4	1	3	2
3	4	1	8	2	9	6	7	5
2	5	7	1	6	3	4	8	9
9	2	3	6	1	8	7	5	4
8	7	4	2	9	5	3	6	1
1	6	5	4	3	7	9	2	8

7	1	9	4	3	5	8	2	6
5	3	8	1	6	2	7	4	9
4	6	2	8	9	7	1	5	3
8	5	6	2	1	4	3	9	7
9	2	1	6	7	3	4	8	5
3	4	7	5	8	9	2	6	1
1	9	4	7	5	8	6	3	2
2	7	3	9	4	6	5	1	8
6	8	5	3	2	1	9	7	4

6	5	7	8	3	4	2	1	9
8	4	2	9	1	6	7	3	5
3	9	1	7	2	5	6	4	8
2	6	9	5	4	8	3	7	1
1	8	4	2	7	3	5	9	6
5	7	3	6	9	1	8	2	4
9	3	8	1	6	7	4	5	2
7	1	6	4	5	2	9	8	3
4	2	5	3	8	9	1	6	7

9	5	4	7	3	1	2	6	8
6	1	3	8	2	5	4	9	7
2	7	8	9	6	4	5	1	3
5	8	1	4	7	9	3	2	6
3	6	7	1	5	2	8	4	9
4	9	2	3	8	6	7	5	1
1	3	9	2	4	8	6	7	5
8	2	6	5	1	7	9	3	4
7	4	5	6	9	3	1	8	2

6	9	5	1	2	8	4	7	3
8	7	3	4	9	6	1	2	5
2	4	1	7	5	3	8	6	9
1	8	4	5	6	2	3	9	7
3	6	7	9	4	1	5	8	2
5	2	9	3	8	7	6	1	4
4	5	8	6	7	9	2	3	1
7	3	2	8	1	4	9	5	6
9	1	6	2	3	4	7	4	8

4	6	3	9	1	7	5	8	2
7	9	2	5	4	8	6	1	3
5	8	1	6	3	2	9	4	7
8	7	9	1	6	3	2	5	4
3	2	5	8	7	4	1	9	6
1	4	6	2	9	5	7	3	8
9	5	7	3	8	6	4	2	1
6	1	8	4	2	9	3	7	5
2	3	4	7	5	1	8	6	9

5	7	4	3	8	9	6	2	1
1	3	8	5	2	6	9	7	4
2	6	9	4	1	7	3	8	5
3	2	6	1	9	4	8	5	7
9	1	7	8	3	5	4	6	2
4	8	5	7	6	2	1	9	3
7	5	3	6	4	8	2	1	9
8	4	2	9	7	1	5	3	6
6	9	1	2	5	3	7	4	8

★ ★ ★ ★

9	6	4	5	7	1	3	8	2
2	5	7	4	8	3	1	6	9
8	3	1	2	6	9	4	7	5
7	8	9	1	3	4	2	5	6
5	2	3	6	9	8	7	4	1
1	4	6	7	5	2	9	3	8
4	7	5	9	1	6	8	2	3
6	1	8	3	2	7	5	9	4
3	9	2	8	4	5	6	1	7

Sub
op

★ ★ ★ ★

9	1	6	2	7	8	4	3	5
3	2	5	1	6	4	7	8	9
4	7	8	9	3	5	2	6	1
8	6	7	5	2	1	9	4	3
5	9	3	8	4	6	1	2	7
2	4	1	7	9	3	8	5	6
7	5	9	6	8	2	3	1	4
1	3	2	4	5	7	6	9	8
6	8	4	3	1	9	5	7	2

★ ★ ★ ★

5	6	8	2	4	9	7	3	1
2	4	7	1	3	6	8	5	9
9	1	3	8	5	7	4	2	6
8	2	6	3	7	4	9	1	5
3	9	1	5	6	8	2	4	7
7	5	4	9	2	1	6	8	3
4	8	5	7	9	3	1	6	2
1	3	9	6	8	2	5	7	4
6	7	2	4	1	5	3	9	8

4	4	6	9	7	3	2	8	5
3	5	7	2	8	1	6	4	9
8	9	2	4	6	5	3	7	8
1	7	8	5	3	4	9	2	6
2	6	3	1	9	7	8	5	4
5	4	9	8	2	6	7	1	3
9	8	1	6	5	2	4	3	7
6	3	4	7	1	8	5	9	2
7	2	5	3	4	9	1	6	8

1	5	7	6	8	9	4	2	3
2	6	4	7	5	3	8	9	1
9	3	8	4	2	1	6	7	5
8	7	1	3	9	6	2	5	4
6	2	5	8	7	4	3	1	9
3	4	9	2	1	5	7	6	8
7	1	2	5	4	8	9	3	6
4	9	6	7	3	7	5	8	2
5	8	3	9	6	2	1	4	7

7	6	8	5	4	9	1	2	3
3	1	2	7	8	6	9	4	5
9	5	4	1	2	3	7	8	6
1	7	3	4	5	8	2	6	9
2	4	6	9	3	7	8	5	1
5	8	9	2	6	1	3	7	4
8	2	5	3	9	4	6	1	7
6	9	1	8	7	5	4	3	2
4	3	7	6	1	2	5	9	8

1	4	5	7	8	3	9	6	2
2	8	6	1	4	9	3	7	5
7	9	3	6	5	2	4	1	8
3	7	2	8	1	4	5	9	6
9	6	4	2	3	5	1	8	7
5	1	8	9	7	6	2	3	4
8	2	1	5	9	7	6	4	3
6	3	7	4	2	1	8	5	9
4	5	9	3	6	8	7	2	1

9	48 8x	6	7	2	3	14	45 4	85 5
3	5	1	4	8	6	2	9	7
49 4	2	7	95 9	91 1	15 5	64 6	3	86 8
7	648 4	2	1	346 6	84 85	36 3	56 5	9
45 58	9	345 8 8	234 265	346 3	845 4	7	1	23 665
15 1	16 6	35 3	235 56	7	9	8	256 2	4
25 24	7	59 54 5	369 6	134 996	14 1	436 4	8	23 36
6	3	94 9	8	94 4	2	5	7	1
28 841	814 1	84 4	36 3	5	7	9	42 66	23 26

4	2	1	7	8	5	6	3	9
3	8	9	2	1	6	4	7	5
7	5	6	3	4	9	1	2	8
9	7	4	1	3	8	2	5	6
2	6	3	5	9	4	7	8	1
8	1	5	6	7	2	3	9	4
6	4	2	9	5	7	8	1	3
1	9	8	4	2	3	5	6	7
5	3	7	8	6	1	9	4	2

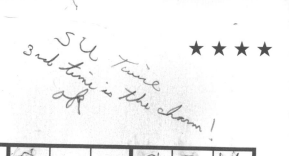

★ ★ ★ ★

2	5	6	8	1	7	9	3	4
7	8	4	6	3	9	2	5	1
9	1	3	2	4	5	7	6	8
6	3	2	1	8	4	5	9	7
4	7	8	9	5	6	1	2	3
1	9	5	3	7	2	8	4	6
3	4	1	5	9	8	6	7	2
8	6	9	7	2	3	4	1	5
5	2	7	4	6	1	3	8	9

8	2	7	9	4	1	3	6	5
6	1	9	7	5	3	4	2	8
4	5	3	6	8	2	1	7	9
1	4	2	3	6	9	8	5	7
7	9	8	4	2	5	6	3	1
5	3	6	1	7	8	2	9	4
9	8	5	2	3	4	7	1	6
3	6	1	8	9	7	5	4	2
2	7	4	5	1	6	9	8	3

7	8	2	9	5	3	4	1	6
1	5	6	7	4	2	9	8	3
4	9	3	1	6	8	5	7	2
6	4	9	5	7	1	2	3	8
8	2	7	4	3	9	6	5	1
5	3	1	2	8	6	7	4	9
2	1	4	3	9	7	8	6	5
9	7	8	6	1	5	3	2	4
3	6	5	8	2	4	1	9	7

★ ★ ★ ★

2	5	6	4	7	8	3	1	9
4	1	8	3	9	6	5	2	7
9	7	3	5	1	2	8	4	6
5	8	9	2	4	3	7	6	1
7	3	4	6	5	1	9	8	2
6	2	1	7	8	9	4	3	5
3	4	7	1	6	5	2	9	8
1	9	2	8	3	7	6	5	4
8	6	5	9	2	4	1	7	3

★ ★ ★ ★

6	4	5	1	7	2	8	9	3
1	9	8	6	3	4	7	5	2
2	7	3	5	8	9	6	1	4
5	2	7	4	1	8	3	6	9
8	6	1	3	9	7	4	2	5
9	3	4	2	5	6	1	7	8
7	8	6	9	2	3	5	4	1
3	1	9	7	4	5	2	8	6
4	5	2	8	6	1	9	3	7

7	5	6	3	4	1	9	8	2
1	9	2	6	7	8	4	5	3
3	8	4	5	9	2	7	6	1
9	3	7	8	6	5	2	1	4
2	6	1	7	3	4	8	9	5
5	4	8	1	2	9	6	3	7
6	1	3	2	8	7	5	4	9
4	7	5	9	1	6	3	2	8
8	2	9	4	5	3	1	7	6

★ ★ ★ ★

2	8	9	5	7	1	3	6	4
4	4	5	6	3	9	2	8	7
7	3	6	8	2	4	5	1	9
3	7	8	1	9	6	4	2	5
9	5	2	7	4	8	6	3	1
1	6	4	2	5	3	9	7	8
6	9	1	4	8	2	7	5	3
8	4	7	3	6	5	1	9	2
5	2	3	9	1	7	8	4	6

★ ★ ★ ★

7	2	9	1	4	3	8	5	6
1	3	8	5	7	6	4	9	2
4	6	5	9	2	8	1	7	3
6	8	3	4	5	9	7	2	1
2	9	4	7	3	1	6	8	5
5	1	7	6	8	2	3	4	9
8	4	2	3	1	5	9	6	7
3	7	6	2	9	4	5	1	8
9	5	1	8	6	7	2	3	4

★ ★ ★ ★

1	3	2	4	5	6	7	9	8
5	6	7	8	9	1	2	4	3
4	9	8	2	3	7	5	1	6
2	7	6	9	4	8	3	5	1
9	4	3	1	7	5	8	6	2
8	1	5	3	6	2	9	7	4
3	5	1	6	8	9	4	2	7
6	8	9	7	2	4	1	3	5
7	2	4	5	1	3	6	8	9

2	3	7	4	6	8	5	1	9
1	5	8	9	2	3	4	6	7
6	9	4	7	5	1	2	3	8
8	4	6	2	1	9	7	5	3
5	2	1	3	7	6	9	8	4
9	7	3	5	8	4	6	2	1
7	6	9	1	3	5	8	4	2
3	8	2	6	4	7	1	9	5
4	1	5	8	9	2	3	7	6

Sub
cellmates
OR

4	6	8	5	2	1	3	9	7
7	1	9	6	3	8	5	2	4
3	5	2	9	4	7	1	8	6
8	4	1	7	6	9	2	3	5
6	2	3	8	5	4	7	1	9
9	7	5	2	1	3	6	4	8
1	8	4	3	7	5	9	6	2
5	3	6	4	9	2	8	7	1
2	9	7	1	8	6	4	5	3

1	3	4	6	8	2	5	9	7
6	7	5	3	4	9	1	8	2
8	9	2	7	5	1	6	3	4
7	8	1	4	2	3	9	5	6
5	4	6	1	9	8	2	7	3
3	2	9	5	6	7	8	4	1
2	5	7	9	3	6	4	1	8
4	1	8	2	7	5	3	6	9
9	6	3	8	1	4	7	2	5

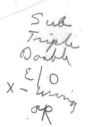

Sub
Triple
Double
3/0
x – wing
or

SU again
DO
Find SU
There

2	1	8	4	3	7	6	9	5
9	6	4	8	2	5	7	1	3
3	7	5	1	9	6	4	8	2
5	3	9	6	1	8	2	4	7
7	8	1	2	5	4	9	3	6
4	2	6	3	7	9	8	5	1
6	46	2	59	59	5	31	7	8
8	9	7	1	6	3	5	2	4
	4	5	7	8	2	31	6	9

(2) all mate
Triple 1 4 9
X-wing

4	7	9	5	8	1	2	6	3
6	1	2	3	7	4	9	5	8
8	3	5	2	6	9	7	4	1
1	5	7	6	4	2	8	3	9
3	8	6	1	9	7	5	2	4
9	2	4	8	3	5	6	1	7
7	6	1	4	5	8	3	9	2
2	9	3	7	1	6	4	8	5
5	4	8	9	2	3	1	7	6

add up
all mate
No 9's

	7				5	6		4
	8		6	4	9			
4	6			7	1	2		5
	4		9		8		2	
9	5		4	2	6		3	7
	2		1		7		6	
7		5		9	2		4	6
	9	4			3		1	2
2					4			

7	4	1	5	3	8	9	2	6
8	9	5	6	7	2	4	1	3
6	3	2	9	1	4	8	5	7
5	8	7	3	9	1	6	4	2
2	6	9	7	4	5	1	3	8
4	1	3	2	8	6	7	9	5
3	7	4	8	5	9	2	6	1
1	2	8	4	6	3	5	7	9
9	5	6	1	2	7	3	8	4

★ ★ ★ ★ ★

multiple all matts
Triples
Sub
ok
It took me over 3 hrs

4	2	6	1	5	7	9	3	8
7	9	8	4	2	3	5	6	1
1	5	3	6	8	9	4	2	7
8	3	4	5	9	1	6	7	2
5	6	2	3	7	8	1	9	4
9	7	1	2	6	4	3	8	5
6	1	7	8	3	5	2	4	9
2	4	9	7	1	6	8	5	3
3	8	5	9	4	2	7	1	6

★ ★ ★ ★ ★

9	4	5	6	8	2	3	7	1
6	1	7	4	3	5	2	9	8
8	3	2	1	9	7	4	5	6
2	6	4	3	7	8	5	1	9
5	8	3	9	1	4	6	2	7
7	9	1	2	5	6	8	3	4
3	7	8	5	4	1	9	6	2
1	2	9	8	6	3	7	4	5
4	5	6	7	2	9	1	8	3

Sub
all matis
a ℰ/0
op

4	1	9	8	5	7	3	2	6
3	5	6	2	1	9	8	4	7
7	2	8	46	43	46	5	1	9
6	9	5	4	43	8	2	7	1
1	3	2	5	7	6	4	9	8
8	7	4	1	9	2	6	3	5
9	8	3	7	2	5	1	6	4
2	6	1	9	8	4	7	5	3
5	4	7	3	6	1	9	8	2

216

5	1	2	3	4	6	7	9	8
9	3	6	5	7	8	1	4	2
7	8	4	1	9	2	6	5	3
3	9	1	8	6	4	2	7	5
6	7	5	9	2	1	3	8	4
2	4	8	7	3	5	9	1	6
4	5	7	6	1	3	8	2	9
1	2	3	4	8	9	5	6	7
8	6	9	2	5	7	4	3	1

★ ★ ★ ★ ★

129

38 4	19	384 9	615 9	2	619	7	34	58
6	5	7	3	4	8	12	12	9
238 4	219	384 9	715 9	75	719	58	34	6
238	6	138 9	127 98	378	412 973	248 9	5	347 8
7	29	358 1	58	6	4 3	48	29	1
235 8	4	1358 9	125 987	357 8	123 97	628 9	627 9	378
9	38	45	286 7	387	236 7	145 6	167	457
1	7	6	4	9	5	3	8	2
45	38	2	867	1	367	945 6	97 6	457

1	8	6	4	5	7	2	9	3
3	4	7	2	8	9	6	5	1
5	2	9	3	1	6	8	7	4
6	3	2	8	7	1	9	4	5
9	1	8	5	4	2	3	6	7
7	5	4	6	9	3	1	8	2
2	9	3	7	6	5	4	1	8
4	6	5	1	3	8	7	2	9
8	7	1	9	2	4	5	3	6

7	3	1	6	8	4	5	9	2
6	4	2	1	9	5	7	8	3
9	5	8	7	3	2	1	4	6
4	9	6	8	5	1	3	2	7
1	8	5	2	7	3	4	6	9
3	2	7	9	4	6	8	1	5
8	1	9	3	2	7	6	5	4
5	6	3	4	1	9	2	7	8
2	7	4	5	6	8	9	3	1

Sub
up

★ ★ ★ ★ ★

8	5	1	6	3	7	4	9	2
2	4	9	8	1	5	3	7	6
6	7	3	4	2	9	1	8	5
9	1	2	3	5	4	7	6	8
4	8	6	9	7	2	5	3	1
5	3	7	1	6	8	9	2	4
3	2	4	5	9	6	8	1	7
1	6	8	7	4	3	2	5	9
7	9	5	2	8	1	6	4	3

4	5	8	3	6	2	7	1	9
3	7	6	9	1	4	2	8	5
9	2	1	7	5	8	6	3	4
8	9	4	6	7	3	5	2	1
1	6	7	2	4	5	8	9	3
5	3	2	1	8	9	4	7	6
7	4	9	5	2	1	3	6	8
2	1	5	8	3	6	9	4	7
6	8	3	4	9	7	1	5	2

6	3	7	8	5	2	9	4	1
9	14	248	714 6	346	713 4	5	63	28 2
512 8	54 5	248	146	9	134	28	63	7
235 7	8	623 644	245 976	346 36	345 97	367 67	1	93 736
235 7	7	9	256	1	3 8	4	5	36 8
1	45 64	634 64	456 97	346 88	345 987	367 678	2	93 86
4	62	38	159	7	158 87	236	9	235 6
38	62	1	459 59	48 4	458 599	723 6	7	235 6
7	9	5	3	2	6	1	8	4

93

★ ★ ★ ★ ★

223

Sub
Triple
Sub
OR

1	3	6	2	5	7	8	9	4
5	8	9	6	4	1	3	7	2
4	2	7	8	9	3	5	6	1
7	4	3	1	2	6	9	5	8
2	9	5	7	8	4	1	3	6
6	1	8	9	3	5	2	4	7
9	6	1	3	7	2	4	8	5
3	7	4	5	1	8	6	2	9
8	5	2	4	6	9	7	1	3

★ ★ ★ ★ ★

4	6	9	1	5
1	5	3	4	6	2
5	6	1	3	9
4	2	5	6	9	7
5	2	1	9	4	7	6	8	3
9	6	7	1	3	8	2	5	4
6	5	4
8	5	7	9	3	2	6
6	5	9	7

Solutions

1

8	7	3	2	4	5	6	1	9
1	9	5	8	6	7	2	4	3
2	6	4	9	3	1	8	7	5
6	8	9	3	1	2	7	5	4
3	5	2	7	8	4	1	9	6
4	1	7	6	5	9	3	8	2
9	3	6	4	7	8	5	2	1
7	4	1	5	2	3	9	6	8
5	2	8	1	9	6	4	3	7

2

1	6	8	4	5	7	3	9	2
4	3	5	8	9	2	1	7	6
9	2	7	1	6	3	4	8	5
2	5	9	6	3	4	7	1	8
7	1	6	2	8	9	5	3	4
3	8	4	7	1	5	2	6	9
5	4	1	9	7	8	6	2	3
8	7	3	5	2	6	9	4	1
6	9	2	3	4	1	8	5	7

3

5	2	7	3	9	8	4	1	6
8	9	6	5	1	4	7	2	3
4	1	3	7	2	6	8	9	5
7	5	1	4	8	3	2	6	9
2	4	9	1	6	5	3	7	8
3	6	8	9	7	2	5	4	1
9	8	4	6	5	7	1	3	2
6	3	2	8	4	1	9	5	7
1	7	5	2	3	9	6	8	4

4

8	5	1	6	2	3	9	4	7
4	3	9	8	1	7	5	6	2
6	7	2	5	4	9	3	1	8
1	6	4	9	5	2	8	7	3
5	9	7	4	3	8	6	2	1
2	8	3	7	6	1	4	5	9
3	4	8	1	7	5	2	9	6
7	2	6	3	9	4	1	8	5
9	1	5	2	8	6	7	3	4

5

1	8	4	9	5	6	7	3	2
7	3	2	1	8	4	9	6	5
6	9	5	2	7	3	1	4	8
5	2	3	6	4	7	8	9	1
8	6	9	3	2	1	4	5	7
4	7	1	8	9	5	3	2	6
3	5	6	7	1	9	2	8	4
2	4	7	5	3	8	6	1	9
9	1	8	4	6	2	5	7	3

6

8	6	2	3	9	7	4	5	1
4	9	5	1	2	6	7	3	8
3	7	1	8	5	4	9	6	2
9	8	4	7	3	2	5	1	6
1	2	6	5	8	9	3	4	7
7	5	3	6	4	1	2	8	9
6	4	8	2	7	5	1	9	3
2	3	9	4	1	8	6	7	5
5	1	7	9	6	3	8	2	4

7

7	1	5	2	4	8	9	6	3
4	6	2	1	3	9	8	5	7
9	3	8	5	6	7	2	1	4
3	8	6	7	1	2	5	4	9
1	4	9	3	8	5	6	7	2
2	5	7	6	9	4	1	3	8
5	9	3	4	2	1	7	8	6
8	7	4	9	5	6	3	2	1
6	2	1	8	7	3	4	9	5

8

7	2	5	9	6	3	8	1	4
3	9	8	1	4	2	6	7	5
4	1	6	8	5	7	9	2	3
1	3	9	6	7	4	5	8	2
8	7	4	5	2	9	3	6	1
5	6	2	3	8	1	4	9	7
2	4	3	7	9	6	1	5	8
6	8	1	2	3	5	7	4	9
9	5	7	4	1	8	2	3	6

Solutions

9

9	8	5	3	2	7	4	6	1
7	1	2	9	4	6	5	3	8
6	4	3	1	5	8	9	7	2
4	3	9	6	1	5	8	2	7
2	6	8	4	7	3	1	9	5
1	5	7	2	8	9	6	4	3
8	7	6	5	9	2	3	1	4
5	9	1	7	3	4	2	8	6
3	2	4	8	6	1	7	5	9

10

3	7	9	8	4	2	5	1	6
6	2	4	3	1	5	7	8	9
5	1	8	9	6	7	3	2	4
2	8	6	7	9	4	1	3	5
7	9	1	5	3	6	8	4	2
4	3	5	2	8	1	9	6	7
8	4	3	6	7	9	2	5	1
9	6	2	1	5	3	4	7	8
1	5	7	4	2	8	6	9	3

11

9	2	1	7	3	5	6	4	8
6	8	7	4	9	2	1	3	5
4	3	5	6	1	8	9	2	7
5	7	9	2	4	3	8	1	6
3	6	8	5	7	1	2	9	4
1	4	2	8	6	9	5	7	3
7	9	4	1	8	6	3	5	2
8	5	3	9	2	4	7	6	1
2	1	6	3	5	7	4	8	9

12

2	3	5	7	6	1	9	8	4
1	9	7	4	8	2	5	3	6
6	4	8	9	3	5	2	1	7
5	6	2	3	4	9	1	7	8
9	7	3	8	1	6	4	2	5
8	1	4	2	5	7	6	9	3
4	2	9	5	7	3	8	6	1
3	5	1	6	9	8	7	4	2
7	8	6	1	2	4	3	5	9

13

6	1	4	7	3	8	5	9	2
7	8	9	4	5	2	1	3	6
2	3	5	1	6	9	7	4	8
5	9	2	3	7	4	8	6	1
4	7	1	6	8	5	3	2	9
3	6	8	9	2	1	4	5	7
1	2	3	5	9	7	6	8	4
9	5	7	8	4	6	2	1	3
8	4	6	2	1	3	9	7	5

14

7	2	4	3	1	5	6	9	8
9	3	5	8	2	6	7	4	1
1	8	6	4	9	7	2	5	3
2	6	8	5	3	4	1	7	9
4	1	3	6	7	9	8	2	5
5	9	7	1	8	2	4	3	6
3	7	2	9	6	1	5	8	4
8	4	1	7	5	3	9	6	2
6	5	9	2	4	8	3	1	7

15

6	5	8	7	9	3	1	2	4
9	4	7	5	2	1	6	3	8
2	1	3	8	6	4	7	9	5
1	3	9	4	8	2	5	7	6
5	2	4	6	3	7	8	1	9
7	8	6	1	5	9	3	4	2
4	7	5	9	1	8	2	6	3
3	6	1	2	4	5	9	8	7
8	9	2	3	7	6	4	5	1

16

1	8	6	4	2	9	7	3	5
5	2	7	8	6	3	9	1	4
4	9	3	5	7	1	2	8	6
9	7	5	1	4	2	8	6	3
2	4	1	6	3	8	5	7	9
3	6	8	7	9	5	1	4	2
6	1	4	9	5	7	3	2	8
8	5	2	3	1	4	6	9	7
7	3	9	2	8	6	4	5	1

Solutions

17

6	7	9	8	2	4	5	3	1
5	1	8	9	6	3	2	7	4
4	3	2	7	1	5	8	9	6
7	9	5	3	4	8	6	1	2
1	8	6	2	5	7	9	4	3
3	2	4	6	9	1	7	8	5
8	4	7	5	3	6	1	2	9
9	6	3	1	8	2	4	5	7
2	5	1	4	7	9	3	6	8

18

8	4	3	6	9	1	5	2	7
5	2	9	7	3	8	4	1	6
1	7	6	2	5	4	8	9	3
9	6	2	4	8	7	1	3	5
3	1	4	5	6	2	7	8	9
7	8	5	9	1	3	6	4	2
4	5	8	3	2	6	9	7	1
6	3	7	1	4	9	2	5	8
2	9	1	8	7	5	3	6	4

19

4	6	9	2	1	7	3	8	5
2	5	7	3	9	8	6	4	1
8	3	1	6	5	4	2	9	7
6	2	8	4	3	1	7	5	9
1	9	3	5	7	2	8	6	4
5	7	4	8	6	9	1	2	3
3	8	5	7	4	6	9	1	2
9	4	6	1	2	3	5	7	8
7	1	2	9	8	5	4	3	6

20

8	5	9	7	4	1	3	6	2
6	7	2	3	5	8	9	1	4
3	1	4	2	9	6	8	5	7
2	9	6	1	7	5	4	3	8
7	4	1	8	3	9	6	2	5
5	3	8	6	2	4	1	7	9
1	8	5	9	6	2	7	4	3
4	6	7	5	8	3	2	9	1
9	2	3	4	1	7	5	8	6

21

3	2	6	7	1	4	5	8	9
8	4	5	3	2	9	1	6	7
9	7	1	6	8	5	4	3	2
5	9	3	2	4	1	8	7	6
6	1	2	5	7	8	9	4	3
4	8	7	9	3	6	2	5	1
7	6	9	4	5	2	3	1	8
1	3	4	8	9	7	6	2	5
2	5	8	1	6	3	7	9	4

22

1	3	2	4	5	8	9	6	7
4	5	6	9	7	3	2	1	8
7	8	9	2	6	1	4	3	5
2	9	1	7	4	5	6	8	3
6	4	5	8	3	2	1	7	9
3	7	8	1	9	6	5	4	2
9	1	3	5	8	4	7	2	6
5	6	4	3	2	7	8	9	1
8	2	7	6	1	9	3	5	4

23

8	3	4	9	2	5	1	6	7
2	7	6	8	1	3	4	5	9
9	1	5	7	4	6	8	2	3
3	6	9	2	5	4	7	1	8
5	2	7	1	8	9	3	4	6
4	8	1	3	6	7	2	9	5
6	4	8	5	3	2	9	7	1
7	5	3	4	9	1	6	8	2
1	9	2	6	7	8	5	3	4

24

5	2	8	9	6	3	4	7	1
3	7	4	1	5	8	6	2	9
1	9	6	2	7	4	5	8	3
7	4	3	6	9	5	8	1	2
2	6	5	7	8	1	3	9	4
9	8	1	3	4	2	7	6	5
8	5	7	4	1	9	2	3	6
4	1	2	8	3	6	9	5	7
6	3	9	5	2	7	1	4	8

Solutions

25

4	5	2	7	1	8	6	9	3
3	1	7	2	9	6	5	8	4
6	9	8	3	4	5	1	2	7
2	7	1	4	8	3	9	6	5
5	3	4	6	2	9	8	7	1
8	6	9	1	5	7	3	4	2
1	8	5	9	7	2	4	3	6
7	4	6	8	3	1	2	5	9
9	2	3	5	6	4	7	1	8

26

6	2	1	9	7	3	5	8	4
5	3	8	4	1	2	7	6	9
9	7	4	8	6	5	2	1	3
3	8	9	6	5	1	4	7	2
2	4	6	7	8	9	1	3	5
1	5	7	3	2	4	6	9	8
8	1	3	2	4	7	9	5	6
7	9	2	5	3	6	8	4	1
4	6	5	1	9	8	3	2	7

27

3	1	9	6	4	8	7	5	2
2	4	6	9	7	5	3	8	1
8	5	7	1	2	3	4	9	6
4	6	3	8	5	1	9	2	7
9	7	1	4	3	2	8	6	5
5	8	2	7	6	9	1	3	4
1	2	4	3	8	6	5	7	9
6	9	8	5	1	7	2	4	3
7	3	5	2	9	4	6	1	8

28

4	3	8	6	1	5	2	9	7
6	5	2	4	7	9	8	3	1
1	7	9	8	3	2	6	5	4
3	9	6	5	4	8	1	7	2
5	8	1	7	2	6	9	4	3
7	2	4	1	9	3	5	8	6
9	6	3	2	5	7	4	1	8
8	4	7	9	6	1	3	2	5
2	1	5	3	8	4	7	6	9

29

7	9	3	5	4	2	8	1	6
8	6	5	3	9	1	4	2	7
2	4	1	6	7	8	3	9	5
9	1	7	8	3	5	2	6	4
3	5	2	7	6	4	9	8	1
4	8	6	1	2	9	5	7	3
1	3	9	2	5	6	7	4	8
6	7	4	9	8	3	1	5	2
5	2	8	4	1	7	6	3	9

30

4	7	2	3	5	8	9	1	6
8	3	6	1	9	2	7	4	5
9	5	1	4	6	7	2	3	8
6	8	7	2	4	9	1	5	3
1	2	9	5	8	3	4	6	7
5	4	3	7	1	6	8	9	2
2	6	8	9	3	4	5	7	1
7	9	5	6	2	1	3	8	4
3	1	4	8	7	5	6	2	9

31

7	5	4	6	3	1	2	9	8
6	9	1	4	2	8	7	5	3
2	3	8	5	9	7	6	1	4
8	7	5	3	4	2	9	6	1
3	1	2	9	8	6	4	7	5
4	6	9	7	1	5	3	8	2
9	4	6	8	5	3	1	2	7
5	2	7	1	6	4	8	3	9
1	8	3	2	7	9	5	4	6

32

5	3	4	7	6	8	2	9	1
7	2	6	4	9	1	8	5	3
1	8	9	5	2	3	4	6	7
6	4	8	1	7	5	3	2	9
9	7	2	6	3	4	5	1	8
3	5	1	2	8	9	7	4	6
8	6	7	9	4	2	1	3	5
4	1	3	8	5	6	9	7	2
2	9	5	3	1	7	6	8	4

Solutions

33

4	9	2	5	3	7	1	6	8
5	7	8	1	6	2	3	4	9
3	1	6	4	8	9	5	7	2
2	3	4	8	1	5	7	9	6
1	6	7	9	2	4	8	3	5
9	8	5	3	7	6	4	2	1
7	5	9	6	4	1	2	8	3
8	4	1	2	9	3	6	5	7
6	2	3	7	5	8	9	1	4

34

2	9	1	8	7	3	5	4	6
7	6	4	2	5	9	8	3	1
8	5	3	4	1	6	2	9	7
9	4	8	7	2	5	1	6	3
3	2	5	9	6	1	7	8	4
1	7	6	3	8	4	9	2	5
4	3	2	1	9	7	6	5	8
5	1	9	6	3	8	4	7	2
6	8	7	5	4	2	3	1	9

35

4	2	9	6	8	3	5	7	1
3	6	5	4	7	1	9	2	8
7	1	8	5	2	9	3	4	6
5	8	4	9	3	6	7	1	2
1	9	7	8	5	2	6	3	4
2	3	6	7	1	4	8	9	5
8	7	2	1	9	5	4	6	3
9	4	1	3	6	8	2	5	7
6	5	3	2	4	7	1	8	9

36

2	9	5	7	6	4	8	1	3
3	4	6	5	1	8	9	2	7
1	7	8	2	3	9	6	5	4
9	2	3	8	5	6	7	4	1
8	5	1	4	7	3	2	6	9
4	6	7	9	2	1	5	3	8
6	8	4	3	9	2	1	7	5
7	3	2	1	8	5	4	9	6
5	1	9	6	4	7	3	8	2

37

9	3	7	5	6	1	2	8	4
2	6	8	9	4	3	1	5	7
1	4	5	8	7	2	6	9	3
8	1	9	2	5	4	7	3	6
4	5	6	7	3	9	8	1	2
7	2	3	1	8	6	9	4	5
5	7	1	3	2	8	4	6	9
3	9	4	6	1	7	5	2	8
6	8	2	4	9	5	3	7	1

38

2	8	3	4	6	7	9	1	5
6	7	5	1	8	9	4	2	3
1	9	4	2	5	3	7	6	8
7	5	2	6	4	1	8	3	9
9	4	1	3	2	8	5	7	6
3	6	8	7	9	5	2	4	1
5	2	6	8	1	4	3	9	7
4	3	9	5	7	6	1	8	2
8	1	7	9	3	2	6	5	4

39

3	8	2	1	5	7	6	9	4
5	9	1	4	2	6	3	7	8
7	6	4	8	3	9	1	5	2
8	2	9	5	6	4	7	1	3
1	7	5	2	9	3	8	4	6
6	4	3	7	8	1	9	2	5
9	1	8	3	4	5	2	6	7
4	3	7	6	1	2	5	8	9
2	5	6	9	7	8	4	3	1

40

2	8	5	6	7	9	1	3	4
1	7	9	4	5	3	6	2	8
3	6	4	8	2	1	9	5	7
7	4	2	1	8	6	3	9	5
5	1	8	9	3	7	4	6	2
9	3	6	2	4	5	8	7	1
8	9	7	5	6	4	2	1	3
6	2	3	7	1	8	5	4	9
4	5	1	3	9	2	7	8	6

Solutions

41

4	6	9	1	7	2	3	5	8
3	2	8	9	5	4	7	1	6
1	7	5	3	8	6	4	9	2
8	9	7	4	6	3	1	2	5
5	3	4	2	1	8	6	7	9
6	1	2	5	9	7	8	3	4
7	4	1	8	2	5	9	6	3
9	5	3	6	4	1	2	8	7
2	8	6	7	3	9	5	4	1

42

7	1	2	8	9	3	4	6	5
8	4	9	6	5	1	2	7	3
6	3	5	7	4	2	8	1	9
1	5	3	4	8	7	6	9	2
4	2	7	9	3	6	5	8	1
9	8	6	2	1	5	3	4	7
3	9	1	5	6	8	7	2	4
2	6	4	3	7	9	1	5	8
5	7	8	1	2	4	9	3	6

43

2	8	3	9	7	6	5	4	1
4	6	5	1	3	2	8	7	9
9	7	1	8	5	4	2	3	6
1	4	7	6	8	9	3	2	5
5	2	9	3	1	7	6	8	4
8	3	6	4	2	5	1	9	7
3	5	8	7	4	1	9	6	2
7	9	2	5	6	8	4	1	3
6	1	4	2	9	3	7	5	8

44

4	1	7	5	3	9	2	8	6
8	9	3	4	2	6	7	1	5
5	6	2	1	7	8	3	4	9
2	7	8	9	6	4	5	3	1
6	4	1	3	8	5	9	2	7
3	5	9	2	1	7	8	6	4
7	3	4	8	5	1	6	9	2
9	8	6	7	4	2	1	5	3
1	2	5	6	9	3	4	7	8

45

9	5	8	3	7	2	1	6	4
6	2	7	9	1	4	8	5	3
3	4	1	5	8	6	7	9	2
7	3	2	1	5	8	6	4	9
4	9	5	7	6	3	2	1	8
1	8	6	2	4	9	3	7	5
8	7	9	6	3	5	4	2	1
2	6	4	8	9	1	5	3	7
5	1	3	4	2	7	9	8	6

46

2	4	5	1	9	3	7	8	6
8	3	1	4	6	7	9	5	2
6	7	9	8	5	2	4	1	3
4	6	7	3	1	5	2	9	8
5	8	2	7	4	9	3	6	1
9	1	3	2	8	6	5	7	4
1	9	4	5	2	8	6	3	7
3	5	8	6	7	4	1	2	9
7	2	6	9	3	1	8	4	5

47

7	1	6	8	4	3	5	2	9
2	3	5	9	7	6	4	8	1
4	9	8	1	5	2	6	7	3
9	8	4	5	6	7	3	1	2
1	2	7	4	3	9	8	6	5
6	5	3	2	8	1	7	9	4
8	4	2	6	1	5	9	3	7
3	6	1	7	9	4	2	5	8
5	7	9	3	2	8	1	4	6

48

8	1	4	3	5	2	6	7	9
5	3	7	6	1	9	8	2	4
9	6	2	4	7	8	3	5	1
2	9	5	7	8	3	1	4	6
4	8	1	9	6	5	7	3	2
6	7	3	1	2	4	5	9	8
3	2	8	5	9	6	4	1	7
1	4	6	2	3	7	9	8	5
7	5	9	8	4	1	2	6	3

Solutions

49

5	8	1	7	4	3	6	2	9
9	3	2	6	1	5	8	7	4
7	6	4	8	9	2	3	1	5
4	7	6	9	5	1	2	8	3
1	2	8	4	3	6	9	5	7
3	9	5	2	7	8	4	6	1
2	4	7	5	8	9	1	3	6
8	5	3	1	6	4	7	9	2
6	1	9	3	2	7	5	4	8

50

4	7	9	3	2	5	8	6	1
6	3	1	8	7	9	4	5	2
5	2	8	6	4	1	9	7	3
8	9	4	2	5	3	6	1	7
3	1	6	4	8	7	2	9	5
7	5	2	9	1	6	3	4	8
9	4	5	7	3	2	1	8	6
1	6	3	5	9	8	7	2	4
2	8	7	1	6	4	5	3	9

51

4	2	3	7	8	9	6	5	1
1	8	5	2	6	4	7	9	3
7	6	9	1	5	3	4	2	8
9	3	2	6	4	8	1	7	5
5	7	4	9	2	1	3	8	6
8	1	6	3	7	5	2	4	9
3	9	8	4	1	2	5	6	7
2	5	7	8	3	6	9	1	4
6	4	1	5	9	7	8	3	2

52

5	6	4	7	2	8	9	3	1
2	9	8	1	4	3	7	6	5
7	3	1	9	5	6	8	2	4
8	7	2	6	1	5	3	4	9
9	4	3	8	7	2	5	1	6
6	1	5	4	3	9	2	7	8
3	2	9	5	6	1	4	8	7
1	5	7	2	8	4	6	9	3
4	8	6	3	9	7	1	5	2

53

7	4	3	9	2	6	5	1	8
5	2	9	8	7	1	4	3	6
6	1	8	3	4	5	2	7	9
2	5	6	7	3	8	1	9	4
1	8	7	4	5	9	6	2	3
3	9	4	1	6	2	8	5	7
8	3	2	6	1	7	9	4	5
4	6	5	2	9	3	7	8	1
9	7	1	5	8	4	3	6	2

54

1	8	4	9	6	5	7	3	2
5	9	3	2	1	7	8	4	6
2	7	6	3	8	4	9	5	1
4	6	8	7	5	2	3	1	9
7	3	2	1	4	9	6	8	5
9	1	5	6	3	8	4	2	7
6	4	1	5	9	3	2	7	8
8	5	7	4	2	6	1	9	3
3	2	9	8	7	1	5	6	4

55

9	7	5	4	2	8	3	6	1
2	3	4	5	6	1	9	7	8
6	1	8	3	9	7	2	4	5
4	9	3	2	1	5	7	8	6
8	5	2	7	3	6	4	1	9
7	6	1	9	8	4	5	3	2
1	2	9	6	7	3	8	5	4
5	8	7	1	4	9	6	2	3
3	4	6	8	5	2	1	9	7

56

9	4	7	3	2	5	8	6	1
2	6	8	1	9	7	5	4	3
1	3	5	6	8	4	9	7	2
3	5	6	2	7	8	4	1	9
8	7	1	9	4	3	6	2	5
4	2	9	5	1	6	7	3	8
6	1	2	4	5	9	3	8	7
5	8	4	7	3	2	1	9	6
7	9	3	8	6	1	2	5	4

Solutions

57

1	7	9	6	4	3	5	2	8
5	4	6	9	2	8	7	3	1
8	3	2	7	1	5	4	6	9
4	1	8	3	6	9	2	5	7
3	6	5	8	7	2	1	9	4
2	9	7	4	5	1	3	8	6
7	5	3	1	9	6	8	4	2
6	2	1	5	8	4	9	7	3
9	8	4	2	3	7	6	1	5

58

1	6	8	5	9	3	4	7	2
3	2	4	7	1	8	6	5	9
5	7	9	2	4	6	3	8	1
2	5	7	4	6	9	8	1	3
9	8	1	3	7	2	5	4	6
4	3	6	1	8	5	2	9	7
8	4	3	9	2	1	7	6	5
6	1	2	8	5	7	9	3	4
7	9	5	6	3	4	1	2	8

59

7	9	4	2	6	3	5	1	8
5	3	2	8	1	7	4	6	9
8	6	1	5	4	9	2	7	3
1	8	9	6	3	2	7	5	4
6	2	3	4	7	5	9	8	1
4	5	7	9	8	1	3	2	6
2	7	6	3	9	8	1	4	5
3	1	8	7	5	4	6	9	2
9	4	5	1	2	6	8	3	7

60

4	5	9	6	7	1	2	3	8
2	6	1	3	4	8	5	9	7
3	8	7	2	5	9	4	6	1
5	3	6	1	9	4	8	7	2
1	7	4	8	2	3	6	5	9
9	2	8	5	6	7	1	4	3
6	1	5	7	3	2	9	8	4
7	4	2	9	8	5	3	1	6
8	9	3	4	1	6	7	2	5

61

9	7	8	1	3	4	5	6	2
4	5	6	8	2	7	9	3	1
3	2	1	5	9	6	4	7	8
7	6	3	2	4	5	1	8	9
1	4	9	7	8	3	2	5	6
5	8	2	9	6	1	3	4	7
2	9	5	3	7	8	6	1	4
6	3	7	4	1	9	8	2	5
8	1	4	6	5	2	7	9	3

62

2	3	5	1	8	7	9	4	6
6	4	8	5	3	9	7	2	1
9	7	1	2	4	6	8	5	3
8	2	4	9	6	1	3	7	5
5	9	6	3	7	8	2	1	4
7	1	3	4	5	2	6	8	9
3	8	7	6	1	4	5	9	2
1	5	9	8	2	3	4	6	7
4	6	2	7	9	5	1	3	8

63

4	5	8	9	3	2	6	7	1
1	3	2	5	6	7	4	8	9
6	7	9	4	1	8	5	3	2
2	9	3	8	4	6	1	5	7
7	6	5	2	9	1	3	4	8
8	1	4	7	5	3	2	9	6
3	2	7	1	8	4	9	6	5
9	4	1	6	7	5	8	2	3
5	8	6	3	2	9	7	1	4

64

8	7	1	3	5	9	4	6	2
3	5	6	2	4	7	9	8	1
9	4	2	1	8	6	3	5	7
5	2	9	6	3	4	7	1	8
1	3	4	7	2	8	5	9	6
7	6	8	5	9	1	2	3	4
6	9	5	8	7	2	1	4	3
4	8	7	9	1	3	6	2	5
2	1	3	4	6	5	8	7	9

Solutions

65

6	8	9	7	1	3	4	2	5
2	1	5	8	4	9	6	7	3
7	4	3	2	6	5	8	9	1
1	6	8	4	5	7	2	3	9
3	7	2	9	8	1	5	4	6
9	5	4	6	3	2	7	1	8
8	2	1	5	9	4	3	6	7
5	3	7	1	2	6	9	8	4
4	9	6	3	7	8	1	5	2

66

7	1	2	8	6	9	5	3	4
3	4	6	1	5	7	8	2	9
8	5	9	4	3	2	1	6	7
2	8	4	5	7	3	9	1	6
5	6	1	9	2	8	4	7	3
9	7	3	6	4	1	2	8	5
1	3	7	2	9	5	6	4	8
4	9	8	7	1	6	3	5	2
6	2	5	3	8	4	7	9	1

67

4	8	1	2	5	7	9	3	6
6	7	5	3	9	4	1	2	8
9	3	2	1	6	8	5	4	7
1	6	8	7	3	9	4	5	2
3	9	7	5	4	2	8	6	1
2	5	4	6	8	1	7	9	3
8	4	3	9	1	6	2	7	5
7	1	6	4	2	5	3	8	9
5	2	9	8	7	3	6	1	4

68

5	9	6	1	8	4	7	2	3
4	2	3	7	9	6	1	8	5
7	8	1	5	2	3	4	9	6
2	3	5	9	1	8	6	4	7
6	1	7	2	4	5	9	3	8
9	4	8	3	6	7	2	5	1
1	5	9	6	3	2	8	7	4
3	6	4	8	7	9	5	1	2
8	7	2	4	5	1	3	6	9

69

6	1	9	3	8	5	4	7	2
7	8	4	1	6	2	3	9	5
5	3	2	9	7	4	1	8	6
9	2	6	7	4	1	8	5	3
3	5	8	2	9	6	7	4	1
1	4	7	5	3	8	6	2	9
4	7	3	6	2	9	5	1	8
8	9	5	4	1	3	2	6	7
2	6	1	8	5	7	9	3	4

70

4	2	6	8	1	7	9	5	3
8	3	1	9	4	5	2	6	7
9	7	5	6	2	3	4	8	1
6	5	2	4	9	1	7	3	8
1	9	3	7	8	2	5	4	6
7	4	8	5	3	6	1	2	9
3	6	9	2	7	4	8	1	5
2	1	7	3	5	8	6	9	4
5	8	4	1	6	9	3	7	2

71

4	5	8	9	2	6	3	1	7
2	3	6	5	1	7	9	8	4
7	1	9	4	3	8	6	2	5
3	7	1	2	6	5	8	4	9
6	2	5	8	4	9	7	3	1
9	8	4	1	7	3	2	5	6
5	6	7	3	8	4	1	9	2
8	4	2	7	9	1	5	6	3
1	9	3	6	5	2	4	7	8

72

3	7	1	2	5	8	4	9	6
9	2	6	3	4	7	1	8	5
4	5	8	1	6	9	7	3	2
6	4	3	7	8	5	9	2	1
5	1	2	4	9	3	6	7	8
7	8	9	6	2	1	5	4	3
2	6	5	8	7	4	3	1	9
8	3	7	9	1	6	2	5	4
1	9	4	5	3	2	8	6	7

Solutions

73

9	6	3	5	1	8	2	4	7
1	2	8	7	4	6	3	9	5
7	5	4	2	3	9	6	8	1
5	8	2	6	7	4	1	3	9
6	4	7	3	9	1	8	5	2
3	9	1	8	5	2	7	6	4
8	1	5	9	2	3	4	7	6
4	3	9	1	6	7	5	2	8
2	7	6	4	8	5	9	1	3

74

7	5	9	2	8	3	1	6	4
1	8	3	4	6	7	9	2	5
2	6	4	5	9	1	3	7	8
4	9	6	7	1	5	8	3	2
8	3	2	9	4	6	7	5	1
5	7	1	8	3	2	4	9	6
3	2	7	1	5	8	6	4	9
9	1	5	6	7	4	2	8	3
6	4	8	3	2	9	5	1	7

75

7	9	5	8	3	6	4	2	1
2	6	8	1	7	4	9	5	3
4	3	1	9	5	2	7	6	8
1	2	9	3	8	7	6	4	5
8	7	4	6	2	5	3	1	9
3	5	6	4	9	1	2	8	7
9	1	7	2	6	8	5	3	4
5	8	2	7	4	3	1	9	6
6	4	3	5	1	9	8	7	2

76

9	5	7	2	1	4	3	8	6
6	3	2	7	8	9	1	5	4
1	8	4	5	6	3	7	9	2
7	2	8	6	4	1	5	3	9
4	9	1	8	3	5	6	2	7
5	6	3	9	2	7	8	4	1
8	1	5	4	7	2	9	6	3
3	4	9	1	5	6	2	7	8
2	7	6	3	9	8	4	1	5

77

5	3	7	9	6	8	2	4	1
6	1	9	2	7	4	8	3	5
2	4	8	3	5	1	9	6	7
4	8	2	1	9	6	5	7	3
7	5	3	8	4	2	1	9	6
1	9	6	7	3	5	4	8	2
9	7	1	5	8	3	6	2	4
8	6	5	4	2	7	3	1	9
3	2	4	6	1	9	7	5	8

78

9	7	5	6	8	1	4	3	2
4	3	2	5	7	9	1	8	6
1	8	6	2	3	4	9	7	5
3	2	9	1	5	7	8	6	4
7	5	1	4	6	8	3	2	9
8	6	4	9	2	3	7	5	1
2	9	7	8	1	5	6	4	3
6	4	3	7	9	2	5	1	8
5	1	8	3	4	6	2	9	7

79

9	7	2	4	6	8	5	1	3
6	4	8	5	3	1	7	2	9
3	5	1	7	9	2	4	8	6
8	6	7	3	1	4	9	5	2
2	9	5	6	8	7	3	4	1
1	3	4	9	2	5	6	7	8
7	8	9	1	4	6	2	3	5
4	1	6	2	5	3	8	9	7
5	2	3	8	7	9	1	6	4

80

8	7	4	9	1	5	2	3	6
2	9	1	3	6	7	5	8	4
3	6	5	4	2	8	9	1	7
9	1	8	6	3	4	7	5	2
5	3	6	7	9	2	1	4	8
4	2	7	5	8	1	3	6	9
7	5	9	8	4	3	6	2	1
6	8	2	1	5	9	4	7	3
1	4	3	2	7	6	8	9	5

Solutions

81

5	6	2	1	3	7	8	9	4
1	7	3	9	8	4	2	5	6
9	4	8	5	2	6	3	1	7
3	5	7	8	4	1	6	2	9
8	1	4	2	6	9	7	3	5
2	9	6	3	7	5	4	8	1
4	3	1	6	9	8	5	7	2
6	8	9	7	5	2	1	4	3
7	2	5	4	1	3	9	6	8

82

4	1	7	6	2	9	3	5	8
8	3	5	4	7	1	2	9	6
2	9	6	8	3	5	7	4	1
1	2	9	3	4	8	6	7	5
3	5	4	7	9	6	1	8	2
7	6	8	5	1	2	9	3	4
6	7	3	2	8	4	5	1	9
9	8	2	1	5	7	4	6	3
5	4	1	9	6	3	8	2	7

83

2	3	4	7	8	1	6	5	9
1	5	9	3	6	2	8	7	4
8	7	6	9	5	4	2	1	3
6	1	7	8	2	3	9	4	5
5	2	3	6	4	9	7	8	1
9	4	8	5	1	7	3	6	2
7	6	2	4	9	5	1	3	8
4	8	1	2	3	6	5	9	7
3	9	5	1	7	8	4	2	6

84

9	5	2	3	1	4	8	6	7
3	1	6	7	8	2	5	9	4
4	7	8	6	9	5	1	2	3
1	2	9	8	6	7	4	3	5
7	3	5	2	4	9	6	8	1
8	6	4	1	5	3	2	7	9
5	8	7	9	2	1	3	4	6
2	9	1	4	3	6	7	5	8
6	4	3	5	7	8	9	1	2

85

1	5	6	2	7	9	3	4	8
2	8	3	1	4	5	6	9	7
7	4	9	3	8	6	5	2	1
8	3	5	4	2	7	9	1	6
4	9	1	6	5	8	2	7	3
6	2	7	9	3	1	8	5	4
3	6	2	5	1	4	7	8	9
9	1	8	7	6	2	4	3	5
5	7	4	8	9	3	1	6	2

86

2	6	7	3	5	8	9	1	4
1	4	8	7	6	9	2	3	5
9	5	3	1	4	2	7	6	8
6	1	2	9	8	5	4	7	3
4	8	5	2	7	3	6	9	1
3	7	9	4	1	6	5	8	2
7	2	4	8	9	1	3	5	6
5	9	1	6	3	4	8	2	7
8	3	6	5	2	7	1	4	9

87

7	8	4	5	3	6	1	9	2
9	3	2	1	8	4	7	5	6
6	1	5	7	9	2	3	8	4
2	9	8	3	5	7	6	4	1
3	4	1	2	6	8	5	7	9
5	7	6	4	1	9	2	3	8
8	5	3	6	4	1	9	2	7
4	6	7	9	2	3	8	1	5
1	2	9	8	7	5	4	6	3

88

8	9	5	6	7	2	4	1	3
4	2	6	3	9	1	5	7	8
7	3	1	4	5	8	2	9	6
5	4	2	7	8	9	6	3	1
1	7	3	5	4	6	9	8	2
6	8	9	2	1	3	7	4	5
2	1	8	9	6	4	3	5	7
3	5	4	8	2	7	1	6	9
9	6	7	1	3	5	8	2	4

Solutions

89

6	1	3	4	9	2	8	5	7
7	4	2	8	3	5	6	9	1
9	5	8	6	1	7	4	3	2
8	3	4	2	6	9	1	7	5
1	6	7	3	5	8	9	2	4
2	9	5	7	4	1	3	8	6
3	2	1	9	7	6	5	4	8
4	8	6	5	2	3	7	1	9
5	7	9	1	8	4	2	6	3

90

2	6	3	8	1	7	4	5	9
7	8	5	9	6	4	2	1	3
1	9	4	3	5	2	7	6	8
6	2	1	4	9	5	8	3	7
3	7	9	2	8	6	1	4	5
5	4	8	7	3	1	9	2	6
9	5	7	1	2	3	6	8	4
4	1	6	5	7	8	3	9	2
8	3	2	6	4	9	5	7	1

91

5	3	7	4	8	6	2	1	9
8	1	9	5	3	2	6	4	7
6	4	2	9	1	7	5	3	8
7	6	8	1	2	4	9	5	3
1	2	5	7	9	3	8	6	4
3	9	4	6	5	8	1	7	2
2	5	1	3	7	9	4	8	6
9	7	6	8	4	5	3	2	1
4	8	3	2	6	1	7	9	5

92

2	4	1	9	6	8	3	7	5
3	9	7	4	5	1	8	6	2
6	5	8	7	3	2	9	1	4
7	2	9	6	1	4	5	3	8
8	6	5	2	7	3	1	4	9
4	1	3	8	9	5	7	2	6
9	8	2	3	4	7	6	5	1
1	7	4	5	8	6	2	9	3
5	3	6	1	2	9	4	8	7

93

6	9	8	7	5	3	4	2	1
3	4	2	8	9	1	6	7	5
5	1	7	4	6	2	3	9	8
1	6	3	9	2	5	7	8	4
7	2	9	6	4	8	1	5	3
8	5	4	3	1	7	2	6	9
2	8	6	5	3	4	9	1	7
9	3	5	1	7	6	8	4	2
4	7	1	2	8	9	5	3	6

94

4	8	1	9	3	2	7	5	6
6	3	5	7	8	1	9	4	2
7	2	9	6	5	4	8	1	3
1	7	6	2	4	9	5	3	8
3	5	4	8	7	6	1	2	9
2	9	8	3	1	5	4	6	7
9	4	7	5	2	3	6	8	1
8	1	3	4	6	7	2	9	5
5	6	2	1	9	8	3	7	4

95

9	8	2	5	3	4	1	6	7
3	7	5	2	1	6	9	8	4
6	4	1	7	8	9	5	3	2
8	1	9	4	5	3	2	7	6
2	6	7	8	9	1	4	5	3
4	5	3	6	2	7	8	1	9
5	3	4	9	7	8	6	2	1
1	9	8	3	6	2	7	4	5
7	2	6	1	4	5	3	9	8

96

1	3	8	4	7	2	6	9	5
7	6	5	8	9	3	1	2	4
9	2	4	5	1	6	3	8	7
3	4	7	6	8	1	9	5	2
2	1	9	3	5	7	8	4	6
8	5	6	2	4	9	7	1	3
6	9	1	7	2	4	5	3	8
5	7	2	1	3	8	4	6	9
4	8	3	9	6	5	2	7	1

Solutions

97

6	1	4	8	2	7	5	9	3
8	9	3	5	1	4	7	2	6
7	2	5	3	6	9	8	1	4
1	4	7	9	5	2	6	3	8
9	3	6	1	7	8	4	5	2
5	8	2	6	4	3	9	7	1
4	7	8	2	3	5	1	6	9
2	5	1	4	9	6	3	8	7
3	6	9	7	8	1	2	4	5

98

7	2	1	9	5	4	8	6	3
6	5	8	3	7	1	2	9	4
9	4	3	2	8	6	5	1	7
5	9	7	6	3	2	1	4	8
8	3	2	1	4	5	6	7	9
1	6	4	8	9	7	3	2	5
2	8	5	7	1	9	4	3	6
4	1	9	5	6	3	7	8	2
3	7	6	4	2	8	9	5	1

99

1	6	4	7	2	3	8	9	5
8	7	3	9	5	1	2	4	6
2	5	9	4	6	8	7	3	1
4	9	8	1	7	2	6	5	3
5	3	1	6	8	4	9	7	2
6	2	7	5	3	9	4	1	8
9	4	5	2	1	6	3	8	7
7	8	6	3	4	5	1	2	9
3	1	2	8	9	7	5	6	4

100

9	4	3	5	8	1	6	7	2
2	6	8	4	3	7	9	5	1
5	1	7	6	2	9	3	8	4
3	5	6	7	9	4	2	1	8
1	2	4	8	5	6	7	9	3
8	7	9	2	1	3	5	4	6
7	3	2	9	4	8	1	6	5
4	9	5	1	6	2	8	3	7
6	8	1	3	7	5	4	2	9

101

6	4	7	9	8	2	1	5	3
9	1	3	5	4	6	8	7	2
2	8	5	1	3	7	6	4	9
3	5	6	2	1	8	7	9	4
8	7	4	3	9	5	2	1	6
1	9	2	6	7	4	5	3	8
7	2	9	8	5	3	4	6	1
4	6	1	7	2	9	3	8	5
5	3	8	4	6	1	9	2	7

102

2	9	6	1	4	7	8	5	3
4	7	3	2	8	5	1	6	9
1	5	8	9	6	3	2	4	7
6	2	5	3	9	4	7	1	8
8	3	7	5	1	6	9	2	4
9	1	4	7	2	8	5	3	6
5	4	1	6	7	9	3	8	2
7	8	2	4	3	1	6	9	5
3	6	9	8	5	2	4	7	1

103

4	7	9	6	8	1	2	3	5
8	2	3	7	5	9	6	4	1
5	6	1	2	4	3	8	7	9
3	1	6	4	9	7	5	8	2
7	8	4	5	1	2	3	9	6
2	9	5	8	3	6	4	1	7
1	5	7	3	2	8	9	6	4
9	3	2	1	6	4	7	5	8
6	4	8	9	7	5	1	2	3

104

8	7	5	1	2	4	3	6	9
6	9	3	5	8	7	2	1	4
2	1	4	9	6	3	7	5	8
3	5	2	4	7	6	9	8	1
7	6	1	8	3	9	4	2	5
9	4	8	2	5	1	6	7	3
1	8	6	3	9	2	5	4	7
5	2	9	7	4	8	1	3	6
4	3	7	6	1	5	8	9	2

Solutions

105

9	4	3	6	7	5	8	2	1
5	1	7	3	8	2	9	4	6
2	8	6	9	1	4	7	3	5
1	9	2	5	6	7	3	8	4
4	3	8	2	9	1	5	6	7
6	7	5	4	3	8	1	9	2
7	2	4	8	5	3	6	1	9
3	5	9	1	2	6	4	7	8
8	6	1	7	4	9	2	5	3

106

9	7	4	8	3	6	5	1	2
2	1	5	9	7	4	6	8	3
3	6	8	5	1	2	9	7	4
6	8	3	4	2	7	1	5	9
7	9	1	3	5	8	4	2	6
4	5	2	6	9	1	7	3	8
1	2	6	7	4	3	8	9	5
8	3	9	1	6	5	2	4	7
5	4	7	2	8	9	3	6	1

107

6	9	4	1	7	8	3	5	2
3	2	8	6	5	4	7	9	1
1	7	5	9	2	3	6	4	8
8	3	9	4	6	7	2	1	5
5	1	7	2	3	9	4	8	6
2	4	6	5	8	1	9	7	3
9	8	1	3	4	2	5	6	7
4	6	3	7	1	5	8	2	9
7	5	2	8	9	6	1	3	4

108

3	7	4	9	6	2	8	5	1
6	9	8	1	5	3	7	2	4
5	1	2	8	7	4	6	3	9
8	4	3	6	9	1	2	7	5
9	5	1	2	8	7	4	6	3
7	2	6	4	3	5	9	1	8
4	6	5	7	1	8	3	9	2
2	3	9	5	4	6	1	8	7
1	8	7	3	2	9	5	4	6

109

8	6	9	1	2	3	4	5	7
2	7	1	5	9	4	6	3	8
5	4	3	8	6	7	9	1	2
3	1	6	2	7	8	5	4	9
4	2	5	9	3	1	8	7	6
7	9	8	6	4	5	1	2	3
1	5	2	7	8	6	3	9	4
6	3	7	4	5	9	2	8	1
9	8	4	3	1	2	7	6	5

110

4	9	5	7	6	8	3	1	2
8	1	2	5	3	4	6	9	7
7	3	6	1	2	9	8	5	4
1	2	8	3	7	6	5	4	9
6	7	3	9	4	5	2	8	1
9	5	4	8	1	2	7	6	3
5	4	7	2	8	1	9	3	6
2	6	9	4	5	3	1	7	8
3	8	1	6	9	7	4	2	5

111

6	9	4	7	5	3	2	8	1
1	3	8	2	4	6	5	7	9
7	2	5	8	1	9	3	4	6
5	7	1	3	9	8	6	2	4
2	4	6	1	7	5	8	9	3
9	8	3	4	6	2	1	5	7
3	6	2	9	8	4	7	1	5
4	5	7	6	2	1	9	3	8
8	1	9	5	3	7	4	6	2

112

6	4	5	7	8	2	9	3	1
8	2	1	4	9	3	6	5	7
9	3	7	6	5	1	2	4	8
4	6	3	2	1	8	7	9	5
1	9	8	5	4	7	3	2	6
7	5	2	3	6	9	1	8	4
3	1	4	9	7	5	8	6	2
5	7	9	8	2	6	4	1	3
2	8	6	1	3	4	5	7	9

Solutions

113

1	9	3	7	6	8	5	2	4
6	8	7	5	2	4	9	3	1
5	2	4	3	1	9	7	8	6
7	3	6	9	8	1	2	4	5
8	4	9	2	7	5	6	1	3
2	5	1	4	3	6	8	9	7
9	1	8	6	4	7	3	5	2
4	6	2	8	5	3	1	7	9
3	7	5	1	9	2	4	6	8

114

9	8	3	2	1	7	4	5	6
5	7	2	6	3	4	8	9	1
6	4	1	5	9	8	2	3	7
1	5	7	9	8	3	6	4	2
8	3	4	1	6	2	5	7	9
2	6	9	7	4	5	1	8	3
3	1	5	8	2	9	7	6	4
4	2	8	3	7	6	9	1	5
7	9	6	4	5	1	3	2	8

115

6	7	4	9	3	5	8	1	2
2	8	1	4	6	7	5	9	3
3	5	9	1	2	8	7	4	6
9	3	7	5	1	2	6	8	4
1	2	5	8	4	6	3	7	9
4	6	8	7	9	3	2	5	1
8	4	2	6	7	9	1	3	5
5	1	3	2	8	4	9	6	7
7	9	6	3	5	1	4	2	8

116

5	6	2	9	8	3	7	1	4
7	1	3	4	5	6	8	2	9
9	8	4	2	1	7	6	3	5
1	5	7	6	4	2	3	9	8
3	9	8	1	7	5	4	6	2
4	2	6	3	9	8	1	5	7
6	4	5	7	2	1	9	8	3
2	3	9	8	6	4	5	7	1
8	7	1	5	3	9	2	4	6

117

2	1	6	4	9	8	3	5	7
7	4	5	6	3	2	1	8	9
3	9	8	7	1	5	6	2	4
1	8	3	2	5	4	9	7	6
9	2	4	3	7	6	5	1	8
6	5	7	9	8	1	2	4	3
4	3	9	1	2	7	8	6	5
8	6	1	5	4	3	7	9	2
5	7	2	8	6	9	4	3	1

118

3	7	9	1	5	4	6	8	2
1	4	6	8	9	2	7	3	5
2	8	5	6	3	7	1	9	4
9	3	7	4	8	5	2	1	6
6	5	2	3	1	9	4	7	8
4	1	8	7	2	6	3	5	9
8	9	3	2	4	1	5	6	7
7	2	1	5	6	8	9	4	3
5	6	4	9	7	3	8	2	1

119

4	8	2	9	6	1	7	5	3
3	7	6	2	5	4	1	8	9
5	1	9	3	8	7	4	6	2
1	3	5	6	4	9	8	2	7
7	9	4	8	1	2	5	3	6
6	2	8	5	7	3	9	4	1
8	6	3	1	9	5	2	7	4
9	5	7	4	2	6	3	1	8
2	4	1	7	3	8	6	9	5

120

4	2	1	6	8	7	3	5	9
5	9	8	3	1	2	6	4	7
6	7	3	5	4	9	1	2	8
8	6	7	2	9	3	5	1	4
1	4	9	8	6	5	7	3	2
3	5	2	4	7	1	8	9	6
2	8	6	1	3	4	9	7	5
9	3	5	7	2	8	4	6	1
7	1	4	9	5	6	2	8	3

Solutions

121

5	3	4	7	9	2	6	1	8
8	2	1	4	5	6	3	9	7
7	9	6	1	3	8	4	5	2
6	1	8	3	7	9	5	2	4
4	5	2	6	8	1	7	3	9
3	7	9	2	4	5	1	8	6
2	4	7	8	1	3	9	6	5
9	6	3	5	2	4	8	7	1
1	8	5	9	6	7	2	4	3

122

7	5	9	1	8	3	2	6	4
1	4	8	5	6	2	9	3	7
6	2	3	9	4	7	1	8	5
4	1	2	6	7	9	8	5	3
9	6	7	8	3	5	4	1	2
8	3	5	4	2	1	7	9	6
5	7	6	2	9	8	3	4	1
3	8	4	7	1	6	5	2	9
2	9	1	3	5	4	6	7	8

123

8	6	5	1	4	9	2	7	3
9	7	2	3	6	5	4	8	1
1	4	3	7	2	8	5	9	6
4	5	8	9	1	7	6	3	2
6	3	9	5	8	2	1	4	7
7	2	1	4	3	6	8	5	9
3	9	6	8	5	1	7	2	4
5	1	7	2	9	4	3	6	8
2	8	4	6	7	3	9	1	5

124

3	1	8	2	5	7	4	9	6
7	2	5	6	4	9	1	8	3
4	9	6	8	3	1	7	2	5
1	8	3	5	7	2	9	6	4
9	6	4	3	1	8	2	5	7
2	5	7	4	9	6	8	3	1
6	4	9	1	8	3	5	7	2
8	3	1	7	2	5	6	4	9
5	7	2	9	6	4	3	1	8

125

8	4	2	9	6	5	1	7	3
6	3	7	8	1	2	9	5	4
5	1	9	4	3	7	6	2	8
1	7	6	5	2	4	3	8	9
3	5	4	6	8	9	2	1	7
9	2	8	3	7	1	5	4	6
2	8	5	7	9	3	4	6	1
4	6	3	1	5	8	7	9	2
7	9	1	2	4	6	8	3	5

126

6	9	8	3	7	2	1	5	4
4	3	5	9	1	8	7	6	2
1	7	2	4	6	5	3	9	8
7	4	9	5	8	3	2	1	6
8	2	1	6	9	4	5	7	3
5	6	3	7	2	1	8	4	9
9	5	7	8	3	6	4	2	1
2	8	4	1	5	9	6	3	7
3	1	6	2	4	7	9	8	5

127

8	1	7	6	3	9	4	5	2
9	4	6	2	5	7	8	1	3
3	5	2	1	8	4	9	6	7
6	3	9	5	4	1	2	7	8
1	8	4	3	7	2	5	9	6
2	7	5	8	9	6	3	4	1
7	9	3	4	1	8	6	2	5
4	6	8	7	2	5	1	3	9
5	2	1	9	6	3	7	8	4

128

4	2	9	1	5	6	8	7	3
6	8	1	3	7	4	9	5	2
3	5	7	8	9	2	1	6	4
2	1	4	5	8	9	7	3	6
8	9	3	4	6	7	5	2	1
7	6	5	2	3	1	4	8	9
1	4	8	7	2	3	6	9	5
9	7	2	6	1	5	3	4	8
5	3	6	9	4	8	2	1	7

Solutions

129

4	7	3	1	5	2	8	9	6
9	5	2	6	3	8	1	7	4
6	8	1	9	7	4	2	3	5
2	9	5	7	4	3	6	8	1
7	3	4	8	6	1	9	5	2
1	6	8	5	2	9	7	4	3
3	2	9	4	1	7	5	6	8
5	1	7	3	8	6	4	2	9
8	4	6	2	9	5	3	1	7

130

9	5	3	8	6	7	1	4	2
4	8	1	2	5	9	7	6	3
7	2	6	4	3	1	8	5	9
2	9	5	1	8	6	4	3	7
1	6	8	7	4	3	2	9	5
3	7	4	9	2	5	6	8	1
5	1	7	6	9	8	3	2	4
6	3	2	5	1	4	9	7	8
8	4	9	3	7	2	5	1	6

131

2	1	8	4	6	7	9	5	3
6	9	4	5	2	3	7	8	1
3	5	7	1	9	8	2	6	4
8	7	5	9	3	1	4	2	6
4	3	1	2	8	6	5	7	9
9	2	6	7	5	4	3	1	8
5	8	3	6	4	2	1	9	7
1	6	2	3	7	9	8	4	5
7	4	9	8	1	5	6	3	2

132

8	6	7	4	2	5	3	9	1
5	1	9	8	7	3	6	4	2
3	4	2	6	9	1	7	5	8
1	7	4	3	5	2	8	6	9
6	3	5	9	8	7	2	1	4
9	2	8	1	4	6	5	3	7
4	5	6	2	1	8	9	7	3
7	8	1	5	3	9	4	2	6
2	9	3	7	6	4	1	8	5

133

5	4	1	9	3	6	7	8	2
9	8	7	5	1	2	6	3	4
6	2	3	7	8	4	5	9	1
8	5	2	1	6	9	4	7	3
1	6	4	3	2	7	9	5	8
3	7	9	8	4	5	2	1	6
7	3	6	2	9	1	8	4	5
2	1	5	4	7	8	3	6	9
4	9	8	6	5	3	1	2	7

134

5	2	7	3	1	4	8	9	6
8	1	4	9	7	6	3	2	5
9	3	6	5	8	2	1	4	7
7	6	3	8	4	9	5	1	2
2	5	1	7	6	3	4	8	9
4	8	9	1	2	5	6	7	3
3	9	8	4	5	7	2	6	1
1	7	2	6	3	8	9	5	4
6	4	5	2	9	1	7	3	8

135

1	4	5	8	7	3	2	6	9
2	9	3	4	1	6	5	7	8
6	7	8	9	5	2	1	4	3
8	3	1	7	6	4	9	5	2
7	2	9	5	3	8	4	1	6
5	6	4	1	2	9	8	3	7
3	1	6	2	9	5	7	8	4
9	8	7	6	4	1	3	2	5
4	5	2	3	8	7	6	9	1

136

5	1	3	6	4	2	7	8	9
8	6	7	9	1	5	2	4	3
4	9	2	8	7	3	5	6	1
1	2	4	3	8	9	6	7	5
6	8	9	2	5	7	1	3	4
3	7	5	1	6	4	8	9	2
2	5	6	4	3	8	9	1	7
7	4	1	5	9	6	3	2	8
9	3	8	7	2	1	4	5	6

Solutions

137

5	7	3	1	4	6	2	9	8
8	4	1	3	2	9	6	7	5
6	2	9	5	8	7	1	3	4
4	8	7	9	5	2	3	1	6
1	6	2	4	7	3	8	5	9
3	9	5	8	6	1	4	2	7
2	3	4	6	9	5	7	8	1
9	1	8	7	3	4	5	6	2
7	5	6	2	1	8	9	4	3

138

5	3	2	1	8	6	4	7	9
4	9	1	3	7	2	5	6	8
6	7	8	5	9	4	3	1	2
9	1	7	4	2	5	6	8	3
8	6	4	7	3	1	9	2	5
2	5	3	9	6	8	7	4	1
1	4	6	8	5	9	2	3	7
7	2	5	6	1	3	8	9	4
3	8	9	2	4	7	1	5	6

139

6	4	8	2	5	7	3	1	9
3	5	2	1	8	9	6	7	4
9	1	7	3	6	4	5	8	2
7	6	3	4	2	8	9	5	1
1	9	5	7	3	6	4	2	8
2	8	4	9	1	5	7	3	6
4	2	9	8	7	3	1	6	5
5	7	1	6	9	2	8	4	3
8	3	6	5	4	1	2	9	7

140

1	3	2	5	9	4	7	6	8
5	6	9	7	8	3	1	2	4
8	7	4	1	6	2	3	9	5
4	5	6	9	2	1	8	7	3
2	1	8	6	3	7	4	5	9
3	9	7	8	4	5	2	1	6
9	4	3	2	1	6	5	8	7
6	2	5	3	7	8	9	4	1
7	8	1	4	5	9	6	3	2

141

5	9	3	7	1	4	2	6	8
2	4	6	3	9	8	7	5	1
7	8	1	5	6	2	3	9	4
6	3	5	9	8	7	4	1	2
1	2	8	6	4	3	5	7	9
9	7	4	1	2	5	8	3	6
8	5	9	2	7	6	1	4	3
3	6	2	4	5	1	9	8	7
4	1	7	8	3	9	6	2	5

142

2	6	3	7	4	9	8	5	1
9	8	4	6	1	5	3	7	2
7	5	1	8	3	2	9	4	6
3	9	7	2	5	6	1	8	4
6	4	5	1	8	7	2	3	9
8	1	2	4	9	3	7	6	5
4	2	9	5	7	8	6	1	3
1	7	6	3	2	4	5	9	8
5	3	8	9	6	1	4	2	7

143

6	8	4	3	1	7	9	5	2
1	2	3	5	8	9	7	6	4
5	7	9	6	2	4	3	8	1
7	1	5	8	9	3	2	4	6
4	3	2	1	7	6	8	9	5
9	6	8	2	4	5	1	3	7
3	9	1	4	6	2	5	7	8
2	4	7	9	5	8	6	1	3
8	5	6	7	3	1	4	2	9

144

7	6	8	1	9	2	5	4	3
1	9	3	4	5	6	2	8	7
2	4	5	3	7	8	9	6	1
4	5	9	2	3	1	6	7	8
8	7	2	6	4	9	1	3	5
3	1	6	5	8	7	4	9	2
5	8	7	9	2	4	3	1	6
6	2	4	8	1	3	7	5	9
9	3	1	7	6	5	8	2	4

Solutions

145

2	4	7	5	6	8	9	3	1
1	5	3	7	9	4	8	2	6
6	8	9	2	3	1	5	7	4
5	6	8	4	7	3	1	9	2
3	2	1	8	5	9	4	6	7
9	7	4	1	2	6	3	8	5
7	9	5	3	1	2	6	4	8
8	1	6	9	4	7	2	5	3
4	3	2	6	8	5	7	1	9

146

9	8	3	1	5	4	7	2	6
1	6	7	8	9	2	5	3	4
4	5	2	3	7	6	8	9	1
5	3	9	6	2	7	1	4	8
6	4	8	9	1	3	2	7	5
7	2	1	4	8	5	3	6	9
3	9	5	2	4	1	6	8	7
8	7	6	5	3	9	4	1	2
2	1	4	7	6	8	9	5	3

147

8	5	2	3	7	1	4	6	9
4	3	7	8	6	9	2	1	5
9	6	1	4	5	2	8	3	7
3	8	4	7	1	5	9	2	6
5	2	9	6	8	3	7	4	1
1	7	6	9	2	4	5	8	3
2	4	3	1	9	7	6	5	8
6	9	5	2	3	8	1	7	4
7	1	8	5	4	6	3	9	2

148

7	8	6	3	9	1	2	5	4
4	5	3	7	2	6	1	9	8
9	2	1	8	5	4	3	6	7
3	6	7	5	4	2	9	8	1
1	9	8	6	7	3	4	2	5
2	4	5	9	1	8	6	7	3
6	7	9	4	3	5	8	1	2
8	1	4	2	6	7	5	3	9
5	3	2	1	8	9	7	4	6

149

9	2	4	3	7	8	1	6	5
8	6	3	5	9	1	2	7	4
1	5	7	6	4	2	3	9	8
7	4	9	2	8	6	5	3	1
3	1	2	4	5	7	9	8	6
6	8	5	1	3	9	4	2	7
2	9	6	8	1	5	7	4	3
5	3	8	7	2	4	6	1	9
4	7	1	9	6	3	8	5	2

150

9	1	8	3	2	7	4	5	6
2	4	6	1	5	9	7	8	3
3	7	5	8	6	4	2	9	1
7	2	9	4	1	5	3	6	8
8	5	4	6	7	3	1	2	9
1	6	3	9	8	2	5	4	7
4	8	7	2	9	1	6	3	5
5	9	2	7	3	6	8	1	4
6	3	1	5	4	8	9	7	2

151

3	1	2	9	4	6	5	8	7
9	4	8	5	7	1	3	6	2
5	7	6	2	8	3	9	1	4
7	3	4	1	2	8	6	9	5
2	8	5	4	6	9	1	7	3
1	6	9	7	3	5	2	4	8
4	9	7	6	5	2	8	3	1
8	5	1	3	9	7	4	2	6
6	2	3	8	1	4	7	5	9

152

2	5	3	8	7	6	9	4	1
1	6	8	5	9	4	2	7	3
7	9	4	1	3	2	5	8	6
4	2	9	3	8	1	7	6	5
3	8	6	7	2	5	4	1	9
5	7	1	6	4	9	3	2	8
8	1	2	9	5	7	6	3	4
6	4	5	2	1	3	8	9	7
9	3	7	4	6	8	1	5	2

Solutions

153

2	3	9	6	4	7	1	5	8
8	7	5	1	2	9	4	6	3
1	6	4	8	5	3	9	2	7
3	9	7	5	1	2	8	4	6
6	5	8	9	7	4	3	1	2
4	1	2	3	8	6	7	9	5
9	8	3	2	6	1	5	7	4
7	2	1	4	3	5	6	8	9
5	4	6	7	9	8	2	3	1

154

3	6	7	1	9	5	4	8	2
1	5	9	2	8	4	7	6	3
4	8	2	7	6	3	9	1	5
8	9	5	6	4	1	2	3	7
2	7	1	5	3	9	8	4	6
6	3	4	8	7	2	1	5	9
5	4	3	9	2	8	6	7	1
7	2	8	3	1	6	5	9	4
9	1	6	4	5	7	3	2	8

155

6	1	4	3	5	9	7	2	8
8	7	3	2	4	6	1	9	5
2	9	5	7	1	8	4	3	6
3	5	9	6	7	4	2	8	1
1	8	2	9	3	5	6	4	7
7	4	6	1	8	2	9	5	3
4	3	7	5	9	1	8	6	2
5	2	8	4	6	7	3	1	9
9	6	1	8	2	3	5	7	4

156

3	8	1	5	9	6	4	2	7
9	6	5	2	7	4	8	1	3
7	4	2	1	3	8	6	5	9
5	9	4	8	2	7	3	6	1
2	7	8	6	1	3	9	4	5
1	3	6	4	5	9	7	8	2
8	2	3	9	6	1	5	7	4
6	1	9	7	4	5	2	3	8
4	5	7	3	8	2	1	9	6

157

1	3	6	8	5	9	4	2	7
5	9	2	7	4	1	6	8	3
7	4	8	3	6	2	9	5	1
4	2	5	6	8	3	1	7	9
3	7	9	2	1	5	8	6	4
6	8	1	4	9	7	2	3	5
2	5	4	1	7	8	3	9	6
8	1	7	9	3	6	5	4	2
9	6	3	5	2	4	7	1	8

158

6	5	3	4	7	1	9	2	8
9	7	4	8	2	5	1	6	3
2	1	8	6	3	9	7	4	5
7	2	6	1	4	8	3	5	9
5	3	1	2	9	7	4	8	6
4	8	9	3	5	6	2	7	1
1	9	5	7	8	2	6	3	4
8	4	7	9	6	3	5	1	2
3	6	2	5	1	4	8	9	7

159

8	9	5	2	1	7	3	6	4
7	2	3	4	9	6	1	5	8
1	4	6	8	3	5	9	7	2
6	1	8	9	7	4	2	3	5
5	7	4	3	6	2	8	1	9
9	3	2	1	5	8	7	4	6
3	8	9	6	4	1	5	2	7
2	6	7	5	8	3	4	9	1
4	5	1	7	2	9	6	8	3

160

9	4	5	2	3	8	1	7	6
6	1	7	5	4	9	2	3	8
2	3	8	7	6	1	5	4	9
8	5	9	1	2	4	3	6	7
3	2	4	6	5	7	8	9	1
1	7	6	8	9	3	4	5	2
5	8	3	9	7	2	6	1	4
4	9	1	3	8	6	7	2	5
7	6	2	4	1	5	9	8	3

Solutions

161

3	4	5	7	1	2	8	6	9
9	1	7	6	8	5	4	3	2
8	2	6	4	9	3	1	5	7
2	9	8	5	4	6	3	7	1
7	6	1	2	3	9	5	8	4
5	3	4	1	7	8	2	9	6
4	5	9	3	2	7	6	1	8
6	7	2	8	5	1	9	4	3
1	8	3	9	6	4	7	2	5

162

1	9	8	6	7	5	2	4	3
3	2	6	8	4	1	5	7	9
4	5	7	3	2	9	8	1	6
6	3	9	4	5	2	7	8	1
8	1	5	7	6	3	9	2	4
7	4	2	1	9	8	3	6	5
5	7	3	2	1	4	6	9	8
9	6	4	5	8	7	1	3	2
2	8	1	9	3	6	4	5	7

163

9	6	3	5	7	8	4	2	1
2	5	1	4	3	9	8	7	6
4	7	8	1	2	6	5	3	9
6	8	2	3	4	5	1	9	7
1	3	9	7	8	2	6	4	5
5	4	7	6	9	1	2	8	3
7	2	5	8	1	3	9	6	4
8	1	4	9	6	7	3	5	2
3	9	6	2	5	4	7	1	8

164

8	5	2	1	3	4	6	9	7
4	9	6	7	8	5	1	3	2
1	3	7	9	2	6	5	4	8
9	6	1	3	4	2	7	8	5
7	4	5	8	9	1	2	6	3
2	8	3	6	5	7	9	1	4
5	2	9	4	1	8	3	7	6
3	7	8	2	6	9	4	5	1
6	1	4	5	7	3	8	2	9

165

2	3	7	6	8	1	9	5	4
8	1	6	5	4	9	3	7	2
4	9	5	7	2	3	1	6	8
3	5	2	8	1	7	6	4	9
1	7	8	4	9	6	5	2	3
9	6	4	2	3	5	7	8	1
5	4	3	1	7	2	8	9	6
7	2	1	9	6	8	4	3	5
6	8	9	3	5	4	2	1	7

166

7	5	2	8	3	6	4	9	1
8	6	9	4	1	7	2	3	5
1	4	3	5	2	9	7	8	6
3	9	7	1	6	2	8	5	4
6	1	5	3	8	4	9	7	2
2	8	4	9	7	5	1	6	3
5	7	8	6	4	1	3	2	9
9	2	1	7	5	3	6	4	8
4	3	6	2	9	8	5	1	7

167

6	8	5	4	1	3	9	2	7
7	2	4	6	5	9	8	3	1
1	9	3	2	8	7	5	6	4
2	3	7	8	4	1	6	9	5
4	6	9	3	7	5	1	8	2
5	1	8	9	6	2	4	7	3
8	7	6	5	3	4	2	1	9
9	5	1	7	2	8	3	4	6
3	4	2	1	9	6	7	5	8

168

2	4	9	8	3	1	6	7	5
7	5	6	4	2	9	8	1	3
1	3	8	5	7	6	4	9	2
8	1	3	7	6	5	2	4	9
6	7	5	2	9	4	3	8	1
9	2	4	3	1	8	5	6	7
4	9	2	1	8	3	7	5	6
5	6	7	9	4	2	1	3	8
3	8	1	6	5	7	9	2	4

Solutions

169

1	8	4	2	9	6	7	3	5
7	9	6	1	5	3	2	8	4
5	2	3	4	7	8	1	6	9
2	4	8	3	1	9	6	5	7
3	7	1	6	8	5	4	9	2
9	6	5	7	4	2	8	1	3
6	1	9	5	2	4	3	7	8
8	3	2	9	6	7	5	4	1
4	5	7	8	3	1	9	2	6

170

4	2	7	3	1	6	5	9	8
5	9	3	7	2	8	4	1	6
1	6	8	9	4	5	7	3	2
9	1	5	4	6	2	3	8	7
2	8	4	1	3	7	9	6	5
3	7	6	5	8	9	1	2	4
7	5	2	6	9	1	8	4	3
8	3	9	2	5	4	6	7	1
6	4	1	8	7	3	2	5	9

171

6	5	7	9	2	1	8	4	3
1	3	9	5	8	4	2	7	6
2	4	8	3	7	6	5	1	9
8	7	3	6	5	9	1	2	4
5	6	1	2	4	7	3	9	8
4	9	2	1	3	8	7	6	5
7	2	4	8	9	3	6	5	1
3	1	5	4	6	2	9	8	7
9	8	6	7	1	5	4	3	2

172

1	4	5	6	2	9	8	7	3
7	3	8	4	5	1	9	6	2
2	9	6	3	8	7	5	4	1
6	8	2	9	3	5	4	1	7
9	7	1	2	4	6	3	5	8
3	5	4	7	1	8	6	2	9
8	1	7	5	9	4	2	3	6
4	6	3	8	7	2	1	9	5
5	2	9	1	6	3	7	8	4

173

6	1	7	5	3	4	9	8	2
4	5	9	2	7	8	1	6	3
2	8	3	1	6	9	4	7	5
7	6	1	3	8	5	2	4	9
9	3	2	7	4	6	5	1	8
5	4	8	9	2	1	6	3	7
8	7	6	4	5	2	3	9	1
1	2	4	8	9	3	7	5	6
3	9	5	6	1	7	8	2	4

174

1	2	6	5	4	3	9	7	8
4	7	3	6	8	9	5	1	2
8	5	9	7	1	2	6	3	4
9	8	1	2	7	4	3	6	5
6	4	5	3	9	1	8	2	7
7	3	2	8	6	5	1	4	9
5	6	7	1	2	8	4	9	3
3	1	4	9	5	7	2	8	6
2	9	8	4	3	6	7	5	1

175

8	9	5	7	1	2	3	6	4
6	2	7	8	3	4	9	5	1
4	3	1	9	5	6	8	2	7
9	4	6	2	8	7	1	3	5
1	8	3	4	6	5	7	9	2
7	5	2	3	9	1	4	8	6
5	1	9	6	4	8	2	7	3
2	6	8	1	7	3	5	4	9
3	7	4	5	2	9	6	1	8

176

8	9	1	3	2	6	5	4	7
3	6	5	4	9	7	1	2	8
4	7	2	8	1	5	6	3	9
6	2	3	5	4	8	7	9	1
9	1	4	7	6	2	3	8	5
7	5	8	1	3	9	2	6	4
5	4	7	2	8	3	9	1	6
2	8	6	9	5	1	4	7	3
1	3	9	6	7	4	8	5	2

Solutions

177

7	9	1	4	5	2	6	8	3
5	2	4	3	6	8	1	7	9
3	8	6	9	1	7	2	4	5
4	5	2	1	3	9	8	6	7
1	6	7	2	8	5	3	9	4
9	3	8	6	7	4	5	1	2
2	7	5	8	4	6	9	3	1
6	4	3	5	9	1	7	2	8
8	1	9	7	2	3	4	5	6

178

4	9	6	3	7	2	5	1	8
5	7	2	6	8	1	3	9	4
3	1	8	9	4	5	6	2	7
8	4	5	7	1	9	2	3	6
1	2	7	4	6	3	9	8	5
6	3	9	2	5	8	4	7	1
2	6	1	8	9	4	7	5	3
7	8	3	5	2	6	1	4	9
9	5	4	1	3	7	8	6	2

179

8	9	2	6	4	7	3	5	1
4	7	3	5	1	8	9	6	2
6	1	5	3	9	2	8	4	7
7	2	1	4	3	9	6	8	5
5	6	4	7	8	1	2	3	9
3	8	9	2	6	5	7	1	4
9	5	8	1	7	6	4	2	3
1	3	7	8	2	4	5	9	6
2	4	6	9	5	3	1	7	8

180

5	9	8	3	4	6	2	1	7
7	1	6	9	5	2	8	4	3
4	3	2	7	8	1	5	9	6
6	8	9	5	7	4	1	3	2
3	4	1	8	2	9	6	7	5
2	5	7	1	6	3	4	8	9
9	2	3	6	1	8	7	5	4
8	7	4	2	9	5	3	6	1
1	6	5	4	3	7	9	2	8

181

7	1	9	4	3	5	8	2	6
5	3	8	1	6	2	7	4	9
4	6	2	8	9	7	1	5	3
8	5	6	2	1	4	3	9	7
9	2	1	6	7	3	4	8	5
3	4	7	5	8	9	2	6	1
1	9	4	7	5	8	6	3	2
2	7	3	9	4	6	5	1	8
6	8	5	3	2	1	9	7	4

182

6	5	7	8	3	4	2	1	9
8	4	2	9	1	6	7	3	5
3	9	1	7	2	5	6	4	8
2	6	9	5	4	8	3	7	1
1	8	4	2	7	3	5	9	6
5	7	3	6	9	1	8	2	4
9	3	8	1	6	7	4	5	2
7	1	6	4	5	2	9	8	3
4	2	5	3	8	9	1	6	7

183

9	5	4	7	3	1	2	6	8
6	1	3	8	2	5	4	9	7
2	7	8	9	6	4	5	1	3
5	8	1	4	7	9	3	2	6
3	6	7	1	5	2	8	4	9
4	9	2	3	8	6	7	5	1
1	3	9	2	4	8	6	7	5
8	2	6	5	1	7	9	3	4
7	4	5	6	9	3	1	8	2

184

6	9	5	1	2	8	4	7	3
8	7	3	4	9	6	1	2	5
2	4	1	7	5	3	8	6	9
1	8	4	5	6	2	3	9	7
3	6	7	9	4	1	5	8	2
5	2	9	3	8	7	6	1	4
4	5	8	6	7	9	2	3	1
7	3	2	8	1	4	9	5	6
9	1	6	2	3	5	7	4	8

Solutions

185

4	6	3	9	1	7	5	8	2
7	9	2	5	4	8	6	1	3
5	8	1	6	3	2	9	4	7
8	7	9	1	6	3	2	5	4
3	2	5	8	7	4	1	9	6
1	4	6	2	9	5	7	3	8
9	5	7	3	8	6	4	2	1
6	1	8	4	2	9	3	7	5
2	3	4	7	5	1	8	6	9

186

5	7	4	3	8	9	6	2	1
1	3	8	5	2	6	9	7	4
2	6	9	4	1	7	3	8	5
3	2	6	1	9	4	8	5	7
9	1	7	8	3	5	4	6	2
4	8	5	7	6	2	1	9	3
7	5	3	6	4	8	2	1	9
8	4	2	9	7	1	5	3	6
6	9	1	2	5	3	7	4	8

187

9	6	4	5	7	1	3	8	2
2	5	7	4	8	3	1	6	9
8	3	1	2	6	9	4	7	5
7	8	9	1	3	4	2	5	6
5	2	3	6	9	8	7	4	1
1	4	6	7	5	2	9	3	8
4	7	5	9	1	6	8	2	3
6	1	8	3	2	7	5	9	4
3	9	2	8	4	5	6	1	7

188

9	1	6	2	7	8	4	3	5
3	2	5	1	6	4	7	8	9
4	7	8	9	3	5	2	6	1
8	6	7	5	2	1	9	4	3
5	9	3	8	4	6	1	2	7
2	4	1	7	9	3	8	5	6
7	5	9	6	8	2	3	1	4
1	3	2	4	5	7	6	9	8
6	8	4	3	1	9	5	7	2

189

5	6	8	2	4	9	7	3	1
2	4	7	1	3	6	8	5	9
9	1	3	8	5	7	4	2	6
8	2	6	3	7	4	9	1	5
3	9	1	5	6	8	2	4	7
7	5	4	9	2	1	6	8	3
4	8	5	7	9	3	1	6	2
1	3	9	6	8	2	5	7	4
6	7	2	4	1	5	3	9	8

190

4	1	6	9	7	3	2	8	5
3	5	7	2	8	1	6	4	9
8	9	2	4	6	5	3	7	1
1	7	8	5	3	4	9	2	6
2	6	3	1	9	7	8	5	4
5	4	9	8	2	6	7	1	3
9	8	1	6	5	2	4	3	7
6	3	4	7	1	8	5	9	2
7	2	5	3	4	9	1	6	8

191

1	5	7	6	8	9	4	2	3
2	6	4	7	5	3	8	9	1
9	3	8	4	2	1	6	7	5
8	7	1	3	9	6	2	5	4
6	2	5	8	7	4	3	1	9
3	4	9	2	1	5	7	6	8
7	1	2	5	4	8	9	3	6
4	9	6	1	3	7	5	8	2
5	8	3	9	6	2	1	4	7

192

7	6	8	5	4	9	1	2	3
3	1	2	7	8	6	9	4	5
9	5	4	1	2	3	7	8	6
1	7	3	4	5	8	2	6	9
2	4	6	9	3	7	8	5	1
5	8	9	2	6	1	3	7	4
8	2	5	3	9	4	6	1	7
6	9	1	8	7	5	4	3	2
4	3	7	6	1	2	5	9	8

Solutions

193

1	4	5	7	8	3	9	6	2
2	8	6	1	4	9	3	7	5
7	9	3	6	5	2	4	1	8
3	7	2	8	1	4	5	9	6
9	6	4	2	3	5	1	8	7
5	1	8	9	7	6	2	3	4
8	2	1	5	9	7	6	4	3
6	3	7	4	2	1	8	5	9
4	5	9	3	6	8	7	2	1

194

9	8	6	7	2	3	1	4	5
3	5	1	4	8	6	2	9	7
4	2	7	9	1	5	6	3	8
7	4	2	1	6	8	3	5	9
5	9	8	2	3	4	7	1	6
1	6	3	5	7	9	8	2	4
2	7	5	6	9	1	4	8	3
6	3	9	8	4	2	5	7	1
8	1	4	3	5	7	9	6	2

195

4	2	1	7	8	5	6	3	9
3	8	9	2	1	6	4	7	5
7	5	6	3	4	9	1	2	8
9	7	4	1	3	8	2	5	6
2	6	3	5	9	4	7	8	1
8	1	5	6	7	2	3	9	4
6	4	2	9	5	7	8	1	3
1	9	8	4	2	3	5	6	7
5	3	7	8	6	1	9	4	2

196

2	5	6	8	1	7	9	3	4
7	8	4	6	3	9	2	5	1
9	1	3	2	4	5	7	6	8
6	3	2	1	8	4	5	9	7
4	7	8	9	5	6	1	2	3
1	9	5	3	7	2	8	4	6
3	4	1	5	9	8	6	7	2
8	6	9	7	2	3	4	1	5
5	2	7	4	6	1	3	8	9

197

8	2	7	9	4	1	3	6	5
6	1	9	7	5	3	4	2	8
4	5	3	6	8	2	1	7	9
1	4	2	3	6	9	8	5	7
7	9	8	4	2	5	6	3	1
5	3	6	1	7	8	2	9	4
9	8	5	2	3	4	7	1	6
3	6	1	8	9	7	5	4	2
2	7	4	5	1	6	9	8	3

198

7	8	2	9	5	3	4	1	6
1	5	6	7	4	2	9	8	3
4	9	3	1	6	8	5	7	2
6	4	9	5	7	1	2	3	8
8	2	7	4	3	0	6	5	1
5	3	1	2	8	6	7	4	9
2	1	4	3	9	7	8	6	5
9	7	8	6	1	5	3	2	4
3	6	5	8	2	4	1	9	7

199

2	5	6	4	7	8	3	1	9
4	1	8	3	9	6	5	2	7
9	7	3	5	1	2	8	4	6
5	8	9	2	4	3	7	6	1
7	3	4	6	5	1	9	8	2
6	2	1	7	8	9	4	3	5
3	4	7	1	6	5	2	9	8
1	9	2	8	3	7	6	5	4
8	6	5	9	2	4	1	7	3

200

6	4	5	1	7	2	8	9	3
1	9	8	6	3	4	7	5	2
2	7	3	5	8	9	6	1	4
5	2	7	4	1	8	3	6	9
8	6	1	3	9	7	4	2	5
9	3	4	2	5	6	1	7	8
7	8	6	9	2	3	5	4	1
3	1	9	7	4	5	2	8	6
4	5	2	8	6	1	9	3	7

Solutions

201

7	5	6	3	4	1	9	8	2
1	9	2	6	7	8	4	5	3
3	8	4	5	9	2	7	6	1
9	3	7	8	6	5	2	1	4
2	6	1	7	3	4	8	9	5
5	4	8	1	2	9	6	3	7
6	1	3	2	8	7	5	4	9
4	7	5	9	1	6	3	2	8
8	2	9	4	5	3	1	7	6

202

2	8	9	5	7	1	3	6	4
4	1	5	6	3	9	2	8	7
7	3	6	8	2	4	5	1	9
3	7	8	1	9	6	4	2	5
9	5	2	7	4	8	6	3	1
1	6	4	2	5	3	9	7	8
6	9	1	4	8	2	7	5	3
8	4	7	3	6	5	1	9	2
5	2	3	9	1	7	8	4	6

203

7	2	9	1	4	3	8	5	6
1	3	8	5	7	6	4	9	2
4	6	5	9	2	8	1	7	3
6	8	3	4	5	9	7	2	1
2	9	4	7	3	1	6	8	5
5	1	7	6	8	2	3	4	9
8	4	2	3	1	5	9	6	7
3	7	6	2	9	4	5	1	8
9	5	1	8	6	7	2	3	4

204

1	3	2	4	5	6	7	9	8
5	6	7	8	9	1	2	4	3
4	9	8	2	3	7	5	1	6
2	7	6	9	4	8	3	5	1
9	4	3	1	7	5	8	6	2
8	1	5	3	6	2	9	7	4
3	5	1	6	8	9	4	2	7
6	8	9	7	2	4	1	3	5
7	2	4	5	1	3	6	8	9

205

2	3	7	4	6	8	5	1	9
1	5	8	9	2	3	4	6	7
6	9	4	7	5	1	2	3	8
8	4	6	2	1	9	7	5	3
5	2	1	3	7	6	9	8	4
9	7	3	5	8	4	6	2	1
7	6	9	1	3	5	8	4	2
3	8	2	6	4	7	1	9	5
4	1	5	8	9	2	3	7	6

206

4	6	8	5	2	1	3	9	7
7	1	9	6	3	8	5	2	4
3	5	2	9	4	7	1	8	6
8	4	1	7	6	9	2	3	5
6	2	3	8	5	4	7	1	9
9	7	5	2	1	3	6	4	8
1	8	4	3	7	5	9	6	2
5	3	6	4	9	2	8	7	1
2	9	7	1	8	6	4	5	3

207

1	3	4	6	8	2	5	9	7
6	7	5	3	4	9	1	8	2
8	9	2	7	5	1	6	3	4
7	8	1	4	2	3	9	5	6
5	4	6	1	9	8	2	7	3
3	2	9	5	6	7	8	4	1
2	5	7	9	3	6	4	1	8
4	1	8	2	7	5	3	6	9
9	6	3	8	1	4	7	2	5

208

5	8	9	2	1	6	7	4	3
7	2	3	5	4	9	6	8	1
6	1	4	3	8	7	2	9	5
4	7	5	9	6	1	3	2	8
2	9	6	7	3	8	1	5	4
8	3	1	4	2	5	9	6	7
9	4	8	1	7	2	5	3	6
3	5	7	6	9	4	8	1	2
1	6	2	8	5	3	4	7	9

Solutions

209

1	5	8	9	3	7	6	4	2
9	6	4	8	2	5	7	1	3
3	7	2	6	1	4	8	5	9
5	3	9	1	4	8	2	6	7
7	8	1	2	5	6	9	3	4
4	2	6	3	7	9	1	8	5
6	1	3	5	9	2	4	7	8
8	9	7	4	6	3	5	2	1
2	4	5	7	8	1	3	9	6

210

4	7	9	5	8	1	2	6	3
6	1	2	3	7	4	9	5	8
8	3	5	2	6	9	7	4	1
1	5	7	6	4	2	8	3	9
3	8	6	1	9	7	5	2	4
9	2	4	8	3	5	6	1	7
7	6	1	4	5	8	3	9	2
2	9	3	7	1	6	4	8	5
5	4	8	9	2	3	1	7	6

211

1	7	3	2	8	5	6	9	4
5	8	2	6	4	9	1	7	3
4	6	9	3	7	1	2	8	5
6	4	7	9	3	8	5	2	1
9	5	1	4	2	6	8	3	7
3	2	8	1	5	7	4	6	9
7	1	5	8	9	2	3	4	6
8	9	4	5	6	3	7	1	2
2	3	6	7	1	4	9	5	8

212

7	4	1	5	3	8	9	2	6
8	9	5	6	7	2	4	1	3
6	3	2	9	1	4	8	5	7
5	8	7	3	9	1	6	4	2
2	6	9	7	4	5	1	3	8
4	1	3	2	8	6	7	9	5
3	7	4	8	5	9	2	6	1
1	2	8	4	6	3	5	7	9
9	5	6	1	2	7	3	8	4

213

4	2	6	1	5	7	9	3	8
7	9	8	4	2	3	5	6	1
1	5	3	6	8	9	4	2	7
8	3	4	5	9	1	6	7	2
5	6	2	3	7	8	1	9	4
9	7	1	2	6	4	3	8	5
6	1	7	8	3	5	2	4	9
2	4	9	7	1	6	8	5	3
3	8	5	9	4	2	7	1	6

214

9	4	5	6	8	2	3	7	1
6	1	7	4	3	5	2	9	8
8	3	2	1	9	7	4	5	6
2	6	4	3	7	8	5	1	9
5	8	3	9	1	4	6	2	7
7	9	1	2	5	6	8	3	4
3	7	8	5	4	1	9	6	2
1	2	9	8	6	3	7	4	5
4	5	6	7	2	9	1	8	3

215

4	1	9	8	5	7	3	2	6
3	5	6	2	1	9	8	4	7
7	2	8	6	4	3	5	1	9
6	9	5	4	3	8	2	7	1
1	3	2	5	7	6	4	9	8
8	7	4	1	9	2	6	3	5
9	8	3	7	2	5	1	6	4
2	6	1	9	8	4	7	5	3
5	4	7	3	6	1	9	8	2

216

5	1	2	3	4	6	7	9	8
9	3	6	5	7	8	1	4	2
7	8	4	1	9	2	6	5	3
3	9	1	8	6	4	2	7	5
6	7	5	9	2	1	3	8	4
2	4	8	7	3	5	9	1	6
4	5	7	6	1	3	8	2	9
1	2	3	4	8	9	5	6	7
8	6	9	2	5	7	4	3	1

Solutions

217

8	1	4	6	2	9	7	3	5
6	5	7	3	4	8	2	1	9
3	2	9	7	5	1	8	4	6
2	6	3	1	7	4	9	5	8
7	9	8	5	6	3	4	2	1
5	4	1	9	8	2	6	7	3
9	8	5	2	3	7	1	6	4
1	7	6	4	9	5	3	8	2
4	3	2	8	1	6	5	9	7

218

1	8	6	4	5	7	2	9	3
3	4	7	2	8	9	6	5	1
5	2	9	3	1	6	8	7	4
6	3	2	8	7	1	9	4	5
9	1	8	5	4	2	3	6	7
7	5	4	6	9	3	1	8	2
2	9	3	7	6	5	4	1	8
4	6	5	1	3	8	7	2	9
8	7	1	9	2	4	5	3	6

219

7	3	1	6	8	4	5	9	2
6	4	2	1	9	5	7	8	3
9	5	8	7	3	2	1	4	6
4	9	6	8	5	1	3	2	7
1	8	5	2	7	3	4	6	9
3	2	7	9	4	6	8	1	5
8	1	9	3	2	7	6	5	4
5	6	3	4	1	9	2	7	8
2	7	4	5	6	8	9	3	1

220

8	5	1	6	3	7	4	9	2
2	4	9	8	1	5	3	7	6
6	7	3	4	2	9	1	8	5
9	1	2	3	5	4	7	6	8
4	8	6	9	7	2	5	3	1
5	3	7	1	6	8	9	2	4
3	2	4	5	9	6	8	1	7
1	6	8	7	4	3	2	5	9
7	9	5	2	8	1	6	4	3

221

4	5	8	3	6	2	7	1	9
3	7	6	9	1	4	2	8	5
9	2	1	7	5	8	6	3	4
8	9	4	6	7	3	5	2	1
1	6	7	2	4	5	8	9	3
5	3	2	1	8	9	4	7	6
7	4	9	5	2	1	3	6	8
2	1	5	8	3	6	9	4	7
6	8	3	4	9	7	1	5	2

222

6	3	7	8	5	2	9	4	1
9	1	2	4	6	7	5	3	8
8	5	4	1	9	3	2	6	7
5	8	3	2	4	9	7	1	6
2	7	9	6	1	8	4	5	3
1	4	6	7	3	5	8	2	9
4	6	8	5	7	1	3	9	2
3	2	1	9	8	4	6	7	5
7	9	5	3	2	6	1	8	4

223

1	3	6	2	5	7	8	9	4
5	8	9	6	4	1	3	7	2
4	2	7	8	9	3	5	6	1
7	4	3	1	2	6	9	5	8
2	9	5	7	8	4	1	3	6
6	1	8	9	3	5	2	4	7
9	6	1	3	7	2	4	8	5
3	7	4	5	1	8	6	2	9
8	5	2	4	6	9	7	1	3

224

3	7	4	6	2	9	8	1	5
1	9	8	5	7	3	4	6	2
2	5	6	8	1	4	7	3	9
4	8	3	2	5	6	1	9	7
5	2	1	9	4	7	6	8	3
9	6	7	1	3	8	2	5	4
7	1	9	3	6	2	5	4	8
8	4	5	7	9	1	3	2	6
6	3	2	4	8	5	9	7	1